Invitation to Public Speaking

4th Edition

Cindy L. Griffin

CENGAGE
Learning™

Australia • Brazil • Japan • Korea • Mexico • Singapore • Spain • United Kingdom • United States

CENGAGE
Learning™

Invitation to Public Speaking: 4th Edition

Executive Editors:
Maureen Staudt
Michael Stranz

Senior Project Development Manager:
Linda deStefano

Marketing Specialist:
Courtney Sheldon

Senior Production/Manufacturing Manager:
Donna M. Brown

PreMedia Manager:
Joel Brennecke

Sr. Rights Acquisition Account Manager:
Todd Osborne

Cover Image:
Getty Images*

*Unless otherwise noted, all cover images used by Custom Solutions, a part of Cengage Learning, have been supplied courtesy of Getty Images with the exception of the Earthview cover image, which has been supplied by the National Aeronautics and Space Administration (NASA).

Invitation to Public Speaking, 4th Edition
Griffin

© 2011 Cengage Learning. All rights reserved.

ACP CIVIC ENGAGEMENT CHAP, 3E
GRIFFIN

© 2008 Cengage Learning. All rights reserved.

ACP IMPROMPTU SPEAKING CHAPTER
GRIFFIN

© 2010 Cengage Learning. All rights reserved.

For product information and technology assistance, contact us at
Cengage Learning Customer & Sales Support, 1-800-354-9706

For permission to use material from this text or product,
submit all requests online at **cengage.com/permissions**
Further permissions questions can be emailed to
permissionrequest@cengage.com

This book contains select works from existing Cengage Learning resources and was produced by Cengage Learning Custom Solutions for collegiate use. As such, those adopting and/or contributing to this work are responsible for editorial content accuracy, continuity and completeness.

Compilation © 2011 Cengage Learning
ISBN-13: 978-1-133-23487-6

ISBN-10: 1-133-23487-9

Cengage Learning
5191 Natorp Boulevard
Mason, Ohio 45040
USA
Cengage Learning is a leading provider of customized learning solutions with office locations around the globe, including Singapore, the United Kingdom, Australia, Mexico, Brazil, and Japan. Locate your local office at:
international.cengage.com/region.

Cengage Learning products are represented in Canada by Nelson Education, Ltd.
For your lifelong learning solutions, visit **www.cengage.com/custom.**
Visit our corporate website at **www.cengage.com.**

Printed in the United States of America

Brief Contents |

Interactive Video Activities

Sample Speech Video for *Invitation to Public Speaking*

The following sample student speech video is featured in the *Invitation to Public Speaking* Interactive Video Activities.

- Each full-length speech is accompanied by a preparation outline, a speaking outline, sample note cards, and critical thinking questions with responses written by the author, available when students answer the questions themselves and submit them to their instructor.
- Each clip illustrates a specific speech element and is accompanied by critical thinking questions.

Chapter & speaker	Speech	Speech type	Full or clip	Related topics
Chapter 1 Mike Piel	"Foothills Gateway: Vote YES on Referendum 1A"	Persuasive	clip	• Remaining audience centered • Persuasive speaking
Chapter 1 Tiffany Brisco	"Self-Introduction"	Introductory	full	• Giving your first speech • Speeches of self-introduction
Chapter 2 Tiffany Brisco	"Child Abandonment Laws"	Invitational	clip	• Encouraging effective listening • Invitational speaking
Chapter 3 Rebecca Ewing	"The Case for Graduated Licensing"	Persuasive	clip	• Effective thesis statements • Persuasive speaking
Chapter 3 Jesse Rosser	"Preventing School Violence"	Persuasive	clip	• Effective thesis statements • Persuasive speaking
Chapter 3 Ogenna Agbim	"This Is Dedicated . . .: A Tribute to the Women of History"	Commemorative	full	• Speech topic and purpose • Special occasion speaking
Chapter 5 Carol Godart	"Fat Discrimination"	Persuasive	clip	• Using a variety of sources • Persuasive speaking
Chapter 5 Damien Beasley	"Deceptive Prescription Drug Advertisements"	Entertaining	clip	• Oral citation of source • Speaking to entertain
Chapter 5 Tiffany Brisco	"Child Abandonment Laws"	Invitational	clip	• Citing sources • Invitational speaking
Chapter 6 Chelsey Penoyer	"11 Lives a Day: Youth Suicide in America"	Informative	clip	• Using narratives • Informative speaking
Chapter 7 Lisa Alagna	"Breast Cancer Awareness"	Invitational	clip	• Deductive reasoning • Invitational speaking
Chapter 7 Brent Erb	"Stay on Designated Hiking Trails"	Persuasive	clip	• Causal reasoning • Persuasive speaking

Interactive Video Activities (continued)

Chapter & speaker	Speech	Speech type	Full or clip	Related topics
Chapter 8 Cindy Gardner	"U.S. Flag Etiquette"	Informative	clip	• Organization of main points • Informative speaking
Chapter 8 Jeff Malcolm	"History of Fort Collins, Colorado"	Informative	clip	• Chronological organization • Informative speaking
Chapter 8 Katy Mazz	"Why Pi?"	Informative	full	• Speech organization • Informative speaking
Chapter 9 Brandi Lafferty	"Feeding the Wild-life: Don't Do It!"	Persuasive	clip	• Story in an introduction • Persuasive speaking
Chapter 9 Mike Piel	"Foothills Gate-way: Vote YES on Referendum 1A"	Persuasive	clip	• Preview in an introduction • Persuasive speaking
Chapter 9 Mike Piel	"Foothills Gate-way: Vote YES on Referendum 1A"	Persuasive	clip	• Conclusions • Persuasive speaking
Chapter 9 Chelsey Penoyer	"11 Lives a Day: Youth Suicide in America"	Informative	clip	• Credibility in conclusion • Startling conclusion • Informative speaking
Chapter 10 Brandi Lafferty	"Feeding the Wild-life: Don't Do It!"	Persuasive	clip	• Casual style of speaking • Persuasive speaking
Chapter 10 Stacey Newman	"Fallen Soldiers"	Commemorative	clip	• Language techniques • Special occasion speaking
Chapter 11 Eric Daley and Shelley Weibel	• "Mountain Biking in Colorado" (Eric) • "Preserving Our National Resources" (Shelley)	Persuasive	clip	• Comparison of written and conversational styles • Persuasive speaking
Chapter 11 Brandi Lafferty, Amy Wood, Carol Godart, and Hans Erian	• "Feeding Wild-life: Don't Do It!" (Brandi) • "Voting Age" (Amy) • "Fat Discrimina-tion" (Carol) • "No More Sugar" (Hans)	Persuasive	clip	• Comparison of delivery methods • Persuasive speaking
Chapter 12 Cindy Gardner	"U.S. Flag Etiquette"	Informative	clip	• Use of object as visual aid • Informative speaking
Chapter 12 Tony D'Amico	"Springtime for Musicians"	Communication analysis	clip	• Use of a poster as visual aid
Chapter 12 Carol Godart	"Fat Discrimination"	Persuasive	clip	• PowerPoint presentations • Persuasive speaking

Interactive Video Activities (continued)

Chapter & speaker	Speech	Speech type	Full or clip	Related topics
Chapter 12 Chelsey Penoyer	"11 Lives a Day: Youth Suicide in America"	Informative	clip	• PowerPoint presentations • Informative speaking
Chapter 12 Joshua Valentine	"The Dun Dun Drum"	Informative	full	• Use of visual and audio aids • Informative speaking
Chapter 13 Rachel Rota	"Tap"	Informative	full	• Informative speaking
Chapter 13 Chung-yan Man	"Chinese Fortune Telling"	Informative	full	• Informative speaking
Chapter 13 Elizabeth Lopez	"The Three C's of Down Syndrome"	Informative	full	• Informative speaking
Chapter 13 Shana Moellmer	"The African Serval"	Informative	full	• Informative speaking
Chapter 14 Shelley Weibel	"Cloning Endangered Animals"	Invitational	clip	• Condition of equality • Invitational speaking
Chapter 14 Melissa Carroll	"Education in Prisons"	Invitational	clip	• Condition of self-determination • Invitational speaking
Chapter 14 Amanda Bucknam	"Funding for HIV/AIDS in Africa and the United States"	Invitational	full	• Invitational speaking
Chapter 14 Cara Buckley-Ott	"Creationism versus the Big Bang Theory"	Invitational	full	• Invitational speaking
Chapter 14 David Barworth	"Federal Minimum Wage"	Invitational	full	• Invitational speaking
Chapter 14 Courtney Felton	"Four-Day School Week"	Invitational	full	• Invitational speaking
Chapter 14 Jennifer N. Dragan	"Bilingual Education"	Invitational	full	• Invitational speaking
Chapter 15 Courtney Stillman	"Light Pollution"	Persuasive	clip	• Persuasive organizational patterns • Persuasive speaking
Chapter 15 Brent Erb	"Stay on Designated Hiking Trails"	Persuasive	clip	• Immediate action (solutions) • Persuasive speaking
Chapter 15 Brandi Lafferty	"Feeding Wildlife: Don't Do It!"	Persuasive	clip	• Causes • Persuasive speaking
Chapter 15 Dana Barker	"No Child Left Behind: Addressing the School Dropout Rate among Latinos"	Persuasive	full	• Persuasive speaking

Interactive Video Activities (continued)

Chapter & speaker	Speech	Speech type	Full or clip	Related topics
Chapter 15 Renee DeSalvo	"The U.S. and the World Peace Crisis"	Persuasive	full	• Persuasive speaking
Chapter 15 Hans Erian	"Too Much Sugar!"	Persuasive	full	• Persuasive speaking
Chapter 16 Maria DiMaggio	"You Have My Deepest Sympathy: You Just Won the Lottery"	Persuasive	full	• Persuasive speaking
Chapter 16 Jessica Fuller	"Colorado Prison Reform: A Solution to Reduce Recidivism and Overcrowding"	Persuasive	full	• Persuasive speaking
Chapter 16 Carol Godart	"Fat Discrimination"	Persuasive	full	• Persuasive speaking
Chapter 16 Amanda Konecny	"Stop Animal Testing"	Persuasive	full	• Persuasive speaking
Chapter 17 Tara Flanagan	"My Grandfather, John Flanagan Sr."	Commemorative	full	• Special occasion speaking
Chapter 17 Brandon Perry	"Water"	Commemorative	full	• Special occasion speaking

Civic Engagement in Action and Ethical Moment boxes featured in the *Invitation to Public Speaking* online resources

The following library of Civic Engagement in Action and Ethical Moment boxes is featured in the Speech Communication CourseMate for *Invitation to Public Speaking*. Click on the link "Library of CEA and EM Boxes." These boxes are in addition to the Civic Engagement in Action and Ethical Moment boxes that appear in this new edition of the text.

CIVIC ENGAGEMENT IN ACTION BOXES

Subject	Title	Synopsis
Ishmael Beah	A Boy Soldier Tells His Story	Ishmael Beah's story about his experiences as a boy soldier in Sierra Leone inspires him to speak out for the rights of children around the world.
Margaret Gibney	I Always Believed Things Would Change	At the age of thirteen, Margaret Gibney of Belfast, Ireland, wrote a letter to British Prime Minister Tony Blair to request peace. Her letter, and subsequent work for peace, caught the attention of the world's leaders.

Rodolfo "Corky" Gonzales	Say What You Got to Say and Say It Directly	Former boxer Corky Gonzales became a leading voice in "one of the most influential and controversial Chicano civil and humanitarian rights organizations" of the 1960s.
Daniel Lubetzky	Food for Peace	Entrepreneur Daniel Lubetzky uses food as a vehicle for speaking out against the violence in the Middle East.
Matt Roloff	Against Tall Odds	Star of TLC's *Little People, Big World*, Matt Roloff raises awareness about the lives of little people in mainstream America.
Wingspread Summit on Student Civic Engagement	The New Student Politics	Students assert that they can use both politics and other, nontraditional means to campaign for positive change in their communities.

ETHICAL MOMENT BOXES

Subject	Title	Synopsis
Animal Liberation Front	How Graphic Is "Too Graphic"?	Do the militant actions and graphic images used by the animal rights group Animal Liberation Front go too far in persuading the public that the abuse of animals should be stopped?
Barry Bonds	When Must We Speak?	Barry Bonds's testimony about his use (or not) of steroids in 2003 raised the issue of what our ethical obligations are when we're required to speak.
Angelina Grimke	Must We Listen to Others?	In 1838, American activist Angelina Grimke broke the law to speak out about the wrongs of slavery and the importance of the vote for women.
Don Imus	Did Don Imus Go Too Far	How far is too far regarding humor that makes fun of others?
Marilyn Manson	What's in a Master Status?	Shock rocker Marilyn Manson uses his image to challenge audiences.
The Patriot Guard Riders	Free Speech and Reasoning	The actions of the Westboro Baptist Church and the Patriot Guard Riders at the funerals of soldiers killed in combat raise questions about free speech and responsibility.
Cindy Sheehan	What Are Good Reasons?	Mother-turned-peace-activist Cindy Sheehan's participation in the public dialogue inspires praise and criticism.
Larry Summers	What Evidence Should a Speaker Use to "Provoke a Debate"?	Former Harvard University president Larry Summers sparks controversy with his statements about women versus men in the fields of math and science.

Preface

Our best public speaking courses focus their efforts on teaching students the skills needed to speak effectively in public settings. To accomplish this goal, public speaking texts follow a familiar and practical framework that teaches students to give informative, persuasive, and special occasion speeches. Public speaking texts are designed to expose students to the wide array of steps and components involved in public speaking and to allow students to practice these various elements in the classroom.

Invitation to Public Speaking, Fourth Edition, not only grounds itself in this successful approach, but expands it to focus on public speaking as public dialogue, encouraging students to see themselves as significant contributors to their larger communities. In this expanded context, public speaking reflects the many changes that have been taking place in our society, changes that call for an exploration of many perspectives (Ellinor & Gerard, 1998). When framed as a public dialogue, public speaking emphasizes the right to be heard and the responsibility to listen to others (Public Dialogue Consortium, 1998). Thus, *Invitation to Public Speaking* explores public speaking in relation to a modern definition of eloquence, in which differences, civility, narratives, visual aids, and even self-disclosure play a larger role than they tend to in traditional rhetoric.

Invitation to Public Speaking encourages students to see public speaking as a meaningful and useful skill beyond the classroom by expanding the range of venues for public speaking. The text prompts students to speak not only in required classroom speaking situations, but also when they are asked to do so (for example, in the workplace) and when they decide to do so (perhaps as voices of their communities). Thus the text exposes them to the wide range of situations that encourage us to contribute to the public dialogue. It also allows instructors, if they desire, to incorporate a service learning component into their course. Additionally, the text's pragmatic approach—in combination with numerous dynamic, real-life examples—allows working students to design speeches with their employment settings in mind.

Invitation to Public Speaking also emphasizes the ethical and audience-centered nature of public speaking. Throughout the text, students are reminded that they speak to and for an audience, and they are encouraged to consider their audience at every step of the speechmaking process. This audience-centered approach reminds students of the responsibilities associated with speaking publicly and the importance of advanced planning and preparation. It also eases some of the familiar speech anxiety students have, because it turns their attention toward speech preparation and effective communication with others and away from the performance aspect of public speaking.

Most existing texts focus primarily on informational and persuasive speaking, often also preparing students to give speeches that entertain or celebrate others. *Invitation to Public Speaking* includes this focus, but also introduces students to invitational speaking, a type of speaking that is becoming increasingly common. In invitational speaking, speakers enter into a dialogue with an audience in order to clarify positions, explore issues and ideas, or share beliefs and values. When we speak to invite, we want to set the stage for open dialogue and exploration of ideas and issues—we want to come to a fuller understanding of an issue, regardless of our different positions. This speech type is introduced when other speech types are defined and discussed, and is included in discussions of the speechmaking process throughout the text.

Finally, *Invitation to Public Speaking* emphasizes interconnections not only among each of the components of the speechmaking process, but also between the speaker and the audience. In this way, the text helps students view public speaking as a layering of skills and issues rather than as a series of actions existing in isolation. Although the speaking process is presented systematically and in discrete steps, the end result is a smooth integration of material and speaking techniques. Additionally, the text's audience-centered approach, focus on ethics, and thorough integration of diversity help students better understand their audiences so they can establish credibility and communicate effectively.

Features of the Book
Extensive Coverage of Civility and Civic Engagement

By emphasizing the "how" and the "why" of public speaking, *Invitation to Public Speaking* demonstrates the impact that participating in public dialogue can have on students' lives and communities. Civility and the importance of civic engagement are emphasized throughout the book. For example, Civic Engagement in Action boxes, included in almost every chapter, highlight the ways in which students, average citizens, and celebrities have used their public speaking skills to affect the public dialogue in meaningful and satisfying ways. Students can look to these vignettes as examples of how to apply public speaking and civic engagement to their own lives as they become more active members of their communities. Even the photo captions emphasize the importance of civic engagement and civility in the public dialogue. The text's thoughtful attention to these issues continually reminds students of the important role that public speaking plays in our diverse society.

Focus on Skills

Invitation to Public Speaking prepares students to give speeches and enter the public dialogue via a solid, pragmatic, skills-based foundation in public speaking. Beginning with Chapter 2, "Effective Listening," and continuing through Chapter 12, "Visual Aids," each chapter guides students through specific speech construction, delivery, or strategy steps. The text provides straightforward instruction in speechmaking that is based on the author's classroom experience and knowledge of students' expectations for skill training.

Practicing the Public Dialogue boxes provide assignable exercises that expose students to each component of the speechmaking process and gives them strategies for tackling the informative, invitational, persuasive, and special occasion speeches found in Chapters 13 through 17. Speech models included throughout the text are consistent with the principles presented.

Additionally, Review Questions conclude each chapter and give students the opportunity to further hone their skills. These questions range from straightforward true-false statements to activities that require more research, student involvement, and reflection.

Speaking Venues and Service Learning

Invitation to Public Speaking covers a variety of speaking venues and provides ample opportunity to incorporate a service learning component into the course. The text's flexible organization allows instructors who do not want to include service learning to easily maintain the traditional classroom-based speaking situation throughout the term.

Chapter 1, "Why Speak in Public?" offers students a comprehensive view of public speaking as public dialogue and discusses speaking when someone is asked to speak, decides to speak, or is required to speak. In addition, Public Speaking and Service Learning: Engaging Community boxes appear in select chapters. Based on actual projects, these narratives reinforce for students the role and power of public speaking outside the classroom and in the public dialogue. Finally, the *Invitation to Public Speaking* Instructor's Resource Manual provides a definition of service learning and instruction for how to use service learning projects as a source for speech topics, speech research, and possibly an environment for delivery.

These options allows students and instructors to step outside the speech classroom if they desire, and take the public speaking skills taught and learned in the classroom into their communities. However, if instructors choose to stay with the traditional classroom speech format, the service learning information can be used simply to prompt students to select and deliver speeches that address larger social issues and dilemmas.

Expansive Coverage of Speech Types

Some courses emphasize particular speech, but *Invitation to Public Speaking* was specifically developed to cover and support the entire array of public speaking types. The text's coverage of multiple speaking forms invites students to discuss audience centeredness and difference, as well as the ways that speakers can acknowledge, incorporate, and respond to difference with respect and integrity.

Beginning with the quick-start guide, "Ten Steps to Entering the Public Dialogue," (pages xxxii–xxxvii) the text presents a synopsis of five types of speaking: informative, invitational, persuasive, speaking on special occasions, and speaking in small groups. Each type of speech previewed in the quick-start is covered in depth in Chapters 13 through 17 and the appendix on group speaking, and is given equal attention with regard to examples and tips in Chapters 2 through 12, furthering the text's goal of preparing readers for public speaking in a range of venues beyond the classroom.

Coverage of Social Diversity

Through reviewer-praised examples and discussion of key concepts, the text makes a comprehensive yet subtle integration of diversity. *Invitation to Public Speaking* offers meaningful coverage of diversity by exploring culture and speaking styles, culture and listening styles, speaking to diverse audiences, and language and culture.

Rather than isolate issues of diversity into separate chapters, *Invitation to Public Speaking* presents ideas and issues of diversity in examples, discussions, activities, and exercises throughout the text. In the process, the text provides sufficient information so that instructors do not need to do additional research in order to have meaningful conversations with their students. This "learn-as-you-go" approach benefits students and instructors as they add to their layers of knowledge about difference.

Coverage of Ethics

Ethical issues are discussed throughout the text to help students understand how ethical considerations affect every aspect of the speechmaking process. For example, the importance of practicing ethics in regard to listening, Internet research, interviewing, reasoning, citing sources, and in informative, invitational, and persuasive speaking are covered thoroughly. In addition, select chapters feature Ethical Moment boxes, which highlight ethical dilemmas related to the public dialogue.

Coverage of Reasoning

The text emphasizes the important skill of reasoning in informative, invitational, and persuasive speaking situations. Chapter 7, "Reasoning," encourages students to recognize the validity of sound reasoning and evidence in any speaking context, while Chapter 16, "Persuasion and Reasoning," provides superior coverage of the critical importance of sound reasoning in persuasion.

Coverage and Use of Relevant Technology

Invitation to Public Speaking was written with technology use in mind. Thoughtful integration on nearly every page continually helps the student understand the links between the text and technology. The text not only covers technology as it relates to speechmaking, but also incorporates the use of technology as a powerful learning tool. The Internet and online databases are discussed as tools for speech topic selection, research, and support, while presentation technology such as Microsoft® PowerPoint® is presented as a resource for creating professional visual aids. Each chapter points students to relevant websites, video clips of student and professional speakers, and other online activities that can be accessed via the online resources for *Invitation to Public Speaking*. (To learn how to use the text in conjunction with its online resources, see the How to Use This Book guide on page xxx.)

What's New in the Fourth Edition

- **New Quick-Start Guide at the beginning of the book.** Last edition's Chapter 2, "Entering the Public Dialogue with Confidence: Your First Speech," has been converted to a streamlined quick-start guide, "Ten Steps to Entering the Public Dialogue," that gets students speaking right away. The material on managing public speaking anxiety has been moved to a new section in Chapter 1, "Why Speak in Public?" titled "Building Your Confidence as a Public Speaker."

- **New bonus chapter on impromptu speaking.** At the request of reviewers, a new bonus chapter that provides guidelines and tips for impromptu speaking can be included in custom versions of the book. For more about Cengage's customization program, see Resources for Instructors on page xxiv.

- **All-new Speaking Visually boxes.** Featured in select chapters, all-new Speaking Visually boxes highlight the powerful effects of visual communication in our society. Topics discussed include street artist Banksy's visual commentary on political and social issues around the world, the surprising success a series of anti-meth ads have had in appealing to fear without alienating viewers, and YouTube's growing influence on young activists who prefer to speak their minds online with video.

- **New and updated Civic Engagement in Action boxes.** Featured in almost every chapter, updated Civic Engagement in Action boxes showcase the work of people who have used public speaking as a means to engage in meaningful public dialogue. New speakers include celebrities such as actors and humanitarians George Clooney and Don Cheadle, and average people who've chosen to make a difference, such as Zainab Salbi, who was so moved by the plight of women victimized during the Yugoslav Wars that she and her husband used their honeymoon money to found an organization to help women survivors of war. Each box includes Web Connect links that direct students to additional information and opportunities to get involved in the public dialogue.

- **New Ethical Moment boxes.** Featured in chapters that include discussion about ethics and public speaking, these case studies ask students to think critically about ethical principles and lapses in the public dialogue. Highlighted issues include how far is too far when spotlighting controversial issues in certain venues (Kanye West), what types of statements are ethical within the realm of free speech (Rush Limbaugh), and whether it's okay to say whatever you want online (Julia Wilson, Megan Meier, Phoebe Prince). Each box includes critical thinking questions that can be assigned or discussed in class.

- **New Public Speaking and Service Learning boxes.** Almost every chapter includes a new Public Speaking and Service Learning: Engaging Community box. These boxes, based on actual student service learning projects, help students make the connection between service learning and public speaking skills. In addition, each box now includes tips for incorporating service learning experiences into the speechmaking process.

- **In Chapter 5, "Gathering Supporting Materials," guidelines for citing sources moved to accompany discussion of bibliographies.** The discussion of citing sources in speeches has been moved from the chapter on developing and supporting ideas to Chapter 5, "Gathering Supporting Materials," so that students can better understand the relationship between their bibliographies and the sources they choose to cite orally.

- **In Chapter 5, "Gathering Supporting Materials," increased resources to help students understand the basics of research.** Many students come to the public speaking course with a good understanding of how to conduct research. But for those students who need help with the basics, tips and links to information are available via the *Invitation to Public Speaking* online resources. These resources can be used to supplement Chapter 5, "Gathering Supporting Materials."

- **In Chapter 15, "Persuasive Speaking," new coverage of the elaboration likelihood model.** A discussion of Petty and Cacioppo's elaboration likelihood model has been added to Chapter 15, "Persuasive Speaking," highlighting how important it is for speakers to make a meaningful connection with their audiences.

- **In Chapter 15, "Persuasive Speaking," increased coverage of organizational patterns for persuasive speaking.** Coverage of cause-effect, effect-cause, and narrative patterns of organization has been added to the discussion of organizational patterns for speeches on questions of policy in Chapter 15, "Persuasive Speaking."

- **In Chapter 16, "Persuasion and Reasoning," increased coverage of logical fallacies.** The discussion of logical fallacies in Chapter 16, "Persuasion and Reasoning," now includes two new fallacies: false cause and hasty generalization. In addition, a new table briefly describes ten additional fallacies, including straw man, appeal to ignorance, and non sequitur.

- **New student speeches.** The text features nine full-length student speeches, presented as either a transcript (Chapters 3, 9, 14, 17), a preparation outline (Chapters 8, 12, 13, 15, 16), or a speaking outline (Chapter 8) so that students can read the speeches in a variety of formats. Three of these speeches are new and highlight the African serval (informative), the four-day school week (invitational), and the virtues of water (special occasion). Video-taped versions of each of the speeches in the text, as well as another thirteen full-length speeches, are included in the Interactive Video Activities, and all are accompanied by a transcript, a preparation outline, a speaking outline, sample note cards, and critical thinking questions. In addition, the Interactive Video Activities feature twenty-nine clips of specific speech elements that students can watch, read, and critique. See the table on page xi for a complete list of all the speeches and snippets that accompany this book.

- **New and updated examples and research.** Throughout the book, examples have been updated to include more that students will recognize and relate to. In addition, research has been updated throughout the book as appropriate.

- **New chapter summaries.** Each chapter summary has been organized into lists that make it easy to study for quizzes and exams.

Resources for Students

Invitation to Public Speaking, Fourth Edition, features an outstanding array of supplements to assist in making this course as meaningful and effective as possible. **Note:** If you want your students to have access to the online resources for *Invitation to Public Speaking*, please be sure to order them for your course—if you do not order them, your students will not have access to them on the first day of class. These resources can be bundled with every new copy of the text or ordered separately. Students whose instructors do not order these resources as a package with the text may purchase them or access them at **cengagebrain.com**. *Contact your local Wadsworth Cengage Learning sales representative for more details.*

- **Speech Communication CourseMate for *Invitation to Public Speaking*.** This site provides students with easy access to the integrated technology resources that accompany the book. These resources include learning, study, and exam preparation tools such as the interactive eBook, student workbook, Audio Study Tools, flashcards, chapter notepads, Web Connect links, the end-of-chapter review questions that support the printed textbook, and a library of the Civic Engagement in Action and Ethical Moment boxes featured in past editions. (For a complete list of the boxes included in this library, see page xiv.) In addition, CourseMate's Engagement Tracker tracking tools allow you to monitor the progress of the class as a whole or of individual students. Engagement Tracker helps you identify students at risk early in the course, uncover which concepts are most difficult for your class, monitor time on task, and keep your students engaged.

- **Interactive Video Activities.** Presented within Wadsworth Cengage Learning's unique interactive user interface, the speech videos help students gain experience evaluating and critiquing introductory, informative, invitational, persuasive, and special occasion speeches so that they can more effectively provide feedback to their peers and improve their own speeches and delivery. This highly praised resource includes the following features:
  - Transcripts and closed-captioning for all speech videos.
  - Preparation outlines, speaking outlines, and note cards for full-length student speech videos so students can recognize the connection between creating an effective speech outline and delivering a speech.

- A "scroll" function that students may choose to turn on or off for full-length speech videos. When the scroll feature is on, synchronized highlighting tracks each speaker's progress through an outline or transcript of the speech as the video of the speaker's delivery plays alongside.
- A "notes" function that lets students insert written comments while watching the video. At a student's command, the program pauses, enters a time-stamp that indicates where the video was paused, and offers students the ability to write their own critiques of the video or choose from a set of pre-written rubrics that teach students how to effectively evaluate speeches.
- Assignable analysis questions with responses written by the text's authors, available when students answer the questions themselves and submit them to their instructor.

- **Audio Study Tools.** This text's Audio Study Tools provides a fun and easy way for students to download audio files and review chapter content whenever and wherever. For each chapter of the text, students will have access to a chapter review consisting of the learning objectives for the chapter, a brief summary of the main points in the text, audio of a sample student speech, and five to seven critical thinking questions. Students can go to the CourseMate for *Invitation to Public Speaking* to listen to or download the Audio Study Tools.

- **Speech Studio™.** With Speech Studio, students can upload video files of practice speeches or final performances, comment on their peer's speeches, and review their grades and instructor feedback. Speech Studio's flexibility lends itself to use in traditional, hybrid, and online courses. It allows instructors to save valuable in-class time by conducting practice sessions and peer review work virtually; combine the ease of a course management tool with a convenient way to capture, grade, and review videos of live, in-class performances; and simulate an in-class experience for online courses.

- Many of the Practicing the Public Dialogue activities can be completed with **Speech Builder Express 3.0™.** This interactive web-based tool coaches students through the speech organization and outlining process. By completing interactive sessions, students can prepare and save their outlines, formatted according to the principles presented in the text. Text models of speech elements reinforce students' interactive practice.

- **InfoTrac College Edition with InfoMarks™.** This virtual library's more than 18 million reliable, full-length articles from 5,000 academic and popular periodicals allow students to retrieve results almost instantly. They also have access to InfoMarks—stable URLs that can be linked to articles, journals, and searches to save valuable time when doing research—and to the InfoWrite online resource center, where students can access grammar help, critical-thinking guidelines, guides to writing research papers, and much more.

- **CengageBrain Online Store.** CengageBrain.com is a single destination for more than 15,000 new print textbooks, textbook rentals, eBooks, single eChapters, and print, digital, and audio study tools. CengageBrain.com provides the freedom to purchase Cengage Learning products à-la-carte—exactly what you need, when you need it. Visit **cengagebrain.com** for details.

- *A Guide to the Basic Course for ESL Students.* Written by Esther Yook, Mary Washington College, this guide for non-native speakers includes strategies for accent management and overcoming speech apprehension, in addition to helpful web addresses and answers to frequently asked questions.

Resources for Instructors

Invitation to Public Speaking, Fourth Edition, also features a full suite of resources for instructors. These resources are available to qualified adopters, and ordering options for student supplements are flexible. Please consult your local Wadsworth Cengage Learning sales representative for more information, to evaluate examination copies of any of these instructor or student resources, or to request product demonstrations.

- **Instructor's Resource Manual,** by Cindy L. Griffin of Colorado State University and Louis Serio of Bristol Community College. The Instructor's Resource Manual provides a comprehensive teaching system. Included in the manual are suggested public speaking assignments and criteria for evaluation, chapter outlines, and in-class activities. All of the Web Connect links and activities listed at the end of each chapter of the student edition are included in detail in the Instructor's Manual in the event that online access is unavailable or inconvenient.

- **Instructor Website.** The password-protected site allows you to view all the assets your students can view, helps you determine what you can assign and encourage your students to use, and includes electronic access to the Instructor's Resource Manual, downloadable versions of the book's Microsoft PowerPoint presentations, and more. Visit the Instructor Website by accessing **http://login.cengage.com** or by contacting your local sales representative.

- *The Teaching Assistant's Guide to the Basic Course.* Written by Katherine G. Hendrix, University of Memphis, this resource was prepared specifically for new instructors. Based on leading communication teacher training programs, this guide discusses some of the general issues that accompany a teaching role and offers specific strategies for managing the first week of classes, leading productive discussions, managing sensitive topics in the classroom, and grading students' written and oral work.

- **PowerLecture.** This CD-ROM contains an electronic version of the Instructor's Resource Manual, ExamView computerized testing, and ready-to-use Microsoft PowerPoint presentations. The PowerPoint slides contain text, images, and cued videos of the Speech Buddy and sample speech videos, and they can be used as is or customized to suit your course needs. This all-in-one lecture tool makes it easy for you to assemble, edit, publish, and present custom lectures for your course.

- **Instructor Workbooks:** *Public Speaking: An Online Approach, Public Speaking: A Problem Based Learning Approach,* and *Public Speaking: A Service-Learning Approach for Instructors.* Written by Deanna Sellnow, University of Kentucky, these instructor workbooks include a course-syllabus and icebreakers; public speaking basics such as coping with anxiety, learning cycle and learning styles; outlining; ethics; and informative, persuasive, and ceremonial (special occasion) speeches.

- *Teaching the Invitational Speech Resource Guide* **and Accompanying Video and DVD.** This resource, featuring an introduction by author Cindy L. Griffin, shows you how to effectively teach the invitational speech to your students.

- **Wadsworth Communication Video and DVD Library.** Wadsworth's video and DVD series for Speech Communication includes Student Speeches for Critique and Analysis as well as Communication Scenarios for Critique and Analysis.

- **Videos for Speech Communication 2010: Public Speaking, Human Communication, and Interpersonal Communication.** This DVD provides footage of news stories from BBC and CBS that relate to current topics in communication, such as teamwork and how to interview for jobs, as well as news clips about speaking anxiety and speeches from contemporary public speakers, such as Michelle Obama and Senator Hillary Clinton.

- **ABC News DVD: Speeches by Barack Obama.** This DVD includes nine famous speeches by President Barack Obama, from 2004 to present day, including his speech at the 2004 Democratic National Convention; his 2008 speech on race, "A More Perfect Union"; and his 2009 inaugural address. Speeches are divided into short video segments for easy, time-efficient viewing. This instructor supplement also features critical thinking questions and answers for each speech, designed to spark class discussion.

- *Guide to Teaching Public Speaking Online.* Written by Todd Brand of Meridian Community College, this helpful online guide provides instructors who teach public speaking online with tips for establishing "classroom" norms with students, utilizing course management soft ware and other eResources, managing logistics such as delivering and submitting speeches and making up work, discussing how peer feedback is different online, strategies for assessment, and tools such as sample syllabi and critique and evaluation forms tailored to the online course.

- *Service Learning in Communication Studies: A Handbook.* Written by Rick Isaacson and Jeff Saperstein, this is an invaluable resource for students in the basic course that integrates or will soon integrate a service learning component. This handbook provides guidelines for connecting service learning work with classroom concepts and advice for working effectively with agencies and organizations. It also provides model forms and reports and a directory of online resources.

- **CourseCare Training and Support.** Get trained, get connected, and get the support you need for the seamless integration of digital resources into your course. This unparalleled technology service and training program provides robust online resources, peer-to-peer instruction, personalized training, and a customizable program you can count on. Visit **cengage.com/coursecare/** to sign up for online seminars, first days of class services, technical support, or personalized, face-to-face training. Our online and onsite trainings are frequently led by one of our Lead Teachers, faculty members who are experts in using Wadsworth Cengage Learning technology and can provide best practices and teaching tips.

- **Custom Chapters for *Invitation to Public Speaking*.** Customize your chapter coverage with bonus chapters on impromptu speaking, civic engagement, and service learning. You can access these chapters online within the Instructor Website, or you can order print versions of the student text that include the extra chapter of your choice. Contact your local sales representative for ordering details.

- **Flex-Text Customization Program.** With this program you can create a text as unique as your course: quickly, simply, and affordably. As part of our flex-text program, you can add your personal touch to *Invitation to Public Speaking* with a course-specific cover and up to thirty-two pages of your own content—at no additional cost.

Acknowledgments

I believe writing and scholarship are both individual and collaborative efforts. Acknowledging the individuals who assisted me throughout the process of writing this book is one small way of recognizing that collaboration and thanking those who offered invaluable assistance and endless support. To Monica Eckman, executive editor; and Greer Lleuad, senior development editor, I express my deepest and heartfelt appreciation. For their invitation to embark on this journey, their incredible vision and talent, their endless guidance, support, kindness, and laughter, I am honored and grateful. My writing process and life are richer because of the two of them. To Lyn Uhl, senior publisher; Amy Whitaker, senior marketing manager; Rebekah Matthews, assistant editor; Colin Solan, editorial assistant; Jessica Badiner, media editor; Michael Lepera, senior content project manager; Katie Huha, senior rights specialist, text; Mandy Groszko, rights specialist, images; Megan Lessard, photo researcher; and Autumn Burger, project manager at Lachina Publishing Services, I express my sincerest thanks. These amazing people shared their talents, time, and energy enhancing the book every step of the way. They also generously offered insight, wisdom, and expertise in response to my never-ending requests and questions.

To Dr. Linda Scholz, assistant professor at Eastern Illinois University, and Dr. Jennifer Emerling Bone, special assistant professor at Colorado State University, friends in every way and collaborators on various aspects during various stages of this book, I am forever indebted. Their excellent ideas and insights, love and support, steady stream of laughter, smiles, and hugs, and willingness to test out the early versions of this book in their own classes are acts of courage and connection that never went unnoticed or unappreciated. The speeches of their students grace the chapters of this book, which reflects not only the talents of those students but also the extraordinary skill Linda and Jennifer possess as teachers. I am lucky to have them in my life.

To Kristen Slattery, Matt Petrunia, Anne Trump, and Beth Bonnstetter, lecturers and former graduate students at Colorado State University, many, many thanks. Their hours and hours in the library, on the Internet, and in my office assisting me with research are invaluable. Working with the three of them gave me the confidence to complete this project on time and the assurance that the ideas in this book are supported by the very best of scholarship, both historical and contemporary.

Many thanks to all the reviewers of this fourth edition for their invaluable feedback and support of this book. They are Todd Brand, Meridian Community College; Elizabeth Brierley, Ocean County College; Ferald Bryan, Northern Illinois University; Steven Grant, Florida State College; Nichelle McNabb, Otterbein College; Michael Polites, Indiana University–Purdue University Indianapolis; Rasha Ramzy, Georgia State University; Erin Reser, Rocky Mountain College; Roberta Steinberg, Mount Ida College; and David Williams, Texas Tech University.

And a warm thank you to all the reviewers, focus-group participants, and class testers of the first, second, and third editions, who are too numerous to list here.

Thanks also to former and current Colorado State University lecturers, graduate students, and special-appointment faculty Cara Buckley-Ott, Kathleen Creamer, Erin Cunningham, Ian Dawe, Brian DeVeney, Alicia Ernest, Holly Gates-Peters, Jeremy Grossman, Bill Herman, Jeffery Ho, Lori Irwin, Keli Larson-Flewell, Jill

Lippman Mellott, Katheryn Maguire, Jeremy Mellott, Beth Myers-Bass, Sonja Modesti, Kirsten Pullen, Raena Quinlivin, Virginia Ramos, Mark Saunders, Heather Scheumann, Allison Searle, Elizabeth Sink, Jamie Skerski, Kristin Slattery, Derek Sweet, Elizabeth Terry, and Toni-Lee Viney, who at various times (and sometimes without even realizing it) shared speech ideas, outlines, assignments, and stories that added to the depth and strength of this project.

Many thanks also to their students, whose speeches are found in pages of this text. And a very special thanks to Mary Triece of the University of Akron, not only for her invaluable class-test feedback, but also for so graciously providing us with the speeches of some of her students, which are also incorporated throughout this text.

And finally, a sincere thank you to my public speaking students and to the students from other parts of the country whose voices enhance this text, for their creativity, flexibility, and talents.

Without a doubt, the strongest collaborative force in my life comes from my family. My husband, Mike Harte; my son, Joseph Griffin-Harte; my sisters, Tracy Zerr and Wendy Stewart; my brother, John Griffin; my father, John Griffin; and my extended family, Jana Webster-Wheeler, Scott Wheeler, and Joseph Wheeler keep strong and steady the flame that fuels my energy. Their unending love and support have enriched this project and reminded me daily that the public dialogue is enhanced by our willingness to listen to others and by our commitment to speak as clearly and honestly as possible. To them, I offer my love and thanks, and the acknowledgment that their care for me gives me great strength and peace.

—Cindy L. Griffin

About the Author

Cindy L. Griffin is a Professor of Speech Communication at Colorado State University. She received her B.S. from California State University, Northridge, her M.A. in Communication from the University of Oregon, and her Ph.D. from Indiana University. Cindy teaches Public Speaking; Women and Communication; Contemporary Rhetorical Theory; Feminist Rhetorical Theory; Communication, Language and Thought; and Rhetoric and Civility. A proponent of service learning, civic engagement, and civility, Cindy integrates these ideas and assignments into her coursework and research. In addition to her teaching and research, she served as editor of the journal *Women's Studies in Communication* from 2007 to 2010 and is a member of the Women's Studies faculty at CSU. She and her husband, Mike Harte, have a son, Joseph, and live in Fort Collins, Colorado.

How to Use This Book

Invitation to Public Speaking provides you with a full suite of online resources that you can use to complete your assignments, study for quizzes and exams, and get more information about topics you're interested in. These resources include

- Sample speech videos
- Sample speech outlines and note cards
- An online speech organizing and outlining tool
- Web Connect links

- A workbook
- Study aids such as glossary flashcards and review quizzes
- And much more

If your instructor ordered these resources with your textbook, go to **http://login.cengage.com** to access them. If your instructor didn't order them but you'd like to use them, you can purchase them at **www.cengagebrain.com**.

Here's how these online resources are integrated into the book:

When you see the CourseMate icon, log on to your online resources and click on the CourseMate link. This link gives you access to several tools, including the Interactive Video Activities, an interactive eBook, a student workbook, Audio Study Tools (downloadable study files), flashcards, and the Web Connect links featured in each chapter.

The text includes several prompts to watch the video of the sample student speeches that accompany this book. You'll find these prompts near the ends of Chapters 3, 8, 9, 12, 13, 14, 15, 16, and 17, along with the in-text examples of speeches. You'll also see additional prompts throughout the book in boxes that appear in the margins. You can access all the videos through your CourseMate.

Each chapter includes at least one Practicing the Public Dialogue box. These boxes provide you with opportunities to practice speaking skills and prepare your speeches. Almost every box includes a prompt called "Online Resources," which suggests online resources that can help you prepare more effective speeches.

References to Web Connect links throughout the text direct you to web links that can help you with your research, brainstorm for speech topics, get involved with causes and issues that interest you, and much more. You can access all the Web Connect links through your CourseMate.

When you see this icon, log on to your online resources and click on the Speech Builder Express link. With Speech Builder Express, you can develop and organize your speeches online.

When you see this icon, log on to your online resources and click on the Speech Studio link. With Speech Studio, you can upload video files of your practice or final speeches, comment on other students' speeches and get their feedback on your speeches, and review your grades and your instructor's feedback.

Quick-Start Guide
Ten Steps to Entering the Public Dialogue

Whether your speaking goal is to inform, invite, persuade, speak to a small group, or to give a special occasion speech, you can use these ten steps for giving speeches as a guide and helpful tool to prepare your presentations.

Step 1
Analyze your audience.

Your first step as a speaker is to identify and analyze your audience (Chapter 4). You can do this by asking yourself these questions:

- Who is my audience?
- What are their interests, views, and experiences?
- What is the size of my audience?
- What do they know about me?

Are they required to listen, or do they have a choice? The audience is your reason for speaking, so you must consider them in each step of your speech preparation process.

Step 2
Determine your topic, purpose for speaking & thesis statement.

Your second step is to consider the topic, or the subject, of your speech (Chapter 3). To do this, you can ask yourself these questions:

- Why would my audience be interested in this topic?
- How they feel about this topic?
- What previous experience might they have with that topic?
- How much time do I have?

Your goal with your topic is to stay audience centered and ethical. Remember, you are entering the public dialogue and want your audience to be legitimately interested in your subject. Table S2.1 will help you develop your topic.

Table S2.1

Two Techniques for Selecting a Speech Topic

Develop a topic of public relevance based on your interests, hobbies, and skills	Do you want to know more about something (a political issue, a culturally significant craft or activity, an event in history, even a person, place, or thing)? Are you actively involved in something (an art or skill, a club or group, a blog or message board that is politically relevant)? Are you good at some task or activity that can be linked to the public dialogue (music, electronics, sports, working with animals)?
Develop a topic of public relevance by brainstorming using free association, categories, or technology	Sit with paper and pen or at a computer and look around the room. Pick one item and then list everything that comes to mind, whether it is related or not. Link one of those topics to a political or social issue. Jot down category headings like "events," "natural phenomena," "concepts," "objects," "problems," or "processes," and brainstorm under these categories. Write down whatever comes to mind within each of the categories. Link one of the topics to a political or social issue. Log on to a search engine (Chapter 8) and review the list of subjects displayed on the home page. Link one of these topics to the public dialogue.

After you've considered your topic, determine your purpose, or reason, for speaking (Chapter 3). Table S2.2 lists the most common general purposes for public speaking. When you identify the *general purpose* of a speech, use an infinitive verb (a verb used with *to*, such as *to inform*) to express this purpose.

After you identify your general purpose, state your specific purpose and your thesis statement (Chapter 3).

A *specific purpose* helps you refine your topic and speaking goal so you will be more focused as you move forward with your speech.

> Example:
> To inform my audience of the volunteer opportunities at the American Red Cross

Your *thesis statement* allows you to state, in a single sentence, the content of your speech.

> Example:
> Three important and meaningful ways to volunteer at the American Red Cross are emergency relief, shelter assistance, and public information and outreach.

> Helpful tip:
> The specific purpose states your broader goals. The thesis statement states the main idea of your speech and helps you identify your main points.

Here's how Missy expressed her specific purpose and thesis statement for her speech "The Mysterious World of Hiccups":

> **Topic:**
> Hiccups

> **General purpose:**
> To inform

> **Specific purpose:**
> To inform my audience of the "anatomy" of a hiccup.

> **Thesis statement:**
> Hiccups, or involuntary spasms of the diaphragm, are most often caused by food, beverages, and medicines but can be cured easily with a few simple techniques.

Crafting your specific purpose and a fully developed thesis statement at the beginning of the speechmaking process provides you with a specific and focused plan for your speech.

Step 3
Identify your main points.

The third step in the speechmaking process is to identify your main points (Chapter 8). Your *main points* should reflect your thesis statement, and they are the most important claims, arguments, or concepts in your speech. For example, in Missy's speech about hiccups, she used her specific purpose and thesis statement to develop the following main points:

I. Hiccups are involuntary spasms of the diaphragm that cause the space between the vocal cords to close suddenly and make a peculiar sound.
II. Hiccups are most often caused by the foods we eat, the beverages we drink, and the medicines we ingest.
III. Mild cases of hiccups can be cured with a few simple techniques.

Table S2.2

The Most Common General Purposes for Public Speaking

To inform	Share with an audience an area of expertise or body of knowledge.
To invite	Gain a fuller understanding of all perspectives by establishing a dialogue with your audience to clarify positions, explore issues and ideas, or share beliefs or values.
To persuade	Advocate or encourage an audience to adopt a particular view, position, or plan.
To introduce	Acquaint an audience with someone, something, or some event.
To commemorate	Share with an audience praise, honor, tribute, or recognition for a person, event, idea, or institution.
To accept	Express gratitude, appreciation, and pleasure at being recognized for an award or nomination.
To speak in or as a small group	Lead or facilitate a discussion with a small group of three to twelve people or speak collectively as a small group to inform, invite, persuade, or all three.

She identified these main points by breaking her thesis down into her primary ideas (definition of hiccups, causes of hiccups, cures for hiccups) and asking herself how she could elaborate on those ideas.

Step 4
Gather your supporting materials.

Your fourth step is to gather supporting material for your speech (Chapter 5). As you gather materials from the library, Internet, interviews, and personal experiences, look for the following types of information so that you can develop your ideas ethically and effectively (Chapter 6):

Examples:
Specific instances used to illustrate a concept, experience, issue, or problem.

Helpful hint:
Examples help you clarify a point or argument, specify the nature of something, or support your explanation.

Narratives:
Stories that recount real or fictional events.

Helpful hint:
The characters, events, and settings of narratives can help draw an audience into your speech, and can illustrate, develop, or clarify a claim you are making. Narratives can be very short or longer, and they can be told in segments over the course of the speech or told at one interval. They may even make up most or all of a speech.

Statistics:
Numerical summaries of facts, figures, and research findings.

Helpful hint:
Statistics numerically quantify, estimate, measure, and represent events, issues, positions, actions, beliefs, and the like.

Testimony:
The opinions or observations of others.

Helpful hint:
Testimony, often in the form of quotations, can come from an authority, an average person who has relevant experience with your topic, or from your own experiences.

Definitions:
Statement of the exact meaning of a word or phrase.

Helpful hint:
Definitions help clarify claims and ideas, especially when new terminology is introduced or when a topic is controversial or emotional.

Presentational aids:
Materials or objects that display your ideas so the audience can see or hear your points.

Helpful hint:
Presentational aids include handwritten and computer-generated images, displays, demonstrations, sound recordings, and the like. They are important because they clarify and reinforce your claims and help to stimulate the audience's interest in your speech.

As you gather your materials, remember to keep your audience, topic, purpose, and main points in mind. Doing so will help you gather enough relevant and interesting material to develop your speech fully.

Step 5
Organize your ideas.

You are now ready to organize your speech (Chapter 8). The three most basic components of almost every speech are the introduction, body, and conclusion.

When you begin to organize your ideas, it is helpful to start with the introduction of the speech (Chapter 9). *Introductions* set the stage for a speech and should accomplish four objectives:

- Introduce you and your topic to the audience.
- Capture the audience's attention and get them interested in or curious about your topic.
- Establish your credibility.
- Preview the main ideas of the speech.

In her speech on hiccups, Missy followed these four principles to come up with the following introduction:

I'm here today to share information about one of life's great mysteries. *(introduces topic)* No, I'm not referring to Stonehenge or the Great Pyramids, but to something everyone in this room has experienced: hiccups! Yes, I'm talking about the mysterious world of hiccups, which seem to be a universal occurrence. However, although this mystery is universal, hiccups appear to serve no physiologic function. *(catches interest)*

I recently was blessed with an overwhelming occurrence of the hiccups, and this sparked my interest and curiosity in the subject. *(establishes credibility)* This "blessing" caused me to do some research and investigation, during which I discovered some interesting information about hiccups. *(establishes credibility)* I would like to share this information with you today. Specifically, my focus will be on three aspects of hiccups that I find especially informative. First, I'll explain the anatomy of a hiccup, or what a hiccup is and how it occurs. Second, I'll explain the three most common causes of hiccups, which are food, beverages, and medicine. Third, I'll share some simple techniques for curing those milder cases of hiccups. *(previews main points)*

The body of the speech is the longest part of a speech and contains the information you have gathered to develop your main ideas (Chapter 8). There are many ways to organize your main ideas, but the most common *organizational patterns* are chronological, spatial, causal, problem-and-solution, and topical. There are two basic rules you can follow to organize your ideas:

Rule 1:
Identify your main ideas and arrange them according to an appropriate organizational pattern. To do this, ask yourself:

- Which ideas must be discussed before others?
- Which ideas will most interest the audience?

Helpful hint:
Remember, your main ideas should follow a systematic, logical, or natural progression that supports and develops your thesis statement.

Rule 2:
Link your ideas together with words and phrases called *connectives*.

- Connectives help you transition from one point to another.
    Example: "The *second way* you can volunteer with the American Red Cross is assisting those who stay at Red Cross shelters."

- Connectives introduce new points and preview or summarize ideas
    Example: "*However*, these two options for volunteering—emergency rescue assistance and shelter care—could not happen without the *third volunteer option*: public information and outreach."

- Connectives call attention to particularly important ideas
    Example: "The *most important* thing about emergency rescue, however, is that only those fully and properly trained can provide this service to the Red Cross."

The conclusion of a speech brings closure to your ideas and it is often the shortest part of your speech (Chapter 9). In your *conclusion*, you want to accomplish two things:

- Signal to the audience that you are finished.
- Summarize or restate your thesis statement.

Let's take a look at the conclusion to Missy's speech:

So, now you see that there is more to learn about the mysterious world of hiccups than you might have imagined. In this speech, I've shared some very enlightening information about what a hiccup is, the reasons hiccups occur, and the process of curing them. *(signals end of speech)* Now, if someday you find yourself in the mysterious world of hiccups, you'll be well prepared to fight back with several of the remedies you've heard about today. *(summarizes thesis)*

Step 6
Create visual and other presentational aids.
In step six you create your visual or other presentational aids (Chapter 12). There are five reasons to use presentational aids:

1. To help gain and maintain audience attention.
2. To help audiences recall information.
3. To help explain and clarify ideas.
4. To help increase your persuasiveness and enhance your credibility.
5. To help reduce your nervousness.

Presentational aids can take many shapes and forms, including images or video clips from the Internet, audio clips, lists of ideas, diagrams, objects or models, photographs or drawings, and charts or maps. Here are some tips to help you decide what kind of presentational aid to use for different types of information:

- For a group or series of names, key features, or procedures, use a **list**.
- For steps in a process, use a **flow chart, model, or Internet download**.
- For the structure of a group, use an **organizational chart**.

- For comparison of quantities at a specific time, use a **bar graph**.
- For trends over time, use a **line graph**.
- For relative sizes of parts of a whole, use a **pie graph**.
- For comparison of quantities, use a **picture graph or model**.
- For a thing or process unfamiliar to your audience, use **an Internet clip, a model, a drawing or a photograph**.
- For the physical layout of a place, use a **map**.

Step 7
Outline your speech.

Preparing your outline is the seventh step of the speechmaking process (Chapter 8). Outlines help you organize your ideas, discover missing points or arguments, and determine whether the speech is balanced and within your time limits.

When you are developing your speech, you create what is called a *preparation outline*, which includes the following elements:

- Speech title.
- Specific purpose.
- Thesis statement.
- Introduction.
- Main points and subpoints.
- Connectives.
- Conclusion.
- Source citations listed in a Works Cited section.

In addition, your preparation outline has the following characteristics:

- Complete sentences.
- Clear labels for introduction, body, connectives, and conclusion.
- Consistent pattern of symbols and indentation (roman numerals for main points, capital letters for subpoints, Arabic numerals for sub-subpoints, and lowercase letters for sub-sub-subpoints: I, A, 1, a).
- At least two supporting subpoints under a main points.
- Approximately equal development of points and subpoints.

See Chapter 8, pages 175–178, for an example of an effective preparation outline.

Speakers also often create a second, shorter outline called a *speaking outline* to use when they deliver their speeches. A speaking outline (or *note cards*) is a condensed version of the preparation outline and includes the following:

- Keywords and phrases only—not the full text of your speech.
- Clear, legible, and large font or handwriting.
- Cues for delivery, such as "make eye contact," "pause," "slow down," "look up," "show visual aid."
- Correct pronunciation of words or names you stumble on.
- One-or-two-word prompts for stories, examples, and concepts you tend to forget.

See Chapter 8, pages 180–183, for an example of note cards and a speaking outline.

Step 8
Consider language and figures of speech.

In step eight, you consider how to use language effectively, appropriately, and ethically (Chapters 2 and 10). Because you will probably use different styles of speaking for different audiences and different speaking goals, ask yourself the following questions as you select the language style for your speech:

- What types of vocabulary, imagery, and rhythms best match my audience, topic, and goals?
- Have I included vocabulary, imagery, and rhythms that draw my audience into my speech and help me express my ideas vividly and appropriately?
- Do any of the vocabulary, imagery, and rhythms have the potential to offend, hurt, or alienate my listeners?
- What vocabulary needs to be defined, explained, or illustrated by examples?
- Am I speaking at a level appropriate for my audience?
- Have I omitted slang, euphemisms, or other unfamiliar or inappropriate words and phrases?
- Have I paraphrased confusing or highly technical terms and phrases?

Step 9
Practice your speech.

In step nine you practice your speech before you deliver it (Chapter 11). So that you'll be very familiar with your speech before you give it in front of an audience, follow these steps:

- Begin your practice sessions alone. *At first, practice only segments of your speech.* For example, try getting the introduction down, then the body, and then the conclusion. You may even find it useful to break the body down by practicing each main point separately.

- *Make notes on your speaking outline* to help you remember your material and delivery techniques. If you plan to use presentational aids, practice using them until you can manage them easily as you speak.
- Once you've practiced each segment of your speech individually, *practice the speech as a whole*. Try practicing in front of a mirror. Go back and *rehearse the places where you stumble* or get lost. Make sure your presentational aids work as planned.
- Before you give your speech, *practice it three to six times from start to finish*, depending on the level of spontaneity or polish you want in your speech.
- Finally, *practice your speech in front of an audience*. Rehearsing your speech in front of your family or friends is a great way to gain some practice and get feedback on your presentation.

Step 10
Give your speech.
The final step in the speechmaking process is a reminder to relax and give your speech with confidence. Here are some guidelines for managing your voice, gestures, posture, facial expressions, and presentational aids as you give your speech:

- Visualize a successful speech before you deliver it.
- Know your introduction well so you can begin your speech feeling confident.
- Use your notes as prompts and as a source of security.
- Make eye contact with audience members during the speech.
- Remember to breathe, gesture naturally, and pause as needed during your speech.

Final hints
If you take the time to select a relevant topic, gather your supporting materials, and organize your speech, you can minimize some of the nervousness that most people feel with public speaking. The more you practice, the more confident you will feel on your speaking day. And if you listen respectfully to the speeches of your classmates, they probably will listen respectfully to you (Chapter 2).

Good luck, and have fun!

Why Speak in Public?

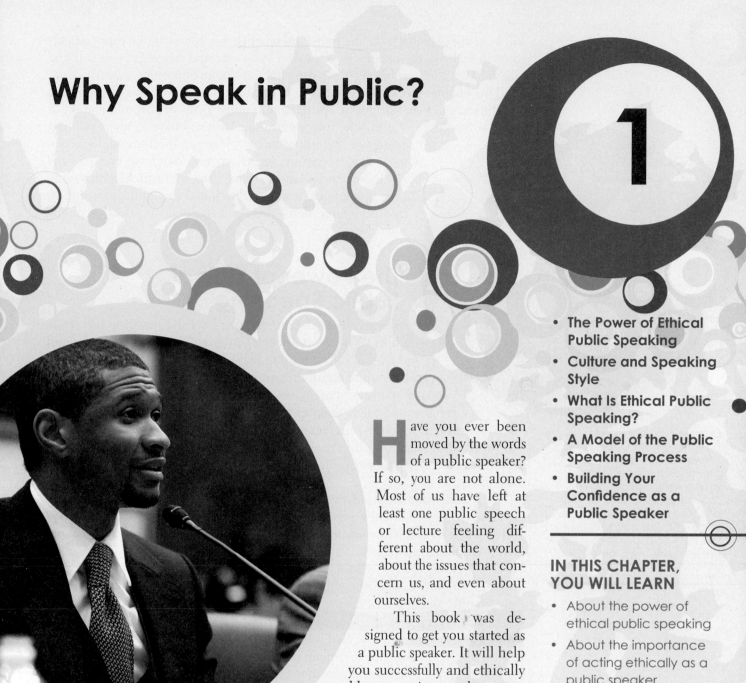

1

- **The Power of Ethical Public Speaking**
- **Culture and Speaking Style**
- **What Is Ethical Public Speaking?**
- **A Model of the Public Speaking Process**
- **Building Your Confidence as a Public Speaker**

Rafael Suanes/MCT/Landov

Have you ever been moved by the words of a public speaker? If so, you are not alone. Most of us have left at least one public speech or lecture feeling different about the world, about the issues that concern us, and even about ourselves.

This book was designed to get you started as a public speaker. It will help you successfully and ethically add your voice to the many public conversations and debates of our democratic society. In these pages, you will learn about a range of settings where public speaking occurs and a variety of reasons for speaking. The chapters that follow break down the components of the public speaking process into discrete steps, which you will follow in crafting your own speeches. As you gain confidence in using these techniques, you can adapt them to your real-life speaking experiences at work and in your community. You'll find that you will speak in any number of instances to provide instructions, explain procedures, share information, encourage or influence decisions, and more.

Public speaking is a learned skill that gets more rewarding as our experience with it grows. No one was born a public speaker. Every speaker had to learn how to give effective speeches—even renowned speakers such as Abraham Lincoln, Martin Luther King Jr., U.S. Secretary of State Hillary Clinton, and the many others you

IN THIS CHAPTER, YOU WILL LEARN

- About the power of ethical public speaking
- About the importance of acting ethically as a public speaker
- About the influence of culture on speaking styles
- What makes public speaking different from other kinds of communication
- The most common reasons for nervousness associated with giving a speech
- Six techniques for reducing speech-related nervousness

will read about in this text. The more you practice this new skill, the more quickly you will feel you are a competent speaker. With care and diligence, you will find that you can add your own voice to the public dialogue in positive ways.

This chapter introduces you to the power of ethical public speaking and the differences between public speaking and other forms of communication. It invites you to consider the opportunities you will have to speak publicly and to recognize the importance of learning the basic skills necessary to do so successfully and effectively. When we consider the power these actions have to shape lives, we begin to gain a sense of the challenges, responsibilities, and thoughtfulness that go into designing, delivering, and listening to effective public speeches.

Even skilled speakers like President Barack Obama had to learn how to give effective speeches. Here the President speaks at his inauguration on January 20, 2009, an event that affected the entire nation. Even if you didn't hear his speech, do you think you have been influenced by it? In what way?

The Power of Ethical Public Speaking

When you speak publicly, you have the power to influence others. With every speech you give, you make choices about the kind of influence you will have. All of us are familiar with hostile public arguments and debates. We are used to politicians taking partisan stances on issues and "doing battle" with their "opponents." Such debates turn social policy questions into "wars," as groups position themselves on either side of the "dispute," offering "*the* solution" while negating the views of the "other" side. We even watch, read about, or listen to people engaging in hostile or threatening exchanges over their differences.

Angry opposition may be a common style of public speaking today, but there are other ways to influence people when you give speeches. As you've watched and listened to combative exchanges, you may have heard some call for more civility in public exchanges. The word *civility* comes from a root word meaning "to be a member of a household." In ancient Greece, *civility* referred to displays of temperance, justice, wisdom, and courage. Over time, the definition has changed only slightly, and in public speaking, **civility** has come to mean care and concern for others, the thoughtful use of words and language, and the flexibility to see the many sides of an issue. To be civil is to listen to the ideas and reasons of others and to give "the world a chance to explain itself."[1] To be uncivil is to show little respect for others, to be unwilling to consider their ideas and reasons, and to be unwilling to take responsibility for the effect of one's words, language, and behaviors on others.

Deborah Tannen, author of *The Argument Culture: Moving from Debate to Dialogue*, offers one of the most compelling descriptions of many people's views about the incivility that characterizes much of our present-day public debates.[2] She explains that in an argument culture, individuals tend to approach people and situations with a me-against-you frame of mind. Since they see each issue, event, or situation as a contest, they begin with the idea that the best way to discuss any topic is by portraying it through opposing positions, rallying to one side of the cause, and attacking the other side. Although conflict and disagreement are familiar parts of most people's lives, the seemingly automatic nature of this response is what makes the argument culture so common today.

Good to Know!

civility: Care and concern for others, the thoughtful use of words and language, and the flexibility to see the many sides of an issue.

Tannen and others concerned with the argument culture recognize that there are times when strong opposition and verbal attack are called for.[3] Nevertheless, this form of communication isn't the only way people can discuss issues, offer solutions, or resolve differences. We can view public speaking not only as engaging in a public argument but also as participating in a public dialogue.

A dialogue is a civil exchange of ideas and opinions between two people or a small group of people. The **public dialogue** is the *ethical* and *civil* exchange of ideas and opinions among communities about topics that affect the public. To participate in the public dialogue is to offer perspectives, share facts, raise questions, and engage others publicly in stimulating discussions.[4] When we enter the public dialogue, we become *active and ethical citizens* who participate in our nation's democratic process and consider the needs of others in our communities as well as our own needs. The ethical dimension of our participation in the

Public Speaking and Service Learning: Engaging Community

As part of his public speaking class at Colorado State University, Connor Mcinerney was required to do a service learning project. He chose to do his project at W.O.L.F. (Wolves Offered Love & Friendship), a nonprofit sanctuary dedicated to saving homeless wolves and wolf-dogs. In this account of his service learning experience, he explains how he believes service work is a valuable way to enter the public dialogue because it stimulates empathy and provides motivation for people to speak for a cause.

The W.O.L.F. sanctuary not only helps animals that have been abandoned but also helps the people who work and volunteer, thereby giving them a sense of connection to the broader public dialogue. Making a lasting difference in this world seems like a nearly impossible task. But my service has shown me that one voice, one helping hand, does make a difference. With the current situation our country is in, I feel W.O.L.F. is an organization that offers a great starting place for people who want to make such a difference. Working with the wolves and being outdoors promoted some soul-searching and thinking that would not likely have happened to me in any other situation—it caused me to think about myself and my views in more complex ways. Through this time of personal reflection, I have dedicated myself to spending more time speaking on behalf of these animals who cannot speak for themselves. Because humans have put Colorado wolves into their current situation, I feel that it is partly my responsibility to better their chance of survival and speak on behalf of their right to live in this area. My service to W.O.L.F. motivates me to be informed and to speak proudly on behalf of their cause.

"MY SERVICE TO W.O.L.F MOTIVATES ME TO PROUDLY SPEAK ON BEHALF OF THEIR CAUSE."

Tips for Incorporating Service Learning into Public Speaking

- Service learning can help you find an issue that concerns, motivates, or angers you. You can use that energy to fuel your inspiration to speak out about the issue. You can also use it as motivation to complete all steps of the speechmaking process, such as the research process.
- By getting involved in your community, you can be part of positive change. Your speeches in class can help you begin that process.
- Realize that delivering your speech is a concrete way of getting involved in your community—through your speech, you're educating and motivating yourself and your audience.

Good to Know!

public dialogue: Ethical and civil exchange of ideas and opinions among communities about topics that affect the public.

Many reform efforts proposed by the U.S. government have been a matter of public debate recently, such as proposals to reform health care, immigration laws, and the financial system. These complex, far-reaching efforts have sparked passionate and sometimes contentious dialogue. How difficult do you think it would be to respond civilly to an audience that doesn't seem open to your topic? What could you do to make your audience receptive to your views?

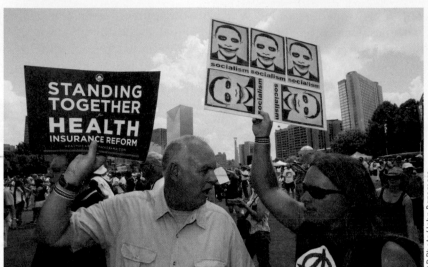

AP Photo/John Bazemore

Practicing the Public Dialogue

1.1

Choose a Civil, Ethical Approach to Public Speaking

Make a list of five topics you might use for a speech in this class. How does each topic contribute to the public dialogue? Now identify how you might discuss each of these topics in a civil, ethical way. For example, would it be more ethical to approach one of your topics from a two-sided perspective and another from a multisided perspective? Why do you think so? Save these as possible topics for your in-class speeches.

Online Resources

CourseMate To learn more about what the public dialogue is and how your participation in this unending conversation can help shape community, access **Web Connect 1.1: Public Dialogue Consortium** online via your CourseMate for *Invitation to Public Speaking.* The Public Dialogue Consortium believes that public communication powerfully influences the world we live in and can positively affect the lives of everyday people.

public dialogue becomes apparent when we participate in the global dialogue, speaking about issues that affect the entire world, such as human rights, hunger, access to medical care, and the environment. To be an **ethical public speaker**, you must consider the moral impact of your ideas and arguments on others when you enter the public dialogue.

Giving a speech is a natural way to enter the public dialogue because it gives us a chance to clearly state our own perspectives and to hear other people's perspectives. In this sense, giving a speech can be like participating in an ongoing conversation. Kenneth Burke describes this conversation as follows:

> Imagine that you enter a parlor. You come late. When you arrive, others have long preceded you, and they are engaged in a lively discussion, a discussion too passionate for them to pause and tell you exactly what it is about. In fact, the discussion had already begun long before any of them got there, so that no one present is qualified to retrace for you all the steps that had gone before. You listen for a while, until you decide that you have caught the tenor of the argument; then you put in your oar. Someone answers; you answer them; another perspective is shared. The hour grows late; you must depart. And you do depart, with the discussion still vigorously in progress.[5]

Throughout this book, you will encounter the power of public speaking. As you engage with this power yourself, you should always strive to give speeches that help clarify issues and stimulate thinking even as you inform, persuade, or invite others to consider a perspective.

Good to Know!

ethical public speaker: Speaker who considers the moral impact of his or her ideas and arguments on others when involved in the public dialogue.

Although you may have strong views on issues, a civil and ethical approach to public speaking often is the most powerful way to present those views.

Culture and Speaking Style

Culture has a powerful effect on communication. Whether the culture derives from our nationality, race, ethnicity, religion, work environment, peer group, or even gender, we can't ignore its effect on communication. When we give or listen to speeches, we bring our cultural styles with us. Consider a few examples of ways that culture influences public speaking:

> The traditional West African storyteller, called the *griot*, weaves a story with song and dance, and enlivens a tale with all sorts of sound effects. He or she changes the pitch to suit the characters and the action and adds all kinds of popping, clicking, clapping sounds to dramatize the events of the story. The members of the audience respond like a chorus. They interpose comments at convenient intervals, add their own sound effects, and sing the song of the tale along with the griot.[6]

> To this day, poets are held in the highest esteem in Arab societies. The Arab poet performs important political and social functions. In battle, the poet's tongue is as effective as is the bravery of the Arab people. In peace, the poet might prove a menace to public order with fiery harangues. Poems can arouse a tribe to action in the same manner as the tirade of a demagogue in a modern political campaign. Poetry frequently functions in a political context to motivate action, and, as such, it is accorded as much weight as a scholarly dissertation.[7]

> The late Texas governor Ann Richards's speaking style [was] dominated by the use of inductive and experiential reasoning, folk wisdom, and concrete examples and stories as the basis for political values and judgments. A favorite line she use[d] [was], "Tell it so my Mama in Waco can understand it." Her accessible style…encourage[d] audience participation and reduce[d] distance between the speaker and audience.[8]

These examples come from cultures that may be different from your own or may be familiar to you. What they suggest is that the ways we approach a public speech often reflect our cultural backgrounds.

Research on cultural styles of communication helps explain some of these differences. In general, many white males, for example, are comfortable with the direct, competitive style of interaction found in public presentations. Because white males have held more public offices and positions of power in the United States historically, it makes sense that their preferred style of communication has become the norm for public speaking. However, there are many other communication styles. African American men, for example, tend to be more comfortable with a complex style of speaking that may be competitive but is more subtle, indirect or exaggerated, intense, poetic, rhythmic, and lyrical. Hispanic or Latino males usually reject the competitive style, favoring a more elegant, expressive, or intense narrative form of public communication. Similarly, Arab American males tend to use an emotional and poetic style (poets often respond to and interpret political events in Middle Eastern countries and rely on rhythm and the sounds of words to express their ideas).[9]

Other research suggests that in most Native American cultures, framing an issue from a two-sided perspective is rare. Many Native American cultures welcome multiple perspectives and discourage competition, preferring cooperation when discussing important matters. In addition, a more circular and flexible style

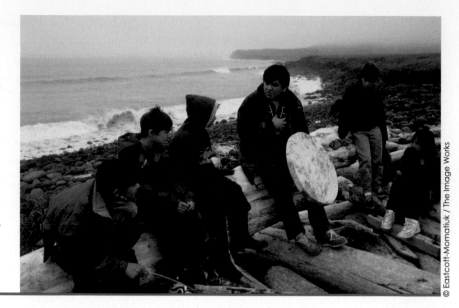

The elder is a well-respected storyteller in Native American culture. Is storytelling a style of speaking familiar to you? What style, or combinations of styles, of speaking do you think you'd like to use in a speech?

© Eastcott-Momatiuk / The Image Works

of presentation is common, as is the use of stories, humor, and teasing to explain ideas or teach beliefs. In many Native American cultures as well as some Asian and Asian American cultures, direct eye contact is a sign of disrespect, and publicly proving that someone else is wrong is considered a serious insult.[10]

The research on styles of speaking specific to women is slight. We do know that, in general, African American and Hispanic or Latina women may use a style of speech similar to the lyrical, rhythmic, or poetic style used by the males of their cultures, but it may be more collaborative than adversarial. White and Asian American women seem to share this sense of comfort with collaboration but do not often incorporate the poetic or lyrical forms into their speaking. In general, we also know that women from many different cultural backgrounds tend to incorporate a personal tone and use personal experiences and anecdotes alongside concrete examples as evidence; they establish a connection and common ground with their audiences in their public speeches.[11]

In reading about these differences, you may have recognized your own culture's influence on your style of communication. These differences suggest there is more than one way to approach public speaking. Public speaking can occur when we argue with others or take sides on an issue. It can take place when we connect, collaborate, and share stories or humor with our audience. It also happens when speakers use various styles of language or delivery. To enter the public dialogue is to recognize the many different styles of speaking and to use those that fit you and the audience best.

What Is Ethical Public Speaking?

Every day, we are bombarded with information from computers, televisions, radios, newspapers, magazines, movies, billboards, and logos on clothing and cars. Bosses, teachers, friends, and family also fill our days with words, sounds, symbols, and conversations. Researchers estimate that we spend as much as 70 to 80 percent of the day listening to others communicate. In fact, so much communication crosses our paths every day that this era has been called the *information age*. Where does public speaking fit into this environment? Consider the different sources of communication in which we can engage:

Intrapersonal communication: Communication with ourselves via the dialogue that goes on in our heads.

Interpersonal communication: Communication with other people that ranges from the highly personal to the highly impersonal. Interpersonal communication allows us to establish, maintain, and disengage from relationships with other people.

Group communication: Communication among members of a team or a collective about topics such as goals, strategies, and conflict.

Mass communication: Communication generated by media organizations that is designed to reach large audiences. This type of communication is transmitted via television, the Internet, radio, print media, and even the entertainment industry.

Public communication: Communication in which one person gives a speech to other people, most often in a public setting. This speech has predetermined goals and is about a topic that affects a larger community. In public speaking, one person—called the _speaker_—is responsible for selecting a topic and focus for the speech, organizing his or her ideas, and practicing his or her delivery. The speaker is also responsible for acting ethically and for responding to audience questions and feedback.

Jon Parker Lee / Alamy

Tim Hall/Digital Vision/Getty Images

Unlike casual conversations with friends and family, public speaking contains a structure and purpose that add a level of responsibility not found in most other everyday interactions. Similarly, the ability of the audience to respond directly sets public speaking apart from mass communication. And unlike private conversations with oneself or with friends, public speaking is directed at specific groups of people and is designed to be shared with those outside the immediate audience.

From these definitions, we can see that public speaking is unique because the responsibility for the organization, delivery, and flow of communication falls mostly on one person. However, if we think of public speaking as participating ethically in the public dialogue, additional differences between public speaking and other forms of communication emerge.

Public Speaking Creates a Community

We often think of public speaking as an individual act. We imagine one person standing in front of a group of people presenting information to them. We forget that public speaking occurs because individuals belong to a community and share social relationships. We speak publicly because we recognize this connection. When we share ideas and information and consider questions and possibilities with others, we

How does the communication in the photo on the top differ from that in the photo on the bottom? How does the communication in both of these photos differ from intrapersonal, group, or mass communication?

Good to Know!

intrapersonal communication: Communication with ourselves via the dialogue that goes on in our heads.
interpersonal communication: Communication with other people that ranges from the highly personal to the highly impersonal.
group communication: Communication among members of a team or a collective about topics such as goals, strategies, and conflict.
mass communication: Communication generated by media organizations that is designed to reach large audiences.
public communication: Communication in which one person gives a speech to other people, most often in a public setting.

are creating a civil community. We recognize we are "members of a household," and even if we disagree with members of that household (our audience), we acknowledge that we are connected to them. We create a community when we speak because we are talking about topics that affect us and each member of the audience.

At times, we may forget our connections to others and think our interests and needs are not important to society. However, we are members of a larger social community, and when we make our voices heard, we recognize the need to stimulate the public dialogue, to answer the claims or statements of those who have spoken before us, and to offer our audience ideas for consideration and discussion.

Public Speaking Is Audience Centered

Public speaking also stands apart from other forms of communication because speakers recognize the central role of their audience. Speakers speak to audiences, and without them, we are not engaged in public speaking. Moreover, in public speaking, the makeup of the audience directly influences the speaker's message. Consider the following scenarios:

> Su Lin's older brother was recently almost hit by a car while riding his bike across town. Upset by motorists' lack of awareness, Su Lin wants to speak out at the next city council meeting to argue for motorist education programs.

> Gretchen's brother recently had a near miss while riding his bike across town. Upset by motorists' lack of awareness, Gretchen has decided to give a speech on motorist safety in her public speaking course.

> Arturo rides his bicycle to work every day and has persuaded many of his coworkers to do the same. He recently had a near miss with a distracted motorist, and he wants to speak to his coworkers about what they can do to stay safe while riding to work.

The audiences in these three scenarios dictate the choices each speaker will make. Each of the audiences—the city council, the public speaking class, and the other cyclists—has different positions, beliefs, values, and needs regarding cyclist safety. City councils have financial limitations, time constraints, and voter preferences that Su Lin will need to consider. Gretchen's classmates, unless they are cyclists, may not readily see the relevance of her concerns and may also resent any efforts to curb their driving habits. At Arturo's workplace, the other cyclists probably also worry about their own vulnerability and wonder whether riding to work is really worth the risk.

These three examples suggest that public speaking is distinctly **audience centered**, or considerate of the positions, beliefs, values, and needs of an audience. To be audience centered is to keep your audience in your mind during every step of the public speaking process, including your research, organization, and presentation.

Public speaking is also audience centered because speakers "listen" to their audiences during speeches. They monitor audience *feedback*, the verbal and nonverbal signals an audience gives a speaker. Audience feedback often indicates whether listeners understand, have interest in, and are receptive to the speaker's ideas. This feedback assists the speaker in many ways. It helps the speaker know when to slow down, explain something more carefully, or even tell the audience

Good to Know!

audience centered: Considerate of the positions, beliefs, values, and needs of an audience.

that she or he will return to an issue in a question-and-answer session at the close of the speech. Audience feedback assists the speaker in creating a connection of mutual respect with the audience.

Public speaking differs from other forms of communication not only because it is done in front of an audience but also because of the ways the speaker relates the ideas of the speech to the audience.

Public Speaking Encourages Ethical Dialogue

A final difference between public speaking and other kinds of communication is that public speaking sets the stage for the ongoing conversation Kenneth Burke described earlier in this chapter. For this conversation to be meaningful, the speaker must present ideas ethically, with fairness and honesty. This ethical aspect of speaking means that the speaker is responsible for framing the conversation, or dialogue, honestly and for laying the foundation for future discussions. Public speaking encourages ethical dialogue because speakers want the people who hear the speech to engage others—and perhaps even the speaker—in a conversation about the topic or issue after the speech is given. Public speaking encourages this ethical dialogue because the speaker is interested in presenting ideas fairly, in discussing issues openly, and in hearing more about them from the audience.

Ethical Moment

CAN BREAKING THE LAW BE ETHICAL?

On April 12, 1963, civil rights activist Martin Luther King Jr. and fellow activists were arrested for intentionally disobeying an Alabama Supreme Court injunction against public demonstrations. While in solitary confinement that day, King read a letter published in the *Birmingham News* by eight white Birmingham clergymen who asked the activists to work through the courts for the change they sought rather than protesting in the streets. In their letter, the clergy accused King and other civil rights advocates of "failing to negotiate," "using extreme measures," and "choosing an inappropriate time to act."

King responded with his "Letter from Birmingham Jail," which explained his unsuccessful attempts to negotiate with unwilling merchants and economic leaders of Birmingham, his conviction that "one has a moral responsibility to disobey unjust laws," and his unwillingness to wait any longer for freedom. In his letter, King made the point that "Injustice anywhere is a threat to justice everywhere" and went on to suggest that "We are caught in an inescapable network of mutuality,

AP Images

tied in a single garment of destiny. Whatever affects one directly affects all indirectly."

What Do You Think?

1. Do you think King acted ethically when he broke the law by disobeying the Alabama Supreme Court injunction? Why or why not?

2. Do you think the Birmingham clergy were correct in labeling King and other civil rights advocates as extremist and unwilling to negotiate? Why or why not?

3. Do you think King was correct when he wrote that we are "caught in an inescapable network of mutuality"? What might be the ethical implications of this claim? How does this idea relate to the discussions about public dialogue in this chapter?

A Model of the Public Speaking Process

Consider the following components of the public speaking process as it has been discussed thus far (Figure 1.1 can help you visualize this process):

Practicing the Public Dialogue

1.2

Consider the Unique Aspects of Public Speaking

Choose one of the five speech topics you identified in Practicing the Public Dialogue Activity 1.1. Think about giving a speech on this topic in class.

- What are two ways your speech could create a sense of community with your audience?
- What are two ways you could stay audience centered while speaking about this topic?
- What are two ways your cultural background might affect your speaking style when giving a speech about this topic?
- What are two ways your speech could encourage dialogue with your in-class audience or with your campus community?

Save this topic and analysis to possibly use for an in-class speech later in the course.

Online Resources

CourseMate You can learn more about how to analyze an audience and stay audience centered by accessing **Web Connect 1.2: Thinking about Your Audience** online via your CourseMate for *Invitation to Public Speaking*. In addition, watch a video clip of a student speaker, Mike Piel, as he makes a relevant connection with his audience and remains audience centered. As you watch Mike speak, consider the strategies he uses to communicate the importance of his topic to his audience. What does Mike say to connect his topic to his audience?

Speaker: A person who stimulates public dialogue by delivering an oral message. The speaker researches the topic of the speech, organizes the material that results from the research, presents the message, and manages discussion after or, in some cases, during a speech. Throughout this process, the speaker is civil, considering the needs and characteristics of the audience.

Message: The information conveyed by the speaker to the audience. Messages can be verbal or nonverbal. For example, a speaker giving a speech about his recent experiences in the military would use words to describe those experiences and facial expressions and gestures to convey the emotional aspects of those experiences. Most of our messages are intentional, but sometimes, we send an unintentional message, such as an unplanned pause, a sigh, or a frown that conveys an idea or a feeling we had not planned to communicate. When we speak, we convey messages by **encoding**, or translating ideas and feelings into words, sounds, and gestures. When we receive the message, we **decode** it, or translate words, sounds, and gestures into ideas and feelings in an attempt to understand the message.

Audience: The complex and varied group of people the speaker addresses. Because of the ethical and audience-centered nature of public speaking, the speaker must consider the positions, beliefs, values, and needs of the audience throughout the design and delivery of a speech.

Channel: The means by which the message is conveyed. A message can be conveyed through spoken words, vocal tone and gestures, and visual aids. The channel might include technology like a microphone, a CD-ROM, a video, or PowerPoint slides.

Noise: Anything that interferes with understanding the message being communicated. Noise may be external or internal. External noise, interference outside the speaker or audience, might be construction work going on outside the classroom window or a microphone that doesn't work in a large lecture hall. Internal noise, interference within the speaker or audience, might be a headache that affects one's concentration or cultural differences that make it hard to understand a message.

Good to Know!

speaker: Person who stimulates public dialogue by delivering an oral message. **message:** Information conveyed by the speaker to the audience. **encoding:** Translating ideas and feelings into words, sounds, and gestures. **decoding:** Translating words, sounds, and gestures into ideas and feelings in an attempt to understand the message. **audience:** Complex and varied group of people the speaker addresses. **channel:** Means by which the message is conveyed. **noise:** Anything that interferes with understanding the message being communicated.

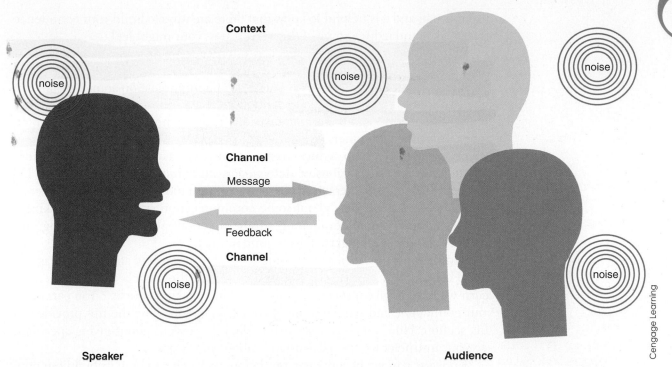

Context

Channel

Message

Feedback

Channel

Speaker

Audience

Feedback: The verbal and nonverbal signals the audience gives the speaker. Feedback from an audience indicates to the speaker the need to slow down, clarify, respond to questions, alter delivery, and the like.

Context: The environment or situation in which a speech occurs. The context includes components such as the time of day and the place the speech is given, the audience's expectations about the speech, and the traditions associated with a speech. For example, a commemorative speech would likely be given in a formal setting, such as during a banquet or at a wedding reception. A speech given as part of a service learning assignment might be given in a very informal setting, such as in your classroom or at the agency itself.

Although we describe each of these components separately, they are interconnected. Notice that the speaker is both a "speaker" and a "listener," sending a message but also attending to feedback from the audience. The audience members also have a key role, reducing external and internal noise whenever possible and listening to the message so they can contribute to the discussion that may occur when the speech is finished.

Building Your Confidence as a Public Speaker

Even the most experienced speakers get a little nervous before they give a speech, so it is normal that you might feel a bit nervous, too. One reason we become anxious is that we care about our topic and our performance. We want to perform well and deliver a successful speech. Another reason we might be nervous before a speech is because we fear the unknown; we anticipate the speaking event and imagine that it will be stressful long before we actually give the speech. These are

Figure 1.1

A model of the public speaking process

Good to Know!

feedback: Verbal and nonverbal signals an audience gives a speaker. **context:** Environment or situation in which a speech occurs.

also normal, and it is helpful to know that there are ways to build your confidence as a speaker and reduce some of the nervousness your might feel.

Our nervousness before a speech is often called **communication apprehension**, "the level of fear or anxiety associated with either real or anticipated communication with another person or persons."[12] Communication apprehension can take two forms. People who are apprehensive about communicating with others in any situation are said to have **trait anxiety**. People who are apprehensive about communicating with others in a particular situation are said to have **state, or situational, anxiety**. To help reduce your nervousness, take a moment to consider whether you are trait anxious or state anxious in communication situations. Do you fear all kinds of interactions or only certain kinds? Most of us experience some level of state anxiety about some communication events, such as asking a boss for a raise, verbally evaluating another's performance, or introducing ourselves to a group of strangers. This is quite normal.

Most people also experience some level of state anxiety about public speaking. This is called *public speaking anxiety (PSA)*, the anxiety we feel when we learn we have to give a speech or take a public speaking course.[13] You can build your confidence and reduce some of your PSA by following the tips provided in this section. However, if you are extraordinarily nervous about giving speeches, see your instructor for special assistance about your fears.

Knowing why we become nervous before a speech can help us build our confidence. Research suggests that most people's state anxiety about public speaking exists for six reasons. Many people are state anxious because public speaking is

- *Novel*: We don't do it regularly and lack necessary skills as a result.
- *Done in formal settings*: Our behaviors when giving a speech are more prescribed and rigid than usual.
- *Often done from a subordinate position*: An instructor or boss sets the rules for giving a speech, and the audience acts as a critic.
- *Conspicuous or obvious*: The speaker stands apart from the audience.
- *Done in front of an audience that is unfamiliar*: Most people are more comfortable talking with people they know. Also, we fear that audiences won't be interested in what we have to say.
- A *unique situation in which the degree of attention paid to the speaker is quite noticeable*: Audience members either stare at us or ignore us, so we become unusually self-focused.[14]

It helps to know that research also suggests people are usually nervous only about specific aspects of public speaking. When people ranked what they fear while giving a speech, here's what they said:[15]

Trembling or shaking	80%
Mind going blank	74%
Doing or saying something embarrassing	64%
Being unable to continue talking	63%
Not making sense	59%
Sounding foolish	59%

Good to Know!

communication apprehension: Level of fear or anxiety associated with either real or anticipated communication with another person or persons. **trait anxiety:** Apprehension about communicating with others in any situation. **state or situational anxiety:** Apprehension about communicating with others in a particular situation.

When we combine this research, a pattern emerges that helps us understand our nervousness. Because public speaking is novel and usually done in a formal setting, our nervousness can make us shake or tremble. Then, when the spotlight is on us as the speaker, we fear our minds will go blank, we will say something embarrassing, or we will be unable to continue talking. Finally, we often don't know our audience well, which can make us fear evaluation, not making sense, or sounding foolish more than we ordinarily would. As you can see, some of our nervousness is legitimate. Even so, we can get past it and build our confidence as speakers.

The suggestions offered here should help you build your confidence and turn your nervous energy to your advantage.

Public Speaking and Service Learning: Engaging Community

Samantha Kroll, a public speaking student at Colorado State University, did her service learning project at KRFC 88.9 FM, a local community radio station. She was nervous about the experience prior to starting at the station. But after some brief training, she found the service enjoyable and exciting because of her freedom to choose topics that interested her.

A t first, I completely dreaded working a whole fifteen hours of community service throughout the duration of the semester. But after I started working at the station, two hours a week was really not that big a commitment—plus it was fun!

I chose to work with a radio station because I thought it would improve my public speaking skills and get me out of my comfort zone. When I first came to the studio, I did not know exactly what to expect. I thought they would have tasks that needed to be done and they would assign them to us, maybe give us a script they had already written and approved for us to read. That was probably the main reason I was nervous—fear of the unknown. I was surprised to realize how much freedom they gave me! I had the freedom to report on topics that I was personally interested in, and they expected me to write my own scripts. On my first day, I was trained for a few hours, and then they put me to work. That first day, I wrote my own script by myself and recorded it. My 30-second segment was aired that following

"THAT WAS PROBABLY THE MAIN REASON I WAS NERVOUS— FEAR OF THE UNKNOWN."

Wednesday. The best part about it was that my anxiety lessened for two reasons: I asked the experienced volunteers for advice, and I felt empowered because I was speaking my own words.

Overall, my experience at the radio station has been so much fun—I have learned important skills and stepped out of my comfort zone. My initial apprehension has turned into a pleasurable challenge. I still get nervous when I go on the air, just as I do when I am giving a speech in class. But I now know that with a bit of guidance and a whole lot of guts, public speaking is not that frightening, especially if I am speaking about something that I care about. I wouldn't be surprised if I spent over 15 hours volunteering at the radio station this semester.

Tips for Incorporating Service Learning into Public Speaking

- Everyone gets nervous speaking, and it helps to realize that being fearful of public speaking is completely normal.
- As you volunteer, ask successful speakers (such as DJs, pastors, teachers, parents) for their tips on how to reduce nervousness. You might be surprised at how down-to-earth and helpful their answers are.
- Take time to fine-tune your script or speech, and be proud to perform your own work.

Do Your Research

One way to build your confidence before giving a speech is to prepare as well as you can.[16] Careful preparation will help you feel more confident about what you will say (and what others will think) and ease fears about drawing a blank or not being able to answer a question. Speakers who research their topics thoroughly before they speak feel prepared. As a result, they tend to be much more relaxed and effective during their presentations.

Practice Your Speech

You can build your confidence and reduce the nervousness associated with the formality of a speech by practicing. And the more times you practice, the more confident you can become. Here is an example of how this can be done.

Randy was terrified to give his first speech. His instructor suggested a solution he reluctantly agreed to try. Feeling a little silly, Randy began by practicing his speech in his head. Then, when no one else was home, he began to present his speech out loud and alone in his room. He then stood in front of a mirror and delivered his speech to his own reflection. After several horrifying attempts, he began to feel more comfortable. Soon after, he began to trust his speaking ability enough to deliver his speech to his older sister, whom he trusted to be kind and constructive. First, he asked her to look interested, even if she wasn't. After doing this a few times, he asked her to give him honest nonverbal feedback. Then he asked her to share her suggestions and comments verbally. Finally, he practiced once more in the clothing he planned to wear and delivered his speech in his kitchen, which he arranged so it resembled, as closely as possible, his classroom.

When speakers practice their speech before they give it, they become more familiar with the process of speaking and the formality of the situation. As they gain comfort by practicing alone, they can move to rehearsals before an audience. They also have time to make changes in their presentation and to smooth out the rough spots before they actually give the speech. This practice is part of a process known as **systematic desensitization**, a technique for reducing anxiety that involves teaching your body to feel calm and relaxed rather than fearful during your speeches. This technique can help you give successful speeches and build your confidence, thus breaking the cycle of fear associated with public speaking. Talk to your instructor if you'd like to learn more about this technique.[17]

Even experienced performers get nervous when they speak in public. After Reese Witherspoon won an Oscar for her role as June Carter in Walk the Line, she revealed that one of her biggest challenges in the role was talking and singing in front of a large group of people.

GARY HERSHORN/Reuters /Landov

Have Realistic Expectations

A third way to build your confidence is to set realistic expectations about your delivery. Very few speakers sound or look like professional performers. When real people give real speeches, they sound like real people who are invested in their topic and speech. So rather than worry about delivering a flawless performance, adjust your expectations to a more realistic level.

Good to Know!

systematic desensitization: Technique for reducing anxiety that involves teaching your body to feel calm and relaxed rather than fearful during your speeches.

Remember, speakers pause, cough, rely on their notes for prompts, occasionally say "um," and even exhibit physical signs of nervousness, such as blushing or sweating. As we give more speeches, these "flaws" either go away, become less noticeable, or we learn to manage them effectively. Here are a few realistic expectations for beginning speakers:

- Take a calming breath before you begin your speech.
- Remember your introduction.
- Strike a balance between using your notes and making eye contact with your audience.
- Make eye contact with more than one person.
- Gesture naturally rather than hold on to the podium.
- Deliver your conclusion the way you practiced it.

Practice Visualization and Affirmations

Sometimes, we increase our nervousness by imagining a worse-case scenario for the speech, and these images often stay in our minds. We've set up what is called a self-fulfilling prophecy: If you see yourself doing poorly in your mind before your speech, you set yourself up to do so in the speech. There are two ways to turn this negative dynamic around and build your confidence as a speaker: visualization and affirmations.

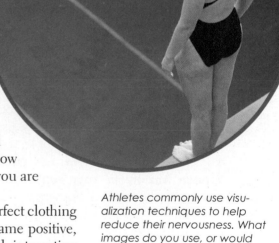

Ryan McVay /Getty images

Visualization. Visualization is a process in which you construct a mental image of yourself giving a successful speech. Research on the benefits of visualization suggests that one session of visualization (about fifteen minutes) has a significant positive effect on communication apprehension.[18] The techniques of visualization are used by a wide range of people—athletes, performers, executives—and can range from elaborate to quite simple processes. For public speakers, the most effective process works like this.

Find a quiet, comfortable place where you can sit in a relaxed position for approximately fifteen minutes. Close your eyes and breathe slowly and deeply through your nose, feeling relaxation flow through your body. In great detail, visualize the morning of the day you are to give your speech.

You get up filled with confidence and energy, and you wear the perfect clothing for your speech. You drive, walk, or ride to campus filled with this same positive, confident energy. As you enter the classroom, you see yourself relaxed, interacting with your classmates, full of confidence because you have thoroughly prepared for your speech. Your classmates are friendly and cordial in their greetings and conversations with you. You are *absolutely* sure of your material and your ability to present that material in the way you would like.

Next, visualize yourself beginning your speech. You see yourself approaching the place in your classroom from which you will speak. You are sure of yourself,

Athletes commonly use visualization techniques to help reduce their nervousness. What images do you use, or would you use, when you visualize yourself giving a successful speech?

Good to Know!

visualization: Process in which you construct a mental image of yourself giving a successful speech.

eager to begin, and positive in your abilities as a speaker. You know you are organized and ready to use all your visual aids with ease. Now you see yourself presenting your speech. Your introduction is wonderful. Your transitions are smooth and interesting. Your main points are articulated brilliantly. Your evidence is presented elegantly. Your organization is perfect. Take as much time as you can in visualizing this part of your process. Be as specific and positive as you can.

Visualize the end of the speech: It could not have gone better. You are relaxed and confident, the audience is eager to ask questions, and you respond to the questions with the same talents as you gave your speech. As you return to your seat, you are filled with energy and appreciation for the job well done. You are ready for the next events of your day, and you accomplish them with success and confidence.

Now take a deep breath and return to the present. Breathe in, hold it, and release it. Do this several times as you return to the present. Take as much time as you need to make this transition.[19]

Research on visualization for public speakers suggests that the more detail we give to our visualizations (what shoes we wear, exactly how we feel as we see ourselves, imagining the specifics of our speech), the more effective the technique is in building our confidence and reducing apprehension. Visualization has a significant effect on building our confidence because it systematically replaces negative images with positive images.

Affirmations. Speakers sometimes undermine their confidence through negative self-talk; they listen to the harsh judgments many people carry within themselves. When we tell ourselves, "I'm no good at this," "I know I'll embarrass myself," or "Other people are far more talented than I am," we engage in negative self-talk. We judge ourselves as inferior or less competent than others. Although it is natural to evaluate our own performances critically (that's how we motivate ourselves to improve), negative self-talk in public speaking situations often is unhelpful. When our internal voices tell us we can't succeed, our communication apprehension only increases.[20]

To build your confidence, however, and counter the negative self-talk that might be going on in your head before a speech, try the following technique. For every negative assessment you hear yourself give, replace it with an honest assessment reframed to be positive. This technique, sometimes called **cognitive restructuring**, is a process that builds confidence because it replaces negative thoughts with positive thoughts called affirmations.[21] **Affirmations** are positive, motivating statements. They are very helpful in turning our immobilizing self-doubts into realistic assessments and options. Consider the following examples:

Good to Know!

cognitive restructuring: Process that helps reduce anxiety by replacing negative thoughts with positive ones, called affirmations.
affirmations: Positive, motivating statements that replace negative self-talk.

Negative	Positive
I'll never find an interesting topic.	I can find an interesting topic. I am an interesting person with resources. I have creative ideas.
I don't know how to organize this material.	I can find a way to present this effectively. I have a good sense of organization. I can get help if I need it.
I know I'll get up there and make a fool of myself.	I am capable of giving a wonderful speech. I know lots of strategies to do so.
I'll forget what I want to say.	I'll remember what I want to say, and I'll have notes to help me.
I'm too scared to look at my audience.	I'll make eye contact with at least five people in the audience.
I'm scared to death!	I care about my performance and will do very well.
I'll be the worst in the class!	I'll give my speech well and am looking forward to a fine presentation. We are all learning how to do this.

Positive affirmations build confidence because they reframe negative energy and evaluations and shed light on your anxieties. To say you're terrified is immobilizing, but to say you care about your performance gives you room to continue to develop your speech. It is also a more accurate description of what is going on inside. Affirmations can assist you in minimizing the impact of your internal judgments and, along with visualization, can help build your confidence about public speaking.

Connect with Your Audience

A final way to build your confidence is to connect with your audience—getting to know them in class or gathering information about them before a more formal speaking situation. As you prepare your speech, identify what you know about them, the ways you are similar to your audience, and the ways you might be different. The similarities may be as general as living in the same town or working for the same company or as specific as sharing the same views on issues. Whatever the level of comparison, finding out about your audience reminds you that we all share many aspects of our daily lives. This helps you see that, despite differences, we do share similar views and experiences.

You can also build your confidence by being a good member of the audience when others are speaking. Although this might seem unusual, ask yourself the following questions: When you are listening to a speech, do you make eye contact with the speaker? Do you sit with an attentive and alert posture, taking notes or showing interest in the presentation? Do you ask relevant questions of the speaker when the speech is over or offer constructive comments if you have the opportunity to evaluate his or her performance? Speakers who fail to behave as engaged and interested audience members often fear the very same response to their speeches.

One way to overcome this fear of disrespectful audiences is to behave as an audience member as you would want others to behave when you speak. Doing so helps establish rapport (if you are kind to a speaker, she or he likely will respond similarly to you). It also helps you learn about how to put together and deliver an effective speech.

The solutions offered in this section may help you reduce some of the speech anxiety so common to beginning public speakers. Preparing, practicing, being realistic, visualizing and affirming, finding connections, and modeling appropriate audience behavior are options that even experienced public speakers use to build their confidence. Learning to relax while giving speeches enhances your ability to contribute to the public dialogue.

Civic Engagement in Action

"WHAT'S YOUR ORANGE-BAND?"

At lunch one day in 2003, a group of friends at James Madison University decided to try to engage students, faculty, staff, and administrators in a meaningful discussion about one important issue: the war in Iraq. They didn't want a rally, protest, or debate, "just a community-wide conversation." For one week, the students passed out simple bands of orange fabric that could be tied to a backpack or jacket to symbolize a desire to talk about the war. They wanted to spark the question "What's your OrangeBand?" and invite conversation about the war.

Five weeks later, more than 2,000 students, professors, and community members had chosen to wear OrangeBands, attend forums, and discuss their views. Dialogue soon turned to a number of other core issues, and the question became "What's your OrangeBand today?" In 2004, the nonprofit OrangeBand Initiative, Inc., was formed, and by 2010, OrangeBand had coordinated dozens of forums and several action campaigns designed to facilitate conversations on a wide range of topics, and inspired more than 10,000 OrangeBand wearers.

The organizers think OrangeBand taps into three things that people are hungry for:

- **Civil discourse (respectful conversation).** There is desire out there to talk about issues we care about with other people and to try to learn from them when we disagree rather than dismiss and disrespect them.
- **Social capital (community).** OrangeBand is not just about having a conversation with someone but also about feeling connected to them. The "relationship building aspect of a quality conversation on an important topic" is just as important as the conversation itself.

Evan Dyson/AP Photo

- **Civic engagement (citizenship).** Whether we call it getting involved, citizenship, or civic responsibility, OrangeBand taps into a desire to participate in democracy. When OrangeBand conversations start up, talking quickly turns to taking action.

OrangeBand chapters or groups are springing up across the nation, and the organization has only one rule: "to be successful in providing a neutral space for dialogue, the organization must remain neutral itself. We vigorously work to protect this political impartiality by inviting people of diverse perspectives to participate on staff and in our forums." OrangeBand is "not interested in advocating for any particular stance"; rather, the goal is to "generate a better understanding of why a person thinks" what she or he thinks.[22]

You Can Get Involved

CourseMate   To learn more about OrangeBand and to get involved, access **Web Connect 1.5: The OrangeBand Initiative** and **Web Connect 1.6: What's Your OrangeBand?** online at your CourseMate for *Invitation to Public Speaking*. And to think more about topics you can address as a public speaker in your community and how you can go about sparking a dialogue, access **Web Connect 1.7: Convening Public Dialogue.**

Chapter Summary

Public speaking is unique.

- Public speaking has a structure, purpose, and role that are different from the other types of communication we engage in regularly: intrapersonal, interpersonal, group, and mass communication.
- Public speaking places a lot of responsibility on the speaker, seeks to address issues that affect the larger community, and relies heavily on one speaker to convey a message. It also creates community, is audience centered, and encourages ethical and civil dialogue in ways that other types of communication do not.
- The model of the public speaking process highlights the role of the speaker and explains the message, audience, and channel as well as the influence of noise and feedback.

Public speaking is powerful.

- Speeches have the power to influence people and to shape actions and decisions. The ideas expressed in speeches enter and shape the public dialogue for years to come.
- The public dialogue is the open and honest discussion that occurs among groups of people about topics that affect those groups. It allows speakers to offer perspectives, share facts, raise questions, and engage others in stimulating discussions. When we join that dialogue, we rely on and respond to these earlier speakers.

Culture influences public speaking style.

- Your speaking style is shaped by your culture as well as your gender.

- As you enter the public dialogue, you will be exposed to speaking styles different from your own. This range of styles is essential to the health of the public dialogue, and understanding these differences assists you in responding civilly to others.

Civil, ethical speakers participate in the public dialogue productively.

- Participating in this dialogue civilly means you must display care, respect, thoughtfulness, and flexibility.
- Participating in this dialogue ethically means you must consider the moral impact of your ideas on your audience and contribute to the public dialogue in productive ways.

Several methods can help build your confidence about public speaking.

- Research your speech topic thoroughly so you feel confident about the material and are prepared to answer questions.
- Practice your speech to work out any problems with it and to feel comfortable giving it in front of an audience.
- Have realistic expectations about your delivery so you don't feel you have to give a perfect presentation.
- Visualize yourself giving a successful speech, and replace any negative self-talk with positive affirmations.
- Find points of connection with your audience. Model good behavior when you are an audience member so you establish rapport with the people who may be members of your audience.

Invitation to Public Speaking Online

CourseMate Now that you have read Chapter 1, use your Speech Communication Course-Mate for *Invitation to Public Speaking* for quick access to the electronic resources that accompany this text. These resources include

- **Study tools** that will help you assess your learning and prepare for exams (*digital glossary, key term flash cards, review quizzes*).
- **Activities and assignments** that will help you hone your knowledge and build your public speaking skills throughout the course (*Practicing the Public Dialogue activities, review questions*).

- **Media resources** that will help you explore public speaking concepts online (*Web Connect links, Enhanced eBook*), develop your speech outlines (*Speech Builder Express 3.0*), watch and critique videos of sample speeches (*Interactive Video Activities*), upload your speech videos for peer reviewing and critique other students' speeches (*Speech Studio online speech review tool*), and download chapter review so you can study when and where you'd like (*Audio Study Tools*).

This chapter's key concepts and review questions are also featured in this end-of-chapter section.

Key Concepts

affirmations (16)
audience (10)
audience centered (8)
channel (10)
civility (2)
cognitive restructuring (16)
communication apprehension (12)
context (11)
decoding (10)

encoding (10)
ethical public speaker (4)
feedback (11)
group communication (7)
interpersonal communication (7)
intrapersonal communication (7)
mass communication (7)
message (10)

noise (10)
public communication (7)
public dialogue (3)
speaker (10)
state, or situational, anxiety (12)
systematic desensitization (14)
trait anxiety (12)
visualization (15)

Review Questions

1. Who are the most compelling speakers you have encountered? Why did they speak: Did they decide, were they asked, or was it required? What issues did they discuss? How do these issues relate to the public dialogue discussed in this chapter? What made these speakers such strong presenters?

2. This chapter presented Deborah Tannen's notion of the argument culture. What is your perception of this culture? Have you been exposed to public communication as an argument? What were your reactions to this kind of interaction? If the people engaged in this interaction were to communicate civilly, what specifically would change?

3. Make a list of issues you find interesting and have followed for some time. Who spoke publicly on these issues? If you don't know who gave speeches on the issues, spend time in the library and on the Internet finding several speeches. How do these speeches affect your own positions on these issues? How did this activity shape your perception of the unending conversation discussed in this chapter?

4. What cultural or gender influences do you think will become (or already are) a part of your speaking style? Are these similar to those discussed in this chapter? If they are different, identify the differences and how they affect communication. Discuss this topic in your public speaking class so that you and your classmates begin with a recognition of the differences you will encounter as you all give speeches.

5. Set aside fifteen minutes of alone time the day before your first speech. Take time to visualize that speech as the process is described in this chapter. Go through each step carefully and in detail. Do not rush or overlook any aspect of the speech process. After you give your speech, compare having visualized the speech and your level of nervousness to a situation in which you were nervous but did not visualize. Was the visualization helpful in reducing your nervousness? Why or why not?

6. Either alone or with a friend, list or discuss the negative self-talk you use to describe your ability to give speeches. Identify the specific negative phrases you use and turn them into positive affirmations. Be realistic in reframing your negative self-talk into positive self-talk using the examples in this chapter as a guide.

7. As you listen to other students give their speeches, see if you can find similarities and differences between them and you. This will help you find points of connection with your audience, one of the techniques for reducing your nervousness before a speech. It will also help you stay audience centered.

8. When you are assigned your first speech, check out Speech Studio to see other students' first speeches. Or record your speech and upload it to Speech Studio. Ask your peers for their feedback. What feedback could you use to help improve your speech before you give it in class? ☑ Speech Studio

Effective Listening

© Mark Richards / PhotoEdit

IN THIS CHAPTER, YOU WILL LEARN TO:

- Explain why listening to others is important
- Identify the reasons we sometimes fail to listen to others
- Implement strategies for becoming a more careful listener
- Implement strategies for becoming a more critical listener
- Implement strategies for becoming a more ethical listener
- Describe how your roles as a speaker and as a listener are related

Can you recall the last speech you heard? How much of its content do you remember? Now think of the last presentation you gave. How much of that information did you want your audience to remember? Is it inevitable that listeners lose so much information? As speakers, we definitely want our audiences to retain more than one-quarter of the information we worked so hard to present. And as listeners, most of us want to make the time we spend listening more profitable. In this chapter, you'll learn about how you listen as an audience member, why our listening sometimes fails, and how to listen carefully, critically, and ethically. You'll then explore how, as a speaker, you can listen to your audience and adapt to their needs, helping them listen to your speech more effectively.

Why Listen to Others?

Listening to others is a very powerful act of communication. When we listen to others, we confirm their humanity, presence, and worth. When we listen and **confirm**, we recognize, acknowledge, and express value for another person. So central is the act of listening that philosopher Martin Buber claimed in the 1920s, "A society may be termed human in the measure to which its members confirm one another."[1] Note that listening is different from hearing. **Hearing** refers to the vibration of sound waves on our eardrums and the impulses that are then sent to the brain. When you listen to someone, you do more than simply receive sound waves—you actively engage with the information you hear.

To confirm others by listening to them is not necessarily to agree with them or even to be persuaded by them. **Listening** is simply the process of giving thoughtful attention to another person's words and understanding what you hear. By listening to another's words, you recognize those words as expressions of that person's experiences, values, and beliefs. If we are to participate in the ethical and civil public dialogue of our communities and make a space for others to do so, we must listen. If we are to be effective public speakers and audiences, we must also understand why we sometimes fail to listen.

Gilbert Carrasquillo/Getty Images Entertainment /Getty Images

One of former President Bill Clinton's strengths as a speaker was his ability to confirm others. In what ways does Clinton appear to be confirming his audience here?

Why We Sometimes Fail to Listen

Why do we ignore some messages but tune into others, opening ourselves up to new ideas and ways of thinking? Why do we willingly confirm some people but refuse to consider confirming others? Similarly, why are we sometimes surprisingly good at understanding some speakers but unable to follow others? Listening researcher Michael Nichols explains that we sometimes fail to listen because "the simple art of listening isn't always so simple." Rather, it is often work. The "sustained attention of careful listening—that may take heroic and unselfish restraint. To listen well we must forget ourselves" and give our focused attention to another.[5]

As listeners, we fail to focus our attention for three reasons: listener interference, speaker interference, and an inability to get beyond differences. **Interference** is anything that stops or hinders a listener from receiving a message. Interference can be external to the listener (auditory or visual distractions) or internal (distracting thoughts or feelings). As you read this section, see if you recognize some of your own weaknesses as a listener or as a speaker.

Listener Interference

You may be surprised to learn that most challenges to listening stem from poor listening habits. Consider the following list of bad listening habits. Can you identify times you've done some of the following?

Good to Know!

confirm: To recognize, acknowledge, and express value for another person. **hearing:** Vibration of sound waves on our eardrums and the impulses then sent to the brain. **listening:** Process of giving thoughtful attention to another person's words and understanding what you hear. **interference:** Anything that stops or hinders a listener from receiving a message.

- Think you're not interested in the subject before the speech really gets going.
- Assume you know what the speaker is going to say before it's even said.
- Get so focused on the details that you miss the bigger point.
- Adopt a passive physical stance—slouching, reclining, making no eye contact.
- Adopt a defensive physical stance—turning away, crossing arms, making hostile eye contact.
- Pay attention to distractions—or create them yourself.
- Be so preoccupied with the messenger that you miss the message.
- Tune out difficult information.
- Tune out information you don't agree with or argue with the speaker's message in your own mind.
- Prepare your response while the speaker is speaking.
- Daydream or pretend you are listening when you really aren't.

At one time or another, most of us have fallen into many of these habits. We may think we've heard all there is to hear on a subject, so we begin daydreaming or simply pretend to listen. We become so enamored of or so frustrated with a speaker that we forget to listen to the content of a speech. We find the material too challenging or difficult to understand, so we give up listening, begin talking to the person next to us, or even open the newspaper and begin to read. Although we might want to blame the speaker for these lapses in listening, we really are responsible for practicing these bad habits. We will learn how to replace these bad habits with more productive ones later in this chapter.

Speaker Interference Caused by Information

As speakers, we can create speeches that are "listenable," speeches that help our audiences focus and pay attention. A **listenable speech** is considerate and delivered in an oral style. This type of speech uses words meant to be heard (oral style) rather than words meant to be read (written style).[6] **Considerate speeches** help our audience process information. Listeners generally stop listening, or become frustrated, when we present information that is overly complicated, challenging, or simple.

When we share ideas that are too complicated, audiences can have difficulty following our line of reasoning. We've probably all heard speakers who try to explain complicated procedures or tell detailed stories in too short a time. When audience members don't have the time or the knowledge to absorb a speaker's ideas from the beginning of a speech, they may just give up listening. Similarly, when our ideas seriously challenge an audience's belief systems, the audience can get caught up in the differences in values and lose sight of the point we are trying to make. This is particularly true when the speaker's topic brings up strong emotions, such as in speeches about polarizing social issues or traumatic events. For an example of an idea that was both too confusing and too challenging to be heard, see the Ethical Moment box "Supporting Material That Sends an Unintended Message" in Chapter 6.

On the other hand, when we present stories or arguments that are too simple, our audiences may become bored and stop listening. Consider the following

Good to Know!

listenable speech: Speech that is considerate and delivered in an oral style. **considerate speech:** Speech that eases the audience's burden of processing information.

Civic Engagement in Action

Colombian singer Shakira may be one of the most driven people in the entertainment industry. Since 1995, she's released several best-selling albums (she's the highest-selling Colombian artist of all time), has won a couple of dozen major music awards (including two Grammy Awards), and collaborated with the South African group Freshlyground to sing the official song of the 2010 World Cup. Oh, and she also performed with superstars Stevie Wonder and Usher at President Obama's inaugural ceremonies in 2008.

But Shakira is also driven to succeed as a humanitarian. When she was eight years old, her father experienced some financial trouble and had to sell much of what her family owned. No longer were they living the comfortable middle-class life she was used to. "In my childish head, this was the end of the world." To help her see that their circumstances weren't as dire as they could be, her father took her to the park to see the homeless kids who lived there, addicted to sniffing glue. "From then on, I gained perspective, and realized that there were many underprivileged children in my country. The images of those kids, with their tattered clothes and bare feet, have stayed with me forever. I said to myself back then, one day I'm going to help these kids when I become a famous artist."

She's certainly made good on that promise to herself. With the money she made from her first successful album, she founded the Pies Descalzos (Barefoot) Foundation, a Columbian charity that provides education and meals for impoverished Columbian children. Shakira also founded the ALAS Foundation (Fundacion América Latina en Acción Solidaria), an organization dedicated to launching "a new social movement that will generate a collective commitment to comprehensive early childhood development programs for the children in Latin America." In 2007, she used her humanitarian clout and persuasive skills to secure

AP Photo/Ramon Espinosa

commitments of an impressive 200 million dollars for the ALAS Foundation from Mexican philanthropist Carlos Slim and U.S. philanthropist and conservationist Howard Buffett. This is no small achievement for an entertainer!

Shakira decided to engage with her community because she wanted to help kids like those she saw in the park. But she also has a larger goal in mind, which she described in a 2008 speech to the Oxford Union about her humanitarian work in Latin America:

Now I want to be clear about this, this isn't about charity. This is about investing in human potential. From an ethical point of view, from a moral point of view, it accomplishes a purpose. But also from an economic point of view, this could bring enormous benefits to all mankind. Universal education is the key to global security and economic growth.[7]

You Can Get Involved

CourseMate To learn more about Shakira's Pies Descalzos Foundation, access **Web Connect 2.1: Barefoot Foundation** at your CourseMate for *Invitation to Public Speaking*. The "How You Can Help" link provides opportunities to volunteer, sponsor a child, lobby your government, and more. Also check out **Web Connect 2.2: Artists for Charity**. to explore a nonprofit organization made up of artists and volunteers all over the world who raise awareness and secure funds for humanitarian causes.

example: Katherine, a graduating senior, was the student speaker at her recent college graduation. Recognizing that graduation is a time of huge transition and uncertainty but also a time of excitement, she decided to read lengthy passages from one of her favorite books, Dr. Seuss's *Oh, the Places You'll Go!* After a while, people stopped listening to her speech because the language was too simple. Her audience began to shift and shuffle, to lose interest, and to strike up small side conversations while she was speaking. Although it can be interesting and meaningful for adults, *Oh, the Places You'll Go!* is written for children. Thus, Katherine's speech on change and the excitement of the unknown used language that was too simple for college graduates and their families.

Speaker Interference Caused by Language

Another way we can help our audience listen is by reducing interference caused by language. Listening can fail simply because the speaker's language is unclear. The language may be too formal or technical, too casual, too noninclusive, or too cluttered.

Formal or technical language. Most of us have heard the following phrases or sayings many times in our lives. Can you recognize them?

1. Scintillate, scintillate, asteroid minific.
2. Members of an avian species of identical plumage congregate.
3. Surveillance should precede saltation.
4. Pulchritude possesses a solely cutaneous profundity.
5. It is fruitless to become lachrymose over precipitately departed lacteal fluid.
6. Freedom from encrustations of grime is contiguous to rectitude.
7. Eschew the implement of correction and vitiate the scion.
8. It is fruitless to attempt to indoctrinate a superannuated canine with innovative maneuvers.
9. The temperature of aqueous content of an unremittingly ogled saucepan does not reach 212 degrees F.
10. All articles that coruscate with resplendence are not truly auriferous.[8]

You may not recognize these common sayings because they are expressed in very formal and technical language. In some situations, this style of language may be quite appropriate, but most audiences stop listening when the speaker's language is more formal or technical than they can understand. These ten very formal sentences simply say:

1. Twinkle, twinkle, little star.
2. Birds of a feather flock together.
3. Look before you leap.
4. Beauty is only skin deep.
5. Don't cry over spilled milk.
6. Cleanliness is next to godliness.
7. Spare the rod and spoil the child.
8. You can't teach an old dog new tricks.

9. A watched pot never boils.

10. All that glitters is not gold.

A specific type of language that is often too technical is **jargon**, language used by a special group or for a special activity. You've probably used jargon if you play sports (a bogey is a type of score in golf) or are a member of a specialized group (in the military, a bogey is an unidentified, possibly hostile, aircraft). You also may have used jargon on your job to identify processes or objects specific to your occupation (truck mechanics know a bogie is a type of wheel assembly used in some automotive trucks). Jargon can be confusing because your audience may not know what a particular word means. As a speaker, use jargon only if it will help your audience better understand your message.

Casual language. Language also can be difficult to listen to if it is too casual. We often fall into our familiar, everyday language patterns, which can be too informal for our audience. Three types of commonly used casual language include slang, colloquialisms, and euphemisms. **Slang** is an informal nonstandard vocabulary, usually made up of arbitrarily changed words. A **colloquialism** is a local or regional informal dialect or expression. A **euphemism** substitutes an agreeable or inoffensive expression for one that may offend or suggest something unpleasant. When our language is too casual, audiences might not be able to follow the main ideas of the speech, or they become confused or uncomfortable. Either way, they stop listening to our message. Consider these examples:

Gary Irving/Stone/Getty Images

Firefighters use jargon to communicate efficiently with one another. How might these firefighters describe this scene to someone who isn't a firefighter? What jargon do you use in your profession that you might need to explain to an audience?

Slang:	Dude, don't call me before college morning. I'm trying to get some shut eye.[9]
	(Dude, don't call me until after noon. I'm trying to get some sleep.)
	That concert was awesome sauce!
	(That concert was the best it could possibly be! It went beyond my expectations.)[10]
Colloquialism:	He done flew off his chair at the news.
	(He was so surprised by the news that it seemed as though he'd fall out of his chair.)
Euphemism:	I'm going to go powder my nose.
	(I have to use the bathroom.)
	Due to changing market forces, the company will be downsizing.
	(Because the company is not making enough profit, employees will be laid off.)

In some settings, such as at a party with your friends, casual language is easily understood. However, in public speaking settings, translate slang, colloquialisms, and euphemisms into expressions an audience is more likely to understand. Some casual language may even be offensive to some members of an audience, causing them to stop listening or to focus on the speaker's language rather than the speak-

Good to Know!

jargon: Technical language used by a special group or for a special activity. **slang:** Informal nonstandard vocabulary, usually made up of arbitrarily changed words. **colloquialism:** Local or regional informal dialect or expression. **euphemism:** Word or phrase that substitutes an agreeable or inoffensive expression for one that may offend or suggest something unpleasant.

er's ideas. Or it may be very confusing to people from cultures other than your own. Remember, when your audience is confused or offended by your language, they won't hear the message you want to send.

Noninclusive language. Listening can break down when you use noninclusive language, or words that seem to refer only to certain groups of people. Such language excludes people who are not in the "in-group" and who are likely to be offended by and tune out speakers who use it. A common example of noninclusive language is language that seems to describe only men, not both men and women. **Gender-inclusive language** recognizes that both women and men are active participants in the world. Using gender-inclusive language is one of the simplest ways you can improve listening, yet some people criticize and resist it. They argue that the pronoun *he* includes both women and men, and using *man* to describe all people is perfectly acceptable. For others, worrying about "gender stuff " is an issue that was resolved years ago. Yet research indicates that when we use noninclusive nouns and pronouns, listeners visualize men far more often than they do women or men and women together (see Table 2.1 on page 28).

Additionally, gender-biased language can be quite ambiguous and thus confusing. When we use the "universal he" to say, "If a person wants to be treated as an adult, he must earn the respect worthy of such treatment," is the "person" a man (only), a woman (only), or a human being of either sex?[11] How is the listener to know for sure? What if Jane wants to be treated as an adult? Can she earn the respect worthy of such treatment? How would a listener know? It is easier to include Jane in the argument—and reduce the work for the listener—by saying, "If people want to be treated as adults, they must earn the respect worthy of such treatment." Regardless of your own stance on the position of women in the world relative to men, avoiding noninclusive terms can help clarify ambiguous arguments or claims. It also helps listeners understand the intended message.

Noninclusive language also includes language that does not acknowledge cultural diversity. **Culturally inclusive language** respectfully recognizes the differences among the many cultures in our society. Although it may seem obvious that we need to consider diversity when we speak to diverse audiences, at times our language does not reflect our attention to diversity.

A common example of language that is not culturally inclusive is **spotlighting**, the practice of highlighting a person's race or ethnicity (or sex, sexual orientation, physical disability, and the like) during a speech. Speakers who spotlight describe a lawyer as a Hispanic lawyer, a doctor as an Asian American doctor, and a friend as an African American friend. Spotlighting is most common among members of the dominant culture in a society, and it marks differences as being unusual. Consider the following examples:

The jury includes five men and two African American women.

The panel includes three professionals and a disabled lawyer.

The meeting is going to be chaired by a Hispanic professor and a university administrator.

He's a talented gay artist.[12]

Good to Know!

gender-inclusive language: Language recognizing that both women and men are active participants in the world.
culturally inclusive language: Language that respectfully recognizes the differences among the many cultures in our society.
spotlighting: Practice of highlighting a person's race or ethnicity (or sex, sexual orientation, physical disability, and the like) during a speech.

Table 2.1

Research on Gender-Inclusive Language

Year	Study
1973	• Children were asked to select photographs for textbook chapters titled "Urban Man" and "Man in Politics" or "Urban Life" and "Political Behavior." • The children nearly always chose pictures of men when the titles included the male nouns. • When the titles were not specifically male oriented, the children chose more pictures that contained both women and men.[13]
1984	• First-grade through college students were asked to write a story about an average student. • When the researchers used the word "he" to describe the assignment, only 12 percent of the students wrote a story about a female. • When researchers used "he or she," 42 percent of the students wrote stories about females.[14]
1995	• College students were asked to fill in the blanks to sentences such as, "Before a judge can give a final ruling, _____," and "Before a doctor can make a final diagnosis, _____." • Even though women today participate in almost all aspects of public and professional life, students chose predominantly masculine pronouns to finish the sentences.[15]
1996, 1998	• Subjects were asked to read a report, written in the style of a newspaper article, about a meeting of athletes and a meeting of scientists. • When neutral and masculine pronouns were used in the report, the subjects described both events as being attended predominantly by men. • When the events were given a female context (a meeting of gymnasts versus hockey players, a meeting of nutritionists versus geophysicists), the subjects described the events as being attended by only slightly more women.[16]
2008	• Students in England, France, and Germany assigned predominantly male images to sentences containing supposedly generic masculine pronouns. • Again, this confirms the overriding power of pronoun choice to influence perceptions.[17]

Spotlighting identifies people thought to belong to a special, and hence an unusual, category. As a result of spotlighting, differences get marked as abnormal, slightly strange, or surprising. A speaker using culturally inclusive language would describe the people in these examples as five white men and two African American women (or as seven people), four professionals (a lawyer is professionally employed), two employees of the university (or a Hispanic professor and a white administrator), and a talented artist.

Sometimes, speakers fail to be culturally inclusive when they neglect information that acknowledges important cultural differences. Using culturally inclusive language helps a speaker tell the whole story. For example, in his speech on equity in the workplace, Howard used culturally inclusive language by including statistical information beyond the familiar "a woman earns about 80 cents to every dollar a man earns." He told his audience that Asian American women earn approximately 95 cents to every dollar a white man earns, white women earn approximately 80 cents, African American women earn approximately 70 cents, and Hispanic women earn approximately 62 cents to every dollar a white man makes. This culturally inclusive language recognized important cultural differences that gave Howard's audience more insight into this complex topic.[18]

Using culturally inclusive and gender-inclusive language communicates to an audience that you are aware of the diversity in our society and of the influence of culture. Your speech becomes more listenable because audiences gain a more holistic view of an issue. Your goal as a speaker is to connect with your audience and to share your ideas with them, so make listening as easy as possible. Using language that includes all members of your audience assists you in doing just that.

Ethical Moment

WHAT DEFINES CULTURALLY INCLUSIVE LANGUAGE AND SPOTLIGHTING?

Former Virginia Senator George Allen found his language in the spotlight during his reelection campaign in 2006. During a rally in Breaks, Virginia, Allen told his audience that he planned to run his campaign on "positive, constructive ideas." To help illustrate how his strategy was different from that of his opponent, James Webb, Allen pointed to a member of the audience, S. R. Sidarth, a 20-year-old senior at the University of Virginia who is of Indian American descent. Allen said, "This fellow here, over here with the yellow shirt—*macaca*, or whatever his name is. He's with my opponent. He's following us around everywhere. And it's just great." A few moments later, Allen turned his attention back to Sidarth and said, "Let's give a welcome to *macaca*, here. Welcome to America and the real world of Virginia."

Based on the color of Sidarth's skin, Allen made an assumption that he was not native to America. Yet, Sidarth was born and raised in the state of Virginia.

The word *macaca* has denotative and connotative definitions. The denotative definition is "rhesus monkey." However, the word is also a racial slur for dark-skinned people, commonly used by French colonists in northern parts of Africa. After much publicity surrounding Allen's remarks, Allen issued an apology and said that he was unclear about the meaning of the term and that it had no derogatory meaning for him. He said he was sorry if Sidarth was offended by

the use of the word. Sidarth responded by saying, "I think [Allen] was doing it because he could, and I was the person of color there and it was useful for him in inciting his audience. . . . I'm disgusted he would use my race in a political context."

Allen lost the election to James Webb.[19]

What do you think?

1. Do you think Allen spotlighted Sidarth by pointing him out in a crowd filled with mostly Anglo-Americans?

2. Allen denied intentionally using the term *macaca* in a derogatory way. Do you think he therefore should have been forgiven for making a mistake in his language choices?

3. Many speculate that Allen lost the election because he used the word *macaca* to refer to an audience member. Do you believe this incident should have been enough to cost Allen the election? Why or why not?

4. How could Allen have used culturally inclusive language to include Sidarth in his speech?

Verbal clutter. Sometimes, audiences have a difficult time listening to a speaker because of **verbal clutter**, extra words in sentences that don't add meaning. Even though listeners can mentally process far more words than speakers can speak per minute (the average speaker speaks at a rate of 125 to 175 words per minute, but a trained listener can process 350 to 450 words per minute), verbal clutter impedes listening because listeners must process words that are unnecessary or redundant.[20]

Examples of verbal clutter are such common words and phrases as "you know," "it's like," "I'm like," "um," "and all," and "stuff like that." These small additions to a speech, although commonly used in casual conversation, distract listeners and add no useful meaning.

Similarly, descriptions loaded with adjectives and adverbs act as verbal clutter. Hard to spot sometimes, we often use this type of verbal clutter when we try to create vivid descriptions. Consider the following cluttered sentences and their uncluttered alternatives.

Cluttered:	Good, effective public speakers use carefully selected and chosen words, sentences, and phrases, correctly and accurately.
Uncluttered:	Skilled speakers present their ideas clearly.
What's improved?	A few strong words are used rather than several adequate, but less focused, words.
Cluttered:	If nothing else, he was first and foremost, above all, a man of considerable honor and principled integrity.
Uncluttered:	Above all, he was a man of integrity.
What's improved?	The redundant words have been edited out (for example, honor and principled), leaving a focused message.

The uncluttered sentences are much easier on the ears. They hold our attention and focus our listening efforts. Without the clutter, audiences have a far easier time listening for our main points and ideas. But how much clutter do you really want to eliminate? Notice the differences in the level of clutter in the next three examples:

Cluttered:	At some point during the day, every single day of her life, no matter the weather or the distractions, she would make the long, steep trek three miles one way to the distant, far-off waterfall.
Less cluttered:	At some point during the day, every day of her life, she made the three-mile trek to the waterfall.
Uncluttered:	Every day, she hiked three miles to the waterfall.

Notice that some of what might be called "clutter" in one speech adds richness and detail to another, setting a particular tone or mood. Go back and reread the cluttered example. If we simply took out the words "distant, far-off," we might have a nice description for a commemorative speech or a speech of introduction. But in a persuasive or informative speech, the focus might be on the daily hike to a waterfall, not on the characteristics of the woman. Thus, the less cluttered or uncluttered versions might make the point far more effectively.

Ask yourself two questions when you want to eliminate verbal clutter. First, do the words you use help develop your argument or make more work for the listener? Second, how many words in your speech are redundant?

Good to Know!

verbal clutter: Extra words that pad sentences and claims but don't add meaning.

Speaker Interference Caused by Differences

Differences between a speaker and an audience can also cause problems with listening. Although we are all similar in many ways, none of us exactly matches our audience in appearance, mannerisms, values, or background. When we are faced with differences, we sometimes see them in terms of a hierarchy (such as seeing a person of a certain age or sex as more trustworthy or credible than another person). When we see differences in this way, we become preoccupied with questions of right and wrong and have trouble focusing on what a speaker is saying. Table 2.2 shows some of the ways speakers and audiences are different and the ways those differences can prevent effective listening.

Table 2.2	
How Differences Can Prevent Listening	
Difference	**How It Affects Listening**
Speech style	Accents, tonal and rhythmic qualities, stuttering, nonnative speakers of a language, and gendered speech differences affect listening. We sometimes see these differences as strange, funny, or inappropriate and have trouble paying attention to the message.
Background and occupation	Differences in race, ethnicity, nationality, regional upbringing, religion, education, occupation, and economic status can affect listening. When we see these differences as right or wrong, we forget to be open to the value of other experiences and influences and often stop listening.
Appearance	Styles of dress, height, weight, hair, body adornment, and even a speaker's posture affect listening. Audiences sometimes have difficulty listening because they are so focused on the speaker's appearance that they can't focus on the message.
Values	When a speaker holds values that are different from members of the audience, listening sometimes is difficult. When listeners are so convinced that certain values are "worthy" and "good" and others are "wrong" and "bad," they rarely listen to understand why that position makes sense to the speaker.

How do we minimize our differences, or explain and account for them, so audiences and speakers can more easily confirm one another? We can go a long way toward that goal by defining *difference* as meaning simply *different*, as not the same but still worth listening to. Thus, we can open up the possibility for listening that confirms others rather than listening that means we must agree with everything they say.

© Neal Preston/CORBIS

As a member of an audience, what about this speaker might cause interference for you as a listener? What could you do to reduce this interference? What could the speaker do?

Although listeners are responsible for interference caused by differences, as speakers we also contribute to this listening problem. Here are a few ways we can minimize the impact of differences:

- Acknowledge and explain differences in speech styles or appearance. Act as an interpreter for the audience, explaining what those differences mean.
- Explain your background and how it affects your position or presentation of information. In this way, you become a source of information regarding your differences, not just someone unusual or unfamiliar.
- Invite others to consider your values without attempting to persuade.
- Assume an invitational stance that attempts to confirm the audience as well as offer your own perspective. (See Chapter 14 for more about invitational speaking.)

Even though differences can seem like permanent obstacles to listening, both audiences and speakers must recognize that difference is the foundation of a healthy public dialogue. Once we invite dialogue rather than monologue, we encourage the exchange of ideas, information, perspectives, and even creative solutions to many of the dilemmas we face. Both audiences and speakers are responsible for creating this healthy dialogue, and a public speaking course is an excellent place to practice listening and speaking in ways that confirm and respect differences.

How to Listen Carefully

As listeners, we can improve our skills and increase the amount of information we retain. In the process, we will also become better speakers. In fact, the listening strategies you'll read about in this and the next two main sections involve listening for many of the components you will incorporate later into your own speeches.

One of the most important obstacles to overcome as a listener is your own interference, or the bad habits discussed earlier in this chapter. However, if you learn to listen carefully, these bad habits are relatively easy to minimize. A careful listener overcomes listener interference to better understand a speaker's message. To minimize your own bad listening habits and reduce interference, try the following strategies.

- **Listen for the speaker's purpose:** <u>Determine the speaker's goal.</u> Is the speaker attempting to introduce, inform, invite, persuade, or commemorate? What are you being asked to learn, consider, think, or agree to?

Practicing the Public Dialogue

2.1

Help Your Audience Listen to Your Speech

Find a partner in your speech class. With your partner, choose a topic that both of you would be interested in giving a speech about. Imagine that each of you is going to give a speech to your classmates on a different aspect of this topic and that you want to ensure that each speech is listenable. With your partner, identify information you could use that would be too complex for the audience. Next, identify language you could use that would be too technical, too casual, and noninclusive. What information and language could you use instead that would be more audience centered? Now, each of you write a short paragraph about your topic with as much verbal clutter included as you can. Then rewrite that paragraph, taking out the clutter. Share your paragraphs with each other. Were you each successful in reducing the clutter? What else might each of you do as a speaker to stay audience centered and create a listenable speech?

Online Resources

CourseMate To learn more about one remedy for a specific kind of noninclusive language, gender-neutral language, check out **Web Connect 2.3: Some Notes on Gender-Neutral Language** online via your CourseMate for *Invitation to Public Speaking*.

Good to Know!

careful listener: Listener who overcomes listener interference to better understand a speaker's message.

- **Listen for the main ideas:** Identify each of the speaker's main points or arguments. Are there two, three, or more main points or arguments? How does the speaker connect each main point or idea? How well can you follow the development of the ideas? Try to find a relationship among the main ideas by listening for previews before main ideas, transitions, connectives from one idea to the next, and summaries that follow main ideas.

- **Listen for supporting evidence and sources:** What kind of evidence does the speaker use to support ideas—narratives, personal disclosure, statistics, comparisons, or expert testimony? Does the speaker use enough evidence, and does it help the speaker make the argument?

- **Write down new words, ideas, and questions:** Write down any unfamiliar words, phrases, or ideas. Keep notes as you listen, writing down main points and important ideas. Write down your questions so you remember what to ask the speaker at the end of the speech.

- **Listen for the conclusion:** Listen to see if you can discover the moment the conclusion begins. How does the speaker summarize the main points? Does the speaker end by telling a story, asking the audience to participate in some action, or using a quotation?

- **Offer nonverbal feedback:** Listen by sitting in an upright (but relaxed) posture. Engage the speaker by making eye contact (if it is culturally appropriate). Use other culturally appropriate nonverbal cues, such as smiles of encouragement and head nods that signal understanding and attention.

How to Listen Critically

To listen critically to a speech is to check it for accuracy as you listen, assessing the strengths and weaknesses of the speaker's reasoning and supporting materials. Note that listening critically is different from listening to judge or find fault with a message. Rather, **critical listeners** listen for the accuracy of a speech's content and the implications of a speaker's message. Critical listeners remain open to new ideas, but they also listen carefully to how speakers develop those ideas into arguments. Additionally, they consider the impact of a speaker's ideas on the immediate audience as well as the larger community.

©Syracuse Newspapers / Michelle Gabel / The Image Works

To help you listen to speeches critically, ask yourself the questions in Table 2.3 on page 34 and then follow the suggested guidelines. Asking these questions will help you assess a speaker's claims and arguments before you make decisions about their value or strength.

When we listen critically, we allow for dialogue because we avoid making quick decisions about good and bad, right and wrong. Listening critically encourages us to ask questions about ideas so we are better able to respond to claims and explore issues with others.

Does it seem that some members of this audience are not listening carefully? What nonverbal cues give you the impression that one person is paying less attention than another? Do you recognize your listening habits in any members of this audience?

Good to Know!

critical listener: Listener who listens for the accuracy of a speech's content and the implications of a speaker's message.

Table 2.3

Guidelines for Critical Listening

Question	Guideline
• How fully has the speaker developed an idea? Is something left out, exaggerated, or understated? Does the speaker use sound reasoning? Are claims based on fact or opinion? (Chapters 7 and 16)	• Speakers must develop all major arguments fully rather than present them without explanation and development. Speakers should not exaggerate arguments or understate their importance. Major ideas should be supported by evidence in the form of examples, statistics, testimony, and the like.
• What sources does the speaker rely on? Are they credible? How are they related to the speaker's topic? Will the sources benefit if facts are presented in a certain way? For example, is the tobacco industry arguing that smoking isn't harmful? (Chapter 6)	• Speakers must use credible sources that are as unbiased as possible. Speakers must cite sources for all new information. Sources should be cited carefully and with enough detail so the audience knows why the source is acceptable.
• Are the claims the speaker makes realistic? What are the implications of those claims? Who is affected by them? In what way? Has the speaker acknowledged these effects, or are they left unstated? Are there other aspects of the issue the speaker should address?	• Speakers must make realistic and logical claims and acknowledge different perspectives. They must also acknowledge those affected by their arguments and acknowledge the effects of their proposed solutions. When speakers take a position, they must not present their position as absolute or as the only one possible.
• How does this speech fit with what I know to be true? What is new to me? Can I accept this new information? Why or why not?	• When speakers make claims that go against your personal experience, see if you can discover why. Sometimes, the answer lies in cultural differences or in a speaker's research. Try to be open to different views of the world while at the same time assessing the speaker's evidence and reasoning objectively. Before you reject a speaker's claims, engage the speaker in a civil discussion to find out why your perspective differs.
• What is at stake for the speaker? How invested is the speaker in the topic and the arguments being made? How will the speaker be affected if the audience disagrees?	• All speakers are invested in some way in their topics and arguments. However, some arguments benefit a speaker more than anyone else. Identify the speaker's motives so you can better understand why she or he is making particular claims.

How to Listen Ethically

Listening ethically encourages audiences to pay attention to the moral implications of a message. Ethics refers to the study of moral standards and how those standards affect our conduct. When we speak of ethics, we are talking about the moral principles we use to guide our behaviors and decisions. An **ethical listener**, then, considers the moral impact of a speaker's message on one's self and one's community. Ethical listeners attend to the standards and principles advocated by a speaker. To listen ethically, listeners must suspend judgment, assess the information they hear, and at times, respond to the speaker's message.

Suspend Judgment

Ethical listeners suspend judgment throughout a speech. To gather as much information as they can, they are willing to listen to a speaker's message, without assigning "right" or "wrong" to it, until the speech is complete and they've had adequate time to evaluate its arguments. Ethical listeners consciously avoid reacting immediately to a statement they disagree with. This allows them to take in the speech's complete message and not jump to conclusions before the speaker is finished. And when they hear the complete message, they can contribute to the public dialogue in more informed ways.

Consider an example. Two students are listening to a speaker on their campus argue for free speech and the right of hate groups to say or print anything they want. Early in the presentation, the speaker says, "It's our constitutional right to express ourselves; this country was founded on that principle. Two hundred plus years later, I argue we are guaranteed the right to say anything we want to anyone."

> *Listener who rushes to judgment:* "That's ridiculous. How can he say that? People don't have the right to say anything they want whenever and wherever they want. That's harassment, and we don't have the right to do that to anyone!"

By rushing to judgment, this listener may stop listening altogether or may focus on a response to the speaker rather than listening to more of what the speaker has to say. By doing so, she may miss the speaker's later claim that our right to express ourselves also guarantees that we can freely criticize hate speech, a freedom not all societies enjoy.

Now consider the speaker who listens ethically, suspending judgment to listen to the full message:

> *Listener who suspends judgment:* "Wow, that sounds extreme to me, but maybe he's got a reason for making that claim. Let me see if I can understand why he makes such a strong statement."

Practicing the Public Dialogue

2.2

Practice Listening Critically

Listen critically to the next speech you hear and ask yourself the questions in Table 2.3. When you listen critically, do you find you better understand the speaker's position and retain more information than when you don't listen critically? Are you able to engage the speaker in the question-and-answer session more meaningfully? Now listen critically to your own speech before you give it in class. Ask yourself the first two groups of questions in Table 2.3. Are you satisfied with the arguments you make and the sources you cite? How do you think your audience will respond to the last three groups of questions?

Online Resources

CourseMate For more practice listening critically to speeches, select one or two of the political speeches featured in your CourseMate for *Invitation to Public Speaking* and evaluate them using the questions in Table 2.3.

Good to Know!

ethical listener: Listener who considers the moral impact of a speaker's message on one's self and one's community.

Even though this student disagrees with the speaker, he's willing to put aside his disagreement until he's heard all the speaker has to say. Thus, he'll have an easier time following the speaker's ideas, confirming them, and responding intelligently to them. Suspending judgment does not mean that we as listeners sit passively without scrutinizing whatever a speaker says. You can still question and disagree with a speaker's message. Suspending judgment is simply a tool to help you listen more effectively and take in a speaker's entire message.

Assess Information and Respond to the Speaker's Ideas

Ethical listening also requires that listeners assess a message (listen critically) first and then respond to the speaker's ideas. When ethical listeners respond to a speaker's ideas, they participate in a constructive dialogue with a speaker. Even if they do not agree with a speaker's position, ethical listeners join the public dialogue so they can better understand a position, explore differences, and share their own views. In their attempts to understand, ethical listeners recognize, acknowledge, and show value for others, even if their positions are vastly different from the speaker's.

Speakers as Listeners: Adapting to Your Audience

Although this chapter has focused extensively on how we as members of an audience can improve our listening skills, speakers are also listeners. In front of an audience, speakers do more than produce a steady stream of words. They listen to their audiences during the presentation by monitoring their expressions, posture, feedback, and level of attention. Speakers use this information to adapt to audience needs throughout the speech by slowing down or speeding up, taking more time to explain, omitting information, or adding extra examples to clarify. In Chapter 4, you'll learn more about your relationship to your audience. Here we'll focus on how you can listen effectively to your audience.

When you give a speech, remember that audience members bring with them many bad listening habits. What follows are some examples of problematic audiences and ways you can counter their bad habits to help them listen better.

Audiences Who Think They Aren't Interested

Sometimes, audience members appear uninterested in your speech from the start or seem to assume they already know what you will say.

Cengage Learning

CourseMate

To see another student speaker attempt to gain her audience's attention in her introduction, watch the video clip of Tiffany Brisco. What does she say in her introduction that makes it easy for her audience to listen to her speech? You can use your CourseMate for *Invitation to Public Speaking* to watch the video, respond to analysis questions, and compare your answers to those provided by the author.

- **Here's how you can address this behavior:** Make your introduction and first main points <u>compelling</u>, innovative, and attentive to your audience's particular biases.
- **Here's an example of a speaker who addressed this behavior successfully:** Genet began his speech by saying, "You say you already know. You say, 'There's nothing new here!' You might even be thinking, 'This will never happen to me,' and maybe—just maybe—you're right. But what if you're wrong? What if you're *probably* wrong? Are you willing to be the two out of three who didn't listen?" After this introduction, he had the full attention of the class and was able to maintain their attention throughout his speech on alcohol and drug addiction.

Practicing the Public Dialogue

2.3

Listening Carefully, Critically, and Ethically

Using the Speech Evaluation Checklist for this activity, evaluate any of the following speakers: one of your instructors, a public figure or student speaker giving one of the speeches featured in the CourseMate, or someone else speaking publicly. Bring your completed checklist to class and discuss the strategies you used to be a careful listener and the ways that listening critically and ethically helped you evaluate the strength of the speaker's ideas and claims.

CourseMate You can access and print this checklist from the Chapter 3 resources of your CourseMate for *Invitation to Public Speaking*.

Speech Evaluation Checklist

Speaker _____   Topic _____

Introduction

_____ Is the purpose of the speech clear? What is the purpose?
_____ Does the speaker establish credibility?
_____ Are the topic and purpose relevant to the audience?
_____ Does the speaker preview the speech?
_____ Does the speaker present ideas that might require me to suspend my judgment while I listen? Identify those ideas.

Body

_____ Are the main points clearly identified? What are the main points?

_____

_____

_____ Are the main points fully supported? Why or why not?
_____ What might be the moral impact of the main points on me and other people?
_____ Are the sources credible? Why or why not?
_____ Is the reasoning sound? Why or why not?
_____ Are other perspectives addressed?
_____ Is the speech listenable? Why or why not? (Consider language, organization, and interference.)

At what points do I suspend judgment to listen ethically and effectively?

_____

_____

Conclusion

_____ Does the speaker signal the end of the speech?
_____ Does the speaker summarize the main points?
_____ Does the speaker appear open to dialogue about the topic?

Discussion

What questions would I like to ask the speaker? _____
What information would I like clarified? _____
What would I like the speaker to talk more about? _____
What would I like the speaker to think more about? _____
What information do I have that I want to share with the speaker?

_____

_____

Audiences Who Are Distracted or Disruptive

Some audience members may slouch, fail to make eye contact, and daydream. Others make or attend to distractions.

- **Here's how you can address this behavior:** Ask questions of the entire audience or of particular members. Or ask the audience to complete an activity related to your topic, such as making a list or jotting down what they already know about the topic. Bring particularly disruptive people into your speech verbally or by bringing them to the front of the audience for a legitimate reason (for example, to give a demonstration or to record discussion ideas on a whiteboard). Note that you want to be careful about singling out audience members. Make sure you aren't embarrassing people or making the rest of the audience feel uncomfortable.

- **Here's an example of a speaker who addressed this behavior successfully:** Noticing that several of his audience members were reading the newspaper during his speech, Seth paused midsentence to catch his audience's attention and said, "You know, I bet that whatever's in that paper isn't as current or relevant to our lives as my next point. Because, at this moment in time, our government is spending billions of dollars to cover up . . . ," and he continued with his topic. At that point, he had the full and respectful attention of the audience.

Sometimes, audience members are distracted by the speaker—by how he or she dresses, unusual hair styles, differences in speech styles, and so on.

Thomas Barwick/Riser/Getty Images

- **Here's how you can address this behavior:** Explain the distraction. In addition, be sure to dress appropriately for the speaking situation—Chapter 11 explains how personal appearance affects the way audiences see you.

- **Here's an example of a speaker who addressed this behavior successfully:** Angelique, a student with a strong accent, shared with her audience that she was from the Dominican Republic. She explained that her husband kept trying to correct her accent, but she told him, "It's my accent and I like it." Sharing this story in the introduction of her speech made her audience laugh and helped reduce the focus on her accent. It also helped her audience listen to her message.

  Approaching this type of situation with good-natured humor can go a long way toward reducing distractions and resistance to your message. It can also help your audience feel that you value them.

Audiences Who Are Confused

You can use a number of strategies to help audiences who appear confused by the information in your speech.

- **Here's how you can address this behavior:** Slow down and explain with more detail. Reduce your number of main points. Alter your language to be more inclusive, less complex, or even less simple. Improvise visual aids: Use an available flip chart or whiteboard, or ask someone from the audience to demonstrate your ideas.

- **Here's an example of a speaker who addressed this behavior successfully:** When Marilyn saw her audience looking confused, she outlined her main points on a whiteboard and jotted down key words and phrases. The audience applauded her efforts and acknowledged that her speech was much easier to follow with a visual map.

These hecklers disrupted a speech given by President George W. Bush in praise of local volunteering efforts. How could he have adapted to these audience members during his speech to help them listen to his message more effectively?

Audiences Who Plan Their Responses Rather Than Listen

Sometimes, particular audience members appear to be planning their responses to you during your speech.

- **Here's how you can address this behavior:** Both verbally and nonverbally, acknowledge their eagerness to participate and approach it as a positive sign of interest.

- **Here's an example of a speaker who addressed this behavior successfully:** When Hallie watched a member of her audience react with dismay to one of

Public Speaking and Service Learning: Engaging Community

Derek Cole, a public speaking student at Colorado State University, did his service learning project with the P.A.L.S. mentoring program sponsored by the Asian/Pacific American Cultural Center at Colorado State University. There, he worked with three "little pals," who helped him realize how powerful the act of listening can be. He continued his mentor role with this organization long after completing his 15 hours for credit.

For my service, I chose to work with the P.A.L.S. mentoring program sponsored by the Asian/Pacific American Cultural Center (APACC) at Colorado State University. I have learned much about the benefits of service work and, more specifically, about the importance of listening and interacting with children. I have found that if children are listened to, they are more likely to value listening to others. I currently work with three "little pals": Cole, Eric, and Glenn. Being Asian/Pacific American, I feel a great connection and responsibility for these boys—a lot of my problems relate closely to the obstacles and conflicts they encounter. Simply asking the children how their day or week was, and being ready to genuinely listen, gives them great satisfaction that someone actually cares. This is easily illustrated through their behavior and the smiles we both share.

Before working with these three, I didn't understand what a powerful tool listening is. Real listening requires effort, and you know you are doing it when you are concerned about understanding the other, not just making up your own reply as they talk. I have learned to be a better listener, adjusting what I say to the children as I see their reactions. I have taken these skills into the public speaking classroom by adjusting my rate of speaking, volume, animation level, and eye contact to the reactions I get from my audience. I learned how important this is from working with my little pals.

> **"REAL LISTENING REQUIRES EFFORT, AND YOU KNOW YOU ARE DOING IT WHEN YOU ARE CONCERNED ABOUT UNDERSTANDING THE OTHER, NOT JUST MAKING UP YOUR OWN REPLY AS THEY ARE TALKING."**

Tips for Incorporating Service Learning into Public Speaking

- Service learning can help you see the importance of being audience centered and of listening to others.
- Use your service learning experiences to help you learn how to listen to others. Then practice your listening skills in class, especially during speeches centered around social conflict. This kind of listening is hard work because it requires humility and patience, but it's worth the effort.
- A speaker has to "listen" just as attentively as audience members do during a speech, paying attention to their faces and body postures. These are indicators that the speaker might need to adjust his speaking style. Use your service learning experience to practice the skill of listening as you speak to others.

her claims and then fidget and sit on the edge of his seat, she knew she had to respond somehow. She acknowledged his desire to respond by saying, "I see I've struck a chord with some of you. If you'll hang on to your questions and hear me out, I'd love to hear your reactions at the end of the speech." Her resister relaxed a bit and was able to put his opposition aside long enough to listen to her full arguments and reasons. The conversation at the end of the speech was lively and dynamic, and both Hallie and the audience member benefited from it.

In Chapter 4, you will discover other excellent ways to help your audience listen to you. As a speaker, when you listen to your audience, you make your message more listenable and memorable, and you make it easier for your audience to give you the attention and respect you deserve.

Chapter Summary

We listen to others for very important reasons.

- We listen to others so we can confirm their ideas and enter the public dialogue in ways that are intelligent and rewarding.
- Listening is one of the most important communicative acts.

We sometimes fail to listen.

- Bad listening habits cause listener interference, which stops or hinders us from receiving messages.
- Our failure to listen well is also caused by speaker interference due to information, language, or other differences in style, background, appearance, and values.

There are many ways to improve our listening.

- To listen carefully, listen for supporting evidence and for the speaker's purpose, main ideas, and the links between ideas. Take notes and write questions you have for the speaker. Provide positive nonverbal feedback. Listen for the conclusion of the speech, and review the material you have just heard.
- To listen critically, assess the strengths and weaknesses of a speaker's reasoning and evidence, and remain open to new ideas and information.
- To listen ethically, listen for the moral implications of a message.
- Ethical listeners practice two listening behaviors: (1) suspending judgment and (2) assessing and responding to the speaker's ideas.

Speakers are also listeners and can adapt their messages so their speeches are listenable.

- When you give a speech, listen to your audience for signs of disinterest, hostility, or opposition.
- Also listen to make sure your style and mannerisms aren't confusing or distracting.
- Finally, listen for signs that your audience is confused by the information in your speech.

Invitation to Public Speaking Online

CourseMate Now that you have read Chapter 2, use your Speech Communication Course-Mate for *Invitation to Public Speaking* for quick access to the electronic resources that accompany this text. These resources include

- **Study tools** that will help you assess your learning and prepare for exams (*digital glossary, key term flash cards, review quizzes*).
- **Activities and assignments** that will help you hone your knowledge and build your public speaking skills throughout the course (*Practicing the Public Dialogue activities, review questions*).

- **Media resources** that will help you explore public speaking concepts online (*Web Connect links, Enhanced eBook*), develop your speech outlines (*Speech Builder Express 3.0*), watch and critique videos of sample speeches (*Interactive Video Activities*), upload your speech videos for peer reviewing and critique other students' speeches (*Speech Studio online speech review tool*), and download chapter review so you can study when and where you'd like (*Audio Study Tools*).

This chapter's key concepts and review questions are also featured here.

Key Concepts

careful listener (32)
colloquialism (26)
confirm (21)
considerate speech (22)
critical listener (33)
culturally inclusive language (27)

ethical listener (35)
euphemism (26)
gender-inclusive language (27)
hearing (22)
interference (22)
jargon (26)

listenable speech (22)
listening (22)
slang (26)
spotlighting (27)
verbal clutter (30)

Review Questions

1. Identify the times you have listened to confirm others. Were you able to recognize, acknowledge, and express value for another individual? Did you do this verbally or nonverbally? Now identify the times you listened with judgment. What are the differences between the two types of listening? Do you prefer one to the other? Why?

2. Monitor your listening for a day and write down five ways your listening failed. How might you change these bad listening habits?

3. Attend, watch, or listen to a speech given by someone very different from you. Pay attention to how you manage the listening interference that comes from differences. Can you listen nonjudgmentally? Can you accommodate different speech styles, mannerisms, dress, and backgrounds? How are you able to listen even though differences may be present?

4. What kinds of slang, jargon, or euphemisms do you use in your everyday interactions at school, at work, or at home? Make a list of some of the unique expressions you use and define each word or phrase on your list. Now think about your next speech topic and your audience. What would be the benefits or the drawbacks of using slang, jargon, or euphemisms in your speech?

5. Review the definition of ethical listening. What is the role of ethical listening in the public dialogue? Do you believe it is your responsibility to listen ethically? Do you think you can suspend judgment and listen to assess and respond to the information? Explain your answers.

Developing Your Speech Topic and Purpose

IN THIS CHAPTER, YOU WILL LEARN TO:

- Identify how context influences your speaking goals

- Choose a speech topic whether you decide to speak, are asked to speak, or are required to speak

- Develop clear statements of purpose for your speech

- Develop the thesis statement of your speech

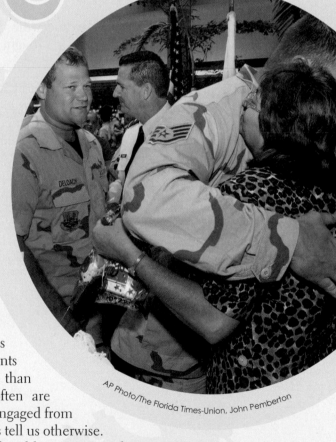

AP Photo/The Florida Times-Union, John Pemberton

In March 2001, thirty-three students from twenty-seven different colleges and universities gathered in Wisconsin for the Wingspread Summit on Student Civic Engagement. The students were invited to participate in a discussion about student political and civic engagement—to talk about what motivated them to speak out and get involved in their local communities. The summit was called because, although students have been volunteering more than ever in recent years, they often are described as apathetic and disengaged from civic life. However, their voices tell us otherwise. They are, in fact, very engaged and have a strong desire to speak out on issues that are important to them.

The Wingspread students said they felt moved to volunteer and participate in civic activities as a result of their personal experiences and interests. It wasn't self-interest that motivated them but rather a recognition of the uniqueness of other people and a desire to promote inclusiveness. Although their activities might not fit the familiar standards for political engagement, that didn't mean they weren't civically involved. Each student often became involved with a number of different issues. For example, one student identified three areas in which she engaged politically and participated in the public dialogue: She organized students against sweatshops, lobbied her state legislature to replace the Native American mascot at her school, and volunteered to teach English as a second language to new immigrants.[1]

Whether you'd like to engage in what the Wingspread students called "participatory democracy" or use public speaking skills in a different way, this chapter will help you select interesting and relevant topics for your speeches. It will also help you determine the best way to frame a topic so you fulfill your speaking purpose, or what you want to accomplish with your speech.

Successful public speaking is usually the result of careful planning and forethought rather than any so-called intuitive or natural speaking ability. No doubt, we can and do find ourselves in front of audiences without much advance notice. However, we are more likely to find ourselves speaking on topics we care about after we've had time to prepare our ideas. Although preparation means work, careful planning before you speak helps you choose speech topics and then narrow them and your purpose to accommodate three speaking contexts: when you decide to speak, when you have been asked to speak, and when you are required to speak.

How Context Influences Your Speaking Goals

There are many different contexts for speaking—formal or informal settings, large or small audiences, serious or lighthearted issues, and so on. Identifying the context in which you speak publicly will help you understand the connection between why we speak publicly and what we speak about.

Deciding to Speak

The most common reason to speak is because we find an issue so important or our experience so relevant that we decide to speak about it. This is also perhaps the most powerful reason people become public speakers. Before the advent of television and radio, people used a variety of platforms to share their opinions and ideas. They spoke in churches and town halls, at street corners, in town squares or centers, and on soapboxes—wooden platforms made out of empty boxes of soap that people stood on to give a speech. So important was the power of public speech in shaping opinions and influencing actions that until the 1850s, legislation in the United States prevented certain people, such as women, from speaking publicly.

Today, people often view mass media as the voice of the public, forgetting we still can and do insert our own voices into public discussions. Although most of us do not have free and easy access to the airwaves—or carry soapboxes around with us—we do decide to speak on many occasions. In educational settings, we give class presentations and participate in student government. In social gatherings, we offer toasts and congratulations to others, or we debate current issues. In business and professional meetings, we discuss ideas and create plans. And in community forums, we speak about the environment, population growth, education, and the like.

When people decide to speak, as the Wingspread students did, they generally speak about issues central to their lives and well-being. To decide to speak publicly is to decide you can offer an audience important knowledge or a valuable perspective.

Being Asked to Speak

To be asked to speak is probably the most flattering context for a public speaker. When we are asked to speak, we are asked to share important experiences, our expertise, or our perspectives with others. When we are asked to speak, we are recognized as experts or at least as a person who has information others want. As you move through life, you might find you are asked to speak in educational settings, at service clubs, or at formal or professional gatherings. But remember that although you may be considered an expert, you'll be a more successful speaker if you follow the principles of speech preparation discussed in this book. Expertise in a particular subject area does not always guarantee you are an expert at giving speeches.

After Hurricane Charley hit Florida in 2004, six-year-old Zach Bonner was motivated to help out by distributing water to families in need. He's been helping people ever since. Now thirteen, one of his most recent—and impressive—feats has been a solo cross-country walk from Florida to California to raise awareness and funds for homeless kids. As a result of his work and his experiences, he has been asked to speak publicly many times. For what reasons do you think you might be asked to speak? Can you think of experiences or expertise you have that you might be asked to speak about? If you weren't asked, would you decide or choose to speak about them in a required setting, such as your speech class?

Being Required to Speak

Being required to speak can be a regular part of our lives. For example, you're now taking a public speaking course that requires you to give speeches. But outside the public speaking class, you may have a job that requires public speaking, such as in marketing or as a tour guide. Occasionally, you may have to fulfill a civic or legal obligation, such as speaking before a Senate hearing or as part of a jury.

When you are required to speak, you often must follow strict guidelines. For example, in a professional setting, your boss may provide you with a topic, a specified amount of time, and a speaking goal and then ask you to give a presentation at a meeting. In a typical public speaking assignment, you may be asked to give an informative speech that is three minutes long, cites two sources, and includes a visual aid. Although we may not like required public speaking, learning to give speeches in a public speaking course can be invaluable. If you view a classroom speaking requirement as an opportunity to prepare for other speaking contexts, you can make the most of the time you spend in class. In a public speaking course, you are given structure and guidance that can help you improve your presentational skills and participate in the public dialogue.

These three contexts—deciding, being asked, and being required to speak—are the reasons people enter the public dialogue. Understanding how you become a public speaker is the first step in preparing a successful presentation. Once you recognize why you are speaking, you can turn your attention to selecting and narrowing your speech topic and deciding on your purpose for speaking.

Choosing Your Speech Topic

Your **speech topic** is the subject of your speech. Selecting a topic for a speech can be a very creative and energizing part of putting a speech together. With a little systematic thought and inventive organization, speakers often come up with a wide range of interesting speech topics. By now, you've probably discovered in your public speaking course that you need to choose a topic of interest to both you and your audience. The steps described in this section will help you find interesting and relevant speech topics for your required speeches. When you decide or are asked to speak, your topic is usually predetermined. Your task in these contexts is to make sure you understand your topic fully. You can do this by asking yourself several questions, which are discussed at the end of this section.

Good to Know!

speech topic: Subject of your speech.

The Classroom Setting

Before you can select an appropriate and interesting topic for your assigned speech, you must consider the requirements of your assignment. Assigned speeches usually have several constraints because they are presented in a classroom setting.

- *Preselected purpose.* An instructor usually tells you to give a particular type of speech such as a speech to inform or persuade. You do not have the freedom to select your speech purpose, and you must select a topic compatible with the purpose.

- *Time limits.* Class size determines speech length; your instructor wants to make sure everyone in the class has time to give their speeches. Classroom speeches often last only a few minutes, and you may be penalized for going over time. You must select and narrow your topic to satisfy the assignment's time limits.

- *Highly structured assignment.* You're usually asked to incorporate several specific speech components. You may be required to cite a specific number of outside sources, use visual aids, incorporate a specific style of language, or use a particular organizational pattern. The structure of an assigned speech often influences topic selection.

- *Instructor as an audience.* You give your classroom speeches to an instructor who is already a skilled public speaker. You must select a stimulating topic that your instructor, who has listened to many other speeches, will appreciate.

- *Class members as an audience.* Your classmates may become the best audience for you as a beginning public speaker. They're also learning the ropes of public speaking, and they'll appreciate your diligent efforts. But they can also be a challenge because they may be interested in topics your instructor doesn't want to hear about. Additionally, they're also searching for interesting topics, so try to avoid commonly used topics.

So how do you select a manageable, interesting, and dynamic topic for your required speeches? The process takes a bit of planning and effort, but you will discover that you have a wealth of usable ideas once you organize your thoughts about who you are, what you know, and what issues and events capture your own attention.

SOPHIE DUVAL/PA Photos /Landov

Suppose you were required to speak and selected the art of British graffiti artist Banksy as your general topic. Some more specific topics could be the importance of his art, the long history of graffiti, the recent emergence of graffiti as an art form versus a form of vandalism, and the importance of graffiti in hip-hop and gang culture. What other topics can you think of that relate to Banksy?

Choosing Your Topic When You Are Required to Speak

One of the most basic ways to select a topic for a required speech is to make a list of your interests and give a speech about one of them. In this section, you'll discover that with some care and time, you can build on this basic process to come up with unique and exciting slants on topics that at first may seem uninteresting.

In a public speaking classroom, the first step in selecting a topic is to outline the requirements of the speech assignment. Write down your speech requirements at the top of your computer screen page or a piece of paper. Your assignment might look like this:

Informative purpose; four minutes long; three to four sources; one statistic; one of the following: metaphor, analogy, narrative, or alliteration; inclusive language.

The second step is to match your interests or expertise to these requirements.

Matching your interests to a speaking assignment. Before you can match your interests to a particular assignment, you must determine what they are. Divide your interests into the following categories: what you like to do, what you like to talk about, and what you would like to know more about.

Most people can identify many activities they like to participate in. Make a list of them, including those that seem serious as well as playful or silly. Try to be as detailed as possible. Krista, a twenty-three-year-old college senior, likes to do the following:

- swim, run, cycle
- play soccer, volleyball, tennis, and Frisbee golf
- snowboard, skateboard, and hike
- watch television and movies
- Facebook

- spend time with her friends
- coach children in sports during the summer
- get good grades
- stay up late
- eat pizza, hamburgers, anything barbecued, and some vegetables

With a little adjustment and creativity, any of these interests could be turned into an interesting informative topic. Krista could inform her audience about any of the following:

- the top ten medal-earning swimmers in the world
- how to play Frisbee golf
- the longest-running television sitcom
- gender differences in friendship styles
- medical research on optimal sleeping patterns

- the history of marathon running
- who invented skateboards
- the first chat room on the Web
- the relationship between grades and annual income
- the origins of pizza

These are just a few of the many informative topics Krista could speak about, all relevant to her instructor, her classmates, and the public dialogue.

Another good way to find speech topics is to take inventory of what you like to talk about. To do this, ask yourself the following questions:

- When do you find yourself participating in discussions?
- When do you feel like you have a lot to say about an issue but don't speak up?
- What topics do you raise in conversations?
- What topics do you repeatedly return to or seek more information about?

For example, Keenan loves to talk about basketball. He could turn this very broad topic into a dynamic speech by going beyond the obvious. What does he love about the sport? Is it the players' skill, the strategy of the game, the politics of athletics, or the behaviors of sports fans? He could fashion a speech out of any of these topics:

- evolution of basketball as a sport
- advantages and disadvantages of starting children in the sport at a young age
- money behind the game

- balance between athletic talent and game strategy
- role of sports fans in supporting individual teams

With some creativity and effort, Keenan could turn his love of basketball into an informative, invitational, or persuasive speech.

Issues, events, people, and ideas you are curious about also often make excellent speech topics. You could give a speech that informs others of a particular event, or you could persuade them to participate in that event. If you are intrigued by a famous person, you could give a commemorative or informative speech about that person's life and accomplishments. If you are curious about a place, an idea, an object, or an animal, you could explore it with others in an informative or invitational speech. If you participate in an activity or have always wanted to do so, you could give a persuasive, informative, or invitational speech about it. Speeches that grow out of a speaker's curiosity often capture the attention, interest, and curiosity of an audience as well.

Matching your expertise to a speech assignment. *Expertise* can be an intimidating label, but whether we realize it or not, almost everyone is an expert in some area of life. Some people are experts in obvious ways, such as playing a musical instrument, painting, or computer programming. Other people are experts in less obvious ways. They may have an unfailing sense of direction, know the right gift to buy for any occasion, or tell hilarious jokes. Dynamic speech topics can come from your own skills and talents. Consider the following examples:

- Tomás is an excellent cook. He decides to give an informative speech on the differences between traditional Bolivian and Spanish foods.
- April is fluent in American Sign Language. She decides to give a speech persuading her audience to learn a second language.
- Rachael comes from a family of artists. She decides to give a speech inviting her audience to support the arts.
- Gardner is a mechanic. He decides to give a commemorative speech on nineteenth-century French inventor Gustave Trouvé, the creator of the first automobile powered by electricity.

These are interesting speech topics about activities or skills that may seem mundane to the person who has them. You can identify areas in which you may be considered an expert by asking yourself the following questions:

- What comes naturally to me?
- What runs in my family?
- Do I often get compliments when I do a particular thing?
- Do others repeatedly ask me to take the lead, take care of some situation, or solve a problem for them?
- Have I ever had special training or lessons?
- Have I spent years studying, practicing, or doing something?
- Do I have degrees, certifications, licenses, or other markers of my accomplishments?

If you answered yes to any of these questions, you may be an expert in some area that would make an interesting topic for a required speech. Although not all of our experiences make us experts, you might find you have expertise because of an event you've witnessed or an environment you've been in. Consider these possibilities:

- Did you live or grow up in another country?
- Did you play sports in high school or college?
- Is there something about your family that is unique or unusual?
- Have you had unexpected or momentous experiences in your life?
- Have you been exposed to other cultures, religions, and philosophies?

Situations like these can generate short speeches that satisfy the requirements of an assignment, capture the attention of your instructor and classmates, and relate directly to the public dialogue. A few final tips: As you translate your

Public Speaking and Service Learning: Engaging Community

Peter R. Baldwin, a public speaking student at Colorado State University, did his service learning project at the Northern Colorado AIDS Project (NCAP). His participation in service learning within the context of his speech class sparked interest in a topic he'd not been interested in before, HIV/AIDS. His passion for this topic, which has great relevance in the public dialogue, inspired him to put the time into his research and really try to relate to his audience so he could "pass on the message" about his interactions and experiences.

Working for the Northern Colorado AIDS Project was an amazing experience that taught me a lot about society as a whole and how diverse the world truly is. Community service, along with this speech class, has not only opened my eyes but caused me to become a lot more enthusiastic about helping out the community. Community service in a learning environment is a wonderful idea because it helps students learn through firsthand experience.

In working for NCAP, I realized how many people actually had AIDS. While delivering food and talking to those affected with this devastating disease, I became more satisfied with myself. I also think that these interactions made me a more open-minded person. I now feel less judgmental when I first see someone, and I feel like I better understand how AIDS affects people's lives.

The great thing about service learning is that your community service draws you in and makes you

"I GAINED INTEREST IN THE TOPIC, WHICH CAUSED ME TO DO MORE RESEARCH AND TRY HARDER TO RELATE TO MY AUDIENCE."

very interested in your topic and your research. In my case, I originally wasn't very interested in the topic of HIV/AIDS, but when I found out how prevalent the disease is, I gained interest in the topic, which caused me to do more research and try harder to relate to my audience. I personally think everyone should give their services to the community if they have time. A speech class is perfect to make into a service learning class because the students get passionate about the subject, and they can pass on the message they get from experience and research to others.

Tips for Incorporating Service Learning into Public Speaking

- Your service learning assignment can provide you with many excellent speech topics. As you identify topics, make sure they fit the goal of your speech assignment. Don't feel you need to cling to a topic, especially if you know you'll struggle to make it fit a particular speech format.
- Once you decide on a topic you're interested in, think about your specific audience and ask yourself if they also would be interested in it. Try to frame your topic so that it will appeal to them as much as it does to you.
- In your introduction, the audience will want to hear how you relate personally to your topic, so don't be afraid to explain how your service learning work led you to your topic.

experiences into speech topics, be certain you can talk about them easily without getting upset or revealing more than you are comfortable with. And note that although you might know a lot about a topic, you should still research it to discover interesting aspects about which you might be unaware.

Brainstorming

Brainstorming is the process of generating ideas randomly and uncritically, without attention to logic, connections, or relevance. This process requires you to free-associate rather than plan, and it is often used as a problem-solving strategy in business settings. Brainstorming can be an effective tool for coming up with speech topics in required speaking situations, and you can use this technique by yourself, in pairs, or in groups. Here are some tips for successful brainstorming:

- Let your thoughts go where they will. Don't censor yourself or others. Allow all ideas, even those that seem trivial or odd.

- Write down your ideas quickly. Don't worry about spelling or punctuation, and abbreviate whenever you can.

- Keep your list handy over the course of several days, and add to it as new thoughts come to you.

There are several ways to approach brainstorming: by free association, by clustering, by categories, and by technology.

Brainstorming by free association. Brainstorming can be as unstructured as sitting at your desk with a pencil and paper, or at your computer with a blank screen, and recording all ideas that come to your mind. Although it might take a moment for the first idea to come to mind, more will follow in rapid succession.

Brainstorming on a computer is especially effective because many people can type faster than they can write in longhand. When you record your ideas quickly, your thoughts also flow quickly. If you use a computer, consider starting by free-associating with the computer screen turned off. Sometimes, the blank screen allows you to free-associate without the pressure of filling up a blank page. At other times, seeing your ideas on the screen stimulates your thinking and spurs additional ideas.[2] After only a minute, a typical free association list might look like this:

© Rudi Von Briel / PhotoEdit

Using a busy image like this as a basis for brainstorming can yield a lot of good ideas for speech topics. What possible topics come to mind when you consider the details of this photo? Can you narrow your ideas down to one interesting topic that would interest your audience and contribute to the public dialogue?

hands, keyboard, letters, movement, running, wind, kites, children, play, laughter, skinned knees, Band-Aids, nurses, hospitals, sterile, feral cats, tiger, cougars, wilderness, encroachment, farming, ranching, cows, cowboys, rodeos, circus, clowns, entertainment, containment, buckets, garage, car, war, peace, hostility, conflict, harm, warm, cold, snow skiing, skis, lifts, chairs, dining rooms, meals, holidays, families, celebration, gifts

A free association list can go on and on until you run out of ideas. When you're trying to come up with a speech topic, try to spend at least several minutes brainstorm-

Good to Know!

brainstorming: Process of generating ideas randomly and uncritically, without attention to logic, connections, or relevance.

Developing Your Speech Topic and Purpose

ing by free association to generate as many ideas as possible. Once you've compiled your list, explore it to determine if one of your ideas might be an appropriate speech topic. The free association list here could generate the following interesting speech topics:

- the inventor of Band-Aids
- what to do when you encounter a feral cat
- different kinds of clowns
- how different countries celebrate holidays or the starts of new seasons

If brainstorming by free association doesn't generate the kinds of topics you think might make an interesting speech, other techniques might help.

Brainstorming by clustering. Clustering is a visual way to brainstorm. Write down an idea in the center of a piece of paper and then draw four or five lines extending from it. At the ends of these lines, write down other ideas that relate to your first idea. Then extend lines from these new ideas to even more ideas. Let's take a look at Jeret's clustering diagram. He began scuba diving at a very young age, so he used this as his general idea and developed the cluster of ideas in Figure 3.1.

Figure 3.1

Cluster diagram

The figure shows that from scuba diving, his general idea, Jeret was able to branch out to many additional ideas. Brainstorming by clustering is a good way to generate speech topics because it gives some structure to the brainstorming process without limiting your possibilities too much.

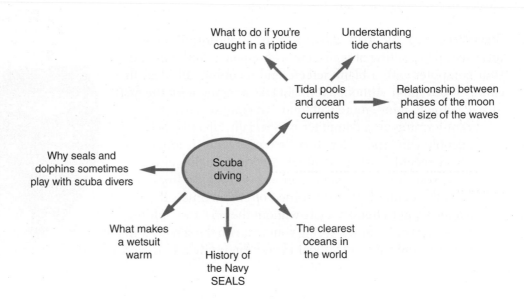

Brainstorming by categories. Most speeches given in public speaking classrooms are about concepts, events, natural phenomena, objects, people, places, plans and policies, problems, and processes. As you've probably noticed, these topics represent different categories. Brainstorming by categories is an excellent way to generate a speech topic, and it provides more structure than free association or clustering. To brainstorm by categories, list the following nine categories on your computer screen or a piece of paper. Then list five or six different words under each heading that fit into the indicated categories. Two students working together came up with this list:

Concepts

socialism
tourism
sustainability
astrophysics
dieting
long-distance
relationships

Objects

cell phones
guitars
TiVo
films of M. Night
Shyamalan
Japanese teapots
mountains

Plans and policies

universal health
care
government
stimulus plans
No Child Left
Behind Act
sex education
censorship laws

Events

Haitian earthquake
relief
Gulf Coast oil spill
Walk for the Cure
Mardi Gras
Inti Raymi (Incan
Festival of the Sun)
Oktoberfest

People

Barack Obama
Sarah Palin
Tiger Woods
Lindsay Lohan
Kanye West
Apollo Ohno

Problems

terrorism
sexism
racism
cancer
obesity

Natural phenomena

tornadoes
eclipses
monsoons
geysers
mudslides
glaciers

Places

my hometown
Machu Picchu
Germany
China
Tanzania
Stonehenge

Processes

brewing beer
building a house
preparing a meal
debating versus
dialoguing
making jewelry

If none of the words you write down immediately strikes you as a good speech topic, select one or two and use free association or clustering to narrow your scope, generate new ideas, or frame the topic in a way that is interesting and fits the requirements of your assignment.

Similarly, if none of your brainstormed topics catches your interest, link several of them together. Can you find a connection among Mexico, India, and your hometown? What about these locations and tsunamis or earthquakes? How about laptops, espresso machines, and theme dining? Linking any of these topics, randomly or with purpose, gives you additional opportunities to develop interesting speech topics.

Brainstorming by technology. You can use technology in a number of ways to find a suitable speech topic. If you have access to the Internet, you can discover possible topics by browsing a search engine's subject indexes. Google, Yahoo!, Bing, and Ask are popular search engines that many people are familiar with. By accessing this resource, you can explore an array of topics, click a general subject, and link to more and more specific websites until you find a topic that interests you and fits the requirements of your speech assignment.

Libraries also provide many online indexes for journals, newspapers, magazines, and the like. Browse through the *Reader's Guide to Periodical Literature*, InfoTrac College Edition, *The New York Times Index*, or subject-specific indexes about medicine, physics, science, or women's studies. (In Chapter 5, you'll explore how to use these types of resources more fully.)

Narrowing Your Topic When You Are Asked to or Decide to Speak

When we decide to speak, we are responding to an issue we are interested in or concerned about. When we are asked to speak, we are usually given a topic that a specific audience wants to hear about. Even though your speech topics in these contexts are predetermined, when you decide or are asked to speak, you want to be sure you clearly understand what your topic is and what's expected of you as a speaker. Sometimes, we decide to speak about issues that are complex or controversial, and when we are asked to speak, the exact topic isn't always very clear. When you decide or are asked to speak, take a moment to ask yourself, or the person who's asked you to speak, the following questions:

- What *exactly* is the topic of my speech? If I have decided to speak, what specific topic do I want to talk about? If I have been asked to speak, what specific topic does my audience want to hear about?

- Can I discuss this topic in the time allowed, or do I need to narrow or broaden my scope? Is there some aspect of this topic that I might be better able to cover in the time allowed?

- Who is my audience? What is my relationship to them? If I've decided to speak, am I qualified to speak about this topic? Will my audience see me as qualified? If not, could I change my topic or strengthen my qualifications in some way? If I've been asked to speak, why am I qualified to speak about this topic?

These questions will help you focus and narrow your topic so it is appropriate for your speaking situation. They'll also help you better understand why you want to speak or why you've been asked to speak and what you're most qualified and prepared to speak about.

Whether you take inventory of your interests and skills, use brainstorming techniques, decide what you are motivated to speak about, or are given a topic to speak about, recognize that you are capable of generating any number of speech topics. With a little bit of creativity and organization, you can come up with speech topics that are interesting and relevant to the public dialogue.

Articulating Your Purpose

There are many different types of speaking: speaking to inform, invite, or persuade and speaking on special occasions and in small groups. For each of these speaking types, the speaker has a different goal: to inform, invite, and persuade or to introduce, commemorate, and accept. These are the goals we focus on in this chapter. Note that as a speaker in or as part of a small group, your speaking goal generally falls into one of these six categories. As such, we'll save the discussion of small group speaking's unique components until the appendix at the end of this book.

Speaking goals can be explained in terms of general purposes and specific purposes. The **general purpose** of a speech is its broad goal: to inform, invite, or persuade or to introduce, commemorate, and accept. The **specific purpose** is a

Good to Know!

general purpose: Speech's broad goal: to inform, invite, persuade, introduce, commemorate, or accept. **specific purpose:** Focused statement that identifies exactly what a speaker wants to accomplish with a speech.

focused statement that identifies exactly what a speaker wants to accomplish with a speech. Let's take a look at how you use each of these purposes to organize your thoughts about your speeches.

General Speaking Purposes

Suppose your instructor asks you to speak about organic farming. You could speak about many aspects of this topic. Without knowing your purpose for your speech, it can be difficult to know where to begin. Do you describe organic farming, what it is, and who practices it (informative)? Do you ask your audience to explore the impact of organic farming on the environment and the average family's grocery bills (invitational)? Do you attempt to convince your classmates that organic farming is the most efficient type of farming (persuasive)? Do you commemorate organic farming or something about it (commemorative)? Your first step toward answering these questions is to determine the overall goal for your speech, or your general purpose:

To inform: describe, clarify, explain, define

To invite: explore, discuss, exchange, understand

To persuade: change, shape, influence, motivate

To introduce: acquaint, present, familiarize

To commemorate: praise, honor, pay tribute

To accept: receive an award, express gratitude

Notice that each of these overall goals is quite different from the others. For example, the goal of acquainting is different from the goal of praising, which is different from the goal of clarifying. So by determining your general purpose, you begin to find a focus for your speech.

Specific Speaking Purposes

Once you determine your general purpose, you must then determine what exactly you want to communicate to your audience, or your specific purpose. Specific speaking purposes help you narrow the focus of your speech. A specific purpose states exactly what you want to accomplish in the speech. To understand the importance of a speech's specific purpose, consider Ashley's speaking situation.

For her service learning assignment, Ashley tutored fourth graders in an after-school math homework program. This experience prompted her interest in several topics related to the public school system in her state, including possible gender bias in math education and the Pledge of Allegiance. She decided that she wanted to talk about the Pledge and that her general speaking purpose was to persuade. She knew she wanted to convince her classmates to change their views on the Pledge, but how exactly did she want them to change? What did she want to persuade them to do or think? If she hadn't figured this out,

Practicing the Public Dialogue

3.1

Generate a List of Possible Speech Topics

Make a list of what you like to do or want to know more about. Make this list as detailed as you can, including what you find yourself discussing with friends or what people say you're good at. Now brainstorm additional topics using one of the techniques you read about in this chapter. Next organize the topics you've listed by categories to help you see connections among your topics and possibly generate more. If you are doing a service learning project in your speech class, make a list of possible topics related to your volunteer experience. Choose ten possible speech topics for your next speech. Set them aside for now.

Online Resources

CourseMate Brainstorming with technology can help stimulate your thinking about contemporary topics. Do your own brainstorming with technology by completing **Web Connect 3.1: Brainstorming with Technology** online via your CourseMate for *Invitation to Public Speaking*.

she would have found herself going in circles as she prepared her speech. She would have researched supporting material she didn't need, and she would have gotten frustrated as she lost sight of what she wanted to accomplish with her speech.

Civic Engagement in Action

A MILLION THANKS

In 2004, Shauna Fleming was a freshman in high school. One day, her father challenged her to motivate her school to do something positive for National Military Appreciation Month, celebrated each May, as a way of honoring the men and women who serve in the military. Fleming decided on a letter campaign and set a goal of sending a million letters. Her decision was influenced by her experience the previous year, when she'd assisted her father in collecting and distributing more than 300,000 valentines to the March Air Reserve Base. "Many of the pilots had tears in their eyes reading the messages. I know the appreciation letters we'll deliver in May will help to lift [soldiers'] spirits."

Her campaign received a boost when a disc jockey from Knoxville interviewed her by phone and introduced her to musician John Michael Montgomery, whose song "Letters from Home" was the inspiration for her campaign. "John Michael had not heard about my letter campaign for the military, so I talked to him on the phone and told him what I was trying to do," said Fleming. "We talked about his song and how he feels the same way I do, that Americans need to show more appreciation for what our service men and women do to protect our freedom."

By July 1, 2004, Fleming had received and sent 800,000 letters and had corresponded with numerous military women and men via e-mail. In addition to sending letters, she began to campaign for donations of movie and music DVDs and CDs to send to troops to help them pass the time as their tours were extended. In October 2004, Fleming framed the millionth letter for President George W. Bush.

When she learned from the Pentagon that a total of 1.4 million military personnel were overseas, Fleming explained, "I wanted to find a way to thank all of

AP Photo/Chris Carlson

our service members, so I decided to continue collecting letters and e-mails until I reached 1.4 million." The Million Thanks organization reached that number in May 2005. Fleming then sent a framed copy of the 1.4 millionth letter to General Richard B. Myers, Chairman, Joint Chiefs of Staff.

Fleming continues to use the public dialogue to let people know about her letter campaign and to encourage them to support our military men and women. In May 2007, her book, *A Million Thanks*, was published; she has partnered with General Motors to film commercials asking viewers to thank our troops by writing a thank-you letter; she's established a website and a Twitter account for her organization; and A Million Thanks has collected and distributed over 4.5 million thank-you letters, cards, and e-mails to U.S. military members.[3]

You Can Get Involved

CourseMate To learn more about A Million Thanks and write a thank-you letter yourself, access Web Connect 3.2: A Million Thanks at your CourseMate for *Invitation to Public Speaking*. Also check out **Web Connect 3.3: Iraq War Veterans** and **Web Connect 3.4: Afghanistan and Iraq War Veterans**. These links provide information and support for U.S. veterans of the conflicts in Afghanistan and Iraq. Many of the links at these sites direct you to information about how you can help U.S. soldiers readjust to civilian life.

Ashley needed to develop a specific-purpose statement. How did she do this? First, she identified her **behavioral objectives**, the actions she wanted her audience to take at the end of her speech. After some thought, she decided that she wanted her classmates to change their view of the Pledge. She wrote on a piece of paper, "I want my classmates to believe differently about the Pledge of Allegiance." Her speech purpose still was fairly broad, but it was more focused than her general purpose of persuading her classmates to change.

Ashley's next step was to narrow the focus of her behavioral objective even further. She defined what she meant by "believe differently." Based on her experiences in the public school and her research, she gained increased understanding of what the Pledge means and why she thought it should be recited with the phrase "under God" by children in school. After some thought, Ashley realized that more specifically than wanting her classmates to believe differently, she wanted them to adopt her views about the Pledge.

So while Ashley generally wanted to persuade her audience to believe differently, she specifically wanted to persuade them to support the Pledge. Thus, her specific-purpose statement was, "I want to persuade my audience that the Pledge, including the phrase 'under God,' should be recited in schools." At this point, she had a very focused idea of what she wanted to communicate to her audience. She then found it much easier to prepare a speech with a specific purpose than if she'd stopped at her general purpose of wanting her audience to change.

Table 3.1 on page 56 shows more examples of general and specific purposes. Notice the differences between them. From the six general purposes, you could generate specific purposes for at least twelve very different speeches.

When you state your specific speaking purpose, state it clearly and remain audience centered. Consider the following tips.

State your specific speaking purpose clearly. Begin your specific-purpose statements with the infinitive phrases *to inform, to invite, to persuade, to introduce, to commemorate*, or *to accept*. These phrases clearly indicate what your general purpose is and what you hope to accomplish with your speech. Compare the following correct and incorrect statements of purpose:

Correct	Incorrect
To introduce Master Cho and three of his most noteworthy accomplishments to my audience.	Master Cho's talent
To inform my audience of the history of martial arts in the United States.	I'm going to talk about martial arts.

Correct	Incorrect
To invite my coworkers to explore ways we could support local community gardens.	Supporting community gardening
To persuade my audience that practicing martial arts is an excellent form of exercise.	The martial arts are good for you.

Good to Know!

behavioral objectives: Actions a speaker wants the audience to take at the end of a speech.

Table 3.1
General and Specific Speaking Purposes

General Purpose	Specific Purpose
To inform	• To inform my audience of the services offered by our campus counseling center. • To inform my audience of the process of planting, harvesting, and preparing organic produce.
To invite	• To invite my audience to consider the merits of the three martial arts experts who have interviewed for our school. • To invite my audience to explore the implications of turning the city's abandoned municipal lot into a clean, safe skatepark.
To persuade	• To persuade my audience to use the services offered by our campus counseling center. • To persuade my audience to buy organic produce.
To introduce	• To introduce my audience to Dr. A. J. Johnson, director of our counseling center. • To introduce my audience to today's schedule for our tour of the Martial Arts Center.
To commemorate	• To commemorate for my audience my grandparents and the values they taught me during my summers on their organic farm. • To commemorate for my audience Wong Fei Hung, one of the first well-known masters of the martial arts.
To accept	• To accept an award from my employer for our highly successful peer counseling program. • To accept the city council's Outstanding Community Project award for my efforts at constructing a clean, safe skatepark in the city's abandoned municipal lot.

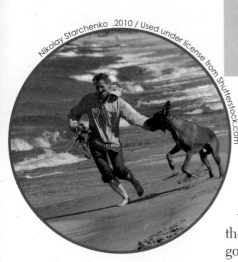

Nikolay Starchenko ,2010 / Used under license from Shutterstock.com

Many general subjects, such as humans' relationship to animals, can generate a seemingly infinite number of speech topics. By narrowing your focus and keeping your audience in mind, you can prepare a manageable speech and let your audience know what to expect.

Notice that the incorrect statements are unfocused and don't indicate the overall goal of the speech. Although it may seem that the incorrect statements leave greater room for a speaker's creativity, they are too vague to be of much help when you prepare your speech. For example, the statement "Master Cho's talent" functions better as a speech topic than a statement of purpose. The statement "I'm going to talk about martial arts" won't help the speaker focus on a particular aspect of martial arts and prepare a manageable speech. Nor will it give an audience a sense of what direction the speech will take. Similarly, the phrase "supporting community gardening" doesn't indicate the speaker's speech goal at all. In contrast, each of the correct statements provides you with a focused, solid framework from which to prepare your speech, and each lets audiences know what they can expect to hear in your speech.

Keep your audience in the forefront of your mind. Remember, you are speaking to and for a particular audience, and you research and organize your speech with this fact in mind. Your specific purpose should clearly reflect the presence of your audience. To this end, be sure your specific-purpose statement includes the words *my audience* or a more specific synonym. Compare the following correct and incorrect statements of purpose:

Correct	Incorrect
To inform my audience of the process of planting, harvesting, and preparing organic produce.	The methods of growing organic produce
To invite my coworkers to consider altering our current training program.	Shall we alter our training methods?
To persuade my audience of the importance of growing and eating organic fruit.	We should grow and eat organic fruit.
To commemorate for my audience Native American hero Chief Joseph, peacemaker and humanitarian.	Chief Joseph was a Native American peacemaker and humanitarian.
To accept and express my gratitude to the city council and my neighbors for the Outstanding Community Project award.	Thank you for this Outstanding Community Project award.

Notice how the correct examples encourage you to reflect on the makeup of your audience in ways that the incorrect examples do not. The words "my audience," "the city council and my neighbors," and "my coworkers" encourage the speaker to focus on a specific group of people with particular traits and characteristics, not on some unspecified entity.

As you begin to organize the materials for your speech, write your general and specific statements of purpose at the top of all your research notes. Like any good road map, clear statements of purpose help you select and navigate the path toward putting the final touches on your presentation.

Stating Your Thesis

So far in this chapter, you've explored how context affects your speaking goals, how to select a speech topic, and what your general and specific purposes are. Now you are ready to take the final step to complete this initial part of the speech preparation process. Every successful speech has a *thesis statement*, sometimes called a *central idea*. A **thesis statement** summarizes in a single declarative sentence the main ideas, assumptions, or arguments you want to express in your speech. It adds focus to your specific purpose because in a thesis statement you state, in a single sentence, the exact content of your speech.

Practicing the Public Dialogue

3.2

Write a General-Purpose Statement and a Specific-Purpose Statement

With three or four other students in class, look over the lists of topics you selected in Practicing the Public Dialogue 3.1. Select one or two topics from each person and write a general-purpose statement and a specific-purpose statement for each. Consider which topics would work best for informative, persuasive, invitational, or commemorative speeches.

Online Resources

You can use Speech Builder Express to help you create these statements. Select "Goal/Purpose" from the left menu and follow the instructions. For short reminders about general- and specific-purpose statements, click the "Tutor" button.

Good to Know!

thesis statement: Statement that summarizes in a single declarative sentence the main ideas, assumptions, or arguments you want to express in your speech.

Note that the thesis statement is closely related to the specific purpose. Recall that the specific-purpose statement indicates what you want your audience to understand or do as a result of your speech. The thesis statement helps you accomplish this goal by allowing you to state in a single sentence the specific ideas you will cover in the speech. The thesis statement helps you identify the main ideas of your speech, which will become your main points for the speech (Chapter 8).

Let's look again at some specific-purpose statements to see how they relate to thesis statements (see also Table 3.2):

Specific purpose: To inform my audience of the different belts in the martial arts

With this statement, Oscar claims it is useful to understand the different belt levels in the martial arts. To focus his speech on a manageable aspect of this topic, he must determine exactly what he wants the audience to know about the martial arts belt systems. He considers what he is asked most often about this topic. Thus, his thesis statement looks like this:

Thesis statement: In the three most common schools of martial arts in the United States—judo, karate, and tae kwon do—the black belt is the most esteemed belt level among the slightly differing belt systems.

With his thesis statement, Oscar considers how much common knowledge there is about the martial arts as well as what people are most curious about. Additionally, his thesis statement summarizes and previews two main points:

1. Judo, karate, and tae kwon do are the most common schools of martial arts in the United States.
2. Each school has a slightly different belt system, but the black belt is the most esteemed belt level in all the schools.

Consider a second example:

Specific purpose: To persuade my audience to eat healthy organic fruit

This statement makes the claim that organic fruit is good for you. To persuade your audience to eat it (what you want to accomplish), you must refine this statement to explain why eating organic fruit is good for you (what you will say to accomplish your goal). In explaining why, your thesis statement begins to take shape:

Thesis statement: Because organic fruit does not contain the dangerous chemicals found in nonorganic fruit, it is far healthier for people to eat and better for the environment.

This thesis statement indicates that the speech will consist of three main points:

1. Organic fruits do not contain dangerous chemicals.
2. Organic fruits are healthier to eat than nonorganic fruits.
3. Organic fruits are grown in ways that are safe for the environment.

Some instructors like to divide a thesis statement into two sentences: one that states your thesis (your main idea) and one that lists the main points of your speech (your preview). You can see examples of this method in the persuasive speeches "No More Sugar!" and "Fat Discrimination," both accessible online via your CourseMate for *Invitation to Public Speaking*. In addition, you can read a more detailed discussion of previews in Chapter 8.

CourseMate

Table 3.2

General and Specific Purposes and Thesis Statements

Informative Speech

General purpose	To inform
Specific purpose	To inform my audience of the three most important ways to avoid getting lost while traveling
Thesis statement	The three simple ways travelers can avoid getting lost are to carry maps, plan out the route beforehand, and ask directions from knowledgeable sources.
General purpose	To inform
Specific purpose	To inform my audience about where to seek shelter during a tornado
Thesis statement	When a tornado strikes, seek shelter in a storm cellar, a fortified storm closet, or your bathtub.

Invitational Speech

General purpose	To invite
Specific purpose	To invite my audience to explore ways to support the arts in our community
Thesis statement	The arts have played a very important role in my life, enhance the quality of life in any community, and I'd like to explore with my audience whether or not there are simple ways to support them.
General purpose	To invite
Specific purpose	To invite my audience to explore the reasons for and against retaining the death penalty in our state.
Thesis statement	I'd like to describe the many benefits and drawbacks of retaining the death penalty in our state and then explore with my audience whether this punishment is still appropriate for serious crimes.

Persuasive Speech

General purpose	To persuade
Specific purpose	To persuade my audience to spay or neuter their pets
Thesis statement	Spaying or neutering pets is easy and affordable, and it helps prevent having to put down thousands of unwanted kittens and puppies each year.

continued

General purpose	To persuade
Specific purpose	To persuade my audience to learn a second language
Thesis statement	When we learn a second language, not only do we learn to appreciate the culture of the people who speak that language, but we also increase our understanding of our own culture.

Speaking Visually

Banksy and Above: Elusive Street Artists Have Their Say

Graffiti artist Banksy uses his art to create satirical commentaries on politics, culture, and ethical issues. Although this London-born artist is elusive—no one knows his true identity—his street art has appeared in cities around the world. Some of his images mock corporate culture and government power. Others call attention to physical spaces that have been damaged by political strife or neglect. For example, in 2005, Banksy painted a series of images on the Israeli West Bank barrier, most of them suggesting ways to break through the wall. And in 2008 he painted a series of images on buildings in New Orleans left derelict by Hurricane Katrina, calling attention to the drawn-out cleanup process. Other Banksy images ""are just silly and amusing. On the wall of the penguin enclosure at the London Zoo, he painted seven-foot-high letters that stated, "We're bored of fish."[4] Banksy doesn't sell his work, but you can find photos of it simply by googling his name.

Above is another street artist who keeps his identity a secret. Born in California and now living in Paris, Above's signature is an "arrow logo." He paints his arrows on surfaces such as store fronts and produce trucks, and he installs wooden versions—both static and in spinning mobile form—on walls and just about any other surface in towns around the world.

Aram Boghosian for The Boston Globe

He explains that the logo is an "upward pointing arrow that represents 'Above' or the mentality 'rise above,'" but he offers that its meaning "is open to interpretation to others." His goal with the arrows is to engage in word play, and he explains

When I was stenciling the word/play on the arrow mobiles, I would brainstorm to where I was going and try and think of words that would relate to each city, or country. I made some arrow mobiles in French (J'ai/faim, chez/vous), Spanish (Hace/sol, como/esta), German (uber/alle), and Italian (ciao/ciao), knowing that I was going to those countries where the viewer could relate even more to the arrow. To be even more specific I would think of word/plays that would relate to a certain environment or structure of a city.[5]

Both Banksy and Above challenge their audiences with visual communication. Banksy's work, although often erased or sprayed over by authorities, challenges his viewers to consider social issues in visual snap shots. He encourages them to take in large amounts of information quickly, and to link these snapshots to cultural and political issues. Above's work, also erased or removed by authorities, blends the visual message of the arrow with simple word play. In this way, he prompts his audience to consider a familiar space or moment in new and amusing ways.[6]

The clarity and focus you get when you develop your thesis statement and main points guide your research efforts and supporting materials, your reasoning, and your organizational patterns (Chapters 5, 6, 7, and 8). Use your thesis statement in combination with your general and specific statements of purpose to help you identify your main points. You can then move to the next steps of putting your speech together.

Now watch a video clip of a student speaker Ogenna Agbim as she delivers a commemorative speech about a topic she's very interested in. As you watch Ogenna speak, notice how her passion about the topic affects her delivery. You can go to your CourseMate for *Invitation to Public Speaking* to watch the video, respond to analysis questions, and compare your answers to those provided by the author.

Practicing the Public Dialogue

3.3

Write a Thesis Statement

In a small group or as a class, choose five of the topics you wrote purpose statements for in Practicing the Public Dialogue 3.2. Write a thesis statement for each. Is your thesis statement a single declarative sentence? Does it state the main ideas, assumptions, or arguments you want to express in your speech? Review the completed thesis statements and select the one for the speech you're most interested in. Why do you like this one more than the others? Does it best fit the assignment your instructor has given you, your audience, or your own personal preferences?

Online Resources

To help you distinguish between effective and ineffective thesis statements, access **Web Connect 3.5: Identifying Thesis Statements** online via your CourseMate for *Invitation to Public Speaking*. To create your own thesis statement, go to Speech Builder Express, select "Thesis Statement" from the left menu, and follow the instructions. For short reminders about thesis statements, click the "Tutor" button. In addition, use your CourseMate to watch the video clips of two student speakers, Rebecca Ewing and Jesse Rosser, as they deliver thesis statements. To see additional speech videos, go to Speech Studio and see how your peers delivered their thesis statements in their speeches. Or upload your own speech and ask others to give you feedback on your thesis statement.

STUDENT SPEECH with Commentary

© Cengage Learning

This Is Dedicated . . . : A Tribute to the Women of History

by Ogenna Agbim

Specific purpose: To commemorate important women in history who have come before my generation

Thesis statement: Throughout history, women's struggle for equality has provided opportunities for women today, and the women of the past deserve our recognition.

Commentary

Ogenna catches her audience's attention with a dedication, setting a tone of optimism and recognition. She also uses rhyming language ("pass you on," "much too long") and repetition ("We have to combine, and we have to keep moving on") for effect and emphasis. By identifying the women in her speaking environment specifically as members of her audience, Ogenna makes the speech relevant to them.

Ogenna continues to draw her audience in by tracing some of women's experiences in history. She also helps her audience listen to her speech by using language that creates pleasing rhythms, such as alliteration ("priceless piece," "happy hearts").

By using specific women in history as examples, Ogenna fulfills her specific purpose and supports the claims she made in her thesis statement that women throughout history have paved the way for women today and deserve to be commemorated.

As she reminds her audience of the significance of past accomplishments and brings herself back into the speech, Ogenna begins to bring her speech around full circle, transitioning from women of history to women of today.

 CourseMate *If you have been assigned a speech in your class, such as an introductory, narrative, or commemorative speech, you can use the following speech as a model. Go to your CourseMate for* Invitation to Public Speaking *to watch the video clip of Ogenna Agbim's commemorative speech. Ogenna gave this speech in an introductory public speaking class. The students' assignment was to give a two- to four-minute speech commemorating an important person or important people in their lives. Notice that even though this speech was required, Ogenna chose a topic that is different enough to keep her audience engaged and listening.*

Introduction

This is dedicated to all the women out there who have gone through the struggle: You're not going through it alone; it's our time to shine. Ladies, don't you hang your heads low. I can see you're feeling bad because you're trying to make it on your own. Ladies, it seems everything for us has gone wrong, but if you believe in me, you will find bad times will pass you on. It's our time to shine. We've been down for much too long. But we have to combine, and we have to keep moving on. We have to combine, and we have to keep moving on.

Body

I want to ask every woman gathered here today to stand up. You, you, and you. My women in front, my women in the middle, and my women in back. If no one has told you, it's your time to shine. You've been down for much too long. For the last couple of hundred years, we women: What have we not endured? We've been slaves, we've been seen through the earth's eyes in every way but our own. We've been told how to act, and how to behave, and what makes us beautiful, and what doesn't. Hundreds of years we've spent, and decades of years, fighting for equal pay and equal opportunities and voting rights. We've supported our men, and our families, our brothers and sisters. Through it all, we haven't been appreciated. We haven't been honored, both entirely appreciated and honored enough. And without crying a river still we stand. As you stand, you represent a priceless piece of the voice that was never heard. You stand for the opportunities missed. You stand for the oppression where our happy hearts were broken and for the things that make us who we are—and made us dismissed. For what you've been through for me, and for us all, I thank you. Without you today, where would we all be?

Now for my ladies who took a stand, take a seat for the future. As I have said, it's our time to shine. Take a front seat and count your accomplishments. Take a seat and view the laws that have been passed because of women. Take a seat and watch every seed women have planted in the concrete grow into beautiful roses. Women, we salute you. We are proud of you. You are an inspiration. You are our mentors, you are our saviors, our motivation, and I commend you. Bessie Coleman, the first African American woman to fly a plane; Zora Neale Hurston, first African American woman graduate of Barnard College; and you, Eleanor Roosevelt, who broke the rules in 1933 for women to be allowed in press conferences; Rosa Parks; Toni Morrison: With so many other women to name, the branches you have built over time will forever give me light to shine. You have been oppressed but have risen as organization presidents, artists, dancers, and dreamers that have led your way and mine. Women, your small steps are like giants in history. Forever you will be a heroine to those you never thought you would touch, and you will be a heroine for saving us throughout the drowning madness.

Women, you motivate me in this age to become a better woman, because without your contributions, today there may not have been a history for me. There may have been no gateway for me to college, and in music, in sports, in politics, and so very much more.

Conclusion

Ladies, it is your time to shine. Your efforts never go unnoticed, at least not in my eyes. Your small impacts make a huge impact on us all, even if it's one body at a time. To my women out there, if you ever find yourself going through a struggle, remember to keep your head held high. You're not going through it alone. We have been down for much too long. But like Maya Angelou once said, "We rise, we rise, we rise." And from this day forward, it is our time to shine.

Ogenna concludes her speech with a memorable quote by a famous woman of today, author and poet Maya Angelou, who is especially appropriate since she's written extensively about her own history.

Chapter Summary

Understanding the context in which you speak will help you prepare effective speeches.

- When you decide to speak, you do so because an issue is so important that you feel drawn to speak out about it.
- When you are asked to speak, you do so because you have been asked to share information with others.
- When you are required to speak, you do so because you are obligated to give a speech.
- Although you are required to speak in your public speaking class, it is more likely you will decide or be asked to give speeches in the future.

When you choose a speech topic, consider the purpose of your speech, your time constraints, and your audience.

- If you are giving a speech in a classroom setting, also consider the specifics of your assignment.
- Choose a speech topic by taking stock of your interests (e.g., what you like to talk about or what people say you're good at) or by brainstorming with a variety of methods: free association, clustering, categories, or using technology.

- Narrow the focus of your speech by matching your interests and expertise to your speech assignment.

Determine the general and specific purposes for your speech.

- Most often, the general purpose for your speech will be to inform, to invite, to persuade, to introduce, to commemorate, or to accept.
- Identify your specific purpose by stating exactly what you want to accomplish with your speech.
- Write specific-purpose statements so your speaking purpose is clear, keep the audience in the forefront of your mind, and use definitive and complete sentences.

Write your thesis statement.

- Your thesis statement is a single declarative sentence that summarizes the main points of your speech.
- Thesis statements indicate what you want to say in your speech to accomplish your speaking goal. They also preview the content of your speech for your audience.

Invitation to Public Speaking Online

CourseMate Now that you have read Chapter 3, use your Speech Communication CourseMate for *Invitation to Public Speaking* for quick access to the electronic resources that accompany this text. These resources include

- **Study tools** that will help you assess your learning and prepare for exams (*digital glossary, key term flash cards, review quizzes*).

- **Activities and assignments** that will help you hone your knowledge and build your public speaking skills throughout the course (*Practicing the Public Dialogue activities, review questions*).

- **Media resources** that will help you explore public speaking concepts online (*Web Connect links, Enhanced eBook*), develop your speech outlines (*Speech Builder Express 3.0*), watch and critique videos of sample speeches (*Interactive Video Activities*), upload your speech videos for peer reviewing and critique other students' speeches (*Speech Studio* *online speech review tool*), and download chapter review so you can study when and where you'd like (*Audio Study Tools*).

This chapter's key concepts and review questions are also featured here.

Key Concepts

behavioral objectives (55)
brainstorming (49)

general purpose (52)
specific purpose (52)

speech topic (44)
thesis statement (57)

Review Questions

1. Use the strategies suggested in this chapter to make a list of four different speech topics you might like to speak about. How do you think the classroom setting would affect what you would say about these topics? What would you do to make these topics suitable for a classroom setting?

2. Rewrite the following incorrect specific-purpose statements so they are correct:

   a. To give 10 percent of your annual income to charity

   b. Barack Obama

   c. Olympic gold medals

   d. Natural disasters

   Isn't the level of water pollution in our local river too high?

3. Make a list of speech topics you might decide to speak about. For each topic, identify why you've decided to speak and who your audience would be.

   How might your reasons for speaking and your audience affect what you say about your topics? Write a general-purpose and a specific-purpose statement for at least one of these topics. Is this a speech you might give in your speech course? Why or why not?

4. Practice writing a general and a specific statement of purpose for a speech on each of the following topics: relief efforts in Haiti, mandatory military service, bilingual education, hybrid cars. Now write a thesis statement for each of these possible speeches and identify the main points for each. Could you choose one of these topics for your next speech? Why or why not?

5. Check out Speech Studio to see speeches about various topics. Do any of them give you ideas for your own speech topics? Or record a speech you're working on, upload it to Speech Studio, and ask your peers for their feedback. What feedback could you use to fine-tune your topic before you give your speech in class? ✓Studio

Your Audience and Speaking Environment

4

Ronald Karpilo / Alamy

- **Considering an Audience as a Group of Diverse People**
- **Considering an Audience as a Community**
- **Considering Your Speaking Environment**
- **Adapting to Audience Expectations**

IN THIS CHAPTER, YOU WILL LEARN TO:

- Define what an audience is
- Conduct a demographic audience analysis
- Adapt to an audience that is both a group of diverse people and a unique community
- Identify the influence of a speaking environment on an audience
- Identify strategies for adapting to audience expectations for a speech

When you give a speech, you add your voice to the public dialogue. To engage in a **dialogue** is to interact, connect, and exchange ideas and opinions with others. When you engage in the public dialogue, you recognize that the speaker and the audience are equally important; both have opinions, feelings, and beliefs. To be a successful public speaker, you must acknowledge these realities and listen carefully to your audience before, during, and after your speech. One of the most effective ways you can listen to your audience is by adopting an audience-centered perspective. To be **audience centered** is to acknowledge your audience by considering and listening to the unique, diverse, and common perspectives of its members before, during, and after your speech. Being audience centered does not mean you must compromise your message to appeal to your audience. Nor does it mean that you can use your knowledge of the audience to manipulate its members. Rather, being audience centered means you understand the positions and perspectives of your audience so you can craft an appropriate, listenable message.

But what is an audience? We often use the term *audience* without much thought. We prepare our speeches with our "audience in mind," we want to "persuade our audience" of something, and we "sit in the audience" as we listen. In terms of public speaking, **audience** is defined as a complex and varied group of people the speaker addresses. Although this definition is simple, we recognize that audiences are far more complex than the definition suggests. Modern audiences are composed of a group of diverse people exposed to endless messages from the media, their workplaces, their families and friends, and many other sources. Despite all these demands on the listening time of a group of highly diverse people, you can learn a number of skills to help you address an audience effectively.

In Chapter 2, you learned how to listen to your audience during a speech to better respond to their needs. In this chapter, you will build on those skills and learn how to best understand your audiences by exploring what an audience is, why there are different types of audiences, how speaking environments affect audiences, and how you can apply what you learn about your audience and speaking environment to help others listen to your speech.

Considering an Audience as a Group of Diverse People

Have you ever noticed that for each similarity you find you have with someone, you also find a difference? Perhaps you and a friend love action films, popcorn, and state-of-the-art theaters. Yet one of you loves a bargain matinee, to sit up close, and to pour on the butter, whereas the other is happiest settling in the balcony for the late night show with no butter at all. You are similar, yet you are different.

People are unique for a variety of reasons that relate to some combination of culture, upbringing, experiences, personality, and even genetics.[1] Like you and your movie-going friend, no two people are alike, and this uniqueness sets us apart and makes us interesting. But groups of people are often similar to one another in many ways. As public speakers, how can we give a speech that takes into consideration an audience's conflicting differences and similarities? First, try to consider how your audiences view the world by analyzing their master statuses and their standpoints.

Master Statuses

Groups of people share common experiences, perspectives, and attitudes because they occupy certain master statuses. **Master statuses** are significant positions a person occupies within society that affect that person's identity in almost all social situations.[2] A person's master statuses might include race or ethnicity, gender, physical ability, sexual orientation, age, economic standing, religion or spirituality, and educational level. They could include positions in society like being a parent, child, or sibling, being employed or unemployed, and so on if those positions affect someone's identity in almost every social situation. Here's how one public speaking student, Miranda, described her master statuses and how they influenced her life and speaking experiences:

> I have many master statuses. I am a daughter dedicated to her family and her family values. I am forever a student, always craving new knowledge. I am a first-generation student, boldly going where no one else in my family has gone

Good to Know!

dialogue: Interaction, connection, and exchange of ideas and opinions with others. **audience centered:** Acknowledging your audience by considering and listening to the unique, diverse, and common perspectives of its members before, during, and after your speech. **audience:** Complex and varied group of people the speaker addresses. **master statuses:** Significant positions occupied by a person within society that affect that person's identity in almost all social situations.

before—college. I am a Mexican American living life for my ancestors. Last but not least, I am curious, always searching for new adventures in life. All of this makes up who I am and affects every decision I make each day, from what clothes I choose to wear to the books I choose to read. It also affects what topics I choose to speak about and how effectively I listen to other speakers.

A status is a *master* status when it profoundly influences a person's identity and the way he or she is perceived by others. Whether we intend to or not, we often respond to other people based on one or more master statuses. For example, teenagers with rumpled and baggy clothes are often treated differently in a grocery store than neatly dressed adult mothers with children. Whether or not our

Ethical Moment

WHAT'S IN A MASTER STATUS?

Grammy-winning rapper and producer Kanye West receives a great deal of attention for his controversial comments and actions. For example, in 2005, West appeared on a live telethon broadcast on several major television networks to raise money for victims of Hurricane Katrina. Speaking live, West went off script to declare that America's bureaucracy was set up "to help the poor, the black people, the less well-off as slow as possible" and that government authorities had given permission "to go down [to New Orleans] and shoot us." He later added that "President Bush doesn't care about black people." His comments aired live on the East Coast but were edited from subsequent broadcasts.

In 2009, West created another stir at the MTV Video Music Awards when he unexpectedly stormed the stage during Taylor Swift's acceptance speech for best music video. West grabbed the microphone from Swift and claimed that "Beyonce had one of the best videos of all time," suggesting that Swift's video was not deserving of the award. At the end of the night, West apologized to Swift and admitted it was wrong to go on stage and take the moment away from her.

In a very different vein, West has spoken publicly about what he calls the "tradition of homophobia" in the black community. In particular, hip-hop artists are known for controversial lyrics that often degrade women and members of the gay community. But West claimed in a 2006 interview published in *Entertainment Weekly* that his level of consciousness about the use of the word *fag* has shifted, and

Brad Barket/PictureGroup/AP Images

he is starting to speak out against using this type of derogatory language. He admits that "standing up for gays was even more crazy than bad-mouthing the president" because being labeled "gay" in the hip-hop community could potentially ruin a career. Thus, Kanye West reveals many complex, and even contradictory, sides of himself, stimulating the public dialogue and placing controversial issues in the spotlight.[9]

What do you think?

1. What are the master statuses Kanye West presents publicly? Make a list of these master statuses and then discuss why they might challenge or be unfamiliar to audiences.

2. Do you think Kanye West uses his master statuses to push "too far" on issues? Why or why not?

3. Does West have an ethical obligation to tone down his image and show respect for others? Why or why not?

4. Name other public figures who challenge audiences as West does. Do you think the actions of these public figures add to or detract from the public dialogue? Why?

assumptions about these people are correct (teenagers will cause problems, mothers are responsible and will manage their children), we categorize and respond to people based on the positions they hold in society.

Master statuses affect our view of the world because we make judgments based on them, and hence, we see some master statuses as more valuable than others. For example, whether we are comfortable acknowledging such differences or not, American culture tends to rank whiteness, heterosexuality, and masculinity higher than color, homosexuality, and femininity. Because the first three statuses are considered more valuable, they are generally rewarded with higher salaries, more acceptance and protections, and more personal freedoms, whereas the last three, on average, receive lower salaries, less acceptance and fewer protections, and greater threats to physical safety.[3]

Standpoints, Attitudes, Beliefs, and Values

The impact of different treatment because of master statuses can affect an individual's **standpoint**, the perspective from which a person views and evaluates society. Members of your audiences have different standpoints because they have different master statuses and thus different experiences. For example, teenagers often see life as unfairly biased against them, and mothers often see the world as expecting them and their children to behave perfectly in all situations.

Note that although master statuses can have a powerful influence on a person's view of the world, they do not *determine* a person's standpoint. For example, not all women believe they need to have children to fully experience womanhood, just as not all men believe their masculinity is weakened if they are not the primary breadwinners for their families. Additionally, we all occupy numerous master statuses throughout our lives, and each influences us in different ways. For example, although we maintain our ethnicity throughout our lives, if we move to a new country, adapt to a new culture, and learn a different language, our experience of our ethnic identity can evolve. Moreover, we all move from young to old and experience changing family and job roles, shifting from child to parent, unemployed to employed, and so on.

Our standpoints influence our attitudes, beliefs, and values. An **attitude** is a general positive or negative feeling a person has about something. Attitudes reflect our likes and dislikes, our approval or disapproval of events, people, or ideas.[4] A **belief** is a person's idea of what is real, not real, true, or not true. Beliefs are more conceptual than attitudes and reflect what we think we know about the world. A **value** is a person's idea of what is good, worthy, or important. Our values reflect what we think is an ideal world or state of being. Values help us determine whether we think a person, idea, or thing is acceptable in our worldview.[5]

Conversations, debates, and arguments held as part of the public dialogue are heavily influenced by the different attitudes, beliefs, and values that result from our different standpoints and master statuses. In particular, attitudes, beliefs, and values are often influenced by our cultural backgrounds. All cultures have unique ways of explaining and organizing the world. Audience-centered speakers recognize these different worldviews and guard against ethnocentrism. **Ethnocentrism** is the belief that our own cultural perspectives, norms, and ways of organizing society are superior to others. When we hold ethnocentric views, we see other

Good to Know!

standpoint: Perspective from which a person views and evaluates society. **attitude:** General positive or negative feeling a person has about something. **belief:** Person's idea of what is real, not real, true, or not true. **value:** Person's idea of what is good, worthy, or important. **ethnocentrism:** Belief that our own cultural perspectives, norms, and ways of organizing society are superior to others.

cultures as odd, wrong, or deficient because they do not do things the way we do. Speakers who let ethnocentric views come through in their speeches run the risk of alienating audience members who do not hold similar views.

To be audience centered, speakers must consider the significant influence of master statuses, standpoints, attitudes, beliefs, and values on audiences. When speakers take these factors into consideration, they increase their chances of giving effective speeches.

Demographic Audience Analysis

How does recognizing your audience's master statuses and standpoints help you become a better, more ethical speaker? By using master statuses as guideposts for crafting your speech, you can try to anticipate the potential impact your speech topic, language, and so on might have on your audience. Are members of your audience first-year high school students or seniors in college? Are they of a certain ethnicity? What types of jobs do they hold? Are they grandparents? What are their educational backgrounds? How might each of these master statuses influence the standpoints of your audience members? Once you've answered these types of questions, you can consider the attitudes, beliefs, and values of your audience more completely. This will help you adapt the message of your speech to your audience.

A common way to determine the master statuses of an audience is to conduct a **demographic audience analysis**, an analysis that identifies the particular population traits of an audience. These traits, or demographic characteristics, include age, country of origin, ethnicity and race, physical ability or disability, family status (parent, child), religion, and gender (male or female). You can gather demographic information by interviewing your audience personally, through a survey, or by researching the Internet. Using the Internet is best when you want to find information about a large general group of people, such as the citizens of a town, county, or region. However, to gather targeted information about your specific audience, you must interview your audience directly or conduct a survey.

You can conduct a demographic analysis before your speech by asking your audience to fill out a survey that asks about demographic information and attitudes, beliefs, and values. Surveys ask two primary types of questions: open ended and closed ended. An **open-ended question** allows respondents to answer in an unrestricted way. An example of an open-ended question is "What are your reactions to the president's economic reforms?" People asked this question are free to respond with any answer they like. A **closed-ended question** requires respondents to choose an answer from two or more alternatives. Examples of closed-ended questions are "Do you support the president's attempts at economic reform?" (requires a yes or no answer) and "On a scale of 1 to 5, with 5 indicating the highest support, how do you rate the president's success at economic reform?" (requires one rating of five possible alternatives).

© Michael Newman / PhotoEdit

Surveys are an excellent way to gather information about your audience's attitudes, beliefs, and values. What kind of information would you want to gather about your audience? Would you use open-ended or closed-ended questions to obtain this information?

Good to Know!

demographic audience analysis: Analysis that identifies the particular population traits of an audience. **open-ended question:** Question that allows the respondent to answer in an unrestricted way. **closed-ended question:** Question that requires the respondent to choose an answer from two or more alternatives.

When you construct your survey, follow these guidelines:

- Keep your survey short (one or two pages).
- Keep your questions short and focused on one idea at a time.
- Use clear and simple language.
- Keep your own biases out of the survey.
- Provide room for respondents to write their comments.

Keep your speaking goals in mind as you construct your survey. What would you like your audience to do or know after you've given your speech? Do you want them to understand a concept or a process? Explore an issue? Take some action? Appreciate another person? Whatever your goal, conducting a thorough and accurate analysis of your audience will help you accomplish your goals in a civil and ethical manner.

Remember that your primary goal in analyzing your audience is to give an ethical, audience-centered speech. Although master statuses can be powerfully influential, people can experience them in very different ways. Speakers must understand that we are all unique, that we experience life differently, and that we grow and change over time. When conducting a demographic analysis and considering master statuses, it can sometimes be easy to forget individual differences and resort to stereotyping. A **stereotype** is a broad generalization about an entire group based on limited knowledge or exposure to only certain members of that group. Stereotyping is harmful because we make assumptions based on incomplete information. It may seem comforting to predict certain behaviors based on a stereotype, but we can usually find many exceptions to any stereotype. Remember, audiences are a collection of people with unique experiences and personalities, and you cannot lump them into one universal category.

Practicing the Public Dialogue

4.1

Conduct a Demographic Audience Analysis

To learn about the group of people who make up your classroom audience, use the sample survey form, Demographic Audience Analysis: General Survey of a Class, to conduct a demographic analysis before your next speech. Using the information you gather, identify your audience's master statuses, standpoints, attitudes, beliefs, and values. As you prepare your speech, remain flexible about the influences of master statuses on your audience and do what you can to avoid stereotyping.

Online Resources

CourseMate You can find the Demographic Audience Analysis form online under the Chapter 4 resources in your CourseMate for *Invitation to Public Speaking*. You can also explore a wide range of audience analysis tools by accessing **Web Connect 4.1: Learning about Your Audience**. If you'd like to widen your exploration of demographic statistics, go to the website of the U.S. Bureau of the Census via **Web Connect 4.2: U.S. Census**. To see an example of a speech given by a student who used her demographic audience analysis to determine how thoroughly she needed to explain her topic to her audience, use your CourseMate to access the speech "Chinese Fortune Telling." You can find this speech in the Interactive Video Activities for Chapter 13.

Considering an Audience as a Community

Although audiences begin with individuals who bring various standpoints to a presentation, they rapidly become a community of people joined together in some way, if only temporarily. Understanding how an audience comes together as a temporary community helps speakers stay audience centered.

Voluntary Audiences

Just as speakers decide something is significant enough to speak out about, people come together as audiences

Good to Know!

stereotype: Broad generalization about an entire group based on limited knowledge or exposure to only certain members of that group.

because they find something significant enough to listen to. These audiences are voluntary: They have chosen to be present. Examples of voluntary audiences are the delegates who attend the Democratic and Republican national conventions every four years, which bring citizens from across the country together to nominate and confirm candidates for office. Public celebrations and commemorations, such as Super Bowl victories or the return of a famous person to a hometown, also bring audiences together voluntarily. And tragedies, like the September 11 terrorist attacks or the Virginia Tech school shootings, often draw people together.

The need to listen unites people with various master statuses and standpoints. This means that most audiences are quite diverse. As a result, they may agree or disagree with a speaker or with one another. Although it is tempting to think that voluntary audiences are easier for speakers to address, this is not always true. Consider city council meetings, where community members hold vigorous debates about school funding, land development, and similar topics. However, voluntary audiences usually have an active interest in your topic. This fact certainly works to your advantage as a speaker, and staying audience centered will help you deliver your message effectively, no matter what your speaking situation.

Involuntary Audiences

Just as speakers are sometimes required to give a speech, people sometimes form an audience because they must. These audiences are involuntary: They might prefer not to be present. Examples of involuntary audiences are students in required public speaking courses and employees in mandatory business meetings. Some involuntary audiences have little or no interest in your topic. Thus, they may display open hostility toward you and your topic or a disconcerting lack of attention and involvement. For example, in your public speaking class, some of your classmates would rather not hear about certain topics because of their own strong beliefs, yet they are forced to sit and listen. Others seem only to stare blankly at you. Still others ignore you and e-mail or text while you are speaking. Unfortunately, you may encounter the same behaviors in your professional and social worlds; some audiences attend a speech only because their job requires it or because of family or social obligations. However, with a little forethought and effort, most involuntary audiences can be brought into the public dialogue.

For the speaker facing an involuntary audience, being audience centered may mean the difference between an ineffective and a successful speech. Before you give your speech, talk with the person who asked you to speak. Discover why your audience is required to attend. Or at the beginning of your speech, ask your audience members why they've been asked to listen to you. Then address those issues in your speech. For example, if you are presenting to an audience that is part of a mandatory training program, ask about the rationale for the training, the goals of the training, and what your audience hopes to gain by the training. Knowing this information will help you design and present a message that is relevant and useful.

Similarly, if an audience opposes your topic, learn why so you can confirm (Chapter 3) and be confirmed by an involuntary audience. Before you speak, ask your audience to write down their concerns and pass them to you, or gather this information several days earlier. The feedback you receive will help you thoughtfully address an audience's concerns, frustrations, or resistance. This audience-centered approach opens up dialogue rather than forcing ideas on people. You let your audience know you are working to understand them as you ask them to do the same for you.

Finally, if you are speaking to an involuntary audience, use a little **empathy** by trying to see and understand the world as another person does. What would motivate you to listen to a topic you disagreed with or a presentation you were required to listen to? If you adopt this empathic, audience-centered approach, your involuntary audience may be delightfully surprised by your presentation and welcome you as a speaker.

So far, you've discovered you must consider both the individual and collective nature of audiences, you've explored why audiences come together at all, and you've learned how you can engage an involuntary audience. Audience-centered speakers keep all these factors in mind as they prepare and present their speeches. In the next section, you'll learn techniques to help you manage your speaking environment effectively.

Considering Your Speaking Environment

Before audience-centered speakers give a speech, they must discover as much as they can about their **speaking environment**, or where and when they will speak, so they can manage their speaking situation with relative ease. Effective speakers must consider such situational factors as the size of the audience and the physical arrangement of the speaking site, the availability of technology, the time of day they'll be speaking, where their speech falls in a series of presentations, and the length of time they have to speak.

Size and Physical Arrangement

The size of an audience and the physical arrangement of a speaking situation may seem like minor matters, but they can have a powerful effect on a speaking environment. You can enhance your ability to connect with your audience if you consider these matters carefully before your speech and adapt to them during your speech. Consider the following example:

> I found [him] alone in an empty basketball locker room moments before he was to speak before a crowd of six thousand at Arizona State University, calmly sipping tea. "Your Holiness, if you're ready . . ."

> He briskly rose, and without hesitation he left the room, emerging into the thick backstage throng of local reporters, photographers, security personnel, and students—the seekers, the curious, and the skeptical. He walked through the crowd smiling broadly and greeting people as he passed by. Finally passing through a curtain, he walked on stage, bowed, folded his hands, and smiled. He was greeted with thunderous applause. At his request, the house lights were not dimmed so he could clearly see his audience, and for several moments he simply stood there, quietly surveying the audience with an unmistakable expression of warmth and good will. For those who had never seen the Dalai Lama before,

---

Practicing the Public Dialogue

4.2

Determine Whether Your Audience Is Voluntary or Involuntary

Consider the audience of a speech you might give sometime in the near future. Are they a voluntary audience, present because they are interested in your topic and want to hear what you have to say? Or are they involuntary, present because they have to be? If they are a voluntary audience, adapt to your audience by identifying the various perspectives they have about your topic. If they are an involuntary audience, discover why and adapt your speech to better suit their needs. What are some ways you can communicate your empathy for them?

Good to Know!

empathy: Trying to see and understand the world as another person does. **speaking environment:** Time and place in which a speaker will speak.

his maroon and saffron monk's robes may have created a somewhat exotic impression, yet his remarkable ability to establish rapport with his audience was quickly revealed as he sat down and began his talk.

"I think that this is the first time I am meeting most of you. But to me, whether it is an old friend or new friend, there's not much difference anyway, because I always believe we are the same; we are all human beings. . . ."[6]

It might seem that a large audience, a group of journalists and security guards, and a wide stage would mean distance and disruption for a speaker, but not necessarily. Despite these potentially difficult physical settings, the Dalai Lama stayed audience centered by engaging with his audience personally. He asked that the house lights be left on, and he took the time to make eye contact with his audience, acknowledging a connection to each audience member. He took advantage of his setting rather than letting it control him. But how does a speaker do this?

To establish rapport with our audiences, we must consider the dynamics of audience size and physical arrangement before we speak, and we must adjust to any changes immediately before or during our speech. To stay audience centered with respect to size and place, ask yourself the following questions:

- How many people will be present?
- Will they stand or be seated? Where will they stand or sit?
- From where will I be speaking?
- Does this arrangement help or hinder the speaking environment I wish to create?
- What adjustments will I want to make before the presentation begins?
- What will I do if I cannot make these adjustments?
- What kinds of adjustments might I make during a presentation if I want to alter the environment?

You probably won't be able to change the size of most audiences, but you should be able to work with the physical setting to create the kind of speaking environment you want. Consider whether you want to stand or sit, where you want your audience to sit (for example, in rows, in a circle, on chairs, on the floor), and how these decisions will affect your ability to connect with your audience. Ideally, you would make arrangements to establish your speaking environment ahead of time, as well as plans to make adjustments during your speech as needed. Remember, your speaking goal is to connect with your audience before, during, and after the speech.

Index Stock Imagery/PhotoLibrary

Strong speakers take stock of their environment before they begin to speak. What questions might you ask yourself to prepare to speak in this environment? If you're planning to use technology, what will you do to make sure your speech is successful even if your technology fails?

Technology

Technology refers to the tools speakers use to help them deliver their message. Technology can be as elaborate as a computer and LCD panel or as simple as a pen and a flip chart. Table 4.1 on page 74 presents a list of technologies speakers typically use. When you're thinking of using technology for your speech, stay audience centered by asking yourself the following questions:

- Have I asked what types of technology will be available for me to use?
- Do I have time to prepare the materials I need to use that technology?
- Do I have the time to practice using the technology? Have I worked out any glitches?
- Am I prepared to speak if the technology fails?

- Am I sure that my decision to use or not use technology helps me create the kind of environment I want?
- Does the technology help me communicate my messages clearly? Does it enhance my speech or detract from it?

Note that audience-centered speakers use technology to do more than simply enhance or project their message. They also make a commitment to their audience to use that technology competently. Consider the importance of this commitment in the following example:

Mike wanted to include several YouTube clips in his speech. He identified the clips he wanted a day or two before he spoke, and he figured he could just pull them up during his speech. When he set up his computer on the day of his speech, he had trouble getting Internet access because the network was not running smoothly that day. After several tries, he was finally able to log on. But he couldn't locate his YouTube citations easily because he had searched for them by subject and failed to record the URLs. Then, because he was not familiar with the projection technology in the room, he discovered the hard way that the volume on the projector had been turned up to its highest level. When he played his first clip, everyone in the audience winced and covered their ears.

Mike did what he could to recover, but after his speech, he felt he didn't really create the kind of environment he wanted. He wanted people to get excited by his material, but he felt they simply were patient with him instead.

In Chapter 12, you will learn more about presentational aids that rely on technology. Remember, although technology is a tool that can help you give a more effective speech, it has its drawbacks. If your speech relies on technology to be effective but the technology you need is not available when you arrive to speak, your presentation will be negatively affected. That's why you need to take the time to consider how to present your speech without technology. Putting this time into your speech before you give it will help you stay audience centered by keeping your attention focused on delivering your message to your audience in a way they appreciate.

Table 4.1

Technologies for Speakers

Traditional Technologies	Electronic Technologies
Podiums for notes	Microphones
Tables or easels for displays	Laptop computers and LCD projectors
Presentational aids such as posters	Overhead projectors and screens
Handouts	Slide projectors and screens
Chalk, chalkboards, and erasers	Presentational aids such as PowerPoint slides
Ink markers, whiteboards, and erasers	Televisions, VCR players, and DVD players
Markers, pens, and flip charts	CD-ROM players
Tacks, pins, or tape	Audio cassette players

Temporal Factors

Audience-centered speakers also consider issues of time, sometimes called *chronemics*, when they think about connecting with their audiences. Three important time considerations are the time of day you'll be speaking, where your speech falls in a series of presentations (will you speak first, last, or somewhere in the middle?), and how much time you'll have to speak.

Time of day. The time of day a speech is scheduled is significant. Take a moment to consider your moods throughout a day. Is your energy different in the morning than it is in the evening? How about before or after a meal? Just as our levels of energy are affected by the time of day, so too is the mood of an audience.

In the morning, audiences tend to be fresher, but they may also be anxious about the responsibilities they have that day. In the evening, audiences may be weary, tired from all the work they've done. Around lunchtime, they are hungry and preoccupied with getting some food, or they have just eaten and may be drowsy as their bodies work to digest food rather than your message. Let's consider Julio and how he adjusts his message about the services his product design company offers according to what time of day he speaks.

In the morning, Julio begins by encouraging his audience to refill their cups of coffee and tea as he speaks. He then acknowledges the demands on their time by speaking for fifteen minutes, asking them to participate in an activity for twenty minutes, and then breaking for fifteen minutes so they can check voice mail and e-mail. When they reconvene, they follow up on the activity for about an hour.

After lunch, Julio also engages his audience verbally because he knows their energy will be a bit lower than it was in the morning. When he speaks for longer than half an hour or so, he incorporates a break so audiences can check messages. If he speaks before lunch, Julio clearly defines his speaking schedule so his audience knows when they can expect to eat.

In the evening, Julio acknowledges that it's the end of a workday that was probably very busy for most audience members. Rather than beginning by explaining the program, he immediately engages them verbally by asking them a few questions about a typical workday that they can answer by raising their hands. This strategy keeps them connected to him in a more direct way—he knows they are probably tired, and he wants them to stay actively involved in the speech rather than sitting back passively.

Julio stays audience centered, regardless of the time of day, by acknowledging the audience's needs at specific times of the day and by organizing his presentations accordingly.

Speaking order. To be audience centered, you must also consider speaking order, or the place you occupy in a series of speakers. If you are the first speaker, you get the audience when they are fresh, listening more actively, and usually more willing to process your message. You also can set the stage for later speakers, make the first impression, and direct the audience's energy without interference by previous speakers. Additionally, you connect with an audience before anyone else does, especially because audiences sometimes ask more questions of first speakers.

If you are the last speaker or near the end of a series, your audience may be tired and weary of processing the information presented by previous speakers. They

Bob Daemmrich/PhotoEdit

A day-long training that features a number of speakers is fairly common in the workplace. If you are asked to present at this kind of speaking event, consider your speaking order, or the place you occupy in a series of speakers.

will have had their attention pulled in lots of different directions, and they may be more inclined to tune out a speaker or leave than to sit and listen to another speech. Therefore, start by acknowledging previous speakers and the information they presented. Then try to use your speech to reenergize the audience and redirect their focus as needed. At the end of your speech, the audience may have asked previous speakers most of their questions, so don't be disappointed if they have none for you. Or be prepared to share the stage with previous presenters who will also be answering the audience's questions.

If you are in the middle, you have the advantage of a warmed-up audience that isn't yet anxious to leave, but such an audience is also able to compare the information in your speech to the information given in previous speeches. Thus, engage an audience by making connections to previous speakers. As needed, recast or reshape the audience's mood or tone so they're able to hear your message more effectively. At the end of your speech, keep in mind that the audience may ask questions that attempt to pull together information from prior speeches or to rectify discrepancies in claims. If you can help audiences synthesize the information from your speech and previous speakers' speeches, you stand a better chance of sticking in their memories; people tend to remember beginnings and endings rather than what comes in the middle.

Length of speech. Students of public speaking often groan when an instructor sets a specific time limit to a speech and refuses to accept an infraction of that limit without penalty to the student. Why the strict time limits? What's the big deal? Time limitations, although invisible to the audience, are an important structural component of a speech.

When speakers exceed the time constraints, they communicate several things. If others are scheduled to speak after them, they communicate to their audience that their presentations are more important than those of the speakers that follow. If they are the only speaker, they communicate their lack of concern that the audience may have other places to be. Speakers who go over time limits also appear disorganized, suggesting they cannot prioritize material to fit into a predetermined time. In the same vein, a speech that is far too short suggests that the speaker has not prepared fully. Finally, speakers who do not prepare a speech that fits within time limits risk not being able to give their entire speech, which means their audience won't receive their complete message.

The responsibility for staying within time constraints falls on the speaker. When you agree to speak, find out how much time you will have for your presentation and stay within that time frame. If your audience wants more of your information, they can ask you to continue, elaborate, or engage you later in a question-and-answer session. (Question-and-answer sessions are discussed at the end of this chapter.) If you decide to speak for far less time than you have been allotted, explain to the audience that you will only deliver a short speech to allow more time for discussion with the audience. If you do not know what your time limitations are and there are other speakers who want to speak, do some quick mental math: Divide the

Practicing the Public Dialogue

4.3

Consider Your Speaking Environment

For your next speech, think about the size of your audience, the physical arrangement of the room, and the technology you want to use. What elements of your speaking environment will help you stay audience centered? What problems might come up during your speech? How could you solve them? Now consider the time of day you will give your speech, your speaking order, and the length of your speech. How will you work with these temporal factors to stay audience centered?

Online Resources

CourseMate To learn more about how physical location affects a speech, check out **Web Connect 4.3: Advanced Public Speaking Institute** via your CourseMate for *Invitation to Public Speaking.*

total time for the event by the number of speakers, allowing time for questions and discussion. Remember, audience-centered speakers manage their time efficiently and responsibly; they create an environment in which audiences feel respected and appreciated. For more information about time limits, see Chapters 9 and 11.

Adapting to Audience Expectations

What expectations do you bring when you go to a ball game? When a friend takes you to dinner? When you attend a dance performance? When you watch a favorite television program or listen to a new song on your iPod? We usually have certain expectations about how these types of activities and events will progress. For example, when we attend a ball game, we expect bleachers, announcers, players, referees, rules, a scoring system, and an end to the game. We expect the game to progress in a certain way, and we know when it doesn't progress properly.

When audiences attend public speaking events, they also bring their expectations. They expect speakers to perform in certain ways, expect public speaking events to follow a certain structure, and they base their interpretation of a speaker's message on those expectations. Audiences have expectations about the credibility of the speaker, the form of a speech, and how the speaker interacts with the audience in discussions. Audience-centered speakers must address these expectations because audiences use them to help decide whether or not a speaker "did a good job."

Expectations about the Speaker

When audiences take the time to listen to a speech, they want the speaker to be competent (qualified) and credible (believable). You'll explore competence and credibility in more detail in Chapters 7, 9, and 16, but here you'll learn how audiences use master statuses to assess whether or not a speaker is qualified and believable.

As you learned earlier in this chapter, master statuses are the positions people hold in society that affect their identities in almost all social situations. Whether we like it or not, once an audience identifies a speaker's master statuses, they usually form expectations about that speaker based on their beliefs concerning those master statuses. For example, Dennis is a fifty-five-year-old white attorney. A Georgia native, he travels to law schools across the country to meet with and speak to prospective new hires for his law firm. At many presentations, he is asked about racism and sexism in the South. He is often challenged, both overtly and subtly, about whether he recognizes forms of discrimination that could be present in his firm. Audiences often don't expect Dennis, a white male from the south, to be able to speak credibly about issues of race and gender.

To understand what an audience might expect of you as a speaker, take a moment to identify your own master statuses. Are you a woman or a man? What is your age and physical state? What is your race and ethnicity? Do you have an accent or particular style of speech? Will you acknowledge your marital status, parental status, or sexuality in your speech? What is your educational level? Are you often labeled or marked by society in a particular way? Your answers to questions like these will help you adjust to your audience's expectations of you as a speaker.

Consider how Carolyn Calloway Thomas, a professor in the Department of Communication and Culture at Indiana University, has addressed the issue of audience expectations of her as a speaker. She once asked a group of students,

"What do you notice about me?" They listed a number of items—her height, dress, style of presentation, occupation, and so on. "Yes, yes," she said, "those all are significant. Go on." Finally, one student said, "You are a black woman." "Yes," she responded, "and although that affects almost every aspect of my life, as well as almost every aspect of how you respond to me, if you can't get past the fact that I am black, if that's all you see about me, we've got a communication problem. You'll get stuck there. I am a black woman, yet I also am a very complex human being."

Civic Engagement in Action

"I WANTED TO UNDER- STAND"

If you conduct a Google search for award-winning actor Angelina Jolie, you'll get literally millions of hits, almost all highlighting her many children, her relationships with famous men, her sexy image, and her movies. However, many people outside the reaches of Hollywood know her primarily for her humanitarian work. Through her efforts as a goodwill ambassador for the United Nations High Commissioner for Refugees (UNHCR), she has assisted the United Nations in providing relief to more than 20 million refugees displaced by violence, war, and poverty around the world. Not only does she engage directly with the men, women, and children who are affected, but she also assists in building shelters for refugees, has released many of her journals that document her travel experiences, and visits U.S. detention centers so she can more effectively advocate for the reunion of families separated while escaping their home countries.

Jolie became interested in the plight of refugees after visiting Cambodia to film *Lara Croft: Tomb Raider*. "I started to travel and realized there was so much I was unaware of," she explains. "There were many things I hadn't been taught in school and daily global events I was not hearing about in the news. So I wanted to understand." Her belief in what the United Nations has always stood for—equality and the protection of human rights for all people—has resulted in her commitment to use her status as an A-list celebrity to learn as much as she can and speak out about the refugee crisis. For example, she says, "When I read about the 20 million people under the

UNHCR/Handout/Reuters/Corbis

care of UNHCR, I wanted to understand how in this day and age that many people could be displaced."

Jolie's focus is on the humanity and heroism of those who have been forced to leave their homes and live in overcrowded and dangerous refugee camps: "What was really shocking was that every individual person you meet will tell you that their immediate family was [affected]. Somebody's child was killed, somebody's husband. Someone was beaten.... You go to these places and you realize what life's really about and what people are really going through.... These people are my heroes."[10]

You Can Get Involved

CourseMate To learn more about UNHCR, access **Web Connect 4.5: UN Refugee Assistance** at your CourseMate for *Invitation to Public Speaking*. Also check out **Web Connect 4.6: ReliefWeb** to explore how you can get involved with global humanitarian issues. This site provides information about humanitarian emergencies and disasters around the world, including the "forgotten" ones.

Professor Calloway Thomas offers speakers a useful strategy for working with audience assumptions about master statuses: Simply acknowledge them. Master statuses do affect us, but help your audience move beyond them because they are not the totality of who we are. Speakers can use many nonthreatening phrases to help audiences move beyond their assumptions. They include phrases such as "I'm often asked that question," "Audiences generally assume," "As a woman (or other master status), people expect me to," and "Now, you might be wondering why someone like me is speaking on this topic today." Phrases that can help audiences shift their focus from unfamiliar styles or mannerisms include "Let me explain the symbolism behind the clothing I'm wearing today," "I'll be using an interpreter today and, as fascinating as they are to watch, I'd love it if you look at me as I speak and ask your questions directly to me," and "Even though I've lived in the United States for ten years now, the English language still stumps me at times. I hear it occasionally stumps some of you native speakers as well, so maybe we can help each other out with some of what we don't understand."

These kinds of phrases acknowledge, directly and kindly, that an audience's assumptions may prevent them from hearing a speaker's message. They also acknowledge differences in a positive way and encourage audiences to better understand those differences. As an audience-centered speaker, you certainly want to understand the positions of your audience, but you also want your audience to understand your positions. To help audiences understand you, encourage them to move beyond simply defining you by your master statuses and ask them to recognize you as a unique individual.

Expectations about the Form of a Speech

Communication scholar and theorist Kenneth Burke defines *form* as "the creation of an appetite" in the minds of an audience and the "adequate satisfying of that appetite." He suggests that a speech has form when one part of it leads an audience to "anticipate another part, to be gratified by the sequence."[7] That is, audiences expect a speech to follow a certain structural progression. For audiences with a Western cultural background, audiences often expect speeches to take the following form:

- The speaker will do most of the speaking or facilitating and share information the audience does not already have.
- The audience will listen during the speech and ask most of their questions at the end of the speech.
- Certain types of speaking will follow certain sequences: At the opening of an event, speeches of introduction are given; at public lectures, speeches of information, invitation, or persuasion are likely; at a celebration, speeches of commemoration or acceptance are given; and at business meetings, speeches take the form of presenting ideas, facilitating discussions, or gathering information.

To stay audience centered, do your best to recognize which form your audience will expect for your speech. Then try to follow that form or explain your reasons for altering it. If you don't, your audience's expectations will be violated, and they may react negatively to your speech. For example, if you are asked to commemorate a colleague, be sure to prepare a speech that praises the person and highlights her contributions. Even if you don't feel your colleague has contributed as much as the company thinks she has, try to focus on the positive aspects of your interactions with her so your speech is appropriate for the occasion. Don't take the opportunity to give a persuasive speech that tries to convince the audience your colleague isn't at all praiseworthy. By violating the form of a commemorative speech, you'll only frustrate your audience's expectations and make them feel uncomfortable. In our next example, the speaker doesn't follow the form he knows his audience expects, but he explains why he doesn't and so gives a successful speech.

Jeff Ho had been invited to speak to a class on communication and culture about representations of race in the media. As an Asian American who had studied the subject fairly extensively and was a dynamic and engaging speaker, Jeff had often been asked to give similar presentations. As a result, he was quite familiar with his material and with his audiences' expectations about how he should present it. Students expected him to lecture and present facts and research so they could take notes. But he really wanted to connect with his audience and create a dialogue, so he decided to violate his audience's expectations.

When he began his presentation, he told the students that he knew they expected him to lecture and they were prepared to sit back and maintain a certain distance. He said, "I'm going to make it really hard for you to stay distant, because I can't be distant from the issue of race and the media—and neither can you. You see, how the media present us as individuals, as people engaged with one another, affects us too powerfully to pretend we can understand by simply listening to someone lecture for fifty minutes. So, I am going to tell you some of my stories, experiences, and perspectives, and I'm asking that you tell me some of yours during this time we have together."

Jeff's presentation was a huge success. His audience understood why he violated their expectations of form because he explained why. In fact, he set up new expectations—the exchange of stories and experiences. He created a new appetite, which he satisfied during his time with them.

Audiences often ask questions because they want to know more about a speaker's viewpoint. What kinds of questions do you think you might get in your next speech? How might you respond to them?

Expectations about Discussions

An important part of the public dialogue is responding to an audience when they ask questions or want to discuss the ideas you present. Speakers are often expected to make time for question-and-answer sessions at the end of a speech or to manage brainstorming sessions and discussions. This type of audience interaction can be challenging because when you share the floor with others, you lose some of the control you had when you were presenting, and you cannot always predict what will happen or what the audience will ask or say.

Despite the unpredictability of discussions and question-and-answer sessions, there are several strategies to stay audience centered and manage this flow of information effectively. First, consider why people ask questions. They usually ask because they want you to clarify points you raised, get more information about a position you advocate, satisfy their curiosity about an issue or an idea, identify or establish connections between ideas, or support or challenge you or the ideas you presented.[8] In addition to asking questions, audience members participate in discussions for many of the same reasons that they ask questions. They also may want to share specific information with the group, restate information in a way that may be easier to understand, or even dominate the conversation.

Identifying which of these reasons motivates someone to participate in a speaking event can help you enormously. If an audience asks you for more information or to clarify a point, try to recognize that they are interested in your topic, not commenting on your ability to present information clearly. If an audience attempts to make connections between what they previously believed and the new information you've presented, help them make those connections rather than get frustrated because they just don't "get it." Similarly, when audience members try to organize their thoughts about a complicated topic, work with them rather than against them and perhaps incorporate their ideas into your plan for the discussion. If they try to dominate the conversation, set some time limits for each question and explain that, although their views are important, you want to hear from as many people in your audience as possible.

Recognizing what motivates an audience to attack or challenge a speaker is a particularly valuable tool. Addressing attacks or challenges from an audience during a question-and-answer session is often a speaker's greatest fear. When an audience attacks or challenges you, it is usually because they doubt the validity of your information or your credibility as a speaker. When you recognize why audiences do these things, you are more likely to respond appropriately rather than feel intimidated or engage in unproductive sparring. Consider the following example:

> Ramón is a small young-looking man with a graduate degree in communication. Fluent in both Spanish and English, he works as an interpreter for a health-care collective that serves migrant workers in his community. The collective consists of physicians, physician's assistants, nurses, and interpreters. Ramón is the only minority at the collective and the only one who has had extensive conversations with the migrant workers the collective serves.

> At a recent meeting Ramón attended, he gave a presentation addressing some of the problems people on his staff were having managing cases. Ramón offered a solution based on his experiences with the workers. He was immediately challenged by one of the physicians, who questioned his suggestions and labeled them "impractical." He told Ramón that there were factors at work he couldn't possibly recognize and then quickly moved the discussion in another direction. Although Ramón had the knowledge, education, and experience to make useful suggestions, he was challenged by someone who had more "credibility" than he did.

The challenge to Ramón's credibility was the result of his master statuses. As a small, young-looking minority, Ramón occupied a less authoritative position than the other people at the meeting, who were all older looking, white, and seen as having more credible credentials. Although Ramón's facts were correct, his audience could not see past his status, and so, however unconsciously, they labeled him as less knowledgeable than they. Ramón understood why his coworker challenged him and responded by saying, "You know, I often get overlooked as a source of ideas because of my age, and I realize that being a minority can sometimes throw people off. But I've lived in this community all my life and am quite familiar with the migrant and farming culture. I've also spoken with many of our clients outside the context of the clinic, and they've told me what they think would help them. I still think there might be ways to translate their suggestions into a feasible plan." Once Ramón explained how his experience and communication skills lent his ideas credibility, the other members of the group were able to move beyond their assumptions and work with his ideas and suggestions.

Despite the unpredictable nature of question-and-answer sessions, speeches that allow time for questions or incorporate discussion can be particularly rewarding for both audiences and speakers. In these speeches, speakers communicate that they're interested in the audience's thoughts, beliefs, and concerns. They also communicate that they want to interact with the audience to provide more information if necessary or perhaps learn something new themselves. They are engaging in a healthy public dialogue by making a space for conversation, confirmation, and the exchange of perspectives. For more information about question-and-answer sessions, see the appendix at the end of this book.

Chapter Summary

Audience-centered speakers consider several things about their audiences before, during, and after their speeches.

- An audience is a collection of people who have gathered to listen to a speaker's message.
- Audience members have various master statuses, standpoints, attitudes, values, and beliefs. You can gather this information by conducting a demographic audience analysis, a survey that provides information about the population traits of a particular audience.
- Audiences form a community, and it's important to acknowledge why people have gathered as an audience. Some audiences are voluntary and are interested in your topic and what you have to say. Other audiences are involuntary and are required to listen to you.

Audience-centered speakers also pay careful attention to their speaking environments and the expectations of their audiences.

- The speaking environment includes the size and physical arrangement of the speaking situation, the available technology, and temporal factors such as the time of day and the speaking order.
- You will be able to give a more effective speech in almost any environment if you assess the environment beforehand and adapt to it during your speech.
- Audience expectations focus on how qualified and believable the speaker is, the form of the speech, and the speaker's ability to lead discussions.

Invitation to Public Speaking Online

CourseMate Now that you have read Chapter 4, use your Speech Communication Course-Mate for *Invitation to Public Speaking* for quick access to the electronic resources that accompany this text. These resources include

- **Study tools** that will help you assess your learning and prepare for exams (*digital glossary, key term flash cards, review quizzes*).
- **Activities and assignments** that will help you hone your knowledge and build your public speaking skills throughout the course (*Practicing the Public Dialogue activities, review questions*).

- **Media resources** that will help you explore public speaking concepts online (*Web Connect links, Enhanced eBook*), develop your speech outlines (*Speech Builder Express 3.0*), watch and critique videos of sample speeches (*Interactive Video Activities*), upload your speech videos for peer reviewing and critique other students' speeches (*Speech Studio online speech review tool*), and download chapter review so you can study when and where you'd like (*Audio Study Tools*).

This chapter's key concepts and review questions are also featured here.

Key Concepts

attitude (68)
audience (66)
audience centered (66)
belief (68)
closed-ended question (69)

demographic audience analysis (69)
dialogue (66)
empathy (72)
ethnocentrism (68)
master statuses (66)

open-ended question (69)
speaking environment (72)
standpoint (68)
stereotype (70)
value (68)

Review Questions

1. Identify the following statements as true or false:

___ A dialogue is simply taking turns in a conversation.

___ When preparing my speech, I need to think more about what I want to say than the background and experiences of my audience.

___ All cultures and subcultures have the same basic idea of how the world works.

___ Audiences will interpret my message in just the way I want them to.

___ To be audience centered, I must say only what the audience wants to hear.

___ Temporal and situational factors have little effect on my speech.

___ When I open up my speech for questions or discussion, I lose all control of the flow of communication.

Each of these statements is false. Can you explain why?

2. Consider the times when as an audience member you held a very different standpoint from the other audience members. Consider the times you held a very similar standpoint to the other audience members. How did these situations affect your experience? Did the speaker address these differences or similarities? What was the effect of the speaker's actions?

3. Discuss with your classmates the differences between voluntary and involuntary audiences. In your public speaking class, you will speak to involuntary audiences. What strategies will you use as a speaker to communicate an audience-centered perspective to your audience?

4. Imagine you are giving a speech to introduce your audience to rock climbing and to encourage them to take up the sport. Describe how your speech might change for each of the following audiences:

- Thirty sixth graders, voluntarily present
- Thirty corporate executives, asked to attend by their bosses
- Seven pregnant women and their partners, voluntarily present
- Fifteen people over the age of sixty, voluntarily present
- Twelve lower-income teenagers who are part of an environmental education program and quite frightened by the prospect of rock climbing
- Your boss at the sporting goods store (you want her to invest more money in supplies for rock climbers)

With your classmates, discuss the changes you would make in your approach, content, and presentation.

5. Consider the room in which your public speaking class is held. Describe the physical setting, options for the placement of speakers, time constraints, and other temporal factors. How is your audience limited or enhanced by these environmental factors? How are you limited or enhanced? Identify specific strategies you can use to enhance this environment so your audience is more open to your message and better understands it.

6. Do discussions and question-and-answer sessions make you nervous? If so, what are your biggest fears regarding these speech elements? Using this chapter as your guide, identify three ways you might ease some of your fears.

7. Check out Speech Studio to see how other students acknowledge their audience and speaking environment in their speeches. Or record a speech you're working on, upload it to Speech Studio, and ask your peers for their feedback. What feedback could you use to make your speech more audience centered before you give your speech in class? Studio

Gathering Supporting Materials

© David Young-Wolff / PhotoEdit

One of our primary responsibilities as public speakers is to provide audiences with accurate information. In addition to expressing our opinions on the topics we speak about, we must also provide facts, examples, and evidence. We can find this type of information, called supporting material, by consulting our own experiences and knowledge, by doing research over the Internet and at the library, or by interviewing the right people.

Conducting research may seem intimidating at first, but if you organize your efforts, the process should be efficient and productive, and in less time than you might imagine, you can fill notebooks and folders with an impressive range of supporting materials. Research not only ensures that your ideas and arguments are accurate and that your audience is appropriately informed, but the insights it offers you on your subject can also keep you excited about your speech up until you deliver it and beyond.

This chapter will help you collect the supporting materials you need to enter the public dialogue successfully. You will learn how to organize your research efforts into three categories: determining what types of information you need, identifying where you can find this information, and assessing the strengths and weaknesses of the information you find. If you approach your research in an organized way, you will spend your time productively, reduce your frustration, and increase your chances of finding excellent materials to support your ideas.

Determine What Types of Information You Need

Before you begin your research in earnest, take some time to organize your thoughts about what types of supporting material you already have and what types you still need. Start by asking yourself the following kinds of questions (note that in Chapter 6, we'll discuss examples, narratives, statistics, testimony, and definitions in detail):

- What examples and stories do I have?
- What statistics will my audience want to know?
- What kinds of testimony will they want to hear?
- What terms and phrases can I define clearly on my own?
- Is the information I already have accurate, relevant, and credible?
- How will I evaluate the accuracy, relevance, and credibility of the information I find?
- What ideas or points can I develop or support from my own experiences?

As you consider these questions, you can construct a **research inventory**, a list of the types of information you have and the types you want to find. A research inventory helps you focus your research efforts and identify areas that need special attention. It is your first step toward making the time you spend gathering materials productive.

Consider the sample research inventory in Figure 5.1 on page 86. This inventory was developed by Alena, who gave a speech on incarcerated parents and their struggles parenting from jail to her public speaking class. The thirty minutes she spent identifying what information she had and what she still needed saved her hours of time on the Internet, in the library, and in interviews. In addition to saving you time, preparing a research inventory before you start to gather supporting materials helps you avoid experiencing what futurist Alvin Toffler calls information overload. In his famous book *Future Shock*,[1] Toffler explained that **information overload** happens when we take in more information than we can process but realize there still is more information we must know.

Educators believe the problem of information overload will grow worse in the future because the amount of information we need to know continues to increase, so much so that by the year 2020 the "available body of information [will] double every 73 days!"[2] However, Toffler offers a useful strategy for managing this overload: Classify information so it fits into manageable units. This is what you do with your research inventory. You organize the information for your speech into two classifications: what you have and what you need. The next step is to determine where you'll find the information you need.

Notice that the last item on the Research Inventory Worksheet is "Sources for this information." Once you know what types of information you want, you can

Good to Know!

research inventory: List of the types of information you have for your speech and the types you want to find.
information overload: When we take in more information than we can process but realize there still is more information we are expected to know.

Speech topic: Incarcerated parents

General purpose: To invite

Specific purpose: I want to invite my audience to consider the issues regarding incarcerated parents and when they should or shouldn't be permitted to parent.

My audience is: My public speaking classmates

I currently have:

Examples and stories:

A story Li wrote from the juvenile corrections facility

Stories from Sandra Enos, _Mothering from the Inside_, 2001

Statistics:

The number of children in the U.S. who have parents in prison, and the number of mothers and fathers released each year to return home. (Silja J. A. Talvi, _Women Behind Bars: The Crisis of Women in the U.S. Prison System_, 2007)

Testimony:

My own experiences working with a correctional facility.

Definitions:

This information is relevant, accurate, and credible because:

The story really catches the emotion and sadness of kids with incarcerated parents.

The book, _Mothering from the Inside_, is foundational, and _Women Behind Bars_ is fairly current.

My audience will want to hear:

Examples of the following:

Specific examples of incarcerated parents.

Statistics for the following:

Statistics to illustrate the kinds of crimes and lengths of sentences that keep parents away from children.

Statistics to illustrate the different lengths of times fathers and mothers are separated from children.

Testimony about the following:

The experiences of mothers and fathers who are currently incarcerated.

The experiences of children with incarcerated parents and of parents who have been released.

Definitions of the following:

Kinship (who takes care of children when a parent is incarcerated)

Incarceration

Correctional facility

The kinds of sources they will find trustworthy are:

People who work in correctional facilities

Legal services

Periodicals and journals that publish articles on the impact of incarceration on families

I need to find the following information:

Specific definitions

More statistics, especially about the effects on families

More testimony (from a range of perspectives)

Sources for this information:

Library database

InfoTrac College Edition (articles about incarceration)

Government websites (statistics)

Websites about barriers incarcerated parents face

Possibly interview a local correctional officer

Figure 5.1

Sample research inventory

classify that information even further by identifying where you are most likely to find it. In the next few sections, you will explore four common sources of information: your own experiences and knowledge, the Internet, libraries, and personal interviews. Understanding how best to access information from these sources and what you can gather from each will help you evaluate each source's strengths and weaknesses.

Use Your Personal Knowledge and Experience

After reading Chapter 3, you probably recognized that you have personal, firsthand knowledge about a number of subjects that would make excellent speeches. After you've selected your topic, use this personal experience as a source of research. Before you begin other research, take a moment to consider what knowledge you already have about your topic. This knowledge can come from your own experiences and training, your family background, hobbies, job or profession, and even things you have read or observed.

For example, the information in Cindy's speech on folding the American flag (Chapter 12) relies on her personal experience in the military and with folding the flag during ceremonial events. Similarly, Carol's source of research for her speech on fat discrimination (Chapter 16) was her own personal experiences. If you're interested in a topic but don't have personal experience with it, you can gain personal experience as part of your research. For

example, suppose you wanted to give a speech about a particular agency in your community. You could visit that agency and observe someone for a day to get the personal experience you need.

Practicing the Public Dialogue

5.1

Prepare Your Research Inventory
Bring a copy of the Research Inventory Worksheet to class. With a partner, discuss the kinds of research you both need for your next speech as well as the types of research you already have. Discuss where you might find the research you need and develop a timeline for gathering this material. Consider the advantages and disadvantages of your sources for the material you might find. Remember to consider your speech goals, your audience, and the need to vary your sources of information.

Online Resources

CourseMate You can download a Research Inventory Worksheet from the Chapter 5 resources in your CourseMate for *Invitation to Public Speaking*.

Search for Materials on the Internet

The Internet is the most popular research tool for college students in the United States. For public speaking students, the Internet offers information on local, regional, national, and international events and issues. It provides a truly staggering range of ideas to pick from in selecting your supporting materials.

The Ethics of Internet Research

The Internet is not without its weaknesses. Because it is easy to access and is open to anyone, information from all sorts of sources is posted that may not be accurate. Many websites are maintained and regularly updated by reputable people, companies, and institutions, but just as many others are not. Websites are regularly abandoned, and thus never updated, by operators who lose funding or simply lose interest. As a result, websites range dramatically in accuracy, complexity, and usefulness. Many sites include information that is old, incomplete, or based on personal opinions and biases. Additionally, identifying credible Internet sites can be difficult because many sites are well designed and look professional even if they're not.

Challenges like these place particular ethical responsibilities on you when you use the Internet to find supporting materials. Although the Internet can be an excellent source of information, you must use this tool properly to get information you can use ethically in your speech. To act in good faith with your audience, use only reliable and relevant information from the Internet and accurately credit the

Public Speaking and Service Learning: Engaging Community

Jordan Tranel, a public speaking student at Colorado State University, did his service learning project at Homeless Gear. This nonprofit organization collects outdoor camping equipment and clothes and manages clothing distributions for homeless people in different cities across Colorado. Jordan collected a variety of sources as supporting materials for his speech, including Colorado census data and the testimony of Homeless Gear staff, volunteers, and homeless people who benefited from the organization. In gathering these materials, he not only learned more about the issue but also acquired strong sources that helped lend credibility to his speech.

Public speaking has never been a strong skill of mine until I took the public speaking service learning class, where I was able to incorporate my passion of community service to help the homeless in Colorado. As the due date for the first speech approached, it was time to start gathering supporting material. As I volunteered for Homeless Gear, my knowledge about the homeless expanded. My main objective in obtaining supporting materials for my speech was to understand as many viewpoints of the different groups associated with the homeless as possible. These groups consisted of average citizens of Fort Collins, volunteers, and even homeless people. After gathering facts and testimonies from a representative from each of these groups, I browsed the Internet to find interesting statistics to support the main points in my speech. One shocking statistic that fueled my passion for this service work and influenced my speech greatly was that the average age of a homeless person in Colorado is 9 years old.

"MY MAIN OBJECTIVE IN OBTAINING SUPPORTING MATERIALS WAS TO UNDERSTAND AS MANY VIEWPOINTS OF THE DIFFERENT GROUPS ASSOCIATED WITH THE HOMELESS AS POSSIBLE."

My extensive research caused my passion for helping the homeless to increase dramatically. And experiencing the gratification of helping others through my internship encouraged me to start my own organization at Colorado State University called Homeless Awareness Team (HAT). The organization hosts gear-drives and fundraisers for the homeless while connecting students with weekly volunteer opportunities. As my involvement with the homeless increased, so did my enthusiasm for speaking about it. When it came time for my speech, I knew it was not only influenced by my passion and experience but was also well balanced with factual statistics and personal testimonies of others working for the same cause.

Tips for Incorporating Service Learning into Public Speaking:

- Incorporate a wide variety of supporting material in your speeches. Using sources from the Internet, periodicals, and personal interviews helps to keep your audience tuned in to your topic.
- Remember that the staff, volunteers, and clients at your service organization are often excellent sources of supporting information to use in your speeches.
- Before interviewing people, it helps to know what the main points of your speech will be so that you can collect the most applicable testimony possible.
- Always remember to explain the purpose of your interview to the interviewee and respect issues of confidentiality. If it's necessary to protect an interviewee's anonymity, label the testimony as "anonymous" in your bibliography and when you cite the testimony in your speech.

sources for this information in your speech. Knowing how to evaluate the quality of information you find on the Internet is crucial and ensures that you develop your speech ideas responsibly.

Evaluating Internet Information

Given the fluid nature of the Internet, how do you know whether a source found there is one you can use in your speech? As you would with any other source of information, evaluate your data according to the following criteria.

Is the information reliable? Check the domain in the URL. Is it .com (a commercial enterprise that might be trying to sell something), .org (a nonprofit organization, more interested in services and issues than in commerce), .edu (an educational institution), or .gov (a government agency)? What bias might those operating the site have about your topic? Do they make any disclaimers about the information they post on the site? What makes this information reliable or not?

Is the information authoritative? URLs that include a tilde (~) often indicate that a single individual is responsible for the information on a website. Can you find the person's credentials posted on the site? Can you contact the person and ask for credentials? Can you find the person's credentials in any print sources, such as a *Who's Who* reference? Regardless of whether the material was authored by a single person, an organization, an institution, or a company, is the author an expert on the subject of the site?

How current is the information? Many web pages include a date that tells you when it was posted or last updated. If you don't see such a date, you may be able to find it in your browser's View or Document menu. If you determine that the website is current, is the time frame relevant to your subject or arguments? You may find great information, but if it doesn't relate to the time frame of your speech, it's not relevant or ethical to use.

How complete is the information? Much of the text posted on the Internet consists of excerpts from printed material, and what is left out may be of more use than what is included. For example, a site may contain one paragraph from a newspaper article, but that paragraph may not reflect the overall message of the article. If you want to use an excerpted portion of a printed work, you must locate the complete work to ensure you are using that material accurately.

Is the information relevant? Many interesting facts and stories appear on the web, but be sure those you use as supporting material do more than just tell a great story. Your information must help you develop your thesis (Chapters 7 and 16). Ask yourself whether the information fits your needs. Does it help develop your main ideas, or does it take you in a different direction?

Is the information consistent and unbiased? Is the information you find consistent with information you find on other sites, from printed sources, or from interviews? Can you find other sources to support the statements, claims, and facts provided by a website? If the information is inconsistent with other sources, it may reflect new findings about a topic, but it also may reflect an unfounded or unsubstantiated claim. Many sites present only one side of an issue. To guarantee

Newscom

Assess the information you see on the home page of the White House. Does the information on this site look current and complete? How reliable do you think the information on this site is compared with the information on, say, TMZ.com, a celebrity-gossip site?

a less biased presentation and more comprehensive picture of your topic, search at a number of different sites and be sure to cross-check what you find against the information you obtain from more established sources such as books and other print documents. Be wary of outrageous or controversial claims that can't be checked for accuracy or aren't grounded in reasonable arguments or sources.[3]

If you keep these six criteria in mind as you research your speech topic on the Internet, you'll be more likely to use supporting materials that are credible. Recall from Chapter 4 that you increase your chances for giving a successful speech by remaining audience centered, and audiences expect information that is reliable, authoritative, current, complete, relevant, and consistent. The Internet is certainly a source of much credible material, but it should be only one of many tools you use to gather materials for your speech.

Research Materials at the Library

The library is your most comprehensive tool for gathering materials. There you have access to librarians, databases, indexes, journals, magazines, newspapers, books, documents, and many other useful resources, including the Internet. These materials cover an extensive range of topics and time frames. And although libraries might not be as easy to access as the Internet, their sources are usually reliable, routinely evaluated, and systematically organized.

But libraries also have their weaknesses. Unless you are familiar with how libraries organize their materials, you can find yourself confused—and even lost. One library may not have the exact source you want, so you have to look for other sources or visit another library. Until you get to know them, libraries can seem quite foreign. However, once you understand the strengths and weaknesses of a library, you can easily combine Internet research with library research to gather a wide range of useful and credible materials for your speeches.

Orientations and Librarians

If you are new to library research or are unfamiliar with the library you will be using, schedule a tour of the library before you begin your research. Getting a library orientation may sound silly or boring, but it can save you countless hours wandering around a place you don't understand. Most orientations take about an hour, and they can give you the confidence you need to begin your research on the right foot.

Librarians are also excellent resources. Consider what a librarian is trained to know: how materials are cataloged or stored, what materials are on databases, how to search through databases, how to refine subject and word searches, where materials are located, and how to request materials from other libraries. These skills can be invaluable to someone who is looking for supporting materials for a speech. Surprisingly, though, many students ask a librarian for assistance only as a last resort. If you find yourself spending more than half an hour searching for materials you can't find, ask for assistance. Remember, librarians won't do the work for you, but they can make the work you do much more efficient and fruitful. When you do seek a librarian in the course of your research, consider the following tips:

- *Fill out your research inventory before you begin your search and bring it with you to the library.* Refer to it as you work with the librarian.
- *Ask specific questions.* For example, rather than asking, "Where can I find information on incarcerated parents?" ask where you might find statistics on

the number of children with incarcerated parents. Or ask where you can find testimony by social workers about the effects of incarceration on families or examples of the most common problems faced by families with one or both parents incarcerated.

- *Share the specifics of your assignment with the librarian.* "It's only a four-minute speech," "My instructor wants three sources from this year and two from within the last ten years," "My audience is a potential source of funding for my proposal," "I want a really dramatic story for my introduction," and so on. Information like this will give the librarian the same focus you have for your speech and will help you avoid information overload.

- *Treat the librarian with respect.* Librarians are highly trained people whose specialty is finding information. They are eager to help but only if you recognize their talents and worth.

Creatas Images/Jupiter Images

To access librarians at the New York Public Library through the Internet, check out **Web Connect 5.3: Online Librarians** via your CourseMate for *Invitation to Public Speaking.* You don't have to live in New York for these librarians to answer questions you have about specific topics via e-mail.

Library Catalogs

A library's catalog allows you to search your topic by title, author, or subject in books, journals, magazines, and many other print and electronic materials. When you log into your library's home page, the catalog is one of the first headings you'll see. Library catalogs allow you to perform keyword and subject searches and will tell you the location of the book, magazine, or other material you want to find. Each page about a source indicates that source's call number, an alphanumeric code that indicates exactly where that material is stored in the library. To learn more about call numbers and how they can help make your research more efficient, check out **Web Connect 5.4: Understanding Call Numbers** through your CourseMate for *Invitation to Public Speaking.*

Don't be shy about asking librarians to help you navigate your school's library or find information. They love to help and can save you a lot of time in your search for supporting materials.

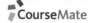

CourseMate

Keyword searches are helpful if you don't know the full title of the source you want. When you search with a word that you know is included in the title, search results will list all titles that include that word. Subject searches allow you to find all the sources that include information about a particular topic. For example, Lin's speech topic was road rage, and she wanted to know if any recent books or magazine articles had been written about her subject. She didn't have a specific author or title, so she searched on the subject of driving. This search produced far too many sources to look through. She then searched on a more specific term, road rage. The results of this search were much more manageable. (If your subject is more than two words, like road rage, put quotation marks around the words: "road rage." The quotation marks tell the computer to search for the words together, not separately.)

Lin later used a Boolean operator to refine her search further. **Boolean operators** are words you can use to create specific phrases that broaden or narrow your search. Three of the most commonly used are AND, OR, and NOT. In her search for links on road rage, Lin used the Boolean operator AND to link her topic with the broader issue of antisocial behavior. As a result, she got a listing of sites on

Good to Know!

Boolean operators: Words you can use to create specific phrases that broaden or narrow your search on the Internet.

both road rage and antisocial behavior. If she had used OR, she would have called up a listing of sites on either road rage or antisocial behavior. If she'd searched on "road rage NOT antisocial behavior," she would have gotten only links to sites about road rage that made no reference to antisocial behavior. Boolean operators help you focus your searches to find as much or as little information as you need.

Databases and Indexes

Databases are collections of information stored electronically so they are easy to find and retrieve. They are useful research tools for several reasons. Computer searches are quick, saving you valuable research time, and they are efficient because you can search using keywords and subjects. Databases allow you to access materials from other libraries, and most can usually be accessed from any computer connected to the Internet. Sources are current because records can be entered into a computerized database as soon as they are available, and they are updated regularly. Finally, databases present their information in a format that is easy to copy.

But databases also have their drawbacks. The so-called logic of databases is sometimes hard to understand, so searches can yield false hits, or citations unrelated to your topic. For example, a search for articles on "road rage" may yield articles on road construction and even anger management techniques. Additionally, many electronic databases (except catalogs) do not include older materials. So, if you are looking for historical trends, you will need to consult other sources of information.

You will find two kinds of databases in libraries. **Bibliographic databases** index publishing data for books, periodical articles, government reports, statistics, patents, research reports, conference proceedings, and dissertations. **Full-text databases** index the complete text of newspapers, periodicals, encyclopedias, research reports, court cases, books, and the like. (An example of a full-text database is InfoTrac College Edition, which is included in the online resources for this book.) Bibliographic databases help you find a specific source of information, such as the title of a journal article, and a full-text database provides the entire text of that item. Note that because full-text databases store so much text, they are more likely to yield false hits.

Some databases provide abstracts of documents. An **abstract** is a summary of the text in an article or publication. An abstract can be very useful because it tells you whether or not a document includes the information you need, which can save you from reading text you can't use. Most abstracts are about a paragraph long, but some are longer. However long the abstract is, you need to track down the full text of the article or publication if you want to cite it in your speech. Abstracts help you find relevant sources, but they are not the sources themselves.

When you want to search through materials that are published regularly, such as magazines, newspapers, yearbooks, scholarly journals, and proceedings from conferences, an index can be very helpful. An **index** is an alphabetical listing of the topics discussed in a specific publication, along with the corresponding year, volume, and page numbers. Many indexes are computerized, but some libraries still rely on the print versions. You can find indexes from almost every academic discipline and area of interest. Figure 5.2 presents a list of commonly used indexes. Keep a few tips in mind when you search indexes for materials:

Good to Know!

database: Collections of information stored electronically so they are easy to find and retrieve. **bibliographic database:** Database that indexes publishing data for books, periodical articles, government reports, statistics, patents, research reports, conference proceedings, and dissertations. **full-text database:** Database that indexes the complete text of newspapers, periodicals, encyclopedias, research reports, court cases, books, and the like. **abstract:** Summary of the text in an article or publication. **index:** Alphabetical listing of the topics discussed in a specific publication, along with the corresponding year, volume, and page numbers.

- Subject and keyword searches are crucial to finding what you want in an index, so be as specific and concise as you can.
- Indexes vary in how they classify topics, so a particular search term might not yield useful results from all indexes.
- You can usually find something on your topic in almost any index, so be sure you are searching indexes relevant to your topic.

Figure 5.2

Indexes

InfoTrac and InfoTrac College Edition	Citations, abstracts, and full-text articles from thousands of magazines, journals, and newspapers.
LEXIS/NEXIS	Full-text database for legal, business, and current issues. Includes U.S. Supreme Court and lower court cases.
Academic Search Premier	Scholarly academic multidisciplinary database. Covers a broad range of disciplines, including general academic, business, social sciences, humanities, general sciences, education, and multicultural topics.
IngentaConnect	Indexes scholarly journals and delivers documents. A fee is charged for document delivery.
Readers' Guide to Periodical Literature	Indexes almost 300 popular and general interest magazines, including *The New Yorker*, *Newsweek*, and *National Geographic Traveler*.
DataTimes	Online newspaper database, including *Washington Post*, *Dallas Morning News*, and *San Francisco Chronicle*.
Christian Science Monitor	Indexes the *Christian Science Monitor International Daily Newspaper*.
New York Times Index	Indexes the *New York Times* newspaper.
NewsBank	Microfiche collection covering current events from newspapers in over 100 cities.
The Times Index (London)	Index to the daily *Times*, the *Sunday Times*, the *Times Literary Supplement*, the *Times Educational Supplement*, and the *Times Higher Education Supplement*.
Wall Street Journal Index	Emphasizes financial news from the Journal. Includes *Barron's Index*, a subject and corporate index to *Barron's Business and Financial Weekly*.
Washington Post Newspaper	Index of the newspaper from our nation's capital.

Government Documents

Government documents can help you make a well-informed contribution to the public conversation. They contain all kinds of useful information:

- Statistics on population, personal income, education, crime, health, and the like
- Information about social issues such as employment, hunger, teen pregnancy, and the environment
- Issues discussed in Congress, such as gun control, seat belts, and education

- Information about historical events, such as wars and elections
- Information on local issues, such as funding for public education or charter schools, land disputes, water rights, and so on
- Research sponsored by the government
- Maps, charts, and posters that you can download or photocopy to make excellent visual aids for your speeches (Chapter 12)

You can find government documents in print, on CD-ROM or DVD, and sometimes on database indexes. Most government information now is available on the Internet thanks to a 1996 mandate by Congress to cease publishing government information in microfiche and paper formats.[4] To find this information on the Internet, check out USA.gov, which you can access at **Web Connect 5.5: U.S. Government Websites and Documents** via your CourseMate for *Invitation to Public Speaking*. This comprehensive website lets you search by subject or by agency.

CourseMate

Reference Works

What is the definition of the word *metamorphosis*? When and where was Oprah Winfrey born? Who was the first person to fly around the world? What was the worst storm in recorded history? When you are looking for simple facts and answers to general questions like these, consult the reference works in the reference section of your library. Reference works contain useful facts and information and can provide you with quick answers, thus saving you hours of time searching the Internet or digging through indexes and abstracts. If you are unsure of exactly which reference work to consult, ask your librarian for guidance. These are some of the more commonly used references and examples of each:

InfoTrac College Edition features millions of up-to-date full-text articles from thousands of journals and magazines. You can access InfoTrac College Edition through your CourseMate for Invitation to Public Speaking.

- *Almanacs:* Collections of facts on various subjects, such as the depth of Lake Michigan (*The World Almanac and Book of Facts*).
- *Atlases:* Books of maps and geographical information (*The Times Atlas of World History, Goode's World Atlas*).
- *Biographical dictionaries:* Information about famous and important people (*Dictionary of American Biography, Who's Who*).
- *Dictionaries:* Compilations of words and their definitions, correct spellings and pronunciations, origins, and synonyms and antonyms (*Oxford English Dictionary; Collins German-English, English-German Dictionary*).
- *Encyclopedias:* Overviews or surveys of a wide range of topics, such as butterflies, chemical warfare, or Toronto (*Encyclopedia Britannica, World Book Encyclopedia*).
- *Gazetteers or guidebooks:* Dictionaries or descriptions of geographical places. Guidebooks contain maps; gazetteers do not (*Chambers World Gazetteer: An A–Z of Geographical Information, Baedeker Guidebooks, Fodor's Travel Guides*).
- *Handbooks:* Summaries or surveys of a single broad subject, such as meetings (*Robert's Rules of Order*).
- *Manuals:* Works that explain how to do something or how an organization operates (*United States Government Manual*).

Cengage Learning

- *Quotation dictionaries:* Compilations of historical and contemporary quotations (*The Oxford Dictionary of Quotations*).

- *Reviews:* Analyses and comments on the work of another, often authors of books, movies, plays, or other performances; artists; or people who make significant public arguments or claims (*Book Review Digest, Index to Scientific Reviews*).

- *Yearbooks:* Summaries of trends and events of the previous year. Can be limited to one subject or to one geographical area (*Information Please Almanac, Atlas and Yearbook; Americana Annual: An Encyclopedia of Events; Statistical Abstract of the United States*).[5]

Reference works can be helpful because they are quick to use and can give you a jump-start on your research efforts. They can provide an overview of a topic and get you started on gathering supporting materials. Reference sources can help you cross-check information you find on the Internet or in another source. They can help you track down someone's credentials or present the specific details of a person's life. They tend to be timely or to give you the information you need for a specific time frame. And they can suggest ideas for other places to look for the materials you need.

Practicing the Public Dialogue

5.2

Research and Evaluate Internet and Library Sources

Bring the research you've found for your speech on the Internet and at the library to class. Share your research with the class and discuss whether your sources are credible, ethical, and audience centered and whether your research supports your speaking goals. Discard any information that does not seem ethical, reliable, authoritative, current, complete, relevant, consistent, or audience centered.

Evaluating Library Resources

Although the information in libraries is generally more reliable than materials on the Internet, you still must evaluate library sources and use them ethically. Not all the sources you find will be credible or appropriate for your particular speech and audience. Evaluate library sources by checking that the source is reliable, authoritative, current, complete, relevant, and consistent. For a summary of how to use Internet and library research to the best advantage, see Table 5.1.

Table 5.1

Internet and Library Research

Use the Internet When You	Use the Library When You
Want an overview of your topic	May want assistance with your search
Want the most current ideas	Want comprehensive materials
Want to explore less established sources	Want established sources
Want shortened versions of print documents	Want the full text of a document
Know your specific subject or URL	Want to review databases
Can verify the accuracy and credibility of the information found	Can evaluate the appropriateness and relevance of the information found

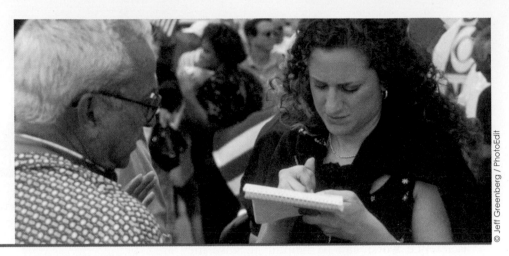

Reporters often use interviews to gather information to be sure their stories are accurate and interesting. If you're planning to conduct an interview for your next speech, who might you interview? How could the information this person provides make your speech more interesting and relevant?

Conduct Research Interviews

Using the words of other people in a speech can supply important information, provide a sense of immediacy, bring abstract concepts and arguments to life, and make seemingly distant issues hit home. Therefore, including the results of an interview in your speech can be a powerful way to present your ideas. An **interview** is a planned interaction with another person that is organized around inquiry and response, with one person asking questions while the other person answers them.[6] Interviews require planning, and productive interviews involve more than simply asking a few questions. You must first decide whom you'll interview, then schedule the interview, decide what questions to ask, conduct the interview in a professional and ethical manner, and then follow up with a letter of thanks.

Determine Whom to Interview

Your first step in conducting interviews is to determine whom you want to interview. There are several criteria you can use to identify the best interview subjects for your speech. Who are the experts on my speech topic? Who has personal experience with the topic? Who will my audience find interesting and credible? Who has time to speak with me? Who do I have the time to contact?

As you gather other supporting materials from the Internet and the library, also keep your eyes open for people in your area who might be excellent sources of information. If you have time, you might consider contacting people who live outside your area via e-mail or the telephone. Choose interview subjects who have credentials and experiences relevant to your topic and so can speak intelligently about it. A good interview subject might be a well-known expert or scholar, a head of an agency or company, someone on staff or in a support position, or a member of a community group, club, or organization.

Schedule the Interview

Although there are exceptions, most people are flattered when asked for an interview and will agree if you present yourself and your request respectfully. To ensure that a potential source sees you as credible and professional, take a moment to consider why you want the interview and why this person is an appropriate

Good to Know!

interview: Planned interaction with another person that is organized around inquiry and response, with one person asking questions while the other person answers them.

interview subject, what specific types of information you want to gather, roughly what questions you'll ask, and approximately how much time you want to spend with this person. When people are asked for an interview, they want to know the answers to all of these questions. Before you contact someone to request the interview, rehearse what you'll say a few times (like you would a speech) so you sound organized and professional. In your request, include the following:

- Identify who you are, providing your full name, where you're from (school, place of business), the public speaking course you're in, and your instructor's name.
- Specify the requirements of your assignment, such as its purpose, length, and topic.
- Describe why you've chosen to contact the person (for example, she's an expert in the field, he's the head of an agency).
- Request the interview, letting the person know how much time it will take and what kinds of questions you'll ask. Include two or three of your most important or engaging questions.

Note that by describing the types of questions you'll ask, your interview subjects can determine whether they can answer them and if they need to prepare before you arrive. And by letting them know how long you need for the interview, they can schedule time for you.

Prepare for the Interview

Preparing for interviews often takes longer than conducting them, but the payoff of careful preparation is worth the extra time you spend. The two components of preparing for interviews are designing your questions and deciding how you will record your interview.

Designing interview questions. Take time with your interview questions because they are your guide for an interview. Showing up with a plan to "just see how it develops" may be a good strategy for meeting a new friend, but it usually does not get you what you need in an interview. Even seasoned interviewers plan their questions carefully before they begin an interview, and most of them also research their interview subjects extensively.[7]

The goal of your interview questions should be to obtain information that you couldn't find through your Internet and library research. For example, in her speech on road rage, Lin couldn't find information about the personality profiles of people prone to road rage. When she interviewed a driving instructor, she asked him about his experiences with students who fell into road rage. Thus, she was able to get the information she needed.

Three kinds of questions are commonly used in interviews: open-ended questions, closed-ended questions, and probes. Most research on interviewing suggests that a combination of open-ended and closed-ended questions yields the best results. Open-ended questions give you more stories and details than closed-ended questions, but when you just need facts, there's nothing like a closed-ended question to prompt the specific answer you need.[8] A **probe** is a question that fills out or follows up an answer to a previous question. Probes are useful for obtaining

Good to Know!

probe: Question that fills out or follows up an answer to a previous question.

more far-reaching or comprehensive answers. Table 5.2 provides examples and the advantages of each of these kinds of questions. (Open-ended and close-ended questions are also discussed in Chapter 4.)

Table 5.2

Examples and Advantages of Different Types of Interview Questions

Question type	Examples	Advantages
Open-ended questions invite a wide range of possible responses.	• How did you become a driving instructor? • What are your thoughts on this most recent form of legislation?	• Usually nonthreatening and so prompt interviewees to do most of the talking. • Do not restrict the form or content of an answer, and they allow interviewees to offer information voluntarily. • Encourage interviewees to pull together ideas, knowledge, and experiences in interesting ways.
Closed-ended questions invite brief, focused answers and allow the interviewer to keep tighter control of the direction of the conversation.	• How long have you been a driving instructor? • Do many of your students display road rage?	• Can be answered easily and quickly. • Encourage interviewees to give you specific information. • Result in shorter answers for you to process.
Probes are questions that fill out or follow up an answer to a previous question.	• *Nonverbal:* Head nods or questioning eyes that indicate interest and a request to continue. • *Minimal responses:* Slight vocalizations such as "Oh?" "Really?" "Um-hmm," and "Is that so?" • *Direct requests for clarification:* "Let me see if I've got this right. Did you say that . . . ?" or "Could you explain what those figures mean for our community?" • *Direct requests for elaboration:* "Why do you say you're angry about this new legislation?" or "When that first driver went crazy with you in the car, what was your reaction?"	• Allow you to take an initial question further than you'd planned. • Allow you to get a more comprehensive answer.

Recording the interview. As you prepare for an interview, consider whether you want to tape-record your conversation or record it on paper. Both methods have advantages and disadvantages. On tape, you have a record of your exact conversation, but you have to transcribe the whole thing to find the exact quotes you want, which can be time consuming. A tape recorder can also sometimes make an interviewee nervous and less prone to share stories and ideas. However, with a tape recorder, you are free to relax a bit during the interview and make more extensive eye contact because you aren't busy writing things down.

When you record your interview on paper, you have the advantage of being able to make notes about nonverbal aspects of the interview that may help you when you repeat a quote in your speech, and when it is over, you already have a written transcript of your conversation. However, because you are trying to record the highlights of what is said, it can be harder to relax and simply engage in a conversation with your interviewee. Whether you plan to take notes on paper or record on tape, ask your interviewee if you have permission to record your conversation.

Conduct the Interview

The guidelines for conducting interviews are essentially grounded in the rules of common courtesy, so they are not difficult to follow. Dress appropriately, show up on time for your interview, and begin by introducing yourself to your interviewee. Restate the purpose of the interview and your speech assignment, and request permission to record the interview. Start with questions that will put the interviewee at ease and then follow those with your most important questions. As the interview progresses, remember that although you are having a conversation with your interviewee, you need to listen more than you talk; you are there to get the other person's perspectives and ideas.

At the end of your interview, ask your interviewee if she or he would like to add any information. You may get a piece of information or a story you did not think to ask for directly but that fits into your speech perfectly. Finally, thank the interviewee verbally for his or her time, and be sure you have recorded names, professional titles, and addresses correctly so you can cite them accurately and send a letter of thanks.

Follow Up the Interview

Review your notes or transcribe your tape as soon after the interview as you can, filling in details that are fresh in your mind and spelling out abbreviations you might have used in recording words on paper. Make notes of ideas that came to you as you listened to your interviewee, such as places in your speech that a particular quote or story might go or ways you might use some of the interview information in your opening and closing comments. And remember, always send formal letters of thanks to your interviewees, communicating your appreciation for their time and willingness to share information with you. You might even share with them some of the interview material you've decided to include in your speech.

Ethical Interviews

Ethical interviewing means preparing for interviews, asking appropriate questions, using quotes and information honestly, including only what was said and staying true to the intention of the speaker, and giving credit to interviewees for the words and ideas you include in your speech. At times, it may be tempting to alter a statement, embellish a story, or change a number or example just slightly to fit your needs. However, if the public dialogue is to function in any meaningful way, we must present material that is accurate and true. Information is inaccurate even if it's been changed only slightly, and people cannot make rational and reasonable choices if they have incorrect information.

Of course, ethics also apply to interviewees. If an interviewee provides information that seems inconsistent with what your other research supports, take the time to double-check your own research and the credentials of your interview subject, and ask your interviewee for documentation or sources that support unusual claims. If an interviewee provides information that is highly personal or would compromise the integrity or reputation of others, do not use that information in your speech. And of course, if an individual shares something with you "off the record," that information should stay out of your speech and out of your conversations with others.

Conducting an ethical interview can be a detailed, time-consuming process. However, all your hard work will result in a conversation with someone who may give you the information you need to make your speech come alive. The supporting materials you gather from interviews also supplement and confirm the materials you find in your Internet and library research.

Research Tips

To make the research process manageable, remember to give yourself plenty of time and consider the following tips for doing research.

Begin by Filling Out Your Research Inventory

Take the time to fill out your research inventory so you can figure out and remember what you need. Update your inventory as you begin finding information and discovering other sources.

Take Notes and Keep Copies

Keep careful, complete notes and records of sources to ensure you have accurate information. This will help you find the information again if you need to and will provide all the information you need to cite your sources correctly in your speech. Include in your notes the following information:

- For all sources, full name of the author; the title of the source (book, magazine, article, document, and so on); the edition, issue, or volume; the publisher; the place and year of publication; and the page numbers where you found the information.
- For Internet sources, the exact URL of a website or page, the publication or posting date, and the date you accessed it.
- For interviews, the full name of the interviewee, his or her title and place of business, and the date of the interview.
- The exact, complete phrases or words you are citing or quoting.

In addition to taking notes, download or photocopy and print pages of the more extensive material you want to cite, paraphrase, or quote. When you record a URL, make sure it is absolutely accurate. Any mistake, even a missing period or a misspelling, may lead to an incorrect site or a dead end, which is why with longer and more complicated URLs it can be worth your time to download or print the pages on which you find information.

Finally, review your notes for completeness and accuracy by asking yourself these questions:

- Is the material *permanent*? This indicates whether you or a member of your audience can find the material again, especially if it comes from an Internet source.

- Is the material from an *authority*? This means that the source is not paid to promote the subject, is not self-published, or is not biased in other ways.

- Did you *include all the bibliographic details* you need for a hard copy citation?

© Michael Newman/PhotoEdit

Avoid Plagiarism

Plagiarism is presenting another person's words and ideas as your own. That is, plagiarism is stealing someone else's work and taking credit for it. This is a serious issue in public speaking because it's dishonest and detrimental to a healthy public dialogue. There are three types of plagiarism. **Patchwork plagiarism** is constructing a complete speech that you present as your own from portions of several different sources. **Global plagiarism** is stealing an entire speech from a single source and presenting it as your own. **Incremental plagiarism** is presenting select portions from a single speech as your own.

All three forms of plagiarism are extremely unethical. However, they are easy to avoid. As you do your research, avoid unintentional plagiarism by taking careful notes and accurately documenting the source of each idea. Remember to cite these sources in your speech, even if you are paraphrasing an idea or borrowing only one phrase. Sometimes, you'll find, especially when researching on the Internet, that some of the basic information you need to cite a source is missing, such as the author's name. This doesn't mean you can't use the source, but if you do, you still must cite it in your speech. Simply cite as much information as you can, such as the name of the site, the URL, or the name of the article. Also be sure to include as much of the citation as you can in your bibliography. (Note that if the author's name is not included on a website, you can use "Anonymous" instead.)

Consider the consequences of plagiarizing: loss of credibility, failing the assignment or course, and perhaps even expulsion from your school. The most obvious way to avoid plagiarism is simple: Do your own work and give credit to others for their ideas and words. For additional information about plagiarism, check out **Web Connect 5.6: Plagiarism: Its Nature and Consequences** through your CourseMate for *Invitation to Public Speaking*.

Keeping your research well organized from the start helps you avoid plagiarism, prepare your preliminary bibliography, and cite sources appropriately when you give your speech. How will the research you use to support your next speech reflect your participation in the public dialogue?

CourseMate

Set Up a Filing System

As you gather information, it is tempting to put it all in one folder and wait to organize it when you sit down to draft your speech. This may save you time initially, but it will cost you time later in the process. It is much more efficient to organize

Good to Know!

plagiarism: Presenting another person's words and ideas as your own. **patchwork plagiarism:** Constructing a complete speech that you present as your own from portions of several different sources. **global plagiarism:** Stealing an entire speech from a single source and presenting it as your own. **incremental plagiarism:** Presenting select portions from a single speech as your own.

your information while you are in the process of collecting it. One of the best ways to do this is by using a filing system. Filing as you go helps you keep track of the information you've already found and ensures that it fulfills the needs you had originally intended for it.

Begin by organizing your materials according to your research inventory. Set up separate files for examples and stories, statistics, testimony, and definitions (Chapter 6) or color-code your materials by type of evidence with a highlighter or other system. Create summaries of your notes and copies, identifying the type of evidence they contain, the date you recorded them, the point the material makes, and where you might use it in your speech (for example, "good for introduction"). As you gather more material, organize it by main points and subpoints (Chapters 3 and 8).

Gather More Material Than You Think You'll Need

We often underestimate the amount of material we need to support our ideas. Or we think we've found the perfect example, only to discover that when we put the speech together, we can't use it after all. For these reasons, gather more information than you think you'll need. Collect several possibilities for your introduction and conclusion, and if your instructor asks for three sources from one time frame, gather six and use the best three. If you need one great example of what a statistic really means, ask your interviewee for a few and choose the one that best illustrates your point. Although you probably won't use all this information in your speech, having it will help you feel more prepared and thus more confident, and you'll be better able to conduct a question-and-answer session because you'll have a deeper understanding of your topic.

Begin Your Bibliography with Your First Source

A bibliography is a record of each of the sources you use in your speech, and accuracy is the key to a good bibliography. There are many different styles for bibliographies. Two styles that are often used for public speaking are the APA (American Psychological Association) and MLA (Modern Language Association) styles. Figure 5.3 shows these styles applied to common types of sources. Be sure to check with your instructor, or your employer if a work presentation requires a bibliography, for which academic or professional style to follow.

Start your bibliography the moment you collect your first source, and apply the appropriate style to all your entries consistently. By doing so, you will have the citations you need before you log off the Internet or leave the library or interview. And when you've finished your research, you will have a **preliminary bibliography**, a list of all the potential sources you'll use as you prepare your speech. (Figure 5.4 on page 104 shows a sample of a preliminary bibliography.) As you organize your speech, you'll decide which information to include or not include and remove entries you don't need. When you finish putting your speech together, you will find your final bibliography is complete, and you won't have to rush to finish it just before your speech.

Good to Know!

preliminary bibliography: List of all the potential sources you'll use as you prepare your speech.

	MLA style	APA style
Book	Isaacson, Walter. *Benjamin Franklin: An American Life*. New York: Simon and Schuster, 2004. Print.	Isaacson, W. (2004). *Benjamin Franklin: An American life*. New York: Simon and Schuster.
Edited book	D'Emilio, Sandra, and Udall, Sharyn. "Inner Voices, Outward Forms: Women Painters in New Mexico." *Independent Spirits: Women Painters of the American West, 1890–1945*. Ed. Patricia Trenton. Berkeley: U of California P, 1995. 153–82. Print.	D'Emilio, S., and Udall, S. (1995). Inner voices, outward forms: Women painters in New Mexico. In P. Trenton, Ed., *Independent spirits: Women painters of the American West, 1890–1945* (pp. 153–182). Berkeley: University of California Press.
Academic journal	Agyeman, Julian. "Communicating 'Just' Sustainability." *Environmental Communication* 1 (2007): 119–22. Print.	Agyeman, J. (2007). Communicating "just" sustainability. *Environmental Communication*, 1, 119–122.
Magazine	Kristal, Marc. "True Hollywood Story." *Dwell* 10 Oct. 2007: 199–214. Print.	Kristal, M. (2007, October). True Hollywood story. *Dwell*, 199–214.
Newspaper	Parker-Pope, Tara. "A Problem of the Brain, Not the Hands: Group Urges Phone Ban for Drivers." *New York Times* 13 Jan. 2009: D5. Print.	Parker-Pope, T. (2009, January 13). A problem of the brain, not the hands: Group urges phone ban for drivers. *The New York Times*, p. D5.
Electronic article based on print source	DiFilippo, Dana. "Experts Puzzled, Worried by Youngsters' Suicides." 15 May 2010. *Philadelphia Inquirer*. Web. 20 Aug. 2010.	DiFilippo, D. (2010, May 15). Experts puzzled, worried by youngsters' suicides [Electronic version]. *Philadelphia Inquirer*. Retrieved from http://www.philly.com/philly/news/home page/20100515_Experts_puzzled__worried_by _youngsters__suicides.html
Electronic article from Internet-only publication	Zelman, Kathleen M. "Expert Q&A: Eating with Food Allergies: An Interview with Stanley Cohen, MD." Web M.D. Web. 30 June 2009. <http://www.webmd.com/diet/ features/expert-q-and-a-eating-with-food -allergies>.	Zelman, K. M. (2009, June 30). Expert Q&A: Eating with food allergies: An interview with Stanley Cohen, MD. Web M.D. Retrieved from http://www.webmd.com/diet/features/expert -q-and-a-eating-with-food-allergies
Electronic article retrieved from database	Grabe, Mark. "Voluntary Use of Online Lecture Notes: Correlates of Note Use and Note Use as an Alternative to Class Attendance." *Computers and Education* 44 (2005): 409–21. ScienceDirect. Purdue U Lib., West Lafayette. Web. 28 May 2006. <http://www .sciencedirect.com/>.	Grabe, M. (2005). Voluntary use of online lecture notes: Correlates of note use and note use as an alternative to class attendance. *Computers and Education* 44, 409–421. Retrieved from ScienceDirect.
Movie	*The Dark Knight*. Dir. Christopher Nolan. Perf. Christian Bale, Heath Ledger. Warner Home Video, 2008. DVD.	De La Noy, K. (Executive Producer), & Nolan, C. (Director). (2008). *The Dark Knight* [Motion picture]. United States: Warner Brothers Pictures.
Television program	"Beyond Here Lies Nothin'." *True Blood*. HBO. 13 Sept. 2009. Television.	Ball, A. (Executive Producer). (2009, September 13). Beyond here lies nothin'. *True Blood* [Television series episode]. New York: Time Warner/ HBO.
Music recording	Nirvana. "Smells Like Teen Spirit." *Nevermind*. Geffen, 1991. CD.	Nirvana. (1991). Smells like teen spirit. On *Nevermind* [CD]. Santa Monica, CA: Geffen.
Personal interview	Sykes, Anna. Personal interview. 19 Feb. 2011.	APA style dictates that no personal interview is included in a reference list. Rather, cite this type of source orally in your speech, mentioning the name of the person you interviewed and the date of the interview.

Figure 5.3

Examples of the MLA and APA bibliographic styles

Figure 5.4

Sample preliminary bibliography

> **Preliminary Bibliography**
>
> Enos, Sandra. <u>Mothering from the Inside: Parenting in a Women's Prison.</u> New York: State University of New York Press, 2001.
>
> <u>Every Door Closed: Facts about Parents with Criminal Records.</u> Center for Law and Social Policy and Community Legal Services, Inc. 29 Sept 2003. Accessed 12 Oct 2006. http://www.clasp.org/publications/EDC_fact_sheets.pdf.
>
> Poehlmann, Julie. "Children's Family Environments and Intellectual Outcomes during Maternal Incarceration." <u>Journal of Marriage and Family</u> 67 (2005): 1275–1285.
>
> "The Beat Within: A Weekly Publication of Writing and Art from the Inside." Pacific News Service. Accessed 10 Oct 2006. http://thebeatwithin.org/news/view_article.html.

Citing Sources

When you incorporate your sources into your speech to support your ideas, you must cite them properly. There are two reasons to cite sources: It is ethical and it adds credibility to your ideas.

Practicing the Public Dialogue

5.3

Prepare Your Preliminary Bibliography

Bring to class several samples of the supporting materials you've collected for your speech, including your Internet research, library research, and interviews. Working as a class, help one another prepare your preliminary bibliography. To format your bibliography correctly, use the citation style required by your instructor.

Online Resources

You can use Speech Builder Express to help you prepare your preliminary bibliography with whatever citation style you are assigned. Go to your CourseMate for *Invitation to Public Speaking* and access Speech Builder Express. Select "Works Cited" from the left menu and follow the instructions. For short reminders from this chapter about bibliographies, click the "Tutor" button.

Citing Sources Is Ethical

In public speaking, our own ideas often grow from the ideas of others. When you cite your sources, you acknowledge this debt, fulfilling your ethical responsibilities to give credit to others for their work and their contributions to your own thinking. If you cite your sources properly, there should be no uncertainty among audience members about which ideas are your own and which ideas come from others. If you do not cite your sources, you risk committing plagiarism.

Citing Sources Adds Credibility

When you cite sources in a speech, you indicate that you have done research on your topic, have some understanding of it, and that your ideas about it have the backing of experts. Citing sources also shows your audience that you value the public dialogue and that you recognize others have something to offer to this dialogue. When you want to bolster the credibility of a point you make, cite the source so your audience recognizes the authority from which it came.

Rules for Citing Sources

Although your instructor may have specific rules for the number and format of sources you are to cite in a speech, there are three general guidelines for citing sources during your speech. These guidelines rely on ethical principles and an audience-centered approach.

Give credit to others. When you rely on the specific ideas or words of others, give them credit during your speech. The guideline works like this: The more specifically you rely on someone else's ideas or words, the more responsible you are for citing them. If you use someone's research, quote or paraphrase someone, or share information from a magazine, book, newspaper, or other news source, you need to cite your source in your speech. You can use phrases like the following:

Last week's *New York Times* tells us that . . .

According to the 2010 Census, . . .

The director of the Center for Applied Studies in Appropriate Technology responded to my question in this way . . .

The Old Farmer's Almanac reports that this will be the wettest year this area has experienced since 1938.

Jane Kneller, professor of philosophy at this university, writes, . . .

Note that even though much of what we already know grows out of the research and work of others, we do not need to provide a citation for every claim we make. Some claims are based on common knowledge, information that is generally known by most people. For example, the statement "Eating a balanced diet is good for your health" is common knowledge and does not require a citation. But the statement "Eat at least three ounces of whole grain bread, cereal, crackers, rice, or pasta every day" requires a source citation such as "according to the U.S. Department of Agriculture's food pyramid."

Give specific information about your source. General phrases such as "research shows," "evidence suggests," and "someone once said" are usually not enough to lend credibility to your speech. If your audience is listening with care, they'll want to know more about your sources. They'll be asking "what research?" "whose evidence?" and "who said?" When you cite a source, include the following information:

- The name of the person or the publication
- The credentials of that person or publication
- The date of the study, statistic, or piece of evidence

These three pieces of information generally are enough to show your audience that your source is valid and your statistics are reliable and relevant to your topic. You can usually omit details such as page numbers and place of publication from your actual speech, but you will want to include them in your bibliography.

Deliver all information accurately. When you cite a source, you must do so accurately. This means giving the name and title of the person correctly, pronouncing any unfamiliar words clearly, and delivering all statistics

Practicing the Public Dialogue 5.4

Cite Your Supporting Evidence
Working in pairs or with a group, practice citing the sources listed in your preliminary bibliography aloud, using the rules provided in this chapter.

Online Resources
CourseMate Watch video clips of student speakers Tiffany Brisco and Damien Beasley as they cite sources in their speeches. Assess the degree to which they accurately cite their sources and provide information about them. Use your Course-Mate for *Invitation to Public Speaking* to watch the videos, respond to analysis questions, and compare your answers to those provided by the author. To see additional speech videos, go to Speech Studio and see how your peers cited sources in their speeches. Or upload your own speech and ask others to give you feedback on how you cited your sources. **Studio**

and quotations accurately. Mispronouncing names and titles, stumbling over dates and quotes, and leaving out important elements of a citation can reduce your credibility. It can even alter the facts you are sharing with your audience. So before you give your speech, check to be sure you have all your source citations recorded correctly and rehearse them until they smoothly fit into your speech. (You'll learn more about delivery in Chapter 11.)

Speaking Visually

Remarkable CD Covers

According to *Smashing Magazine*, an online magazine about the latest trends and techniques in Web development, the "most striking [album cover] designs are those that capture both a buyer's attention and the essense of the music." Remarkable designs range from obscure to graphic, vintage to surreal, and comic to unforgettable.[9] What separates a remarkable cover from one that is just serviceable is that, although some make obvious reference to the music or musician they promote, most rely on obscure references and images. The artists who create these album covers are speaking visually to their audiences, deftly using principles of visual processing, graphic and artistic design, and drama, mystery, and humor.

When CDs first started replacing vinyl albums in the 1980s, the original case for the CD was one half the size of an LP vinyl album, thus allowing more space for an artist to promote the music.[10] Today's CD covers are considerably smaller, and now that we have the ability to download most of the music we like, CD covers face new challenges. According to The Album Cover Network,

For a while, there was a true "marriage" of two very distinct and different media—art and music. In their heyday, LP covers were an outlet for experimentation, art, fun, social comment, and the power of the visual image to sell you the music that was contained therein. It's over, I guess. The "cover" of a CD is about 14 percent of the size of a record album; the artwork on the cassette box is just 7 percent as big. That's barely enough space to put the name of the artist, much less some breathtaking or unusual artwork.[11]

If you are considering adding a clip of music to one of your speeches, or are speaking about a particular artist or genre of music, or even speaking about a political or social movement, you might want to "speak visually" and show images of the cover art that accompanied the musician's songs and music. These images, if appropriate and ethical, can add a visual dimension that may interest your audience. As visual scholar Paul Martin Lester explains, the "most powerful, meaningful, and culturally important messages are those that combine words and pictures equally and respectfully."[12]

CourseMate To see a number of remarkable album covers created for CDs, use your CourseMate for *Invitation to Public Speaking* to access **Web Connect 5.1: Obscure and Remarkable** and **Web Connect 5.2: Sleevage**.

GAB Archive/Redferns/Getty Images

Chapter Summary

Gathering a wide, relevant range of supporting materials for your speech ensures that you help the public dialogue remain responsive, lively, and healthy.

- You can find information to use as supporting material by consulting your own knowledge and experience, doing research over the Internet and in libraries, and conducting interviews.
- The tools to aid you in the research process include the research inventory, search engines, librarians, catalogs, databases and indexes, government documents, reference works, and professional interviewing practices.
- To present ethical arguments and proposals to your audiences, learn to evaluate the strengths and weaknesses of your sources by assessing their reliability, authoritativeness, currency, completeness, relevance, and consistency.

With a bit of planning, you can make the research process efficient and productive.

- Start your research by filling out your research inventory.

- As you gather materials, take notes, make copies, and download material from the Internet. By accurately recording the critical details about each of your sources, you can easily avoid plagiarism and get an early start on your preliminary bibliography.
- To give yourself more options when you're in the final stages of preparing your speech, gather more information than you think you'll need.
- Set up a filing system at the start of your research effort to keep careful track of your materials.

Citing sources properly is ethical and adds credibility to your ideas.

- Cite the sources you rely on specifically or quote directly.
- Provide enough specific information about your source so that your audience knows the source is valid, reliable, and relevant.
- Cite sources accurately by recording all your research carefully and practicing your delivery.

Invitation to Public Speaking Online

CourseMate Now that you have read Chapter 5, use your Speech Communication Course-Mate for *Invitation to Public Speaking* for quick access to the electronic resources that accompany this text. These resources include

- **Study tools** that will help you assess your learning and prepare for exams (*digital glossary, key term flash cards, review quizzes*).
- **Activities and assignments** that will help you hone your knowledge and build your public speaking skills throughout the course (*Practicing the Public Dialogue activities, review questions*).

- **Media resources** that will help you explore public speaking concepts online (*Web Connect links, Enhanced eBook*), develop your speech outlines (*Speech Builder Express* 3.0), watch and critique videos of sample speeches (*Interactive Video Activities*), upload your speech videos for peer reviewing and critique other students' speeches (*Speech Studio online speech review tool*), and download chapter review so you can study when and where you'd like (*Audio Study Tools*).

This chapter's key concepts and review questions are also featured here.

Key Concepts

abstract (92)
bibliographic database (92)
Boolean operators (91)
database (92)
full-text database (92)

global plagiarism (101)
incremental plagiarism (101)
index (92)
information overload (85)
interview (96)

patchwork plagiarism (101)
plagiarism (101)
preliminary bibliography (102)
probe (97)
research inventory (85)

Review Questions

1. If you are doing service learning in your public speaking course, take time to consider your speech topic and the supporting materials you will need. If you are gathering information for an agency, set up time to talk with someone there to help you identify what kind of material you should gather. If you are presenting your speech about the agency, what information sources will you use? Will you use the Internet, the library, personal interviews, or all three?

2. Use the evaluation criteria described in this chapter to evaluate the strengths and weaknesses of the information you have gathered for your next speech. Is it reliable, authoritative, current, complete, relevant, and consistent? Based on your assessment, identify information you might discard, and consider whether you need to do more research for your speech.

3. Draft a list of questions you would like to ask a personal contact for your next speech. Keep in mind your speech goals, time limitations, and audience. Now organize that list so the most important questions are first and the least important ones are last. Next consider how you will begin your interview. Will you start with your most important questions or some warm-up questions? What questions will you use to close the interview?

4. Bring three or four of the sources you will use in your next speech to class. In small groups, practice delivering the citation of those sources with each other. Focus on those sources with especially long titles, with names that are difficult to pronounce, or that are just confusing. Work with one another to find the most comfortable way to cite these sources in your next speech.

Developing and Supporting Your Ideas

6

Bill Aron / PhotoEdit

In public speaking, a **claim** is an assertion that must be proved. When we make claims, we "call out" to others so that we can explore and exchange ideas, respond to one another, and we clarify, refine, and revise our positions. When we communicate our claims ethically and effectively, we stimulate and enhance the public dialogue.

We prove our claims with **evidence**, the materials speakers use to support their ideas. Evidence comes from the information you already know and gather in your research on the Internet, at the library, and in interviews. Ethical evidence allows you to explain a process with confidence, share a perspective in a way that encourages understanding, identify a problem and pose a solution, motivate an audience to action, or acknowledge someone's accomplishments. And strong evidence helps build your credibility, or believability. In Chapter 7, you'll learn how you can enhance your personal credibility. In this chapter, you'll learn how to assess the credibility of your evidence. Credible and ethical evidence is the foundation of the common language in the public sphere.

The five most common types of supporting material are examples, narratives, statistics, testimony, and definitions. You are probably familiar with these types of evidence, but you may not be sure when to use them or how to evaluate their strengths and weaknesses. Let's start with examples as evidence.

- **Examples**
- **Narratives**
- **Statistics**
- **Testimony**
- **Definitions**

IN THIS CHAPTER, YOU WILL LEARN TO:

- Explain the importance of supporting materials in a speech
- Identify and provide examples of the five main types of supporting materials
- Apply tips for using each of the five types of supporting materials effectively

Examples

Examples are specific instances used to illustrate a concept, experience, issue, or problem. Examples can be brief, only a word or a sentence or two, or they can be longer and more richly detailed. Examples can also be real or hypothetical. A **real example** is an instance that actually took place. A **hypothetical example** is an instance that did not take place but could have. Generally, real examples are more credible and convey a sense of immediacy. Consider the following real examples from student speeches:

> In her speech on binge drinking on college campuses nationwide, Eileen used a powerful example of a binge drinker by describing her friend who "consumed twelve to fifteen beers combined with shots of hard liquor each evening, and stopped only because she ran out of alcohol, time, or money."

> In his speech on the dangers of exotic pets, Kyle used an example provided by the head of his city's Pest Control and Wildlife Department: "According to the department's head, one man had a Gaboon viper, a cobra, a black-tailed rattle-snake, a copperhead, three large boas, and a full-grown alligator that acted as a 'guard dog.'" Kyle explained to his audience that these pets were hazardous because the owner was "bitten by his Gaboon viper and died from the bite. The remaining so-called pets? They went to the Humane Society to be adopted by other people or to be euthanized."

These students used examples to help clarify exactly what they meant when they used the terms *binge drinker* and *hazardous pets*.

Occasionally, you can clarify a point with a hypothetical example. A hypothetical example usually begins with words like *imagine*, *suppose*, or *let's say that*. For example, when Clara addressed a group of teenagers in an after-school program on proper eating for her service learning project, she could have simply said, "Skipping breakfast isn't good for you." Instead, to be a more effective speaker, she supported her claim with a hypothetical example:

> Suppose you skipped breakfast this morning. Let's see what that would do to your energy level by about 9 or 10 o'clock—that's during second period, right? If you haven't eaten by then, you'll probably feel bored or restless, and maybe sad or unmotivated. You might also feel angry or irritable, kind of grouchy and crabby. And maybe you'll feel a little lightheaded or dizzy if you stand up fast. You might have a headache. You'll definitely have trouble concentrating on your schoolwork because your blood sugar is low or because all you can think about is how hungry you are. Sound familiar to any of you?

Clara's hypothetical example, although not real itself, grew out of research that was grounded in real experience. It helped her audience understand more clearly why skipping meals isn't good for them.

Several criteria can help you decide when using an example would be most effective. Consider the following guidelines, all of which help you answer in advance any questions your audience may have about your topic.

Use Examples to Clarify Concepts

Identify the concepts in your speech that your audience might consider complex or unfamiliar, and then use an example to help you frame those concepts

Good to Know!

claim: Assertion that must be proved. **evidence:** Materials that speakers use to support their ideas. **example:** Specific instance used to illustrate a concept, experience, issue, or problem. **real example:** Instance that actually took place. **hypothetical example:** Instance that did not take place but could have.

in terms your audience will understand. That is, try to anticipate what parts of your speech might prompt your audience to ask, "What do you mean by that?" Examples frame abstract concepts and experiences in terms of concrete actions, events, people, and things. Thus, an example can make an abstract or complex point clearer.

Civic Engagement in Action

"IN WHAT AREA OF YOUR LIFE DO YOU WIELD INFLUENCE?"

Many celebrities are known for their charity work and for using their money to help people less fortunate than themselves. But some celebrities raise the bar and become respected humanitarians on the international stage. George Clooney and Don Cheadle are two of these stars. Made famous by hit movies such as *The Perfect Storm* and *Up in the Air* (Clooney), *Traffic* and *Hotel Rwanda* (Cheadle), and the *Ocean's* franchise (both of them), Clooney and Cheadle have used their wealth and influence to bring attention to a number of humanitarian causes, most notably the crisis in Darfur, Africa.

Darfur is a region in Sudan, a country in northeastern Africa. The Darfur conflict began in 2003. Since then, warring factions have killed hundreds of thousands of people and have forced more than 2.5 million people from their homes into "displaced people" and refugee camps. Civilians living in these camps are consistently and brutally attacked by rebels, militias, and government forces. In addition, they suffer from malnutrition, disease, and the threat of starvation. In 2004, then–U.S. Secretary of State Colin Powell described the Darfur conflict as the worst humanitarian crisis of the twenty-first century.

The devastation in Darfur moved Clooney and Cheadle to speak out in a number of public forums to raise awareness about the crisis and support for the people affected:

- Along with fellow actors Brad Pitt, Matt Damon, and movie producer Jerry Weintraub, Clooney and Cheadle founded Not On Our Watch, an organization that focuses "global attention and resources towards putting an end to mass atrocities around the world."
- Cheadle co-authored a book titled *Not on Our Watch,* which explains how ordinary citizens can

take action to end ongoing crises in Darfur and elsewhere.
- Clooney was involved in two documentaries, *Sand and Sorrow* and *Darfur Now*, both of which served as international calls to action to help the people of Darfur.

For their efforts, Clooney and Cheadle were presented with the Summit Peace Award by the Nobel Peace Prize Laureates in Rome in 2007.

When asked in a 2007 Time.com interview how average Americans can make a difference in Darfur, Cheadle said,

"In what area of your life do you wield influence? Are you a member of a church group? A book club? There are many ways, and none of them can be overlooked when you are talking about trying to create a collective awareness."[1]

You Can Get Involved

CourseMate To learn more about Clooney and Cheadle's humanitarian organization, access **Web Connect 6.1: Not on Our Watch,** at your CourseMate for *Invitation to Public Speaking*. The "What you can do" link in the top-left menu provides opportunities for advocacy and action. Also check out **Web Connect 2.2: Students for Darfur,** an organization that uses Facebook to help bring attention to the Darfur crisis and spark action.

AP Images/Fred Kaufman

In Clara's case, she anticipated her audience's question "what does she mean by 'isn't good' for me?" Her detailed example about the physical and mental impacts of skipping breakfast clarified what she meant.

Use Examples to Reinforce Points

What parts of your speech might prompt the audience to say, "I don't see how this point matters"? Examples help an audience see your points in terms of the larger case you're making in your speech. Therefore, examples help audiences recognize the relevance and importance of your points as support for your claims. Kyle used an example of how hazardous exotic pets can be to reinforce his point that owning exotic pets is a dangerous hobby. By describing what happened to one owner of such pets, and then what happened to the animals after the owner died, Kyle encouraged his audience to consider the potentially deadly consequences of this hobby.

Use Examples to Bring Concepts to Life or to Elicit Emotions

When someone says, "I'm not affected by that issue," an example helps bring a concept to life by providing specific images audience members can picture in their minds. When they're able to create a mental picture, one that is filtered through their own thoughts and experiences, they can better understand how an issue affects them or someone they know. Eileen's example of the sheer amount of alcohol consumed by her friend brought the reality of binge drinking to life for her audience. Specifically, Eileen's reference to drinking that "stopped only when [her friend] ran out of alcohol, time, or money" highlighted just how out of control and self-destructive binge drinking can become, adding emotional weight to her claim. Similarly, Kyle's example of the exotic pets being euthanized brought out the emotions in his audience. No longer were the exotic pets curiosities; they became real animals that died through no fault of their own.

Use Examples to Build Your Case or Make Credible Generalizations

When someone says, "It's not as common or prevalent as you say," using a number of examples helps them see that it is. A series of examples can help you build a case or help you make a plausible generalization. For example, if Eileen cited numerous examples of binge drinking on college campuses throughout the country, those in her audience who think binge drinking is an isolated problem might be compelled to reconsider their views and see the issue as a nationwide concern.

Not all examples are equal. Some don't illustrate your point well, and others won't resonate with your audience. See Table 6.1 for tips that will help you evaluate an example for its strengths and weaknesses.[2]

Narratives

A **narrative** is a story that recounts or foretells real or hypothetical events. Narratives help us explain, interpret, and understand events in our lives or the lives of

Good to Know!

narrative: Story that recounts or foretells real or hypothetical events.

Table 6.1

Tips for Using Examples Ethically and Effectively

Ask yourself this . . .	And do this . . .	Example
Is the example relevant?	Make sure your example refers to the point you are making, not to something else.	In her speech about binge drinking, Eileen offers an example of treatment programs for older adults as her "success story solution." But her example won't be relevant because her target population consists of students in their teens and early twenties, not older adults. It's a great example of a solution but not the solution to her specific problem.
Is the example appropriate?	Avoid examples that are too graphic, emotional, detailed, or personal for an audience. Use caution with examples that contain violent details, the manipulation of emotions, overly technical material, or the use of explicit personal details.	In his speech on the damage caused by the earthquake in Chile, Trenton used many images and verbal descriptions of the devastation caused. As he attempted to persuade his audience to support the relief efforts there, he was careful not to prey on his audience's emotions by showing only overly graphic images of children who had been killed or hurt. Instead, he showed a range of examples of the devastation so that his audience had a realistic sense of the magnitude of the relief efforts needed.
Is the hypothetical example ethical?	Make sure your hypothetical example represents events or information grounded in fact. Audiences should believe it really could be true or have happened. And tell your audience the example is hypothetical. Don't mislead your audience into believing that a made-up example, however plausible, is real when it isn't.	In his speech about humans being able to adapt to and survive in harsh environments, Colin provided a dramatic description of how we would have to adapt to live on Venus. However, it would be impossible for almost all life on Earth to survive on Venus. Its average surface temperature is 860 degrees Fahrenheit, and the clouds rain sulfuric acid. Thus, this example didn't give his audience much insight into how humans have adapted to harsh conditions on Earth, such as barren deserts and ice ages.
Are there enough examples to support your claim?	Determine whether one example is enough or whether you need several. •If you can't find more than one example to support your point, perhaps your claim is unfounded. •If you want to suggest something is common but can't find examples of it, it may not be as common as you thought. One example suggests an isolated incident, not a trend, so avoid generalizing from a single example.	When Eileen described the extent of the problem of binge drinking, she used quite a few examples to make her case. But earlier in her speech, when she was simply illustrating what constitutes binge drinking, she knew just one example would be sufficient.
Have you accounted for the counterexamples?	Be sure to consider counterexamples that refute your claims. Counterexamples are specific instances that contradict your claims; they make your assertions appear false or at least weaken them.	If Kyle found that many exotic pets were safe to own, he'd have to explain why this is so. If he can't explain these counterexamples, he has to adjust his claim to "some exotic pets, such as poisonous snakes, are dangerous to own." He can't ethically claim that all exotic pets are dangerous because he has counterexamples that refute this claim.

One of Ronald Reagan's strengths as a speaker was his ability to personalize his speeches with narratives. For example, he personalized a speech commemorating the Allied soldiers who landed in Normandy, France, during World War II in an effort to defeat the German army in Europe by telling the stories of individual soldiers who exhibited courage and strength during a battle that took many lives. What stories might you use to personalize your ideas and draw your audience into your speech?

AP Photo

others.[3] Speakers can use **brief narratives**, sometimes called vignettes, to illustrate a specific point or **extended narratives** to make an evolving connection with a broader point. Whatever their length, narratives can be valuable aids to public speakers. When used in speeches, stories can give historical context to events, make strong connections between ideas and experiences, and add emotional depth to characterizations. They can also describe subjects, settings, and actions with sensory details that can captivate an audience.

Stories often reference other stories or rely on parts of other stories to be complete. This process, called **intertextuality**, is very common in television programs, movies, and computer games. For example, one TV show refers to another or relies on part of a narrative from another show to make its point. Today, because many of our stories come from entertainment media, intertextuality in everyday communication is becoming very common. Make sure your audience has the references necessary to follow these types of intertextual narratives.

Because narratives are so appealing to audiences, always search for stories you can use in your speech as you gather your supporting material. A carefully selected and well-told story can add a personal touch, make a point, or move an audience in significant ways. There are several criteria to follow when you are thinking about incorporating a narrative into your speech.

Use Narratives to Personalize a Point

Former U.S. President Ronald Reagan was an expert at using stories to make his point in personal ways. An advocate of private initiative rather than government assistance, he told the story of Jose Salcido, whose wife had died of cancer.

> [Her death left Jose] both father and mother of thirteen children. In an accident only the Lord can explain, one day the brakes on his truck didn't hold and he was crushed against a brick wall as he walked in front of the vehicle. The children who had lost their mother now had lost their father. But even they were not orphaned.

Good to Know!

brief narrative: Short story or vignette that illustrates a specific point. **extended narrative:** Longer story that makes an evolving connection with a broader point. **intertextuality:** Process in which stories reference other stories or rely on parts of other stories to be complete.

Reagan went on to tell of extended family, neighbors, members of their church parish, and even strangers who stepped in to help the Salcido children in the absence of their parents. He finished his story by reading a letter from one of the people who assisted the children: "This is for the children of Jose Salcido. It is for them to know there are always others who care; that despite personal tragedy, the world is not always the dark place it seems to be." In this one story, Reagan drew his audience personally into his argument. As they listened to his story, they actually could see themselves assisting the children.[4]

Use Narratives to Challenge an Audience to Think in New Ways

A narrative can challenge an audience to think differently or to understand the world in new ways. Curtis began his speech on the various kinds of racism in the following way: "Let me tell you the story of Ishmael."

> Ishmael was sitting at a restaurant in town, minding his own business, eating dinner with some of his friends. At another table nearby, he and his friends heard snickering and laughter but ignored it because they didn't think it related to them. Pretty soon, the laughter got louder, and two guys from that table began to address Ishmael and his friends. At first, they thought it was going to be a friendly exchange but soon realized they were the butt of the jokes being told—racist jokes, about the shape of Ishmael's eyes and the color of his skin. The so-called jokes soon turned to taunts and verbal abuse, with the girlfriends joining in. Not sure what to do, Ishmael and his friends were saved, so to speak, by the owner of the restaurant, who asked Ishmael and his friends to leave.

Curtis paused here to let the story sink in. He began again: "You think I might be making this up? It happened to my best friend a couple of years ago while he was a student at this very university."

With his narrative, Curtis compelled any listeners in his audience who might have believed that racism no longer exists to rethink their views. As we tell a story, we share our perspectives with an audience in personal, yet organized, ways. In listening to our story, an audience may find a commonality not recognized before or gain a new or deeper understanding of an issue.

Use Narratives to Draw an Audience in Emotionally

Facts, statistics, and examples can prove the claims you make in your speech, but they lack the emotional appeal of a story. If your audience can't connect with your speech on an emotional level, your listeners may not feel that its subject is important enough for them to care whether you prove your claims or not. Use a story, then, when you want to draw your audience into the speech emotionally. Josiah used this brief story, found as he gathered materials for his speech on the history of battles portrayed in theatrical productions:

> Planned stage combat reduces the level of danger that is part of any battle scene in a play. According to William Hobbs in *Fight Direction for the Stage and Screen*, in early sixteenth-century Stockholm, the actor who played the part of Longinus in *The Mystery of the Passion*, and who had to pierce the crucified Christ, was so carried away with the spirit of the action that he actually killed the other actor. The king, who was present, was so angry that he leapt onto the stage and cut off the head of Longinus. And the audience, who had been pleased with the actor's zeal, were so infuriated with the king that they turned upon him and slew him.

Cengage Learning

CourseMate

Watch a video clip of student speaker Chelsey Penoyer as she uses narratives to bring emotion to her speech. As you watch Chelsey speak, consider how effectively she uses narratives. Do they draw you into her speech? You can use your CourseMate for *Invitation to Public Speaking* to watch the video, respond to analysis questions, and compare your answers to those provided by the author.

Josiah could have made his point by offering statistics on the number of deaths and accidents in stage fights over some period of time, but instead, he drew his audience in emotionally with a brief story about the implications of unrehearsed fights in theatrical battle scenes.

Use Narratives to Unite with Your Audience

Stories can describe common, profound, or dramatic experiences that you can use to create unity between yourself and your audience. When you share a story about an experience that is just like everyone else's, you establish common ground with your audience. When you relate a powerful moment in your life, you reveal a personal aspect of yourself that allows your audience to identify with you more fully. When you tell dramatic or exciting stories, you can connect with your audience by sharing a way of thinking about the world that may be new to them. Stories, because of their human element and the personalized way they are told, can create a sense of togetherness between speakers and their audiences.

In speeches, narratives are more than stories that entertain: They convey something specific to an audience. See Table 6.2 for tips that can help you determine whether the narrative you want to use in your speech does more than simply "tell a good story."

Table 6.2

Tips for Using Narratives Ethically and Effectively

Ask yourself this . . .	And do this . . .	Example
Does your narrative make a specific point?	Have a specific reason for telling a story. For example, you may want to reaffirm values, challenge perspectives, remind your audience of important events and beliefs, or teach ways of being and thinking. Be sure your narrative has a clear point. Remember, there are a lot of great stories, but not every one makes your point well.	President Reagan told the story of the orphaned children in such a way that his point could not be missed—without assistance from everyday people, the children would have suffered more than they already had.
Is the length appropriate?	Make sure your story fits within the time limit for your speech. Brief stories allow you to make your point quickly and often fit better into speeches. But don't discard an extended story without considering how it might fit in your speech. An extended story offers more detail and can keep the audience listening throughout the speech to "hear how the story ends."	In her speech about wildlife conservation, Mariah wanted to use an extended story about Christian the lion, famously purchased from a department store in London, reintroduced to the wild, and then reunited with his former owners.[5] She opened with a part of the story (how Christian came to be purchased from a department store), added pieces of it as she developed her speech (his being raised in London and then reintroduced to the wild), and then concluded with the remainder of the story (the reunion).

Is the language you use vivid?	Use language not only to relate the story's details, but also to bring the story's message to life. • You don't need to use flowery or complicated language to present your story, nor should you exaggerate or change a story to meet your needs. • Rather, think about the language you choose and the images and messages it conveys and creates.	Remember that you have an ethical obligation to tell the truth with your story. Language facilitated the story's message in both Josiah's and Reagan's speeches. When Josiah said the audience "turned upon him and slew him," he created a visual image and evoked sixteenth-century speech. Reagan's phrase the "world isn't always a dark place" conveyed a sense of hope during troubled times.
Is the delivery appropriate to the story?	Ensure that your delivery of the story is appropriate. Practice telling your story several times until you get your pauses, emphasis, gestures, and expressions the way you want them.	When Josiah told the story about stage fighting gone wrong, he was appropriately dramatic yet somber. He didn't tell the story in a flippant or joking way that would have made light of a tragic situation.
Is the story appropriate for my audience?	Consider how your listeners will respond to your story; not all people respond to stories in the same way. How listeners do respond depends on many factors, including their cultural background. • Make sure the stories you tell ring true for your audience. • Your story shouldn't be too graphic, too personal, or simply inappropriate for a particular audience. Some stories don't tell a familiar tale or recount a common experience. If you suspect parts of your story will be too culturally unfamiliar to your audience, make sure you explain those parts. Or choose a different story altogether.	When Marie gave her speech about her experience as an exchange student in Africa, she told the traditional parable of a European missionary who felt guilty that he was able to live in a much nicer house than his African neighbors. One day, the missionary confessed this to one of his neighbors, who responded in surprise, "But, Father, you're the poorest man in the village. You have no grandchildren!" She explained that this story illustrated the importance of family over individual wealth in African culture.

Statistics

Statistics are numerical summaries of facts, figures, and research findings. They help audiences understand amounts (100 individuals participated), proportions (that's almost half the people in this organization), and percentages (fully 50 percent said they'd participate again). Numbers summarize and help audiences make sense of large chunks of information (eight glasses of water a day, every day of the year, is the equivalent of almost 3,000 glasses of water a year). They also help people see where something is in relation to other things (he's the third-fastest runner in the world). See Figure 6.1 on page 118 for a visual representation of statistics that could help an audience understand how the U.S. government classifies people who immigrate to the United States.

Good to Know!

statistics: Numerical summaries of facts, figures, and research findings.

Figure 6.1

Visual representation of statistics

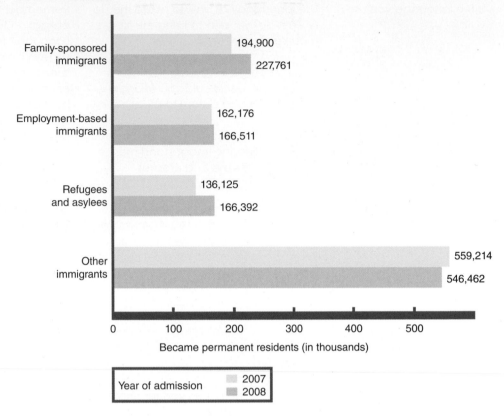

Class of admission

Visual representations of statistics help an audience understand complex or abstract information. This graph shows the number of immigrants to the United States who became permanent residents in 2007 and 2008 by class of admission.

Source: U.S. Department of Homeland Security, Office of Immigration Statistics, *2008 Yearbook of Immigration Statistics*. See also http://www.dhs.gov/ximgtn/statistics/publications/yearbook.shtm.

Numbers and statistics may seem less glamorous than a story or a clever example, but relevant, surprising, or little-known statistics can grab an audience's attention. Statistics can help you synthesize large amounts of data, point out exceptions to trends or generalizations, or express the magnitude or impact of an event or issue. Statistics can also help you make and refine your claims, and they can highlight certain aspects of your topic that other types of evidence cannot. According to Cynthia Crossen, author of *Tainted Truth: The Manipulation of Fact in America*, 82 percent of people surveyed said statistics increase a story's credibility.[6] One of the best sources of statistics is the Statistical Abstract of the United States. This resource includes statistics related to crime, population, health, and many other topics. You can access it online via **Web Connect 6.3: Statistical Abstract** through your CourseMate for *Invitation to Public Speaking*.

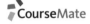 CourseMate

Types of Statistics

Common statistics include totals and amounts, costs, scales and ranges, ratios, rates, dates and times, measurements, and percentages. Other more technical statistics are the mean, median, and mode. The mean, median, and mode are numbers that summarize sets of numbers. When you use them correctly, they can be an important source of evidence, but why, how, and when to use them isn't always clear. The descriptions that follow will help you determine the type of statistics you need in your speech. Also see Figure 6.2 for a visual representation of the differences between mean, median, and mode.

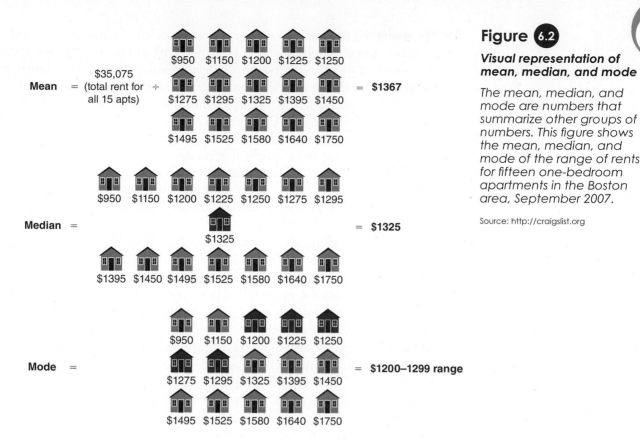

Figure **6.2**

119

Visual representation of mean, median, and mode

The mean, median, and mode are numbers that summarize other groups of numbers. This figure shows the mean, median, and mode of the range of rents for fifteen one-bedroom apartments in the Boston area, September 2007.

Source: http://craigslist.org

Cengage Learning

The **mean** tells you the average of a group of numbers. Find it by adding all the numbers in your data set and then dividing by the total number of items. Use the mean when you want to describe averages, patterns, tendencies, generalizations, and trends, especially for large groups of data. For example, the mean is what you need if you want to find the average weight of a group of teenagers, like Clara did in her speech to the after-school youth in our earlier example. To find her mean, Clara added together the weight of each of the teens in her audience (they weighed 115, 121, 126, 132, 154, 159, 163, 167, and 170) and then divided that number by the total number of teens she had weighed (9). This gave her the mean, 145 pounds, the average weight in her audience. She used that average, or mean, to compare her audience's average to the average weight of teenagers fifty years ago and then to teen athletes and nonathletes. She and her audience then entered into a discussion about average weights of teenagers in general.

When your data sets include extreme values, or what are called outliers, using the mean to generalize about the data is misleading.[7] A group of students speaking to county commissioners about affordable housing illustrates why this is so. The students presented information about the average cost of housing in their area. Most of the houses rented for $900 to $1,500 a month, but one particular home rented for $2,250 a month. In this case, the students couldn't have used the mean because the outlier in this set of data ($2,250) would have distorted the picture of housing costs in their area. To provide a more accurate statistic, the students need to use the median or the mode or leave out the $2,250 rental and explain why.

Good to Know!

mean: Average of a group of numbers.

The **median** is the middle number in a series or set of numbers arranged in a ranked order. A median tells you where the midpoint is in your set of data. It shows you that one-half of your observations will be smaller and one-half larger than that midpoint. Use the median when you want to identify the midpoint and make claims about its significance or about the items that fall above or below it. For example, the median weight of Clara's teens is 154. This means that half the teens weighed more than 154 and half weighed less. Both Clara and her audience now have more information than simply the average weight of teens (145 pounds). For example, Clara can begin to explain weight in relation to body type or height (those below the median ranged in height from four feet eleven inches to five feet eight inches and those above the median ranged from five feet six inches to six feet one inch).

The students speaking about affordable housing used the median to explain that one-half of the homes they assessed rented for less than $1,100 a month and one-half rented for more than $1,100. They then explained that once the housing that rented for less than the median had been rented, families looking for rentals in their area had to pay more than $1,100 a month. They discussed the monthly income necessary to support such housing costs. Using the median in this way helped them make a case for building Habitat for Humanity homes in a particular neighborhood so more families could afford to live there.

The disadvantage of using the median is that significant numbers below and above the midpoint might not be discussed. For example, is it significant for a teen to weigh 39 pounds lighter than the median weight, as the lightest person does, or 16 pounds heavier than the median, as the heaviest does? Similarly, if the students failed to explain that below the median rent of $1,100, houses rented for only as low as $950, their audience could get the sense that some housing was much more affordable than that. And if they didn't note that above the median, homes rented for as high as $2,250 their audience might not understand that about half of the housing in the area was too expensive for most families. Thus, their audience could get the impression that families easily could afford to live in a certain neighborhood, when actually they could not.

The **mode** is the number that occurs most often in a set of numbers. Use the mode when you want to illustrate the most frequent or typical item in your data set to establish the occurrence, availability, demand, or need for something. For example, if Clara found that of the nine in her group, seven ate five times a day and the two others ate four times a day, then the modal rate of food consumption is five times a day—that's the most common number of meals her audience eats in a day. She then could talk about metabolism during growth spurts and the need for many teens to eat more than three times a day as they are growing. Similarly, if the students showed that the most common monthly income for people looking for rental homes was $1,500, they could use the mode to show that most of the homes for rent in their area were priced too high for these people. Thus, they could argue that Habitat for Humanity homes were crucial.

Numbers help you make claims and establish the importance of your ideas. Because audiences give numbers so much credibility, consider the following guidelines when you want to use statistics ethically and appropriately.

Good to Know!

median: Middle number in a series or set of numbers arranged in a ranked order. **mode:** Number that occurs most often in a set of numbers.

Use Statistics to Synthesize Large Amounts of Information

Statistics allow you to present large amounts of data in a very precise way. For example, in a speech on the process of newspaper production, Josh explained that in his hometown of approximately 1 million people, 31,000 copies of the local paper were printed each weekday, and 37,000 copies were printed on Sunday. And he explained, "if you took one average-sized newspaper and cut it into the size of a paperback book, you have a book about 350 pages thick." Use statistics when you want your audience to appreciate the numerical force behind something or when you want them to understand the size or quantity of an event.

But be careful about using too many statistics. Audiences have a hard time remembering numbers. In fact, the more numbers you use, the fewer your audience is likely to remember. How difficult do you think it would be to remember the numbers in the following example?

> Based on these 2008 figures, we can say of the 1,393 males between the ages of eighteen and twenty-one with incomes above $24,000 a year and less than two years of training who attended this event more than three times but less than five, 743 drove their own vehicles, 259 rode with friends, 128 took the bus, and 11 walked. This leaves 252 unaccounted for. Now, let's look at the 2010 data. These figures change slightly.

Although this is a hypothetical example, it illustrates how beginning speakers sometimes tend to use too many numbers and use them randomly. The result is more information than audience members can remember, presented without a systematic structure to help them.

Use Statistics When the Numbers Tell a Powerful Story

In a speech on cradle-to-grave marketing, Jess could have told the story of a child heavily influenced by television advertising. Instead, he chose to use statistics:

> The average twelve-year-old spends four hours a day watching television—the equivalent of two months of nonstop TV watching per year. They see 40,000 commercials a year—the equivalent of 100 commercials a day. The result is what marketers call the "nag factor," children badgering their parents to buy products, culminating in 2 billion children-influenced dollars spent on products in 2000. So powerful is the nag factor that U.S families spend 54 billion of their, and their children's, dollars on toys, sweets, food, electronics, shoes, clothes, sports, and movies.

The story Jess told with these numbers, two months total television watching, 100 commercials a day, that resulted in parents spending an enormous amount of money and increased focus on this market by advertisers, is far more powerful than the story of one child begging a parent to buy products on a shopping trip.

Use Statistics When Numerical Evidence Strengthens a Claim

Statistics can strengthen a claim, especially one made in an example or a story, because they quantify or measure the impact of an event. They also allow you to make the same claim in a new way. After Rupert gave verbal and visual examples to describe the damage done by Hurricane Katrina, he used statistics to strengthen his claim that the storm caused an almost incomprehensible amount of damage:

> You can see why this hurricane is still a topic of conversation, concern, and relief efforts today. Katrina flooded 57 miles of coastline along the St. Tammany Parish. The hurricane created a storm surge 16 feet high, or deep, that traveled a full 6 miles inland. By August 31, 2005, 80 percent of New Orleans had been flooded, with the famous French Quarter somehow being spared damage.

Rupert's description and examples affected the audience on one level, his visual aids influenced them on another, and his dramatic statistics reinforced his claims about the damage caused by the storm.

There are many ways to misuse statistics. Recall from our housing example that the mean rent misrepresented the affordability of housing in a particular neighborhood. Similarly, if Clara suggested that the modal number of meals for teens is five per day, we can easily overlook the thousands of teens who go without food each day because of poverty or eating disorders. Because statistics can be manipulated, see Table 6.3 for guidelines that will help you use them responsibly and accurately.

Table 6.3

Tips for Using Statistics Ethically and Effectively

Ask yourself this . . .	And do this . . .	Example
How accurate are my statistics?	Be certain the sources of your statistics are credible, the data are current, and the statistics represent what you claim they do. • Avoid manipulating a statistic to say what you want. • Be wary when a source that is overly invested in a particular outcome provides a statistic. See if you can find other sources that confirm your statistic, or if that isn't possible, present statistics from various perspectives to make your claim more accurately.	When only 10 percent of those surveyed say they would try a product again but only twenty people were sampled, you don't have a very credible statistic. Using outdated statistics about unemployment rates can mislead the audience into thinking that the economy is better or worse than it actually is. Data on global warming compiled by the petroleum industry are likely to be influenced by the industry's views on the issue.
Can I make my statistics easier to remember by displaying them visually?	Display statistics visually on an overhead, in a PowerPoint slide, in a handout, or on a board or flip chart.	Take another look at Figure 6.1. Imagine a speaker presenting those numbers only verbally. Displaying the immigration statistics visually reinforces the verbal presentation by helping the audience keep track of and visualize the statistics.
Can I make my statistics easier to remember by rounding numbers up or down?	Round your numbers up or down wherever possible, especially when you want to emphasize general size rather than the exact amount.	Rupert rounded his numbers about the damage caused by Hurricane Katrina to whole numbers. He spoke of 57 miles, 6 miles, and 16 feet rather than providing the exact measurements of the damage caused.

| Can I make my statistics easier to remember by grouping similar numbers together? | When you must present a lot of numbers to make a point, find ways to group similar categories together so your audience can digest them more easily. Although your audience will still have to keep track of quite a few numbers, "chunking" makes them easier to follow. | In our hypothetical example, demographic data, mode of transportation, and insignificant data could be grouped so the audience could remember numbers that are related to one another: "Based on these 2008 figures, we can say that about 1,100 of the 1,400 males under age twenty-one, with basic training and making more than $24,000 a year, traveled to this event. This leaves about 300 unaccounted for." |
| Can I make my statistics easier to remember by translating them into relatable numbers? | Translate your statistics into numbers that your audience can easily recognize and relate to. | • How big is 57 miles of shoreline? It's the distance between two familiar points, say, your own college campus and the next town or point of significance. It's also the distance of more than two marathons.
• What does it mean to say a surge of 16 feet? Show this distance by asking two members of your audience to stand 16 feet apart. Or explain that it is the height of approximately three people who are 5 feet 4 inches.
• How large is 80% of New Orleans? Show a map of the city with that 80% shaded in blue. Then explain how much of your own town would have been covered by the same amount of water. |

Testimony

When speakers use the opinions or observations of others, they are using **testimony** as a source of evidence. Testimony is sometimes called "quoting others" or "citing the words of others." We usually think of testimony as coming from an authority, an expert, or a person who has professional knowledge about a subject. This is often true, but testimony can also come from average people who have relevant experience with your topic. Speakers sometimes also provide their own testimony—their own words and experiences as sources of evidence.

Testimony often takes the form of a **direct quotation**, an exact word-for-word presentation of another's testimony. At other times, speakers **paraphrase** the words, or provide a summary of another's testimony in the speaker's own words. Direct quotations often are seen as more credible than paraphrasing, but sometimes, a person's words or stories are too long, too complex, or contain inappropriate language for a particular audience, making paraphrasing a better option.

Generally, use someone else's testimony when his or her words make your point more clearly, powerfully, or eloquently than your own. When you use the testimony of someone considered an authority in a particular field, you are using **expert testimony**. When you use the testimony of someone who has firsthand knowledge of

Good to Know!

testimony: Opinions or observations of others. **direct quotation:** Exact word-for-word presentation of another's testimony. **paraphrase:** Summary of another's testimony in the speaker's own words. **expert testimony:** Opinions or observations of someone considered an authority in a particular field.

Ethical Moment

SUPPORTING MATERIAL THAT SENDS AN UNINTENDED MESSAGE

In January 2010, nine students of Arab descent at Dearborn High School in Detroit, Michigan, received national attention when they arrived to school wearing sweatshirts that referenced the September 11, 2001, attacks on the World Trade Center. The group of students, all from the class of 2011, wore sweatshirts that depicted the number 11, representing the twin towers; the school's mascot, a thunderbird, flying directly toward the numerals; and the slogan "You can't bring us down."

After teachers, staff, and other students reported feeling offended by the image, the sweatshirts were confiscated. Dearborn Public Schools spokesperson David Mustonen stated that "teachers and kids were obviously upset," and senior Donovan Golich felt the group should be suspended. The school later held a public meeting for parents, staff, and area residents so they could discuss the situation.

Meanwhile, the students involved in the incident told school officials that they were simply showing pride for their class of 2011. One of the students, Hiab Mussad, stated that the public was overreacting. He claimed, "[W]e just wanted to show our support (to our class)." Even so, many angry parents called upon school officials to suspend the group. However, the administrators determined that the incident was a matter of "kids not thinking, not realizing the consequences of something they thought was pretty innocent," and no disciplinary action was taken against the students. Instead, educators emphasized the need for a public dialogue between parents and the school.

The shirts worn by these students raise questions about master statuses, our ability to consider the many connotative definitions of the message on the shirts, visual images, and the ethical use of supporting material, particularly real-life and emotionally charged examples and narratives.[8]

What Do You Think?

1. Do you think the images and slogan on the sweatshirts were appropriate to wear to school? Why or why not?

2. What are some of the denotative and connotative associations with the September 11, 2001, attacks? In what ways can connotative understandings of the attacks differ among cultures and be affected by master statuses?

3. The image of the number 11 as the twin towers of the World Trade Center and the thunderbird as a plane draws an audience in emotionally. Was the message on the sweatshirts an ethical appeal to emotions? Why or why not?

4. What are different interpretations for the slogan "You can't bring us down"?

5. When using supporting material, ethical speakers are encouraged to ask themselves, "Is this example or story appropriate for my audience?" Do you think the sweatshirts were appropriate for the audience of students at Dearborn High School? Why or why not?

a topic, you are using **peer testimony**, sometimes called *lay testimony*. You also can use your own testimony to convey your point. This is called **personal testimony**. To use each type of testimony ethically, always give credit to the person you are quoting or paraphrasing, including his or her name and credentials.

Good to Know!

peer testimony: Opinions or observations of someone who has firsthand knowledge of a topic (sometimes called *lay testimony*).
personal testimony: Your own opinions or observations that you use to convey your point.

Use Testimony When You Need the Voice of an Expert

Sometimes, an audience may be interested in our descriptions of an issue or event, but we might not have enough credibility to make our claims believable. Expert testimony can give our ideas an extra boost. Phrases like "according to the surgeon general" add the voice of authority to a speech. Darian enhanced his credibility by using expert testimony in his speech on the shortage of qualified schoolteachers:

"We have good people coming in," said Sandra Feldman, president of the American Federation of Teachers, "but we lose almost 50 percent of them in the first five years." Why? The reason is money, according to Ms. Feldman: "If someone lasts four or five years, they see that they can teach, but they can't support themselves or their families."[9]

Incorporating the testimony of recognized experts lends an air of credibility to your own testimony and helps you build a stronger case. Just be careful about using testimony from biased sources. **Bias** is an unreasoned distortion of judgment or prejudice about a topic, and a biased source will have an unreasoned personal stake in the outcome of an issue.[10] In contrast, an **objective** source is someone who does not have a personal stake in an issue and can provide a fair, ethical, and undistorted view of a topic. Although objective sources certainly have preferences and feelings, they are not so strongly influenced by their own stake in an issue that they distort information.

Obviously, no one can be completely objective. In fact, sometimes we want to use the testimony of someone who has a personal stake in an issue because that person understands the issue as an insider. For example, in his persuasive speech on transportation options for people who are legally drunk, Eric cited DUI officer Kirsten Innes as stating, "After 10 o'clock on a weekend evening, almost 50 percent of drivers are alcohol impaired." However, more often, it's preferable to use testimony from sources who are not personally invested in an issue and do not stand to gain from a particular outcome.

Use Testimony to Illustrate Differences or Agreements

Speakers often use testimony when they want to illustrate the range of opinions about a topic. Testimony from several different sources gives an audience a sense of the diversity—or lack of it—on opinions circulating in the public dialogue. If you can cite a variety of expert opinions on your subject, you illustrate the complexity of an issue. Or if all the experts agree and offer a unified voice, you illustrate the strength of a particular opinion. Consider statements like these: "In my review of the minutes for the planning commission meetings from January to September of this year, I found only one person on the nine-member city planning commission who disagreed. Let me share what Joel Phillips, the dissenting voice, said and then tell what the other eight individuals had to say." Or "There seems to be incredible diversity on this issue. Of the five professors

Good to Know!

bias: Unreasoned distortion of judgment or prejudice about a topic. **objective:** Having a fair, ethical, and undistorted view on a question or issue.

I interviewed, none offered the same solution to the problem I posed. Here are some of their suggestions." When used in these ways, testimony sheds light on agreements or disagreements over issues that affect your audience.

Use Your Own Testimony When Your Experience Says It Best

Although the words of an expert can lend credibility to a speech, sometimes your own experiences make a stronger impression. In a speech on the peer pressure that contributes to the prevalence of eating disorders in young women, Rachael used her own testimony. She said to her audience, "No one has ever come up to me and said, 'Wow, Rachael, you look great! Have you gained ten?' It's always the opposite, isn't it? 'Have you lost ten?'" She could have used the testimony of a doctor or a psychologist, but her personal testimony about her own experiences strengthened her point about the peer pressure many young women encounter.

Luke Sharrett/The New York Times/Redux Pictures

In 2010, executives from energy company BP and its drilling partners gave testimony in Washington, D.C., for a Senate inquiry into the massive oil spill in the Gulf of Mexico. When asked by lawmakers why the companies hadn't been better prepared to prevent the accident, the executives tried to shift the blame to one another. Do you think they were able to give credible testimony about how they could have prevented the crisis? How could they have strengthened their credibility?

Paraphrase Testimony to Improve Listenability

The exact words of an expert may not always be appropriate for an audience because they may be too complex or too vulgar. However, you can still use that person's words if you paraphrase, summarizing statements rather than repeating them exactly. For example, when Joel Phillips, the dissenting commissioner, explained, "residential zoning factors historically have an inverse effect on the growth this sector of the community feasibly can accommodate," Shatanna paraphrased his words by saying, "Mr. Phillips, the dissenting commission member, explained that, historically, zoning ordinances have a negative effect on the growth of our community." Her paraphrasing allowed her to use the commissioner's testimony without confusing her audience by using his specialized terminology.

Similarly, try paraphrasing when your source uses profanity or vulgar language that may not be appropriate for a particular audience. But note that if your source feels strongly enough about an issue to use profanity, or if the use of profanity is an important part of that person's personality, your paraphrase should reflect this without repeating his or her exact words. Tell your audience that your source feels strongly enough about an idea to swear about it or that the person uses profanity liberally in discussing the idea. Remember, paraphrasing is a summary of what was said, not a recasting of someone's feelings or beliefs. Also note that although profanity may not always be inappropriate in a speech, you should still think carefully about your reasons for including it and your audience's possible reactions to hearing it.

Testimony enhances a claim or adds to a position much like a second opinion would. It brings in outside voices, adds other perspectives, and illustrates what others are thinking and saying about your issue. But to use testimony ethically and effectively, it must meet certain criteria. See Table 6.4 for tips on how to use testimony best.

Table 6.4

Tips for Using Testimony Ethically and Effectively

Ask yourself this . . .	And do this . . .	Example
Is the source of your testimony credible?	Determine the credibility of your testimony by asking these questions: • Does it come from people who are knowledgeable about your subject? • Have these people been trained in its particular area? Do they have the proper credentials or experiences? • Have they earned the respect of other experts in their field? Make sure your testimony comes from someone who actually knows about your subject, not just from someone people might like or find interesting. Similarly, when using testimony from a nonexpert, make sure the person has some legitimate connection to the issue you are speaking about.	Advertisements often provide excellent examples of the unethical use of testimony because they rely on how much consumers admire a spokesperson, not on what the spokesperson knows about the product. Yusef noted this fact in his speech about the rise of consumerism in China. He discussed that because it has become a symbol of status to buy celebrity-endorsed products, celebrities are banned from endorsing medical products such as drugs and nutritional supplements.[11]
Is the testimony biased?	To determine if a source is biased, ask these questions about the person: • What is this person's connection to the issue? How does that connection affect her or his perspective? Does he or she have a personal stake in the issue? • Are this person's ideas about this topic so firmly rooted that she or he would be unable to speak credibly on another aspect of the topic? • Are this person's words informed and reasoned? Is he or she making claims based on adequate exposure to the issue?	In his speech about how to cope with depression, Sean used testimony from his sister—an executive at a pharmaceutical company—about how effective a medication her company manufactured was in treating depression. Although his sister wasn't trying to sell the product her company manufactured, Sean's audience was skeptical about her testimony because they perceived it as being biased. Sean could have increased his credibility by also citing unbiased studies that indicated how well the medicine worked. Or he could have discussed the medication his sister's company manufactured as just one of many effective medications on the market.
Have you paraphrased accurately?	Be careful when you paraphrase another person's testimony or change some of the language so it is more suitable to your audience. It is unethical to change the intended meaning of testimony, change its tone, or place it in a context that your source did not intend.	One of the commissioners Shatanna interviewed said, "It's very complicated. Let me outline some of the issues for you." He then described seven distinct issues. Shatanna's paraphrasing reflected this complexity. In her speech, she said, "Commissioner Fields presented seven different issues. The issue that most directly affects my topic today is the first one he mentioned, the conflict between what residents and retailers want."

continued

Developing and Supporting Your Ideas

| Is the testimony connected to your point? | When you use personal testimony, make sure it enhances your speech and that you're not using it simply because you want to share your or someone else's perspectives and experiences. If you think testimony about your or someone else's experience fits into your speech perfectly, connect it to the larger issue you are speaking about.[12] | Rachael's testimony about the pressure to be thin was connected to her speech topic. She used her experiences not to draw attention to herself but to illustrate a common experience for many young women. Rachel didn't just tell her own story. She also told the story of other women. |

Public Speaking and Service Learning: Engaging Community

Geoff Dodge, a public speaking student at Colorado State University, did his service learning project at the Food Bank for Larimer County. The speech he gave about his experience with service learning included as evidence his own testimony and that of some of the employees at the Food Bank. When he used his own testimony, he was able to convey his insights about how one might solve the problem of hunger in his community. And when he solicited the testimony of the Food Bank employees, he not only learned more about the issue but also acquired supporting evidence that helped lend credibility to his speech.

I felt pretty strongly about the topics of all my speeches, and through my service, I found things that I wanted to make my peers aware of. Without having had the experience of working at the Food Bank, I don't think I could have spoken nearly as effectively on behalf of the agency or on the topic of hunger. Most of the material I put into my speeches came directly from experiences I had at the Food Bank or from the opinions of some of the employees there. Speaking on the topic of my service learning project was also good because I could discuss the issues I planned to speak on with Food Bank employees and get their opinions. I wanted to include their opinions because these people dealt with the issue every day and have an even greater insight than I do on how things can be improved.

"I WANTED TO INCLUDE THEIR OPINIONS BECAUSE THESE PEOPLE DEALT WITH THE ISSUE EVERY DAY."

Tips for Incorporating Service Learning into Public Speaking:

- Don't be afraid to use your own experiences with your subject matter as evidence. Doing so helps enhance your credibility and conveys the material more personally.
- Choose your testimony carefully. Take time to understand the work that individuals do within your service learning organization. This will help ensure that the people you get supporting material from will be fully qualified to answer your questions and provide information.
- When you interview people, take the time to paraphrase what your interviewee says as you conduct the interview. Although this practice seems awkward at first, it helps clarify comments and encourages more in-depth descriptions.

Definitions

Definitions are essential to public speaking. Without them, the common language shared by speaker and audience breaks down quickly. A **definition** is a statement of the exact meaning of a word or phrase. Definitions can make terms, whether simple

Good to Know!

definition: Statement of the exact meaning of a word or phrase.

or complex, clear and meaningful for your audiences. Provide a definition of a word in a speech when its meaning may be ambiguous and confusing to your audience.

Every word has both a denotative and a connotative definition. The **denotative definition** is the objective meaning you find in a dictionary, the definition of a word on which most everyone can agree. In contrast, a **connotative definition** is the subjective meaning of a word or a phrase based on personal experiences and beliefs. Be aware that providing the dictionary definition of a word may not always be enough to get your point across; definitions come from personal experiences as well as from the dictionary.

An example illustrates how powerful a connotative definition can be. Abolitionist Sojourner Truth, born a slave in New York in approximately 1797 and freed in 1827, focused one of her most famous speeches on the definition of the word *woman*. In "Ain't I a Woman?" she repeatedly questioned the definition of this word, asking her audience to decide whether or not she actually was "a woman."

Hulton Archive/Getty Images

> That man over there says that women need to be helped into carriages, and lifted over ditches, and to have the best place everywhere. Nobody ever helps me into carriages, or over mud-puddles, or gives me any best place. And, ain't I a woman? Look at me, look at my arm. I have plowed and planted and gathered into barns, and no man could head me—and ain't I a woman? I could work as much and eat as much as a man (when I could get it) and bear the lash as well—and ain't I a woman? I have borne thirteen children and seen them most all sold off into slavery, and when I cried out with a mother's grief, none but Jesus heard. And ain't I a woman?[13]

As this example illustrates, connotative definitions can move an audience in a way that denotative definitions sometimes can't. However, because connotative definitions are based on emotions and personal experiences, they can cloud an issue or confuse an audience. Therefore, be sure to identify the connotative definitions you use in your speech and take into account the varying connotations one word may have. Truth did this when she questioned the audience's connotative definitions of *woman*.

Although some speeches are built around a definition, as in Truth's example, others incorporate definitions to clarify words for audiences. The guidelines for using definitions in your speeches are as follows.

Even familiar terms have both denotative and connotative definitions. As a result, they can convey meanings you may not intend. To minimize this problem, identify some of the familiar terms you plan to use in your speech and look them up. Do you think the connotative meanings of those terms match the dictionary definitions? How will you make sure your own meaning is clear to your audience?

Use Definitions to Clarify and Create Understanding

Use a definition when you anticipate your audience will say, "I don't know what that word means" or "I've never heard the word used that way before." For technical terms, a denotative definition often suffices. For familiar words used in new ways, connotative definitions are a must. For example, in a speech to students at Moscow University, Ronald Reagan defined the word *freedom* as the recognition that no single authority has a monopoly on truth. At the time, democracy was new to the Soviet Union, so Reagan's definition helped his audience see more clearly what he believed are the benefits of a democracy.

Good to Know!

denotative definition: Objective meaning of a word or a phrase you find in a dictionary. **connotative definition:** Subjective meaning of a word or phrase based on personal experiences and beliefs.

Use Definitions to Clarify an Emotionally or Politically Charged Word

Many words in our language have become emotionally and politically charged. Words like *race, sexism, disability, discrimination, equality, liberal,* and *conservative* have become hotbeds of dispute. When you use words like these, provide a definition. Explain how you are using the word so you can minimize some of the emotions and politics associated with it. Otherwise, your audience may not be able to understand or even listen to you.

Use Definitions to Illustrate What Something Is Not

Definitions also explain to an audience what something isn't. In a student speech on the hostile environment created by sexual harassment, Hillary defined *hostile environment* and *harassment* first by what they are and then by what they are not:

According to the *Webb Report: A Newsletter on Sexual Harassment,* behavior is sexual harassment if it (1) is sexual in nature, (2) is unwelcome by the person it is directed at, and (3) is sufficiently severe or pervasive that it alters the conditions of that person's employment and creates an abusive working environment. This means it's not sexual harassment nor is it seen as creating a hostile environment if the behavior: (1) isn't sexual in nature, (2) is welcomed by the person it's directed at, and (3) doesn't negatively affect that individual's working environment and create an abusive climate. The behavior may be offensive, unproductive, or even harmful, but if it doesn't meet all three criteria, then it's not considered sexual harassment.

Hillary defined what sexual harassment is by illustrating for her audience what it isn't.

Use Definitions to Trace the History of a Word

The history of a word, called its **etymology**, allows you to trace the original meaning of a word and to chart the changes it has undergone over time. In speeches, tracing the history of words offers your audience insight into the words' origins and the ways those origins affect our understanding and use of the words today. Etymologies, then, can help you build an argument for a position or tell a more comprehensive story about an issue. Many dictionaries provide the etymology of words, but *The Oxford English Dictionary* is a particularly good source for tracing a word's origins. Another good resource is the Word Origins website, which you can access with **Web Connect 6.5: Word Origins** via your CourseMate for *Invitation to Public Speaking.* Both sources define words and give you their original meanings, and they are useful when you want to know why words we use today have the meanings they do.

Using definitions seems fairly straightforward and simple, and it usually is. But as with all forms of evidence, you must consider the credibility, clarity, and accuracy of your definitions. See Table 6.5 for tips that will help you ensure that your definitions are ethical and effective.

 CourseMate

Good to Know!

etymology: History of a word.

Table 6.5

Tips for Using Definitions Ethically and Effectively

Ask yourself this . . .	And do this . . .	Example
Is the source of the definition credible?	Consider whether the dictionary or other source you are using for your definition is credible. • Some sources are more extensive than others, offering recent definitions as well as a comprehensive history of a word. • Examples of credible sources include encyclopedias, textbooks, and books about specific topics such as music, law, or engineering. If you are using a particular person's definition of a word, make sure that person is a credible and qualified source.	In her speech about the role of the U.S. military in the twenty-first century, Erin didn't rely only on definitions of terms in her regular English dictionary. She confirmed that her definitions were accurate in a military context by using an even more credible source, the U.S. Department of Defense's DOD Dictionary of Military and Associated Terms. With the DOD dictionary, she was able to confirm the meaning of terms such as *healthcare provider* and *campaign*, which have specific meanings in military jargon.
Have you avoided proper meaning superstition?	If you decide to use a term without defining it, be sure your listeners have the same understanding of the term that you do so you can avoid proper meaning superstition. *Proper meaning superstition*, a term coined by I. A. Richards and C. K. Ogden in the late 1920s, is the belief that everyone attaches the same meaning to a word and that you are using that meaning. With proper meaning superstition, speakers use words believing their audiences will have exactly the same referent, which isn't always the case.[14]	In his speech about feminism in India, Sanjay avoided proper meaning superstition by explaining how the concept of feminism was understood by different people in different contexts and cultures. For example, he provided a basic definition found in most dictionaries, that feminism is a movement for social, cultural, political, and economic equality of men and women. He also defined *feminism* as a global struggle for the end to discrimination and a means for attaining individual liberation.[15]
Have you actually defined the term?	Avoid using a term to define itself, using unfamiliar words in a definition, and using circular definitions. To ensure a fair and ethical public dialogue, our definitions must clarify our arguments rather than confuse our audiences.	• Sharon used a term to define itself when she said, "By *younger* I mean people who aren't very old—they're still young." With this definition, her audience still didn't know what she meant by "young." Is it five years of age, twenty years, or something else? • When Fernando said, "By *septifragal*, I mean to say dehiscing by breaking away from the dissepiments," the words he used were familiar to the scientists in his audience but not to anyone else. • Nelson used a circular definition when he said, "By *masculine*, I'm referring to those traits not feminine, and by feminine, I mean those not masculine." With this definition, his audience still didn't know what he meant by either "masculine" or "feminine."

Chapter Summary

Ethical and effective speakers support their claims with evidence that is credible, relevant, appropriate, and organized.

- Each type of supporting material has strengths and weaknesses, and each is important to the common language of public speaking.
- Use a variety of evidence types to build and strengthen your claims, develop your ideas, communicate ethically, and appeal to your audiences.

Examples are specific instances that illustrate a concept, experience, issue, or problem.

- Examples can be real or hypothetical.
- They should help clarify or reinforce a claim or bring an idea to life.

Narratives are stories that recount or foretell real or hypothetical events.

- Narratives can be brief or extended.
- They help you personalize your claims, challenge your audience to think in new ways, evoke emotions, or unite with your audience.

Statistics are numerical summaries of facts, figures, and research findings.

- The three types of statistics most commonly used in speeches are the mean (or average), the median (or middle point), or the mode (or most frequently appearing).
- Use statistics to synthesize large amounts of information, help you tell a powerful story, or strengthen your claims.

Testimony uses your own or others' opinions or observations to support your claims.

- Peer or expert testimony can add the weight of authority to your speech and help you illustrate differences and agreements.
- Use your own testimony (personal testimony) when your voice illustrates your point best.
- Paraphrase complex testimony to improve its listenability.

Definitions are statements of the exact meaning of a word or phrase.

- Definitions can be denotative (commonly agreed on) or connotative (based on personal experiences or beliefs).
- They can clarify or create understanding for your audience or explain an emotionally or politically charged term.
- They also can be used to explain what something is not or to trace the history of a term.

Invitation to Public Speaking Online

CourseMate Now that you have read Chapter 6, use your Speech Communication Course-Mate for *Invitation to Public Speaking* for quick access to the electronic resources that accompany this text. These resources include

- **Study tools** that will help you assess your learning and prepare for exams (*digital glossary, key term flash cards, review quizzes*).
- **Activities and assignments** that will help you hone your knowledge and build your public speaking skills throughout the course (*Practicing the Public Dialogue activities, review questions*).

- **Media resources** that will help you explore public speaking concepts online (*Web Connect links, Enhanced eBook*), develop your speech outlines (*Speech Builder Express 3.0*), watch and critique videos of sample speeches (*Interactive Video Activities*), upload your speech videos for peer reviewing and critique other students' speeches (*Speech Studio online speech review tool*), and download chapter review so you can study when and where you'd like (*Audio Study Tools*).

This chapter's key concepts and review questions are also featured on the next page.

Key Concepts

bias (125)
brief narrative (114)
claim (110)
connotative definition (129)
definition (128)
denotative definition (129)
direct quotation (123)
etymology (130)
evidence (110)

example (110)
expert testimony (123)
extended narrative (114)
hypothetical example (110)
intertextuality (114)
mean (119)
median (120)
mode (120)

narrative (112)
objective (125)
paraphrase (123)
peer testimony (124)
personal testimony (124)
real example (110)
statistics (117)
testimony (123)

Review Questions

1. Consider the examples or narratives you have gathered for your speech. Are they real or hypothetical, brief or extended? Out loud, practice delivering one of your examples or narratives. Do you feel comfortable with your delivery? Why or why not? Practice delivering this material until it sounds natural and conversational.

2. Bring the statistics you have found in your research to class. In groups, discuss how you might work with these statistics to present them clearly and ethically to your audience. Identify your means, medians, and modes. Discuss what each of these types of statistics tells or illustrates for your audience, including a discussion of how to avoid misrepresenting an issue with your statistics.

3. In what instances might you be an expert and offer your own testimony in a speech? What makes you an expert in this situation and not in others? How could you establish your credibility as an expert if you were to use this testimony?

4. Check out Speech Studio to see how other students use supporting materials in their speeches. How appropriate and credible did their materials seem? Or record a speech you're working on, upload it to Speech Studio, and ask your peers for their feedback. What feedback would help you fine-tune how you use your supporting materials before you give your speech in class? ☑Studio

Reasoning

©James Nubile / The Image Works

Whether your speaking goal is to inform, invite, or persuade, sound reasoning plays a central role in your preparations to enter the public dialogue. Only through sound reasoning can you ensure that you have fully and ethically supported your claims with convincing evidence. Speakers accomplish sound reasoning when they use the three forms of proof that the Greek philosopher Aristotle labeled *logos*, *ethos*, and *pathos*. **Logos** refers to the logical arrangement of evidence in a speech, **ethos** to the speaker's credibility, and **pathos** to the emotional appeals made by a speaker.[1] (For more information about and examples of these three forms of proof, access **Web Connect 7.1: Aristotle's Forms of Proof** through your CourseMate for *Invitation to Public Speaking*.)

In the public dialogue, we share our knowledge and views most effectively when we reason with our audience. When you reason, you use logos, ethos, and pathos to justify the connections between your evidence and your claims. That is, you arrange your evidence logically, establish and build your credibility, and appeal to emotion to show that your evidence supports your idea, position, or perspective. Reasoning helps an audience make **inferences**, the mental leaps we make when we recognize that a speaker's evidence supports his or her claims.

- **Patterns of Reasoning**
- **A Map of Reasoning**
- **Tips for Reasoning Ethically**

IN THIS CHAPTER, YOU WILL LEARN TO:

- Identify Aristotle's three modes of proof
- Describe the five patterns of reasoning used to construct sound arguments
- Test the strength of your claims with Toulmin's model of reasoning
- Apply tips for reasoning ethically

When you reason logically, you offer evidence that you think most people in your audience would accept as legitimate and appropriate.[2] Evidence is the material you use to support your ideas, and it consists of the examples, narratives, statistics, testimony, and definitions you gather through research and interviews (Chapter 6). This evidence helps you develop what is often called an *argument*. Although the term argument may bring to mind an angry dispute, in the public dialogue, an **argument** is a set of statements that allows you to develop your evidence to establish the validity of your claim.[3]

Each time you develop a main point or link ideas together logically in a speech, you use evidence and reasoning to develop a sound and ethical argument for your perspective. Just as you use organizational patterns to arrange your main points in a speech, you use patterns of reasoning to help you organize your evidence and claims.

Even Aristotle was unclear about how many examples to use for inductive reasoning. In one of the oldest surviving treatises on rhetoric, he stated, "If you put your examples first you must give a large number of them; if you put them last, a single one is sufficient; even a single witness will serve if he is a good one."[5]

Patterns of Reasoning

Although scholars have developed more than twenty-five different patterns of reasoning, we limit the discussion here to five of the most useful for beginning public speakers: reasoning by induction, deduction, cause, analogy, and sign.[4] These patterns can help you develop logical arguments in all of your speeches, whatever their goals. You probably are already familiar with most of these patterns because we use them commonly every day without giving them much thought. What makes them unique in public speaking is that speakers consciously employ the patterns to arrange their evidence and develop the logic of their main points and subpoints.

Induction, or Reasoning from Specific Instances

James is an excellent basketball player.

His brother Jeff is an excellent swimmer.

Their sister Julia is the star of the track team.

Jenny, the youngest of the family, will be a fine athlete, too.

Throughout our lives, we often observe regularities, patterns of behavior, and trends. We can point to these repeating patterns to make a claim about something we expect to happen or be true. When we do so, we reason inductively. **Inductive reasoning** is a process of reasoning that uses specific instances, or examples, to make a claim about a general conclusion (Figure 7.1).[6]

Inductive reasoning, sometimes called argument by example, is best used when you can identify patterns in evidence that indicate something is expected to happen again or should hold true based on previous experience.[7] For example, in the scenario at the beginning of this section, the claim that Jenny, the youngest in a family of athletes, is likely to be a talented athlete is based on the trend her siblings have established.

Let's look at how inductive reasoning can be used in a speech. In her invitational speech on becoming a vegetarian, Karyl used inductive reasoning to

Good to Know!

logos: Logical arrangement of evidence in a speech; the first of Aristotle's three types of proof. **ethos:** Speaker's credibility; the second of Aristotle's three types of proof. **pathos:** Emotional appeals made by a speaker; the third of Aristotle's three types of proof. **inferences:** Mental leaps we make when we recognize that a speaker's evidence supports his or her claims. **argument:** Set of statements that allows you to develop your evidence to establish the validity of your claim. **inductive reasoning:** Process of reasoning that uses specific instances, or examples, to make a claim about a general conclusion.

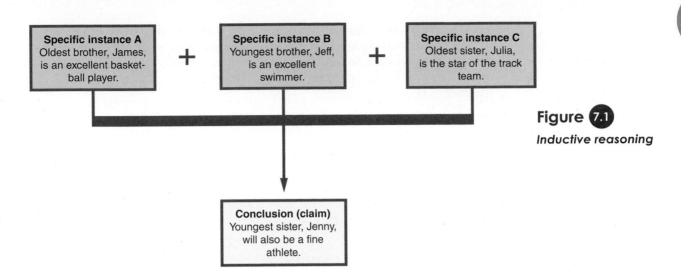

Figure 7.1
Inductive reasoning

describe her switch from eating meat to avoiding it. She gave examples from six slaughterhouses to illustrate the treatment of the animals and the reasons she chose to stop eating meat. This series of examples allowed Karyl to reason as follows:

> Animals in the six slaughterhouses I researched experience harsh conditions and unnecessary cruelty (*her series of specific examples*). Animals in slaughterhouses throughout the United States are treated inhumanely (*her generalization based on her examples*), and I decided not to support this treatment by not eating animals (*her personal decision based on her inductive reasoning*).

When you reason from specific instances, you can state your claim (general observation) first and then offer your supporting instances, or you can present the instances first and then make your claim. In the following example, Ruby stated her claim first and then provided specific instances:

> The amount of privacy we are allowed to keep is under siege every day (*claim*). Beverly Dennis, an Ohio grandmother, completed a questionnaire to get free product samples. Instead, she got a sexually graphic and threatening letter from a convict in Texas who was assigned the task of entering product data into computers for the company (*specific instance*). Similarly, the dean of the Harvard Divinity School was forced to resign after downloading pornography to his home computer. He asked a Harvard technician to install more memory to his computer at home, and in the process of transferring files, the technician discovered, and reported, the pornography (*specific instance*).

Ruby used inductive reasoning again later in her speech. In the following example, she withheld her claim until after she had described her specific instances. Also notice how she used statistics to reinforce the pattern in her specific instances:

> Like many of you, I thought my own life was safe because I do not download pornography or request free product samples. But as I continued to do research for my speech, I learned that my medical records, phone calls, and faxes to my doctor aren't as private as I thought. Nor are my e-mails at work. Medical records are passed along to numerous individuals and recorded or filed electronically—accessible to any determined employee or computer hacker (*specific instance*). And phone calls and faxes can be monitored or picked up by anyone from the office staff to the other doctors (*specific instance*).

And according to this year's report by the American Management Association, nearly three-quarters of U.S. companies say they are monitoring employees electronically. In fact, according to *The Unwanted Gaze*, some companies even use computer software that monitors and records every keystroke an employee makes. Using this software, called Spector, an employee at a Nissan dealership was fired after her employer opened one of her e-mails, a sexually explicit note to her boyfriend (*specific instance*). Can you imagine your boss reading your e-mails to your boyfriend? Our privacy has gone public in ways we are only beginning to imagine (*claim*).

Expressed as a formula, an inductive argument looks like this:

Specific instance A	or	Claim you want to establish
Specific instance B		Specific instance A
Specific instance C		Specific instance B
Specific instance D		Specific instance C
Claim based on the specific instances		Specific instance D

Guidelines for inductive reasoning. There are three guidelines for reasoning from specific instances:

- Make sure you have enough examples to make your claim.
- Make sure your generalizations are accurate.
- Support your inductive arguments with statistics or testimony.

Let's take a closer look at each of these guidelines. First, be sure you have enough examples to make your claim. For instance, if only one person in Jenny's family is a fine athlete, you cannot claim she likely will be because you do not have enough specific instances to back that claim. Similarly, if only one or two slaughterhouses treat animals inhumanely, you cannot claim that most of them do.

Therefore, to reason ethically, avoid *anomalies*. Anomalies are exceptions to a rule, unique instances that do not represent the norm. When speakers rely on anomalies or use too few examples to make a claim, they may be guilty of making **hasty generalizations**, or reaching a conclusion without enough evidence to support it. To support your claim, find more than three instances before you make any inferences about larger patterns. However, your audience probably needs no more than four specific instances, even if you have identified far more than that.

Second, make sure your generalizations are accurate. Although it can be tempting to make a claim about only a few instances, be careful not to overgeneralize. For example, if people in your community are buying hybrid vehicles and this trend seems to be catching on in your region, you can predict that many people in your community will replace their current vehicles with a hybrid in the coming year. But you probably can't extend that prediction to other parts of the country unless you have specific examples to support your claim. Don't be too hasty in extending examples from one area or group to another unless your data support that claim.

Third, support your inductive arguments with statistics or testimony. Although you cannot produce an endless list of examples without boring your audience, you can develop your case by supplementing your examples with statistics or testimony. For example, if you want to explain that organic farms produce competitively priced, high-quality crops, offer examples of two or three farms that do so. Then strengthen your inductive process with statistics showing that organic farmers are successfully competing with nonorganic farms at a county, state, or national level. You also could support your examples with testimony from the

Good to Know!

hasty generalization: Error in reasoning in which a speaker reaches a conclusion without enough evidence to support it.

head of the Department of Agriculture, validating the profitability of organic farming. Statistics and testimony help your audience better understand the validity of the larger trend you are describing.

Deduction, or Reasoning from a General Principle

Grade inflation negatively affects all college students.

Jody is a college student.

Jody is affected negatively by grade inflation.

When speakers reason from general principles to specific instances (the opposite of inductive reasoning), they reason deductively. **Deductive reasoning** is a process of reasoning that uses a familiar and commonly accepted claim to establish the truth of a very specific claim (Figure 7.2). The first statement above, "Grade inflation negatively affects all college students," is called the **major premise**, or the general principle, and states a familiar, commonly accepted belief. The combination of the major premise with the second statement, " Jody is a college student," called the **minor premise**, or the specific instance, establishes the truth of the third statement, "Jody is negatively affected by grade inflation," called the **conclusion**.

Expressed as a formula, a deductive argument looks as follows:

Major premise, or general principle

Minor premise, or specific instance of the general principle

Conclusion based on the combination of the major and minor premises

Guidelines for deductive reasoning. Reasoning from general principles to specific instances is an effective way to build a case for your claims. When your general principle is firmly established or commonly accepted, your reasoning should unfold smoothly. For example, some clearly established and commonly accepted general principles are that asbestos causes lung cancer, driving drunk is dangerous, and elected officials should act with integrity.

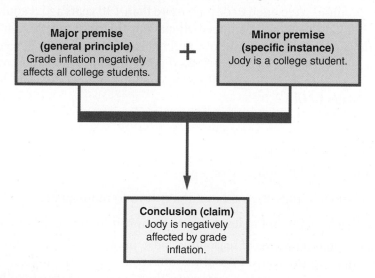

Figure 7.2

Deductive reasoning

Good to Know!

deductive reasoning: Process of reasoning that uses a familiar and commonly accepted claim to establish the truth of a very specific claim. **major premise:** Claim in an argument that states a familiar, commonly accepted belief (also called the general principle). **minor premise:** Claim in an argument that states a specific instance linked to the major premise. **conclusion:** Logical outcome of an argument that results from the combination of the major and minor premises.

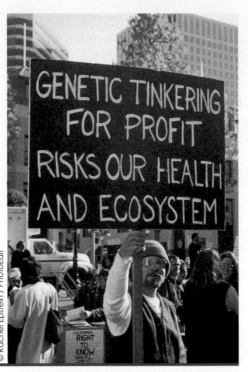

This protestor's sign illustrates a general principle that is not accepted by everyone. Do you accept this principle? If not, what additional evidence would you need to accept it as valid?

© Rachel Epstein / PhotoEdit

Sometimes, audiences won't accept your general principle. When they don't, you will need to strengthen it with additional evidence or reasoning. This process is called *establishing the validity of the major premise*. For example, if you assert that raising cattle for beef consumption is cruel and unethical, juvenile crime is out of control, or pornography is a violation of women's rights, your audience is more likely to need proof. If your audience does not accept your major premise, they are less likely to accept your conclusion. You will need to use careful reasoning to develop your case.

We often enter the public dialogue precisely because we want to establish the truth of a general principle. Let's see how one very famous speaker, Susan B. Anthony, worked from a controversial general principle. Anthony spoke in favor of women's right to vote in the 1870s. She built her reasoning for women's right to vote on the premise that the U.S. Constitution guarantees all citizens the right to vote. Her full line of reasoning looked as follows:

Major premise:	The U.S. Constitution guarantees every citizen the right to vote.
Minor premise:	Women are U.S. citizens.
Conclusion:	The U.S. Constitution guarantees women the right to vote.

Although this deductive argument makes sense to us today, Anthony's major and minor premises were open to dispute more than 140 years ago. People did not agree that the Constitution guaranteed all citizens the right to vote, nor did they agree about who was a citizen. Anthony and many other suffragists devoted much of their speeches to trying to convince their audiences of their major and minor premises. Despite their passionate efforts, women did not get the right to vote in the United States until 1920.[8]

Causal Reasoning

If I don't study, then I'll do poorly on my exam.

If I use recreational drugs, then I'll eventually turn to more addictive ones.

If I study self-defense, then I'm less likely to be hurt if someone attacks me.

Causal reasoning is a process of reasoning that supports a claim by establishing a cause-and-effect relationship. Causal reasoning identifies an "if-then" relationship that suggests "if" one factor is present, "then" another is sure to follow.[9] The statements at the beginning of this section are examples of causal relationships.

Good to Know!

causal reasoning: Process of reasoning that supports a claim by establishing a cause-and-effect relationship.

Each of them establishes a cause-and-effect relationship: lack of preparation (the cause) results in poor grades (the effect); use of recreational drugs (the cause) leads to the use of addictive ones (the effect); and learning self-defense (the cause) lessens the risk of harm in the event of an attack (the effect).

Speakers often use causal reasoning to develop their ideas with great success. In the following example, Kameron uses causal reasoning to develop his argument that zebra mussels, native to the Caspian Sea in Europe but not to the waters of the United States, are seriously damaging the aquatic environment:

> Zebra mussels cause damage to every aspect of any aquatic ecosystem they encounter. They destroy the natural balance of the ecosystem by filtering the food from water at an insane rate of one liter of water each day. Not much you think? Well, these mollusks can live in colonies of up to 70,000 mussels. That's 70,000 liters of water cleared of all food each day. This means the zebra mussels consume all the food usually eaten by animals lower in the food chain. The result is catastrophic repercussions on down the line. For example, a body of water whose food is filtered away cannot support any kind of life. The larger fish then have nothing to eat, resulting in fewer fish for anglers.

Speaking Visually

Disturbing Images Dissuade People from Trying Meth—Not Even Once

In 2007, the U.S. Office of National Drug Policy Control (ONDCP) joined with the media and several states in a campaign to prevent methamphetamine use and raise awareness about the treatment of meth addiction. Two years later, the ONDCP launched an aggressive advertising campaign targeted at people aged 18 to 34 in the sixteen states with the highest levels of reported meth use and lab seizures: Alaska, Washington, Oregon, Nevada, Wyoming, Arizona, New Mexico, Oklahoma, Arkansas, Missouri, Iowa, Minnesota, Illinois, Indiana, Kentucky, and Nebraska.[10] The ads for this campaign—created in conjunction with various state campaigns such as the Montana Meth Project's "Not Even Once" campaign and Alabama's "Zero Meth" campaign—are described as graphic and disturbing. Yet, they also seem to be effective in reducing meth use among young users.[11] To see many of the most disturbing ads, log on to blogger Brian Lovin's website "40+ Most Powerful Anti-Meth Advertisements." Use your CourseMate for *Invitation to Public Speaking* to access **Web Resource 7.2: Anti-Meth Advertisements.**

Persuasive speakers are cautioned to curb their use of graphic images (Chapters 12 and 16). Indeed, much research suggests that if fear appeals are too graphic and cause an audience to feel immobilized, speakers lose the support of the audience.[12] However, compared with appeals that cause an audience to shut down and dismiss the speaker, something unusual and effective is happening with the anti-meth ads. The ads are appealing to fear by using fairly graphic and disturbing images with success. What do you think the difference is, and how might you model the success of these campaigns in your own speeches?

The Meth Project Foundation, Inc.

MY FRIENDS AND I SHARE EVERYTHING. NOW WE SHARE HEPATITIS AND HIV.

METH NOT EVEN ONCE.

Kameron's causal reasoning allows him to argue compellingly that zebra mussels (the cause) lead to aquatic devastation (the effect).

Guidelines for causal reasoning. Causal reasoning is an effective form of reasoning because it allows you to link two events together. But because causal relationships are sometimes difficult to prove, select your causal evidence carefully. Consider the following three guidelines:

- Avoid false causes.
- Avoid assuming an event has only one cause.
- Cite supporting evidence to strengthen your cause-and-effect relationships.

Ethical Moment

FREE SPEECH OR "ADVOCATING DEATH"?

Conservative political commentator Rush Limbaugh is known for speaking his mind and criticizing liberal politicians and policies. On his radio show that aired October 20, 2009, Rush Limbaugh criticized a blog written by Andrew Revkin, a journalist for *The New York Times*. In Revkin's blog post "Are Condoms the Ultimate Green Technology?" he claimed that an increase in the human population correlates directly with an increase in carbon dioxide emissions. He wrote that "recent research has resulted in renewed coverage of the notion that one of the cheapest ways to curb emission in coming decades would be to provide access to birth control for tens of millions of women around the world who say they desire it." He raised the question of implementing a "baby-avoidance carbon credit," similar to selling "CO_2 credits for avoiding deforestation," and stated that this idea was "purely a thought experiment, not a proposal."

AP Photo/Photo courtesy of Rush Limbaugh

After learning of Revkin's thought experiment, Rush Limbaugh called Revkin, and others who believe humans are ultimately to blame for climate change, "environmental wackos." Limbaugh lamented, "This guy from *The New York Times*—if he really thinks that humanity is destroying the planet, humanity is destroying the climate, that human beings in their natural existence are going to cause the extinction of life on Earth—Andrew Revkin, Mr. Revkin, why don't you just go kill yourself and help the planet by dying?" After ten days of media stories questioning Limbaugh's

integrity for making the comments, Limbaugh (re)framed his position. On his show, he stated, "Mr. Revkin, for crying out loud, I'm making a point. I'm not advocating death. I do not advocate death on this program. I do not advocate control over anybody else's life."[13]

What Do You Think?

1. What is the definition of free speech? What does free speech mean to you?

2. Were Rush Limbaugh's original comments regarding Andrew Revkin in the realm of free speech? Why or why not?

3. If you, or others, found either Limbaugh's or Revkin's remarks offensive, do you still think they should be protected by free-speech principles?

4. What are the ethical implications of Limbaugh's statement that Revkin should "just go kill" himself?

5. Do you think Revkin was ethical in expressing his thought experiment on using birth control as a means to reduce carbon emissions? Why or why not?

Let's take a closer look at each of these guidelines. First, avoid false causes.[14] A **false cause** is an error in reasoning in which a speaker assumes that one event caused another simply because the first event happened before the second. It can be easy to assume a false cause. You pick up your "lucky" pen from your desk, and five minutes later, you get a creative brainstorm for the project you are working on.

Did the lucky pen cause the creative brainstorm? Perhaps, but it's hard to tell. Similarly, your nephew watches two hours of violent cartoon programming in the morning. When he sits down to lunch, he points his hot dog at his sister and makes shooting noises. Did the violence in the cartoons cause the behavior? Perhaps his behavior was prompted by the game he played with neighbors the day before or the joke his father told while making similar gestures. Again, the connection is not certain.

Although it is tempting to assume direct causes when one event happens shortly after another, the two events may not be directly related. When one event happens *immediately* after another, there may be a link, but you would need to investigate further to be sure. To remain ethical, if you make a causal claim in a speech, you must be certain one event did in fact cause the other.

Second, avoid assuming that an event has only one cause. Events often have many causes, especially those that become topics in the public dialogue. For example, it is unrealistic to try to pin the cause of teen suicide on one factor. It is far more appropriate to address the multiple factors that contribute to teen suicide: the home and school environment, social pressures, individual personality traits, and the teen's support system and friendships. Similarly, it is inaccurate to suggest that watching violent television is the sole cause of violence in children. Many other factors contribute to violent behaviors, and a speaker's reasoning must address all these causes.

Third, strengthen your cause-and-effect relationships by citing strong supporting evidence. For example, in his informative speech about zebra mussels, Kameron identified a very strong connection between the overpopulation of zebra mussels and the damage done to boats, buoys, docks, and anchors. He was able to support his connection by providing testimony from local fishers who had seen buoys sink from the weight of too many mussels! However, in a persuasive speech about the relationship between power lines and cancer in people who live close to them, Christina could make only a very weak connection: Her father, who died of cancer, had lived near power lines for years. However, the scientific evidence she provided to establish a strong link between cancer and proximity to power lines was sketchy and inconclusive. Thus, no matter how hard she tried, her audience would not accept her claim that power lines caused her father's cancer.

Analogical Reasoning

The American Academy of Pediatrics, partnering with First Lady Michelle Obama, is urging its doctors to write exercise and eating "prescriptions" for their patients. "Just as we give immunizations," says AAP president Judith Palfrey, "we're going to give healthy eating and exercise advice at every visit."

Public-health advocates are taking on Big Food just as their predecessors took on Big Tobacco. Dr. David Kessler, the former head of the FDA, argues that

Good to Know!

false cause: Error in reasoning in which a speaker assumes that one event caused another simply because the first event happened before the second.

the fattening of America has happened by design as food companies intentionally manufactured irresistible cocktails of sugar, fat, and salt. Manufacturers' efforts to do better don't assuage Kelly Brownell, head of Yale's Rudd Center for Food Policy and Obesity. "The country defaults to giving industry the benefit of the doubt," he says. "Industry says you don't need to regulate us; we'll police ourselves." The tobacco industry abused that with [who knows] how many lives as a consequence. To expect the food industry to be different may be wishful thinking.[15]

When we compare two similar things and suggest that what is true for the first will be true for the second, we are reasoning analogically. **Analogical reasoning**, or reasoning by way of comparison and similarity, implies that because two things resemble each other in one respect, they also share similarities in another respect. For example, when Newsweek writers compare the U.S. food industry to the so-called Big Tobacco corporations, the writers argue that the food industry, like major tobacco companies before they began to be regulated in the late 1990s, cannot be trusted to put the health of consumers before its own profits.

We also reason analogically when we contrast differences in two similar conditions or events and draw inferences about what should be true for both but isn't. Consider how Stephanie used analogical reasoning to inform her audience about the differences in the way crimes against minorities are treated in contrast to those against whites:

> I was living in Oak Harbor, Washington, when JonBenet Ramsey was killed. . . . Like everyone else, I was appalled and followed the coverage of her death for three months. Then, in my town of Oak Harbor, a seven-year-old girl named Deborah Palmer disappeared while walking to school one morning. . . . Her lifeless body was found washed up on a local beach six miles from her house. Do you know who Deborah Palmer was? Well, JonBenet's murder ran as a cover story in almost every national newspaper and magazine. Her little face looked back at me for over a year every time I went into a grocery store. Deborah's story ran in the *Seattle Times*, the *Skaggit Valley Herald*, and the *Whidbey Island News* for a total of nine articles. In a very short period of time, Deborah's story disappeared completely.
>
> Why the difference when the crimes were so similar and neither murderer was ever found? JonBenet was a crowned beauty queen with blond hair and blue eyes. Deborah was the child of an African American father and a Filipino mother.

The analogy Stephanie used to draw her audience into her compelling speech is that JonBenet Ramsey and Deborah Palmer had much in common. They were little girls who died brutally and tragically within three months of each other. Police have yet to find either murderer. If one child received extensive news coverage, shouldn't the other one have, too?

Although Stephanie held the audience's attention as she developed her analogy, analogies also can be short and straightforward. For example, when speaking to her audience about the importance of more than direct care, physician Deborah Prothrow-Stith used this simple and effective analogy: "We were just stitching them up and sending them back out on the streets, back to the domestic equivalent of a war zone."[16]

Good to Know!

analogical reasoning: A process of reasoning by way of comparison and similarity that implies that because two things resemble each other in one respect, they also share similarities in another respect.

Guidelines for analogical reasoning. To increase the effectiveness of analogical reasoning, be sure what you are comparing is truly alike. When you compare two things that don't share characteristics, your analogy is invalid and will seem illogical to your audience. Most of us have heard invalid analogies and thought to ourselves, "That's like comparing apples to oranges." For example, it is invalid to suggest that proposed nonsmoking ordinances will succeed in Kentucky,

Civic Engagement in Action

"I HAD NO IDEA THAT ANYONE WAS LISTENING"

Wangari Maathai, the daughter of a share-cropper father and a farmer mother, can be considered something of a first lady. She is the first woman from East and Central Africa to earn a Ph.D. (in biological sciences), the first woman to become a department chair of the University of Nairobi, the first president of the African Union's Economic, Social, and Cultural Council, and the first African woman to earn a Nobel Peace Prize.

Maathai began her impressive career as an environmental and political activist in the 1970s. As part of her work with the National Council of Women of Kenya, Maathai established the Green Belt Movement in response to her conversations with rural women about their concerns over water, energy, and nutrition. Seeing the connections between the clear-cutting of forests and the diminished quality of life for many in Kenya, she began to lead high-profile campaigns to save Kenya's forests and protect its green spaces. Working with thousands of other women, she planted trees to replenish the soil, protect the watersheds, provide fuel, and enhance nutrition. "If you understand and you are disturbed," she said, "then you are moved to action. That's exactly what happened to me."

The government responded to the movement by harassing Maathai and many other women, holding them in jail and sending them death threats. At one point, Maathai was labeled a "mad woman" and beaten almost to death. However, these setbacks did not stop her. By the late 1990s, the government had abandoned its illegal deforestation and development plans and, to date, more than 30 million trees have been planted throughout Kenya. However, when Maathai received the Nobel Peace Prize in 2004 for her work with the Green Belt Movement, she

AP Photo/Sayyid Azim

was surprised. She said, "I had no idea that anyone was listening."

As the Green Belt Movement's official website states, the movement has evolved into "one of the most prominent women's civil society organizations, . . . advocating for human rights and supporting good governance and peaceful democratic change through the protection of the environment." Maathai explains this evolution by saying, "When you start working with the environment seriously, the whole arena comes: human rights, women's rights, environmental rights, children's rights—you know, everybody's rights. Once you start making these linkages, you can no longer do just tree-planting."[17]

You Can Get Involved

CourseMate If you'd like to learn more about the Green Belt Movement and how you might contribute to its work in Kenya and around the world, access **Web Connect 7.3: Green Belt Movement.** For information about other organizations that work to conserve the environment, access **Web Connect 7.4: Environmental Action Groups.** This resource is sponsored by the National Resources Defense Council, a nonprofit environmental action organization. You can access these resources through your CourseMate for *Invitation to Public Speaking.*

Tennessee, and North Carolina because they succeeded in California, Oregon, and Washington. This analogy is invalid because the public attitudes toward smoking in the three tobacco-growing southern states are different from those in the three western states whose economies do not depend on tobacco. If you make an analogy between two things, they must share true similarities for the analogy to be valid.

Reasoning by Sign

> Even watching their seismographs jump—even if they could have measured the height of the waves at their origin—geologists couldn't have predicted with any certainty that the sea would rise up in Sri Lanka, a thousand miles away from the fault line.[18]

A **sign** is something that represents something else. It is one of the most common forms of reasoning we use in our daily lives: Dark clouds are a sign of a storm rolling in; a decrease in the number of applications for a certain academic program is a sign of declining interest; the bailiff's command "all rise" is a sign that the judge is about to enter the courtroom.[19] Signs have an important function in the reasoning process because they prompt us to infer what is *likely* to be. They help speakers establish relationships and draw conclusions for their audiences based on those relationships. However, as the example about the tsunami that struck Sri Lanka in 2004 suggests, sometimes the connection between a sign—the movement on a seismograph or the height of waves at their origin—that is needed to infer the likelihood of an event—a devastating tsunami in Sri Lanka—can't be made or just isn't there. **Reasoning by sign** assumes something exists or will happen based on something else that exists or has happened.

Signs, like causal relationships, can have strong or weak relationships. Reasoning by sign is strengthened when you can point to the repetition of one example to build a case. For example, *every* time the Richter scale registers above a certain level for an undersea earthquake, a tsunami occurs. Scientists have accurately predicted all five of the significant ocean-spanning tsunamis since 1950, but they also predicted fifteen that turned out to be false alarms.[20] So note that few signs are infallible, and most are open to question.

Guidelines for reasoning by sign. Because signs are fallible, consider three guidelines for using them:

- Think about whether an alternative explanation is more credible.
- Make sure a sign is not just an isolated instance.
- If you can find instances in which a sign does not indicate a particular event, you do not have a solid argument.

Let's take a closer look at each of these guidelines. First, is an alternative explanation more credible? In a speech on the standards for licensing teachers, Seogwan suggested that the low test scores in the nation's public schools were a sign of poorly trained teachers. He reasoned that low scores represented, or sig-

Good to Know!

sign: Something that represents something else. **reasoning by sign:** Process of reasoning that assumes something exists or will happen based on something else that exists or has happened.

naled, poor teaching. However, when his audience questioned him, they raised a number of equally credible explanations. Could the lower scores be a sign of outdated or biased tests? Of overcrowded classrooms? Of the need to restructure our classrooms? Of poor testing skills? Each of these explanations is as likely as the one Seogwan offered, and much evidence supports each of them. As a result, his audience thought Seogwan's reasoning was flawed. To avoid this pitfall, be sure that when you claim one thing is a sign of another, an alternative explanation isn't equally valid or better.

Second, when you reason by sign, make sure the sign is not just an isolated instance. Speaking in favor of pornography, Mark argued that all of his friends, women included, had no problems with pornography. This, he claimed, was a sign that most people accept pornography now. He ignored the nationwide debate over pornography and the many people who are offended by it and campaign against it. He mistakenly assumed that one instance (his friends' support of pornography) represented a larger pattern.

Third, when you reason by sign, you are suggesting the sign almost always indicates a particular event. If you can find instances in which the sign does not indicate that event, you do not have a solid argument. In his speech on our ability to predict natural disasters, Tim offered the evidence that not every undersea earthquake of a certain magnitude results in a tsunami. He added that, in fact, a few quakes of a lesser magnitude did. Thus, blaming scientists for not notifying authorities in the countries affected by the 2004 tsunami was unreasonable. However, Tim argued, the occurrence of that tsunami and the tragedies left in its wake are signs that warning systems, regardless of their overprediction rates, are imperative.

A Map of Reasoning

You can use the patterns of reasoning you've explored in this chapter to assemble your evidence into a logical argument. One way to help you assemble ideas logically and construct your argument is to develop a map of your reasoning process. A solid argument should follow this map of reasoning, which is adapted from Stephen Toulmin's model of a sound argument (Figure 7.3).[21]

Claim	What do you think or want to propose?
Grounds	Why do you think this or want to propose it?
Warrant	How do you know the grounds support the claim?
Backing	How do you know the warrant supports the grounds?

This model of a sound argument helps you both as a speaker and as an audience member. As a speaker, you can use these questions to double-check the logic of your assertions, making a map of your own reasoning. As a listener, you can use the map to assess the reasons speakers give in support of their own claims.

Practicing the Public Dialogue

7.1

Test the Reasoning of Your Arguments

Bring one of your main arguments to your speech to class. Present this argument to the class and determine which pattern of reasoning will help you develop this argument most fully (inductive, deductive, causal, analogical, or by sign). After each person has presented her or his argument and selected a pattern of reasoning to support it, discuss the strengths and weaknesses of each person's approach.

Online Resources

CourseMate To see examples of two types of reasoning, deductive and causal, used in a speech, watch video clips of student speakers Lisa Alagna and Brent Erb. Consider how effectively Lisa uses deduction, paying particular attention to how she establishes the major premise of her argument. Consider how Brent makes a causal claim. Is the stated cause-and-effect relationship accurate or inaccurate? You can use your CourseMate for *Invitation to Public Speaking* to watch these videos, respond to analysis questions, and compare your answers to those provided by the author.

Figure 7.3

Toulmin's model of reasoning

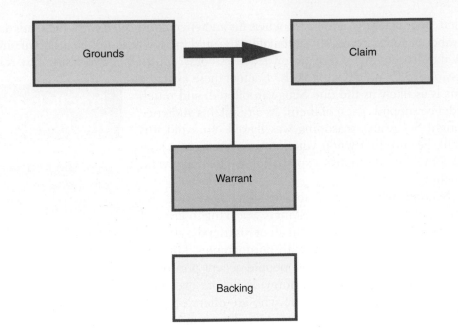

Let's look at a map of the reasoning in Damon's persuasive speech on teen suicide to understand how this model works in an actual argument:

Claim	*What do you think or want to propose?* The high rate of teen suicide for males is now a part of our community.
Grounds	*Why do you think this or want to propose it?* Three boys have committed suicide in our community in the past two months.
Warrant	*How do you know the grounds support the claim?* Three suicides in two months represent a high rate of suicide for male teens in a community of our size.
Backing	*How do you know the warrant supports the grounds?* Research indicates that three suicides in two months are above the average rate for male teens in a community of our size.

This map—a bit like a child's continually asking "why?"—helps speakers and audiences track a line of reasoning and find any flaws or loopholes. The reasoning in Damon's speech is solid, and the map helps us see this. He has acceptable grounds, warrant, and backing for his claim.

This map also can be used to test your reasoning in other types of speeches. In Stephanie's informative speech, she argued that crimes against minorities are treated differently from those against whites (*claim*). She used the murder of Deborah, a child with African American and Filipino heritage, and the murder of JonBenet, a white child, as her examples (*grounds*). Stephanie described the extensive coverage of JonBenet's murder and the minimal coverage of Deborah's murder (*warrant*). She used an implied argument to say that what was true of the coverage of JonBenet's murder (it was extensive and gained a lot of attention) should also have been true of Deborah's murder (*backing*). With this backing, Stephanie relied on the common belief in the United States that all people should be treated equally regardless of their master statuses.

Now let's use the model to uncover flaws in Christina's causal arguments about power lines and cancer. Notice that after the warrant, her backing breaks down:

Claim
: *What do you think or want to propose?*

Living near power lines increases the risk of cancer.

Grounds
: *Why do you think this or want to propose it?*

My father died of cancer and we lived near a power line.

Warrant
: *How do you know the grounds support the claim?*

The reason my father had cancer was because of the power line.

Backing
: *How do you know the warrant supports the grounds?*

Scientific research has yet to confirm the connection between cancer and power lines.

Her causal reasoning fell prey to several problems: circular reasoning, overgeneralizing, and claiming only one cause. Using Toulmin's model, we see that Christina used a circular form of reasoning (you'll learn more about circular reasoning in Chapter 16):

Grounds
: My father died because of the power line.

Warrant
: The power line caused my father's death.

Additionally, her backing discredits her argument; she produced no scientific evidence to support her claim. Her research turned up only speculation and inconclusive evidence (her backing) rather than the definitive connection she needed. Mapping her grounds, warrant, and backing clearly illustrates the weakness of her argument.

How could Christina have improved her argument? If she had reasoned inductively, offering several examples of people who lived near power lines and died of cancer, her warrant would have been acceptable. She also could have offered statistics to support her claim, showing her audience the numerical correlation between power lines and cancer.

When you reason, trace each step of your argument with Toulmin's model. Mapping your arguments before you deliver your speech helps you find any flaws in your reasoning and fix them. As a member of an audience, when you have trouble following a line of reasoning, ask the four questions of Toulmin's model: What is the speaker claiming or proposing? Why does the speaker think or want to propose this? What grounds support the speaker's claim? What backing supports the grounds? These questions should help you spot invalid claims and poorly developed arguments.

Practicing the Public Dialogue

7.2

Apply Toulmin's Model of Reasoning to Your Arguments

Select several of the arguments you presented in Practicing the Public Dialogue 7.1 and, as a class, apply Toulmin's model of reasoning to them. Identify the claims, grounds, warrant, and backing in each argument, verify the logic of these four parts, and make any adjustments in reasoning to strengthen them.

Online Resources

CourseMate To explore more information and illustrations of the Toulmin model, access **Web Connect 7.5: Toulmin Model** through your CourseMate for *Invitation to Public Speaking*.

Tips for Reasoning Ethically

Evidence, reasoning, logic, and arguments are powerful tools in the public dialogue. With them, we can share information, express our perspective and invite dialogue on an issue, make a case for a certain position, and even celebrate someone's accomplishments. However, we can also manipulate, confuse, and misrepresent events, issues, and people. Thus, we must carefully consider the ethics of reasoning. Speaking ethically requires our commitment to giving speeches that are accurate and well reasoned. The following tips will help you reason ethically in your speeches.

When political candidates participate in a debate, they must make sure the evidence they present is accurate, particularly about issues of national interest. Otherwise, voters will doubt their credibility. How might you verify the accuracy of evidence in your speech? What implications for the public dialogue result from the misuse of evidence?

Build Your Credibility

The reasoning in your speech helps build your credibility with your audience. **Credibility** is the audience's perception of a speaker's competence and character. **Competence** is the audience's view of a speaker's intelligence, expertise, and knowledge of a subject. As a speaker, you express your competence through the reasoning, organization, and delivery of your speech. **Character** is the audience's view of a speaker's sincerity, trustworthiness, and concern for the well-being of the audience. You show your character through the honesty and regard for the audience you display.[22]

Through ethical reasoning, as discussed throughout this chapter, you communicate to an audience that you are competent and you care about them. You convey to the audience that you have thought about the best way to express your ideas and you want others to understand them. In short, a careful reasoning process communicates an audience-centered stance that enhances your credibility. This credibility is a critical component of the ethical reasoning process. (For more about credibility, especially in regard to persuasive speaking, see Chapter 16.)

Use Accurate Evidence

Because speakers are adding to the ongoing discussion of issues that affect us all, they want to use accurate evidence. It is just as easy to find examples, statistics, and testimony from unreliable sources as it is to find them from credible sources. It is also possible to misrepresent or alter any statistic, example, narrative, or testimony you do find. However, a healthy public dialogue depends on legitimate evidence to build sound reasoning.

As a speaker, you are ethically obligated to use accurate evidence in all of your reasoning, no matter what pattern you use to present it. Although you may be able to present a fully developed inductive argument based on fabricated examples or a compelling analogy that is false, you would be deceiving your audience.

Verify the Structure of Your Reasoning

Applying Toulmin's model of reasoning to your arguments is the final way you can ensure the ethical nature of your reasoning. (In fact, Toulmin developed this framework to assist average people in discovering weaknesses in their reasoning processes.) By using this model as you develop your speech, you can check the warrants, grounds, and backing for your claims and ensure their accuracy. Note

Good to Know!

credibility: Audience's perception of a speaker's competence and character. **competence:** Audience's view of a speaker's intelligence, expertise, and knowledge of a subject. **character:** Audience's view of a speaker's sincerity, trustworthiness, and concern for the well-being of the audience.

that it is unethical to assert a claim is true if you do not have evidence to support that claim. Similarly, it is unethical to make unfounded arguments that could alarm audiences (recall Christina's speech about power lines and cancer). When you correct weaknesses and potentially disturbing claims before presenting them to your audiences, you are acting ethically.

Public Speaking and Service Learning: Engaging Community

David Rider, a public speaking student at Colorado State University, did his service learning project at La Familia or The Family Center. This nonprofit organization runs a variety of educational programs for parents and children and offers lower-income families low-cost child-care options. David experienced a learning moment with two children in an after-school program when he challenged a youngster's common reasoning patterns and turned a competitive situation into one of mutual learning and cooperation.

I was helping a fourth grade boy, David, with a school project that consisted of decorating paper cheeseburgers, french fries, and milkshakes with stickers. A fifth grade girl, Allison, came over to observe. She politely asked David and me if she could help. David responded "Why? This is my homework."
Before Allison was able to get upset, I explained to David why allowing Allison to help might be both fun and a benefit to him. After a few rebuttals, he accepted. She and David made small talk as I slowly faded out of the situation and helped another student with an assignment. Ten minutes later, I went and peeked over their shoulders to find that now David was helping Allison with her Spanish homework.

This was a learning moment for David, Allison, and me. David learned that accepting help is not a sign of failure and can actually make the task more enjoyable. Allison learned that by giving help, she might

"I LEARNED THAT BY CHALLENGING ANOTHER'S JUSTIFICATIONS, RATIONALLY AND LOGICALLY, I MIGHT HELP OPEN THEM UP TO SURPRISING UNDERSTANDINGS OF HOW A COMMUNITY WORKS."

receive some in the future. Both of them were pleased because it would have taken both David and Allison longer to do their homework individually. Additionally, I learned that by challenging another's justifications, rationally and logically, I might help open them up to surprising understandings of how a community works. I am glad that I have had this service learning opportunity because I would have never learned this while sitting in class.

Tips for Incorporating Service Learning into Public Speaking

- People are often uncomfortable with change. When using reasoning to ground your argument, it is best to stay as simple as possible. Try not to overcomplicate your claims or evidence. This gives people the chance to think through your argument without feeling overwhelmed or as though they can't keep up.
- When presenting your argument, take logic, emotion, and your own credibility into consideration. Also think about your particular audience and consider their various responses to the points you make. Each of your arguments should be tailored to your specific audience.
- When delivering your argument, consider the feedback your audience is giving you. If it looks like you have lost them, try reframing your reasoning with their particular interests in mind.

Chapter Summary

The process of sound reasoning is basic to all speeches.

- Sound reasoning is one of the most powerful aspects of a healthy public dialogue.
- When we reason, we use Aristotle's three types of proofs—logos, ethos, and pathos—to offer explanations and justifications for our ideas and positions.
- The logic of our reasons depends on our evidence—the examples, narratives, statistics, testimony, and definitions we gather during our research process.
- This logic helps our audience make inferences and see the connections between our evidence and claims. Our goal is to develop an argument that our audience will find credible.

Beginning speakers use five common patterns of reasoning.

1. Inductive reasoning, or reasoning from specific instances, relies on a series of examples to develop a claim we expect to be true.
   - When you reason inductively, have enough examples to support your claim.
   - Make sure your generalizations are accurate.
   - Use statistics and testimony to support your arguments.
2. Deductive reasoning, or reasoning from a general principle, begins with a commonly accepted major premise. In combination with a specific instance, or minor premise, it then establishes the truth of a specific claim or conclusion. If your general principle is one the audience will not accept immediately, you will need to establish its validity.
3. Causal reasoning establishes an "if-then" relationship, suggesting that if one event happens (a cause), then another is sure to follow (an effect).
   - When you use causal reasoning, be careful not to claim a causal relationship if it can't be proved.
   - Also be careful not to assume mistakenly there is only one cause for an event.
   - In addition, try to identify the strength or weakness of the relationship you are establishing.
4. Analogical reasoning is a process of reasoning by way of comparison and similarity. It implies that because two things resemble each other in one respect, they also share similarities in another respect. However, be sure the two things you are comparing truly are alike.
5. Reasoning by sign assumes something exists or will happen based on something else that exists or has happened. A sign represents something else, and when the sign is present, speakers reason that the other thing will be, too.
   - When you reason by sign, be sure there isn't a more credible explanation for your claim.
   - Also be sure that the sign is not an isolated instance. The sign should always be present alongside what it represents.

Using Toulmin's model of reasoning, speakers can verify the strength of their arguments.

- The model sets out four questions:
   1. The claim: What do you think or want to propose?
   2. The grounds: Why do you think this or want to propose it?
   3. The warrant: How do you know the grounds support the claim?
   4. The backing: How do you know the warrant supports the grounds?
- Listeners, too, can use this model to assess the strength of a speaker's reasoning.

Like all other aspects of public speaking, reasoning has an ethical component.

- To be ethical during the reasoning process is to establish strong credibility with your audience through sound reasoning.
- Ethical speakers use their evidence accurately and do not make claims their evidence does not support.
- They also take time during the speech writing and research process to verify the structure of their reasoning so they will not confuse or alienate their audience.

Invitation to Public Speaking Online

CourseMate Now that you have read Chapter 7, use your Speech Communication Course-Mate for *Invitation to Public Speaking* for quick access to the electronic resources that accompany this text. These resources include

- **Study tools** that will help you assess your learning and prepare for exams (*digital glossary, key term flash cards, review quizzes*).
- **Activities and assignments** that will help you hone your knowledge and build your public speaking skills throughout the course (*Practicing the Public Dialogue activities, review questions*).

- **Media resources** that will help you explore public speaking concepts online (*Web Connect links, Enhanced eBook*), develop your speech outlines (*Speech Builder Express 3.0*), watch and critique videos of sample speeches (*Interactive Video Activities*), upload your speech videos for peer reviewing and critique other students' speeches (*Speech Studio online speech review tool*), and download chapter review so you can study when and where you'd like (*Audio Study Tools*).

This chapter's key concepts and review questions are also featured here.

Key Concepts

analogical reasoning (144)
argument (136)
causal reasoning (140)
character (150)
competence (150)
conclusion (139)
credibility (150)

deductive reasoning (139)
ethos (136)
false cause (143)
hasty generalization (138)
inductive reasoning (136)
inferences (136)

logos (136)
major premise (139)
minor premise (139)
pathos (136)
reasoning by sign (146)
sign (146)

Review Questions

1. Bring a copy of the newspaper to class. In groups, identify as many different types of reasoning as you can find in the text, photographs, and advertisements. Label each item you find inductive, deductive, causal, analogical, or sign and evaluate the strength of each item's reasoning according to the guidelines discussed in this chapter.

2. Map the reasoning you find in a newspaper editorial or a letter to the editor according to Toulmin's model of an argument. Does the writer make solid arguments, or can you find weaknesses in his or her warrant, grounds, backing, or all three? Based on what you've read in this chapter, can you see ways to strengthen the writer's claims?

3. This chapter suggests that a speaker's credibility is an important part of the ethical process of using reasoning. Do you agree? Why or why not? Can you identify speakers you have heard or read about who do not have much credibility and you would deem unethical? Compare those speakers lacking credibility to a speaker you find credible. Whose arguments do you find more ethical?

4. Check out Speech Studio to see how other students' use reasoning in their speeches Or record a speech you're working on, upload it to Speech Studio, and ask your peers for their feedback. What feedback could you use to fine-tune your reasoning before you give your speech in class? **Studio**

Organizing and Outlining Your Speech

8

- **Organize for Clarity**
- **Main Points**
- **Connectives**
- **The Preparation Outline**
- **The Speaking Outline**
- **Note Cards**

IN THIS CHAPTER, YOU WILL LEARN TO:

- Identify the main points for your speech
- Determine the appropriate number of main points for your speech
- Organize your main points according to five different patterns
- Apply tips for preparing your main points effectively
- Use four different kinds of connectives in your speech
- Create a preparation outline
- Prepare a speaking outline
- Prepare note cards to use as prompts during a speech

David Young-Wolff/PhotoEdit

Once you've gathered the information for your speech, you may be wondering how to organize it into a coherent presentation. There are several ways you can do this. In this chapter, you will learn about the role organization plays in clear and effective speeches, how to structure your main points, the different patterns of organization you can use, and effective ways to move from one idea to the next.[1] You also will learn about outlining and how to use this technique to evaluate the organization of your speech and to prepare for its presentation. Once you master the fundamental steps of organization and outlining, you can branch out to more elaborate techniques. For now, use these basic frameworks to help you build speeches that are clear, interesting, and easy to follow.

Organize for Clarity

Public speakers usually take considerable time to organize their ideas so that their audiences will find their message logical and easy to follow. Like many other aspects of the speechmaking process, organization is an important audience-centered responsibility. Let's look at an example that illustrates the importance of a well-organized speech. See if you can make sense of the following outline of ideas:

1. Take one of the corners and bring it to the center.
   a. The history of this process is an intriguing one.
   b. My mother had the flag given to her family when her brother died in the Vietnam War.
2. The stars on the edge of the flag are highly symbolic.
   a. It should never touch the ground.
   b. She describes the ceremony as quite beautiful and symbolic.
3. You need two people to fold a flag correctly.
   a. There is a correct way to fold a flag.
   b. The flag should always be displayed behind the speaker's left shoulder.

Can you follow this speaker's organizational logic? Although you begin to realize that the speech is about flags by the second subpoint, are you clear about the speaker's thesis? Is her speech informative, invitational, persuasive, or for a special occasion? Can you tell whether she was asked, required, or decided to speak? It is hard to figure out what this speech is about from the outline just presented.

Now consider this speech organized in a way that is more linear and more appealing to an audience:

Specific purpose: To inform my audience about the rules and regulations for handling the U.S. flag.

Thesis statement: The flag, a symbol of much that is great about this nation, should be hung, handled, and folded in a specific manner.

Main points:
    I. Each part of the flag has a specific meaning or purpose dedicated to symbolizing patriotic ideas.

    II. Because of the symbolism of each of these parts, the flag should be hung in a specific manner.

    III. Flag etiquette, more than just stories told from generation to generation, tells us how to handle a flag properly.

    IV. Flags also should be folded in a specific way, with each fold representing important qualities of our country.

Cengage Learning

CourseMate

Watch a video clip of student speaker Cindy Gardner giving a speech about how to fold an American flag. Notice how she organizes her ideas. You can use your CourseMate for *Invitation to Public Speaking* to watch the video, respond to analysis questions, and compare your answers to those provided by the author.

Notice how this outline gives you a much clearer sense of what Cindy will cover and how her ideas relate to one another. **Organization**, the systematic arrangement of ideas into a coherent whole, makes speeches listenable. It makes your ideas and arguments clear and easy to follow.

Main Points

One of the first steps in organizing a speech is to identify your main points. **Main points** are the most important, comprehensive ideas you address in your speech. They give your speech focus and help you decide which information to include and which to leave out. They are your overarching themes or subjects.

Identify Your Main Points

You can identify the main points of your speech in two ways. First, take stock of your speech assignment, list of ideas, and research. You will know you have a main point when you realize that if you do not develop a particular idea, your speech topic will seem incomplete, nonsensical, or will not accomplish your goal for the speech.

Second, if you have already written your thesis statement, you should be able to find your main points within it. Notice in the example about folding a flag that Cindy's thesis statement defines her main points: (1) the symbolism in the U.S. flag and how a flag should be (2) hung, (3) handled, and (4) folded. Without a thesis statement (as in the first version of Cindy's outline), a speaker's ideas are simply a random collection of points.

Your thesis statement may not always be as specific as Cindy's, especially if you are giving a process, or how-to, speech. Nonetheless, even with the broad thesis statement in the next speech, Candice used it to develop her main points. Notice how the four steps Candice mentioned in her thesis statement became the four steps she discussed in her speech.

Specific purpose: To inform my audience of the process of making a scrapbook.

Thesis statement: There are four steps to making a quality scrapbook.

Main points:
   I. Collect the materials you want to put into the book.

   II. Decide on the order of your materials.

   III. Arrange the materials in the book.

   IV. Cover or bind the book.

Your thesis statement and your research should guide your selection of main points for other types of speeches as well. In an invitational speech on the problem of elder abuse, Peter developed the following main points:

Specific purpose: To invite my audience to consider two possible solutions to the problem of elder abuse.

Thesis statement: The problem of elder abuse is quite widespread but may be solved by more thorough background checks of employees in care facilities and increased funding for training and salaries.

Good to Know!

organization: Systematic arrangement of ideas into a coherent whole. **main points:** Most important ideas you address in your speech.

Main points: I. More thorough background checks of employees in care facilities may help solve the widespread problem of elder abuse.

II. Increased funding for training and salaries may also help solve this problem.

In his speech, Peter used his thesis statement to identify the two primary solutions to elder abuse, and he used his research to develop those possibilities.

Use an Appropriate Number of Main Points

Knowing how many main points to include can be difficult because we often gather more information than we need and our subjects can be complex. Additionally, classroom speeches often have other requirements, such as incorporating visual aids, citing a specific number of sources, and engaging in a question-and-answer discussion with the audience. So how do you determine the number of main points to include?

In any kind of speech, your time limit is your most important guideline for determining the number of main points. For even a two- to three-minute speech of introduction, you might start with a long list of main points, as May did:

Specific purpose: To introduce myself to my audience.

Thesis statement: I have lived an interesting life thus far and have goals for the future.

Main points: I. I was born in the air over China, so I have dual citizenship.

II. I've lived in many different cities, states, and countries.

III. I love to do anything that pertains to water.

IV. I'll graduate next June and travel with friends for the summer.

V. After that, I'll join the navy.

VI. From there, I hope to become an aquatic research scientist for a university.

Although each of these points is interesting, there are far too many to cover—even if May had ten minutes. Also notice that her thesis statement is quite vague and does not help focus her ideas. When you have a long list of ideas for any kind of speech, recognize that you'll have to reduce your scope. Most classroom speeches are limited to two to four main points depending on the length of your speech and your speaking goals. You can reduce your scope by returning to your thesis statement and tightening it up (as May needs to do) or by focusing on only the main points that best develop your thesis statement. Here's a solution for May's speech:

Specific purpose: To introduce myself to my audience.

Thesis statement: The first twenty-two years of my life have been nomadic ones, and I will most likely continue with this lifestyle for some time.

Main points: I. My nomadic lifestyle began when I was born in an airplane over an ocean near China.

II. I'll continue to nurture my nomadic spirit and love of water by joining the navy when I graduate.

III. The third step of the safe ascent is the actual ascent: Slowly rotate upward, breathe normally, and release air from your BCD as you go.

Spatial pattern. When ideas are arranged in terms of location or direction, they follow a **spatial pattern** of organization. For example, arranging ideas from left to right, top to bottom, or inside to outside helps your audience visualize the relationship between ideas or the structure of something. Spatial relationships can be abstract, as in the next example from Terri's speech about eating according to the food pyramid. At other times, they indicate the location of real things or places, as in the second example from Demetrious's speech about five Italian villages.

Specific purpose:	To inform my audience of some of the creative ways to eat according to the food pyramid.
Thesis statement:	The food pyramid can be used creatively to eat interesting and healthy foods that incorporate whole grains, vegetables and fruits, protein, and even some fats and sugars.
Main points:	I. At the foundation of the food pyramid are the grain and vegetable servings that you can combine to make dishes from around the world, such as couscous salad with tomatoes and basil.
	II. You can complement this foundation with the middle level of the pyramid—the dairy, fruit, and protein servings—by making dishes such as curried chicken with apricots.
	III. The top of the pyramid includes the stuff we really like to eat, the fats and sweets that can be made into such delicacies as candied almonds.

In the second example, the spatial pattern describes geographical locations:

Specific purpose:	To invite my audience to visit the Cinque Terre, five villages along the Mediterranean coast of Italy that are only accessible by boat or by footpath.
Thesis statement:	The Cinque Terre contains five villages set into a steep hillside that visitors to the Mediterranean coast of Italy may find enchanting: Monterosso, Vernazza, Corniglia, Manarola, and Riomaggiore.
Main points:	I. The farthest village, called Monterosso, is a popular attraction because of the huge statues carved into the rocks overlooking its beaches.
	II. The next two villages, Vernazza and Corniglia, display remarkable vineyards, homes, and a central promenade and piazza.
	III. A hike to the top of the fourth village, Manarola, gives you a stunning view of the ocean and all five of the villages.

Good to Know!

spatial pattern: Pattern of organization that arranges ideas in terms of location or direction.

IV. Riomaggiore, the village of love, completes the Cinque Terre, or five villages, with its captivating display of homes and shops tucked into the final ravine of this remarkable Italian hillside.

Causal pattern. Speeches that describe a cause-and-effect relationship between ideas or events follow a **causal pattern** of organization. When you use this organizational pattern, you will have two main points: one discussing the cause and the other describing its effects. You can present either the cause first or the effects first depending on your topic and your speaking goal. In the next example, Jeremy uses a causal pattern to organize the ideas presented in his informative speech on sibling rivalry.

AP Photo

Specific purpose: To inform my audience of the causes and most serious effects of sibling rivalry.

Thesis statement: Sibling rivalry is caused by competition for attention and can become quite severe if not handled properly.

Main points:
  I. Sibling rivalry is caused by competition for positive attention from parents.

  II. If ignored, sibling rivalry can turn to hatred between siblings.

If the effects have already happened, you might choose to present the effects first followed by the cause. In this next example, Chaundra discusses the effects of worker burnout first, and then she attempts to persuade the audience of one of its possible causes.

Specific purpose: To persuade my audience that the rapid pace of today's workplace is leading to an unusually high level of burnout.

Thesis statement: Today's workers are experiencing high levels of burnout, which is caused by increased demands on their time and energy.

Main points:
  I. Today's workers display levels of burnout that are higher than ever.

  II. Today's working environments contribute to burnout through a constant demand for more output in shorter amounts of time.

A causal organizational pattern is useful when your topic describes an event or situation and its consequences. It is also helpful when you want to describe an event that might happen and what its effects might be.

New York's five boroughs could be discussed using a spatial pattern of organization. What main points could you write for this area that would follow this pattern? Could you also discuss this area using another pattern?

Problem–solution pattern. Speeches that identify a specific problem and offer a possible solution follow a **problem–solution pattern** of organization. This pattern is common in persuasive speeches because we can describe a problem and follow with a call to action. The problem–solution pattern has two main points: the

Good to Know!

causal pattern: Pattern of organization that describes a cause-and-effect relationship between ideas or events.
problem–solution pattern: Pattern of organization that identifies a specific problem and offers a possible solution.

description of the problem followed by a description of the solution. Solutions can be general or specific. In the following example, Molly's solution was a general recommendation:

Specific purpose:	To persuade my audience that beef byproducts have invaded our lives and that awareness is the first step to becoming an educated consumer.
Thesis statement:	Becoming aware of the problem of the presence of beef byproducts in such common items as deodorants, photographic film, marshmallows, gum, and candles is the first step in a solution of raising our awareness to make educated consumer choices.
Main points:	I. Without our knowledge, beef byproducts are included in many of the products we put on and in our bodies, as well as in and around our houses.
	II. The solution to this invasion is to become aware of the presence of these beef byproducts so we can make informed choices about what we buy and use.

In the next example, Brandon called for a very specific solution:

Specific purpose:	To persuade my audience to vote in favor of bond measure 343 in November.
Thesis statement:	Money going to support before- and after-school meal programs is at an all-time low, and this measure will ensure the improvement of these services to students in our public schools.
Main points:	I. There currently is not enough money available to provide adequate before- and after-school meal programs to students in our public schools.
	II. Passing bond measure 343 will provide this necessary money.

In Chapter 16, you'll learn more about the various types of solutions that speakers can suggest to their audiences.

Topical pattern. Speeches that divide their topics into subtopics, each of which addresses a different aspect of the larger topic, follow a **topical pattern** of organization. When you use a topical pattern, you can organize your ideas by following a progression of ideas that suits your own style. You can use the principle of primacy (putting your most important idea first) or recency (putting what you most want your audience to remember last), or you can arrange the ideas in other ways. In the following example, Justin arranged his ideas topically to address the two major types of phobias:

Specific purpose:	To inform my audience of the two major types of phobias.
Thesis statement:	Although there are many specific phobias, these "irrational fears and dislikes" can be categorized in two ways: social and specific.

Good to Know!

topical pattern: Pattern of organization that allows the speaker to divide a topic into subtopics, each of which addresses a different aspect of the larger topic.

Main points:

I. A *social phobia* is a fear of appearing stupid or being shamed in a social situation.

II. A *specific phobia* is a fear of specific objects or situations, like spiders, closed spaces, and so on.

In the following example, Alex uses a topical pattern to persuade her audience that women in "glory sports" are just as talented as the men.

Specific purpose: To persuade my audience that very talented women engage in what are commonly called *glory sports*.

Thesis statement: We know very little about the three most prominent women who participate in glory sports, even though they are as talented as the men who participate in the same sports.

Main points:

I. Layne Beachley is a professional surfer living in Sydney, Australia, who became the Women's ASP World Surfing Champion in 1998 and then won title six more times until she retired in 2008.

II. Cara Beth Burnside, a pioneer of women's skateboarding, resides in southern California and is the first woman to have a signature skate shoe.

III. Tara Dakides, also from California, is "the most progressive and influential female ever to strap on a snowboard," doing tricks "most guy pros haven't even done yet."

Topical patterns help you organize a speech that doesn't fit into a chronological, spatial, causal, or problem–solution organizational pattern. If you try to rearrange the examples in this section into one of these other organizational patterns, you'll find that your ideas won't fit well.

Tips for Preparing Main Points

There are three keys to developing your main points. First, keep each main point separate and distinct— don't combine points. Second, word your points consistently. Finally, devote appropriate coverage to each main point.

Keep each main point separate and distinct. To be as clear as possible, each main point should be a separate idea. Once you've identified your likely main points, double-check them to be sure you have not combined two ideas into one main point. We may be tempted to combine two ideas to cover as much information as we can. But notice what happened when Aaron combined two ideas into a single point:

Practicing the Public Dialogue

8.1

Select an Organizational Pattern for Your Speech

As a class, brainstorm topics for speeches that could conceivably be arranged according to more than one of the organizational patterns discussed in this chapter. Choose one of these topics and then divide into five groups. Assign a different organizational pattern (chronological, spatial, causal, problem–solution, or topical) to each group. In your group, create a specific purpose, thesis statement, and up to five main points for the topic using the organizational pattern you were assigned. Have each group present their results to the class and then, as a class, determine which organizational pattern (or patterns) worked best for the topic. Why was this pattern more successful than the others? Use what you learned from this activity to select the most appropriate pattern for your next speech.

Online Resources

When you're ready to organize the main points of your next speech, you can use Speech Builder Express to help you. Select "Organization" from the left menu and follow the instructions.

Ineffective main points	Effective main points
I. Electronic music is produced from a variety of machines that make noise electronically.	I. Electronic music is produced from a variety of machines that make noise electronically.
II. Electronic music has become more popular in recent years and is performed by many well-known artists.	II. Electronic music has become more popular in recent years.
	III. Electronic music is performed by many well-known artists.

Although both columns cover the same ground, the points in the right column are clearer because each addresses only one idea. By separating the two points, Aaron can avoid confusing or overwhelming his audience.

Word your main points consistently. Try to word your main points as consistently as possible. A parallel structure is easier to organize and remember. In the next example, Michael presented an informative speech on the reasons for stop signs. Notice how the parallel main points in the right column are clearer and more memorable than those in the left column:

Ineffective main points	Effective main points
I. Drivers need to know who has the right of way, and a stop sign tells us that.	I. Stop signs assign the right of way to vehicles using an intersection.
II. Stop signs slow down drivers who are traveling at unsafe speeds.	II. Stop signs reduce the problem of speeding in certain areas.
III. Sometimes, pedestrians need protection from vehicles, and stop signs give them that protection.	III. Stop signs protect pedestrians in busy intersections or near schools.

With a simple reworking of phrasing, Michael made his main points parallel: Stop signs assign, stop signs reduce, stop signs protect. Although this kind of parallel structure is not always possible, your ideas will be clearer and more memorable when you can use it.

Devote the appropriate coverage to each main point. Remember that your main points are your most important ideas. Therefore, each point should receive the same level of development and attention in your speech. If you find yourself spending little time developing a particular point, ask yourself whether it really is as important as you thought and whether it should be a main point in your speech. If, on the other hand, you find yourself putting a lot of development into one point, consider if you should divide it into two points. In preparing a speech on the art of batik, Martha discovered the following imbalance:

Specific purpose: To inform my audience about batik, a beautiful and diverse art form that has been practiced for centuries.

Thesis statement: The art of batik has an intriguing history as well as methods of production and designs that reflect the skill and politics of the artisan.

Main points: I. The history of batik (*65 percent of the speech*)

II. The production of batik (*15 percent of the speech*)

III. The designs of batik (*15 percent of the speech*)

IV. Where to purchase batik (*5 percent of the speech*)

Martha realized she had spent so much time on her first point that she didn't have time to cover her remaining points. Although the history of batik is important, it wasn't the only information she wanted to share with her audience. She also wanted to show them the production process and some of the designs she loved. After some consideration, Martha reduced the scope of her speech by dropping her fourth point (which wasn't really a part of her thesis statement), and she condensed the details of her first point. She reworked her speech as follows, saving 20 percent of her time for the introduction and conclusion:

Specific purpose: To inform my audience about batik, a beautiful and diverse art form that has been practiced for centuries.

Thesis statement: The art of batik has an intriguing history as well as methods of production and designs that reflect the skill and politics of the artisan.

Main points:

    I. The history of batik (*30 percent*)

    II. The production of batik (*25 percent*)

    III. The designs of batik (*25 percent*)

Your goal, as Martha's revised main points suggest, is not necessarily to spend exactly the same amount of time on each point but to offer a balanced presentation of your ideas.

Teen Traffic Crashes in Arkansas

- More than 125 killed in crashes involving teen drivers in 2005
- Teens 7% of driving population but 13% of drivers involved in fatal crashes
- Almost 20% of highway deaths involved 15–20 year old drivers)

AP Photo/Mike Wintroath

By preparing your main points carefully, you'll give an effective speech that your audience will find easy to follow. Consider your next speech. How will you order and present your main points so they have the greatest impact? (On a side note, can you spot the typo in this visual aid? Be sure to check your PowerPoint slides for mistakes!)

Connectives

Your main points are the heart of your speech. Once you have them on paper and supported them with your research, you must find ways to connect them to enhance the audience's understanding. The words and phrases we use to link ideas in a speech are called **connectives**. They show audiences the relationship between ideas.

Before you read the descriptions of the four types of connectives, consider some of the connectives that speakers use unconsciously: "all right," "next," "now," "um," "and," "so," "so then," and "ah." These words or sounds are often called *fillers* because they tell the audience very little about the relationship between ideas. Fillers can be annoying, especially when the same one is repeated often in a speech. The following section offers four useful alternatives to these fillers. Transitions, internal previews, internal summaries, and signposts add meaning and help your audience remember your ideas.

Transitions

Transitions are phrases that indicate you are finished with one idea and are moving to a new one. Effective transitions restate the idea you are finishing and introduce your next one. In the following examples, the transitions are underlined:

Good to Know!

connective: Word or a phrase used to link ideas in a speech. **transition:** Phrase that indicates a speaker is finished with one idea and is moving on to a new one.

Now that you understand how our childhood memories influence our relationship to money, let's explore the relationship we have to money as adults.

Once you've visited Manarola, you're ready to move to the final village, Riomaggiore, also known as "the village of love."

You can consciously insert transitions such as "let's turn to," "now that you understand," "in addition to," and "that brings me to my next point." But many will come naturally as you close one point or idea and begin a new one. Use transitions to link ideas within your main points and to guide your audience from point to point as you deliver your speech.

Internal Previews

An **internal preview** is a statement in the body of your speech that details what you plan to discuss next. Internal previews focus on what comes next in the speech rather than linking two points, as transitions do. Internal previews are very similar to the preview you offer in the introduction of a speech (Chapter 9), but you use them to introduce a new point rather than the entire speech. In the next example, Martha introduces her second point, batik production, with an internal preview:

> In discussing the production of batik, I'll explain the four steps: the preparation of the cloth, the mixing of the dyes, the application of the dye, and the setting of the image in the cloth.

After hearing this preview, the audience is ready for four steps and begins to appreciate the intricacies of the batik process. Internal previews are often combined with transitions, as in Robert's discussion of theatrical lighting:

> As you can see, *(transition)* with the invention of the light bulb came exciting and safer possibilities for theatrical lighting. And the now familiar light bulb takes me to my third point, *(internal preview)* the invention of three instruments that revolutionized lighting in the theater: the ellipsoidal, the fresnel, and the intelabeam.

Not every main point requires an internal preview, but the unfamiliar terminology in Robert's third point lends itself to a preview. Introducing new concepts or terminology before offering the details enhances your audience's understanding of your topic.

Internal Summaries

An **internal summary** is a statement in the body of your speech that summarizes a point you've already discussed. If you've just finished an important or complicated point, add an internal summary to remind your audience of its highlights. In Jeremy's speech on sibling rivalry, he used an internal summary at the end of the first point:

> To summarize, the causes of sibling rivalry—birth order, sex, parental attitudes, and individual personality traits—can cause children to compete for their parents' affection and attention.

Good to Know!

internal preview: Statement in the body of a speech that details what the speaker plans to discuss next. **internal summary:** Statement in the body of a speech that summarizes a point a speaker has already discussed.

Like internal previews, internal summaries can be combined with transitions so you can move efficiently into your next point. Here's an example from Brandon's speech:

> In short, (*internal summary*) the lack of funding for before- and after-school meal programs leads to poor academic performance, increased absences, and behavioral problems. But let's see (*transition*) what this bond issue will do to remedy many of these problems.

Internal summaries are excellent tools when you want your audience to remember key points before you move on to a new idea. When combined with transitions, internal summaries can help audiences move smoothly from one idea to the next.

Signposts

A **signpost** is a simple word or statement that indicates where you are in your speech or highlights an important idea. Signposts tell your audience where you are in the presentation of your main points and help your listeners keep track of a detailed discussion or list of items. These tools add clarity to a speech and can make it flow. Signposts can be numbers ("first," "second," "third"), phrases ("the most important thing to remember is," "you'll want to make note of this"), or questions you ask and then answer ("so, how do we solve this dilemma?"). In Alex's speech on women in glory sports, she asked questions to introduce each of her main points.

© Joseph Sohm/Visions of America/Corbis

Transitions, internal previews, internal summaries, and signposts are like highway signs that help your audience see where you're going in your speech. Where will you include connectives in your next speech to best show your audience how your ideas relate to one another?

For her first main point, she asked,

> How many of you know who Layne Beachley is?

For her second, she asked,

> So, you didn't know Layne Beachley. How about Cara Beth Burnside? Can anyone tell me her accomplishments?

And for her third, she asked,

> Okay, I'll give you one more try. Who knows Tara Dakides's contributions to the world of glory sports?

Although you don't want to overuse these kinds of questions, they can be effective in getting an audience involved in your speech because audience members will try to answer the questions in their own heads before you do.

The final use of signposts is to mark the most important ideas in your speech. When you hear or use any of the following phrases, it's a signpost asking the audience to pay close attention:

1. The most important thing to remember is . . .
2. If you hear nothing else from today's speech, hear this . . .
3. Let me repeat that last figure for you . . .
4. This next point is crucial to understanding my arguments . . .

You should use this kind of signpost only once in a speech. If you use it more often, the audience quickly loses confidence that what you are about to say is really "the most important thing."

Good to Know!

signpost: Simple word or statement that indicates where you are in your speech or highlights an important idea.

The Preparation Outline

The **preparation outline** is a detailed outline of your speech that helps you evaluate the organization of your ideas. The preparation outline consists of your speech's title, specific purpose, thesis statement, introduction, main points and subpoints, connectives, conclusion, and source citations. It contains enough detail for you to verify that your speech is fully organized and complete, but it does not include every word you will say. Note that it's best to begin creating a preparation outline as soon as you begin working on your speech.

Title, Specific Purpose, and Thesis Statement

Because a preparation outline helps focus your ideas and organize your materials, write the title of your speech and your specific purpose and thesis statement at the top of the outline. The title of a speech usually comes from its specific purpose and thesis statement because both indicate the theme of your speech. A good title also reflects the tone of your speech. Let's take a look at how Brooke and Katy titled their speeches.

Brooke:

Title:	The World's Fire
Specific purpose:	To inform my audience about the history and legends of the chili pepper.
Thesis statement:	The history of the chili pepper includes global, national, and personal stories.

Katy:

Title:	Why Pi?
Specific purpose:	To inform my audience about the number pi.
Thesis statement:	Pi, a fascinating number with an unusual history, has become an obsession for some people.

Both speakers chose simple, yet appropriate, titles for their speeches. Their titles reflect the content of their speeches, which is explicitly stated in their specific purposes and thesis statements. (Katy's complete preparation outline for her speech "Why Pi?" is featured at the end of this section.)

Practicing the Public Dialogue

8.2

Prepare the Main Points and Connectives for Your Speech

Bring your thesis statement for your next speech to class. With a partner, discuss the main points you prepared to develop your thesis statement. Are your main points distinct? If you have combined your points, separate them. Next consider the phrasing of your main points. Have you used a parallel structure to word each one? If not, revise your wording so your points are parallel. Now consider how balanced your main points are. If you suspect you're spending too little or too much time on a point, adjust it so the coverage of each point is more balanced. Finally, identify the places within or between your main points where a connective would add clarity or help you move from one idea to the next.

Online Resources

 You can use Speech Builder Express to help you create your main points and connectives for your next speech. Select "Outline" and "Transitions" from the left menu and follow the instructions.

Good to Know!

preparation outline: Detailed outline a speaker builds when preparing a speech that includes the title, specific purpose, thesis statement, introduction, main points and subpoints, connectives, conclusion, and source citations of the speech.

Introduction

You'll read much more about introductions in Chapter 9, but here we'll discuss how to incorporate this part of a speech into an outline. An introduction should do four things: catch your audience's attention, reveal your speech topic, establish your credibility, and preview your main points. Identify these four steps in your preparation outline. This will help you be sure you have included each of them in your introduction. Here's how Nathan and Brooke outlined their introductions.

Nathan:

I. How far do you think you can walk? (*catch attention*)

    A. A hike from Georgia to Maine will put you on the Appalachian National Scenic Trail. (*reveal topic*)

    B. I've hiked this trail twice in my life, the most recent time being last summer. (*establish credibility*)

II. Today, I'd like to share with you a brief history of this trail, some facts about the trail and how it's maintained, and stories from some people who've hiked the trail. (*preview main points*)

Brooke:

I. The words chilly, chili, and Chile refer to cold weather, spicy beans, and a country in South America. (*catch attention*)

    A. Today, I'm speaking about the chili pepper. (*reveal topic*)

    B. The Chile Today website says the chili pepper has conquered taste buds and cuisines for 10,000 years. (*catch attention and establish credibility*)

    C. To me, the chili pepper is a legend, story, and tale. (*establish credibility*)

II. The chili pepper legends I'll discuss come from a variety of stories. (*preview main points*)

    A. Some stories are found across the globe.

    B. Others are the national stories originating in our own country.

    C. My final story is a personal one about my grandfather, the person who introduced me to the chili pepper's legacy. (*also establishes credibility*)

In these examples, the speakers summarized their introductions in outline form. These outlines do not include the full text of the speeches but rather are a synopsis of the main ideas. By using this format, the speakers could see they included the four components of a strong introduction.

Main Points, Subpoints, and Sub-Subpoints

As you learned earlier in this chapter, the most important ideas in your speech are your main points. Your main points make up the body of your speech. When you want to elaborate on your main points, you use subpoints and sub-subpoints. A **subpoint** develops an aspect of a main point. A **sub-subpoint** goes deeper to

Good to Know!

subpoint: Point in a speech that develops an aspect of a main point. **sub-subpoint:** Point in a speech that develops an aspect of a subpoint.

Civic Engagement in Action

PROOF THAT ONE PERSON DOES COUNT

In the early 1990s, the former Yugoslavia was torn apart by bitter ethnic conflicts, known collectively as the Yugoslav Wars. These wars quickly became infamous for the war crimes committed as the wars progressed, including mass ethic cleansing and the systematic rape of women as a tool of warfare. In the United States, Zainab Salbi and her new husband, Amjad Atallah, were horrified by media reports of the women who were being victimized during the wars. They wanted to volunteer to help, but found that there was no organization that addressed the problem. So, instead of spending their honeymoon money on a trip, they used it to found Women for Women International, an organization that works to help women survivors of war from all over the world.

Andrew H. Walker/Getty Images

her neighborhood. And just a month after she moved to the United States at nineteen, Iraq invaded Kuwait and she was cut off from her parents. Her inability to help or be with her family during such a crisis motivated her to find a way to help others affected by war. "Yes, I am only one person," she says, "but I am proof that one person does count."[2]

Women for Women International focuses on helping women recover from their wartime experiences to become fully participating citizens in their communities. The organization offers both direct aid and more lasting help in the form of job training and leadership education. It also puts women in touch with one another with the goal of giving them a voice in regions of the world where women do not traditionally have one. Women for Women's philosophy is that "access of knowledge and expression of voice + access to and control of resources = lasting social and political change."

Salbi's passion for helping women who have survived war stems from her own experiences. Born and raised in Baghdad, Iraq, she tried to live a normal life during wartime. "I learned to coexist with war," she says, often waking up to the sound of missiles hitting

You Can Get Involved

CourseMate To learn more about Women for Women International, access **Web Connect 8.1: Women for Women** at your CourseMate for *Invitation to Public Speaking*. The "Get Involved" link provides many innovative ways to help, including opportunities to volunteer, shop for products made by women the organization helps, and sponsor a "sister." Also check out **Web Connect 8.2: Girls Inc.** to explore a youth organization that helps U.S. girls "confront subtle societal messages about their value and potential, and prepares them to lead successful, independent, and fulfilling lives." Click on the "About Girls Inc." link and then on the "Take Action" and "Support Girls Inc." links to see how you can get involved.

develop an aspect of a subpoint. You can think of main points, subpoints, and sub-subpoints as moving from the whole to the parts, or from the general to the specific. Consider the following example from Kameron's speech on zebra mussels:

I. Zebra mussels cause damage to every aspect of any aquatic ecosystem they encounter.

A. They destroy the natural balance of the ecosystem.

    1. They consume all the food available to those lower on the food chain.

    2. Larger fish no longer have smaller fish to feed on.

B. They form large colonies that attach themselves to any solid object, making it difficult for commercial enterprises.

    1. They congregate on buoys and markers, causing them to sink.

    2. They clog intake ports by attaching themselves to anything solid.

Notice that the main point (I) is developed and supported by the two subpoints (A and B). Additionally, the subpoints are developed and supported by the sub-subpoints (1 and 2 under subpoints A and B). In addition, notice that the points are organized according to the principle of **coordination**, or arranging your points into successive levels, with the points on a specific level having equal importance.

Remember, a main point is the broadest, most comprehensive idea; a subpoint supports and develops the main idea; and a sub-subpoint supports and develops the subpoint.

Conclusion

You'll read much more about conclusions in Chapter 9, but here we'll discuss how to incorporate this part of a speech into an outline. The conclusion has two goals: to signal the end of the speech and to reinforce your thesis statement. As you outline your conclusion, make sure it meets these goals. Like your introduction, the outline of the conclusion isn't a word-for-word transcript. Rather, it's a summary of what you'll say. Let's take a look at how Nathan and Will outlined the conclusions to their speeches.

Nathan:

I. So, now do you think you could walk from New York to Chicago or from Georgia to Maine? (*bring speech to an end*)

II. Even if you're not up for the hike, many people have hiked the 2,200-mile-long footpath to raise funds, overcome disabilities, and seek out spiritual insights. (*reinforce thesis statement*)

Will:

I. As you've seen in these last few minutes, ideas that were once regarded as fiction may soon be reality. (*bring speech to an end*)

II. Although there are ethical questions and concerns, germ-line engineering and cloning may soon be processes that are used every day. (*reinforce thesis statement*)

Connectives

As we discussed earlier, connectives are words and phrases used to link ideas in a speech, and they come in four varieties: transitions, internal previews, internal summaries, and signposts. Because most connectives are only a single sentence, simply write them out rather than outline them. By writing out your connectives, you can easily see if you've overused a phrase (for example, "now let's" again and

---

Good to Know!

coordination: Process of arranging points into successive levels, with the points on a specific level having equal importance.

again), and you can see which points you might clarify with internal previews, summaries, or both. In her speech on crazy lawsuits, Cassie previewed her main points in her introduction, wrote the connective to her first main point, and then outlined her first main point:

Connective: Let's begin by looking at some definitions.

I. Three terms come up in most of these cases.
    A. The first term is tort.
    B. The second term is civil suit.
    C. The third term is frivolous lawsuit.

Similarly, Kelly used a transition in his speech on the Japanese language to get from his first main point to his second:

Connective: Now that I've introduced you to some Japanese body language, I would like to discuss a little bit about spoken Japanese.

And in his speech on germ-line engineering, Will incorporated an internal summary into his preparation outline and then moved on to cloning, his next main point:

Connective: As you've just heard, germ-line engineering combines the age-old idea of manipulating DNA strands through selective breeding of animals and the newer research that is unpacking the human DNA code. But this isn't the only radical idea around today.

Include connectives between the major sections of your preparation outline (introduction, body, and conclusion) and between main points to help track your transitions from one idea to the next.

Works Cited

The final component of your preparation outline is a list of the works you have cited in your speech. Follow the guidelines for preparing a preliminary bibliography in Chapter 5 or those required by your instructor. Your instructor might require an established format for your list of works cited, such as that of the Modern Language Association (MLA) or the American Psychological Association (APA). For guidelines for these bibliographic styles, see Figure 5.3 in Chapter 5.

Unless your instructor indicates otherwise, include only the sources you actually cited orally in your speech. By listing sources, you'll see how many you relied on to build your arguments and establish your credibility. If you discover you have cited only one or two sources and think you need more, you can go back and rework sections of your speech to include additional citations. Remember, citing the work of others not only enhances your ideas and increases your credibility, but it is also ethical.

Tips for the Preparation Outline

Use complete sentences. Always write your ideas in complete sentences. The difference between a full-sentence outline and a keyword outline is obvious when the two are compared, as in Figure 8.1. Although you do get a sense of Javad's topic and ideas in the keyword example, a full-sentence outline is a far more useful tool to help you prepare and track the components of your speech. A keyword outline gives you very little sense of how fully developed your ideas are and whether you have thought them through completely. In contrast,

Keyword outline (incorrect)	Full-sentence outline (correct)

I. The Tuskegee Airmen
  A. Four squadrons
  B. The elite 332nd
  C. Their names
II. Obstacles
  A. The first
  B. No officers
  C. Recognition
	I. The Tuskegee Airmen were an elite group of African American fighter pilots who fought during the Second World War.
	  A. The first five men graduated from four different squadrons at the Tuskegee training center in Alabama.
	  B. The Tuskegee Airmen were considered one of the Allies' strongest weapons.
	  C. Because of their talents, the Tuskegee Airmen were given nicknames in both German and English.
	II. Although history books now recognize these men as heroes, they had to overcome many obstacles to be allowed to fly.
	  A. At first, they were not allowed to form a squadron because "no colored squadrons" were needed.
	  B. They then were told no such unit was allowed because there were "no commissioned Negro officers" in the Air Force.
	  C. Although they never lost a bomber they escorted, it wasn't until 1948 that the first African American pilot received his gold wings.

Figure 8.1

Keyword versus full-sentence outline

a full-sentence outline clearly shows how well your speech is organized, what the contents of each point are, where there are inconsistencies, and where more development might be needed.

Label the introduction, body, conclusion, and connectives. In addition to labeling the title, specific purpose, and thesis statement in your preparation outline, label the introduction, body, conclusion, and connectives. These labels mark each component of your speech and encourage you to consider each one separately. They also help you see how much time you are devoting to each section and avoid an introduction that is overly long or a conclusion that is too abrupt.

Use a consistent pattern of symbols and indentation. Outlines are based on the principles of **subordination**, or ranking ideas in order from the most to the least important. The most common way to indicate subordination in an outline is to use a traditional pattern of symbols and indentations. Main points are labeled with capital Roman numerals (I, II, III, and so on). Subpoints are labeled with capital letters (A, B, C, and so on). Sub-subpoints are labeled with Arabic numbers (1, 2, 3, and so on). Indentations help you visually indicate the subordination of ideas. Your main points are set farthest left, and each level of subpoints is indented progressively farther to the right. In a complex outline, you may need sub-sub-subpoints and even sub-sub-sub-subpoints. Label sub-sub-subpoints with lowercase letters (a, b, c, and so on), and label sub-sub-sub-subpoints with lowercase Roman numerals (i, ii, iii, and so on). Figure 8.2 on page 175 gives examples of traditional and complex outlines.

Good to Know!

subordination: Process of ranking ideas in order from the most to the least important.

When you indent, be sure you indent all the text that corresponds with the point, not just the first line of text. (This type of indent is called a hanging indent. You can use Word's numbering formatting feature or the margin tabs in the ruler at the top of your document to help create hanging indents.) This will help you see the ranking of each point clearly and emphasize the relationship your subpoints have to your main points.

Incorrect

II. Although history books now recognize these men as heroes, they had to overcome many obstacles to be allowed to fly.

A. At first, they were not allowed to form a squadron because "no colored squadrons" were needed.

Correct

II. Although history books now recognize these men as heroes, they had to overcome many obstacles to be allowed to fly.

   A. At first, they were not allowed to form a squadron because "no colored squadrons" were needed.

Divide points into at least two subpoints. When you support broad ideas with more specific ideas, you divide your points. For example, in Javad's speech about the Tuskegee Airmen, he discussed the three obstacles the men overcame in his second point. He divided this main point about overcoming obstacles into three subpoints: (1) the belief that there was no need for a "colored squadron," (2) the fact that there were no commissioned Negro officers in the Air Force, and (3) the fact that they were not formally recognized as pilots until 1948.

Common sense tells us that when we divide a point, we must divide it into at least two parts because you can't divide something into only one part. But what if a point doesn't seem to divide naturally into two or more parts? For example, when Cassie began working on her speech about frivolous lawsuits, she intended to define only one legal term, not three. Thus, she wound up with only one subpoint for her main point about definitions. To solve this dilemma, she could have folded the definition into another point. For example, she could have defined the term tort while describing her first crazy lawsuit. Instead, she decided to expand her original point about important definitions and ended up with three subpoints.

Be careful when you fold one point into another. Make sure you discuss only one idea in each point so that your audience can follow your discussion and reasoning easily. For example, when Shelley spoke about threatened and endangered species, she divided the two ideas "threatened" and "endangered" into separate points rather than collapsing them into one. In doing so, she was able to help her audience understand the differences between the two categories.

Practicing the Public Dialogue

8.3

Build Your Preparation Outline

Using the template provided by your instructor or the sample at the end of this section as a guide, build a preparation outline for your next speech. Start by creating a title and indicating your specific purpose and thesis statement. Then outline your introduction, your main points, subpoints, sub-subpoints, and your conclusion. Add connectives that will help you transition from one idea to the next. Finally, add a section of the works you intend to cite in your speech, following the format provided by your instructor or this book. As you prepare your outline, remember to incorporate the tips you've read in this chapter: Translate incomplete sentences or keywords into full sentences; label the introduction, body, and conclusion of your speech; use the proper symbols to indicate your main points, subpoints, and sub-subpoints; indent your points properly; and correct any imbalances you discover in your points.

Online Resources

You can use Speech Builder Express to help create your outline. Select the appropriate speech parts from the left menu and follow the instructions. When you've entered all your information, click "Completing the Speech Outline" to view your preparation outline. If you like, you can then export your outline to Word and print it.

Figure **8.2**

Traditional and complex outlines

175

Traditional outline	Complex outline
I. Main point	I. Main point
A. Subpoint	A. Subpoint
1. Sub-subpoint	B. Subpoint
2. Sub-subpoint	1. Sub-subpoint
3. Sub-subpoint	a. Sub-sub-subpoint
B. Subpoint	i. Sub-sub-sub-subpoint
II. Main point	ii. Sub-sub-sub-subpoint
A. Subpoint	b. Sub-sub-subpoint
B. Subpoint	2. Sub-subpoint
1. Sub-subpoint	II. Main point
2. Sub-subpoint	

Check for balance. A speaker's goal is to offer an equal presentation of each main point, and your preparation outline will show whether your ideas are complete and balanced. If your presentation outline shows that one or two points get far more discussion than the others, reconsider your speech goals and how you have tried to accomplish them.

Suppose your preparation outline showed the structure illustrated by Figure 8.3. Note that the second main point is developed in far more detail than the first or third main point. Additionally, subpoints B and E are more fully developed than the others are. The outline shows an imbalance that needs to be corrected. Either the speech can be refocused to make the second main point the thesis statement, or some material can be eliminated from the second main point and some material added to the other two main points.

I. Main point
II. Main point
  A. Subpoint
  B. Subpoint
    1. Sub-subpoint
    2. Sub-subpoint
    3. Sub-subpoint
  C. Subpoint
  D. Subpoint
  E. Subpoint
    1. Sub-subpoint
    2. Sub-subpoint
    3. Sub-subpoint
    4. Sub-subpoint
    5. Sub-subpoint
III. Main point
  A. Subpoint
  B. Subpoint

Figure **8.3**

Imbalanced outline

© Cengage Learning

PREPARATION OUTLINE with Commentary

Why Pi?

by Katy Mazz

Specific Purpose: *To inform my audience about the number pi.*

Thesis Statement: *Pi, a fascinating number with an unusual history, has become an obsession for some people.*

CourseMate *Are you ready to build your preparation outline? Use the following outline as a model. You can use your CourseMate for* Invitation to Public Speaking *to watch a video clip of the speech Katy Mazz gave based on this outline. Katy gave this speech in an introductory public speaking class. The assignment was to give a four- to six-minute informative speech about any topic. Students were asked to create a preparation outline, to cite at least four sources, and to speak from a speaking outline or note cards. In addition, they were asked to end on a strong note. (You can read Katy's speaking outline later in this chapter.)*

Commentary

Katy labels her introduction to help keep her place as she gives her speech. The outline of her introduction is very detailed to help her account for and identify the four components of a strong introduction.

She indicates her specific purpose and thesis statement at the beginning of her preparation outline. This helps her stay audience centered, focused on her topic, and reminded of her speech goals.

Katy catches her audience's attention by reciting pi to thirty-one decimal places and by getting them curious about its presence in their lives.

In subpoint E, she reveals the topic of her speech.

Katy adapts her topic to her audience by indicating she knows her audience quite well—she recognizes they are all speech majors. She establishes her credibility by indicating she has researched her topic and is personally interested in it.

In the last point of her introduction, Katy previews the three main points of her speech.

By marking the body of her speech with a heading, she can clearly see where she must shift from her introduction to her first main point.

Notice that she uses complete sentences for each point.

She divides her first main point into two subpoints. In the first one, she explains what pi is and what makes it unusual. Notice how she uses a rhetorical question in her third sub-subpoint to spark her audience's interest.

In subpoint B, Katy continues to explain what pi is. Again, she presents interesting information to help her audience appreciate pi's popularity and intrigue.

In her first transition, Katy briefly restates her last point and introduces her second point, the history of pi. She sets the transition off so she can find it easily and see she is moving on to her second main point.

Introduction

I. 3.1415926535897932384626433832795. (*catch attention*)
   A. Most of you know the name of the number I just recited.
   B. It is found in rainbows, pupils of eyes, sound waves, ripples in the water, and DNA.
   C. It is a ratio that nature and music understand but that the mind cannot comprehend.
   D. This number has sparked curiosity over the past 4,000 years.
   E. I am talking about pi—not the dessert, but the circle ratio. (*reveal topic*)

II. I will try to present pi as the fascinating topic I think it is to a class of speech majors who wonder if they can survive a speech about math.
   A. I have researched this topic, finding information not only technical and historical but also fanatical. (*establish credibility*)
   B. My own interest came about when I was challenged to memorize more digits than a friend of mine.

III. I plan to inform you of what pi is, the history of pi, and how pi has created obsessions in people's lives. (*preview main points*)

Body

I. Even if you don't know what it represents, pi is a number that almost everyone is familiar with.
   A. When you divide the circumference of a circle by its diameter, the result will always equal pi.
      1. No matter the size of the circle, this division results in what is called the circle ratio.
      2. Although we refer to pi as 3.14 or 22/7, it is actually an irrational number, meaning that it cannot be represented as a fraction.
      3. The number pi is never-ending—or is it?
      4. For ages, mathematicians have puzzled, and have been almost ashamed, that it is so difficult to find another value as simple as the circle ratio.
   B. Pi is more than just the circle ratio.
      1. According to David Blatner, who wrote *The Joy of Pi*, this value can be found in all fields of math and science, architecture, the arts, and even in the Bible.
      2. The world record for calculating pi to the greatest number of decimal places is 206 billion decimal places, calculated by Dr. Kanada at the University of Tokyo.

Transition: Although 206 billion digits have been calculated thus far, there was a time in antiquity when there was uncertainty of the second decimal place.

II. Woven among pi's infinite digits is a rich history, ranging from the great thinkers of ancient cultures to the supercomputers of the twentieth century.
   A. Four thousand years ago, there was no decimal system, compass, paper, or pencil, yet people still found ways to calculate pi.
      1. The Egyptians used a stake, a rope, and the sand to approximate pi as a little greater than 3.
      2. The Greeks, Babylonians, Israelites, Chinese, and Mesopotamians also studied the circle ratio, yet none of them were certain of the third decimal place.
   B. Whether pi is an infinite number remained a mystery until the sixteenth century.

1. Petr Beckmann, a former professor of engineering at Colorado University, likes to call this period the age of the digit hunters, with each generation popping out more digits than the next.
   2. Keep in mind that at this point the electronic calculator had not yet been invented.
   3. Famous mathematicians of the time continued to break records for calculating pi.
   C. In the twentieth century, the invention of the computer allowed mathematicians to calculate pi to 16,000 digits, confirming that pi is infinite and totally random.

Transition: What is the fascination with pi that has caused people to be both fanatical and obsessed?

III. Blatner states, "People have calculated, memorized, philosophized, and expounded on" pi more than on any number in history.
   A. The Chudnovsky brothers, Gregory and David, were both mathematicians from Russia who moved to New York to entertain their obsession with pi.
      1. In their own apartment, they built a supercomputer from scrap materials.
      2. With this computer, they were able to calculate more digits and to study its use in various formulas.
   B. Other people try to memorize pi.
      1. Some do it for sport or to be silly, but others are more serious.
      2. Blatner states that in 1995, Hiroyuko Goto spent over nine hours reciting 42,000 digits of pi from memory, far exceeding the world record.
         a. This was a rare case, but there are methods of memorization for the average memory.
         b. Some people remember pi through poems, clever mnemonics, and songs.
         c. Some simply memorize the digits in groups of fours, which is the method I've found easiest.
   C. So many people are obsessed with pi that the number is celebrated on Pi Day every March 14, or 3/14.
      1. The website Ridiculously Enhanced Pi Page suggests that you gather with friends at 1:59 P.M. to celebrate.
      2. At this time, eat pie and share personal stories about pi.

Summary and transition: So ends my analysis of people's obsessions, but my earlier question was not fully answered.

Conclusion

I. No one knows for sure why pi has caused such a craze or why several books, movies, and web pages have been devoted to this subject. (*bring speech to an end*)
   A. What inspired the Chudnovsky brothers to devote their lives to the search for pi?
   B. What inspired me to write a speech on a silly number?
   C. The answer lies in the mystery of pi: People explore pi because it is an adventure to do so.

Katy divides her second main point into three subpoints that help her develop her discussion of pi's rich history. She develops her argument chronologically, from ancient history to the present era. Notice her use of subordination and proper indentation of each new point.

Katy shares interesting historical facts about math that appeal to her audience of speech majors.

Note her interesting language: "the age of the digit hunters" and "each generation popping out more digits." In this point, she uses her research creatively and stays audience centered.

Katy brings her audience up to the present era with subpoint C.

By asking another rhetorical question, she previews her third main point.

In her final point, Katy explains the obsession some people have with the number pi. In her three subpoints, she discusses a different aspect of this obsession.

In subpoint A, Katy tells a story of the Chudnovsky brothers and the lengths to which they went to study pi.

Katy uses Goto as an example of someone obsessed with memorizing pi and then shares some memorization methods that are easier. Notice that subpoint B is slightly more developed than subpoints A or C but that her three subpoints still are fairly evenly balanced.

Her third subpoint wraps up her discussion of the obsession with pi, using a lighthearted story of a tradition she learned on the Ridiculously Enhanced Pi Page website.

Katy includes a transition in her summary by returning to one of her questions from earlier in her speech. Also note that she marks her conclusion as a distinct part of her outline.

Katy begins her conclusion by answering her question about why pi has caused such a craze. She then summarizes her main points.

Notice that the outline of her conclusion includes a lot of detail. This helps her (1) make sure she has incorporated the two aspects of a strong conclusion and (2) see that her conclusion is shorter than her introduction and will take only a few moments to deliver.

Katy ends her speech with a quotation, leaving her audience with a strong sense of the mystique of the number pi.

Katy includes a bibliography of the specific research she references in her speech. She prepared this speech in 2000, and note that her sources range from 1971 to 2000, indicating that she did both historical and current research. She also relies on both Internet and print sources, illustrating that she searched in several places for material rather than relying on only one kind of source.

II. Remember that pi is not only the circle ratio, not only the biggest influence on math over history, but also a number that has a great effect on people and an influence on everything we do. (*reinforce thesis and summarize main points*)

III. William Schaaf, in *The Nature and History of Pi*, concludes that "probably no symbol in mathematics has evoked as much mystery, romanticism, misconception and human interest as the number pi."

Works Cited

Beckmann, Petr. *A History of Pi*. New York: St. Martin's Press, 1971.

Blatner, David. *The Joy of Pi*. New York: Walker and Company, 1997.

Blatner, David. "Pi Facts and Figures." *The Joy of Pi*. Accessed September 20, 2000. http://joyofpi.com/.

Ridiculously Enhanced Pi Page. Posted 1998. *The Exploratorium*. Accessed September 23, 2000. http://www.exploratorium.edu/pi/pi98/.

Schaaf, William. "The Nature and History of Pi." *The Joy of Pi*. Accessed September 20, 2000. http://www.joyofpi.com/schaaf.htm.

Witcombe, Chris. "Notes on Pi." *Earth Mysteries*. Sweet Briar College. Accessed September 23, 2000. http://witcombe.sbc.edu/earthmysteries/ EMPi.html.

© Cleve Bryant/PhotoEdit

You need your speaking outline to remember specific information you plan to use in your speech. Many speakers add delivery cues to their outlines to help them remember to pause, make eye contact, or use a visual aid. What delivery cues do you think you would use in your next speech?

The Speaking Outline

The **speaking outline**, sometimes called *speaking notes*, is a condensed form of your preparation outline that you use when speaking. Remember that you will almost never memorize a speech or read it from a manuscript. Most often, you will choose the exact words of your speech as you are giving it. Therefore, you need a speaking outline to help remember specific information that you plan to include in your speech. For example, your speaking outline might include the full text of quotations, statistics, names, and other material you want to remember exactly. It also includes delivery prompts, such as "make eye contact," "slow down," and "breathe."

The most effective speakers make frequent eye contact with their audience and speak directly to them. Their speaking outlines encourage them to do this. Because speakers do not have the full text written out in front of them, they are not tempted to read to the audience. Instead, they rely on the ideas, words, and phrases in their speaking outline to remind them of what they want to say.

Although you may feel you will give a better speech if much of it is written out fully on your speaking outline, experienced speakers have found this simply isn't so. The most dynamic speakers are those whose speaking outlines only prompt their memories and enable them to engage their audiences directly.

Speaking outlines are very personalized documents. As you gain experience speaking, you will discover what you need to include in your outline and what you can leave out. For now, use the following tips to help build your speaking outline.

Good to Know!

speaking outline: Condensed form of a preparation outline that you use when speaking.

Tips for the Speaking Outline

Use keywords and phrases. When you write your speaking outline, use keywords and phrases or abbreviated sentences. As you prepare this outline, think carefully about what words and phrases will help you remember your complete ideas. In the example here, notice how Graham reduced his full sentences to keywords, working from the larger idea to its most essential component:

Preparation outline

I. Many people are not aware of what a voucher system is.
   A. Voucher programs take taxpayers' money and give it to families.
      1. Families then use money to send children to the school of their choice.
      2. The school of choice could be either a public or private school.
   B. In theory, money that normally goes to public schools now is distributed to a range of schools.
   C. The program is touted as a new solution to the old problem of inadequate public education.

Speaking outline

I. The voucher system
   A. Taxpayers' money to families
   B. Money normally goes to public schools
   C. New solution to old problem

The keywords capture the essence of Graham's ideas and help him remember the full thought when he looks down at his notes. The keywords call to mind the full argument or explanation. They keep him talking and prevent him from reading his speech.

Write clearly and legibly. Many speakers print their speaking outline from a computer because the print is more legible than their handwriting. They also use a plain, easy-to-read font, often in a larger size than normal. (Similarly, speakers who write their outline by hand print larger than they normally do.) Notice the difference between these two font sizes:

Love conquers all.

Love conquers all.

Although in most writing we wouldn't use the larger font size, in a speaking outline the bigger letters make our speech much easier to deliver, especially if we're nervous.

Add cues for delivery. As you practice, notice where you tend to stumble, where you are too tied to the outline and forget to make eye contact, and where you move too quickly or slowly. Also notice where you have trouble with pronunciation or remembering what you want to say. Add cues to help you through these rough spots. Cues are words and phrases like "slow down," "pause," "look up," "show visual aid," and "make eye contact." They also include the correct pronunciation of any words that are hard for you to say, especially names, or a word or two to help you remember a complete idea or a part of a story or example you tend to forget. Add this final component of your speaking outline after you've written it and have practiced your speech a few times. If you've printed your outline from a computer, handwrite your cues. If you've handwritten your speaking outline, use a different color for your cues. Be sure to keep the cues brief so they don't distract you from your audience and your speech.

Note Cards

Some speakers prefer note cards to a speaking outline (Figure 8.4). Note cards (three-by-five or four-by-six inches) are smaller and less obvious than full sheets of paper. They also are sturdier and less likely to shake if a speaker's hands tremble. And they give us something to hold on to, sometimes making us feel a little more secure as we speak. If you feel more comfortable with note cards, follow these guidelines:

- Use keywords and phrases and place no more than five or six lines on each card. As with speaking outlines, do not write the full text of the speech on the cards.
- Write clearly and legibly. Print or type directly on the card, or if you handwrite your notes, use large, clear printing that is easy to read.
- Use only one side of the card. This reduces the likelihood that cards will get out of order during the speech.
- Number each card so you can easily reorder them if they get mixed up.
- Put cues for delivery on your cards so you can see them (use separate cards or different colors for these cues).
- When you deliver the speech, the cards should have a low profile. Try not to gesture with them, play with them, or tap them on the podium. You want the audience to pay attention to you, not the note cards.

Figure **8.4**

Sample note cards

—9—
Transition:

What is the fascination with pi that has caused
people to be both fascinated and obsessed?

(Pause)

III. As <u>Blatner</u> states, "People have calculated,
memorized, philosophized, and expounded
on" pi more than on any number
in history.

—10—

A. The Chudnovsky (chud-NOV-sky) brothers,
Gregory and David.
1. In their apartment, built a supercomputer
from scrap.
2. Calculated more digits and studied the
use of pi in various formulas.

B. Many other people try to memorize pi.
1. Some for sport or to be silly;
others are more serious.

—11—

2. <u>Blatner</u> states that in 1995, Hiroyuko
(he-roy-U-ko) Goto spent over nine hours
reciting 42,000 digits of pi from memory,
far exceeding the world record.

(Make eye contact)

a. This was a rare case

SPEAKING OUTLINE with Commentary

Why Pi?
by Katy Mazz

Are you ready to build your speaking outline? You can use the following outline as a model. Katy based her speaking outline on her preparation outline, and she modified it in places to account for problems she encountered with her delivery as she practiced her speech.

(Breathe)
(Make eye contact)

Introduction
I. 3.14159265358979323846264338332795

(Pause)

  A. Most of you know the name of this number.
  B. In rainbows, pupils of eyes, sound waves, ripples in the water, and DNA.
  C. Nature and music understand, but the human mind cannot quite comprehend.
  D. 4,000 years of curiosity.

(Pause)
(Make eye contact)

  E. I am talking about pi, the circle ratio.
II. Speech majors may wonder if they can survive a speech about math.
  A. My research turned up technical, historical, and fanatical information.
  B. What sparked my own interest.
III. Today, I'll share with you what pi is, the history of pi, and how pi has created obsessions in people's lives.

Body
I. Pi is a symbol that most everyone is familiar with.
  A. The circumference of a circle divided by its diameter.

(Slow)

  1. This number is also called the circle ratio.
  2. We refer to pi as 3.14 or 22/7, but it is an irrational number.
  3. Pi's mysticism is due to the fact it's never ending—or is it?
  4. Mathematicians have long puzzled about values as simple as the ratio of a circle.
  B. Pi is more than the circle ratio.
  1. According to David Blatner, who wrote <u>The Joy of Pi</u>, this value can be found in all fields of math and science, architecture, the arts, and even the Bible.
  2. The world record for calculating pi to the greatest number of digits is **206 billion decimal places**, calculated by <u>Dr. Kanada at the University of Tokyo</u>.

Commentary

At the top of her speaking outline, Katy makes notes to herself to breathe and make eye contact with her audience. She knows she'll be nervous, so she uses these notes to remind her to take a breath and look for friendly faces. She also makes a note to pause after she recites the digits of pi and before she goes on with her introduction.

Note that her introduction is an abbreviated version of the introduction in her preparation outline. She gives herself just enough cues to help her remember the four steps of her introduction.

To help with her delivery, Katy reminds herself to pause and make eye contact here before stating the topic of her speech.

She previews her speech in point III, stating her three main points.

Katy titles the body of her speech to remind her that she is moving to the main points. This is also a visual cue to help find her place after she makes eye contact with her audience.

She writes "slow" as she begins her first point to remind her to not rush through this information, which is new for many of her audience members.

Again, Katy gives herself enough text to remember her ideas, but not so much that she can fall prey to reading her speech to her audience.

Katy underlines the names of her sources and sets the

Organizing and Outlining Your Speech

numbers she wants to remember in bold so she'll deliver them correctly. Notice that she sets entire quotes in bold so she can find them easily and deliver them correctly.

She makes a note to pause before her transition so she can shift her pace a little to signal she is moving to a new point. She also writes out her full transition to remind her to deliver it—she's concerned that her nervousness will cause her to skip it and jump into her second main point.

As she did in her first main point, she underlines sources and sets in bold the facts she wants to remember.

Again, Katy writes out her transition, this time including a signal to pause after the transition before she begins her final main point.

In point III, Katy adds the phonetic spelling (spelled as they should sound) of two names so she will be sure to pronounce them correctly.

Her note to make eye contact signals her to look directly at her audience after she delivers the startling statistics of nine hours and 42,000 digits. This will help emphasize her point that this feat is rare but that people really are obsessed with pi.

When she practiced her speech, Katy noticed she tended to rush through her conclusion. She added notes to slow down and make eye contact so she would take time to wrap up her speech.

Katy ends her speech with

(Pause)

Although 206 billion digits have been calculated thus far, there was a time in antiquity when there was uncertainty of the second decimal place.

II. Pi has a rich history.
    A. Four thousand years ago, people could calculate pi, even without today's resources.
        1. The Egyptians approximated pi as a little greater than 3.
        2. The Greeks, Babylonians, Israelites, Chinese, and Mesopotamians were not certain of the third decimal place.
    B. The infinity of pi remained a mystery until the sixteenth century.
        1. <u>Petr Beckmann</u>, a former professor of engineering at <u>Colorado University</u>, calls this period **"the age of the digit hunters, with each generation popping out more digits than the next."**
        2. Keep in mind there was still no electronic calculator.
        3. Famous mathematicians continued to break records.
    C. In the twentieth century, the invention of the computer allowed mathematicians to calculate pi to **16,000 digits**.

What is the fascination with pi that has caused people to be both fanatical and obsessed?

(Pause)

III. As <u>Blatner</u> states, **"People have calculated, memorized, philosophized, and expounded on"** pi more than on any number in history.
    A. The Chudnovsky (Chud-NOV-sky) brothers, Gregory and David.
        1. In their apartment, built a supercomputer from scrap.
        2. Calculated more digits and studied the use of pi in various formulas.
    B. Many other people try to memorize pi.
        1. Some for sport or to be silly; others are more serious.
        2. <u>Blatner</u> states that **in 1995, Hiroyuko (He-roy-U-ko) Goto spent over nine hours reciting 42,000 digits of pi from memory, far exceeding the world record.**

(Make eye contact)

        a. This was a rare case.
        b. Some people remember pi through poems, mnemonics, and songs.
        c. Some memorize the digits in groups of fours.
    C. The number is celebrated on Pi Day every March 14, or 3/14.
        1. The Ridiculously Enhanced Pi Page suggests gathering at 1:59 P.M.
        2. Eat pie and share stories about pi.

So ends my analysis of people's obsessions, but my earlier question was not fully answered.

Conclusion

(Slow down!)
(Make eye contact)

I. No one knows why pi has caused such a craze.
    A. What inspired the Chudnovsky brothers?
    B. What inspired me?

C. The answer lies in the mystery and adventure.

II. The biggest influence on math over history and influences everything we do.

III. William Schaaf, in <u>The Nature and History of Pi</u>, concludes that "**probably no symbol in mathematics has evoked as much mystery, romanticism, misconception and human interest as the number pi.**"

Source: Adapted with permission from Katy Mazz.

a quote, so she underlines the source's name and sets the quote in bold so she won't stumble when she delivers the final words of the speech.

Practicing the Public Dialogue

8.4

Build Your Speaking Outline

Using the template provided by your instructor or the sample at the end of this section as a guide, build a speaking outline for your next speech. Translate the complete sentences of your preparation outline into keywords and phrases that will help you remember key ideas as you give your speech. Review your outline to make sure your ideas are outlined and easy to follow visually. Also make sure your computer-written text or handwriting is easy to read from a distance. If it isn't, adjust your printing, fonts, or type sizes so they are clear and legible. Finally, save a copy of your outline on your computer or make a few photocopies of it.

As you practice your speech, add your delivery cues. If you find your outline is too messy after several rounds of practice and adjustments, print a new one and add only those cues that you find most helpful (or mark up one of your photocopies). Remember, your speaking outline should be legible. Too many notes and changes will make it hard to read.

Online Resources

CourseMate If you'd like to see more examples of speaking outlines, use your CourseMate for *Invitation to Public Speaking* to access the video resources for this book. All the full-length student speeches are accompanied by speaking (keyword) outlines, preparation (full-sentence) outlines, and note cards. As you watch a speech, let the speaking outline scroll alongside so you can see how the outline compares with the speaker's delivery.

Chapter Summary

Organization is the systematic arrangement of ideas into a clear and coherent whole.

- To achieve this clarity, you must identify the main points of your speech.
- Main points are the most important ideas in a speech, developed from your research or your thesis statement.
- Use the time limit of your speech as a guideline for determining your number of main points. If you have too many points to cover in the time allotted

to speak, return to your thesis statement and narrow the scope of your presentation.

- Be sure each main point is separate and distinct, you use consistent wording for each point, and you devote the appropriate amount of coverage to each point.
- To show the relationships between your main points, use connectives: transitions, internal previews, internal summaries, and signposts.

Main points can be organized in five basic patterns.

1. Chronological

2. Spatial

3. Causal

4. Problem–solution

5. Topical

The preparation outline is the outline you use to prepare a speech.

- It contains your main points, subpoints, and sub-subpoints written out in complete sentences.

- This outline also includes the title of your speech, the specific purpose, and the thesis statement.
- It outlines your introduction and conclusion, labels each part of your speech clearly, and includes your connectives and a list of the research sources you plan to cite in the speech.

The speaking outline is the outline you use when you deliver your speech.

- Speaking outlines contain keywords and phrases rather than full sentences, ensuring that you will deliver your speech in a conversational manner.
- Some speakers prefer note cards to speaking outlines. Note cards are smaller and sturdier than a full sheet of paper.

◯ Invitation to Public Speaking Online

 CourseMate Now that you have read Chapter 8, use your Speech Communication Course-Mate for *Invitation to Public Speaking* for quick access to the electronic resources that accompany this text. These resources include

- **Study tools** that will help you assess your learning and prepare for exams (*digital glossary, key term flash cards, review quizzes*).
- **Activities and assignments** that will help you hone your knowledge and build your public speaking skills throughout the course (*Practicing the Public Dialogue activities, review questions*).

- **Media resources** that will help you explore public speaking concepts online (*Web Connect links, Enhanced eBook*), develop your speech outlines (*Speech Builder Express* 3.0), watch and critique videos of sample speeches (*Interactive Video Activities*), upload your speech videos for peer reviewing and critique other students' speeches (*Speech Studio online speech review tool*), and download chapter review so you can study when and where you'd like (*Audio Study Tools*).

This chapter's key concepts and review questions are also featured here.

Key Concepts

causal pattern (161)
chronological pattern (159)
connective (165)
coordination (171)
internal preview (166)
internal summary (166)

main points (156)
organization (156)
preparation outline (168)
problem–solution pattern (161)
signpost (167)
spatial pattern (160)

speaking outline (178)
subordination (173)
subpoint (169)
sub-subpoint (169)
topical pattern (162)
transition (165)

Review Questions

1. Write a specific purpose, thesis statement, main points, and subpoints for a speech on a topic of your choice. Now mix up those main points and subpoints and try to deliver a sketch of the speech to your classmates. Can they follow your organization? Why or why not?

2. Choose one of the following topics: M&M's® candy, Valentine's Day, or finals week. Using each of the five patterns of organization discussed in this chapter, write a specific purpose, thesis statement, and main points for a speech about the topic you chose. What is the emphasis in each speech, depending on its organizational pattern?

3. In class, write a possible speech topic on a three-by-five-inch card or a strip of paper. Pass your topic to your instructor. Your instructor will select several topics, ask you to get into groups of five, and distribute a topic to each group. With your group, write the specific purpose, thesis statement, and main points for a speech. Also write connectives for the speech, including each of the four types of connectives discussed in this chapter. Now deliver the sketch of your group's speech to the class (be sure to use your connectives).

4. Imagine you're going to give a speech describing your day from breakfast through dinner. Prepare a preparation outline for this speech. Make sure your outline includes the title of your speech, your specific purpose and thesis statement, an introduction, four main points with at least two subpoints per main point, connectives, and a conclusion.

5. Using the preparation outline from question 4, construct a speaking outline for your speech on your day. Add delivery cues as needed. Discuss the differences between your preparation outline and your speaking outline. What are the strengths and weaknesses of each?

6. Check out Speech Studio to see how effectively other students organized their speeches. Can you identify the organizational patterns they used? Or record a speech you're working on, upload it to Speech Studio, and ask your peers for their feedback. What feedback could you use to fine-tune your speech organization before you give your speech in class? ✓Studio

9

Introductions and Conclusions

IN THIS CHAPTER, YOU WILL LEARN TO:

- Describe the four functions of an effective introduction

- Prepare a compelling introduction

- Describe the two functions of an effective conclusion

- Prepare a compelling conclusion

- Identify at least four tips for preparing both an introduction and a conclusion

Introductions, even short ones, make an audience more willing to listen to a speech, think more highly of the speaker, and understand the speech better.[1] At the other end of the speech, conclusions reinforce thesis statements, remind listeners of main points, and frame the speaker's ideas and arguments in just the way he or she wants. Because the introduction and the conclusion are such important parts of a speech, they require special consideration. In this chapter, you will learn the basic techniques for developing each. As you read the following discussions, keep in mind that your introduction and conclusion frame the way you enter and exit the public dialogue.

Alexey Stiop/ Used under license from Shutterstock.com

The Introduction

Your introduction is your first contact with your audience. In the opening words of your speech, you set the stage for what's to come, connect your audience to your topic, and establish your purpose for speaking. Introductions are like first impressions—they are important and lasting. Because of this, introductions require all of your audience analysis skills (Chapter 4). To develop an introduction that allows you to connect with your audience in the way you want, consider the four functions of any introduction:

- Catch the audience's attention
- Reveal the topic to the audience
- Establish credibility with the audience
- Preview the speech for the audience

Notice that each objective is highly audience centered. Thus, you need to design your introduction, like the body of your speech, with your audience in mind. In each of the four components of the introduction, you consider the audience's perspectives and the reason the audience is listening to your speech as well as your own goals. Let's take a closer look at each of these components and then at some techniques for implementing them with effective introductions.

Catch the Audience's Attention

One of the most important tasks you have as a speaker is to capture the attention of your audience. You want your audience to listen to you and to be intrigued and curious about your topic. When you catch the audience's attention, you not only pique their curiosity, but you also show them how the topic relates to them. Keep in mind that however you get your audience interested in your topic, to act ethically, you must be honest, respectful, and behave in a manner consistent with the principles of an open and healthy public dialogue.

Reveal the Topic of Your Speech

In your introduction, you also want to let the audience know the subject of your speech. Although guessing games can be fun, your audience wants to know what you will be discussing. Keeping them in suspense for a moment or two is fine, but your introduction should reveal your topic before you begin your first main point.

Establish Your Credibility

As you've learned, to be credible is to gain the trust of your audience and to communicate to them that you have considerable knowledge of your topic. If your audience regards you as credible and competent, they will believe they have good reasons to listen to your ideas. Establishing credibility contains an ethical dimension. Audiences do not like to be lied to or misled. If you distort your credibility on a subject, your audience is less likely to believe you or be influenced by your speech.

Preview Your Speech

The fourth component of an introduction is to preview the main points of the speech. In your **preview**, you share with your audience a brief overview of each of the main points in your speech. Previews communicate to your audience that you are organized and competent. In setting the stage for the body of the speech, previews help your audience organize their thoughts about your topic and mentally prepare for what you're going to say next.

Good to Know!

preview: Brief overview in the introduction of a speech of each of the main points in the speech.

WILSON

THE APPEARANCE OF INTEGRITY

Establish your credibility early in your introduction so your audience understands why you're qualified to speak on your topic. But be careful to represent your expertise accurately and ethically. Audiences don't like to be misled.

Preparing a Compelling Introduction

There are several creative ways to gain your audience's attention, reveal your topic, establish your credibility, and preview your speech. Let's look at some techniques that will help you prepare compelling, memorable introductions.

Ask a Question

A question can arouse your listeners' curiosity and capture their attention. A question can also reveal the topic of your speech—the answer should relate to your topic. Sometimes, speakers use a **rhetorical question**, a question, used for effect, that the audience isn't supposed to answer out loud but rather in their own minds. At other times, speakers may ask questions to solicit answers directly from the audience. In the next two examples, Nathan asks rhetorical questions and supplies his own answers, and Cassie solicits answers from her audience before revealing the topic of her speech.

Do you think you could walk from New York to just beyond Chicago? How about from Georgia to Maine? If you're up for such a hike, take the route from Georgia to Maine—that will put you on the Appalachian National Scenic Trail, a trail that stretches over 2,000 miles and traverses fourteen states. This trail is also the topic of my speech today.

You've heard of the game "Strange but True"? Play with me for a minute. I'll read the headline, and you tell me if it's true or not. Ready? Okay.

"Surfer Sues Surfer for Theft of Wave." True or false?

"Deaf Bank Robber Wins Suit: Courts Say Alarm Exploited His Disability." True or false?

"College Student Falls Out Fourth-Story Window during Mooning Prank: Sues University for Negligence." True or false?

Each of these lawsuits is real, and these "crazy lawsuits" are the subject of my speech today.

Beginning a speech with a question, whether rhetorical or not, encourages active listening by your audience. Thus, questions can prevent your audience from sitting back passively as you speak. If you open your speech with a question, be sure it relates directly to your topic, and remember to pause after each question so the audience has time to answer it either aloud or in their heads.

Good to Know!

rhetorical question: Question, used for effect, that an audience isn't supposed to answer out loud but rather in their own minds.

Tell a Story

A second way to capture your audience's attention and reveal your topic is to tell a story. Remember from Chapter 6 that stories, or narratives, draw an audience into your speech by offering characters and dramas they can relate to. Stories also personalize topics that might seem remote or disconnected to some audience members. Notice how Brandi uses language creatively to draw her audience into her story.

> It seemed like such a harmless thing to do. What could be wrong with putting out a little food to help the foxes and deer make it through a hard winter? Besides, seeing wildlife in your backyard is one of the many benefits to living in Colorado. Or so thought a family who set out dog food, hamburger, and grains for foxes and deer near their home in the wooded foothills just outside Denver. But guess who also came to dinner? Tasty treats left in the family's backyard lured hungry mountain lions into the neighborhood. Not only did the wild cats like the hamburger, but they also had their eyes on one of their favorite prey, the deer.
>
> It didn't take long for the real trouble to start. Residents' cats and dogs began disappearing from their yards. Fear and anger set in, and people began calling officials to do something about the mountain lions. What started as a well-meaning effort for deer and foxes ended in the death of one of Colorado's favorite wild animals. The mountain lion was killed in a trap set out to make the neighborhood safe again.
>
> Hi, my name is Brandi Lafferty, and today I'd like to describe some of the negative consequences associated with feeding big game wildlife and encourage you to help keep our wildlife wild.

If you use a story in your opening, be sure it relates directly to your topic and clearly connects to the body of your speech. Sometimes, it's tempting to tell a great story just because it's a great story. Avoid this pitfall and use only stories that help introduce your topic.

Cengage Learning

CourseMate

Watch a video clip of student speaker Brandi Lafferty telling a story in her introduction. You can use your CourseMate for *Invitation to Public Speaking* to watch the video, respond to analysis questions, and compare your answers to those provided by the author.

Recite a Quotation or a Poem

You also can catch your audience's interest and reveal your topic through a quotation or poem. Quotations lend your speech the credibility of someone more famous or knowledgeable than you are. They also can teach lessons or illustrate perspectives that are relevant to your speech. Quotations can be quite simple or fairly complex. In a speech on adoption, Chad began with a simple quotation:

> Dennis Rainey, author of the book *One Home at a Time*, states, "I have a wife and six children, two of which are adopted—but I can't remember which ones."

Speaking about the terrorist attacks on New York City and Washington, D.C., in September 2001, Mike began with a more complex quotation:

> Mohandas K. Gandhi said, "When I despair, I remember that all through history the way of truth and love has always won. There have been murderers and tyrants, and for a time they can seem invincible. But in the end they always fail. Think of it: always."

In the next example, Jessica begins her speech with a poem to set the tone and reveal her topic:

© Spencer Grant / PhotoEdit

"May your thoughts be as glad as the shamrocks,

May your heart be as light as the song.

May each day bring you bright happy hours,

That stay with you all year long.

For each petal on the shamrock,

This brings a wish your way—

Good health, good luck, and happiness

For today and every day."

When some hear this Irish blessing, they think of a three-leaf clover. Others think of Ireland or St. Patrick. My family has its roots in Ireland, and we always think of all three. The shamrock has a long history of meaning for the Irish, and it represents the magical number 3. To fully understand the importance of the shamrock, though, you need to know how it became the symbol of Ireland. You must also understand how St. Patrick used it, and how it is represented every year by St. Patrick's Day. Even if you're not Irish, a little bit of information about the shamrock will help you enjoy your next March 17 celebration or understand those who make such a big deal of it.

Most people enjoy a good story, so telling one is a particularly effective way to catch an audience's attention. What are some interesting stories from your life that you could tell in the introduction to a speech? Would one of these stories relate to the topic of your next speech?

CourseMate

Notice, too, how Jessica establishes her credibility early in the introduction by referring to her family's roots in Ireland. She also connects her topic to her audience in the final sentences of the introduction.

When you use a quotation or poem, be sure it relates directly to your topic or illustrates the importance of your subject. Like stories, there are a lot of great quotations and poems, but you should only use one that sums up your topic and grabs your audience's attention. Also remember to cite the source of the quotation or poem and to deliver it so the audience knows it is a quotation or poem rather than your own words (for tips on delivery, see Chapter 11). To explore places on the Internet where you can find quotations for your introduction, access **Web Connect 9.1: Starting with a Quotation** through your CourseMate for *Invitation to Public Speaking*.

Give a Demonstration

When you demonstrate some aspect of your topic, you can capture your audience's interest and make them want to see or hear more. In the following example, Megan began by singing. After she had captured her audience's attention, she revealed the topic of her speech, the author of her song. In the second paragraph, she previewed her speech so her audience knew exactly what she was going to cover.

(*Begin by singing "Amazing Grace."*) Comfort is what I feel when I hear this song. No matter if I am at a funeral service or singing it in a choir, this song overwhelms me with a sense of peace. I know it has the same effect on others as well. But who was the man behind this song? And isn't it, as some say, a bit over-done? Dr. Ralph F. Wilson states that he used to think "Amazing Grace" was just that, overdone. Wilson says, "'saved a wretch like me,' come on, really now. But the author really was a wretch, a moral pariah." Wilson is the author of *The Story of John Newton*, and John Newton is the author of America's most popular hymn, "Amazing Grace."

But what happened to John Newton that made him a "moral pariah"? What happened in this man's life that it was only the "grace of God" that could save him? Well, today I'm going to share with you just how a "wretch" like John Newton wrote such a well-known hymn. I'll begin by telling you a little bit about his early life. Then, I'll tell you how he came to write "Amazing Grace." Finally, I'll conclude by discussing this hymn's legacy.

Speaking Visually

What's in a Tattoo?

According to Smithsonian.com, "Humans have marked their bodies with tattoos for thousands of years. These permanent designs—sometimes plain, sometimes elaborate, always personal—have served as amulets, status symbols, declarations of love, signs of religious beliefs, adornments and even forms of punishment."[2] The earliest examples of tattoos are found on the 5,200-year-old "Iceman" found along the Italian-Austrian border in 1991, and 4,000-year-old Egyptian female mummies. The Iceman's tattoos are thought to be the result of an effort to release pain, as they are found in random spots along his joints. The tattoos on the Egyptian mummies are believed to be artistic markers of status or permanent amulets designed to protect women during pregnancy. Ancient tattoos showed geometrical shapes and patterns, animals, mythical creatures, and plants. These artistic tattoos are thought to have marked status (high or low, depending on the era), and other tattoos were used to identify someone as a slave.

Facial tattoos—most commonly associated with the Maori of New Zealand and some Native American people such as the Cree—have also been found on the bodies of six mummified Greenland Inuit women who lived around 1475 A.D. In the Maori culture,

The head was considered the most important part of the body, with the face embellished by incredibly elaborate tattoos or "moko," which were

regarded as marks of high status. Each tattoo design was unique to that individual and since it conveyed specific information about their status, rank, ancestry and abilities, it has accurately been described as a form of ID card or passport, a kind of aesthetic bar code for the face.[3]

However, tattoos as markers or conveyors of information have also been used by sailors so that they could be easily identified should they drown, to identify prisoners of Nazi concentration camps, and as symbols of gang membership or activities.

A 2006 telephone survey conducted by the Pew Research Center found that 36 percent of Americans aged 18 to 25, 40 percent of those 26 to 40, and 10 percent of those 41 to 64 had a tattoo.[4] Today, the ten most popular tattoo designs are flowers, lettering, symbols, religious signs, skulls, Japanese designs, portraits, symbols of love, birds, and wildlife.[5] And although the excessively tattooed body was once seen as deviant or lower-class and placed on display at fairs and circuses, communication scholar Mindy Fenske argues that today's tattoos are a form of "writing on the body" that communicates a challenge to notions of class, acceptability, and even what a body is for and can do. Today's tattooed bodies, Fenske argues, are a "performance of resistance" and often serve as visual statements about someone's identity and the body's ability to speak out about or for something.[6]

Adam Radosavljevic/ Used under license from Shutterstock.com

Although not everyone has the talent to stand up and sing for their audiences, many speeches can be opened with some type of demonstration. Speeches about activities, sports, and art—about how to do anything—offer good possibilities for demonstrations.

When you use a demonstration to introduce your speech, make sure you can complete it in only a few minutes or even seconds. Introductions and conclusions are a relatively small part of the speech. In fact, as you will see later in this chapter, your introduction and conclusion should make up no more than 20 percent of your speech. Time your demonstration to make sure you'll have enough time for the rest of your speech. If your demonstration seems too long, think about using it in the body of your speech instead. In either case, practice your demonstration before the speech so you can make a positive impression on the audience.

Make an Intriguing or Startling Statement

An intriguing or startling statement is an excellent way to draw your audience in with the unknown or the curious. Let's look at a few examples of this technique:

> *Ohayoo gozaimasu.* You probably don't know what I just said. I just gave you the greeting for "good morning" in Japanese, the ninth most spoken language in the world. Having studied Japanese for over three years now, I would like to share a little bit about this intriguing language with you today. I know you're probably wondering, "Why should I care about the Japanese language when I live in the United States?" Well, according to the *Encyclopedia Britannica*, there are currently over 125 million speakers of Japanese worldwide. In today's world, that means you're more than likely to meet a Japanese speaker at least once in your life. Wouldn't it be a good idea to know at least something about his or her language?

> Today, I'll share some of what I know about the Japanese language with you. I'll first talk about Japanese body language, which is both similar to and different from American body language. Then, I'll discuss spoken Japanese, which requires a lot of practice to learn. Finally, I'll tell you a little about the written language, which contains over 50,000 characters and three alphabets.

In this example, Kelly illustrates all four criteria for a strong introduction. He catches the audience's interest in the first few lines, establishes his credibility in the third sentence, relates the topic to his audience in his final lines of the first paragraph, and previews his speech in the second paragraph.

As you read this next example, see if you can identify all four of the criteria for a strong introduction. Notice how Katy takes a little extra time in her introduction to relate the topic to her audience and to establish her credibility:

> 3.14159265358979323846264338327950. Most of you know the name of the number I just recited. It's a number found in rainbows, pupils of eyes, sound waves, ripples in the water, and DNA—a ratio that both nature and music understand but that the human mind cannot quite comprehend. This number has sparked curiosity in many minds over the past 4,000 years. I'm talking about pi—not the dessert, but the circle ratio.

> Now, a class of speech majors is probably wondering if they can survive a six-minute speech about math. My own interest came about when I was challenged to memorize more digits than a friend of mine could. As a result of that challenge, I have researched this topic, finding information not only technical and historical but also fanatical. Today, I plan to inform you of what pi is, the history of pi, and how pi has created an obsession in people's lives.

When you choose to introduce your speech with a startling statement, use caution. You want to startle rather than offend your audience. Beginning speakers sometimes fall into the trap of thinking that an offensive statement is appropriate because it will, indeed, startle. If you are thinking about using a statement that may be too graphic or inappropriate, find an acceptable alternative. Your startling statement should invite the audience to listen, not shut down communication. The website AmusingFacts.com contains many interesting, unusual, and startling facts. To find a fact that would be appropriate to include in your introduction, access this site via **Web Connect 9.2: Amusing Facts** through your CourseMate for *Invitation to Public Speaking*.

CourseMate

State the Importance of the Topic

Some speakers begin their speeches with clear statements of the significance or magnitude of a topic. When you state the importance of the topic, you tell the audience why they should listen. Tina used this technique to introduce a speech on a topic that seemed fairly ordinary but was actually quite relevant to her audience:

> Okay. Everyone look down at your feet. How many of you have shoes on? Just as I thought. Each of us has a pair of shoes or sandals on our feet. But how many know where those shoes come from? And let's be honest. How many women in the audience have shoes with heels of an inch or more? Um-hmm, don't answer. And for the men, do you steer the women in your lives toward the heels in the shoe stores? Maybe even some of you men own a pair of heels? Well, when I look in my closet, I see one pair of sneakers, two pairs of boots, and a dozen high-heeled shoes. But do I know where these shoes come from or how heels were invented? No. At least not until I did some research into my shoe fetish.
>
> Today, I'd like to share the story of shoes with you. I'd like to discuss the origination of shoes, the changes they've gone through, the invention of high heels (which originally were made for men, by the way), and the troubles those heels have caused.

In this example, Tina states the importance of her topic by reminding her audience that wearing shoes is something almost everyone does but that it can have troubling consequences for some.

You also can state the importance of a topic by showing that although a practice or phenomenon is uncommon, it has a significant impact. Will did this in his speech about germ-line engineering and cloning:

> Imagine a world filled with humans who are genetically perfect, with no flaws or birth defects—humans who are superior to what we know today. Now imagine there's no shortage of body parts for transplants or to repair what we now call "irreparable" injuries, because an exact replica of each person is available—strictly for donation. Although these two notions seem far-fetched, we may be coming closer to this imaginary world than we realize.
>
> The two processes I asked you to imagine are called germ-line engineering and cloning, the topic of my speech. I know most of you are familiar with these ideas from science fiction novels, movies, and television, but in the next few decades, you may be able to visit your local geneticist to create a designer baby or maybe even have yourself cloned. I realize there are serious moral and ethical concerns about genetic engineering. However, I'd like to invite you to consider that the benefits of these two forms of engineering far

Gilbert Garrigue/WireImage/Getty Images

U2 singer Bono is known for giving speeches with particularly memorable introductions, often making intriguing statements to great effect. Think about the last speech you watched or listened to. How well was the introduction presented? Was it interesting or startling or funny? Did it draw you into the speech?

outweigh the disadvantages. Today, I'll describe the two processes for you, germ-line engineering and cloning, and then share the advantages of these processes. I'll then discuss two ways that those of us in this room are likely to be affected by these forms of genetic engineering and then open the floor for discussion.

Share Your Expertise

Although you know your qualifications for speaking on a subject, your audience may not. Establishing credibility does not mean boasting and bragging. Instead, it means you share your expertise with your audience. Recall how Jessica, Kelly, Katy, and Tina stated their credibility in their introductions:

- *Shamrocks.* My family has its roots in Ireland.
- *Japanese Language.* Having studied Japanese for over three years now, I would like to share a little bit about this intriguing language with you today.
- *Why Pi?* As a result of that challenge, I have researched this topic, finding information not only technical and historical but also fanatical.
- *History of Shoes.* Well, when I look in my closet, I see one pair of sneakers, two pairs of boots, and a dozen high-heeled shoes. But do I know where these shoes come from or how heels were invented? No. At least not until I did some research into my shoe fetish.

Establishing your credibility often is a subtle process. In these examples, the speakers revealed their expertise by illustrating their qualifications to speak about their topics. They referred to family, study, research, and personal experience to communicate their competence. Use these same techniques to establish your credibility in your speeches. And remember, your credibility also comes through your research (Chapter 5), the development of your ideas (Chapter 6), your reasoning (Chapters 7 and 16), your organization (Chapter 8), and your delivery (Chapter 11).

State What's to Come

Previewing your speech is a necessary component of your introduction. When you preview your speech, you give your audience an overview of your main points. This is important because even the best listeners need help following and remembering a speaker's ideas throughout a speech. When your audience hears a preview, they will anticipate your main points, be prepared to listen to them, and not be surprised or confused.

The best previews are brief; they set the audience up for what's to come but do not go into too much detail. Here's how Nathan and Cassie previewed their speeches:

- *Appalachian Trail.* First, I'll give you a brief history of the trail's formation. Then, I'll share some facts with you about the trail itself and how it's maintained. Finally, I'll tell you the stories from some of those who have hiked the trail.
- *Crazy Lawsuits.* In my research, I found many crazy cases that actually have gone to court, and today, I'll discuss some of the craziest. I'll begin with some basic legal terms that come up in these cases so you can follow them more easily. Then I'll share with you some of my favorite cases and give you a sample of the kinds of things that tie up our court system. Finally, I'll persuade you that

we should help those who are organizing to control these lawsuits and stop the abuses of our legal system.

In each of these examples, the speakers used variations of "first, then, finally" to identify the order of main points Although this language might seem unimaginative, spoken language is quite different from written language (Chapter 10). Audiences need extra tools to help them absorb and remember a speaker's ideas. (This is also why connectives are so helpful to audiences.) Explicit language like that used in the previews here increases the likelihood that your audience will understand your ideas, follow them throughout the speech, and remember them when the speech is over.

Public Speaking and Service Learning: Engaging Community

In her work at the International House, Brittany Urban, a public speaking student at Colorado State University, was assigned to be a guide for a blind student, Noah, from Oman. Brittany quickly became aware of not only the difficulties a blind person faces on a daily basis but also the appreciation for the external world that sighted people often take for granted. Brittany used this eye-opening experience to create a poignant introduction and conclusion to her in-class speech on her service organization.

Never having been a guide to a blind person, the first days were extremely stressful—with every misstep, stumble, or doorway, I became increasingly tense. However, over time the stress changed to respect and enlightenment. Guiding Noah through a few hours of his day has made me appreciate all the things I can do by myself. During a walk, Noah once commented on the smell of the air and, although he meant little by it, it touched my busy lifestyle and halted the ever-present task list running through my mind.

I was able to use my personal experiences with Noah in the introduction and conclusion for my informative speech on the International House organization. I feel that without interjecting my personal experience and revelations into this speech, the supporting material in the body of my speech would have taken a much more superficial tone. I chose to open with a summary of Noah's average daily difficulties and adaptations and to close the speech by explaining how witnessing his life has made me never take my vision for granted.

"I FEEL THAT WITHOUT INTERJECTING MY PERSONAL EXPERIENCE AND REVELATIONS INTO THIS SPEECH, THE SUPPORTING MATERIAL IN THE BODY OF MY SPEECH WOULD HAVE TAKEN A MUCH MORE SUPERFICIAL TONE."

Tips for Incorporating Service Learning into Public Speaking:

- Often, great ideas for introductions and conclusions come during or even after writing the main body of a speech. Don't become frustrated if you can't "start at the beginning" by writing a great introduction right away.
- When brainstorming your introduction, think of the different ways speakers you've heard have opened their speeches. How did they grab your attention right away? Is there a way to incorporate some of the techniques they used into your speech?
- If you are struggling when writing your conclusion, look back to your introduction and tie up any loose ends. Answer any questions you asked, repeat a powerful phrase, or just bring the audience's attention back to the opening narrative or example. Doing this creates a well-rounded feel to your speech—it brings your audience back to where they began and also helps them see what they've learned along the way.

Introductions and Conclusions

Tips for Your Introduction

Look for introductory materials as you do your research. As you conduct research on your speech topic, look for stories, quotations, startling facts or statements, and other material for your introduction. If you collect material you might use in your introduction, you will have several options to choose from, so you can select the one that suits your audience and your goals best.

Prepare and practice the full introduction in detail. Introductions represent your first opportunity to connect with your audience, so prepare and practice the introduction completely before you give your speech. If you are opening with a story, practice telling the full story until you can tell it with ease and flair. If you are opening with a quotation, memorize it. If you plan to begin with a demonstration, rehearse it until you have it perfected. Introductions set the stage for what's to come, so you want this part of the speech to go flawlessly. Use your notes as infrequently as possible, if at all, and be sure to make maximum eye contact. Practice your full introduction until you can deliver it smoothly and confidently. A well-delivered introduction will not only enhance your credibility but will also increase your confidence as you move into the body of your speech.

Be brief. Remember, introductions tell just a little of what's to come and set the stage for the body of the speech. Introductions should be brief, only 10 to 15 percent of the speech. If they are longer, they become tedious. They also cut into the time you need for your main points. If your planned introduction is longer than 10 to 15 percent of your speech, you probably have included too much detail. Remember, your goal is not to give your speech in the introduction but to get the audience ready to hear your speech.

Be creative. Creativity is one of the best ways to capture an audience's attention and reveal your topic. Creative doesn't necessarily mean "elaborate and artistic." In this case, creativity means simply using your imagination to come up with new ideas and perspectives on how to open your speech until you find something that works just right. Trying out several of the techniques in this chapter will help you prepare a creative and effective introduction.

Practicing the Public Dialogue

9.1

Prepare Your Introduction

In class, generate a list of six to eight possible speech topics. Divide into groups, one for each topic. In each group, write an introduction for a speech on the topic you've chosen. Be sure to include the four parts of an introduction and one of the techniques for making it compelling. Now share this introduction with the class and get feedback on its effectiveness.

Online Resources

You can use Speech Builder Express to help you create your introduction. Select "Introduction" from the left menu and follow the instructions. For short reminders from this chapter about effective introductions, click the "Tutor" button. Once you've created your introduction, Speech Builder Express will save it as part of your overall outline until you are ready to complete the next step in the speech process.

The Conclusion

Your conclusion is your final contact with your audience. Just as the introduction represents the first impression you make on your audience, the conclusion represents your last impression. Because this last impression will linger with your listeners long after your speech is over, take time to prepare your conclusion so you end your speech with as much care as you began it. Then practice that conclusion so you can deliver it in just the way you want. When you deliver your conclusion, you have two primary goals:

- Bring your speech to an end
- Reinforce your thesis statement

Effective conclusions reinforce your thesis statement and indicate clearly that you are ending your speech. For example, if you were speaking about military rituals, you could describe several traditional rituals, present their history, and discuss their obvious and subtle meanings. When you concluded your speech, you could illustrate your thesis by describing an actual ritual, such as the one shown here that was used in 2009 to commemorate the victims of the terrorist attacks on September 11, 2001. In addition, you could use a visual aid, such as a photo like this one, to reinforce the meanings of the ritual.

UPI/David Handschuh/Pool/newscom

End Your Speech

When you end a speech, you are signaling to the audience that your presentation is over. Rather than ending abruptly or just trailing off, you want to communicate clearly that the speech is wrapping up. This signal comes through your words as well as your style of delivery. The more audience centered you are, the more effective your conclusion will be.

Like the close of a conversation, the conclusion of a speech exhibits a shift in style.[7] Generally, closure in conversations is signaled by a pause, a change in the rate of speaking, and even a different tone of voice. In speeches, we use these same cues. When you've concluded your final main point, use these shifts in delivery to signal to your audience that you are about to wrap up.

Another effective way to signal the end of your speech is with a concluding transition. These are simple words and phrases such as "in closing," "in summary," "in conclusion," "let me close by saying," and "my purpose today has been." Although these transitions seem obvious, they alert your listeners that you are moving from the body of your speech to your conclusion. These transitions also will help you incorporate the techniques discussed in the next section.

Reinforce Your Thesis Statement

The second function of your conclusion is to reinforce the thesis statement of your speech. Recall from Chapter 3 that your thesis statement summarizes, in a single declarative sentence, the main ideas, assumptions, or arguments you want to express in your speech. When you restate or rephrase your thesis statement in your conclusion, you remind your audience of the core idea of your speech. Notice how this reinforcement can be very succinct, as in Chad's speech on adoption, or more elaborate, as in Katy's on pi:

> In my family, I have two parents, an older sister, and two younger brothers. One of them is adopted, but in my heart I could not tell you which one.

In conclusion, no one knows why pi has caused such a craze or why several books, movies, and fanatical web pages have been produced on this subject. What inspired the Chudnovsky brothers to devote their lives to the search for pi? What inspired me to write a speech on a silly number? The answer lies in the mystery. Exploring pi is an adventure, which is why people do it. I want you to remember pi not only as the circle ratio, not only as the biggest influence on math over the course of history, but as a number that has an influence on everything we do.

Restating your thesis statement reinforces your arguments and encourages your audience to remember your speech.

Preparing a Compelling Conclusion

There are several techniques for signaling the end of a speech and reinforcing your thesis statement. You likely will combine several of these techniques to deliver a comprehensive conclusion. As you develop your conclusion, remember to continually ask yourself, "What final ideas do I want to leave with my audience?"

Summarize Your Main Points

An effective tool for ending your speech and restating your thesis statement is a summary of your main points. A **summary** is a concise restatement of your main points at the end of your speech. You use it to review your ideas and remind your audience of what's important in your speech. Will used this technique in his conclusion:

> As you've seen in these last few minutes, ideas that have been presented to us as fiction may soon be reality. Germ-line engineering and cloning may soon be processes that are used in our everyday life. Both techniques raise ethical questions and concerns, especially as we consider the advantages and disadvantages of each. I have shared some of my own thoughts about these issues in this presentation; I'd now like to open it up for questions and discussion.

When you summarize your main points, remember to do three things. First, offer only a summary—don't restate too much of your speech. The audience has already heard the details, and you are only trying to reinforce the key ideas and help them remember what you've said. Second, don't introduce new ideas into the summary. If you didn't bring an idea up in the body of the speech, don't raise it in the conclusion. New ideas in a conclusion will only confuse your audience. Finally, try to use the same kind of language in your summary that you used in the body of your speech. Familiar phrasing will help your audience recall your main ideas rather than forcing them to figure out what the new wording means.

Answer Your Introductory Question

If your speech begins with questions, answer them in the conclusion. This technique reminds the audience of what they've learned in the speech. Nathan, who began with questions about hiking the Appalachian Trail, returned to those questions in his conclusion:

> So, now do you think you could walk from New York to Chicago or from Georgia to Maine? Well, even if you're not up for the hike, many others have been.

Good to Know!

summary: Concise restatement of the main points at the end of a speech.

As a result of the efforts to maintain the Appalachian Trail, individuals have hiked the 2,200-mile-long footpath to raise funds, overcome disabilities, and seek out spiritual insights. The next time someone asks you if you want to "take a hike," perhaps you'll say, "why not?"

Refer Back to the Introduction

Occasionally, a speaker opens with a word, phrase, or idea and then returns to it in the conclusion. Like answering introductory questions, this technique brings the speech full circle and provides a sense of completeness. This technique usually is combined with others, such as summarizing the main points. Recall Kelly's speech about the Japanese language. After he summarized his ideas, Kelly returned to his opening as he concluded his speech:

> Thank you for listening, or as they say in Japan, *doomo arigatoo gozaimashita.*

Reggie, who opened his speech with a story of a boy's battles with chronic health problems, finished the story in his conclusion. After restating his thesis, he said,

> And that boy I told you about in the opening of my speech? Well, I'm that boy, I'm now nineteen, doing fine, and in fact, I haven't set foot in a hospital for over four years now.

For more on the methods of creating a speech conclusion, complete the activity at **Web Connect 9.3: Ending Effectively** through your CourseMate for *Invitation to Public Speaking.*

Recite a Quotation

When you conclude with a quotation, you rely on someone else's words to reinforce your thesis statement. A concluding quotation should come from someone you cited in your speech or from a famous person the audience will recognize. In the following example, Tina returns to a source she had cited earlier in her speech:

> As we've heard today, shoes have gone through great changes over time. What started with animal skins and then lace transformed itself into the twenty-four-inch heels worn by both men and women and on to the modern look we know today. But as Dr. Rene Cailet says, "Shoes should protect the foot and not disturb it. Having sore feet is not normal. As in any body part, pain is a signal that something is wrong."

Tips for Your Conclusion

Look for concluding materials. As you research your speech, look for materials you can use in your conclusion. You may find just the right summary or technique if you keep in mind the kind of conclusion you want to create. If you find more quotations than you can use in the body of your speech, try to select one for your conclusion. Or if a story is too long to tell in the introduction, think about saving part of it for the conclusion. As you research and develop your speech, you will come across effective materials for your conclusion. Save them and then draw from these options to create an ending your audience will appreciate.

Courtesy of NASA

Bring your speech around full circle by referring to your introduction in your conclusion. For example, if you were speaking about space exploration, you could begin your speech with the story of Galileo's first vague glimpse of Saturn's rings. You could then end with a description of the Cassini-Huygens mission to Saturn and Titan, which yielded stunning new images of Saturn and its moons unlike any seen before. What ideas do you have for concluding your next speech in a memorable way?

CourseMate To see a good example of a speaker who uses her conclusion to enhance her credibility, watch a video clip of student speaker Chelsey Penoyer. As you watch Chelsey speak, notice the startling statement she makes about her experience with her speech topic. How does her statement enhance her credibility? You can use your CourseMate for *Invitation to Public Speaking* to watch the video, respond to analysis questions, and compare your answers to those provided by the author.

Be creative. Your conclusion is your last contact with your audience. Your creativity should keep your listeners interested until the very end and help them remember your ideas and arguments after your speech is over. A creative conclusion, like Nathan's or Reggie's, can emerge from a clear summary and a reference back to the introduction. Or it may involve sharing a quotation or finishing a story begun in the introduction. Whatever technique you use, it must suit your audience, speech goals, and the tone of your speech.

Be brief. Conclusions should make up only 5 to 10 percent of the total speech. Remember, conclusions don't introduce new information; they bring closure to the ideas already presented. If you find your conclusion is running too long, you may be finishing a main point you did not cover completely in the body or providing too much detail in your summary. If your conclusion is too long, reduce its scope and detail.

Don't leave the conclusion to chance. Take time to prepare the conclusion carefully before you deliver the speech. Your last contact with your audience should be one that enhances your credibility and strengthens your arguments. Make sure you know what you want to say and rehearse your closing words carefully so you can make eye contact with the audience and end your speech with confidence and assurance.

STUDENT SPEECH with Commentary

Foothills Gateway: Vote YES on Referendum 1A
by Mike Piel

Specific purpose: To persuade my audience to vote yes on Referendum 1A.

Thesis statement: Voting yes on Referendum 1A is a good idea because it will save Foothills Gateway, a community organization that serves people with mental disabilities at little cost to the taxpayer.

CourseMate *As you craft the introduction and conclusion of your next speech, you can use the following speech as a model. Use your CourseMate for* Invitation to Public Speaking *to watch the video clip of Mike Piel's speech. As part of a service learning assignment, Mike gave this speech in an introductory public speaking class. The assignment was to give a four- to five-minute persuasive speech about a local issue. After you watch the video, respond to the analysis questions and compare your answers to those provided by the author.*

Commentary

Mike begins with two rhetorical questions and a compelling statistic that captures the audience's attention and relates his topic to his audience.

Introduction

How many of you are planning on having children? How many of you are planning on having a child with a mental disability? None?

Unfortunately, this is a reality that so many people in this world have to face day to day. In fact, one of every four people in Larimer County alone is in some way affected by someone with a mental disability. Luckily for these people, a community organization called Foothills Gateway is here to make their lives a little easier. Unfortunately, this great organization is in danger of losing its funding. The only way to prevent this from happening is to vote yes on Referendum 1A in the upcoming election. To make you more aware of the situation, I'm going to take the next few minutes to inform you of several things. I will let you know what it is exactly that Foothills Gateway does, why passing this referendum is such a good idea, and lastly, how it's going to affect you, the taxpayer.

He reveals his topic and states his goal. He establishes his credibility by explicitly stating this goal and by stating he will address the impact of this vote on taxpayers.

Mike finishes his introduction by previewing his speech. Notice how he clearly states his three main points and adapts his last point to his audience.

Conclusion

Now, over the last few minutes, I have tried to inform you about what Foothills Gateway does, why this referendum is a good idea, and a little bit about how it's going to affect you, the taxpayer. I'll try to appeal to your good sense, your good nature as human beings—don't turn your back on people who are less fortunate than you, because if you don't take care of them, nobody else will. So please vote yes when you go to the ballot. Thank you.

Mike signals the end of his speech with the phrase "over the last few minutes" and by restating his three main points.

He makes a direct appeal to his audience, reinforcing his thesis and reminding his audience of his purpose for speaking—to persuade them to vote yes on the referendum. Notice how he makes a direct, yet simple, appeal to their emotions, ending his speech on a strong note of human interest and compassion.

○ Chapter Summary

A speech's introduction is your first contact with your audience.

- An introduction has four objectives:

  1. To catch your audience's attention.

  2. To reveal your topic.

  3. To establish your credibility.

  4. To preview your speech.

- To accomplish these four goals, use a variety of techniques, such as asking a question, telling a story, reciting a quotation or poem, giving a demonstration, beginning with an intriguing or startling statement, or stating the importance of your topic.

Several tips are useful to remember when you create your introduction.

- Look for introductory materials as you do your research.
- Make the introduction brief, no more than 10 to 15 percent of the speech.
- Be creative.
- Practice the full introduction carefully before you give the speech.

A speech's conclusion expresses the final words in your speech.

- A speech conclusion has two goals:

  1. To signal the end of your speech.

  2. To reinforce your thesis statement.

- To indicate that you have reached the conclusion of your speech, use pauses, shifts in the rate and tone of your delivery, and transitions.
- Several other techniques can help you leave a lasting impression with your audience, including summarizing your main points, providing the ending to a story begun in the introduction, answering a question raised in the introduction, referring back to a comment made in the introduction, and summing up your speech with a quotation.

Several tips will help you with your conclusion.

- As with the introduction, look for effective concluding materials during your research.
- Be creative and brief.
- Conclusions should be no more than 5 to 10 percent of your speech.

- Don't leave your conclusion to chance. Develop it carefully and practice it until you can deliver it with confidence.

To be effective, introductions and conclusions must be audience centered.

- To connect positively with your audience in the opening moments of your speech, consider who your listeners are and what kinds of appeals will be appropriate and interesting to them.
- Similarly, to leave a lasting and effective impression with your audience, consider how they feel about your topic.

Invitation to Public Speaking Online

 CourseMate Now that you have read Chapter 9, use your Speech Communication Course-Mate for *Invitation to Public Speaking* for quick access to the electronic resources that accompany this text. These resources include

- **Study tools** that will help you assess your learning and prepare for exams (*digital glossary, key term flash cards, review quizzes*).
- **Activities and assignments** that will help you hone your knowledge and build your public speaking skills throughout the course (*Practicing the Public Dialogue activities, review questions*).

- **Media resources** that will help you explore public speaking concepts online (*Web Connect links, Enhanced eBook*), develop your speech outlines (*Speech Builder Express 3.0*), watch and critique videos of sample speeches (*Interactive Video Activities*), upload your speech videos for peer reviewing and critique other students' speeches (*Speech Studio online speech review tool*), and download chapter review so you can study when and where you'd like (*Audio Study Tools*).

This chapter's key concepts and review questions are also featured here.

Key Concepts

preview (187) rhetorical question (188) summary (198)

Review Questions

1. Name eight different techniques for catching the attention of the audience and revealing the topic of a speech. Identify the strengths of each technique.

2. Why should speakers establish their credibility and preview the main points of a speech? Are these components of an introduction important?

3. Suppose you have been asked to give a speech on the history of bubble gum. How would you establish your credibility on this topic? How creative do you think you could be in introducing this topic? Give examples of how you would establish your credibility and creativity.

4. Name four different techniques for concluding a speech. Identify the strengths of each technique.

5. In class, write a possible speech topic on a slip of paper and trade that paper with another student. Now write an introduction and a conclusion for a speech on that topic using the techniques discussed in this chapter. Present your introduction and conclusion to the class for feedback on each of their components.

6. Check out Speech Studio to see how other students handled their speech introductions and conclusions. Do the techniques they used give you ideas for your own introductions and conclusions? Or record a speech you're working on, upload it to Speech Studio, and ask your peers for their feedback. What feedback could you use to fine-tune your introduction and conclusion before you give your speech in class? **Studio**

Language

JAMES R. BRANTLEY/The Washington Times /Landov

10

- **Language Is Ambiguous**
- **Language and Culture**
- **Language and Gender**
- **Language and Accuracy**
- **Language and Public Speaking**
- **Language, Imagery, and Rhythm**

IN THIS CHAPTER, YOU WILL LEARN TO:

- Use clear and accurate language in your speeches
- Use culturally inclusive and gender-inclusive language
- Explain the differences between spoken and written language
- Describe at least three ways to use language to create memorable images
- Describe at least four ways to use language to create a pleasing rhythm

Language, the system of verbal or gestural symbols a community uses to communicate, is central to the speech-making process. Yet we often take language for granted, failing to realize how much of our knowledge comes from language rather than from direct experience. Some would say that objects exist in the world around us and that people use language to describe those objects as they truly are. However, most now believe the way we know something is through the words we use to describe it.[1] For example, even though a dog may sit directly in front of a group of people, one person may describe the dog as a large, clumsy, furry, lovable animal; another as an unpredictable, aggressive, frightening nuisance; and another as a hairy, smelly, extra mouth to feed. Language, it seems, can be a tool we use to shape and describe the world around us. Communication scholars agree that language, the systematic code of a group of people, is central to establishing and maintaining societies.

In the public dialogue, language allows us to share our thoughts, question the ideas of others, and invite our audiences to consider our positions. In Chapter 2, we discussed language as it relates to listening. In this chapter, we explore language as it relates to speaking. Specifically, we discuss the ambiguity of language, culture and language, gender and language, the accurate use of language, the importance of language in public speaking, and several of the linguistic devices public speakers use to create memorable images and a pleasing rhythm.

Language Is Ambiguous

If a speaker never utters a word but instead communicates through mime and gesture, how well do you think you would understand the speech? What if a speaker delivered the speech in a different language? Could you grasp the intricacies of the message? Obviously, understanding others when we do not share a common language is difficult. But if we share a common language with our audience, shouldn't communication be easier? Isn't it enough to use the same labels for things to communicate a message? How much attention must we give to the language in our speeches if we speak the same language as our audience? Consider the semantic triangle of meaning, created in 1923 by C. K. Ogden and I. A. Richards,[2] as shown in Figure 10.1.

Figure 10.1

Semantic triangle of meaning

Notice that the line at the bottom of the triangle is broken, reflecting the arbitrary nature of language. There is not necessarily a connection between a symbol and a referent because the words (symbols) we use to name things (referents) are human inventions. For example, the symbol freedom is just an English word we've come up with to name its referent, the state in which someone lives without undue restraints and restrictions. What other symbols for the experience of "freedom" can you think of?

On the left corner of the triangle is the **symbol**, the word or phrase spoken by the speaker. For example, when a speaker says "freedom," as did Martin Luther King Jr. in his "I Have a Dream" speech, or "homeland security," as did George W. Bush when he spoke to the nation about terrorism and security, those words are the symbols. On the right corner of the triangle is the **referent**, the object, concept, or event the symbol represents. In our two examples, the referent is the actual experience of freedom or the importance of national security. You might also think of this as the denotative definition of a word or event. This is the commonly held definition of a word or the actual object or event named by the speaker.

At the top of the triangle is the **thought**, or **reference**. This is the memory and past experiences audience members have with an object, concept, or event. When a speaker offers a word or phrase, audience members recall their own experiences with that word or phrase. These are our connotative definitions, our personalized, subjective interpretations of words, objects, or events. So the symbols "freedom" and "homeland security" call to mind a variety of connotative experiences and memories for the members of an audience.

The semantic triangle of meaning shows us that even though all the audience members might understand the symbol and even have a similar referent for it, they do not have the same thoughts, or references, for the symbol. This difference is what makes language ambiguous. The experience of freedom or the desire for national

Good to Know!

language: System of verbal or gestural symbols a community uses to communicate. **symbol:** Word or phrase spoken by a speaker. **referent:** Object, concept, or event a symbol represents. **thought**, or **reference:** Memory and past experiences that audience members have with an object, concept, or event.

security (or any referent) differs among people and groups depending on their culture, geographical location, and master statuses. For some, freedom is a given. For others, freedom is something that has been fought for over the centuries. Similarly, homeland security means different things to different people depending on their military affiliations, religions, and personal experiences with terrorism.

Public Speaking and Service Learning: Engaging Community

In her service at Special Needs Swim, Natasha Alers worked in a unique program that offers therapeutic aquatic services to a wide range of people with disabilities. When Natasha spent time partnering with three diverse clients, she was able to see how her interactions with them provided her learning opportunities to enhance many of her public speaking skills, particularly her choices of verbal and nonverbal feedback.

The last few weeks I have split my time between three participants: an older blind woman, an energetic young boy, and a teenage girl who shows true exuberance toward every task she takes on.

When I'm partnered with the older blind woman, we simply sit in the warm pool by the jets and she talks. She talks about all the people giving her a hard time, the people who believe she can't take care of herself, the people who move around things in her apartment. She has shown me that there is more to an answer than how you respond physically. Because of her blindness, I am forced to form verbal responses to her words, criticisms, and my impressions of the wonders of her life. This is a challenge because I have a tendency to respond to certain things in life through actions, through my body language, and through physical expressions.

On the days I am paired with the young boy, my adaptation skills are most certainly challenged. This young boy speaks both English and Spanish but doesn't respond to or seem to like English very much. My speaking in Spanish has really helped him open up and actually have fun in the pool. My articulation is not always the best when speaking Spanish or in general, for that matter. Playing in a relaxing, fun environment with this little boy has helped me slow down and not just spew the words out. Speaking to young kids in a fun setting requires more emphasis on certain words to compliment their achievements or simply amuse them. Having to adapt what I say around them has really helped me to think about what I say instead of just saying it, in turn improving my articulation.

Lastly, when I am paired with the teenage girl, I have found it helps her relate to me if I play up all my emotions and react in an extreme way to the funny things she does. This particular girl wants to say "hi" to everyone. This forces me to go out and talk to people I don't know or really have any connection with. This has helped me be more playful and much more comfortable making a fool of myself in front of people I don't really know. This will most certainly help my nerves about public speaking in the future.

> **"HAVING TO DO [SERVICE LEARNING] HAS REALLY HELPED ME TO THINK ABOUT WHAT I SAY INSTEAD OF JUST SAYING IT."**

Tips for Incorporating Service Learning into Public Speaking

- Adapt your language choices to your audience members. For example, using advanced vocabulary when speaking to a group of elementary school students will often result in their disconnecting immediately and will usually be interpreted as demeaning. Be sensitive to the capacities of your audience members.

- Realize that many of your audience members may not have had the same experiences you describe in your speeches. To enhance their understanding and provide more vivid explanations, use metaphors, similes, and personifications to describe your experiences.

- To avoid offending other people by using a label, ask them how they prefer to be referred to.

When speakers forget that words do not have the same meaning for everyone, they unintentionally create ambiguity for their audiences. When they forget that people may share symbols but not experiences with those symbols, they run the risk of confusing or alienating their audiences. One way to clear up some of this ambiguity is to use concrete language. **Concrete language** refers to a tangible object—a person, place, or thing. For example, rather than talking about politicians, speak about specific politicians: Name them or their political parties so your audience knows exactly which politicians you are referring to. This will help you avoid **abstract language**, which refers to ideas or concepts but not to specific objects.

As you think about whether the language you will use in your speech is concrete or abstract, diagram it on Ogden and Richards's semantic triangle of meaning. Ask yourself whether the language you use is as specific as you think it is. If it isn't, search for ways to represent generalized concepts or ideas with specific examples. And if you must use abstract language, take time in your speech to define key concepts or ideas for your audience so your listeners will understand your intended meaning. Review the discussion of definitions in Chapter 6 to familiarize yourself with some of the ways speakers can define words for their audiences to eliminate the ambiguity created by connotations.

Language and Culture

In its most basic sense, language is an organized and learned symbol system. It is used to represent human experiences and to transmit messages. Language allows us to describe, label, and share events with others and to understand each other's perspectives and experiences. However, people in different cultures have different life experiences and thus name and define the world differently.

For example, in American Sign Language, which is a visual rather than spoken language, signs often are subtly altered to reflect the visual aspects of objects and events. The concepts "modest home" and "mansion" begin with the same basic sign for "home" but differ in their execution. In contrast, in spoken English, words are only occasionally modified to emphasize some aspect of appearance (for example, "huuuge house"). Usually, to emphasize some visual aspect, we add more words to the description or choose a different word.

Subcultures, or groups within a larger culture that share its language, may also use the language differently. For example, the language of rap music, which has roots in the African American tradition of "signifying," has clear differences from Standard English. Signifying is governed by its own rules of grammar, semantics, and syntax. It allows people to make statements that have double, and often even multiple, meanings that are not understood by people outside the subculture.[3] The topics of rap music, the words it uses, and the ways those words are put together and delivered reflect these multiple meanings, as well as the experiences and perspectives of members of this subculture.

The culturally bound nature of language requires us to be aware of obvious, as well as subtle, differences. As speakers, we can adapt our language choices to the culture of the people we are addressing, or if we do not know their culture well enough to do so, we can acknowledge the differences as we speak. If we can identify which words our audience might not understand because of cultural or regional differences, then we can offer clarification for those words and promote understanding rather than confusion.

Good to Know!

concrete language: Language that refers to a tangible object—a person, place, or thing. abstract language: Language that refers to ideas or concepts but not to specific objects.

Idioms are especially difficult for people of other cultures to understand. An **idiom** is a fixed, distinctive expression whose meaning is not indicated by its individual words. "I was in stitches" and "they kept me in the dark" are examples of English idioms. In American Sign Language, "the train is gone" is an idiom that means you missed the joke or the heart of the matter. We often use idioms without realizing it: "I don't get it," "it's way over my head," and "go figure" are three common examples. Idioms can be especially difficult for nonnative speakers. To be fully understood, we must "unpack the meanings" (another idiom) of potentially confusing phrases and words.

Cultural differences can interfere with communication in other ways, too. If we do not know how a cultural group prefers to identify itself, we may accidentally offend some members of our audience. Table 10.1 will help familiarize you with some of the preferred labels for different cultural groups.

Table 10.1

Appropriate Labels for People of Different Cultures

Ethnicity	African American or black
	Asian American, or identify the country of heritage: Chinese American, Japanese American, Korean American. (Note that *Oriental* refers to an art object, like a rug, and not a person.)
	Hispanic, Latina or Latino, or identify the country of heritage: Cuban American, Mexican American
	Native American or American Indian, or identify the specific nation: Sioux, Navajo, Hopi. (Note that just *Indian* more often refers to people from India.)
	European American or white
Physical ability	A person with [name of disability]
	A person living with [name of disability]
	A person who has [name of disability]
Age	Boy or girl (a person under the age of twelve)
	Young woman or young man (a person between the ages of twelve and eighteen)
	Man or woman (a person nineteen years old or older)
	Older person (rather than elderly or senior)
Sexual orientation	Bisexual man or woman
	Gay man or lesbian
	Straight or heterosexual man or woman
	Transgendered person (a general term to describe those who have gender identities not traditionally associated with their birth sex)
	Transvestite (someone who adopts the dress of the opposite sex)
	Transsexual (a person who wants to change, or has changed, his or her anatomical sex)

Good to Know!

idiom: Fixed, distinctive expression whose meaning is not indicated by its individual words.

Although the use of appropriate labels sometimes is called "politically correct speech," appropriate labels really are about respecting others. Labels help us shape our perceptions of others, and our perceptions affect how we treat other people. Thus, inappropriate labels, such as labels that perpetuate stereotypes, can

Ethical Moment

IS IT OKAY TO SAY WHATEVER YOU WANT ONLINE?

Although most of us say that technology plays an important role in our communication with others, just how important is that role? We know that blogs, text messages, Twitter, and social networking sites can be used to update friends on the events in our lives, express our ideas, and even spark dialogue. However, we don't often consider how these forms of technology can also be used in illegal and harmful ways.

For example, in 2006, fourteen-year-old Julia Wilson received a visit at her school from FBI agents after posting the words "Kill Bush" and an image of the former president on her MySpace web page. Since her web page was accessible to anyone on the Internet, the FBI believed that her comment could inspire terrorists to act upon it. Yet Julia had already removed the image months prior to the visit by the FBI. And although Julia was removed from class and questioned by the authorities, she was not charged with breaking the law. This incident led many to question Julia's right to free speech and the authorities' right to interrogate her without her parents present. No one died as a result of Julia's message on her MySpace page—unfortunately, that was not the case for Megan Meier and Phoebe Prince.

In 2006, thirteen-year-old Megan Meier believed she was communicating on her MySpace page with a teenage boy named Josh Evans. Little did she know that "Josh" was a fictitious person created by Megan's nemesis, Sarah Drew, and her mother, Lori. After several weeks of communicating with "Josh," Megan received an e-mail from him stating, "The world would be a better place without you." Megan, who had a history of depression, replied, "You're the kind of boy a girl would kill herself over." She hanged herself that same day. Fifteen-year-old Phoebe Prince had a similar experience with cyberbullying in 2009. After she moved from Ireland to Massachusetts

AP Photo/Tom Gannam

to start her freshman year of high school, it did not take long for Phoebe to receive taunting text messages and comments posted on Facebook from other students at the school. Someone even made a hate page about Phoebe on Facebook, and dozens of students joined. The bullying became too much for Phoebe, and she hanged herself in her closet.[4]

What Do You Think?

1. Do you think U.S. free speech laws should have protected Julia Wilson and given her the right to use technology to post "Kill Bush" on her MySpace page? Why or why not?

2. Should all words and phrases be protected by law, or should our government ban some words and phrases from the public dialogue because they are too inflammatory or potentially dangerous? What would those words and phrases be, and why do you think they should be protected or banned?

3. No one was charged with a crime in the death of Megan Meier. Do you think laws should be created that protect individuals from using technology to threaten or bully others? Why or why not?

4. What ethical guidelines should people follow when using technology to communicate? Should these guidelines be the same for people like Julia Wilson as they would be for people who bully others online?

cause an audience to feel disrespected and stop listening. Groups name themselves because they wish to emphasize aspects of their lives that are important to them. Audience-centered speakers are aware of how cultures and subcultures name themselves and the characteristics or histories they are honoring. We show respect for our audience when we use appropriate labels.

Language and Gender

In Chapter 2, you learned that it's important to use gender-neutral language so your speeches address both women and men. To help you do this, consider the guidelines in Table 10.2 for translating some common gender-biased language into gender-inclusive language. These guidelines are from the American Psychological Association.

Increasingly, speakers are using gender-inclusive words and phrases in their speaking. In his speech to the American people after the terrorist attacks on the World Trade Center and Pentagon in 2001, President George W. Bush referred to the "business men and women, mothers and fathers . . ." who lost their lives in the attack, acknowledging the professional as well as the personal roles of the women and men who died. Using gender-neutral and gender-inclusive language reflects your awareness of both men and women as valued and active participants in the world.

Table 10.2

Guidelines for Gender-Inclusive Language

Problematic	Preferred
Man, mankind	People, humanity, human beings, humankind, human species
To man a project	To staff a project, hire personnel, employ staff
Manpower	Workforce, personnel, workers, human resources, staff
Man's search for knowledge	The search for knowledge
Chairman	Chair, chairperson, moderator, discussion leader, facilitator
Foreman, mailman	Supervisor or superintendent, postal worker or mail carrier
Salesmanship	Selling ability
Sportsmanship	Teamwork, cooperation, conduct, respect for others, graciousness
He, his, him (universal "he" as a pronoun that refers to both women and men)	They (used with plural nouns), she or he, his or her, him or her
Dear Sir:	Dear Sir or Madam, To whom it may concern, Dear members of the _____ Committee (name the specific group)
Mr. and Mrs. John Smith	John and Jane Smith
Doctors and their wives	Doctors and their partners or significant others
Woman doctor, lady lawyer	Doctor or physician, lawyer or attorney

Language and Accuracy

Consider the following lists of words:

persecution	prosecution
simple	simplistic
patriarchal	patriarchic
good	well

What are the differences between the words in each column? If someone is *persecuted*, is that the same as being *prosecuted*? If you look in the dictionary, you'll see that to be persecuted is to be subjected to cruel or unfair treatment, whereas to be prosecuted is to be tried in a court of law for a criminal offense. The words have different meanings, yet they often are confused. Similarly, many speakers like to add "-istic" to the end of words because they think it makes a concept sound more complex. Yet *simple* means easy, straightforward, or effortless, and *simplistic* means lacking complexities. Although you should be able to find *patriarchal* in the dictionary, can you find *patriarchic*? It's not a word in the English language, although speakers sometimes use it, confusing it with *patriarchal*. How about *good* and *well*? Do you know the difference between the two? Does your favorite band play good or do they play well? (They should play well and sound good.)

Knowing the correct definitions and usage of words is important because accurate language affects not only your meaning but also your credibility. Three tips will help you improve the accuracy of your language.

- *Check the definitions of the words you are using.* When a word is central to the meaning of a sentence or a claim, look it up in the dictionary to be sure you have the correct word. Looking up words can save you considerable embarrassment. In a commemorative speech, a student described her sister by saying, "She's incredible: She's kind, generous, and always thinks of others; she's notorious for this in my hometown." Although her sister was remarkable, "notorious" means well known for undesirable features, not desirable ones.

- *If your use of language is not as strong as you'd like, work with someone who has <u>strong language skills</u>.* Most colleges and universities have writing and tutoring labs, with people ready to help students with clarity and grammar. (Ask your instructor about the resources available on your campus if you aren't familiar with them.) If you take time to seek this kind of help, you will find that not only will your speeches be clearer and your credibility enhanced, but your writing will improve as well.

- *<u>Study</u> the language.* American civil rights leader Malcolm X copied the dictionary word by word to improve his language skills, but there are other ways to improve yours. Read books, magazines, and newspapers; take courses that focus on language skills; and practice with language and vocabulary workbooks from the library, bookstores, and teaching supply stores. You can even study a foreign language, which will teach you about your own language in the process. Studying

Practicing the Public Dialogue

10.1

Evaluate Accuracy of the Language in Your Speech

Make a list of five to ten words you think everyone in your audience will define in the same way. Exchange lists with a partner in your speech class and write definitions for each other's words, but don't use a dictionary. Share your definitions with each other and see if you agree on them. Now look your words up in a dictionary and see if your and your partner's definitions match the definitions provided in the dictionary.

Online Resources

 CourseMate The Internet offers many sites that can help you improve the accuracy of the language in your speeches. Here are a couple of good ones: To look up the meanings and proper usage of words online, access **Web Connect 10.1: Merriam-Webster Online** through your CourseMate for *Invitation to Public Speaking*. This resource features a dictionary, a thesaurus, and a variety of other features to help you use words correctly. For a list of words that speakers typically have difficulty with, check out **Web Connect 10.2: Words Commonly Misused.**

the language systematically not only will increase your vocabulary but also will help you develop your arguments and ideas more clearly.

Language and Public Speaking

It may be tempting to write out our entire speeches beforehand to get every word right. And then we may be tempted to read the speech to our audience to avoid the ambiguities and errors of language discussed in this chapter. However, when we speak, we want to use language meant to be spoken, not read. Writing out a speech is appropriate only when speaking from a manuscript (see Chapter 11). Even though every speaker makes a mistake now and then, with care and attention to language, you can learn to address your audience with clarity and vividness most of the time.

AP Photo/Al Grillo

The most effective speakers use what is called an **oral style**, a style that reflects the spoken rather than the written word. They "talk" their speeches rather than read them, and this makes them more "listenable" and easier to understand. The differences between the spoken word and the written word are significant: Spoken language is more interactive, more casual, and more repetitive than written language.[5]

Spoken Language Is More Interactive

Written messages are fixed messages whose words are already recorded or written down. However, when we speak to others, we interact with them: We make adjustments as we speak, monitor their interest and understanding, and ask or respond to questions. When we speak publicly, our language reflects the shifts, pauses, and adjustments we make for our audience. We carry on a conversation with our audience in ways that we do not when we write to someone.

Former Alaska Governor Sarah Palin is well-known for her folksy oral style. Think about the language you plan to use in your next speech. What steps will you take to use an oral rather than written style?

Our nonverbal communication also reflects this interactive mode. Our expressions and gestures reinforce our words, giving spoken language a different tone than written language. Written prose doesn't lend itself to this spontaneous nonverbal interaction. Speakers who read written-out speeches usually sound as if they're delivering something the audience should be reading rather than listening to. Although speakers might feel more confident delivering a memorized speech, audiences can get restless and irritated with this style. Remember to stay audience centered and use an interactive style of language and delivery.

Spoken Language Is More Casual

Written language tends to be more formal than spoken language, although there are exceptions. If you open almost any book or magazine and read the text out loud, you will notice that the words sound a little formal. Written and spoken languages differ in formality because writing tends to be more rule governed than speaking. When we speak, we use more contractions (for example, "can't" instead of "cannot") and colloquialisms ("No way!" instead of "That simply is not possible"). We also run our words together when we speak (we read, "I'm going to ask" but say, "I'm gonna ask"). A speaker who delivers a speech in a written style sounds more distant and formal than one who talks to the audience.

Good to Know!

oral style: Speaking style that reflects the spoken rather than the written word.

CourseMate

To see a speaker using a casual style, watch the video clip of student speaker Brandi Lafferty. You can use your CourseMate for *Invitation to Public Speaking* to watch the video, respond to analysis questions, and compare your answers to those provided by the author.

Spoken Language Is More Repetitive

Written messages do not need the repetition that spoken messages do. When a message is written, readers can go back and reread it if they need help remembering what was said. But because public speaking audiences often need help remembering what they hear, public speakers use more repetition than writers do.

Public speakers intentionally repeat main ideas and arguments. They summarize their main points and restate important arguments to help their audiences remember them. Recall from Chapters 8 and 9 that in your speeches you present an overview of your ideas (introduction), state those ideas (body), and then summarize them (conclusion). You also use repetitive tools like transitions, internal summaries, and internal previews to help audiences remember your ideas. This repetitive quality, so necessary to public speaking, is found less often in many forms of written communication. The need for repetition reinforces the importance of speaking rather than reading to audiences.

Language, Imagery, and Rhythm

Because much of what we know comes to us through language rather than direct experience, we want to pay careful attention to the images we create with our words. As you put together the final touches of your speeches, listen to your words and phrases. Do they inspire you? Do they create a picture in your mind of what you are describing? Are they pleasing to your ears? Do they make you want to hear more? If your language draws you into your speech, then it likely will draw in your audience. By carefully choosing the words in your speech, you can use language to create rich images and sensations.

In this section, you will read about a number of verbal techniques that draw your listeners into your ideas. These tools can be divided into two general categories: language that creates memorable imagery and language that creates a pleasing rhythm.

Language That Creates Memorable Imagery

Our language can call to mind engaging sights, smells, tastes, and sounds. With language, we can bring an idea to life and make abstractions seem concrete. Figures of speech, such as similes, metaphors, and personification, can create powerful images for our audiences, making our speeches appealing, interesting, and memorable. In the examples that follow, notice how these devices blend with the words around them. They call up the images without calling attention to themselves.

Simile. A **simile** makes an explicit comparison of two things that uses the word *like* or *as*. Although the two things we are comparing are different, they are similar in a way that we want to highlight to make a specific point. Consider the following examples of similes from speeches given by Patrick and Haley:

> Although he stands only five feet ten to my six feet two, my *father seems like a giant* to me and probably always will. But he's a gentle giant, for the most part, and I look up to him and appreciate many of the lessons he taught me.

Good to Know!

simile: Figure of speech that makes an explicit comparison of two things using the word *like* or *as*.

From the time you first begin to consume it, the sugar in your body scratches the lining of the arteries leading to your heart. *The process is like sandpaper on wood*, and it never reverses itself.

Through similes, Patrick emphasized his respect for his father, and Haley dramatized the hazards of consuming sugar. Patrick could simply have said he respected his father, and Haley's statement that sugar scratches the lining of the heart was enough to make her point. However, by using similes, their audiences could "see" Patrick's respect for his father and the damage sugar does to arteries.

Metaphor. A **metaphor** is a comparison between two things that describes one thing as being something else. Aristotle described a command of metaphors as "the greatest thing by far." The word *metaphor* comes from a Greek term meaning "transference."[6] When we use metaphors, we are transferring the qualities of one thing to another, illustrating their similarities.

Although many metaphors create associations that are obvious (for example, "the war on drugs"), some are subtler, such as Guatemalan human rights advocate Rigoberta Menchú's "we are not myths of the past, ruins in the jungle, or zoos."[7] In the "war on drugs," the comparison is explicit—the government is responding to drug trafficking in a warlike manner. In contrast, Menchú's comparison of the Mayan people to myths, ruins, and zoos is subtler. Menchú is arguing for the rights of the Mayan people today by comparing them to what they are not. In both examples, the metaphors make the comparisons memorable. Two student speakers, Silas and Brooke, used metaphors quite successfully in the following ways:

> Melanoma is one of the most common cancers in Americans between the ages of twenty-five and twenty-nine. If it is caught early and removed, a person lives a normal life. Well, maybe it's normal. According to Matthew Brady, now nineteen, after summers on his boogie board and at the age of only fourteen, "they *cut a steak out of my back*."

> As I ate, my mouth got hotter and hotter . . . and hotter. I took a sip of water. It kept right on heating up. The source of this *fire in my mouth?* The fairly well-known habanero chili.

Like similes, metaphors bring ideas to life with rich associations and comparisons. However, they can go astray sometimes in awkward ways. A **mixed metaphor** makes illogical comparisons between two or more things. When speakers mix their metaphors, they begin with one metaphor and then switch to another midstream. The confusion, if not humor, that results from mixed metaphors is apparent in the following examples:[8]

> It appears as though the *Achilles heel* of the Eagles' defense is about to rear its ugly head.

Good to Know!

metaphor: Figure of speech that makes a comparison between two things by describing one thing as being something else.
mixed metaphor: Metaphor that makes illogical comparisons between two or more things.

I wanted all my *ducks in a row*, so if we did *get into a posture*, we could pretty much *slam dunk this thing and put it to bed*.

In the first example, the speaker asks the audience to associate the metaphor of an Achilles heel (a weak point) with the rearing of an ugly head (an unsightly appearance). However, heels cannot raise their heads. In the second example, the speaker associates a slam dunk (a high probability shot in basketball) with putting something to bed (finishing a task). Combined with the metaphor of ducks in a row (everything in order) and a posture (a bluff), the audience has trouble deciding which image to focus on. In short, mixed metaphors bring together too many or contradictory associations and are difficult to visualize. To avoid mixed metaphors, take a close look at the metaphors you want to use to be sure the words in the phrase refer to the same category, event, or thing.

© Jeff Greenberg / PhotoEdit

Speakers often use language to create powerful visual images for their audiences. Describe this 1959 Chevrolet Corvette using simile, metaphor, and personification. For example, how would you describe what it felt like to drive this car on a scenic highway? What words would you use to describe, say, excitement or apprehension about driving such an expensive car?

Personification. When we use **personification**, we attribute human characteristics to animals, objects, or concepts. Personification assigns sight, speech, hearing, thought, emotion, action, or sensation to objects (such as trees, rocks, buildings) or to concepts (such as love, bravery, sadness). "Confusion spoke," "the trees listen," and "the voice of democracy" are examples of personification. In the following examples, notice how easy it is to accept the traits assigned to things we don't typically see as having these human qualities:

My *bones are tired*. Not tired of struggling, but tired of oppression. (Audley "Queen Mother" Moore, civil rights leader)[9]

With personification, the ideas expressed here come to life. Bones, which can break or weaken, can't become tired. However, the image of deep fatigue is highly effective and stays with the audience long after the words are said.

In a speech about losing his job, Carl used personification to describe the letter he received and his reaction to it:

Those words just sat there staring at me. They wouldn't leave and they wouldn't explain themselves. "You're fired," they said. And they refused to tell me anything else.

The image Carl created conveys the shock of being fired without explanation or recourse. Personification, in sum, can call up vivid images and sensations for your audience.

Language That Creates a Pleasing Rhythm

We can strengthen the images we create with our words by focusing on the way the words sound when put together. When we think of rhythm, we may think of poetry, music, or children's stories, not speeches. However, some of the most effective public speakers in history have used rhythm to strengthen the presentation of their ideas. Consider Jesse Jackson, John F. Kennedy, and Barbara Jordan. These speakers are all known for the power of their ideas and their rhythmic language. In speeches, **rhythm** is the arrangement of words into

Good to Know!

personification: Figure of speech that attributes human characteristics to animals, objects, or concepts. **rhythm:** Arrangement of words into patterns so the sounds of the words together enhance the meaning of a phrase.

patterns so the sounds of the words together enhance the meaning of a phrase. Parallelism, repetition, alliteration, and antithesis are four ways to emphasize your ideas with rhythm.

Civic Engagement in Action

"ALRIGHT HEAR THIS"

Founded in 2001 by former Def Jam head Russell Simmons, the Hip-Hop Summit Action Network (HSAN) is dedicated to using hip-hop as a catalyst for education and advocacy related to the well-being of at-risk youth. HSAN focuses on issues of community development, access to high-quality public education and literacy, freedom of speech, voter education, economic advancement, and youth leadership development. Since its beginnings, HSAN has sponsored a number of civic events, such as a Smackdown Your Vote campaign to register "Two Million More in 2004," the 2008 get-out-the-vote campaign to register "50K in one day" (with the Hip-Hop Caucus), and the 2009 national Hip-Hop Summit on Financial Empowerment entitled "Get Your Money Right." HSAN also works with the Recording Industry Association of America in support of the advisory labels that alert parents to explicit content in music. It has defended hip-hop culture before members of the U.S. Congress and such federal regulatory agencies as the Federal Trade Commission and the Federal Communications Commission.

AP Photo/Rob Widdis

HSAN also seeks to harness the immense popularity of hip-hop to educate others about hip-hop music and culture. "Once an underground, controversial style characterized by gangsta mythology and all-too-real turf wars," says Nelson George, author of *Hip-Hop America*, "rap music is now embraced across the radio dial and across the nation by a diverse, multiracial fan base. . . . Rappers are pop stars, pop stars rap, and the sound is as integral to the cultural landscape as country music or rock." HSAN's goal is to use this mainstream success to encourage the recording industry to establish mentoring programs and forums that will stimulate dialogue between artists, hip-hop fans, and industry leaders and promote understanding and positive change.

Recently, HSAN has been involved in a dialogue with the recording and broadcast industries about forming a coalition to recommend guidelines for lyrical and visual standards. In particular, they recommend that these industries "voluntarily remove/bleep/delete the misogynistic words *bitch* and *ho* and the racially offensive word *nigger*." They maintain that these words are utterly derogatory and show a complete lack of respect for the history of suffering and oppression that women, African Americans, and other people of color have experienced in the United States. They are not advocating censorship. Rather, "[W]e are consistent in our strong affirmation, defense, and protection of the First Amendment right of free speech and artistic expression. . . . Our discussions are about the corporate social responsibility of the industry to voluntarily show respect to [African Americans, other people of color, and to all women]."[10]

You Can Get Involved

CourseMate   To learn more about the work of the Hip-Hop Summit Action Network and see how you can become a part of their efforts, access **Web Connect 10.4: Hip-Hop Summit** at your CourseMate for *Invitation to Public Speaking*. Also access **Web Connect 10.5: Campus Activism** to get involved with issues related to the arts, the media, free speech, and much more. You can use this resource to publicize your own activist events, join an existing campaign, and build networks.

Language

Parallelism. When we arrange related words so they are balanced or arrange related sentences so they have identical structures, we are using **parallelism**. The notion that "beauty is as beauty does" is an example of a simple but effective use of parallelism. Because of its rhythm and symmetry, parallelism helps an audience remember a statement. Here are other, more complex, examples of parallelism:

> *Rich and poor, intelligent and ignorant, wise and foolish, virtuous and vicious, man and woman* — it is ever the same, each soul must depend wholly on itself. (Elizabeth Cady Stanton, nineteenth-century suffragist)

> My parents shared not only an improbable love, they shared an abiding faith in the possibilities of this nation. They would give me an African name, Barack, or "blessed," believing that *in a tolerant America* your name is no barrier to success. They imagined — they imagined me going to the best schools in the land, even though they weren't rich, because *in a generous America* you don't have to be rich to achieve your potential. (then–Illinois Senator Barack Obama, 2004 keynote address to the Democratic national convention)

Repetition. When we use **repetition** in a speech, we repeat keywords or phrases at the beginnings or endings of sentences or clauses. President Franklin D. Roosevelt's "I see one-third of the nation ill-housed, ill-clad, and ill-nourished" is an example of repetition. The repetition of the word *ill* creates a rhythm that helped his audience remember his claims. Representative Barbara Jordan used repetition in her 1976 keynote address to the Democratic national convention:

> *We are a people* in a quandary about the present. *We are a people* in search of our future. *We are a people* in search of a national community.

In the next example, poet Nikki Giovanni used repetition to create a memorable message in her speech "We Are Virginia Tech," given at the close of the memorial ceremony for the 2007 Virginia Tech shooting victims. Notice that in the fourth sentence, "we are" is implied.

> *We are* Virginia Tech. *We are* strong enough to stand tall tearlessly. *We are* brave enough to bend to cry. And sad enough to know we must laugh again. *We are* Virginia Tech.

Repetition is one of the easier verbal techniques for beginning speakers to use. Consider these examples from student speeches:

> Let me talk about my experiences as a first-year teacher. I'll tell you now, I loved it, but *I was not prepared*. For the endless energy of the students? *I was not prepared*. The demands on my time outside the classroom? *Not prepared*. Angry parents? *Not prepared*. Learning disabilities? *Not prepared*. Language differences? Personal tragedies? Trusting faces staring up at me? You got it: *I was not prepared*.

> As *students, we need* to respond. As *students, we need* to care. As *students, we need* to step forward and share our positions.

Good to Know!

parallelism: Arrangement of related words so they are balanced or of related sentences so they have identical structures.
repetition: Repeating keywords or phrases at the beginnings or endings of sentences or clauses to create rhythm.

Speakers often combine repetition with parallelism to reinforce messages rhythmically and ensure that their words stay with us long after a speech is over. In the following example, former Massachusetts Congressman Joe Moakley repeats "it is never a crime" and then uses parallelism to end with "It is always a duty."

> *It is never a crime* to speak up for the poor, the helpless, or the ill; *it is never a crime* to tell the truth; *it is never a crime* to demand justice; *it is never a crime* to teach people their rights; *it is never a crime* to struggle for a just peace. *It is never a crime. It is always a duty.*

Alliteration. **Alliteration** is the repetition of the initial sounds of two or more words in a sentence or phrase. We can use alliteration to emphasize an idea, to create a humorous tone, or as a **mnemonic device** (a verbal device that makes information easier to remember).[11] Alliteration is not just for children's rhyming games (such as *P*eter *P*iper and his *p*ickled *p*eppers). Consider these common phrases: the *W*ild *W*est, *f*east or *f*amine, the *b*allot or the *b*ullet, *c*ompassionate *c*onservatism, *s*trong and *s*ilent, and the *M*illion *M*an *M*arch. These phrases have become familiar in part because alliteration has made them more memorable. When used sparingly, alliteration can give a rhythm to your words that audiences find engaging and easy to remember. Consider these examples of alliteration and the ways the repetition of sounds make it easier to remember the ideas in a speech.

AP Photo

> We are in a transitional period right now—fascinating and exhilarating times, learning to adjust to *changes* and the *choices* we—men and women—are facing. (Barbara Bush, former first lady)

> Now is the time for *repentance, restitution,* and *reconciliation,* and I honor those three functions in the light of the great ethnic, racial diversity in our world today. (Maggie Kuhn, founder of the Gray Panthers)

Antithesis. The word antithesis means "opposite." In a speech, you use **antithesis** when you place words and phrases in contrast or opposition to one another. One of the most famous uses of antithesis comes from John F. Kennedy's inaugural address in 1961: "And so, my fellow Americans: *Ask not what your country can do for you—ask what you can do for your country.*" With this simple phrase, he caused those listening to think about their personal responsibility for preserving the freedoms many Americans had begun to take for granted. Kennedy offered a second example of antithesis in that same speech:

> Let us never negotiate out of fear. But let us never fear to negotiate.

Antithesis is perhaps more complex than alliteration and parallelism, but it still is used with great success. As you put together the ideas in your speeches,

John F. Kennedy is renowned for using eloquent language in his speeches. One of the techniques he's most known for is his use of antithesis. Try to incorporate at least one example of antithesis into your next speech.

Good to Know!

alliteration: Repetition of initial sounds of two or more words in a sentence or phrase. **mnemonic device:** Verbal device that makes information easier to remember. **antithesis:** Placement of words and phrases in contrast or opposition to one another.

see if you might be able to phrase them using antithesis. Here's how Werner used antithesis in his speech:

Some say that people with developmental disabilities only *take from us*, but I say they actually *give to us*.

Other speakers also have used antithesis with great impact:

We can do no *great things*—only *small things* with great love. (Mother Teresa, humanitarian and Nobel Peace Prize laureate)

Words cannot *be remote from reality* when they *create reality*. (John Cowper Powys, English novelist)

Antithesis draws an audience into your speech, adding force and rhythm to your ideas.

These seven devices for engaging your audience in your ideas—simile, metaphor, personification, parallelism, repetition, alliteration, and antithesis—can help you create memorable images and appealing rhythms in your speech. Used thoughtfully, they can help your audience recall sensations and experiences and remember your ideas. As you use these linguistic devices, remember the importance of respecting cultural differences and speaking with gender-inclusive language. Similarly, remember that language can be ambiguous, and your linguistic devices should clarify your ideas, not confuse your audience. If you create appropriate and engaging images with your language, you will enhance the public dialogue.

Practicing the Public Dialogue

10.3

Evaluate the Imagery and Rhythm of Your Speech

As a class, select a speech topic for an imaginary speech. Prepare the general and specific purposes for the speech and the main points. Break into groups and assign each of the following elements to a different group: the introduction, the conclusion, and the main points (one main point per group). In your groups, use as many of the devices for creating memorable images and appealing rhythms as you can for your part of the speech. Make sure your language is culturally inclusive and gender inclusive. Now, in your groups, deliver the parts of the speech to the class and discuss the language strategies you used in your speech part. Why did you make the choices you made? Why were they effective or not?

Online Resources

CourseMate

To see a speaker use linguistic devices in her speech, watch the video clip of student speaker Stacey Newman. Were her uses of these devices effective? Why or why not? You can use your Course-Mate for *Invitation to Public Speaking* to watch the video, respond to analysis questions, and compare your answers to those provided by the author.

Chapter Summary

Language is the system of symbols we use to communicate with one another.

- Language is complex and ambiguous because of our subjective associations with the meaning of words.
- The semantic triangle of meaning reveals this complexity and ambiguity by illustrating how word meaning derives from the relationships among the symbol, the referent, and the thought (or reference).

Culture also affects language and our understanding of the meaning of words.

- To be audience centered, avoid words that are strictly tied to a single culture or explain the meaning of those words that are.
- To better connect with and avoid alienating the diverse members of an audience, use culturally inclusive and gender-inclusive language.

Accurate use of language communicates your credibility to your audiences.

- Inaccurate use of language can harm your credibility and cause unnecessary confusion.
- To ensure accuracy, check the definitions of keywords before you deliver your speech, or improve your use of language by working with someone who has a strong command of the language or by studying English or even another language.

There are several differences between spoken and written language.

- Spoken language reflects an oral style that is more interactive, casual, and repetitive than written language.

- Because of these differences, avoid writing out your speech and reading it to your audience. Instead, work from an outline so you will deliver your speech in a conversational rather than written style.

Many techniques can make your language more appealing to your audience.

- To create vivid and memorable images, use similes, metaphors, and personification.
- *Similes* are explicit comparisons of two things using the word *like* or *as*.
- *Metaphors* are comparisons of two things that describe one as the same as the other.
- *Personification* ascribes human characteristics to nonhuman objects or ideas.
- To create a pleasing rhythm, use parallelism, repetition, alliteration, and antithesis.
- *Parallelism* balances related words, phrases, or sentences by giving them identical structures.
- *Repetition* emphasizes keywords or phrases at the beginning or ending of a sentence or clause.
- *Alliteration* is the repetition of the initial sounds of two or more words in a phrase or sentence.
- *Antithesis* is the contrast of words or phrases.

Invitation to Public Speaking Online

CourseMate Now that you have read Chapter 10, use your Speech Communication CourseMate for *Invitation to Public Speaking* for quick access to the electronic resources that accompany this text. These resources include

- **Study tools** that will help you assess your learning and prepare for exams (*digital glossary, key term flash cards, review quizzes*).
- **Activities and assignments** that will help you hone your knowledge and build your public speaking skills throughout the course (*Practicing the Public Dialogue activities, review questions*).

- **Media resources** that will help you explore public speaking concepts online (*Web Connect links, Enhanced eBook*), develop your speech outlines (*Speech Builder Express* 3.0), watch and critique videos of sample speeches (*Interactive Video Activities*), upload your speech videos for peer reviewing and critique other students' speeches (*Speech Studio online speech review tool*), and download chapter review so you can study when and where you'd like (*Audio Study Tools*).

This chapter's key concepts and review questions are also featured on the following page.

Key Concepts

abstract language (206)
alliteration (217)
antithesis (217)
concrete language (206)
idiom (207)
language (204)

metaphor (213)
mixed metaphor (213)
mnemonic device (217)
oral style (211)
parallelism (216)
personification (214)

referent (204)
repetition (216)
rhythm (214)
simile (212)
symbol (204)
thought, or reference (204)

Review Questions

1. Look up the dictionary definitions of five to seven keywords you will use in your next speech. Do they mean what you thought they meant? Have you been pronouncing them correctly? If you were using an incorrect word, replace it with a correct one.

2. Bring a newspaper or magazine to class and look for language that is sensitive or insensitive to culture and gender. In what ways is the language appropriate or inappropriate? What mistakes do you think the authors of the articles made, if any? What are the implications of these mistakes? What are the implications of the appropriate choices the authors made?

3. Bring a dictionary to class. Look up the following commonly confused pairs of words:

   accept/except, compose/comprise, nauseated/ nauseous, adverse/averse, explicit/implicit, principal/principle, affect/effect, poured/pored, anxious/eager, fewer/less, reign/rein, appraise/ apprise, healthy/healthful, stationery/stationary, between/among, imply/infer, uninterested/ disinterested, compliment/complement, lay/lie, who/whom

   How many of these words did you have confused before you began this exercise?

4. Select a topic for an imaginary speech. Write out your introduction or first main point for that speech. Now read that to a small audience. Put the paper aside and talk that part of your speech in an oral style. What differences do you notice? Is the oral style interactive, casual, and repetitive?

5. Divide into groups and select one of the following terms:

   smoking   greyhound racing   the draft

   Halloween   gasoline

   Using the seven devices for creating imagery and rhythm (simile, metaphor, personification, parallelism, repetition, alliteration, antithesis), write statements about this topic. Share your results with the class. Which devices helped you do a particularly good job conveying your ideas? Why do you think so?

6. Check out Speech Studio to see how other students use language in their speeches. In what ways do they use language accurately, create memorable images, and create pleasing rhythms? Or record a speech you're working on, upload it to Speech Studio, and ask your peers for their feedback. What feedback could you use to fine-tune your language before you give your speech in class? ☑Studio

Delivering Your Speech

11

AP Photo/Evan Vucci

I f you look up the word *delivery* in the dictionary, you will discover the following definitions: (1) the carrying of something to a particular person or address; (2) the process of giving birth; (3) the action and manner of throwing or tossing a ball or punch; (4) the rescue of someone from hardship; and (5) the action or manner in which somebody speaks to an audience. Although this chapter focuses on the fifth definition of **delivery**, the action or manner of speaking to an audience, the other four definitions are also relevant.

When we deliver our speeches, we do carry something to others—our message. Our delivery also gives birth to our ideas as we bring them to life for our audience. Similarly, when we enter the public dialogue, we throw or toss our ideas out to our audiences, hoping they will catch them. Depending on the speaking environment, our passion and engagement, and the beliefs of our audience, our ideas may even feel like punches. Finally, when we share information with our listeners or encourage them to change, we can sometimes help them avoid hardship or confusion.

What these other definitions of *delivery* suggest is that delivery is more complex than simply "giving a speech." It is your way of connecting with your audience and sharing your ideas with them. Because of the importance of delivery,

- **Methods of Delivery**
- **Verbal Components of Delivery**
- **Nonverbal Components of Delivery**
- **Rehearsing Your Speech**

IN THIS CHAPTER, YOU WILL LEARN TO:

- Identify and describe four different methods of delivering a speech
- List and demonstrate the verbal components of delivery
- List and demonstrate the nonverbal components of delivery
- Identify effective strategies for rehearsing your speech

this chapter covers the verbal and nonverbal components of delivery that will help you present your ideas in the most effective way. In the discussion that follows, you will learn about four methods of delivery, the verbal and nonverbal components of delivery, and strategies for rehearsing your speech.

Methods of Delivery

The four types of delivery you use as a public speaker are extemporaneous, impromptu, manuscript, and memorized.[1] Let's look at each of these methods of delivery and the reasons for using them.

Extemporaneous Delivery

Most of your speeches will be extemporaneous. When you give an **extemporaneous speech**, you present a carefully prepared and practiced speech from brief notes rather than from memory or a written manuscript. Because an extemporaneous delivery tends to be more natural than other deliveries, it is one of the more common methods.

An extemporaneous delivery evolves as you work from your preparation outline to your speaking outline. Recall from Chapter 8 that when you work with your preparation outline, you organize all the material you've thoroughly researched. Therefore, you come to know your speech in full detail. You then summarize that detail in the speaking outline. When you practice giving your speech from the speaking outline, words and phrases remind you of the full ideas on the preparation outline. Thus, your speaking outline provides the brief notes you speak from. Because you don't need to read the full text of your speech to remember what you want to say, you can give your speech in a natural way.

The advantages of extemporaneous deliveries are many. The speaking outline or speaking notes prompt your ideas but do not allow you to read every word to your audience. Your eye contact and gestures are natural, and your tone is conversational. Finally, because extemporaneous deliveries encourage direct communication between the speaker and audience, it is easier to stay audience centered.

Delivery tips. Many beginning speakers worry they might forget their speeches if they use an extemporaneous delivery. To help overcome this fear, follow these guidelines:

1. Add more keywords and phrases to your outline (not full sentences). This way, you'll have more cues to aid your memory.
2. Practice your speech often before you give it so you will feel more confident about what you will remember and want to say.

Your goal isn't necessarily to eliminate your fear by reading your speech but to give yourself tools so you can "talk" your speech.

The differences between an extemporaneous delivery and a speech read to an audience are striking. With an extemporaneous delivery, your language follows an oral rather than a written style (Chapter 10). An extemporaneous delivery

Cengage Learning

CourseMate

To compare the differences between a speech delivered in a conversational style and one that is read, watch the video clips of student speakers Shelley Weibel and Eric Daley. Which style of delivery do you think is more effective? You can use your CourseMate for *Invitation to Public Speaking* to watch the video, respond to analysis questions, and compare you answers to those provided by the author.

Good to Know!

delivery: Action or manner of speaking to an audience. **extemporaneous speech:** Speech that is carefully prepared and practiced from brief notes rather than from memory or a written manuscript.

also follows a **conversational style**, which is more formal than everyday conversation but remains spontaneous and relaxed.[2] Additionally, with a conversational style, your posture and gestures are relaxed, and you make frequent eye contact with your audience. In contrast, because reading requires your full attention, you're less able to make eye contact with your audience and gesture spontaneously. Imagine if Dr. Martin Luther King Jr. or Hillary Clinton had read their most famous speeches to their audiences. Their charisma and power would have disappeared.

Public Speaking and Service Learning: Engaging Community

Brandon Gustafson, a public speaking student at Colorado State University, did his service learning project with the Homeless Awareness Team (H.A.T.). This organization collects outdoor gear donated by the general public and redistributes it to local homeless people. He found that his enthusiasm for this service work helped him deliver a successful speech extemporaneously. He carefully prepared and practiced his speech so that he could deliver it in a casual tone that he felt matched the testimony he included in his supporting materials.

I have always thought delivering speeches would be a very nerve-racking experience. But after the first in-class speech, which was delivered to a small group of just three to four students, I realized that it could be a fairly calm and low-key experience that allowed me to get to know some of the kids in my class better. By the time my second speech came around, which was delivered extemporaneously to the whole class while I stood up at a podium, I had already started to do my service at H.A.T. I was more nervous about giving this speech, but I found that my excitement about telling others about my service work actually made my performance more casual.

Before starting this class, I had no connection to homeless populations, and I took a great interest in my service. Because I was so proud of the service I was doing, I was able to deliver a successful extemporaneous speech. I had an important message: I had done interviews with homeless people, and they were relying on me to deliver their words and feelings to my peers. I feel like I did them justice in my casual, yet passionate delivery.

> **"BECAUSE I WAS SO PROUD OF THE SERVICE I WAS DOING, I WAS ABLE TO DELIVER A SUCCESSFUL EXTEMPORANEOUS SPEECH."**

Tips for Incorporating Service Learning into Public Speaking:

- Always practice your speech as you intend to deliver it. For example, if you want to deliver a speech to a large audience while standing at a podium, practice that way—practice while standing and speaking a bit louder than you normally would.
- Practice your speech from start to finish ten times, without stopping. When practicing, public speakers tend to start at the beginning of their speech and continue until they mess up. Then they start over, without continuing on to practice the middle and end of their speech. This results in a well-rehearsed introduction but a sloppy body and conclusion. Always practice giving your full speech, even if you stumble, so that the entire speech is well rehearsed and you feel comfortable with the introduction, body, and conclusion.
- Practice in front of a mirror or other people. This technique allows you to "see" what you are saying and make sure your nonverbal delivery matches your verbal delivery. For example, if you are delivering a speech about a very exciting experience, such as bungee jumping, your delivery should convey the excitement and adventure that matches the experience.

Good to Know!

conversational style: Speaking style that is more formal than everyday conversation but remains spontaneous and relaxed.

Impromptu Delivery

When you give an **impromptu speech**, you present a speech that you have not planned or prepared in advance. Although you may be wondering why anyone would do this—especially in light of the previous discussions about the importance of preparation, planning, and practice—impromptu speaking is quite common. It occurs in meetings or public gatherings when someone is asked to speak or feels the need to share her or his perspective. When you decide to speak, you have the advantage of having a moment or two to organize your ideas. If you suddenly are asked to speak, you may not be able to jot down notes, but you still can organize your ideas. Consider the following scenario:

© Bettmann/CORBIS

As a senior at the university, José was having trouble registering for the courses he needed to graduate. Enrollment on his campus was at an all-time high, and the number of majors in his own department had grown enormously. As a result, classes filled early. He expressed his frustration to his adviser, who suggested José attend a campus open forum on graduation requirements. José's adviser facilitated the discussion, and during the question-and-answer session, he asked José if he would share his frustrating experiences with the audience. José paused and quickly organized his thoughts about his frustrations and how they related to the discussion. His speech was a success not only because it addressed the discussion directly but also because he was candid about his experiences.

José's quick organization in his head gave him confidence and helped him deliver an audience-centered speech that was easy to follow.

American author and speaker Mark Twain joked, "It usually takes more than three weeks to prepare a good impromptu speech." This isn't true, of course, but with a few minutes of thoughtful organization, you can make it seem as if you took three weeks to prepare.

Delivery tips. Although you never have much time to prepare an impromptu speech, you can practice impromptu deliveries. In fact, your speech instructor likely will ask you to give several impromptu speeches during the semester. When you deliver an impromptu speech, use the following guidelines:

1. Quickly but calmly decide on the main points you want to make.
2. Introduce your main points as you would in a speech you had prepared in advance: Offer a preview such as "the three things I'd like to cover are" and use signposts such as "first."
3. Support your main points with subpoints and sub-subpoints.
4. Summarize your main points in a brief conclusion.

If you find yourself in an impromptu situation, stay calm. The skills you learn in your public speaking course are invaluable for such situations. Even though you may be nervous, you have learned to organize ideas, relate them to the audience, and deliver various types of speeches. Remember, too, that when you give an impromptu speech, your audience does not expect elaborate source citations, fancy visual aids, or creative introductions. They are looking for immediate clarity or guidance. If you rely on the fundamental skills you have learned in your public speaking course, you can handle impromptu speeches successfully.

Good to Know!

impromptu speech: Speech that is not planned or prepared in advance.

Manuscript Delivery

When you give a **manuscript speech**, you read to an audience from a written text. Although most speeches are best delivered extemporaneously, some speeches require a manuscript delivery:

- When detailed and exact information must be reported carefully, such as to a professional board or a formal committee
- When your speech will be scrutinized word by word, archived, and referred to later (for example, the president's address to the nation)
- When your speech text will be used later for some other purpose (for example, a keynote address at a conference, which often is published)

A manuscript speech is one of the most challenging forms of delivery. Contrary to what most beginning public speakers think, speaking effectively from a manuscript requires more preparation and skill than extemporaneous or impromptu speaking. Two problems are likely when a speaker reads from the full text. First, the speech often sounds like a written text and not an oral text, or a speech that "reads" well but doesn't "talk" well. Second, the speaker may be inclined to read to the audience rather than talk with them. Let's look at some solutions to these problems.

Delivery tips. When you write your speech in manuscript format, the best way to avoid a written style is to talk the speech aloud as you write it. The following guidelines will help you do this:

1. Working from your preparation outline, sit at your desk and speak the words as you write them on your computer or paper.
2. If you find yourself thinking the speech rather than saying it aloud, go back and speak the part you have just written. You usually will notice that you've slipped into a writer's style instead of a speaker's style.
3. Change the language in these sections to reflect spoken ideas rather than written ideas. Remember, your goal is to write a speech, not an essay.

The second problem with using a manuscript is the temptation to read the manuscript to the audience. This will greatly reduce your eye contact with the audience because you are focusing on the manuscript and not your listeners. Also, your words may sound wooden because you are more concerned about reading your words accurately than how your words might sound with your audience. Finally, your delivery may be too fast because you are more focused on getting the words out than paying attention to how the audience is reacting to you.

The way to overcome the challenges associated with reading a speech is to practice speaking from the manuscript again and again. If you become familiar with your manuscript during practice, you will find your natural rhythm and conversational style. You will notice where you can make eye contact with your audience easily and for extended periods. Like your extemporaneous speeches, you will be able to deliver full ideas or subpoints without reading. You also will discover that you'll want to slow down because, even though the words are in front of you, you feel comfortable enough to speak the words with feeling rather than rush through them.

Good to Know!

manuscript speech: Speech that is read to an audience from a written text.

Memorized Delivery

When you give a **memorized speech**, you present a speech that has been written out, committed to memory, and given word for word. With a memorized delivery, you give the speech without any notes. Orators 2,000 years ago prided themselves on their ability to memorize speeches that were hours long. Today, memorized speeches are usually used only for toasts, blessings, acceptance speeches, introductions, and sometimes in forensics. Use a memorized delivery in these situations:

- When your speech is very short
- When you want to say things in a very specific way
- When notes would be awkward or disruptive

The trick to a memorized delivery is to speak as naturally and conversationally as possible. Rather than focusing on remembering your words, focus on communicating your words to your audience. When you deliver a memorized speech, don't recite it but rather deliver it as though you were talking to your audience.

Delivery tips. To commit a speech to memory, follow these steps:

1. Write a manuscript of the speech using an oral style, not a written one.
2. Commit each line of your speech to memory.
3. Every few lines, set the manuscript aside and practice delivering them to an imaginary audience without reading them. Repeat until you can deliver your entire speech naturally and with confidence.
4. Once you've learned the full speech, practice it over and over, reminding yourself to listen to the meaning of your words. Remember, you want to bring the words to life and connect with your audience.

If you are delivering a long memorized speech, keep your manuscript nearby, if you can, so you can find your place if you get lost. If you can't keep your manuscript near you, someone else may be able to hold it and prompt you if you lose your place. If you lose your place and have no one to prompt you, continue extemporaneously or pause, backtrack to the last line you remember, repeat it in your head, and you should be able to remember what comes next.

Table 11.1 reviews the advantages and disadvantages of the four delivery methods. In addition, watch the video clips of student speakers Brandi Lafferty, Amy Wood, Carol Godart, and Hans Erian as they deliver parts of their speeches. Each of these speakers used a different method of delivery for her or his speech. Which delivery method do you think was most effective? You can use your CourseMate for *Invitation to Public Speaking* to watch these videos, respond to analysis questions, and compare your answers to those provided by the author.

Practicing the Public Dialogue 11.1

Compare Delivery Methods

In class, take an item out of your backpack or from your pocket. Turn to the person next to you and give an impromptu speech about this item. The speech can be informative, invitational, or persuasive and should be no longer than sixty seconds. Now find an example of something written—a paragraph in this textbook, the newspaper, or the like. Give another sixty-second "speech," reading the written material. With your partner, discuss the differences between the delivery styles. Which did you prefer to deliver? Which did you prefer to listen to?

Online Resources

CourseMate To learn more about giving impromptu speeches, check out **Web Connect 11.1: How to Give a Successful Impromptu Speech** through your CourseMate for *Invitation to Public Speaking*. Also consider the benefits and drawbacks of extemporaneous delivery by reading **Web Connect 11.2: Memorize, Read, or Extemporize?**

Good to Know!

memorized speech: Speech that has been written out, committed to memory, and given word for word.

TABLE 11.1

Advantages and Disadvantages of the Four Delivery Methods

	EXTEMPORANEOUS	IMPROMPTU	MANUSCRIPT	MEMORIZED
Definition	A speech that is carefully prepared and practiced from brief notes rather than from memory or a written manuscript.	A speech that is not planned or prepared in advance and uses few or no notes.	A speech that is written word for word and read to an audience.	A speech that is written word for word, memorized, and given word for word.
Advantages	Combines a conversational style with a speaking outline. Encourages careful organization.	Allows for a conversational style with few or no notes.	Helps present very detailed or specific information exactly as the speaker wants.	Frees the speaker to move about the room. No need for notes.
Disadvantages	Requires practice time. Speakers may be tempted to memorize the speech.	Requires thinking and organizing ideas quickly. No time for preparation.	Requires a conversational style that can be hard to achieve because the speaker reads from a full text.	Requires careful memorization. Speaker must remember important points and details without notes.

Verbal Components of Delivery

A speech's power comes not only from its words but also from how they are delivered. Speakers known for their delivery—for example, John F. Kennedy, Barack Obama, Ann Richards, and Martin Luther King Jr.—use **vocal variety**, or changes in the volume, rate, and pitch of a speaker's voice that affect the meaning of the words delivered. We achieve vocal variety by consciously using certain verbal components of delivery: volume, rate, pitch and inflection, and pauses. The proper articulation and pronunciation of words and a consideration of dialect are also important components of delivery.

Volume

Volume is the loudness of a speaker's voice. Common sense tells us that we want to speak loudly enough for our audiences to hear us but not so loudly that we make our listeners uncomfortable. Knowing just how loud to speak can be difficult because our own voice sounds louder to us than to the audience and because the appropriate volume varies with each situation. Culture also affects perceptions about appropriate speaking volume. For example, in some Mediterranean cultures, a loud voice signals sincerity and strength, whereas in some parts of the United States, it may signal aggression or anger. In some Native American and Asian cultures, a soft voice signals education and good manners.[3] However, in some European cultures, a soft voice may signal femininity, secrecy, or even fear.

Pay attention to nonverbal cues from your audience to help you adjust your volume. If you are speaking without a microphone, watch the faces and postures

Good to Know!

vocal variety: Changes in the volume, rate, and pitch of a speaker's voice that affect the meaning of the words delivered.
volume: Loudness of a speaker's voice.

of people in the back of the room as well as those in front as you begin to speak. If the people in the back seem confused, straining to hear, or are leaning forward intently, it's a signal to increase your volume. If the people in front move back in their seats and look uneasy, you likely are speaking too loudly. This is a signal to lower your volume.

When you use a microphone, you still need to pay attention to your volume. Before you begin your speech, test your voice with the microphone. Make sure you are the proper distance from it (neither too far nor too close) so the audience can listen comfortably. Don't turn off or avoid a microphone because it makes you nervous or you think people can hear you without one. Microphones exist to help audiences listen (and speakers speak) comfortably. Stay audience centered and use the microphone.

Rate

Rate is the speed at which we speak. There is no formula for the proper rate at which to deliver a speech. For example, Dr. Martin Luther King Jr. began his "I Have a Dream" speech at a rate of 92 words per minute and finished at a rate of 145.[4] The rate at which we speak conveys different feelings. When we speak quickly, we project a sense of urgency, excitement, or even haste. When we speak slowly, we convey seriousness, heaviness, or even uncertainty. Both a rapid rate and a slow rate have their place in a speech. However, too much of one or the other strains the audience's attention and may cause them to stop listening.

To check your rate, tape yourself for several minutes. Then play back the recording and assess your speed. If you are using a manuscript, each page (typed, double spaced, in a twelve-point font) should take two minutes to deliver. If you are much faster or slower, adjust your rate accordingly. You can also use rhythm (Chapter 10) to help you monitor your rate. Arranging your words into patterns so the sounds of the words together enhance meaning can help you vary your rate in an appealing way. Remember, rate is an audience-centered concern. We want to engage our audience, and our rate of speaking helps us in this effort by communicating certain emotions or energies.

When members of your audience come from varied cultural backgrounds or are nonnative speakers of your language, try to slow your rate so accents and unfamiliar words are easier to follow. Adjusting your rate in this way communicates an audience-centered stance and adds to your credibility.

Pitch and Inflection

Pitch refers to the position of tones on the musical scale, and in public speaking, it reveals itself in the highness or lowness of a speaker's voice. **Inflection** is the manipulation of pitch to create certain meanings or moods. Together, pitch and inflection help us communicate more effectively with our audience. Consider the word *well* and its different meanings when used in spoken language. The control of pitch and inflection allows us to say "well" in ways that suggest joyful surprise or indecision or indignation or pity. All speakers manipulate their pitch to create meaning during their speeches. All of us alter our pitch to ask a question, express

Good to Know!

rate: Speed at which a speaker speaks. **pitch:** Highness or lowness of a speaker's voice. **inflection:** Manipulation of pitch to create certain meanings or moods.

satisfaction or displeasure, convey confidence or confusion, or even communicate threats or aggression. Variations in pitch clarify meaning and help catch and maintain our audience's attention.

Speakers who do not pay attention to their pitch and inflection risk losing their audience. Speakers who do not alter their pitch speak in what is called a **monotone**. Other speakers may say everything in too low or high a pitch. When a speaker says everything in a monotone or a low pitch, the audience senses a lack of interest or energy. When the pitch is too high for too long, every word is communicated with equal enthusiasm, or "excessive zeal,"[5] and the audience begins to wonder which points are the most important. There are solutions to these problems. First, tape yourself so you can hear your pitch. If your pitch is too high, practice breathing more deeply (from the abdomen rather than the throat) and relaxing your throat muscles as you speak. Speak from your diaphragm rather than your throat, and read aloud regularly to practice this technique until you can get your pitch to drop naturally. (Note that proper breathing also helps you increase the volume of your voice and project your voice farther.) If you speak in a monotone or in too low a pitch, practice delivering your speech (or reading something aloud) in an overly dramatic way, using inflection, exclamations, and vocal variation as much as possible. With practice, vocal variation will come naturally and carry over into public speaking situations.

SAUL LOEB/AFP/Getty Images

Pauses

Pauses are hesitations and brief silences in speech or conversation. In speeches, they often are planned, and they serve several useful functions. Pauses give us time to breathe fully and to collect our thoughts during a speech or before we answer a question from the audience. Pauses also give audiences time to absorb and process information—they're like a rest stop, giving the audience a breather before continuing. Finally, pauses before or after a climactic word or an important point reinforce that word or point.

Pauses can also add clarity. Read the passage here without stopping to pause after any of the words.

> The back of the eye on which an image of the outside world is thrown and which corresponds to the eye of a camera is composed of a mosaic of rods and cones whose diameter is little more than the length of an average light wave.

Without pauses, it's hard to understand what's being said here, isn't it? Now read the passage again and note where you would naturally pause. Does the meaning of the passage become clearer?

The four pauses that make this passage easier to understand are after *eye*, *thrown*, *camera*, and *cones*.[6] These are places in written text where we would add commas to indicate meaning. In written text, pauses often are indicated by punctuation, but in speeches, audiences can't see the punctuation. Pause to punctuate your words as well as to establish mood, indicate a transition, take time to reflect, or emphasize a point. For example, in his speech on the pollution caused by using fossil fuels, Pres-

Speakers like Barack Obama incorporate vocal variety in their speeches to engage audiences. Consider the introduction to your next speech. Practice this part of your speech, listening for your vocal variety. Adjust your delivery as needed to make sure you catch your audience's attention and communicate your message clearly.

Good to Know!

monotone: Way of speaking in which a speaker does not alter her or his pitch. **pauses:** Hesitations and brief silences in speech or conversation.

ton used a pause to make a particular impact: "In fact," Preston argued, "according to the Southern California Edison Electric Transportation website, updated only last month, running for half an hour in urban air pollution introduces as much carbon monoxide into your lungs as [pause] smoking a pack of cigarettes."

Learning the art of the pause takes time and practice. Before you become comfortable with the brief moments of silence necessary in a speech, you may have the urge to fill the silence. Avoid **vocalized pauses**, or pauses that speakers fill with words or sounds like "um," "er," or "uh." Vocalized pauses not only are irritating, but they can also create a negative impression of the speaker. When a speaker uses so many vocalized pauses that they intrude into an audience's awareness, listeners may begin to question the speaker's knowledge and speaking capabilities.[7] If you have a habit of vocalizing pauses, try the following process to eliminate them:

1. Listen for vocalized pauses in your daily speech.
2. When you hear one, anticipate the next one.
3. When you feel the urge to say "um" or "er" to fill space, gently bite your tongue and don't let the word escape.
4. Wait until your next word of substance is ready to come out and say it instead.

It may take time to eliminate vocalized pauses from your speech, and you may feel awkward with the silence, but the results are worth the effort.

Articulation

Articulation is the physical process of producing specific speech sounds to make language intelligible to our audiences. Our clarity depends on our articulation—whether we say words distinctly or whether we mumble and slur. Articulation depends on the accuracy of movement of our tongue, lips, jaws, and teeth. This movement produces either "didjago?" or "did you go?" In fact, scholars of performance and delivery argue that poor articulation is a trend across all sectors of U.S. culture.[8]

Audiences expect public speaking to be more clearly articulated than private conversation. Speakers with an audience-centered focus care about clear articulation. Clearly articulated words communicate that you want your audience to understand you and can add to your credibility. For your audience to understand your ideas, they must be able to decipher your words. To improve your articulation skills, try the following exercise:

1. Several days before your speech, select a part of your speech or a short written text you can read aloud.
2. Practice saying each word of your speech excerpt or text as slowly and clearly as possible, exaggerating the clarity of each word.
3. Repeat this exercise once or twice each day before you give your speech.

This exercise will help you recognize how much you slur or mumble and teach you to speak more clearly when you give your speech. Don't worry—you won't speak in this exaggerated way when you finally deliver your speech, but your words will be much clearer.

Good to Know!

vocalized pauses: Pauses that speakers fill with words or sounds like "um," "er," or "uh." **articulation:** Physical process of producing specific speech sounds to make language intelligible.

Pronunciation

Just as you would not turn in an essay you knew was filled with spelling errors, never deliver a speech filled with pronunciation errors. **Pronunciation** is the act of saying words correctly according to the accepted standards of a language. Pronunciation and articulation may seem similar, but pronunciation refers to how *correctly* a word is said, whereas articulation refers to how *clearly* a word is said. For example, saying the word *nuclear* as "nu-cle-ar" (correct) rather than "nu-cu-lar" (incorrect) has to do with pronunciation, and mumbling either pronunciation rather than speaking it clearly has to do with articulation.

Pronouncing words correctly communicates to your audience that you have listened carefully to the public dialogue going on around you. You have taken care to learn the common language and pronounce it correctly. In addition, correct pronunciation of terms and names in a language other than your native one communicates your respect for that culture and enhances your credibility.

Dialect

A **dialect** is a pattern of speech shared by an ethnic group or people from specific geographical locations. Dialects include specific vocabulary that is unique to a group as well as styles of pronunciation shared by members of that group. All people have a dialect, and your own dialect comes from your ethnic heritage as well as the place you grew up. For example, do you say "wash" or "warsh" when you want something clean? How about "soda," "pop," or "coke" when you want a soft drink? Your choices reflect your dialect.

People who use a standard American dialect (the dialect newscasters use when they are on the air) often forget that they, too, have a dialect, and they sometimes view the dialect of others as inferior. For public speaking, dialect is important because speakers need to consider the effect their dialect has on those who are unfamiliar with it. Speakers may use words that aren't familiar to their audience or may pronounce words in ways that sound odd or different.

If you know your dialect will be unfamiliar to your audience, try the following:

1. Acknowledge your region of birth or ethnic heritage.

Practicing the Public Dialogue

Refine the Verbal Components of Your Delivery

If you'd like to get some feedback on the verbal components of your delivery, ask your public speaking class to help you. Here are some exercises you can do in front of the classroom using your classmates as your audience:

- If you are a very quiet speaker, begin speaking as softly as you can and increase your volume until all the people at the back of the classroom nod their heads to indicate they can hear you comfortably.

- If you are a very fast speaker, begin speaking as fast as you can and decrease your rate until your listeners nod to indicate they are comfortable with your rate.

- If you have trouble with vocalized pauses, begin using as many of them as you can while you speak for about sixty seconds. Then continue to speak for another sixty seconds, being careful not to use a single vocalized pause.

- If you struggle with articulation, pronunciation, or dialect, begin speaking as you normally would for about sixty seconds. Then slow your speech and say each word carefully until your listeners nod to indicate they can understand you clearly.

Online Resources

CourseMate For some ideas about how to practice varying your vocal style, access **Web Connect: 11.3: Improving Vocal Variety** through your CourseMate for *Invitation to Public Speaking*. And don't forget to use a dictionary to help you learn how to pronounce words correctly. You can access a dictionary online with Web Connect 10.1 from Chapter 10.

Good to Know!

pronunciation: Act of saying words correctly according to the accepted standards of a language. **dialect:** Pattern of speech that is shared by an ethnic group or people from specific geographical locations.

2. Talk about how that shapes your use of language by giving examples of some of the differences you've encountered between your dialect and those of your audience.
3. Define terms that are unfamiliar to your audience.
4. Soften the accent associated with your dialect if that accent is fairly strong and might hinder understanding.

Nonverbal Components of Delivery

The nonverbal components of delivery are those aspects communicated through our bodies and faces. For public speakers, these include personal appearance, eye contact, facial expression, posture, gestures, and proxemics.[9]

Scholars of interpersonal communication recognize that nonverbal communication has a powerful impact on the meanings exchanged between people. Researchers suggest that between 65 and 93 percent of the total meaning of a message comes to us through nonverbal signals.[10] Additionally, when nonverbal signals contradict verbal signals (for example, you say you're glad to see someone but your facial expression and physical posture suggest you're not), people tend to believe the nonverbal signals more than the verbal ones.[11]

For public speakers, nonverbal communication is especially important because it conveys meaning and it can either enhance or detract from the overall message. Let's look at how the components of nonverbal communication affect a speech.[12]

Personal Appearance

Personal appearance, or the way you dress, groom, and present yourself physically, is an important part of delivery. But how important? Consider the following sayings:

You can't judge a book by its cover.
Beauty is in the eye of the beholder.
Looks are everything.
Beauty is as beauty does.
You can never be too rich or too thin.
You can dress him up, but you still can't take him out.
Good-looking lawyers make more money.

Which statements are true? Does physical appearance matter, or is it irrelevant? Studies show that, indeed, personal appearance matters quite a bit. People deemed "more attractive" earn more money than their "less attractive" peers, and personal grooming plays a large part in our perception of a person's attractiveness for both men and women.[13] Attractive characteristics are defined as "those characteristics that make one person appear pleasing to another."[14] Even though we may say we shouldn't judge people by their looks, it seems that is exactly what we do.

Without a doubt, standards for attractiveness and beauty change with generations as well as with cultures and subcultures. Despite these differences, though, there is a basic standard for acceptable personal grooming in public speaking situations: the speaker's dress should be appropriate to the occasion.[15] If the

Good to Know!

personal appearance: Way speakers dress, groom, and present themselves physically.

occasion is formal, the speaker is expected to dress formally. If the occasion is casual, the speaker's clothing should be less formal. A speaker who shows up at a formal occasion in a T-shirt and shorts not only displays a lack of audience awareness but is likely to lose credibility. Similarly, wearing formal business attire to speak at a casual gathering is also inappropriate. In short, be sure your clothing matches the style and tone of the occasion.

Another standard for appropriate grooming in public speaking situations is to wear attire that is neither too revealing nor too restricting. As fashions change, standards for acceptability change. More than 100 years ago, displaying bare skin in public was considered highly unacceptable. Today, the amount of bare skin or body that can be exposed or accentuated is far greater, and many celebrities accept awards and make speeches wearing very little at all. However, most of us aren't movie stars or pop stars, so when giving a speech in public, we want the audience to listen to our message and not be distracted by our appearance. Dressing simply and tastefully does more than help your audience pay attention to your message. It also helps you move about comfortably and freely as you give your speech.

Delivery begins the moment the audience sees you, so pay careful attention to your personal appearance and present yourself appropriately for the occasion at which you are speaking.

AP/ Wide World Photos

Research suggests that a speaker's dress should be appropriate to the occasion. Actor Matt Dillon is shown here reading a farewell speech by baseball great Lou Gehrig at a New York Mets game to raise awareness of Lou Gehrig's disease. Do you think he is dressed appropriately, given his audience and speaking situation? When you've given speeches in class, have you considered the importance of your appearance? What do you think is appropriate to wear for a classroom speech?

Eye Contact

The second essential component of nonverbal delivery is **eye contact**, visual contact with another person's eyes. Like personal appearance, appropriate eye contact is affected by culture and gender. Most North Americans and Western Europeans expect a speaker to make extensive eye contact. However, in Native American cultures, as in Japan and parts of Africa, extensive eye contact is considered invasive and disrespectful. Gender, too, affects the meaning of eye contact. For men, direct and extended eye contact with another man may be perceived as a challenge or threat. For women, direct and extended eye contact with a man may be interpreted as an invitation to flirt. So knowing what to do with our eyes as we deliver a speech depends on knowing who is in our audience.

Even though the nuances of eye contact are complex, most cultures expect at least some eye contact during a speech. Eye contact has three functions. First, it is a way to greet and acknowledge the audience before the speech begins. Second, eye contact is a way to gauge and keep our audience's interest. We use eye contact to monitor feedback from our audience and adjust our volume, rate, and pitch accordingly. Third, eye contact is a way to communicate sincerity and honesty.

Audiences rate speakers who make eye contact for less than half their speech as tentative, uncomfortable, and even as insincere and dishonest.[16] In contrast, speakers who make eye contact for more than half their speech are viewed as more credible and trustworthy.[17]

For eye contact to be effective, try to do two things as you look out at your audience. First, make eye contact with many people in the audience rather than a few friendly faces. Make eye contact with people in all parts of the room, not just those immediately in front of you. Gather information about level of comprehension, interest, and agreement from as many people as you can.

Good to Know!

eye contact: Visual contact with another person's eyes.

Second, look with interest. Rather than scanning faces in the audience or looking over listeners' heads to the back of the room, really look at individual people in the audience. Slow down the movement of your eyes so you actually make a connection with people through your eye contact. Looking with interest communicates you are pleased to be speaking to your audience and are interested in their responses.

Facial Expression

Your face plays a central role in communicating with your audience, letting them know your attitudes, emotional states, and sometimes even your inner thoughts. Your **facial expression** is the movement of your eyes, eyebrows, and mouth to convey reactions and emotions. Actors are highly skilled at using their faces to communicate, and audiences appreciate this talent. Although you don't need to be as skilled as an actor, you do need to consider your facial expressions as you deliver your speech. A poker face, although useful in a card game, will not help you communicate your ideas.

You can use your facial expressions to communicate your own interest in your topic, your agreement or disagreement with a point, your openness to an idea, and even your feeling about an issue. Take some time to decide which facial expressions might be useful to include in your speech. If these expressions aren't coming naturally to you, practice them until you are comfortable delivering them.

Posture

Posture is the way we position and carry our bodies, and whether we realize it or not, people assign meaning to our posture. We are perceived as confident and relaxed or tense and insecure based, in part, on our posture. A confident speaker is often called "poised," possessing assurance, dignity, and a sense of calm. Nervousness can affect our posture, making us feel awkward and act in ways we'd never do in other situations: grip the podium with both hands, slouch over our speaking notes, pace back and forth, or stand stuck to one spot. These nervous reactions detract from our delivery and communicate a message we probably don't want to send.[18]

But by paying attention during practice to the way we carry our bodies, we can eliminate some nervous postures. To become aware of your posture during a speech, practice your speech in the way you actually will give it. That is, if you will deliver your speech standing, practice while standing up. Devise a makeshift podium if need be. Or if you are to sit while giving the speech, practice the speech while sitting, with chairs beside you and your notes on a table in front of you. Similarly, if you will use a hand-held or attachable microphone, practice with something resembling it so you get the feel of speaking with a microphone.

By practicing the speech in the way you'll actually give it, you can correct your nervous habits before you deliver the speech. For example, if you find that you pace or grip the podium tightly, you can replace the bad habit with a better one. If you discover you stand immobilized when you practice, you can add cues to your speaking outline to remind you to move during your speech. If you slouch, you can practice sitting up straight and looking out at your audience. In sum, your posture during your speech should improve if you pay attention to your body during practice.

Good to Know!

facial expression: The movement of your eyes, eyebrows, and mouth to convey reactions and emotions. **posture:** Way speakers position and carry their bodies.

Finally, pay attention to the way you begin and end your speech. Wait until you are at the podium or have the microphone in your hand before you begin talking. Don't start speaking until you are facing your audience and have made eye contact. Similarly, don't walk off the stage until you have finished the last word of your conclusion. Finishing your conclusion or your final answer before you leave the spotlight communicates confidence and a willingness to give every word the attention it deserves. These guidelines will help you remain audience centered.

Gestures

Gestures are movements, usually of the hands but sometimes of the entire body, that express meaning and emotion or offer clarity to a message. Students of rhetoric in ancient Greece and Rome spent hours learning specific gestures to accompany specific parts of their speeches. For example, certain gestures were used with transitions, and others signaled specific kinds of main points or ideas. These choreographed gestures were used until the eighteenth century.[19] Today, research on gestures in public speaking indicates that gestures should be as natural as possible rather than memorized.

However, beginning public speakers don't always know what gestures will appear natural in a speech. With only minor variations, natural gestures in a speech are the same as those you normally use in personal conversations to complement your ideas and bring your words to life. The same is true for public speeches. Gestures make our delivery lively, offer emphasis and clarity, and convey our passion and interest. Use these tips to help you with gestures:

1. *Vary your gestures.* Try to use different kinds of gestures rather than repeating only one gesture. Some gestures emphasize (a fist on the podium), clarify (counting first, second, third on your fingers), or illustrate (drawing a shape with your hands in the air). Try to incorporate a variety of these gestures into your speech.
2. *Use gestures that fit your message.* Sometimes, a point needs an extravagant gesture; at other times, a more subtle gesture is much more effective. For example, use a relaxed pattern of hand movement as you explain a point but a larger more vigorous movement when you are emphasizing something quite important.
3. *Stay relaxed.* Your gestures should flow with your words. Try to keep your movements comfortable and effortless. If you find a gesture makes you tense, drop it from the speech and replace it with something more casual and familiar.

You will find that as you relax and gain experience speaking, you will stop thinking about your gestures and simply use them as you normally do in conversation.

Proxemics

Effective speakers pay close attention to **proxemics**, the use of space during communication. Be mindful of how far away you are from your audience as well as how elevated you are from them (for example, on a platform or a podium). The

Good to Know!

gestures: Movements, usually of the hands but sometimes of the full body, that express meaning and emotion or offer clarity to a message. **proxemics:** Use of space during communication.

farther away you are, the stronger the idea of separation. The higher up you are, the more the idea of power is communicated.

You can work with proxemics in your delivery. Recall from Chapter 4 that the Dalai Lama worked without a lectern, sometimes even sitting down on stage. Although you don't want to remain too close to your audience throughout your speech, getting close to them at key points allows for greater connection and communicates a desire to be perceived as more of an equal. Try stepping from behind the lectern or down from the podium and moving closer to your audience. If you can't do this because you need a microphone or a place to put your notes, you might be able to move closer during a question-and-answer session. Doing so will help you communicate openness and a willingness to engage in conversation with your audience.

Practicing the Public Dialogue 11.3

Refine the Nonverbal Components of Your Delivery

As a class, discuss the differences in your styles of nonverbal delivery: Are you someone who likes to dress more formally or more casually? Do you have to make adjustments to your nonverbal style because of your cultural background? How much eye contact are you comfortable with? Do you wish you could stand closer to your audience or farther away? Would you prefer to hold the podium, gesture, or put your hands in your pockets? What about your personal preferences enhances your speaking presence and what might detract from it?

Online Resources

CourseMate Your Interactive Video Activities for this book feature dozens of speeches by student and professional speakers. If you'd like to work on improving your nonverbal delivery style, watch a few of these speeches and evaluate how the speakers handle the nonverbal components of delivery. Are there things these speakers do that you'd like to incorporate into your own speech? Are there things these speakers do that you'd like to avoid? For additional pointers about a specific aspect of nonverbal delivery, your personal appearance, access **Web Connect 11.4: Dress for Success** through your CourseMate for *Invitation to Public Speaking*. This resource is meant to help college students dress appropriately for job interviews, but it can also give you a sense of the type of dress that is acceptable for professional presentations.

Rehearsing Your Speech

Although it may sound odd, the more you practice, the more natural you will sound. This is because you will be familiar with your speech on many levels. You'll not only know the ideas but will also have some of the wording worked out. You will be comfortable with the verbal and nonverbal components of your delivery. And you'll feel more confident during your question-and-answer session, if your speech includes one, because you will have prepared and rehearsed the answers to questions you might be asked. (For information about how to handle question-and-answer sessions, see Chapter 4 and Appendix A.) Take a look at these guidelines for rehearsing your delivery. If you follow them, your delivery will communicate your interest in participating in the public dialogue.

1. Practice giving your speech aloud using your speaking outline (Chapter 8).
2. Practice all stories, quotations, statistics, and other evidence until you can deliver them exactly as you want.
3. When you are comfortable with your material, practice your speech in front of a mirror. Monitor your nonverbal communication and make adjustments as needed so you communicate your message clearly.
4. Now tape your speech and listen for vocal variety. Check your volume, rate, pitch and inflection, pauses, and how you articulate and pronounce words. If you think your dialect will hinder your delivery, make adjustments.
5. Practice your speech again, incorporating the verbal and nonverbal changes you worked out in steps 1 through 4.
6. Now practice a few times in front of a friend. Have the person ask you questions at the end of the speech and practice answering them. Incorporate any useful feedback your friend may offer.

7. Stage a dress rehearsal. Consider your personal appearance by wearing the clothing you will wear on the day you speak. Set up your practice area so it resembles the actual speaking situation as closely as possible. Consider proxemics and the space you want between you and the audience.

For more information about how to rehearse your speech effectively, access **Web Connect 11.5: Practicing Your Speech** through your CourseMate for *Invitation to Public Speaking*.

CourseMate

Rehearsing your speech in front of your family or friends is a great way to gain some practice and get feedback on your presentation. Whom would you practice your speech in front of? Why would you choose that person (or those people)?

Speaking Visually

Social Commentary, YouTube-Style

Considered a sort of "Speakers' Corner" that "both embodies and promotes democracy,"[20] YouTube allows its users to create their own videos and to upload and manipulate their favorite movie clips, TV clips, and music videos. Created in 2005 by former Pay Pal employees Chad Hurley, Steen Chen, and Jawed Karim, YouTube is now immensely popular. Every day people watch 2 billion videos and upload hundreds of thousands more to the site.[21] In 2009 *Entertainment Weekly* magazine put YouTube on its end-of-the-decade best-of list, summing up its appeal by describing the site as "providing a safe home for piano-playing cats, celeb goof-ups, and overzealous lip-synchers since 2005."[22]

Aram Boghosian for The Boston Globe

According to the *Boston Globe*, YouTube is also influencing a growing number of activists who use video imagery to speak their minds online. For example, when 23-year-old Elisa Kreisinger wanted to protest the lack of gay characters and story lines on

television, she didn't petition people to boycott HBO or write an angry letter to the *New York Times*. Instead, she remixed scenes from the TV and movie versions of *Sex and the City* into two pro-gay narratives and uploaded them to her blog, drawing 21,000 hits. "I wouldn't have done it if it was text-based," says Kreisinger. "Things are more easily communicated through video ... And there can be more powerful statements."[23]

The trend to use video to speak out about political and social issues has exploded recently, facilitated by Web 2.0 technology and inspired by the entertaining and informative videos created by video bloggers and *The Daily Show*. "Making media now is a powerful way of participating in all kinds of life, including civic and political life," says Lee Rainie, director of the Pew Research Center's Internet & American Life Project. People in their teens and twenties "are now deeply connected to the political process in a way that their parents, at their age, could never be."[24]

Chapter Summary

To deliver a speech to an audience is to share your hard work and well-planned ideas.

- Delivering a speech involves many components: delivery type, verbal and nonverbal considerations, and the rehearsal process.
- When we hear or give a carefully prepared and well-articulated speech, we realize that delivery is the art of clarifying issues and engaging audiences.

There are four types of delivery.

- An extemporaneous speech is delivered from brief notes or an outline.
- An impromptu speech is delivered with little or no advance notice or time for preparation.
- A manuscript speech is written out word for word and read aloud.
- A memorized speech has been committed to memory and is delivered without notes.

As you deliver your speeches, pay attention to both verbal and nonverbal components.

- To achieve vocal variety, be mindful of verbal components such as volume, rate, pitch and inflection, pauses, articulation, pronunciation, and dialect.
- To enhance your verbal message, consider the nonverbal components of your speech, including personal appearance, eye contact, facial expressions, posture, gestures, and proxemics.

Be sure to rehearse your speech.

- Rehearsing your speech helps ensure that your delivery will be smooth and comfortable.
- A well-practiced speech also helps you communicate your interest in your topic and in the public dialogue.

Invitation to Public Speaking Online

CourseMate Now that you have read Chapter 11, use your Speech Communication Course-Mate for *Invitation to Public Speaking* for quick access to the electronic resources that accompany this text. These resources include

- **Study tools** that will help you assess your learning and prepare for exams (*digital glossary, key term flash cards, review quizzes*).
- **Activities and assignments** that will help you hone your knowledge and build your public speaking skills throughout the course (*Practicing the Public Dialogue activities, review questions*).

- **Media resources** that will help you explore public speaking concepts online (*Web Connect links, Enhanced eBook*), develop your speech outlines (*Speech Builder Express 3.0*), watch and critique videos of sample speeches (*Interactive Video Activities*), upload your speech videos for peer reviewing and critique other students' speeches (*Speech Studio online speech review tool*), and download chapter review so you can study when and where you'd like (*Audio Study Tools*).

This chapter's key concepts and review questions are also featured on the following page.

Key Concepts

articulation (230)
conversational style (223)
delivery (222)
dialect (231)
extemporaneous speech (222)
eye contact (233)
facial expression (234)
gestures (235)

impromptu speech (224)
inflection (228)
manuscript speech (225)
memorized speech (226)
monotone (229)
pauses (229)
personal appearance (232)
pitch (228)

posture (234)
pronunciation (231)
proxemics (235)
rate (228)
vocal variety (227)
vocalized pauses (230)
volume (227)

Review Questions

1. Identify speakers you consider to have good delivery. What characteristics make their delivery strong? How many of these characteristics might you incorporate into your style of delivery?

2. Which method of delivery will you choose (or have you been assigned) for your next speech? Why? How will you make that method as audience centered as possible? Now identify the method of delivery that you actually prefer. If the two don't match, what will you do to feel more comfortable with the type of delivery you will use for your next speech?

3. Review the discussion in Chapter 1 about nervousness. Are there any tips that you can incorporate into your delivery? Which ones? Why do you think they are useful?

4. Identify the differences among extemporaneous, impromptu, manuscript, and memorized deliveries. What are the strengths and weaknesses of each type of delivery?

5. Write a quick speech and exchange the speeches among classmates. In groups, give that speech as though it were a tragedy, a surprise, or a hilarious story. Or choose some other approach that will allow you to work on vocal variety. How well are you able to match the verbal aspects of your delivery to the mood you have selected?

6. Check out Speech Studio to see how other students deliver their speeches. Or record a speech you're working on, upload it to Speech Studio, and ask your peers for their feedback. What feedback could you use to fine-tune your delivery before you give your speech in class? ✓Speech Studio

12

Visual Aids

IN THIS CHAPTER, YOU WILL LEARN TO:

- Discuss the importance of using visual aids
- Identify and describe the different types of visual aids
- Determine what to show on a visual aid
- Format visual aids

Tony Avelar/Bloomberg via Getty Images

Because we live in a visual culture, we have come to accept the information we get from visual messages as casually as we accept the sunrise. So prevalent are these images that when we are asked to listen without a visual stimulus, we often lose interest and become restless. Although people once listened to music and politicians without accompanying images and visual distractions, now we are bored by performances that aren't stimulating to the eyes as well as the ears. But what does our visual culture mean for beginning public speakers? In your speeches for your speech class, you probably will be asked to use visual aids. And in many of your speeches outside the classroom, you will want to display parts of your message visually. How do you compete with the sophistication of the images in magazines and newspapers, on television and computer screens, and in live performances? How do you take advantage of technology to craft visual aids that not only enhance your message but appeal to your audience?

speakers want, and often need, to design effective visual aids. To help public speaker, this chapter discusses the reasons for using visual aids, the various types of visual aids, helps you decide what to show on a how to format your visual aids, and offers guidelines for using them.

Why Visual Aids Are Important

You can certainly give an effective speech without visual aids. In fact, many of the speeches you've read about in this book were given without visual aids, including Martin Luther King Jr.'s famous "I Have a Dream" speech. Yet many types of speeches benefit from effective visual aids, especially those that describe a process, include complex information, or are intended to have great impact. Let's take a look at the important functions of visual aids in a speech.

Visual Aids Help Gain and Maintain Audience Attention

In 1996, when attorney Johnnie Cochran displayed the glove said to belong to accused murderer O. J. Simpson and told the jurors, "If it doesn't fit, you must acquit," he had his audience's full attention. Although his words were compelling and he used a memorable rhyme, the visual aid caught the jury's attention and kept them focused on his argument. A visual aid gives an audience something to focus on, and it reinforces your verbal message. If you want to capture your audience's attention, consider using a visual aid to complement your words.

Visual Aids Help Audiences Recall Information

One of the best-known studies of visual aids in speeches assessed the amount of information the audience recalls because of visual aids. Here is what the researchers found:

A *message without visual aids*
- 3 hours later: Audiences recall 70 percent of the information.
- 3 days later: Audiences recall only 10 percent of the information.

A *message delivered with visual aids only*
- 3 hours later: Audiences recall 72 percent.
- 3 days later: Audiences recall 35 percent.

A *message with both words and visual aids*
- 3 hours later: Audiences recall 85 percent.
- 3 days later: Audiences recall 65 percent.[1]

Clearly, visual aids assist with recall.

In another study, researchers asked people to examine a series of photographs and identify those that were repeated. With as many as 200 photographs in a series, people still could pick out the repeat photographs.[2] However, when recall was tested by listening to series of numbers, people begin to forget which numbers were repeated in series of only six or seven numbers. Although common sense tells us that it often is more difficult to remember numbers, this study reinforces the previous one: Visual information greatly improves audience recall. So one of the goals of your visual aids is to help your audience remember information.

Visual Aids Help Explain and Clarify Information

Research also suggests that visual aids can help you explain material and thus enhance the clarity of your information. Complex ideas and numbers can be hard to understand verbally but are much easier to sort out when displayed visually. Presenting an idea visually makes it more concrete. Visual aids such as handouts also increase the audience's continuity of thought because they can go back and check their understanding.[3] So the third goal of your visual aids is to help you explain or clarify your ideas.

Visual Aids May Increase Persuasiveness and Enhance Credibility

Research also suggests that visual aids may increase your persuasiveness and enhance your credibility.[4] Here's how:

- Visual aids clarify your message.
- Visual aids organize information.
- Visual aids identify key points.
- Visual aids facilitate the reasoning process.

In addition, images encourage audiences to make associations, so you can use both text and images to move your audiences toward a particular position.

Visual aids also can add to your credibility by bringing a visual dimension to your speech. Professional-looking and creative visual aids can energize your speech, making you appear more prepared, engaging, and lively. For example, a graph that displays a trend in people's attitudes is an excellent way to display the evidence you're using to back up a claim. It also helps you organize and clarify information, communicating an audience-centered perspective that contributes to your credibility.

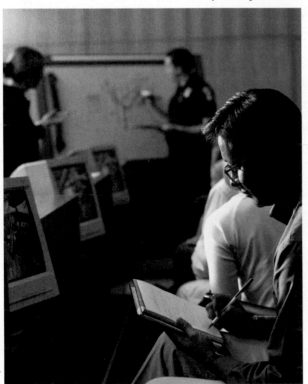

Guy Cali/Corbis

Visual aids can be quite powerful and memorable. Thus, they are often used in legal trials to help persuade juries of a defendant's guilt or innocence. What visual aids will you use in your next speech? How will they help you catch your audience's attention, help you be more persuasive, and enhance your credibility?

Visual Aids May Reduce Nervousness

Finally, visual aids may help reduce your nervousness.[5] When you prepare effective visual aids, you pay more attention to the effectiveness of your speech's organization. Better organization reduces nervousness because you know your ideas are logical and carefully planned. Visual aids also can direct audience attention away from you and give you something to focus on other than your nervousness. Additionally, visual aids give you something to do with your hands, helping you relax in front of your audience. For example, in her speech on fitness, Jemma used a fit ball (a large rubber ball used to stretch and strengthen muscles) as a visual aid. A very nervous speaker, Jemma found that as she demonstrated how to use the ball, her attention was focused on explaining her ideas rather than on her nervousness. Not only was she more relaxed, but the audience learned a great deal from her demonstrations.

Types of Visual Aids

There are various kinds of visual aids you may be required or choose to use. Every type of visual aid has its strengths and weaknesses, so don't settle on any one kind until you've decided what you want to accomplish with the visual aspect of your speech. Here we'll look at several of the most common visual and presentational aids for speeches: objects, models, and demonstrations; handouts; whiteboards and SmartBoards; DVDs and Internet images; and Power-Point presentations. For information about two other types of visual aids that are somewhat outdated but still used at times, slide projectors and overhead projectors, see Appendix B.

Objects, Models, and Demonstrations

An **object** is something that can be seen or touched, and a **model** is a copy of an object, usually built to scale, that represents that object in detail. Objects and models can better help your audience understand certain ideas because they present the ideas visually. However, objects sometimes are impractical or impossible to bring to a speaking situation. For example, when you give a speech about the workings of a car, you could not easily bring a real engine to class. In such cases, models are ideal. Models can be smaller than the objects they represent (a model

Displaying an object or a model can engage an audience immediately, and many speeches lend themselves to this type of visual aid. Several of the speakers in Chapter 8 displayed objects. For example, Candice showed a scrapbook, and Martha displayed different batik patterns.

of a car engine), larger (a model of the mechanics of a wristwatch), or life-size (a model of a human brain). In all these cases, the models allow you to show an object that otherwise would have been difficult to show.

You can also use objects to demonstrate a process. A **demonstration** is a display of how something is done or how it works. For example, Cindy used her flag to demonstrate the process of folding a flag. Candice showed a scrapbook she'd created to demonstrate how to compile a scrapbook. Martha displayed various batik styles as she described how batik is produced. If you can't demonstrate the process yourself, you can show a process from a YouTube (or other) video clip. When you display an object or a model or demonstrate a process, consider the following guidelines.

Make sure your visual aids and demonstrations enhance understanding. Some objects or models may be intriguing, but they won't enhance your speech. Choose an object or a model that clarifies information. Remember, you want to use the object or model to help your audience understand your topic better. When Lee gave his speech on the Vietnam Veterans Memorial, his only visual aid was a T-shirt he had purchased when he visited the memorial. Although the shirt was attractive, it did not help him clarify a point or illustrate the power of the memorial to evoke emotions. Lee would have been better off finding an Internet video of someone visiting the memorial to help him illustrate the memorial's power.

CourseMate

Cindy Gardner demonstrated the process of folding a flag. If you'd like to watch the video clip of Cindy giving her speech and evaluate how effectively she uses a demonstration, you can use your CourseMate for *Invitation to Public Speaking* to watch the video, respond to analysis questions, and compare you answers to those provided by the author.

Good to Know!

object: Something that can be seen or touched. **model:** Copy of an object, usually built to scale, that represents an object in detail. **demonstration:** Display of how something is done or how it works.

Public Speaking and Service Learning: Engaging Community

Candice Andrews, a public speaking student at Colorado State University, did her service learning project at A Turning Point, a substance abuse recovery center. One of Candice's interests outside class was creating scrapbooks, and she decided to incorporate this interest into her service learning experience and her speech. Scrapbooks are a natural visual aid that worked perfectly in the demonstration speech she gave to the young women at A Turning Point. Candice also did a wonderful job matching her own interests with the needs of her audience, creating a fun and informative audience-centered speech.

When I first found out that we had to volunteer as part of the course requirement, I felt a bit apprehensive. Then I discovered that one of the agencies I could volunteer for was a facility that housed juvenile delinquents. This intrigued me. I myself had a difficult childhood. My parents divorced when I was young. A few years later, my father was in a severe motorcycle accident that left him permanently disabled. To make the situation even worse, my brother was diagnosed with cancer when he was only sixteen years old. It took me a little while to find the positives in life and to realize that some people had it worse than I did. The decision to focus on the positives is what led me to making scrapbooks.

I started to collect happy memories in photographs and display them in a scrapbook. Once I had found my passion and creative outlet, I wanted to share it with others. That is what led me to A Turning Point, a facility where I could help troubled teens.

The girls I worked with were challenged teenagers who were trying to turn their lives around, and I wanted to help. I soon discovered that the girls I worked with wanted to learn something new. I began by going to A Turning Point on a Saturday morning and staying for ten hours. I spent the day snapping pictures of the girls having fun and playing. Next, I returned to give an interactive speech on how to make a scrapbook.

I brought along the photos I had taken and gave each girl several photos to include on her own scrapbook page. The girls had a great time designing their own page and learning how to focus their energy on something positive. I also used the photos I took at Turning Point in my own scrapbook and as visual aids in my speeches.

The public speaking class gave me the opportunity to take my creative talents and my public speaking skills and combine them into one. Whether you give a speech because you are asked to or are required to, I believe you can have a profound effect on someone in the audience. What you get out of a service learning project is what you put into it. And for me, it was touching someone's life through words and creativity.

> **"I COMBINED MY CREATIVE TALENTS AND PUBLIC SPEAKING SKILLS INTO ONE."**

Tips for Incorporating Service Learning into Public Speaking:

- Before deciding on what type of visual aid to use in your speech, consider your speaking environment. Is the room set up with a projector? Is there an easel to display posters on? Will you simply have to hold something up for all to see? It is better to create your visual aids with the environment in mind rather than adapt upon arrival.

- Emphasize the *visual* in your visual aids—use them to clarify points, hold your audience's attention, and assist with recall. Try to keep text on your visual aids to a minimum, and utilize them more for pictures, graphs, and other images that highlight your topic.

- E-mail yourself a backup copy of your electronic visual aids so you can access them even if something goes wrong in transit to your presentation.

- Don't forget to practice with your visual aids. As you rehearse, practice changing the slides in your PowerPoint presentation, putting up and taking down your poster, or holding up and walking around with an object or model. Practicing these actions will ensure that your speech flows smoothly.

Also try to avoid demonstrations that are too complex, require a lot of equipment, or might make you look awkward or unprofessional. If your process is complex, simplify it for your demonstration, show only a part of the process, or use the Internet to help you show your audience the process without having to deal with complex equipment. When Brock gave his speech on emergency rescue services, he wanted to talk about the importance of the equipment used and the knowledge that rescue workers need to use the equipment properly. To demonstrate some of the more complex knots rescue workers often use, Brock brought in ropes with knots already begun. He finished tying the knots for his audience, demonstrating their strength as well as their complexity. Rather than take his audience through the entire process, he helped them understand that process by having a part of it prepared and set up before he began his speech.

Choose objects that are legal and nonthreatening. Many interesting objects are illegal, threatening, or dangerous. Avoid displaying weapons, chemicals, drugs, or animals, all of which can be dangerous or difficult to handle. Although you may know how to handle these items outside a speech situation, you can't always predict what an animal, a dangerous substance, or other people will do during the speech. If you're not sure whether an object is appropriate for a classroom speech, check with your instructor.

Practice your demonstration before your speech. Don't leave anything to chance with a demonstration. Rehearse it several times before the speech to be sure your equipment works correctly, your steps are smooth and effective, and your words explain what you are showing the audience. If you are using a video to demonstrate something, download the segment you want before your speech so you can open it without any delays. Consider Oscar's speech on the martial arts. He practiced his demonstration in a small space, so he knew he could show his audience his martial arts moves without hurting someone or knocking things over. He also practiced when and how he would speak as he demonstrated various moves. Practicing his demonstration beforehand helped him decide whether he should demonstrate the moves himself or show images of them.

Handouts

Business speakers often use handouts as visual aids. Examples include bound copies of business plans or year-end summaries; agency or product brochures; maps and photographs; and photocopies of graphs, charts, or articles. Many handouts can be displayed on a PowerPoint slide or distributed to your audience electronically beforehand. But there are times when it's best to hand out a hard copy of your information so the audience can refer to it during a speech or read it later and pass it along to others. Handouts can elaborate on your message and help you spread it beyond your immediate audience. Before you decide to use a handout, check with your instructor to see if you're allowed to use them in your course. If you can use handouts, consider the following guidelines.

Mark the points you want to emphasize. One of the problems with handouts is that the audience sometimes has trouble finding the point you want them to focus on. To prevent this confusion, mark the points you want the audience to locate. Use letters or symbols or a more visual device such as color-coded plastic tabs. For example, if you want your audience to pay attention to one area on a graph or map, identify it with an arrow, symbol, or number. If you want them to turn to specific pages in a report, place tabs on those pages. Another way to help your audience locate specific spots in handouts is to show the page, chart, or map in a PowerPoint slide. Highlight the information or areas you will refer to and direct the audience's attention to those places as you speak. If you find an interesting image in a book or a magazine or on a website, you can isolate the image and reproduce it on a blank piece of paper or transfer it to a transparency or a Power-Point slide. Showing only the image will help you focus your audience's attention and prevent them from getting distracted by extraneous information.

Distribute the handout before or after a meeting. To avoid the disruption of passing out material during your speech, distribute your handouts before the meeting begins or your speech starts. This is less distracting for the audience and does not disrupt your speech. Alternatively, distribute a handout after you've finished speaking if your speech includes information you'd like your audience to take away with them.

Remember that the handout supplements the message. A handout should add information to your speech and not become its text. Do not read lengthy passages from the handout aloud. Just refer to its key points during your speech so your audience will be sure to note them when they read the handout after your speech. To avoid depending on the handout too much, outline its key points in your notes. And to keep your delivery extemporaneous, refer to the outline rather than to the handout itself.

Whiteboards and SmartBoards

Available in many offices and classrooms, whiteboards and SmartBoards are very convenient. They allow you to create a visual aid as you speak, clarify concepts during your speech, or keep track of ideas generated during discussions. They also help you when you need to respond immediately to audience confusion or questions. They keep information in front of the audience rather than having to remove it to make space for new information. With the SmartBoard, you can even duplicate what you write on it and make a handout for the audience at the end of your speech.[6] Used in these ways, whiteboards and SmartBoards can help you stay audience centered throughout your speech. If you use a whiteboard or SmartBoard during a speech, consider the following guidelines.

Write neatly and legibly. What you write on the board is not likely to be as neat as it would be on a prepared visual aid. It also hasn't been proofread for errors in spelling and grammar. So take care to write clearly, use a systematic organizational framework (such as an outline), and watch for spelling errors.

Speak to the audience, not to the board. We sometimes talk while we are writing on the board because we're trying to stay within our time limit and because we're involved in the speech and want to keep the momentum going. However, this means our back is to the audience while we're talking. To avoid this problem, stop talking when you turn to the board to write or repeat your comments when you turn to the audience. Although this may feel awkward the first few times, your audience will appreciate the care you take to speak to them directly.

Poster Boards and Flip Charts

Poster boards and flip charts can be a good choice for speeches because they are durable and can be reused. Like SmartBoards and whiteboards, flip charts allow you to record information during your speech, which is convenient for speaking in groups when brainstorming is a part of your process. Although many images can be shown to audiences electronically, a poster board allows them to see something up close and without the distortion that an electronic image sometimes has.

Because of their size (about twenty-four by thirty-six inches), poster boards and flip charts are not suitable for large audiences. Use them for small groups where everyone will be sitting near enough to read them. If you use a poster board or flip chart as a visual aid, consider the following guidelines.

Make the design as professional as possible. Take time to display your ideas neatly and professionally. Don't just throw something together. Instead, think carefully about what you want to include. Use color and images to attract interest and attention. Use rulers and guides to ensure straight lines for words and sentences. Print neatly and clearly so that you present a professional look. Make sure you will have a stand for the poster board or flip chart. If you plan to hang your visual aids, bring pins or tape with you and think ahead about where you will display the poster board or flip chart so everyone can see it. If you are in a classroom, placing poster boards on the tray of the whiteboard is tempting but can cause problems. The boards tend to fall over, and because the chalk trays are usually behind you, you may block the audience's view of your posters. So consider where you will place them and perhaps ask a member of your audience to display them for you. Finally, think about where you will put poster boards when you've finished discussing them.

Speak to the audience, not to the poster board or flip chart. As with whiteboards and SmartBoards, you may sometimes find yourself speaking to the poster board or flip chart rather than to the audience. To avoid this problem, practice your speech with the visual aid so you are able to glance at or point to it but talk to the audience. Note that the students speaking on affordable housing (Chapter 6) not only prepared visual aids that looked professional, but they also practiced using the poster boards so they were speaking to their audience rather than to the visual aid. They also worked in teams with one student pointing to the visual aids while a second student explained the significance of the numbers.

DVDs and Internet Images

You can use technology to support your speech with images and sounds of your topic. If your audience is unfamiliar with your topic, an image from a DVD or the Internet can help bring it to life like no other presentational aid can. But the power these tools have to captivate audiences also carries some risks. When you rely too heavily on these visual aids, they can take over your presentation and diminish your own significance as a speaker. If you decide to use DVDs or online images, consider the following guidelines.

Keep your clip brief. The longer your clip is, the bigger its presence in your speech becomes, and if you're trying to stay within a tight time limit, the less time you have to speak. For example, if you have five minutes for a speech, a one-minute clip would leave four minutes for your speech. And after you subtract the time for your introduction and conclusion, you'll have less than three minutes to develop your main points. Remember, the shorter your speech, the shorter your clip should be.

Cue and edit your segment. If you are using only one segment of a clip, cue up that segment before your speech. Then, when you deliver your speech, you

Cengage Learning

CourseMate

To see an example of a speaker displaying an image with a poster board, watch the video clip of student speaker Tony D'Amico. How effectively do you think Tony used his visual aid? Use your CourseMate for *Invitation to Public Speaking* to watch the video, respond to analysis questions, and compare your answers to those provided by the author.

only need to push Play to get the exact segment you want. If you are using more than one segment, make a master tape or copy them onto your computer so all of your clips are cued in the correct order in a single place, eliminating the need to switch DVDs or find a segment by fast-forwarding.

Don't compete with your visual or audio clip. Try to let the clip speak for itself. If you can, set the clip up for your audience beforehand and avoid talking over it so that your audience is not distracted.

PowerPoint Presentations

PowerPoint technology allows speakers to create slides containing text, diagrams, and images. The slides, in turn, can be arranged in any sequence, edited to include audio and video clips, printed on paper (for use as handouts), and projected onto screens or a monitor for viewing during presentations. This technology is excellent for large and small audiences.

However, as with all visual aids, you still need to think about what you want to display visually and the best format for that material. It may be tempting to use this technology because it has become so popular, but if it doesn't help your audience understand and recall your message, there is no point using it in your speech. When using Power-Point slides, consider the following guidelines.

Understand the purpose of a visual aid. Even though this technology offers a wide variety of design options (such as graphics, overlays, fadeouts, and sound), you don't need to use them all. Use only those that will help you focus, clarify, and organize your speech. Use this form of visual aid to enhance your message and build your arguments, not to impress your audience with the technology.

David Hartung/Bloomberg via Getty Images

PowerPoint and other multimedia presentations can be powerful, particularly when used to emphasize points and illustrate concepts that are difficult to describe in words. However, because this type of visual aid is so easy to create, it's easy to use it in a way that doesn't necessarily help you give a better speech. Access **Web Connect 12.1: Thinking Critically about PowerPoint** *to read an interesting article about how to best incorporate a computer-generated presentation into your speech, "How to Keep the Audience Awake and Learning" by Sharon Colvin.*

Prepare and practice in advance. As with any visual aid, take time to prepare your slides and the accompanying descriptions. Give yourself enough time to reorganize, add slides, and eliminate those that don't seem to contribute to your speech. Use your preparation time to decide which points (if any) lend themselves to fades, overlays, graphics, or sound. And don't forget to check for errors once you've designed your slides. Practice using and describing your slides so your delivery is fluid and extemporaneous. Finally, familiarize yourself with the projection equipment prior to your speech so that you won't run into any problems and can use technology to its fullest.

What to Show on a Visual Aid

Choosing the best type of visual aid to enhance your speech is your first step in using visual aids effectively. The second is deciding what to show on your visual aids. Remember the purpose of visual aids: to clarify, enhance, and illustrate your ideas and make your key points more memorable. You can accomplish your purpose by using visual aids that are based on text (lists), diagrams (charts and graphs), or images (drawings, photographs, and maps).

Lists

A **list** is a series of words or phrases that organize ideas one after the other. Lists are text-based visual aids, meaning they rely on the written word rather than on images to convey meaning. Use lists when your material lends itself to itemizing a group or a series, such as names, key features, or procedures. Lists help audiences keep track of material and identify the main points of a speech or discussion. The types of visual media best suited to lists are chalkboards and whiteboards, flip charts, poster boards, and computer-generated presentations. When you use lists, consider the following guidelines.

Make your list brief and balanced. A list is a synopsis, so keep your lists brief. Use keywords or phrases rather than full sentences. Your goal is to prompt the memory of your audience members, not to have them read your full text. Here are some examples showing how to shorten sentences to words or phrases:

Full sentences	*List*
Visual aids help audiences recall more information.	Recall
Visual aids help explain and clarify information.	Explain
Visual aids can enhance a speaker's persuasiveness.	Persuade
Visual aids can enhance a speaker's credibility.	Enhance credibility
Visual aids can reduce a speaker's nervousness.	Reduce nervousness

Follow the six-word/six-line rule, which suggests you use no more than six words per line and no more than six items per list.[7]

Note that audiences recall lists best if the items are parallel (Chapter 8). As you develop your lists, try to find balance or symmetry in the wording. For example, in a list of tips for using objects as visual aids, here's how you could balance your wording:

Incorrect	*Correct*
Use objects that illustrate or clarify.	Illustrate or clarify
Illegal and threatening objects may harm your audience.	Legal and nonthreatening

Remember, your goal is to cue your audience visually, not to overload them with text.

Include a heading. To help the audience keep track of your ideas, put a heading in boldface type at the top of your list. Because your audience can't go back and reread your written material, as they can with a full text, help them with recall by naming each list.[8] Here's an example:

The Importance of Visual Aids
- Recall
- Explain
- Persuade
- Enhance credibility
- Reduce nervousness

Good to Know!

list: Series of words or phrases that organize ideas one after the other.

Charts

Charts show steps in a process or parts of a concept. They can help speakers illustrate the relationship between the steps or parts and how each relates to the whole process or concept. The two most common charts used as visual aids are the flow chart and the organizational chart. A **flow chart** illustrates direction or motion—for example, the unfolding of a process or the steps to a goal. An **organizational chart** illustrates the structure of groups, such as organizations, businesses, or departments. Use a chart as a visual aid when you want to represent the parts of a whole or to simplify a complex process. Because charts are usually drawn in advance, the types of visual media best suited to them are handouts, poster boards, and PowerPoint slides. If you select a chart as your visual aid, consider the following guidelines.

Emphasize the visual image. When you create a chart, use single words or short labels for titles and positions and as few words as possible to describe the steps of a process. Help your audience visualize the process and its parts quickly and clearly by keeping it simple. Figures 12.1 and 12.2 are examples of charts that emphasize the visual.

Figure

Flow chart

Figure 12.2

Organizational chart

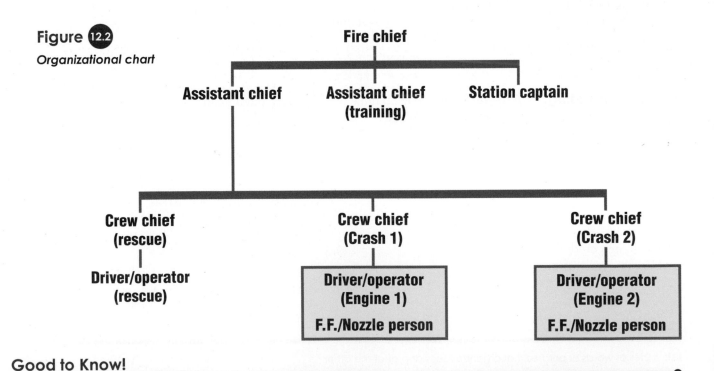

Good to Know!

flow chart: Chart that illustrates direction or motion. **organizational chart:** Chart that illustrates the structure of groups.

Use lines, arrows, shading, and color to show relationships and direction. To keep the audience's attention moving in the direction you want, use lines, arrows, shading, and color to help them follow your points as you explain the steps in a process or the structure of an organization. For example, in Figure 12.1, the yellow boxes show the beginning and the end of a fire department's response to an emergency, the green boxes indicate each step of the response process, and the arrows indicate the progression of the steps from beginning to end.

Graphs

When you want to compare numbers, quantities, or statistics, graphs are excellent visual aids. A **graph** is a visual comparison of amounts or quantities. Graphs help audiences see growth, size, proportions, or relationships. You can use different kinds of graphs for different purposes. **Bar graphs** compare quantities at a specific moment in time. **Line graphs** show trends over time. **Pie graphs** show the relative proportions of parts of a whole. **Picture graphs** present information in pictures or images. Figures 12.3, 12.4, 12.5, and 12.6 show how data from the U.S. Census Bureau could be represented using different graphs.

Figure

Bar graph

Source: U.S. Census Bureau, Population Estimates Program, April 1, 2000, and July 1, 2005.

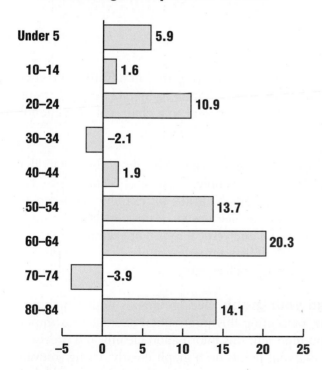

Percent Change in Population by Selected Age Groups: 2000 to 2005

Age Group	Percent Change
Under 5	5.9
10–14	1.6
20–24	10.9
30–34	−2.1
40–44	1.9
50–54	13.7
60–64	20.3
70–74	−3.9
80–84	14.1

Figure

Line graph

Source: U.S. Census Bureau, Current Population Survey, 1968 to 2006 Annual Social and Economic Supplements.

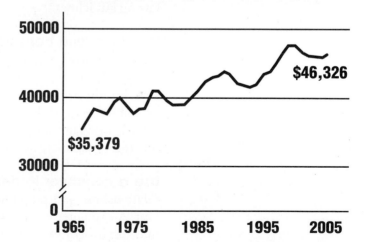

Real Median Household Income: 1967 to 2005

$35,379

$46,326

Good to Know!

graph: Visual comparison of amounts or quantities that show growth, size, proportions, or relationships. **bar graph:** Graph that compares quantities at a specific moment in time. **line graph:** Graph that shows trends over time. **pie graph:** Graph that shows the relative proportions of parts of a whole. **picture graph:** Graph that presents information in pictures or images.

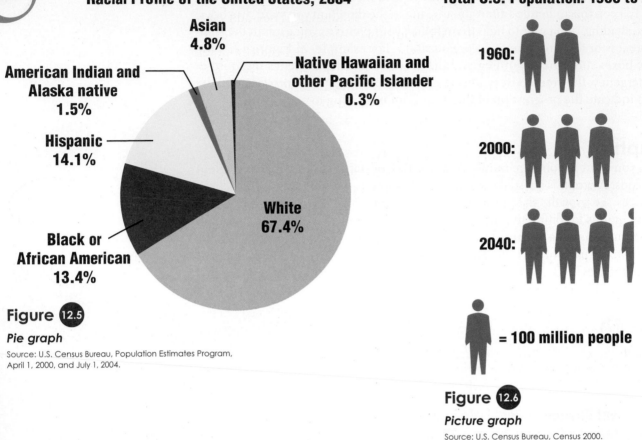

Figure 12.5

Pie graph

Source: U.S. Census Bureau, Population Estimates Program, April 1, 2000, and July 1, 2004.

Figure 12.6

Picture graph

Source: U.S. Census Bureau, Census 2000.

Like charts, graphs are most effective when prepared in advance and used for handouts, poster boards, flip charts, and computer-generated presentations. When you decide to display the figures you present in a chart, consider the following guidelines.

Use clear and consistent labels. Use descriptive headings for graphs that contain horizontal and vertical axes—for example, "Year" and "Percentage." For line graphs, mark equal intervals in the graph's grid—for example, numbers by tens, hundreds, or thousands and dates by decades or centuries. Show the numbers of those intervals on the horizontal and vertical axes. For example, the vertical axis in Figure 12.4 indicates 2005 dollars earned in intervals of $10,000. The horizontal axis indicates time in intervals of ten years.

Use a computer to design your graph. Because graphs display amounts, relationships, and proportions, presenting this information accurately is important. A computer can help you represent this information cleanly and precisely, drawing images to scale and marking points on a graph clearly. Using software such as Microsoft Excel (or an equivalent), simply enter the numbers and labels into the program's data table and select the type of graph you want to depict. You can even experiment with different kinds of graphs to see how they show your information.

Drawings

Drawings are diagrams and sketches of someone or something. They add clarity to your presentation because they help you show your audience what something looks like. You can create your own drawings, select them from computer or online clip art, or copy them from books, magazines, and other sources. The best visual media for drawings are handouts, poster boards, and PowerPoint slides. Simple drawings can also be rendered on a whiteboard or SmartBoard. If you decide to use drawings in your speech, consider the following guidelines.

Simple is best. According to many graphic arts texts, people seem to remember the outline of an image more than its details.[9] These texts advise you to keep your drawings simple. Use line drawings, symbolic representations rather than realistic drawings, simple clip art, and even children's art. When Cory gave a speech about the process of knitting a wool sweater, she used simple line drawings to illustrate how the wool from a sheep is processed into yarn. Remember, your goal is to represent your verbal message visually and not to use or create a great work of art (Figure 12.7).

Make sure the drawing clarifies the verbal message. Although drawings can be used to set the tone or communicate emotion, more often you will use them to explain your ideas and articulate your message clearly. Use drawings to depict shapes (for example, animals, buildings, symbols, and patterns) and to show details (for example, what someone with dyslexia sees or acupressure points on the body). Before you add a drawing to your speech, think about how it helps communicate your message. Does it clarify a concept? Does it illustrate something your audience may not have seen before? Does it simplify something that is complex? Be sure the drawing will enhance understanding for the audience.

Use audience-centered humor. You can use cartoons and funny or unusual drawings to make a humorous statement. However, first consider how your audience might react to the message sent by a drawing you find humorous. Consider the master statuses, standpoints, attitudes, beliefs, and values (Chapter 4) of your audience members. Be certain a humorous drawing will be funny to everyone. Reject drawings you think might offend or insult members of your audience. For more on the topic of humor in speeches, see Chapter 17.

Photographs

Photographs help you show your audience exactly what something looks like or what really happened. They can also add color and drama to your speech. Photographs are most often shown on PowerPoint slides projected onto a screen or a monitor, but you can also use them as handouts. Unless you can print or project a large enough copy of a photograph so that your audience can easily see it, you shouldn't display actual photographs while delivering your speech. If you think a photograph will help clarify your ideas or make your point, consider the following guidelines.

Figure 12.7

Simple line drawing

Source: From http://www.straw.com/ clipart. Used with permission.

Good to Know!

drawing: Diagram or sketch of someone or something.

Describe the photograph. To use a photograph successfully, you need to tell the audience what they are seeing. Call their attention to certain aspects of the photograph by describing them or explaining the action captured by the photograph. Don't be tempted to let the image speak for itself. Use the photograph to help you make your point by talking about it with the audience. For example, when Demetrious used photographs to describe the five villages of the Cinque Terre (Chapter 8), he pointed out the unique aspects of each village to help the audience distinguish them.

Don't pass out photographs. Rather than passing out original photographs to your audience during your speech, copy them and distribute them as handouts before the speech. When you are ready to refer to a photograph, call the audience's attention to the handout (in Chapter 7, Kameron did this to illustrate a zebra mussel colony on a buoy). Passing out individual photographs poses several problems: Original photographs are much more expensive than photocopies, especially if you are reproducing them for a large audience. Your audience will be distracted by them and by the process of passing them around the room. And by the time the last rows get the photographs, you will probably have moved on to a new point.

Do not display photos in a book. Images in books are too small to be seen by anyone but those sitting right in front of you. So instead of showing a picture in a book, reproduce it on a handout or use it to create a PowerPoint slide and project it onto a screen or monitor. Your audience will appreciate your effort to include everyone in the presentation, not just those in the front rows. If for some reason you cannot reproduce images from a particular book or want to show the entire book as well as the images it contains, display the book after the speech so the audience can get close to the images and even talk with you about them.

Maps

Maps are visual representations showing the physical layout of geographical features, cities, road systems, the night sky, and the like. Maps can help you show your audience the physical layout and characteristics of a place, its location in relation to other places, and the route between locations. Use a map to show your audience physical details that are best understood when presented both verbally and visually. The best visual media for maps are poster boards, handouts, and PowerPoint slides. If you decide to incorporate a map into your speech, consider the following guidelines.

Draw your map to scale. Because maps help audiences understand relationships, draw the map to scale so the relative distances are accurate. Put your scale of measurement on a corner of your map so your audience can gauge the actual distances. For example, in drawing a map of a certain neighborhood, the students from Chapter 6 used the scale of 4 inches = 1 city block. This kind of scale doesn't require precise measurements because the students were mapping something generally. A speaker would likely use a published map to illustrate specific geographical or astronomical features.

Good to Know!

map: Visual representation showing the physical layout of geographical features, cities, road systems, the night sky, and the like.

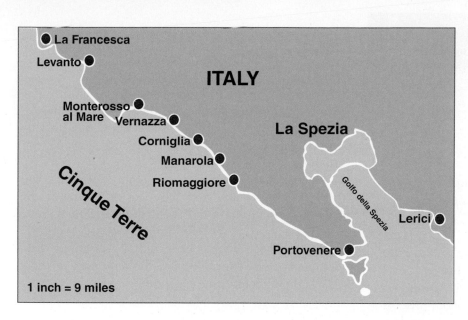

Figure 12.8

Map of the Cinque Terre region in Italy

255

Include the most important details. When you copy a map or draw one yourself, follow the same design principle you would use for drawings: Simple is best. Eliminate unnecessary details so the most important features will stand out. This will help the audience focus on your points and not get distracted by unrelated details. Just as you would when you draw a map for a friend, give your audience only the key points or markers to help them find their way or understand the path they should follow. Mark the parts of the map you want to emphasize using clear identifying features such as arrows, circles, or color. If you are giving directions or explaining movement, such as the migration of birds, mark the path with numbers or arrows (you can do this beforehand, or you can draw on the map with a highlighter or marker as you describe the path). For example, in Demetrious's speech about the Cinque Terre region in Italy, as he described each village, he could have circled it on the map to help the audience see where the villages are in relation to one another (Figure 12.8). If you want to use an image from GoogleMap, make sure it is clear and that you can find the points you want on the map.

If you hand out a map, show a larger visual aid of that same map. Use a PowerPoint slide or a GoogleMap image to explain a handout map to your audience. This way, you can point to or mark areas of the map rather than trying to describe them with words alone. This technique is especially useful when you want to point out several areas of a map and a handout would help your audience follow your discussion.

Speak to the audience, not to the map. As you describe your map, maintain eye contact with the audience rather than look at the map. This can be challenging because we usually want to follow the map with our eyes as we describe it. To prevent this, keep your notes in front of you and refer to places on the map by the number or color you used to highlight them or by pointing briefly to the map and then returning to your notes.

Once you've decided on the type of visual aid you want to use and what you want to show on it, follow some basic principles regarding formats, which are discussed next. These principles will help you design a visual aid that is easy to see and communicates your ideas effectively.

Practicing the Public Dialogue

12.1

Identify Visual Aids to Use in Your Speech

Identify one or two of the main points you will develop in your next speech. Outline that point and then decide what type of visual aid will help you make that point most clearly. Will it be a list, graph, photograph, video clip, or something else? Now decide how you will show the visual aid to your audience. Will you display an object before your audience or demonstrate a process? Will you show your visual aid in a handout or with a PowerPoint presentation? Discuss these choices as a class or in small groups, keeping in mind the question, "How does this visual aid help me establish my credibility and communicate more clearly?"

Online Resources

CourseMate Your online resources for *Invitation to Public Speaking* feature several video clips of student speakers using visual aids in their presentations. As you prepare your own visual aids for your speech, check out some of these videos to help you determine what type of visual aid might work best for you. For example, consider whether Carol Godart's PowerPoint presentation helped increase her persuasiveness and credibility in her speech about weight discrimination. Or evaluate whether Chelsey Penoyer's PowerPoint presentation on youth suicide followed the guidelines in this chapter for effective visual aids. To see an example of a speaker giving a demonstration, watch Cindy Gardner's speech on folding the U.S. flag. Or watch Josh Valentine's speech on African drumming for an example of a speaker using photographs and audio clips. And for an example of a speaker using a poster board to display an image, see Tony D'Amico's speech on Broadway musicals. You can access all of these speeches under the Chapter 12 resources in your CourseMate for *Invitation to Public Speaking.*

Formats for Visual Aids

Understanding a few basic design principles will help you develop professional-looking visual aids yourself or work with a graphic designer to create them. Don't underestimate the influence of these design principles. If you apply them with thought and care, they have the power to enhance your visual aids and, by extension, your verbal message.

Note that if you decide to create visual aids with Microsoft PowerPoint, you have access to many templates that incorporate the ideas discussed in this section. However, some of these templates don't follow the formatting advice offered here and so can detract from your message. Be sure to review the templates provided by PowerPoint before you use them.

Font Style and Size

A **font** is a type or style of print. Fonts range from simple to elaborate. As a rule of thumb, ensure the readability of your text by choosing a simple font over a fancy one. You will also need to choose between *serif fonts* and *sans serif fonts*. Serif fonts show small finishing strokes at the ends of the strokes of the letters and so create a baseline for readers' eyes, leading them easily from letter to letter. (The font you're reading now is a serif font.) Most newspapers and books use serif fonts, and if your visual aid contains a lot of text, this is an excellent font to use. To emphasize words, use a boldface version of your font to make the letters heavier and darker. Some common serif fonts are illustrated here, and you will find others on your own computer.

Times New Roman	**Times New Roman (bold)**
Bookman	**Bookman (bold)**
Palatino	**Palatino (bold)**

Graphic artists suggest you can add variety to your visual aids by using different fonts in your titles or headings. To do this, use *sans serif fonts*, or fonts without the finishing strokes at the ends of the letter strokes.[10] Because of their straight lines, sans serif fonts create a distinctive, crisp look. Thus, they tend to mark titles or headings as more prominent than the text in serif fonts that follows them. Some common sans serif fonts are shown here, and you will find others on your own computer:

Helvetica	**Helvetica (bold)**
Lucida Sans	**Lucida Sans (bold)**
Univers	**Univers (bold)**

Good to Know!

font: Type or style of print.

When you create your visual aids, avoid elaborate font styles, including shadow, embossed, engraved, and outline fonts. Although they look fun and interesting, they are more difficult to read and create extra work for your audience. Notice how your eyes have to slow down to identify each letter in the samples here:

Mistral
Robotik

Zapf Chancery
Handwriting

Save fancy styles for other projects and keep your visual aids simple and easy to read.

Font size is the size of the letters measured in *points*. The general rules for font size on visual aids are as follows. Note the size for headings, main points, and subpoints:

Headings: 30- to 36-point font

Main points: 24-point font

Subpoints: 18-point font

By varying your font size, you help your audience identify your main points and subpoints. Unless your audience will all be sitting close to the visual aid, don't use smaller fonts than these because they are hard to read from a distance. If people struggle to see your text, your ideas become difficult to follow. Note that in most classrooms, audiences start sitting at about two or three feet from the speaker, and they are farther if you are speaking, say, on a stage in an auditorium. To test whether your audience will be able to read the text on a projected visual aid, view it from about fifteen feet away. If you strain to read it, you audience probably will, too.

Color

When you add color to your visual aids, you tap into several design principles. First, color helps an audience make associations. For example, soft tones tend to set a calm mood, whereas bright colors tend to set an exciting mood. Note that the meanings of color, and the moods they evoke, vary across cultures. In Western traditions, red can bring to mind anger or passion. But in China, red often symbolizes good fortune, and in ancient Mexico, red symbolized the sun and its awesome power.[11] Second, different colors help your audience differentiate objects or items in a list. Finally, color creates hierarchies. For example, darker to lighter progressions indicate the level of importance, with the darkest the most important. You can use these three design principles to their advantage in your visual aids.

Notice how the addition of color to a visual aid can create a particular mood. In his speech about melanoma, Silas used Figure 12.9 when he discussed the dangers of spending too much unprotected time in the sun. The reds and oranges create an irritating, uncomfortable mood, implying the burning effects of the sun.

Good to Know!

font size: Size of the letters in a particular font measured in points.

He used Figure 12.10 with the same basic image, but with blues and greens, to create a cooler, soothing mood that implies shade and protection.

Figure 12.11 shows how dark and light tones can indicate levels of importance. In her speech about dangerous earthquake faults in northern California, Janice displayed a map that shows how intensely certain areas of northern California are likely to shake during a major earthquake. The darker colors indicate more intense shaking, whereas the lighter colors indicate milder shaking.

Figure 12.9

Beach in hot colors

Figure 12.10

Beach in cool colors

Figure 12.11

Map that shows earthquake intensity with color

Source: Courtesy U.S. Geological Survey.

When you use color in visual aids, establish a contrast between the text and the background so the text is legible. Avoid combinations of colors that are hard to read, such as bright red on dark green or white on light beige. Also, be careful not to overwhelm your audience with too much color. To find the balance you need, follow these suggestions:

Cool colors: Blue, purple, green. Cool colors are calm and relaxing for most people, and they tend to be easier on the eyes. Use no more than two of these colors per page. Use them for text or graphics (as alternatives to black and brown).

Hot colors: Fuchsia, orange, red. Hot colors are stimulating and grab the audience's attention. Use them sparingly to identify keywords or bullet points, create emphasis, or draw the audience's attention to one particular item.

Background colors: Soft yellow, light blue, lavender, light green, soft orange, and beige. Use soft colors such as these to create backgrounds and borders. Background colors also fill in solid areas that otherwise would have no color. Use them to add interest without grabbing the audience's attention. These colors should help the audience better distinguish and focus on foreground elements such as letters or images.

Balance

Balance is the visual relationship between the items on your visual aid. You establish balance by the way you use space to arrange your ideas. A balanced visual aid helps your audience find information easily and not feel as if their eyes are tipping in a certain direction. With text, it is easy to achieve balance by using bullets and indentation:

Heading
- First point
- Second point
- Third point

You also can achieve balance by dividing your page (or screen) down the center with an imaginary line. Consider the placement of your information carefully. A balanced visual aid sets the audience at ease and makes listening easier. It also helps you communicate your message clearly.

Guidelines for Effective and Ethical Use of Visual Aids

No doubt you will use many different types of visual aids during your speech class and over the course of your speaking career. As you've read through this chapter, you've probably noticed a few guidelines that came up again and again:

- **Prepare in advance.** By giving yourself adequate time to prepare your visual aids, you will avoid rushing to complete them at the last minute, and you can create visual aids that you can be proud of.
- **Practice in advance.** Practicing delivering your speech with your visual aids allows you to ensure that they will fit seamlessly into your presentation without any glitches. Practicing also lets you revise or change the order of the visuals if necessary before you give your speech. It will also be easier for you to maintain eye contact with the audience while you are presenting your visual aids if you have practiced beforehand.
- **Use your visual aids only when you discuss them.** When you're through discussing the point that relates to your visual aid, remove it from the audience's attention. This will help shift the audience's focus back to you and your next point.

Practicing the Public Dialogue 12.2

Design Your Visual Aids
Begin designing your visual aids for your next speech. Make sure you follow the basic design principles of font style and size, color, and balance. Prepare at least a couple of drafts for each of your visual aids, and then check with friends or classmates about which are most effective in presenting information and promoting recall.

Online Resources
CourseMate Most speech instructors ask their students to use PowerPoint to prepare visual aids for at least one in-class speech. If you don't already know how to use PowerPoint or would like some pointers, access **Web Connect 12.2: Creating a PowerPoint Presentation** at your CourseMate for *Invitation to Public Speaking*. This resource was created for teachers, but it is one of the best PowerPoint tutorials available.

Good to Know!

balance: Visual relationship between the items on a visual aid.

- **Explain what is shown on each visual aid.** Take the time needed to explain each visual aid fully rather than showing it quickly and moving on to your next point. Audiences will appreciate having each visual aid explained and will have an easier time understanding the relationship between your visual aid and your point.
- **Speak to the audience, not to the visual aid.** Because audiences look at visual aids briefly before turning back to the speaker, you want to be ready for them when their eyes return to you. By practicing your speech with your visual aids, you will be better prepared to make eye contact with audience members after they have viewed your visual aids.

Another important consideration is the ethical nature of your visual aids. As a guideline, remember that the goal of your visual aids is to clarify or illustrate your points so your audience will better understand your topic. You should avoid visual aids that might shock, disgust, horrify, or offend your audience, particularly within the classroom. One of the best ways to ensure that your visual aids will be appropriate for your audience is to remain audience centered when choosing them. Consider your audience's master statuses and adapt your visual aids to the needs of not only your speech goal but also your audience. Be sure to avoid misleading your audience: Make sure your visual aids are accurate and do not distort or exaggerate your claims. Sometimes, it may be tempting to jolt your audience with an extreme image or sound to gain their attention or make a point, but be careful not to jolt them too much. You want your visual aids to help your audience understand your message more clearly, not to be turned off about your message because of your visual aids.

Preparation Outline with Commentary

© Cengage Learning

The *Dun Dun* Drum

by Joshua Valentine

Specific purpose: To inform my audience about the how and why the dun dun *drum is used.*

Thesis statement: The dun dun *is an African drum with an interesting history that is used both musically and linguistically.*

CourseMate *This informative speech makes good use of photographs and audio to illustrate and clarify points. Use your CourseMate for* Invitation to Public Speaking *to watch a video of Josh Valentine giving this speech and see his transcript and speaking outline. Josh gave this speech in an introductory public speaking class. The assignment was to give a four- to six-minute speech with visual aids. Students were also asked to create a preparation outline that indicated where in the speech the visual aids were to be displayed, that cited the sources of the visual aids, and that included a Works Cited section.*

Commentary

Josh, a drummer, takes his topic from his interest in music. He catches his audience's attention by asking them to imagine using a musical instrument to communicate language, something people in the United States don't typically do.

In the second main point of his introduction, he introduces his topic. He adapts his topic to his audience by using a familiar source, *Webster's Dictionary,* to define what language is and then explains

Introduction

I. Imagine that your friend asks you what you did over the weekend, but instead of using words, your friend beats a drum. (*catch attention*)

II. You will probably never have such an encounter, but in some cultures, music is used for purposes that are different from those we are accustomed to. (*reveal topic*)

A. *Webster's Dictionary* defines language as "any system of symbols, sounds, or gestures used for communication."

B. Our culture does not have instrumental sounds that represent English words, but in other cultures around the world, sounds have meaning.

III. I have been playing percussion since junior high, and I first learned about the *dun dun* while attending a percussion workshop two years ago. *(establish credibility)*

IV. Today, I will explain the history of the *dun dun* as well as its linguistic use and its musical use. *(reveal thesis statement and preview main points)*

Body

I. The Nigerian talking drum, *dun dun* (pronounced *doon doon*), actually does talk, in the Yoruba language. *[Display photograph of dun dun drum downloaded and used with permission from http://media.dickinson.edu/gallery/Sect5.html.]*

A. The *dun dun* originated during the Oyo Empire of Yoruba-land in the fifteenth century A.D. for the purposes of worship.

B. Drums are constructed from trees located near roads where many people pass, which allows the tree to hear human speech.

C. The Yoruba language is easily communicated on the *dun dun*.
   1. Yoruba is a tonal language.
   2. Yoruba speakers use three basic pitches or tones, connected by glides, as an essential element of pronunciation.
      a. Listen to this sound clip and try to identify the three main tones. *[Play a sound clip downloaded for one-time use from the Internet.]*
      b. If you have a sharp ear, you may also be able to pick out some glides essential to the Yoruba language.
   3. Melody is the basis for the Yoruba language since the same word pronounced with a different melody means something different.

D. The *dun dun* functions by changing the tension of two skin heads using the leather straps that hold the heads in place. *[Point out the straps on the PowerPoint slide.]*

II. The *dun dun* was originally created to communicate.

A. The Yoruba from southwestern Nigeria have used drums for spiritual communication throughout their history. *[Show photo of carved drum downloaded from www.hamillgallery.com . . . YorubaDrum01.html.]*
   1. The *dun dun* was originally created as a tool for worship of the gods.
   2. Songs and hymns of praise were created entirely on *dun dun* drums and are still recited today.
   3. Listen to the intensity of this spiritual worship song played on talking drums. *[Play example downloaded for one-time use from http://www.world-beats.com/instruments/dundun.htm.]*

B. The Yoruba also used drums for social communication.
   1. The *dun dun* has been part of day-to-day casual conversation.
      a. According to the World Beats website, "A master drummer can maintain a regular monologue on a talking drum, saying hi to different people, cracking jokes, and telling stories."
      b. *Dun dun* drummers are often heard speaking the names of friends and family on their drums as a greeting and sign of respect.

C. The *dun dun*'s secondary, yet most obvious, use is as a musical instrument.
   1. It became a musical instrument because of its use in worship.

that although Americans don't use music as language, other cultures do.

He establishes his credibility by indicating that he is a musician and that he learned about his topic in a percussion workshop.

In the last point of his introduction, Josh previews the two main points of his speech.

Because his audience is unfamiliar with his topic, Josh uses his first main point to explain what the *dun dun* drum is, where it originated, and what it is used for.

By allowing his audience to see and hear a *dun dun* drum, Josh helps his audience better understand his topic. In particular, the audio clips let the audience hear what is complicated to explain in words alone.

He kept a careful record of where he obtained his visual and audio aids so he could cite his sources accurately in his speech. Note that he downloaded copyrighted material according to the terms of use posted by the websites he accessed—he requested permission or agreed to use the material only for his speech in class.

The visual aid Josh used for subpoint D of his first main point clarifies how the drum works.

In his second main point, Josh explains how the drum is used to communicate. He continues to use his visual and audio aids to enhance and clarify the information in his speech.

In subpoint B, he provides details that his audience can relate to: "saying hi," "cracking jokes," "telling stories." Notice that he cites his sources simply but effectively.

In point II.B.b Josh uses a specific example to explain how the Yoruba "talk" with the *dun dun* drum.

In point 2.C he adapts to his audience by explaining how the *dun dun* drum is used in a way that is familiar to people in the United States, as a musical instrument.

a. At first it was used mainly to communicate ideas, but since worship in the Yoruba culture is a corporate activity, people began coming together, and music on the *dun dun* was born.

b. Religious songs are still recited today, although often only for their musical value.

2. Even everyday speech becomes song when the Yoruba use the *dun dun*.

a. According to the website Drum Talk, the word *kabo*, which means "welcome," is only a two-syllable word, so a more common phrase "spoken" on a *dun dun* is, "Welcome, we are happy that you arrived safely."

b. "Speech" on the *dun dun* is always made rhythmic, even when the spoken word would not be rhythmic.

3. The *dun dun's* use as a musical instrument has spread far beyond Nigeria.

a. Next to the *djembe*, the *dun dun* is the most well-known and recognizable African drum used in America.

b. According to African American musician Francis Awe's drum clinic, "[It] fares well in jazz, blues, R&B, rock and roll, reggae, classical music, even choral music."

c. This clip comes from a song by Francis Awe. *[Play sample clip downloaded from http://www.nitade.com/html/cd1.html.]*

Josh ends the body of his speech with an audio clip that reinforces his final sub-subpoint, that the *dun dun* drum is now an international instrument.

Josh begins his conclusion by reinforcing that the drum is used for both language and music. He then summarizes his main points.

He ends his speech with an intriguing statement that encourages his audience to remember what he's told them about a particular African drum.

Conclusion

I. Whether in language or song, the *dun dun's* sound is always unusually beautiful. *(bring speech to an end)*

II. Today, we have seen the origins of the Nigerian talking drum (*dun dun*), its uses as a linguistic tool, and its uses as a musical instrument. *(reinforce thesis and summarize main points)*

III. So next time you hear music as simple as a beating drum, you might remember that the drummer may be communicating much more than you think.

Works Cited

Awe, Francis. *Talking Drum Clinic by Francis Awe.* 1999. Accessed March 20, 2007. http://www.after-science.com/awe/clinic.html.

BataDrum.com. "How Bata Drums Talk and What They Say." In *Understanding the Purpose and Meaning behind the Rhythms.* 2002. Accessed March 21, 2007. http://www.batadrums.com/understanding_rhythms/talk.htm.

DeSilva, Tamara. "Lying at the Crossroads of Everything: Towards a Social History of the African Drum." *Research, Writing, and Culture: The Best Undergraduate Thesis Essays, 1998–2000* (No. 2), 1997. Accessed March 20, 2007. http://www.artic.edu/saic/programs/depts/undergrad/Best_Thesis_Essay.pdf.

Drum Talk Ltd. *Background Information.* 2000. Accessed March 20, 2007. http://www.drumtalk.co.uk/drum_background.html.

Plunkett, A. "Nigeria (Africa) *Dun Dun.*" *World Beats.* 2002. Accessed March 21, 2007. http://www.world-beats.com/instruments/dundun.htm.

Chapter Summary

Audiences have come to depend on visual images for both information and entertainment.

- Using simple visual aids in your speech responds to this expectation and helps you clarify and communicate your message.
- In the public dialogue, visual messages are as important as verbal ones.

Visual aids have five purposes.

- Gain and maintain audience attention.
- Aid audience recall of information.
- Help you explain and clarify information.
- Increase your persuasiveness and enhance your credibility.
- Aid your preparation and thereby reduce your nervousness.

You can choose from a variety of visual aids.

- Objects, models, and demonstrations.
- Handouts.
- Whiteboards and SmartBoards.
- Poster boards and flip charts.
- DVDs and Internet images.
- PowerPoint presentations.

You can show six different kinds of information on your visual aids.

- Lists of keywords and phrases help you organize ideas sequentially.
- Charts help you break ideas into separate parts.
- Graphs allow you to compare quantities and amounts.
- Drawings show diagrams and sketches of people and things.

- Photographs show audiences how things look in real life.
- Maps help audiences understand places geographically and spatially.

When using any of these types of information on visual aids, pay careful attention to their formatting.

- Use legible font styles and sizes.
- Use color to create a mood that enhances your message; establish a visual hierarchy to help you differentiate among ideas, and create contrast so your visual aids are readable.
- Create visual balance to help your audience find information easily, set them at ease, and make listening easier.

There are several guidelines for using visual aids in speeches.

- Prepare the visual aid in advance. This allows you to make sure the design is effective and to make any necessary changes before the speech.
- Always practice your full speech with your visual aids so you become comfortable using them.
- When you are finished talking about the visual aid, remove it from view so your audience will return their attention to you.
- Always explain each visual aid to your audience so its meaning is clear.
- Speak to the audience when using visual aids so your attention is on them rather than on the visual aid.
- Always consider the ethical nature of your visual aids so that you do not offend or alienate your audience.

Invitation to Public Speaking Online

CourseMate Now that you have read Chapter 12, use your Speech Communication CourseMate for *Invitation to Public Speaking* for quick access to the electronic resources that accompany this text. These resources include

- **Study tools** that will help you assess your learning and prepare for exams (*digital glossary, key term flash cards, review quizzes*).
- **Activities and assignments** that will help you hone your knowledge and build your public speaking skills throughout the course (*Practicing the Public Dialogue activities, review questions*).

- **Media resources** that will help you explore public speaking concepts online (*Web Connect links, Enhanced eBook*), develop your speech outlines (*Speech Builder Express 3.0*), watch and critique videos of sample speeches (*Interactive Video Activities*), upload your speech videos for peer reviewing and critique other students' speeches (*Speech Studio*

online speech review tool), and download chapter review so you can study when and where you'd like (*Audio Study Tools*).

This chapter's key concepts and review questions are also featured here.

Key Concepts

balance (259)
bar graph (251)
demonstration (243)
drawing (253)
flow chart (250)
font (256)

font size (257)
graph (251)
line graph (251)
list (249)
map (254)

model (243)
object (243)
organizational chart (250)
picture graph (251)
pie graph (251)

Review Questions

1. Watch a few speakers outside class, live or taped, give speeches. Which speakers incorporate visual aids and which do not? What are the strengths and weaknesses of each approach?

2. Bring an object or a model to class and practice describing it to your classmates. Try holding it, displaying it, and passing it around. Which techniques work well for you and which do not? Why and why not?

3. Many students believe computer-generated visual aids are superior to other types of visual aids. Additionally, many employers want employees to be familiar with this technology. In light of this emphasis on a single type of visual aid, identify the strengths of computer-generated visual aids (such as PowerPoint slides and online images and video). What kind of material is best suited to this form of presentation? Although you may use this type of visual aid in your future workplace, what other types of visual aids might you also use?

4. Create several drafts of your visual aids using different font styles and sizes, colors, and principles of balance. Bring these to class and, in groups, select those that are most effective. Why are they effective? Why were the others less effective?

5. Select one of the following speech topics. Generate ideas for visual aids you could use for an informative, invitational, or persuasive speech on the topic.

   The Supreme Court

   musical instruments

   bubble gum

   corporate bailouts

   Alexander Graham Bell

6. Check out Speech Studio to see how other students use visual aids in their speeches. Or record a speech you're working on, upload it to Speech Studio, and ask your peers for their feedback. What feedback could you use to fine-tune your visual aids before you give your speech in class? ☑Speech Studio

Informative Speaking

13

Amanda Edwards/Getty Images

ur days are often flooded with information—images, ideas, stories, data, statistics, and more—yet, we don't always receive the full story. We may receive bits of useful information, but we don't always have enough to fully understand an important process, circumstance, or issue. Sometimes, the part of the story we have is inaccurate or incomplete, so our assumptions are skewed, as this quote by Jennifer, a student at Colorado State University, illustrates:

Sometimes people just need more information. Like the time my friends asked me, "Why can't I just leave my trash here? Isn't that what the staff is paid for, to pick up my trash?" or when they said, "Why does it matter if we lose certain species? I'll never see that animal anyway." I knew then that they didn't need persuasion or invitation; they really didn't know why it mattered. They needed information.[1]

To fully understand the world we live in, we need complete and accurate information. To meet that need, speakers in the workplace, in the classroom, and in our communities often speak informatively. An **informative speech** communicates knowledge and understanding about a process, an event, a place or person, an object, or a concept. Informative speakers share what they know or have researched to familiarize audiences with topics they want or need to understand.

- **Types of Informative Speeches**
- **Organizational Patterns for Informative Speeches**
- **Tips for Giving Effective Informative Speeches**
- **Ethical Informative Speaking**

IN THIS CHAPTER, YOU WILL LEARN TO:

- Describe the five types of informative speeches
- Apply the four most common patterns of organization for informative speeches
- Identify three tips for giving effective informative speeches
- Identify three principles for giving ethical informative speeches

Informative speakers create **informative speaking environments**, environments in which a speaker has expertise or knowledge that an audience needs but doesn't already have. When speakers create informative environments, their goal is not to invite (Chapter 14) or persuade (Chapter 15) but rather to illustrate for an audience how something is done or the importance and relevance of a topic. Informative speakers attempt to enhance an audience's understanding of how some part of the world works.

As you enter the public dialogue, you will give many informative speeches.[2] In fact, across professions, demand is growing for employees with strong public communication skills and an ability to share information with others in a wide range of settings.[3] We place such emphasis on informative speaking because we need information every day—for example, to understand how a new medication will affect us, to learn how to parallel park, to deliberate over the governor's proposal for spending a budget surplus, or to complete the complex assignment our boss just gave us.

Types of Informative Speeches

The five types of informative speeches most common in public speaking classes and the workplace are speeches about processes, events, places and people, objects, and concepts. Each type of speech has a different focus, and each is suited to a different occasion.

Speeches about Processes

Commonly called a how-to or a demonstration speech, **speeches about processes** describe how something is done, how something comes to be what it is, or how something works. Process speeches help an audience learn how to complete a task, understand how something develops over time, or comprehend how a process unfolds. The fundamental goal of a process speech is to show your audience how to *perform* a process or how to better *understand* a process. The following are some sample topics for process speeches:

- How to get a passport
- How coal is mined in the United States
- How to protect yourself from harmful sunburns
- How to determine how much to tip a server in a restaurant
- How a solar panel converts the sun's heat into energy

Process speeches are common because most people are constantly learning how to perform new tasks. For example, your boss may ask you to explain to a colleague how to fill out and submit an expense report. Or you may be asked to explain to new staff how an employee incentive program came to be implemented, especially if you have a history with that particular program. In the classroom, you may be required to speak about a process that your classmates will benefit from learning more about.

Good to Know!

informative speech: Speech that communicates knowledge and understanding about a process, an event, a person or place, an object, or a concept. **informative speaking environment:** Environment in which a speaker has expertise or knowledge that an audience needs but doesn't already have. **speech about a process:** Informative speech that describes how something is done, how something comes to be what it is, or how something works.

The following two examples illustrate process speeches about a very familiar topic: coffee. In the first example, Tracee describes how coffee came to be a popular drink in North America.

Specific purpose:	To inform my audience how coffee became one of the most popular drinks in North America.
Thesis statement:	Through a series of historical events beginning in the 1500s, coffee replaced tea as one of the most popular drinks in North America.
Main points:	I. Coffee found its way to North America in the 1500s when trade routes opened between coffee-growing countries and Europe and then expanded to North America.
	II. Coffee began to gain in popularity as tensions with England accelerated in the 1700s and imports of tea decreased.
	III. By the 1900s, international commerce, marketing techniques, and individual lifestyles made coffee one of the most popular drinks in North America.

In the second example, Wynton describes how the process of growing and harvesting a particular kind of coffee works.

Specific purpose:	To inform my audience how shade-grown coffee is grown and harvested.
Thesis statement:	The process of growing and harvesting shade-grown coffee differs from the process used by coffee plantations in three significant ways.
Main points:	I. Shade-grown coffee is grown in small plots, quite unlike the more familiar coffee plantation method.
	II. As the plants grow, these plots provide nonchemical forms of fertilizer and pest control.
	III. When the coffee beans are mature, they are harvested and stored in ecologically friendly ways.

Notice how each of these speeches follows a progression of steps, from first to second to third. Because process speeches describe step-by-step progressions, they are almost always organized chronologically. Recall from Chapter 8 that the chronological pattern traces a development or evolution over time. A chronological pattern of organization allows you to develop your speech from the first step to the last or from the earliest signs to the most recent examples. (Later in this chapter, you'll explore organizational patterns for informative speeches more fully.)

Speeches about Events

Speeches about events describe or explain significant, interesting, or unusual occurrences. These speeches help an audience understand what happened, why it happened, and what effect it had. We often describe what happens in our personal lives so we can better understand the influence of events. Similarly, public speakers

Good to Know!

speech about an event: Informative speech that describes or explains a significant, interesting, or unusual occurrence.

share what happens with audiences to help them understand a significant event in the context of history or society or community. In some ways, speeches about events are mini history lessons that educate audiences about key moments. Some sample topics for speeches about events are

> The eruption of Iceland's Eyjafjallajokull volcano
>
> The 2008 economic collapse
>
> The passing of the Health Care Reform Bill
>
> The death of civil rights leader Dorothy Height
>
> Large-scale food recalls

Speakers are often asked to speak about events, usually in professional settings. Consider Thom, whose boss asked him to speak to his fellow employees at a grocery store about the latest recall of beef in their region.

Specific purpose: To inform our staff of the most recent recall of beef and products that contain beef.

Thesis statement: This most recent recall of beef from our store requires that we identify all beef purchased within the last three months, identify all products containing beef purchased within the last three months, and remove and dispose of these products in very specific ways.

In a community setting, people may decide to speak about local events as a way to inform councils, planning boards, or community service agencies and perhaps assist them with the decisions they make.

Specific purpose: To inform the city council about the high rate of accidents at the corner of College and Elm Streets.

Thesis statement: The intersection of College and Elm is the site of an unusually high rate of accidents during certain hours of the day.

When you are required to speak about an event, select a topic your audience will find interesting and relevant. For example, inform your classmates of an event that affects your own campus (a public hearing to improve public transportation to the campus), the community that houses your campus (an annual jazz festival that showcases successful musicians from the community), or your state or region (a recognition ceremony for local volunteers who helped collect clothing for earthquake victims in Haiti).

Most speeches about events, especially historical events, are arranged chronologically. However, if the way an event unfolds is not the focus of your speech, you can organize your speech topically. Or if you want to analyze why an event occurred and what effect it had, you can use a causal pattern.

Bettmann/CORBIS

Historical events are often interesting topics for informative speeches, especially if they relate somehow to an audience's current experience. For example, the invention of the ENIAC computer in 1945 marked the beginning of a revolution in how we distribute, process, and store information. What historical events do you think might make a good topic for an informative speech?

Speeches about Places and People

Speeches about places and people describe significant, interesting, or unusual places or people. These speeches can be fun to give in a classroom because you can share your experiences with places and people you've visited or have found

Good to Know!

speech about a place or a person: Informative speech that describes a significant, interesting, or unusual place or person.

Chapter 13

fascinating. In the workplace or the community, speeches about places and people help audiences understand the importance, nature, appeal, charm, or integrity of a particular place or person or the contributions a particular person has made to an organization or a community. Some sample topics for speeches about places and people are

Service agencies in your community

Steve Jobs

Tanzania

Pro-democracy Buddhist monks of Myanmar

Michael Jackson

Supreme Court justices

Civic Engagement in Action

TO THE RESCUE!

Often people join the public dialogue to speak for those who can't speak for themselves. Sometimes these unheard voices belong to other people, such as children, or to entities such as the environment. Many times, these voices belong to animals.

Dog owner Lori Weise, a manager at a furniture store in Los Angeles, crossed paths one day with a homeless man named Benny Josephs and his pit bull, Iron Head. The bond between this man and his dog had a profound impact on Weise. "I was so impressed with how the two were really one," she says. "Iron Head was never on a leash and never strayed too far from Benny's sight." Her interactions with Josephs and Iron Head inspired her to found Downtown Dog Rescue in 1996. Since then, this organization has rescued and adopted out more than 3,000 dogs, provided resources for homeless people and their pets, and raised awareness in the Los Angeles area about animal cruelty. Lori is a tireless advocate for healthy and responsible pet ownership, using many channels to get the word out, including community events, letter writing campaigns, speeches at conferences, and Twitter.

Luigi "Shorty" Rossi is another Angelino who's big on bulls—pit bulls, that is. Rossi credits pit bulls with saving his life when he was young, providing loyal companionship during the hardest times of his life, including a stint in prison for gang-related activity. In 2001, after having made a successful career for himself as an entertainer and talent manager, he founded Shorty's Pit Bull Rescue. Just as Downtown Dog Rescue does,

Stephanie Diani/ Discovery Channel/Everett Collection

Shorty's Rescue rescues, rehabilitates, and adopts out neglected and abused pit bulls. The organization also promotes a positive view of this misunderstood breed, using education and activism to help prevent animal cruelty. Shorty's forums for speaking out include short films, public service commercials, and Animal Planet's reality show about his endeavors, *Pit Boss.*[4]

You Can Get Involved

 To learn more about how you can get involved with animal rescue efforts, access **Web Connect 13.4: Animal Rescue Directory** at your CourseMate for *Invitation to Public Speaking*. This Yahoo! directory provides thousands of links to animal rescue resources, searchable by region, type of animal, and organization websites. Also check out **Web Connect 13.5: Downtown Dog Rescue** to explore how you might get involved with Lori Weise's organization in the Los Angeles area. Finally, take a look at **Web Connect 13.6: Best Friends Animal Society**. Best Friends offers lots of opportunities to get involved with animal rescue efforts nationwide. Click around the many links on the site to see what you might be interested in doing with this unique and far-reaching organization.

Because you won't have time in a speech to discuss all there is to know about a place or a person, the goal of this type of speech is to capture the *spirit* of that place or person. You want your audience to understand why this place or person is important or useful to them or their community, important historically, or just interesting and worth learning about. Let's look at an example of a speech that Adrianna gave in her public speaking course.

Specific purpose: To inform my audience about the history and features of the Freedom Trail in Boston, Massachusetts.

Thesis statement: The Freedom Trail, which originated in the late 1950s, is a pedestrian path through downtown Boston that links sites of historical importance to the United States, such as our first public school and the site of the Boston Massacre.

In the next example, Garrett informs his classmates about Captain Nicole Malachowski, the first woman selected to join the Thunderbirds, the Air Force's most elite team of pilots.

Specific purpose: To inform my classmates of Captain Nicole Malachowski, the first woman selected to fly with the Thunderbirds.

Thesis statement: In 2005, the Thunderbirds, a small eight-person team of the best pilots in the Air Force, selected its first woman pilot, Captain Nicole Malachowski, to join them in flying the most advanced aircraft in the world.

Speeches about places or people can be organized topically (how the Freedom Trail was conceived, the importance of the historical sites to which the trail leads), chronologically (events in Captain Malachowski's life that led to her selection), or spatially (Big Bend National Park in Texas features recreational areas in the mountains, the desert, and at the Rio Grande River).

Speeches about Objects

Speeches about objects are about anything that is tangible, that can be perceived by the senses. When we speak informatively about objects, we describe the components or characteristics of something so an audience can better understand it and why it might be important or valued. Some sample topics for speeches about objects are

Nanotechnology   Honeybees

Hybrid automobiles   Poisonous frogs

Speeches about objects are common in the working world. For example, a product development coordinator might speak regularly to his colleagues about new products that come across his desk, describing their qualities, uses, and appeal. Similarly, tour guides often speak about local objects of importance or interest, describing buildings, sculptures, and pieces of art. For a required classroom speech about an object, you might describe something useful, rare, or interesting to your audience. For example, Jun Lee gave a speech about *Mona Lisa's* mysterious smile:

Good to Know!

speech about an object: Informative speech about anything that is tangible, that can be perceived by the senses.

Specific purpose: To inform my audience about the *Mona Lisa* and the many theories about her famous smile.

Thesis statement: One of the most famous paintings of all time, the *Mona Lisa* has inspired several theories about the reason behind her mysterious smile.

A very popular topic for speeches about *animate* objects is animals and their behaviors, habitats, and ways of interacting with humans and other animals. Here is a sample specific purpose and a thesis statement for Shana's speech about the African serval.

Specific purpose: To inform my audience about keeping the African serval as a house pet.

Thesis statement: Although the African serval's legs, ears, and coloration aid in its survival in the wild, these same adaptations have a whole new meaning when taken into the context of keeping a serval as an exotic house pet.

Many speeches about objects are organized topically (the characteristics of poisonous frogs). Others are organized using a causal pattern (possible causes of the colony collapse disorder plaguing honeybees), and sometimes, a speech about an object can be organized chronologically (hybrid automobiles, from the first to the latest model) or spatially (the different features of a hybrid car). Be sure to select the pattern that helps you express your ideas clearly and efficiently.

Speeches about Concepts

Speeches about concepts are about abstractions, things you can't perceive with your senses, such as ideas, theories, principles, worldviews, or beliefs. The goal of a speech about a concept is to help your audience understand your subject, its history, its characteristics, and its effect on society or individuals. Some sample topics for speeches about concepts are

The new frugality	Sustainability
Adult literacy	Theories of adolescent development
No Child Left Behind Act	Global citizenship

When you give speeches about concepts, you help audiences more fully understand or appreciate issues, principles, systems, and the like. Consider Tory's speech about "the new frugality."

Good to Know!

speech about a concept: Informative speech about an abstraction, something you can't perceive with your senses, such as an idea, a theory, a principle, a worldview, or a belief.

Specific purpose: To inform my audience about the new frugality, sometimes called "less is more."

Thesis statement: Because of our recent economic crisis, many people are embracing the values of the new frugality, which involves owning fewer material possessions, being less "possession-identified" and more "self-identified," and of course, spending less money.

Speeches about concepts can be challenging because it might be difficult to explain an abstraction clearly. However, this type of speech is also very helpful because sometimes audiences need to understand concepts before they can understand how something works or why a person is significant.

Speeches about concepts are often organized topically (the principles of the No Child Left Behind Act) or chronologically (early theories of adolescent development to the most recent theories). Sometimes, a speech about a concept can be organized causally (the causes of the idea of global citizenship).

Organizational Patterns for Informative Speeches

Informative speeches can be organized in a variety of ways, and you will probably use a wide range of organizational patterns as you become a proficient public speaker. As a beginning speaker, practice using the most common patterns, discussed in Chapter 8 generally and in this section specifically. These organizational patterns are the chronological, spatial, causal, and topical patterns. Using these patterns, you can organize your main points logically.

Chronological Pattern

With a chronological pattern, you can organize your main points to illustrate how a topic has developed over time or what steps an audience must take to complete a task. Most of us are familiar with the chronological pattern because most stories we tell or hear progress from start to finish chronologically. Chronological patterns are especially effective for process speeches, but as you learned earlier in this chapter, they also are well suited for other kinds of informative speeches. In the following example, Alan gives a speech to explain to his audience how the Ford Mustang set the standard for the muscle cars of the 1960s.

Specific purpose: To inform my audience of the history of the Ford Mustang.

Thesis statement: The Ford Mustang, which quickly became the muscle car to beat in 1964 with its combination of high performance and low cost, continues to be the most popular car of that decade.

Main points: I. Pontiac's GTO—which stands for "gas, tires, oil"—is credited as the first of the muscle cars of the 1960s.

II. Ford quickly took the top spot among muscle cars, releasing the high-performance, low-cost Mustang to the public on April 17, 1964.

III. Ford then added new makes with increasingly attractive features and options to maintain its popularity, among them the Fastback, the Grande, the Mach I, the Boss 302, and the Boss 429.

IV. The muscle cars of the 1960s remain some of the most popular cars of that decade, and the newer Mustangs give us a glimpse into why this is so.

Alan takes his audience through the evolution of muscle cars in the 1960s, beginning with the Pontiac GTO; then moving on to Ford's first Mustangs; its release of newer makes, features, and options; and the current influence of those features on today's cars. By using this pattern, he provides his audience with basic information they can build on as he progresses through his speech.

The next example illustrates how Joseph used the chronological pattern to trace the evolution of a concept. He described a spiritual belief system, its evolution, and the ways the system is integrated into every aspect of life.

Specific purpose: To inform my audience how the Kemetic civilizations of ancient Egypt created a holistic view of existence.

Thesis statement: Even though African civilizations are often thought of as pagan, the Kemetic civilizations of ancient Egypt created a holistic view of existence in which a monotheistic spiritual belief system was integrated into every aspect of life, including architecture and astronomy.

Main points:
I. This religious belief system began with the observation of heavenly bodies.

II. The Kemites began to integrate their knowledge of celestial cycles into their religious beliefs and identified many deities, each worshiped as different aspects of one God.

III. As the Kemites' body of knowledge increased, their society began to integrate their religious beliefs into every aspect of life.

Joseph takes the audience through an evolutionary process, tracing and describing the development of a belief system from its origins to its full development.

Spatial Pattern

The spatial pattern allows you to address topics logically in terms of location or direction. Recall from Chapter 8 that with this pattern you can arrange your main points by the position they represent within a physical space. You can use this pattern to inform your audience of the places that relate to your topic, the activities that occur in those places, or the activities that are necessary to the functioning of your topic. In the following example, Lehla uses a spatial pattern to describe the animal shelter she works for.

Specific purpose: To inform my audience about the animal shelter and the various kinds of animals we care for there.

Thesis statement: Although we care for dogs and cats at the shelter, we also have the capability to care for animals ranging from livestock to fish.

Main points:
I. Dogs and cats, which make up most of our clientele, are housed closest to the entrance for ease of care and visitation.

II. In the cages and containers behind the dogs and cats, we have birds, fish, and small reptiles.

Sigurgeir Sigurjonsson/Nordic Photos/Photolibrary

Many topics of informative speeches can be organized in several different ways. For example, a speech about the effects of extreme geographical events could be organized chronologically (the evolution of a particular geographical event) or spatially (the types of extreme geological events that occur in different parts of the world.) This photograph depicts the eruption of the Eyjafjallajökull volcano, which caused massive flooding in Iceland and grounded flights throughout Europe. How do you think you could organize this subject topically and causally?

III. Outside, in back of the shelter, we house the livestock, which need more space and open air.

IV. At the farthest border of the property, and under tight lock and key, we keep the large reptiles.

By addressing her topic spatially, Lehla guides her audience around the various parts of the shelter. They learn something about the shelter itself as well as about the animals, which was one of her primary speech goals.

In the next example, Scott uses a spatial pattern to describe the different parts of a guitar and how each part works to produce sound.

Specific purpose: To inform my audience of how the different parts of the guitar work together to produce sound.

Thesis statement: The guitar has three main parts—the head, neck, and body—and each works together in intricate ways to produce the sounds we call music.

Main points:
    I. The top of the guitar is the head, which houses the nut and the tuning pegs.

    II. The next part is the neck, which contains three essential parts: the frets, the truss rod, and the fingerboard.

    III. The bottom part is the body, which is made of a reinforced front, back and side panels, a sound hole, and the bridge and saddle.

The spatial pattern is a clear and effective way to describe the different parts of an object.

Causal Pattern

Causal patterns highlight cause-and-effect relationships. A cause is an event that makes something happen, and an effect is the response, impression, or change that results from that cause. When you use causal patterns, you inform your audience about what causes certain events, places, objects, or concepts to come into being.

In the following example, Kelsey describes how onions cause us to cry and methods to prevent tears when cutting an onion.

Specific purpose: To inform my audience about the cause of an onion's tearful effect and methods used to prevent tears when cutting an onion.

Thesis statement: The internal chemistry of the onion is the cause of its tearful effect when being chopped, but various methods may be used to prevent this occurrence.

Main points:
    I. The onion's chemical make-up, along with the human eye, combine to induce tears.

    II. The first method to prevent tears is chilling the onion.

    III. The second method involves using an open flame during onion preparation.

    IV. Using water around the onion is a helpful technique to reduce tears as well.

    V. The last method involves cutting the core from an onion, where most lachrymators are thought to be stored.

Kelsey's use of the causal pattern helped her explain what causes the tears and then how you can cause a reduction in those tears.

Topical Pattern

The topical organizational pattern allows a speaker to address different aspects of a topic. For example, in Shana's speech about the African serval, she organized her ideas topically to address the physical characteristics that make it so suited to life in the wild. Then she spoke about the consequences of bringing it into a domestic setting. Topical patterns work well for informative speeches when topics can be easily and logically divided into subtopics. Using a topical pattern, you can highlight the aspects of a topic that are most useful and important for an audience to understand. In Lauren's speech about the history of nursery rhymes, she used a topical pattern.

Specific purpose:	To inform the audience about the dark history of the origin of nursery rhymes.
Thesis statement:	Nursery rhymes are seen as innocent and lighthearted tales because they are always associated with children, but the truth is that stories like "Ring around the Rosie," "Peter, Peter, Pumpkin Eater," and "Mary, Mary, Quite Contrary" have dark and often gruesome origins that would seem anything but child appropriate.
Main points:	I. The rhyme "Ring around the Rosie" goes all the way back to the year 1350 in Europe, when the Black Plague was at its peak.
	II. The rhyme "Peter, Peter, Pumpkin Eater" is actually a rhyme about a man who forced his mistress to wear a chastity belt.
	III. "Mary, Mary, Quite Contrary" is actually the most gruesome rhyme of the three.

By using this organizational pattern, Lauren was able to use subtopics to inform her audience of the dark origins of many favorite childhood nursery rhymes.

Practicing the Public Dialogue

13.2

Select an Organizational Pattern for Your Informative Speech

Return to the list of possible informative speech topics you prepared in Practicing the Public Dialogue 13.1. In groups, select a single topic and see if you can create a rough thesis statement and main points for four different informative speeches on this topic, using each of the organizational patterns you've just read about. As a class, discuss which of these speeches you would find most interesting and why. As you discuss your favorite topic and organizational pattern, consider the tips for giving effective informative speeches in the next section.

Online Resources

CourseMate To consider the effectiveness of the organizational pattern one student speaker used for her informative speech, watch a video clip of Shana Moellmer giving her speech about the African serval. You can use your CourseMate for *Invitation to Public Speaking* to watch the video, respond to analysis questions, and compare your answers to those provided by the author.

Tips for Giving Effective Informative Speeches

In an informative speaking environment, you contribute to the public dialogue by sharing your knowledge with your audience, illustrating with clarity and detail the relevance of that knowledge to your listeners. Three tips that will help you create informative speaking environments and give effective informative speeches are (1) bring your topic to life, (2) tailor your information to your audience, and (3) use language that is clear and unbiased.

Bring Your Topic to Life

When you give an informative speech, you want your audience to understand your topic in a detailed and dynamic way. Effective informative speakers bring a subject to life for an audience, engaging their listeners so they appreciate the information they receive. Take careful stock of your topic and your audience so you can be sure to share information that is both *engaging* and *relevant*. Engaging material draws an audience in and excites or interests them. An audience finds material relevant if it is useful or something they must know to do their jobs, live in a community, or make informed decisions.

One of the ways to bring a topic to life is to stay audience centered. As you craft your speech, continually ask yourself how your overall topic, main points, and subpoints relate to your audience.

- What does the audience need to know?
- How will they use the information you present?
- How can you make the information clear?

If you keep these questions in mind throughout your preparation process, you will be more likely to present your material in an engaging and relevant way. For example, in a speech about school violence, Aaron brought his second point, perpetrator's manipulation by other students, to life by asking his audience a rhetorical question: "Think back to high school. How many examples of manipulative behavior can you think of? Probably too many. In my junior year, I remember one group of students who constantly picked on my friends and me. It felt like no matter what we did, we were the brunt of their jokes and the focus of their hostility." By sharing his own experience of manipulation, he touched on an experience common to many members of his audience.

Another way to bring your topic to life is to share the human side of your topic. If you are presenting technical information, explaining intricate details, or carefully outlining a process, try to use examples, images, and descriptions that help your audience connect to your topic personally. If you are presenting numbers or statistics, give the figures a human face. As one student asked after hearing

Demonstration speeches are often very engaging because they provide audiences with especially relevant, useful information. When you give this type of speech, remember to avoid overwhelming your audience with too much information. Consider a demonstration speech you might like to give. What is the most important information you think your audience would need?

Susan Van Etten / PhotoEdit

an informative speech about how to avoid the kinds of sunburns that lead to skin cancer, "What do all those SPF factors and fancy names mean for me and my skin tone personally?" As you prepare your speech, anticipate this kind of question and look for opportunities to relate your information to the human experience. For example, in a speech on modern art, you might personalize different techniques and styles by drawing parallels to skills learned in art classes or by asking your audience to attempt the techniques on their own as you describe them.

Tailor Your Information to Your Audience

Recall the discussion of information overload from Chapter 5. Just as you can feel overwhelmed by the abundance of information you find in your research, your audiences can be equally overwhelmed by the information you share with them in your speech—no matter how engaging and relevant you make that information. As an informative speaker, one of your most challenging tasks is to decide how much information to include in a speech and how much to leave out:

- When you present too much information, you run the risk of overwhelming an audience.
- When you present too little information, you run the risk of leaving them unclear or confused about your topic.
- If you present material that is too technical, detailed, and complicated, your audience will have a hard time following it.
- If the information in your speech is too simple, your audience will become bored or feel that you are talking down to them.

Given these dilemmas, the best way to tailor your information to your audience is to *stay audience centered* throughout the speech process. As you develop and present your speech, continually reflect on the needs and interests of your audience. Include information that you think would be of the greatest educational value for your audience, and adjust your presentation of this information so that it matches your audience's level of knowledge, expertise, and experience.

The decisions about what information to include or exclude can seem very subjective, but if you follow the principles of effective listening (Chapter 2), audience centeredness (Chapter 4), and organizing your speech for clarity (Chapter 8), you will find it easier to determine how much information to include in your speech.

Use Language That Is Clear and Unbiased

Because informative speeches focus on describing, defining, and explaining, use language that is descriptive and instructive. To ensure your audience can follow you, define all new terminology, break complicated processes into steps, and explain language specific to a particular field or activity. For example, when Wynton spoke about shade-grown coffee, he explained what the terms *shade grown, fair trade, organic,* and *sustainable* mean. Similarly, when Thom spoke to his colleagues about the beef recall affecting their store, he made sure his audience understood the specific dates and exact methods of disposal. You can also make a point of explaining familiar words you use in new ways. For example, Lauren took time to link what her audience thought were lighthearted phrases and words from the nursery rhymes to their darker historical origins.

Informative language should be as objective as you can make it. Focus on presenting your information as clearly and accurately as you can and avoid expressing your own views (as in invitational speaking) or trying to sway your audience (as in persuasive speaking). Remember that the goal of informative speaking is to pass along information your audience needs or wants. Make sure the language of your speech is fair and unbiased. Use phrases like "my research indicates that" or "according to the experts," rather than "I hope I've convinced you that this is the best way."

Similarly, when you incorporate personal knowledge into an informative speech, which is common when you describe or explain something you have experience with, make sure your language reflects your *experience*, not your biases or preferences. For example, phrases like "after seven years with these machines, I'd recommend the following steps" and "I've been involved in four food recalls since I began in this industry, so I can give you some background and details" are more informative than persuasive.

Ethical Moment

WHEN MUST WE SPEAK?

Republican Representative Joe Wilson received quite a bit of media attention for his response to President Obama's speech about his health-care bill, delivered to Congress on September 9, 2009. Representative Wilson shouted "You lie!" after President Obama stated that his proposed health-care plan would not cover illegal immigrants. In response to Wilson's outburst, boos could be heard from many members of the audience. The outburst caused President Obama to respond "That's not true" before continuing his address.

Immediately after the address, many members of Congress expressed their feelings of disappointment in Wilson's "disrespectful" actions. Wilson called and apologized to President Obama. Even so, members of the House of Representatives felt it necessary to discipline Wilson further for his outburst. Members passed a House resolution that stated, "Whereas the conduct of the Representative from South Carolina was a breach of decorum and degraded the proceedings of the joint session, to the discredit of the House: Now, therefore, be it resolved that the House of Representatives disapproves of the behavior of the Representative from South Carolina, Mr. Wilson, during the joint session of Congress held on Sept. 9, 2009." The Office of the Historian of the House stated that the resolution is the "first time in its 220-year history to discipline a member for speaking out during a presidential speech in the chamber to a joint session of Congress."

Yet Wilson was not the only member of Congress to demonstrate disapproval of the president's address. Republican Representative Louie Gohmert displayed

Chip Somodevilla/Getty Images

a sign around his neck that read, "What bill?" and a small group of Republicans raised a stack of papers in the air in response to President Obama's call to Republicans to share their health-care reform ideas. None of these members were disciplined by the House of Representatives.[5]

What Do You Think?

1. Do you believe Representative Wilson violated the standards of decorum for presidential addresses? Why or why not? Do you think members of Congress should be allowed to speak out during a presidential address to Congress? Why or why not?

2. Ethical informative speaking requires that speakers present information that is accurate, complete, unbiased, and honest. Do you think politicians should follow these guidelines? Why or why not?

3. Do you think the House of Representatives was fair in disciplining Wilson for his actions, but not Representative Gohmert or the group holding up the stack of papers? Why or why not?

The distinctions here may seem slight, but they are important because they set informative speaking apart from other kinds of speaking. For more information on the effective use of language, see Chapter 2 (how language affects listening) and Chapter 10 (language style).

Ethical Informative Speaking

Ethical informative speakers make sure their speeches are based on careful research, unbiased information, and the honest presentation of information. Let's take a look at each of these components of ethical informative speaking.

- Our audiences expect that we have taken the time to find information that is accurate and complete. So we must carefully research the details of our topic and share the full story with our audiences. If we haven't done this, we may wind up giving our audiences inaccurate or incomplete information. (See Chapter 5 for tips on how to gather accurate and complete supporting materials for your speech.)

- As an informative speaker, present unbiased information to your audience. Recall from Chapter 4 that although we all hold biases, we can take steps to minimize them. You can minimize your biases by presenting examples, statistics, testimony, and other materials as fairly and as neutrally as possible regardless of your personal positions. Save your preferences for your persuasive speeches; use your informative speeches to help your audiences gain a full understanding of your topic.

- Present your information honestly. Don't distort your evidence or make up supporting material as you need it. A healthy public dialogue depends on accuracy. If you misrepresent your speech topic, your audience will come away with an inaccurate view of important issues and situations. Ethical informative speaking relies on the honest and accurate distribution of information, which can happen only if speakers present that information truthfully.

Cengage Learning

Preparation Outline with Commentary

The African Serval
by Shana Moellmer

Specific purpose: To inform my audience about keeping the African serval as a house pet.

Thesis statement: Though the African serval's legs, ears, and coloration aid in its survival in the wild, these adaptations take on a whole new meaning in the context of keeping a serval as an exotic house pet.

CourseMate *You may have already given an informative speech in your class. Whether you have or whether this is the first time you've spoken informatively, you can use the following outline as a model. Use your CourseMate for* Invitation to Public Speaking *to watch a video of Shana Moellmer giving this speech and see her transcript, speaking outline, and note cards. Shana gave this speech in an introductory public speaking class. The assignment was to give a*

Commentary

Shana begins her speech with a rhetorical question, engaging her audience early. She piques their curiosity by suggesting they own a typical house cat rather than her unusual subject.

As she reveals her topic, she draws her audience in with a mention of the grassy savannahs of Africa and a brief history of the African serval. She also establishes credibility by citing her sources in her introduction.

Shana continues to draw her audience in to her subject with her positive but cautionary language about the drawbacks of keeping a serval as a pet.

At the end of her introduction, Shana clearly reveals her main points. She then uses a transition to signal to her audience that she is beginning her first main point.

Shana clearly states her first main point and uses several sub- and sub-subpoints to develop her ideas.

By citing relevant, reliable sources and providing interesting facts, she boosts her credibility and builds her argument about how the serval is adapted to a life in the wild rather than someone's home.

four- to six-minute speech, with a minimum of four sources cited. Students were also asked to create a preparation outline that included a Works Cited section and to use at least one visual aid in their speech. (In the video, Tim Estiloz delivered Shana's speech.) Remember that you can use your CourseMate to access videos of several other informative speeches, including Rachel Rota's "Tap," Chung-yan Man's "Chinese Fortune Telling," Elizabeth Lopez's "The Three C's of Down Syndrome," and Josh Valentine's "The Dun Dun Drum."

Introduction

I. By a show of hands, how many of you own a cat? (*attention getter*)
    A. I'm assuming those would be your typical 5- to 15-pound house cats, with the most exotic breeds being a Persian or a Sphinx.
    B. What would you say if I told you that you could own a 40-pound cat the size of a Labrador?
II. I'm talking about the African serval, which is native to the grassy savannahs of southern and middle Africa. (*reveal topic and relate to audience*)
III. The serval has been domesticated and brought into the homes of about 195 Americans, according to the 2000 cat census by the Long Island Ocelot Club, which is part of the Endangered Species Conservation Federation. (*establish credibility*)
    A. Although the serval can be domesticated, potential owners must know that this feline is well adapted to life in the wild.
    B. Bringing it into a domestic setting can have setbacks.
IV. Though the African serval's legs, ears, and coloration aid in its survival in the wild, these adaptations take on a whole new meaning in the context of keeping a serval as a house pet. (*thesis and preview*)

Transition: First, we'll look at how the serval's physical aspects allow it to survive in the wild.

Body

I. The African serval is a creature that is well adapted for life in the wild.
    A. On average, it stands about two feet tall, is three feet long, and has a ten-inch tail.
        1. Most of the serval's height comes from its long legs.
        2. The serval's legs are "the longest legs relative to its body of any cat species" (Nevada Bengals and Savannahs).
    B. The serval's legs benefit its survival.
        1. They allow the cat to stand tall in grasses of the African savannah, giving it a height advantage over its prey.
        2. In addition, they allow it to jump up to ten feet straight up into the air, which is a key hunting strategy (Serval Conservation Organization).
            a. Servals will leap up and crash down onto their prey, crushing it instantly or pinning it until they can get it securely into their mouth.
            b. A serval can even "capture . . . birds in flight by leaping . . . into the air and slapping them to the ground."
    C. The next trait of the serval that aids in its survival is its large, rounded ears, which help it locate prey.
        1. The serval's ears are quite mobile and move like satellites to pinpoint the location of a sound.
        2. The size of the serval's ears allows it to take in even the ultrasonic squeaks of savannah rodents.

3. Without these ears, the rustling of the tall savannah grasses would drown out all evidence of its prey.

D. Finally, the serval's coloration and spotting pattern provide camouflage and help deter its predators.

1. The serval's light brown coat with its scattered, dark-spotted pattern break up its profile, allowing the cat to blend into the shadows of the grasses.

2. In addition, the serval has matching white markings on the backs of its black ears.

   a. These markings are called ocelli.

   b. They deter predators, making it seem as if the serval has spotted the threat with eyes in the back of its head (Syminou—Exotic Cats).

Transition: Though the legs, ears, and coloration of the serval serve as important tools for survival in the wild, they serve a much different purpose when viewed in the light of keeping the serval as a pet.

II. For those who want to keep the serval as a pet, consider the consequences of bringing its wild adaptations into a domestic setting.

A. The serval's long legs and jumping capabilities make it difficult to keep it out of unwanted areas.

1. Jessi Clark, webmaster of ExoticCatz.com and avid serval owner, shares an insight into living with this large cat: "Domestic cats jump on your windowsills and the refrigerator, rarely disturbing household objects. Servals jump on your bookshelves, kitchen counters, tables, computer desks, and any other raised surface leaving a trail of destruction in their wake . . . Knickknacks on the bookshelf? Gone, or later discovered buried in the litter box. Stuff on your kitchen counter? Knocked over and sent flying several feet in random directions."

2. Special precautions must be taken if the serval is kept in an outdoor area.

   a. If the serval is kept in an outdoor enclosure, the enclosure should have a secure roof.

   b. A serval can easily jump and climb out of an inadequate enclosure.

B. The serval's ears, though useful for hunting in the wild, serve as a mood indicator in the domestic setting.

1. When a house cat is upset, it will hiss and raise the hairs on its back and tail.

2. But with servals, "these behaviors are just as likely to mean 'I love you, and I'm excited you're home' or 'Cool bird, Mom! Can I chase it?'" (Jessi Clark)

   a. The key is how the ears are placed.

      i. An upset serval will have its ears pressed flat against its head as it hisses.

      ii. An interested one will have the ears more erect.

   b. To properly assess the mood of this large pet, it's important to recognize that its body language—especially its ears—is different from a house cat's body language.

C. The serval's coat coloration, which kept it from standing out in the wild, instead draws attention in a domestic setting.

1. What common city walker wouldn't pause and stare at the spectacle of someone walking a cheetah-like, dog-sized cat on a leash down the street?

2. That big, colorful coat makes big, colorful hairballs.

Shana uses simple, yet interesting, language ("leap," "crash," "crush") to keep her audience interested in her topic.

In points I.C and I.D Shana uses brief transitions ("the next trait," "finally") to indicate that she is shifting her argument to address additional aspects of the serval's life in the wild.

Shana describes the distinctive markings behind the cat's ears, offers the formal name for those markings, and then explains their function. In following this topical pattern, she is able to present her information clearly and maintain her audience's interest.

Shana uses an internal summary and a preview to transition to her second main point. Using both, she is able to remind her audience of what they just learned and to signal them to get ready for her second point. In addition, she ties her main points together by using the material in her first main point to help her develop her discussion of the consequences of keeping an African serval in the home.

In point II.A.1, Shana supports her argument that it's difficult to keep servals as pets by quoting an authority. The quote uses familiar comparisons that her audience can easily relate to.

In point II.B, Shana again compares servals to the more familiar house cat so that she can inform her audience of the challenges of bringing a serval into a home.

She wraps up her second main point with a rhetorical question that again draws her audience into her topic. This question touches on a humorous aspect of owning a serval—big, colorful hairballs.

Shana provides a summary of her first main point, cites one of her authorities to review her second main point, and finishes her speech with an intriguing quotation, keeping her audience's attention until the very last line of her speech.

Conclusion

I. The African serval's adaptations serve it differently in the wild than in the domestic setting. *(review)*
   A. The serval's long legs allow it to leap and catch prey in the wild, and they let the serval get up onto high places around your house.
   B. Its ears serve to pinpoint the faint noises of its prey or to let you know how your pet is feeling.
   C. The cat's coloration provides camouflage in the wild, while declaring its exotic nature when walking down a suburban street.
II. Although it may seem that keeping a serval is more of a hassle than a privilege, Jessi Clark declares that "a well-raised serval really is incredibly sweet and amazing . . . [and] is worth every bit of the time and effort"—as long as you're willing to put up with the obnoxious moments as well as the cute ones. *(closing line)*

Works Cited

Buckley, K. J. (2000). LIOC-ESCF 2000 cat census. The Long Island Ocelot Club-Endangered Species Conservation Federation. Retrieved from http://efcf.org/Census00.html.

Clark, J. (2005). African serval. *Small cat species*. Exotic Catz: The Resource and Education Site. Retrieved from http://exoticcatz.com/speciesserval.html.

Nevada Bengals and Savannahs. (2009). The African serval. *Savannah cat info: The savannah cat*. Retrieved from http://nevadabengals.com/savannah.html.

Serval Conservation Organization. (n.d.). Servals in the wild. *Wild*. Retrieved from http://servals.org/home.htm.

Syminou Exotic Felines. (2008) The Savannah. *The Savannah/Serval*. Retrieved from http://www.syminou.com/savannah-en.html.

Chapter Summary

Informative speaking may be the most common form of public speaking.

- To speak informatively is to share knowledge with an audience to increase their understanding of a particular topic.
- To create an informative speaking environment is to bring a topic to life for an audience and to illustrate its relevance so an audience better understands its impact on their world.

The five types of informative speeches are about processes, events, places and people, objects, and concepts.

- Process speeches describe how something is done, how something comes to be what it is, or how something works.
- Speeches about events describe or explain a significant, interesting, or unusual occurrence.

- When you give speeches about places and people, you describe something significant, interesting, or unusual about your topic.
- In speeches about objects, you inform your audiences about anything that can be perceived by the senses.
- Speeches about concepts describe or explain abstractions, things you can't perceive with your senses, such as ideas, theories, principles, worldviews, or beliefs.
- These five different types of informative speeches can be organized chronologically, spatially, causally, or topically.

Three tips can help you give an effective speech.

- *Bring your topic to life*: Relate your topic to your audience by sharing the human side of that topic with engaging and relevant details.

- *Tailor your information to your audience:* Determine how much an audience knows about a topic and thus how much information to present.
- *Use language that is clear and unbiased:* Use language that focuses on descriptions, definitions, and explanations so audiences can more easily learn new information. This type of language sets informative speaking apart from invitational and persuasive speaking.

Make a point to commit to the principles of ethical public speaking.

- Research the information in your speech carefully.
- Present the information honestly and without bias.

◯ Invitation to Public Speaking Online

CourseMate Now that you have read Chapter 13, use your Speech Communication Course-Mate for *Invitation to Public Speaking* for quick access to the electronic resources that accompany this text. These resources include

- **Study tools** that will help you assess your learning and prepare for exams (*digital glossary, key term flash cards, review quizzes*).
- **Activities and assignments** that will help you hone your knowledge and build your public speaking skills throughout the course (*Practicing the Public Dialogue activities, review questions*).

- **Media resources** that will help you explore public speaking concepts online (*Web Connect links, Enhanced eBook*), develop your speech outlines (*Speech Builder Express 3.0*), watch and critique videos of sample speeches (*Interactive Video Activities*), upload your speech videos for peer reviewing and critique other students' speeches (*Speech Studio online speech review tool*), and download chapter review so you can study when and where you'd like (*Audio Study Tools*).

This chapter's key concepts and review questions are also featured here.

Key Concepts

informative speaking environment (266)

informative speech (266)

speech about a concept (271)

speech about a place or a person (268)

speech about a process (266)

speech about an event (267)

speech about an object (270)

Review Questions

1. Consider the following as possible informative speaking topics for your next assigned speech:

carpets   making pizza

social media   religion

Rihanna   subways

How many different kinds of informative speeches could you give on each topic? What would be the strengths or advantages of choosing one type of speech over another for these topics? How would your speech be relevant to the public dialogue?

2. Create a preparation outline for an informative speech on the topic of the U.S. response to natural disasters. How many different organizational patterns could you use for this topic? How would each pattern highlight a different aspect of this topic? How would you reduce the scope of your speech to make it manageable for your public speaking course?

3. In groups or as a class, identify five or six of the most commonly used, but poorly defined, terms you hear regularly. Use informative language to define those terms for your classmates. Some terms to define might be

democracy   socialism

free speech   hate speech

gun control   conservation

4. Select one of the topics from question 3 and write a specific purpose and thesis statement for a speech about that topic. Next choose your organizational pattern and develop the main points for this speech. How might you bring this topic to life and manage the information you have about this topic so it is relevant to the audience?

5. Check out Speech Studio to see informative speeches given by other students. Or record a speech you're working on, upload it to Speech Studio, and ask your peers for their feedback. What feedback could you use to fine-tune your informative speech before you give it in class? ✓Studio

15 Persuasive Speaking

IN THIS CHAPTER, YOU WILL LEARN TO:

- Describe the three types of persuasive speeches
- Apply the most common patterns of organization for persuasive speeches
- Identify three tips for giving effective persuasive speeches
- Identify the principles for giving ethical persuasive speeches

Throughout history, people have given persuasive speeches in political arenas, courtrooms, workplaces, community settings, social gatherings, and classrooms. Today, just as our ancestors have, we use persuasive speech in the public dialogue to influence and alter the perspectives, the positions, and even the lives of others. When you understand the principles of persuasive speaking, you too can add your voice to the public dialogue as a persuasive speaker whether you decide to speak, are asked to speak, or are required to speak.

dbtravel/dbimages / Alamy

A **persuasive speech** is one whose message attempts to change or reinforce an audience's thoughts, feelings, or actions. To ask an audience to see things the way we do is quite different from speaking informatively (Chapter 13) or invitationally (Chapter 14). When we speak to inform, we share our knowledge or expertise with an audience, helping them better understand a topic by providing information. When we speak to invite, we set the stage for exploration of a topic, encouraging an open discussion that welcomes different perspectives. In contrast, when we speak to persuade, we ask an audience to think as we do about a topic, to adopt our position, or to support our actions and beliefs. In that sense, we act as advocates for a particular issue, belief, or course of action.

This chapter discusses several aspects of speaking that are central to persuasion. You will explore the three major types of persuasive speeches, the organizational patterns best suited to persuasive speeches, some strategies for gaining audience support, and some of the common challenges and ethical considerations that persuasive speaking presents.

Types of Persuasive Speeches

Attempts at persuasion generally address questions of fact, questions of value, or questions of policy. Each category concerns a different type of change sought from an audience. Knowing which type of change you want to request from your audience members helps you develop a listenable message for them.

Questions of Fact

When we want to persuade an audience about debatable points, we are speaking about questions of fact. A **question of fact** addresses whether something is verifiably true or not. For example, we can determine with certainty who won last summer's Boston marathon by consulting a yearbook or looking up marathon records online, and so the facts concerning this topic are not open to debate. But we cannot absolutely determine the training schedule that will produce the fastest marathon runners in the future. Any claim to such knowledge is speculative and therefore open to dispute. An audience can be persuaded to accept one opinion or another about the best training method by a speaker's use of arguments, evidence, and reasoning (Chapters 7 and 16).

Our understanding of many topics today derives from theories that have not yet been conclusively proven. Whether it is the reason dinosaurs became extinct, the original purpose of Stonehenge, the techniques used to construct the Egyptian pyramids, the way to end the HIV/AIDS crisis, or the most effective methods to improve student reading skills, the facts about these issues are not absolute and leave room for competing theories. Therefore, they make excellent topics for speeches in which you try to persuade audiences that you have the correct answers.

Questions of Value

When we want to persuade an audience about what is good or bad, right or wrong, we are speaking about questions of value. A **question of value** addresses the merit or morality of an object, action, or belief. Is it right to continue offshore drilling for oil even though drilling presents risks to the environment? Is it moral to punish certain crimes with death? Is it ethical to require all children to say the Pledge of Allegiance in school? These are questions of value, as are debates over what constitutes "good" and "bad" art, music, or theater.

When you attempt to persuade your audiences about questions of value, you move from asserting that something is true or false to advocating that one thing is better or worse than another. Questions of value cannot be answered simply by analyzing facts. Rather, they are grounded in what people believe is right, good, appropriate, worthy, and ethically sound. Thus, it can be difficult to persuade

Good to Know!

persuasive speech: Speech whose message attempts to change or reinforce an audience's thoughts, feelings, or actions.
question of fact: Question that addresses whether something is verifiably true or not. **question of value:** Question that addresses the merit or morality of an object, action, or belief.

audiences about questions of value. This is because when we speak on questions of value, we must *justify* our claims. We must provide suitable reasons for accepting a particular action or view. When we justify a claim, we set *standards* and we argue that our view satisfies certain principles or values generally regarded as correct and valid by most people. So when we try to persuade an audience that drilling for oil is worth the risk to the environment, we justify that claim by arguing that the oil from offshore drilling meets a certain standard of necessity that warrants risks to the environment. Or when we attempt to persuade our audience that it is moral to punish certain crimes with death, we try to justify our claim on the basis of a particular standard: that certain actions fall into a specific category that warrants this kind of punishment.

Questions of Policy

When we want to persuade an audience about the best way to act or solve a problem, we are speaking about questions of policy. A **question of policy** addresses the best course of action or solution to a problem. What form of support should employers provide for veterans with disabilities? How should the federal government implement mandatory drug testing? How many credits for graduation should the university require? At what age should people be allowed to drink alcoholic beverages legally? Each of these questions focuses on an issue that cannot be resolved solely by answering a question of absolute fact or debating the morality of an issue.

Although questions of policy might address the facts about the contributions veterans make in the workplace or the morality of mandatory drug testing, they go beyond these questions to offer solutions and plans of action. In sum, speeches about questions of policy present audience members with a specific solution or plan to a problem and try to persuade them that the solution or plan will eliminate the problem satisfactorily.

Because each type of persuasive speech—questions of fact, value, or policy—focuses on different issues and goals for change, each requires a different type of organizational pattern to be most effective. Many persuasive speeches can be organized according to the patterns discussed in Chapter 8, particularly speeches about questions of fact and value. However, because speeches about questions of policy often call on an audience to take a specific action, they sometimes require unique organizational patterns.

Organization of Speeches on Questions of Fact

Speeches on questions of fact can be organized chronologically, spatially, and topically. To help you decide which organizational pattern is best, ask yourself the following questions: Can you achieve your goals best by describing the issue as it developed over time, by describing a spatial arrangement, or by covering distinct topics?

Thomas used the spatial pattern to organize his speech about campus lighting. He traced the layout of the campus from its center to its perimeter to make the case that it is not adequately lit for safety.

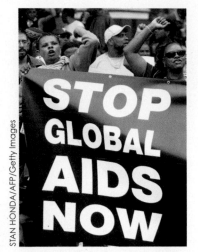

STAN HONDA/AFP/Getty Images

Persuasive speakers often ask audiences to take a course of action that will solve a problem or otherwise benefit a particular community. What problem do you feel needs to be addressed in your community? What course of action could you suggest that would motivate an audience to help you address that problem?

Good to Know!

question of policy: Question that addresses the best course of action or solution to a problem.

Specific purpose: To persuade my audience that the lighting on campus is not adequate

Thesis statement: From the library to the farthest parking lot, the lighting on campus is not adequate to ensure safety after dark.

Main points:
  I. Lighting near the center of the campus casts many shadows in which someone can hide.

  II. Around the perimeter of this center, the lighting is spaced too far apart to offer adequate protection.

  III. The lighting in the parking lots that border the campus should be much brighter than it currently is.

In the next example, Jacki used the topical pattern to develop her speech about the benefits of the school voucher system.

Specific purpose: To persuade my audience that the United States should implement more school choice, through the voucher system, as a way to increase performance and satisfaction for students

Thesis statement: Although there are arguments against it, implementing vouchers to increase school choice encourages schools to use resources more effectively, resulting in a better education for students.

Main points:
  I. A private school choice system means that the federal government gives vouchers, or money, to students to help pay for the cost of attending private schools.

  II. The Milwaukee Parental Choice Program (MPCP), which has been in place since 1990, currently serves 127 schools in Milwaukee, Wisconsin, and benefits both private and public schools.

  III. Vouchers encourage competition and break the stranglehold of teacher's unions, resulting in better education for students.

  IV. Although critics say vouchers pull the brightest students away from our public schools, the benefits and opportunities for all students outweigh this risk.

By organizing her speech topically, Jacki was able to discuss the main issues related to a school voucher system, including its benefits.

Practicing the Public Dialogue

15.1

Select a Persuasive Speech Type

As a class, brainstorm as many different persuasive speech topics as you can. Next, group the topics according to the three types of persuasive speeches you've just read about. Some might fit into more than one group depending on how you phrase your thesis statement for a particular topic. Discuss which of these topics you find most interesting and why. Save this list for the next Practicing the Public Dialogue activity.

Online Resources

CourseMate If you'd like to search for a persuasive topic on your own, access **Web Connect 15.1: 200+ Persuasive Speech Ideas** through your CourseMate for *Invitation to Public Speaking*. To see an example of a good persuasive speech, watch a video clip of Hans Erian giving his speech about the dangers of sugar. You can use your CourseMate to watch the video, respond to analysis questions, and compare your answers to those provided by the author.

Organization of Speeches on Questions of Value

Like speeches on questions of fact, speeches on questions of value can be organized chronologically, spatially, or topically. In the following example, Eiji used the chronological pattern to develop her speech about the value of encouraging girls to participate in the sciences.

Civic Engagement in Action

A FEW CITIZEN ACTIVISTS WITH BUCKETS

When activist Erin Brockovich and attorney Edward Masry—both made famous by the movie *Erin Brockovich*—became ill in 1995 from fumes emitted by an oil refinery that Masry was suing, the Bucket Brigade movement was born. Bucket brigades are community-based groups that use specially designed buckets, commissioned by Masry, to gather and test air samples in neighborhoods near state-owned oil refineries, chemical plants, and similar facilities that emit toxins into the environment. When people in these neighborhoods experience health problems they suspect are caused by pollution, they form bucket brigades to help crack down on facilities that are violating environmental laws.

The Bucket Brigade movement achieved one of its most important successes in 1999 when a Louisiana brigade successfully monitored emissions from more than fifty industrial facilities around Mossville, Louisiana, including vinyl plastic manufacturers, chemical production facilities, oil refineries, and a coal-fired power plant. Mossville residents had long complained of numerous illnesses but were repeatedly told by industry representatives that the facilities' emissions were not harmful. "I've asked [the refinery officials] to solve their problems, but they deny, deny, deny," explained Ken Ford, president of St. Bernard Citizens for Environmental Quality.

Fed up with the companies' total lack of response to their complaints, the community decided to make their problem a "national issue," says Anne Rolfes, director of the Louisiana Bucket Brigade. Mossville residents formed their own bucket brigade and began taking samples of air around the facilities, which revealed extraordinarily high levels of contaminants. Those levels were verified by the Environmental Protection

Louisiana Bucket Brigade

Agency, and offending companies were forced to pay fines and upgrade to state-of-the-art monitoring equipment. In addition, other towns in Louisiana's "cancer alley" took Mossville's cue and formed their own bucket brigades, leading to the establishment of the Louisiana Bucket Brigade. As a result, reports the Louisiana Bucket Brigade's website, "Pollution has been significantly reduced, all of which stemmed from a few citizen activists with their buckets."

Recently, the brigade has partnered with Grassroots Mapping, a group of Gulf Coast residents and activist mappers, who are documenting the effects of the BP oil spill in the Gulf Coast. Their goal is to collect data that will assist in the federal government's assessment and response to the disaster, as well as in the coming litigation over the spill.[1]

You Can Get Involved

CourseMate Check out **Web Connect 15.2: Environmental Issues** through your CourseMate for *Invitation to Public Speaking*. This About .com page features links to articles about environmental issues that would make good topics for persuasive speeches. Also access **Web Connect 15.3: Change.org**, an online hub that launches and promotes movements for social change on the web.

Specific purpose: To persuade my audience that encouraging girls to participate in the sciences is of value to us all

Thesis statement: Throughout history, when women have been encouraged to participate in the traditionally male-dominated world of science, they have made significant contributions that have benefited all of us.

Main points:

I. In the late 1700s, Caroline Lucretia Hershel's father and brother encouraged her interest in astronomy, and she developed the modern mathematical approach to astronomy.

II. In the late 1800s, with the support of her husband and colleagues, botanist Elizabeth Knight Britton built impressive botanical collections and is said to be the first person to suggest the establishment of the New York Botanical Gardens.

III. In the early 1900s, Maria Goeppert-Mayer was encouraged by her university professors to pursue her interest in science, which led to her winning the 1963 Nobel Prize in physics for her groundbreaking work in modeling the nuclei of atoms.

David Young-Wolff / PhotoEdit

Persuading an audience on a question of value can be a challenge, especially if audience members have different opinions about what is good or moral. Therefore, selecting an effective organizational pattern is important. For example, would it be more effective to persuade a group of teenagers that smoking is dangerous by discussing the diseases that smokers typically die of (topical) or by discussing the debilitating progression of a particular disease (chronological)?

The next example illustrates a question of value organized spatially. In this speech, Trevor arranged his main points so they followed specific locations within a city.

Specific purpose: To persuade my audience that the preservation of open space within and between communities should take priority in city planning

Thesis statement: Open space both within and along the perimeter of a city is crucial for a healthy community.

Main points:

I. Open space in the heart of a city creates a friendlier, more relaxed city center.

II. Open space in identifiable areas or districts within a city brings people together, resulting in more familiarity with one's neighbors and safer neighborhoods.

III. Open space between two cities reduces urban sprawl and strengthens people's attachment to their own city.

When we give persuasive speeches on questions of fact or value, we may ask our audience to change their view or agree on what is right or wrong, but we do not ask them to do anything. Therefore, the chronological, spatial, and topical patterns work well for these types of speeches. However, for persuasive speeches about questions of policy, we also ask our audience to agree on what must be done to solve a problem. Thus, we must rely on different types of organizational patterns.

Organization of Speeches on Questions of Policy

Persuasive speeches about questions of policy usually require organizational patterns that clearly define a problem and then offer a well-developed solution. Determining the best pattern for your speech depends on the kind of change you are hoping to get from your audience: *immediate action* or *passive agreement*. The differences between the two are simple, yet the impact they have on a speech is significant.

When you attempt to **gain immediate action**, your goal is to encourage an audience to engage in a specific behavior or take a specific action. You want to move beyond simply asking your audience to alter a belief. When you seek immediate action, you want to be as specific as possible in stating what you want your audience to do. You need a clear **call to action**, an explicit request that an audience engage in some clearly stated behavior. For example, rather than asking audience members to simply agree with you that the lighting on campus is inadequate, you ask them to contact the school administration and urge its staff to provide the funds needed to improve campus lighting in next year's budget.

In contrast, when you want to **gain passive agreement**, your goal is to ask an audience to adopt a new position without asking them to act in support of that position. When you seek passive agreement, you still advocate a solution to a problem, but you don't call your audience to action. Instead, you simply encourage them to adopt a new position or perspective. Consider the differences between requesting immediate action and passive agreement in the following specific purpose statements:

Immediate action

To persuade my audience to vote against placing vending machines in our public schools

To persuade my audience to adopt my aerobics training program

Passive agreement

To persuade my audience that open space in a city benefits that city and its residents by making it more attractive and livable

To persuade my audience that childhood obesity is a serious problem

Notice how the requests for immediate action focus on asking an audience to do something specific, whereas the requests for passive agreement simply ask an audience to alter a belief. Let's look at some organizational patterns that will help you meet your speech goals whether you request immediate action or passive agreement.

Problem-Solution Organization

Speeches that follow a **problem-solution organization** focus on persuading an audience that a specific problem exists and can be solved or minimized by a specific solution. These types of persuasive speeches are generally organized into two

Good to Know!

gain immediate action: Encourage an audience to engage in a specific behavior or take a specific action. **call to action:** Explicitly request that an audience engage in some clearly stated behavior. **gain passive agreement:** Ask an audience to adopt a new position without also asking them to act in support of that position. **problem-solution organization:** Organizational pattern that focuses on persuading an audience that a specific problem exists and can be solved or minimized by a specific solution.

main points. The first point specifies a problem, and the second proposes a solution to that problem. In the problem component of your speech, you must define a problem clearly, and the problem must be relevant to your audience. In the solution component, you must offer a solution that really does help solve the problem and that an audience can reasonably support and implement.

Consider the following examples of problem-solution speeches given by Sheri and Carlos. Notice how they used their thesis statements to state a problem clearly and then how they communicated that problem to their audiences in their first main points. Also notice how they related the problem to their audiences directly and personally. In the first example, Sheri spoke about the issue of light pollution.

Specific purpose: To persuade my audience that although light pollution is a problem that affects us increasingly every day, we can implement simple solutions to reduce the effects of this pollution

Thesis statement: Light pollution disrupts ground-based astronomy, is a costly energy waste, and affects our health and safety, but there are simple solutions to the problem of light pollution.

Main points:

I. Light pollution poses three significant problems.

A. In cities, light pollution causes urban sky glow, which disrupts ground-based telescopes.

B. Light pollution represents an extreme waste of energy, and that waste is costly to all of us.

C. Light pollution causes mild to severe medical conditions and so is unsafe for our communities.

II. The problem of light pollution can be alleviated in two ways.

A. Light pollution can be controlled through government regulations, such as light codes, which are similar to noise codes.

B. Light pollution can be reduced through personal actions, such as using less unnecessary light and purchasing equipment that reduces light directed toward the sky.

Notice how Sheri's first main point clearly defines the specific problems created by light pollution and how her second main point offers reasonable solutions. Also note that she requests both passive agreement and immediate action. She asks for passive agreement when she states that supporting government regulations is a good idea, and she asks for immediate action when she suggests her audience modify the lights in their homes.

In the next example, Carlos wants the U.S. government to replace the current electrical power grid with a smart grid. First, he has to explain the problems associated with the current grid. Then, he proposes a plan to solve the problem.

Specific purpose: To persuade my audience that the U.S. electrical grid needs to be replaced with a smart grid

Thesis statement: Replacing the outdated and overwhelmed U.S. electrical grid with a smart grid will provide more efficient energy use, greater consumer control over their energy use, and increased reliability and security for Americans.

Main points:

I. The current U.S. electrical grid is inefficient and overwhelmed because of our increasing demands for electricity.

II. Power outages have increased over the past decade, causing disruptions in our lives and creating financial strain for businesses and homeowners.

III. Replacing the current electrical grid with a smart grid will provide more efficient and reliable energy to consumers, save money, reduce future power outages, and increase our security by reducing our dependence on other countries for energy.

IV. Contact your local government representatives and ask that they support updating the current electrical grid with a smart grid.

Carlos illustrated the problems caused by the outdated electrical grids. He then offered a viable solution that the government should implement. Finally, Carlos encouraged his audience to take action by contacting their local government officials and asking for their support on fixing this problem. Because problem-solution speeches pose a problem while simultaneously offering a solution, they are excellent vehicles for persuading an audience to support a cause or take an action.

Problem-Cause-Solution Organization

The problem-cause-solution pattern of organization is a slight variation of the problem-solution pattern. Speeches that follow a **problem-cause-solution organization** focus on identifying a specific problem, the causes of that problem, and a solution to the problem. This type of speech is especially effective when you think you will be more persuasive if you explain how a problem came about. Explaining the causes of a problem can help your audience better see the merits of a proposed solution. Describing causes also allows you to explain how an audience came to believe what they do and to clarify any misconceptions they may have about a topic. In either case, you are sometimes more persuasive if you provide an audience with more information about a problem.

Problem-cause-solution speeches generally have three main points: The first identifies a clear and relevant problem, the second identifies the relevant causes of that problem, and the third details a clear and appropriate solution to the problem. Two examples illustrate this pattern of organization:

Specific purpose: To persuade my audience that the problems caused by feeding big-game wildlife can be easily solved

Thesis statement: The problems of wildlife overpopulation, the spread of disease, and other negative consequences caused by feeding big-game wildlife can be solved by keeping food away from wild animals.

Main points:

I. In many areas where people and big-game wildlife live near each other, there is overpopulation in certain species, outbreaks of disease, and a decrease in our acceptance of hunters and hunting.

Cengage Learning

CourseMate

Watch a video clip of student speaker Brent Erb giving a persuasive speech and urging immediate action from his audience. Pay attention to the solutions he proposes. Could you implement them? You can use your CourseMate for *Invitation to Public Speaking* to watch the video, respond to analysis questions, and compare your answers to those provided by the author.

Good to Know!

problem-cause-solution organization: Organizational pattern that focuses on identifying a specific problem, the causes of that problem, and a solution to the problem.

II. These problems are caused by well-meaning people leaving food out for wildlife in the winter and by campers who are not careful to keep their food and food smells away from wild animals.

III. These problems can be solved by simply not feeding wildlife; by protecting our food, washing our dishes, and washing our faces and hands when camping; and by putting our garbage in sealed containers.

Notice how Brandi was able to make a stronger case for her solution by identifying the specific causes of wildlife overpopulation, the spread of disease, and other wildlife-related problems. Once her audience knew the reasons for the problems, they could see the merits of a solution that might have seemed too simple to be effective.

A second example illustrates a different purpose for addressing a cause of a problem:

Specific purpose: To persuade my audience to manage their privacy settings on their social networking sites in order to ensure fairer treatment in the hiring process

Thesis statement: Managing privacy settings on social networking sites can reduce the likelihood that employers will unfairly base hiring decisions on applicants' personal and private information online.

Main points:
I. Many employers unfairly use personal and private information obtained on social networking sites to make hiring decisions.

II. Teenagers and young adults often do not set privacy restrictions on their social networking sites, making themselves vulnerable to repercussions in the hiring process.

III. Setting privacy controls on social networking sites will prohibit employers from accessing personal and private information about employees and ensuring fairer and more equitable treatment in the hiring process.

Problem-cause-solution organizational patterns are useful when you think that providing information about the cause of a problem will help persuade your audience to change their views or beliefs.

Causal Organization

When a problem is based on a cause-and-effect relationship, a causal pattern of organization will work well to persuade an audience. There are two possible ways to arrange a speech using a causal pattern: moving from cause to effect or from effect to cause. For example, Eli wanted to discuss the effects of reintroducing wolves in several western states. He first described the process of reintroducing the wolves (cause) and then focused on the decline in wildlife population (effect).

Specific purpose: To persuade my audience that the reintroduction of the gray wolf has significantly decreased the elk population in Idaho, Montana, and Wyoming

Cengage Learning

CourseMate

Watch a video clip of student speaker Brandi Lafferty giving a persuasive speech. Did her decision to include a discussion of the problem's causes make the speech more effective? You can use your CourseMate for *Invitation to Public Speaking* to watch the video, respond to analysis questions, and compare your answers to those provided by the author.

Thesis statement: Since the reintroduction of wolves in western regions, the elk population has declined dramatically, and farmers' cattle, sheep, and dogs have been killed.

Main points:
I. In 1995, gray wolves were reintroduced to Yellowstone National Park and the surrounding states of Montana and Idaho.

II. Since the reintroduction of wolves in western regions, the elk population has declined dramatically, forcing some regions to ban elk hunting.

III. Other animals, including cattle, sheep, and dogs, have also been impacted by the reintroduction of wolves.

A cause-to-effect pattern worked well for Eli's topic because it emphasized that the wolves were the main reason for the decline in elk populations. In contrast, Rupa chose to arrange her speech using the effect-to-cause pattern of organization. She wanted to make her point by first capturing her audience's attention with a real story of five girls who died in a car accident (effect) and then explaining what caused the horrific accident.

Specific purpose: To persuade my audience that texting while driving can lead to fatal accidents

Thesis statement: When drivers text while driving, they are putting their lives, and their passengers' lives, in danger.

Main points:
I. In 2007, five high school graduates from Rochester, New York, died when their vehicle swerved into oncoming traffic and hit a tractor trailer.

II. Authorities believe the driver became distracted while she was sending text messages, which caused the head-on collision.

In this speaking situation, Rupa's audience were members of the western New York community and had heard about the accident (the effect) weeks before learning of the cause. Rupa believed that reminding the audience members of the deadly outcome of the accident before revealing its cause would help persuade them that texting while driving is a serious issue.

Narrative Organization

Speeches can also be organized using one or more stories to construct an argument. Depending on the topic, a speaker may share an extended narrative to help personalize an argument that may seem difficult for some audience members to fully comprehend. Razz implemented this strategy in his speech on the problem of children being abducted and forced to work as child soldiers in countries such as Sierra Leone, Africa. Razz wanted to share Ishmael Beah's story as an extended narrative to reveal the thoughts, reactions, and experiences of one boy's journey from abduction to rehabilitation.

Specific purpose: To convince my audience that rehabilitation programs work to change child soldiers' lives for the better

Thesis statement: Ishmael Beah is a former child soldier from Sierra Leone, Africa, and his story teaches us that rehabilitation programs can work to give child soldiers a new life.

Main points:

I. Ishmael Beah was a young boy when his village was attacked and burned, forcing him and several other children to wander from place to place to survive.

Public Speaking and Service Learning: Engaging Community

Matt Welte, a public speaking student at Colorado State University, completed his service learning project at Doherty High School in Colorado Springs, Colorado. As a health and exercise science major and an avid athlete himself, he felt very comfortable mentoring young athletes. However, he was shocked to find out how many of these high school athletes were using some sort of nutritional supplement to enhance their performance. Matt decided to do some research and found out some potentially negative affects these supplements could have on a younger body. What he found prompted him to do his persuasive speech on the topic of banning such supplements for those younger than eighteen.

> **"I AM CON-VINCED THAT SOMETHING NEEDS TO BE DONE TO MAKE KIDS MORE AWARE OF WHAT INGREDIENTS ARE IN THE SUPPLE-MENTS THEY'RE TAKING."**

High school sports are something that surrounded my life long before I was in high school. When I was a toddler, my father was a wresting and football coach. When I was in elementary and middle school, my older brothers were playing high school sports, and eventually I ended up spending four years playing sports at Fountain Fort Carson High School. I have only been out of high school sports for a few years, so when I chose to do my service learning in the area high school athletics, I assumed I had nothing more to learn about the topic. I was absolutely wrong.

At Doherty High School, I have learned several things about the social, environmental, physical, and psychological issues that these kids face on a daily basis. I delivered a presentation to the students on the topic of dietary supplements in athletics, pointing out potential dangers as well as their side effects. Over half of the kids present willingly told me everything they were putting into their bodies—not all of it was harmful, but enough was potentially so to raise some alarm. The most surprising aspect of my interaction with the student athletes was that a significant number of them had no clear understanding of the potential dangers to their still-developing bodies.

Overall, I have learned a lot through my service: I am now convinced that something needs to be done to make kids more aware of what ingredients are actually in these supplements that they are taking, and I am willing to speak out about this. I advocate that either a complete ban, or at least an age restriction, should be placed on certain performance-enhancing supplements, and that the FDA needs to better regulate the products that are being put on the market. Because of my service learning, I was more invested in my persuasive speech.

Tips for Incorporating Service Learning into Public Speaking

- Most speakers pick a persuasive topic that they are passionate about. Your service learning can help with this. It also can help you identify facts and evidence that will build a persuasive case.
- Narratives and testimony are useful sources of evidence for a persuasive speech. Consider using some of the stories you gathered from your service learning in your speech, particularly in your introduction. This personal touch can help your audience become more invested in your topic.
- Your service learning gives you personal experience with your topic. When you are developing your persuasive speech, be sure to adapt your service learning experiences to your audience. Show them how your issue affects them specifically and how they can take some realistic action to make a change.

II. At the age of twelve, Beah was captured by the Revolutionary United Front (RUF) and forced to become a child soldier.

III. Beah was rescued by UNICEF, was given counseling and rehabilitation services, and received the opportunity to start a new life in the United States.

By using Beah's story to personalize the problem of child soldiers, Razz made his topic more accessible for his audience. This strategy helped him convince his audience that rehabilitation programs sponsored by UNICEF can work to provide these young children with a better life.

Courtney also chose to use a narrative pattern to convince her audience that the government-funded Special Statutory Program helps those who have type 1 diabetes. To persuade her audience that the funds are necessary, Courtney shared several narratives from family members who have type 1 diabetes.

Specific purpose:	To persuade my audience that the Special Statutory Program is a much needed program to improve the lives of people with diabetes
Thesis statement:	Type 1 diabetes is a serious issue that is often misunderstood by the public, but three personal narratives about family members living with type 1 diabetes illustrate how the disease affects those who have it and that the Special Statutory Program is helping to battle, prevent, and eventually cure type 1 diabetes.
Main points:	I. My dad was diagnosed with type 1 diabetes when he was seventeen years old.
	II. On a family vacation to Florida, my sister, Jamie, was hospitalized and diagnosed with type 1 diabetes.
	III. I began watching my younger brother inject insulin into his body three times every day while still trying to be a "typical" kid.
	IV. My family has benefitted from the Special Statutory Program, so I know firsthand how important the program is in funding research to find a cure for diabetes and hope Congress will continue to authorize this funding.

Comparative Advantages Organization

When your audience agrees with you about a problem but feels the solution is up for debate, a comparative advantages speech is often an excellent choice. Speeches that follow a **comparative advantages organization** illustrate the advantages of one solution over others. In this type of speech, use each main point to explain why your solution is preferable to other possible solutions. If you must criticize alternative solutions to strengthen your explanations, simply explain why the alternatives will not work, taking care not to degrade or belittle them.

Consider Angela's situation. Her coworkers and bosses already knew a problem existed: Sales were down, and they were beginning to lose what had once

Good to Know!

comparative advantages organization: Organizational pattern that illustrates the advantages of one solution over others.

been faithful customers. Therefore, Angela chose to give a comparative advantages speech so she could focus on illustrating the strengths of her proposed training program.

Specific purpose:	To persuade my coworkers that my new training program will increase our sales and enhance our public profile
Thesis statement:	My proposed training program—which includes a longer initial training period, a more detailed assessment and understanding of the strengths of our products, and a stronger mentoring component than our current program—will turn our sales around.
Main points:	I. A longer initial training program will give our staff more time than our current program allows to develop a working knowledge and appreciation of the company and its mission.
	II. A more detailed knowledge of our products and their value will enable our staff to work with our clientele more expertly than our current training allows.
	III. A stronger mentoring program will improve the communication style of our new sales staff and help them respond to unfamiliar situations more effectively than our current mentoring program does.

Angela did not spend time outlining the problem because her audience already knew the training program needed improvement. Instead, she compared the advantages of her program to the weaknesses of the company's current program. She was careful to avoid criticizing the current program too heavily because her boss had been instrumental in bringing that model to the company. Rather, she simply said, "Our current program no longer is meeting our needs. If we make these changes, we'll be back on top."

Monroe's Motivated Sequence

Monroe's motivated sequence is an organizational pattern that helps you address an audience's motives and how those motives could translate into action. Developed in 1935 by Alan Monroe, **Monroe's motivated sequence** is a step-by-step process used to persuade audiences by gaining attention, demonstrating a need, satisfying that need, visualizing beneficial results, and calling for action. Monroe maintained that this pattern satisfies an audience's desire for order and helps a speaker focus on what motivates an audience to action. Monroe's motivated sequence organizes the entire speech, not just the body, and takes listeners through a step-by-step process of identifying a problem and resolving to help solve that problem.[2]

1. **Attention.** In this step, you catch the audience's interest so they take notice of an issue. Your goal is to motivate the audience to listen and see the personal connection they have to a topic. Using statistics or a story can accomplish this task. For example, Sierra began her speech by telling a story to capture her audience's attention. She began, "I was only ten years

Good to Know!

Monroe's motivated sequence: Step-by-step process used to persuade audiences by gaining attention, demonstrating a need, satisfying that need, visualizing beneficial results, and calling for action.

old when I found my mother sitting on her bed crying. Not knowing how to react, I sat down beside her and grabbed her hand. When I asked her what was wrong, she replied, 'I am sick and hope that I can hold your hand for many, many more years.' I soon learned my mother had breast cancer and that she would not be able to hold my hand much longer."

2. **Need.** In this step, you identify the need for a change, meaning a problem that can be solved. You define the problem and how it directly or indirectly affects the audience. Your goal is to encourage your audience to become invested in the problem, feel affected by it, and want to find a solution. Sierra began the need section by proving the severity of the problem. She stated, "The latest study on breast cancer indicates that one in eight women will be diagnosed with breast cancer in her lifetime! That means two of you in this room will be directly affected, and almost everyone else will likely know someone affected by breast cancer."

3. **Satisfaction.** In this step, you define what the specific solution is and why it solves the problem. In doing so, you show the audience how their "need" is "satisfied." Sierra argued in her speech that the Susan G. Komen Breast Cancer Foundation was making important strides in finding a cure for breast cancer and needed more national, state, and local funding to support their research efforts.

4. **Visualization.** In this step, you describe the benefits that will result from the audience's need being satisfied. You can describe what life will be like once the solution is in place, or you can remind the audience what it would be like if the solution were not implemented. Either way, you help the audience visualize how the solution will benefit them. Sierra achieved the visualization step by asking her audience to imagine life without the fear of breast cancer. She described, "Imagine one day you're standing in your bedroom and your daughter walks in and takes your hand. Now imagine being able to tell her that you want to be able to hold her hand for many years in the future, and this time, you can. Reducing the rates of breast cancer will ensure longer, healthier lives for women."

5. **Action.** In this final step, you outline exactly what the audience should do. This is your call to action, the plea for the audience to take immediate action or make a personal commitment to support the changes you're advocating. Sierra asked her class to join her for a breast cancer walk being held in their community. She concluded, "This Saturday at 9 ' ᴛ ., a walk to raise money for breast cancer research will take place right here on campus. I ask that you join me in this fight and join me on the walk."

Practicing the Public Dialogue 15.2

Select an Organizational Pattern for Your Persuasive Speech

Return to the list of possible persuasive speech topics that you prepared in Practicing the Public Dialogue 15.1. In groups, select a single topic and determine whether you want to work on a question of fact, value, or policy. See if you can create a rough thesis statement and main points for a persuasive speech on this topic using one of the organizational patterns you've just read about. Select the pattern that would best help you persuade your audience to take action or modify their thinking about a topic. As you discuss your organizational pattern, consider the tips for giving effective persuasive speeches in the next section.

Online Resources

CourseMate To see another example of a persuasive speech that you can use as a model, use your CourseMate for *Invitation to Public Speaking* to watch the video clip of Sheri's speech about light pollution. Consider the effectiveness of the organizational pattern she uses for her speech. If you had given a speech on this topic, would you have used the same pattern? Why or why not?

For an example of a speech outline that follows Monroe's motivated sequence and a checklist that can help you incorporate this pattern into a speech, access **Web Connect 15.4: Monroe's Motivated Sequence** through your CourseMate for *Invitation to Public Speaking*.

CourseMate

Connecting with Your Audience

Petty and Cacioppo's elaboration likelihood model (ELM) explains that receivers process persuasive messages in either a *central processing* or a *peripheral processing* route depending on how motivated the audience is to think critically about a message. The more a speaker encourages listeners to become consciously engaged to think about a persuasive message, the more likely listeners are processing information in the central route. This means listeners are evaluating the overall quality of the argument, evidence and supporting material included, and any call for action presented in the speech. In this situation, listeners may research additional information on the topic after they listen to the speech because they want more details before deciding if they will support the speaker's argument.

When listeners lack motivation to think critically about a topic, they move toward using the peripheral route. In this situation listeners consume messages in a passive manner. They may focus on parts of the speech without thinking critically about the message in its entirety. In addition, listeners may be influenced by the speaker's style of dress or delivery, not the quality of speech structure and content.

To encourage listeners to process information in the central route, speakers should connect their topic to their audience, explain the reasons that the audience should be concerned about the speech topic, and continuously work toward keeping the audience actively and critically thinking about the speech information. Listeners using the central processing route tend to be more heavily influenced by a speaker than those using the peripheral route.

Tips for Giving Effective Persuasive Speeches

Consider the many times you've wanted to convince others to join with you, think like you, or support you. You may have wanted them to do something as simple as go to a movie or eat a new kind of food or as complicated as join a particular organization or share your passionate social views. Most people are deeply committed to certain things in life, such as their spiritual or political beliefs. Or because of deeply held convictions, they feel a strong sense of right and wrong about certain issues, such as whether women should participate in active combat. It's natural to want others to share our commitments and beliefs, and most of us can think of many times we wanted to convince others to think, feel, and act as we do.

To help you give persuasive speeches, remember the following tips to increase your chances for successful persuasion: (1) be realistic about changing your audience's views, (2) use your evidence fairly and strategically for the best results, and (3) use language that respectfully motivates your audience to change.

Be Realistic about Changing Your Audience's Views

Researchers generally agree that for persuasion to succeed, an audience must be open to change. If an audience is not open to change, even your best persuasive efforts are likely to fail. This means you must consider your audience's perspectives carefully and frame your persuasive attempts around issues that your audience will be open to considering. If you know your audience believes something quite strongly and isn't open to change (views on religion often fall into this category), you probably won't be successful in convincing them to change that view no matter how well reasoned or researched your speech is. However, if the audience is open to considering an alternative perspective (for example, that there is a place in our society for different religious practices), your persuasive efforts are more likely to be successful.

This means you must think carefully about the position your audience holds and choose a realistic argument before you attempt to change their views. It is often tempting to ask an audience to change their views completely, especially if you don't agree with those views. However, successful persuasion involves advocating a position, or some *aspect* of a position, that your audience can be open about. For example, it may be unrealistic to think you can change your audience's views on legalizing certain drugs if your audience has had bad experiences with drugs or people who use drugs. But you may be able to persuade them to see the benefits that some of these drugs offer in medical treatments. That is, you may be able to persuade them to reconsider some part of their position rather than undertake a radical change.[3] Your attempts at persuasion will likely be more successful if you take a realistic, audience-centered approach to changing others. Rather than asking for radical changes, approach your speech goals and your audience with some restraint.

Remember, audiences hold particular beliefs and positions because of their experiences and worldviews. If you respect those positions and experiences as you ask your audience to change, you'll be more likely to give a successful speech.

Use Evidence Fairly and Strategically

Research on evidence and persuasion suggests that besides carefully researching, organizing, and delivering your speech, there are some strategies you can use to help construct effective persuasive arguments. These strategies involve two-sided messages, counterarguments, and fear appeals.

Because persuasive speakers advocate one position over others, they often frame an issue as two sided, even if there are multiple perspectives on the issue (Chapter 14). A **two-sided message** addresses two sides of an issue, refuting one side to prove the other is better. Research suggests that when speakers discuss two sides of an issue, they are more persuasive if they actively refute the side they oppose rather than simply describe it without providing evidence for why the audience should share the speaker's views on it.[4]

Similarly, addressing **counterarguments**, arguments against the speaker's own position, enhances a speaker's credibility. For example, when Tony advocated a policy of controlled burns to prevent forest fires, he increased his believability when he also discussed the argument that controlled burns can get out of control and cause major damage. By acknowledging this counterargument, Tony illustrated why the concerns it raises are unfounded, strengthening his position that controlled burns prevent other fires from burning out of control.

Good to Know!

two-sided message: Persuasive strategy that addresses both sides of an issue, refuting one side to prove the other is better.
counterarguments: Arguments against the speaker's own position.

Note, however, that you must use two-sided messages and counterarguments with care. In persuasion, credibility is important (Chapters 7 and 16), and you must take care that your opposing comments are not too judgmental or inflammatory. If you unfairly attack someone else's view or refute an opposing position too harshly, audiences may perceive you as less likable—and audiences find unlikable

Speaking Visually

Ribbon Campaigns and Awareness Bracelets

Today, we display a yellow ribbon to communicate our support for military troops and their families. However, the meaning of this visual symbol has changed over time. Four hundred years ago, the reference to the ribbon originated in a song about a woman wearing a yellow ribbon to signal that she was waiting for the return of her beloved. In the late 1800s and early 1900s, the yellow ribbon became associated with waiting for the return of a soldier. And in the 1970s, Irwin Levine and L. Russell Brown wrote "Tie a Yellow Ribbon 'Round the Ole Oak Tree," a song about a convict returning home. In the song, if the convict's lover tied a yellow ribbon around the oak tree near a certain bus stop, she communicated that he was welcome to come home.

In addition to communicating support for our soldiers, today's yellow ribbons also communicate our awareness of, and desire to prevent, teen suicide. Other ribbon colors communicate our commitment to different causes: red symbolizes AIDS awareness as well as a drug-free lifestyle; pink expresses our desire for breast cancer awareness; white symbolizes our desire to end men's violence against women; blue refers to either our desire to support free speech or to raise awareness about chronic fatigue syndrome; and green speaks to our desire for open adoption records.

Similar to ribbons, gel bracelets also speak to us visually. A well-known example is the yellow "live strong" band established by Lance Armstrong to promote support for cancer research. Other examples

Paul Vallance/PhotoLibrary

include a white gel bracelet that speaks out against poverty and a half blue–half red gel bracelet that speaks for epilepsy awareness. Jelly bracelets also make statements. Popularized by Madonna in the 1980s, they were once just an inexpensive form of teen fashion. But in recent years, "some teens and pre-adolescents, including elementary school students, know jelly bracelets as sex bracelets. Sex bracelets are a coded form of communication among teens and young people where wearing different colored jelly bracelets indicate what sexual acts the teen is supposedly willing to perform."[5]

When people convey their messages through ribbons and bracelets, they expect their audiences to respond on different levels. First, the audience must respond personally to the object. For example, they might be curious ("What is it about?") or annoyed ("I don't like all these useless ribbons and bracelets!"). Second, the audience places the object into a historical framework, responding with "I know (or don't know) the history of this cause or issue." At this level, the audience relies on mythos and a cultural memory of the issues the object supports and the circumstances that prompted its creation. Finally, the audience responds ethically, assessing the "rightness" of the object's visual communication and the wearer's explanation of it. As a result of the audience's own ethical framework and the arguments and evidence that back up the meaning of the object, the audience responds with, "I support (or don't support) this cause."[6]

speakers less persuasive. Additionally, the audience will focus their attention on assessing the merit of your judgmental claim rather than attending to the rest of your message.[7] So when Tony advocated for controlled burns, he avoided saying, "That's stupid. Anyone knows that the fear of out-of-control prescribed burns is as ridiculous as fearing you'll burn down your house by lighting your barbecue!" Instead, he clearly and directly illustrated why the fear is unfounded—but not stupid—and why his policy is preferable.

Speakers can also use fear appeals to persuade audiences to change or take action. A **fear appeal** is the threat of something undesirable happening if change does not occur. In political ads, politicians frequently employ fear appeals as a way to motivate voters. Research suggests that fear appeals may motivate audiences who are not initially invested in your topic to *become* invested.[8] A fear appeal causes audience members to take notice of an issue and see how it relates to them personally. When audiences already feel connected to the topic, fear appeals simply reinforce that connection. However, if a fear appeal is so extreme that audience members feel immobilized, imagining that there is nothing they can do to solve the problem, they may simply avoid or deny the problem.[9] Thus, if you use fear appeals, temper them so your audience feels there is a solution to the problem that will actually work. For example, if your speech is about the risk of violent crime in your community, speak honestly about it but do not exaggerate it. Then offer practical steps your audience can take to reduce their risk so they feel hopeful and empowered rather than defeated.

Use Language That Encourages an Audience to Change

Just as informative speaking relies on language that is clear and unbiased, and invitational speaking relies on language that fosters openness and a desire to explore an issue, persuasive speaking relies on language that will motivate an audience to think or act differently. The most obvious examples of persuasive language are words and phrases that indicate what an audience "should do," what the "best" solution would be, or how something is "better than" something else. Persuasive language often appeals to emotions, as in "Wouldn't it be tragic if we failed to respond appropriately to this situation?" (See Chapter 16 for more about emotional appeals.) Additionally, audiences should hear strong calls to action such as "I'm asking each one of you to attend the rally tonight" or appeals such as "Imagine what our national park would look like with power lines running through it." However, research indicates that the more invested people are in a position, the less effective phrases such as "Today, I'll persuade you that" or "I'm here to convince you that" are, especially in your introduction.[10] When you tell an audience you will persuade them, they tend to hold more firmly to their positions.

Research on persuasion in conversations suggests that speakers who use words and phrases that show they understand the feelings and motivations of others are generally more persuasive than speakers who don't.[11] This means your language should reflect an appreciation for the positions audience members hold. Use language that helps you clarify your position and its merits without casting a negative light on the views of others. Although persuasive speeches are sometimes used to attack or argue, avoid this tactic when you enter the public dialogue by using respectful language, even if you and your audience disagree.

Good to Know!

fear appeal: Threat of something undesirable happening if change does not occur.

Using respectful language does not mean you should not try to motivate your audiences to change. On the contrary, the goal of persuasive speaking is to encourage an audience to think or act differently, and your language should reflect this challenge. Phrases like "Perhaps you've never thought about the impact of," "I encourage you to consider this evidence carefully," and "How can we let this kind of damage continue?" do not attack or demand but instead urge audiences to reevaluate their positions. Some of our best efforts at persuasion have resulted in speeches that respectfully challenge an audience to think in new ways.

Ethical Persuasive Speaking

Have you ever noticed that sometimes when you try to change someone, that person regularly resists your attempts?[12] Can you recall when your parents tried to persuade you to do (or not do) something, like dress a certain way, date a certain kind of person, or attend a certain function? For many people, as soon as the persuasion began, so did the resistance. Why did this happen when our parents likely had our best interests at heart?

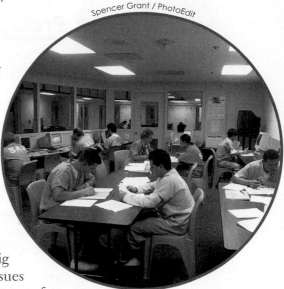

Spencer Grant / PhotoEdit

Research and personal experience tell us that when others try to persuade us, we feel our freedom to choose our own path is threatened. In the United States especially, the freedom to choose is often basic to our sense of self. When someone tries to convince us to think, feel, or do something new or different, many people dig in their heels and hold on to their positions even more firmly. The issues we try to persuade others about are often complicated, making the process of persuasion even more challenging. Questions of fact, value, and policy are rarely simple or clear-cut. When beliefs, preferences, experiences, and habits come into play, these questions can get clouded and emotional, and people often invest in particular outcomes.

Given these characteristics of persuasion, be sure you request change ethically. To persuade ethically is to persuade others without threatening or challenging their sense of freedom to choose what is best for them. Remember, when you persuade, you act as advocate for a particular position, not as a bully who tries to force or threaten an audience to see things your way. Ethical persuasion also requires you to recognize the complexity of the issues you speak about and the possible impact of your proposed solutions on your audience. As you prepare your persuasive speech, keep the following four questions in mind. The first three address the complexity of audiences and issues, and the fourth helps you consider the effect of the changes you request.

Be realistic about what you can or cannot persuade an audience to think, feel, or do. For very personal or controversial issues, focus on some aspect of the issue that an audience could reasonably consider. For example, some audience members may have been victims of crime and may not be receptive to the notion of "prisoners' rights." In this case, you might focus on aspects of prison reform, such as education, that keep prisoners occupied in a constructive way while they're serving their sentences. How can you frame the topic of your next persuasive speech to be realistic about asking your audience to change?

- What is my position on this topic, and why do I hold this position?
- What are my audience's positions on this topic, and why do they hold these positions?
- Why am I qualified to try to persuade my audience on this issue?
- Is my request reasonable for my audience, and how will they be affected by the change?

As an ethical persuasive speaker, you must understand your own position and the positions of your audience. Acknowledge your own master statuses, standpoints, and unique experiences as well as those of each member of your audience.

Similarly, ethical persuasive speaking requires you to *present information* in an ethical way. This means you must tell the truth, avoid distorting or manipulating evidence, and present information accurately and completely. To ensure that you present your evidence ethically, review the research tips in Chapter 5.

Remember, audiences dislike being manipulated and misled. Even if a speaker gains support through the unethical manipulation of evidence or ideas, that support is usually lost when the audience discovers the deceit. Gaining support through ethical means will only increase your credibility.

Preparation Outline with Commentary

No Child Left Behind: Addressing the School Dropout Rate among Latinos
by Dana Barker

Specific purpose: To persuade my audience that our nation must address the high dropout rate among Latinos

Thesis statement: The dropout rate among Latinos in high schools and colleges, caused by low economic status and lack of family support, is too high, and this problem must be addressed with increased funding and teacher training.

CourseMate *Are you ready to practice your powers of persuasion by giving an effective persuasive speech? Use the following speech as a model. Use your CourseMate for* Invitation to Public Speaking *to watch a video clip of this speech and see Dana's transcript and speaking outline. Dana gave this speech in an introductory public speaking class. The assignment was to give a four- to six-minute speech with a minimum of four sources cited. Students were also asked to create a preparation outline that included a Works Cited section. (Remember that you can use your CourseMate to access videos of other persuasive speeches, including "The U.S. and the World Peace Crisis" by Renee DeSalvo.)*

Commentary

Dana begins her speech by sharing an inspiring story about Mabel, a young Latina high school dropout.

With this story, she reveals the topic and problem of her speech: Latino dropout rates. She then establishes her credibility by explaining that she has conducted extensive research on her topic. She completes her introduction by previewing the main points of her speech.

Dana begins the body of her speech by clearly stating her argument: The dropout rate for Latinos in secondary schools must be addressed.

She supports her proposition by citing

Introduction
I. I'll begin with a story from the *Santa Fe New Mexican* about Mabel Arellanes. *(catch attention)*
   A. After becoming pregnant and dropping out of school at sixteen, Mabel has reenrolled in high school and is the junior class president.
   B. Her change in attitude has led her to the hope of becoming a lawyer.
   C. But Mabel's story is not representative of the current trends among Latinos.
II. I have researched trends in Latino socioeconomic status, graduation rate, and population in the U.S. *(establish credibility)*
III. Today I will discuss the problem of a high Latino dropout rate and suggest a solution. *(preview main points)*

Transition: Let me begin by discussing the problem.

Body
I. The dropout rate among Latinos in secondary schools and colleges is too high and must be addressed.
   A. The dropout rate is excessive.

1. Statistics and firsthand accounts attest to the high dropout rate.
   a. According to the *News & Observer*, one in twelve Latino students dropped out of high school in North Carolina during the 2003–2004 school year.
   b. This statistic does not account for the 47.5 percent of Latino students who have not graduated in four years since the beginning of the 1999–2000 academic year.
   c. Gamaliel Fuentes, who dropped out of school at fifteen, said, "We have no money; that's why I dropped out of school. [My father] asked me, but I decided. Now, if I could go back in time, I would stay still in school."
2. The tendency for Latinos to drop out is triggered by low socioeconomic status and a lack of family support.
   a. The *Hispanic Outlook in Higher Education* explains that students coming from families of lower socioeconomic status are less likely to succeed in college because high schools do not prepare them well.
   b. Latino families expect their young people to contribute economically, and work schedules often conflict with studies.

Transition: Next, I will discuss the importance of addressing the Latino dropout rate.

B. Addressing the dropout rate will keep Latinos from remaining at a generally low economic status.
   1. Income is heavily dependent on education level.
      a. According to the *Daily Evergreen* newspaper, a person with a bachelor's degree can earn almost one million dollars more over the course of their lifetime than someone with no college education.
      b. A census report in the *San Antonio Express-News* found that Latinos earned merely 6.2 percent of the bachelor's degrees awarded in 2001.
      c. Yet, the U.S. Census Bureau found that Latinos made up 12 percent of the national population in 2000 and 13.3 percent in 2002.
      d. In her essay "Canto, Locura, y Poesia," Olivia Castellano of California State University, Sacramento, writes, "They [Latinos] carry a deeply ingrained sense of inferiority, a firm conviction that they are not worthy of success."
   2. Ultimately, all who hold the belief that our country is the "land of opportunity" are affected by the Latino dropout rate.
      a. The U.S. Census Bureau states that in 2001 two out of ten Hispanics lived below the poverty line, while only one out of four earned a yearly salary of $35,000 or more.
      b. Comparatively, around 50 percent of non-Hispanic whites earned $35,000 or more that year.
      c. These figures are far from exemplifying opportunity for Latinos.

Transition: But what will happen if the problem is not solved?

C. Since the percentage of Latinos in our population is still climbing, ignoring this issue will lead to a greater gap between the life of the typical American and the life of the Latino American.

recent statistics about the North Carolina school system. Additionally, she uses peer testimony to explain why Latino students are dropping out of high school and to establish pathos.

To support her point that dropout rates contribute to the generally low economic status of U.S. Latinos, Dana provides a source that describes the discrepancy of income levels between high school dropouts and university graduates. She also provides statistics to highlight the low number of Latinos graduating from college.

Next, Dana uses expert testimony to explain why such low graduation rates exist for the Latino population.

Dana also provides statistics from a highly credible source to illustrate the typical disparity between the income level of Hispanics and non-Hispanic whites.

Dana's transition between her points I.B and I.C tells her audience that she is about to explain the consequences of not addressing the problem of Latino dropout rates.

Before moving to her solution, Dana draws her audience in personally by asking them to consider the urgency of the problem. Then Dana presents her solution, explaining that teacher training and educational success programs will help Latinos succeed in school and will help change the Latino mind-set about education.

She uses an example of a successful program, AVID, to support her claim. Note how with this example Dana uses analogical reasoning (Chapter 7) to convince her audience that her solution will be successful, suggesting that the success of this program could be repeated with similar programs. Additionally, in point II.B, she succinctly states how her solution could be implemented.

Dana explains the potential results of implementing her plan. She informs her audience that the results will take time, but the plan could produce a newfound sense of accomplishment and pride among the U.S. Latino community.

Dana completes her speech with a brief conclusion that summarizes her main points and reinforces her thesis.

Dana's bibliography of the specific research she references in her speech shows the currency of her sources. (She created the speech in 2008.) She relies on a variety of sources, including books, newspapers, and the Internet.

Transition: As I proceed to discuss the solutions for this problem, are you beginning to sense the urgency of this situation?

II. To solve the problem of a high dropout rate, we must fund teacher sensitivity training and programs that help Latinos succeed in education, and Latinos must change their perspective on the importance of education and their ability to succeed.

A. Programs that educate teachers about Latino culture and beliefs and that help Latino students succeed in education will have the most impact on the dropout rate.

1. Properly educated teachers will become aware of how they are able to meet the needs of Latino students.

2. The *Santa Fe New Mexican* reported on the success of a program called AVID, which boasts a 95 percent college entrance rate among its Latino students.

Transition: What can we expect from this solution?

B. This solution, which can be implemented at the national, state, and local levels, is dependent on increased funding and the efforts of educators with experience in Latino culture.

1. Increased funding will help reform educational budgets for Latino communities and fund college success programs like AVID.

2. This solution also requires the collective efforts of highly knowledgeable professionals with experience in education and Latino culture who can train other educators.

C. Given proper attention and execution, the plan to address the Latino dropout rate will help the dropout rate begin to fall and will instill pride in the Latino community.

1. Although it will take at least a decade before results are fully apparent, perhaps even a generation, ideally the plan will result in an increase in Latinos earning bachelor's, master's, and doctoral degrees.

2. The sense of accomplishment gained by furthering education will change the typical Latino mind-set regarding education and instill an overall sense of pride in the U.S. Latino community.

Conclusion

I. I have discussed the problem of high dropout rate among Latinos, and I have discussed a possible solution for addressing the issue. *(summarize main points)*

II. Hopefully, you can clearly see that the high Latino dropout rate is an issue of great concern, one that requires prompt and thorough attention. *(reinforce thesis)*

Works Cited

Castellano, Olivia. "Canto, Locura, y Poesia." *Race, Class, and Gender: An Anthology.* Compiled by Margaret L. Andersen. Edited by Patricia Hill Collins. Belmont, CA: Wadsworth, 1997.

Economics and Statistics Administration. *The Hispanic Population in the United States, 2002.* United States Department of Commerce. Accessed March 14, 2005. http://www.census.gov/population/www/socdemo/Hispanic/ho00.html.

Ferry, Barbara. "High School Program Gives Students a Fighting Chance." *Santa Fe New Mexican.* February 15, 2005: p. B-1.

Hannah-Jones, Nikole. "School an Elusive Dream: For Latino Students, Desire for Diploma Often Clashes with Needs of Families." *News & Observer.* February 18, 2005: p. A1.

McGlynn, Angela Provitera. "Improving Completion Rates for Hispanic Students: 'Best Practices' for Community Colleges." *Hispanic Outlook in Higher Education* 14.4 (2003): pp. 21–25.

Silva, Elda. "Latino Grad Rate Still Lags across U.S.: Finances Often Hinder Earning a Four-Year Degree." *San Antonio Express-News.* June 6, 2004: p. 1K.

Turner, Drew. "Four Year Degree Worth the Wait." *Daily Evergreen.* January 10, 2005.

Chapter Summary

When you speak persuasively, you often address questions that are complex and not easily resolved.

- Your goal with a persuasive speech is to alter or influence an audience's thoughts, feelings, or actions about issues that are not easily resolved.

Persuasive speeches generally fall into three categories.

- Questions of fact address the verifiable truth of an issue.
- Questions of value refer to the appropriateness of an action or belief.
- Questions of policy focus on the best solution to a problem.

There are several organizational patterns you can use for persuasive speeches.

- Persuasive speeches on questions of fact and value can be organized with chronological, spatial, and topical patterns.
- Persuasive speeches on questions of policy can be organized with the problem-solution, problem-cause-solution, causal, narrative, comparative advantages, and Monroe's motivated sequence patterns.
- All of these organizational patterns provide different ways to present information about a problem and proposed solutions.
- Which pattern you select depends on your audience and your speech goals.

For policy speeches, you can request immediate action or passive agreement.

- When you seek to gain immediate action, you attempt to encourage an audience to engage in a specific behavior or take a specific action.

- When you seek to gain passive agreement, you try to persuade an audience to adopt a new position without asking them to act in support of that position.

Three important tips will help you give an effective persuasive speech.

- Use persuasion realistically. Don't ask for radical changes if an audience isn't likely to support your proposals. Adapt your request for change to your audience's ability to change.
- Use evidence fairly and strategically to strengthen your arguments and increase your chances for audience support. Address complex issues with two-sided messages and counterarguments so you can refute opposing positions and appear more credible to your audience.
- Similarly, use fear appeals to motivate your audience to change, but don't overuse this strategy to the point of immobilizing your audience with fear.
- Use language that will motivate your audience to change but will not threaten or insult them.

Do your best to give ethical persuasive speeches.

- Request change without threatening or manipulating your audience.
- Make an effort to understand your audience members' positions on an issue as well as you understand it.
- Present information that is honest, accurate, and fair.

Invitation to Public Speaking Online

CourseMate Now that you have read Chapter 15, use your Speech Communication Course-Mate for *Invitation to Public Speaking* for quick access to the electronic resources that accompany this text. These resources include

- **Study tools** that will help you assess your learning and prepare for exams (*digital glossary, key term flash cards, review quizzes*).
- **Activities and assignments** that will help you hone your knowledge and build your public speaking skills throughout the course (*Practicing the Public Dialogue activities, review questions*).

- **Media resources** that will help you explore public speaking concepts online (*Web Connect links, Enhanced eBook*), develop your speech outlines (*Speech Builder Express 3.0*), watch and critique videos of sample speeches (*Interactive Video Activities*), upload your speech videos for peer reviewing and critique other students' speeches (*Speech Studio online speech review tool*), and download chapter review so you can study when and where you'd like (*Audio Study Tools*).

This chapter's key concepts and review questions are also featured here.

Key Concepts

call to action (314)
comparative advantages organization (320)
counterarguments (324)
fear appeal (326)
gain immediate action (314)

gain passive agreement (314)
Monroe's motivated sequence (321)
persuasive speech (309)
problem-cause-solution organization (316)

problem-solution organization (314)
question of fact (309)
question of policy (310)
question of value (309)
two-sided message (324)

Review Questions

1. With other members of your class, develop an imaginary speech to persuade lawmakers to lower the voting age to sixteen. As you develop this speech, consider the implications of the requested change for as many constituencies as possible: sixteen-year-olds, parents, lawmakers, voter registration workers, voting sites, mail ballots, candidates, teachers, the structure of education, and the like. What are the implications of this persuasive request?

2. You have just been informed you have only five minutes of the legislator's time to present your persuasive appeal developed in question 1. How will you revise your speech to account for this time frame? How will you determine what information to keep in and what to leave out?

3. Consider the speeches you have heard that changed your mind or actions regarding an issue. How were you persuaded to change? Can you incorporate

any techniques from these speeches into your own persuasive speeches?

4. Your topic is public transportation. Develop a specific purpose statement, thesis statement, and main points for the following three types of persuasive speeches: a question of fact, a question of value, and a question of policy. Use the discussion of organizational patterns in this chapter to help organize your speech.

5. Write an outline for a persuasive speech on the subject of physical education in schools. Organize this speech according to Monroe's motivated sequence. Pay careful attention to each of the steps in this organizational pattern. What are the advantages of this pattern over, say, a comparative advantages pattern or a problem-solution pattern? What are the disadvantages?

6. Search for "graphic Australian anti-smoking ad" on YouTube. Are the fear appeals used in this anti-smoking campaign legitimate? Do they motivate an audience to action, or are they so strong that they immobilize an audience? Why?

7. Check out Speech Studio to see other students deliver their persuasive speeches. Or record a speech you're working on, upload it to Speech Studio, and ask your peers for their feedback. What feedback could you use to fine-tune your persuasive speech before you give it in class? ☑Speech Studio

16 Persuasion and Reasoning

IN THIS CHAPTER, YOU WILL LEARN TO:

- Use evidence effectively in a persuasive speech
- Enhance your credibility before, during, and at the end of your speech
- Use emotional appeals effectively and ethically to persuade your audience
- Appeal to mythos effectively and ethically to persuade your audience
- Avoid seven of the most common fallacies in persuasive arguments

The arguments you will use in your speeches are based on reasoning. Speakers accomplish sound reasoning when they use logos, ethos, and pathos (Chapter 7). **Logos** is the logical arrangement of evidence in a speech; **ethos** refers to the speaker's credibility; and **pathos** refers to the emotional appeals made by a speaker.[1] In this chapter, you'll learn more about these three components of reasoning as well as a fourth: *mythos*. Speakers appeal to mythos when they want to tap into common cultural beliefs and attitudes to persuade their audience. This chapter also examines fallacies, which are errors in logic and reasoning commonly made in persuasive speaking.

PAUL J. RICHARDS/AFP/Getty Images

In persuasive speeches, your logical use of evidence, appeals to credibility, and appeals to emotion determine the strengths or weaknesses of your arguments. When used effectively, evidence, credibility, and emotion work together to help you move an audience toward a particular position. They help you introduce an issue and increase the audience's awareness of its implications. They also help you secure your audience's agreement and encourage them to take action. Finally, the effective use of reasoning helps your audience integrate their new awareness into their daily lives.[2] The next three sections discuss how you can incorporate evidence, credibility, and emotion successfully in your persuasive speeches.

Evidence and Persuasion

When you speak persuasively, you use evidence in much the same way you use it in other types of speeches. However, for persuasive speeches, three aspects of the effective use of evidence are especially important: the use of specific evidence, novel information, and credible sources.

Use Specific Evidence

When you want to convince your audience that something is true, good, or appropriate, you will be more successful if you use evidence that is *specific* rather than *general*.[3] Your evidence should support your claims as explicitly as possible. For example, in a speech persuading her audience not to smoke, Shannan used the following specific evidence to describe the toxic ingredients in cigarettes:

> You want to make a cigarette? According to Dr. Roger Morrisette of Farmington State College, a single cigarette contains over 4,000 chemicals. If you want the recipe, well, this is what you'll need. You'll need some carcinogens, or cancer-causing agents; some formaldehyde, or embalming fluid; some acetone, which is paint stripper or nail polish remover; benzene or arsenic; pesticides such as fungicides, herbicides, and insecticides; and toxins like hydrogen cyanide, ammonia, and nicotine.

Shannan could have argued "Cigarettes are toxic and contain thousands of poisonous chemicals," but that is far less specific than her list of ingredients. She is more persuasive because she uses specific evidence rather than simply making a general claim.

Present Novel Information

In this age of information overload, it seems that audiences have already heard "all the reasons" to support (or oppose) a position. Still, research indicates that you will be more persuasive when you present new, rather than well-known, information to your audience.[4] When you go beyond what your audience already knows, you capture their attention and cause them to listen more carefully to your ideas.

In a speech on pet overpopulation, Malachi produced new information that was quite persuasive. His audience already knew that unspayed animals cause pet overpopulation, so he presented some novel information on this familiar topic:

> According to the Humane Society of the United States in seven years, one unspayed female cat and her unspayed offspring can theoretically produce 420,000 cats. In six years, one unspayed female dog and her offspring can produce 67,000 dogs.

Malachi used information that was new to his audience as well as specific evidence (the exact figures). He took a familiar topic, pet overpopulation, and helped his audience take notice in new ways.

Good to Know!

logos: Logical arrangement of evidence in a speech; the first of Aristotle's three types of proof. **ethos:** Speaker's credibility; the second of Aristotle's three types of proof. **pathos:** Emotional appeals made by a speaker; the third of Aristotle's three types of proof.

Use Credible Sources

Recall that in research, credibility relates to the potential bias of a source, whereas in reasoning, it relates to the trustworthiness of a source. When you want to persuade your audience, you must use evidence that comes from dependable sources. If you don't, you will be less effective in convincing your audience of your position.

There are two guidelines for using credible sources persuasively. First, provide enough information about your source so that your audience can assess its credibility.[5] This means you must cite as much specific source information as you can: date of publication, author credentials, organizational affiliation, and other significant information. In the following example, Brian's credibility is weakened because he does not provide this information: "Numerous articles have been published explaining the benefits of laser eye surgery. According to one, this procedure is the safest of all available." How many is "numerous"? Who wrote these articles? When were they written? Brian offered no dates, no sources of publication, and no credentials. Although the evidence might be legitimate, the audience has no way of determining if it is. They are less likely to be persuaded than if Brian had offered concrete information about dates, authors, and publications (see Chapter 5 for citing sources in speeches).

Second, select sources your audience will see as trustworthy and fair. Although every source has a perspective, use sources your audience will see as relatively unbiased. For example, even though the Humane Society has a position on animal overpopulation, it also has a reputation for being credible and fair. To be persuasive, choose sources that are reliable and known for expertise in your subject. Avoid sources that may be seen as extreme or overly biased.

Your audience is more likely to consider your persuasive arguments when you strengthen your reasoning with specific evidence, novel information, and credible sources. However, you must go beyond using evidence effectively in a persuasive speech. You must also make appropriate use of ethos, or your credibility as a speaker.

Audiences consider sources that are well respected in their field to be credible. For example, British astrophysicist Stephen Hawking is almost universally seen as a trustworthy and credible source because his research is solid and validated by his peers and because he has the integrity to admit when he has made a mistake. What evidence from a well-respected source could you use to lend credibility to your next speech?

MIGUEL RIOPA/AFP/Getty Images

Credibility and Persuasion

A speaker's **credibility** comes from the audience's perception of a speaker's competence and character. The most important aspect of credibility is that an audience attributes it to a speaker (Chapter 7). No matter how talented, prepared, or polished you are as a speaker, if the audience does not see you as credible, you simply aren't credible.[6]

However, the two most important factors in credibility are the audience's perception of your competence and character. **Competence** is the audience's view of a speaker's intelligence, expertise, and knowledge of a subject, and **character** is the audience's view of a speaker's sincerity, trustworthiness, and concern for his or her well-being (Chapter 7).[7] You express your competence through your research, your organization, and your delivery. If you have taken time to prepare and practice your speech, you are more likely to be viewed as competent. Competence also

Good to Know!

credibility: Audience's perception of a speaker's competence and character. **competence:** Audience's view of a speaker's intelligence, expertise, and knowledge of a subject. **character:** Audience's view of a speaker's sincerity, trustworthiness, and concern for their well-being.

comes from your personal talents and expertise, the experience and knowledge you bring to the speech before your research. You communicate your character by taking the time to analyze your audience and tailor your speech to meet their needs, using inclusive language and convincing logic to express your integrity, values, principles, and attitudes toward others. These actions let your audience know you care about them and can be trusted to give a speech that is thoughtful and worth listening to.

You can manage your credibility by understanding the three types of credibility and when they are established in a speech and by knowing how you can enhance your credibility.

Types of Credibility

Three types of credibility exist in any speech: initial, derived, and terminal. **Initial credibility** is the credibility a speaker has before giving a speech, **derived credibility** is the credibility a speaker develops during a speech, and **terminal credibility** is the credibility given to the speaker at the end of a speech. The following scenario illustrates how these three types of credibility develop:

Jeff Greenberg / Alamy

> You've been assigned to speak to a group of high school students and persuade them to volunteer in their community. When you arrive at the high school auditorium to speak, you've brought your *initial credibility* with you—what the students think about you before you even begin your speech. Their impression might be based on very little information (you're a college student) or on some specific information (their teachers told them who you are, why you're coming to speak, and what you'll be talking about).
>
> You begin your speech. It's well researched and you've thought carefully about your audience and how your topic is relevant to them. You've developed a style of delivery that you think the students will appreciate. You've worked hard on your introduction, knowing you need to catch their attention right away. You've also decided to share your own volunteer experiences with them. As you give your speech, you are establishing *derived credibility*—what you say and do throughout your speech to cause students to see you as competent and trustworthy.
>
> You finish your speech and open up the floor for questions and discussion. At the end of your time with the students, you close your presentation and say good-bye. When the students leave their interaction with you, they've assigned what's called *terminal credibility*; they walk away with some conception of your level of knowledge, expertise, sincerity, and trustworthiness.

Do you see this speaker as credible? Do you think his audience sees him as credible? What do you think this speaker can do to establish common ground with his audience?

As you can see from this scenario, credibility evolves during a speech. You may start your speech with high initial credibility, but if you don't follow through on this by building your derived and terminal credibility throughout your speech, your overall credibility with your audience will drop. Or you may begin with low initial credibility because an audience does not know you but wind up with excellent overall credibility because you worked diligently to build your derived and terminal credibility during your speech. Because credibility is a process, you must work to enhance or maintain it throughout your speech.

Good to Know!

initial credibility: Credibility a speaker has before giving a speech. **derived credibility:** Credibility a speaker develops during a speech. **terminal credibility:** Credibility a speaker has at the end of a speech.

Enhancing Your Credibility

If you begin a speech with little initial credibility because the audience does not know you, you need to build credibility during the speech. You can build your credibility in three ways: explain your competence as you begin your speech, establish common ground with your audience, and deliver your speech fluently with expression and conviction.

Establish your competence. Your introduction (Chapter 9) is an ideal place to establish your competence. Here you can reveal any credentials, training, or experiences that make you competent to speak on your topic. Or you can explain that although you may not be specifically trained, you have done extensive research on the topic. Throughout the speech, you can increase your credibility by citing sources, sharing your experiences, and offering insights based on your background and research. In her speech on teen suicide, Chelsey enhanced her credibility right away by citing statistics and credible sources. Throughout her speech, she used narratives and visual aids to increase her credibility. And at the end of her speech, she used personal testimony to great effect.

> I've been a member of the Yellow Ribbon Organization [a suicide prevention program] for three years now and a survivor for five years. I found this organization at the worst stage of my life when I had completely hit rock bottom. With their help, I recovered and now have made it one of my missions in life to speak out about youth suicide.

At first, Chelsey seemed to be just another speaker with the usual amount of initial credibility. But as she spoke, her research, evidence, and preparation increased her credibility quite effectively. Her startling personal testimony at the end of her speech enhanced her terminal credibility, bringing a personal note to the speech that moved her audience and kept them interested right up to the end.

Establish common ground. A second way to build your credibility is to establish common ground with your audience. To establish **common ground** is to identify similarities, shared interests, and mutual perspectives with an audience. You can establish common ground by showing the audience you share values, experiences, and group memberships with them.[8] You can do so by stating that you belong to similar organizations, appreciate the same activities, or hold certain values as important. You can also establish common ground when you explain your views and positions and why they are in harmony with those held by audience members. When you take time to establish a friendly bond (often called *rapport*) with your audience, they will begin to like, trust, and respect you. Audiences attach higher credibility to speakers they see as similar to themselves.

Barbara Bush is a speaker who is well-known for establishing common ground in one notable speech. In 1990, Bush was asked to give the commencement speech by the senior class of Wellesley College when they found their first choice, author Alice Walker, could not attend. About a quarter of the graduating class protested, claiming that because Bush was famous not for her own accomplishments but because of the man she married, she was not a good role model for the career-oriented students of Wellesley. Knowing how her audience perceived her, Bush established common ground by acknowledging their interest in Walker and relating that interest to their college experience.

Good to Know!

common ground: Similarities, shared interests, and mutual perspectives a speaker has with an audience.

Now I know your first choice today was Alice Walker, known for *The Color Purple*. Instead you got me—known for the color of my hair! Alice Walker's book has a special resonance here. At Wellesley, each class is known by a special color. For four years the class of '90 has worn the color purple. Today you meet on Severance Green to say good-bye to all of that, to begin a new and a very personal journey to search for your own true colors.

Deliver your speech effectively. A third way to enhance your credibility is through your delivery. Research indicates that speakers who are prepared, energetic, speak moderately fast, and appear comfortable in front of their audience are seen as credible.[9] If you practice your speech and work on your delivery (Chapter 11), your credibility should increase. Here's how one student enhanced his credibility by preparing his speech with effective delivery in mind.

> Kip knew his initial credibility for his speech would be low. He'd blown his first speech for the class, and this was the second round. Not only that, he was a member of the football team, and he'd missed some classes because of travel to games. He knew the other students thought he was just a "dumb football player" who didn't care about the class.
>
> However, Kip wanted to get his degree and teach history at a high school. He knew the importance of public speaking and communication skills in his future profession. So he chose a topic he felt really connected to, worked hard on putting his speech together, and practiced delivering his speech as many times as he could before the speaking day. He worked on his speaking rate because he knew he talked too fast when he was nervous. He worked on his eye contact so he could connect with his classmates nonverbally as well as verbally. He was enthusiastic about the topic and found ways to convey that enthusiasm in his delivery and his language. He also wanted to appear comfortable (even though he was really nervous), so he worked on his introduction until he had it just perfect.
>
> On the day of the speech, Kip appeared confident, prepared, and quite engaged with his material and the audience. He went from being a "dumb football player" in the eyes of his classmates to a very credible speaker.

Remember that the audience assigns credibility to a speaker. Speakers with high credibility tend to be more persuasive than those with low credibility, so give this component of your speech careful consideration. You can also strengthen your persuasive message by making appropriate use of pathos, or appeals to emotion.

Practicing the Public Dialogue

16.1

Consider Your Credibility

As a class, make a list of people you think have strong credibility. These people can be anyone—celebrities, historical figures, people you know personally. Discuss the qualities these people have that make them credible in your eyes. Make a list of these qualities and see if they correlate with the qualities of credibility you've been reading about in this chapter. Would you find these people persuasive on all topics or only a few? What qualities do you have that make you credible? How can you use these qualities to enhance your credibility as a speaker?

Online Resources

CourseMate If you'd like to complete a similar activity on your own, use your CourseMate for *Invitation to Public Speaking* to access the videos of professional speakers included in the online resources for this book. Select two professional speakers you think are highly credible and watch their videos. Assess their initial, derived, and terminal credibility. Now select two professional speakers you think are not very credible and assess their initial, derived, and terminal credibility. How could you apply what you observed in the videos about credibility to your own speeches?

Emotion and Persuasion

Emotional appeals, or pathos, can be one of the most challenging aspects of persuasion. On the one hand, research suggests that speakers persuade only when they appeal to emotions because they encourage the audience to relate to an issue on an internal, personal level. On the other hand, because emotions are so personal and powerful, research also suggests that an inappropriate appeal to emotions can cause an audience to shut down in an instant.[10] Appeals to emotions can be complicated, so it's useful to understand what emotions are and which emotions people most commonly experience.

Emotions are "internal mental states" that focus primarily on feelings. Research distinguishes emotions (internal states such as fear, anger, sadness) from bodily states (tiredness, hunger), cognitive states (confusion, uncertainty), and behavioral states (timidity, aggressiveness).[11] Communication research has identified six primary emotions that tend to be expressed similarly across cultures and three secondary emotions that are expressed differently depending on age, gender, and culture.[12] The primary emotions are

- *Fear:* an unpleasant feeling of apprehension or distress; the anticipation of danger or threat
- *Anger:* a feeling of annoyance, irritation, or rage
- *Surprise:* a feeling of sudden wonder or amazement, especially because of something unexpected
- *Sadness:* a feeling of unhappiness, grief, or sorrow
- *Disgust:* a feeling of horrified or sickened distaste for something
- *Happiness:* a feeling of pleasure, contentment, or joy

The secondary emotions are

- *Pride:* an appropriate level of respect for a person, character trait, accomplishment, experience, or value; feeling pleased or delighted
- *Guilt:* an awareness of having done wrong, accompanied by feelings of shame and regret
- *Shame:* a feeling of dishonor, unworthiness, and embarrassment

Another emotion common to persuasive speeches but not identified among the primary or secondary emotions is

- *Reverence:* a feeling of deep respect, awe, or devotion

In persuasive speaking, you make appeals to emotions to accomplish the following goals:

- *Gain attention and motivate listening:* You often catch an audience's attention and motivate them to listen by appealing to their emotions with a compelling short story, testimony, or examples.
- *Reinforce points:* You can use emotional appeals to reinforce main points or subpoints. For example, when you support a point with a statistic and then reinforce the statistic with an example of how some aspect of the statistic has affected a specific person, an audience can understand your point on a more personal level.
- *Express personal commitment:* When you care deeply about an issue and want your audiences to recognize this depth of commitment, you may appeal to emotions by shifting your delivery to a more passionate or intense tone, or you may personalize your claims and arguments.
- *Call to action or conclude memorably:* You can often move an audience to action by asking them to envision the result of that action and how it could affect them personally. You might end your speech with a compelling story or quote and so conclude memorably.

Because emotional appeals engage an audience personally, you'll want to consider a few aspects of emotional appeals to use them effectively: audience centeredness, vivid language, and a balance of emotion and reason.

Stay Audience Centered

Perhaps the most important component of a persuasive emotional appeal is how appropriate that appeal is for the audience. Consider your audience very carefully before you decide what kinds of appeals to use. For example, almost every one of our master statuses (Chapter 4) affects how we respond to the emotional side of an issue; our age, gender, physical ability, religion, ethnicity, and culture greatly influence how we see an issue and thus the acceptability of an emotional appeal. As you consider the emotional appeals you want to make to your audience, ask yourself the following questions:

- Will the members of your audience have firsthand experience with your topic, or will it feel distant to them?
- What kinds of experiences will they have had?
- What emotions might be associated with those experiences? If they haven't had direct experiences, why not?
- In what ways might you be able to draw them into your topic emotionally without offending anyone?

Although no speaker can predict with total accuracy how an audience will respond to an emotional appeal, you can consider your audience carefully and select those appeals to emotions that seem most appropriate. When speakers misjudge the appropriateness of an appeal to an emotion, they generally make one of three errors.

Overly graphic and violent appeals. An overly graphic visual or verbal appeal is one that describes wounds and injuries, deaths, attacks, or harm to another being in extensive detail. The speaker generally is hoping to impress the audience with the horror of an act but carries the description too far and causes the audience to shut down or feel overwhelming revulsion.

Overly frightening or threatening appeals. When a speaker describes something so frightening or threatening that the audience feels helpless or panicked, they will stop listening or they will feel immobilized. These kinds of appeals tend to stay with audience members long after a speech is over and cause them to feel unnecessarily fearful. In contrast, an appropriate fear appeal is one that moves the audience to act but does not immobilize or terrorize them (Chapter 15). A common overly frightening appeal is one in which a speaker argues that if the audience doesn't prevent something from happening or stop some behavior, they or someone they care about will die.

Overly manipulative appeals. An appeal to an emotion, either positive or negative, that relies on theatrics, melodrama, and sensation rather than on fact and research is overly manipulative. Such appeals encourage the audience to feel pity, shame, guilt, or humiliation about something or to become overly excited or enthusiastic. Speakers may make overly manipulative appeals when they want their audience to see a person in a certain way, donate time or money to a cause, or act in a particular way. For example, in a speech asking an audience to give to a charitable organization, Jade showed images of children with cerebral palsy. She asked her audience questions to engage them and then created sad stories about the children based on the answers they gave. Although she received donations, she manipulated her audience's emotions with hypothetical stories to get them to give money rather than relying on true stories or research.

By staying audience centered, you can make appropriate appeals to emotions. If you keep your audience in the front of your mind, you will recognize which appeals are appropriate for them and which ones aren't. An example of a speaker who made appropriate appeals to emotions in a speech is Mary Fisher, who addressed the 1992 Republican national convention as a person with AIDS. In her moving speech, she appealed to the emotions that accompany illness, loss, death, HIV/AIDS, conceptions of evil, risk and safety, and love and care for one another. Although her appeals were powerful, they were appropriate to her audience and not overly graphic, frightening, or manipulative. Fisher is an example of an audience-centered speaker who used pathos to make compelling emotional appeals without misusing the audience's feelings.

Use Vivid Language

Appeals to emotions ask an audience to recall some of their most profound experiences. You can use vivid descriptions and examples to help your audience connect with those experiences. One of the reasons that Martin Luther King Jr. is considered one of the most influential speakers of the twentieth century is the vivid language he used to create images for his audiences. In his "I Have a Dream" speech on the steps of the Lincoln Memorial, his language helped his audience "see" his vision and connect to it emotionally as well as rationally. When he spoke of freedom, he described the "chains of discrimination" and the "manacles of segregation" that "crippled." He used evocative words and phrases, such as "languishing" and "exile," the "magnificent words of the Constitution," and a "promise to all" for the "riches of freedom."[13]

AP Photo

Martin Luther King Jr. is particularly well known for his powerful use of language to inspire and motivate his audiences. Consider your next persuasive speech. What are some images you can use to help your audience see what you're talking about and make an emotional connection to your topic?

The world's most profound speakers have been trained to make the most of vivid language, but even novice speakers can use language to move and inspire. In a speech on American veterans that was both persuasive and commemorative, Darrin created the following emotional appeal through his vivid language:

Imagine sitting down to a peaceful meal with your wife, husband, or children. A "ring," "ring," "ring" is heard, interrupting you like an unwanted guest. The distinct sound of this ring suspends all talk. It's like this illusionary figure drifts across the room, touching the souls of those dear to you. Even before you pick it up, you know your country has gone to war, and this is your call to duty.

Vivid language helps your listeners create images that are rich with feeling. When you speak persuasively, try to find words and phrases that tap into your audience's memories. If you do so, you will have an easier time drawing your audience in emotionally to your claims and arguments.

Balance Emotion and Reason

When you speak persuasively, seek a balance between reason and emotion. Overly emotional speeches may stimulate your audience, but without sound reasoning, they are less likely to be persuaded by your arguments.

Use appeals to emotion to elaborate on your reasons or to show the more personal side of your evidence. If you make a claim with statistics or offer an example of the impact of a plan, support it by drawing out the emotional aspects. Similarly, if you make an appeal to emotions, back it up with sound reasoning. When you balance emotion and reason, your audience will see more than one dimension of your persuasive appeals and can be persuaded on more than one level.

Appeals to emotion are necessary parts of persuasive speeches. If you can avoid overly graphic, frightening, or manipulative appeals, you can tap into powerful emotions. By staying audience centered, paying careful attention to your language, and balancing reason and emotion, you will be able to craft persuasive arguments that encourage your audience to think differently about issues.

Mythos and Persuasion

"No one is immune to the folk knowledge of their culture," state Marian Friestad and Peter Wright, marketing and psychology researchers at the University of Oregon.[14] The folk knowledge of a culture is **mythos**, the interrelated set of beliefs, attitudes, values, and feelings held by members of a particular society or culture. Friestad and Wright explain that we learn mythos not through any formal training but rather through the "whisperings of Mother culture."[15] We listen to these whisperings as children, adolescents, young adults, and adults. They come through anecdotes and customs as well as through events and accepted norms for behavior.

Whether you have grown up in the United States or another culture, you're likely familiar with some of the cultural myths of the United States. These cultural narratives stress the importance of freedom and democracy. They describe the United States as the land of opportunity and tell of journeys from rags to riches. They emphasize the value of progress and the exploration of new frontiers. They celebrate heroes and heroines who have made the United States a world leader. The mythos of any culture communicates who its people are and what values it holds most important.

Mythos and persuasion are tightly interconnected. When we appeal to mythos, we call to mind history, tradition, faith, feelings, common sense, and membership in a community or culture. In doing so, we tap into a rich reservoir of emotions, attitudes, and values. We encourage our audience to accept our claims based on stories told over generations. We personalize an argument beyond making an appeal to an emotion: We tap into larger stories about "the way things are" and "the way things should be." Because mythos is an important part of the persuasive process, consider a few guidelines when you use this appeal in your speeches.

A Part of the Story Can Tell the Whole Story

To tap into the mythos of a culture, you rarely need to tell the full story to the audience. In the 1960s, John F. Kennedy referred to the mythos of the American frontier in many of his speeches, calling forth the complete myth with just a few words:

> The New Frontier of which I speak is not a set of promises—it is a set of challenges. It sums up not what I intend to offer the American people, but what I intend to ask of them.

With these few words, Kennedy was able to call to mind the stories of settling the West, of overcoming odds, and of hard work. With the phrase "New Frontier," he transferred the myths of the "old frontier" to his presidency and drew people into the adventure and its challenges. Similarly, when Martin Luther King Jr. spoke of freedom in his "I Have a Dream" speech, he did not detail the complete

Good to Know!

mythos: Interrelated set of beliefs, attitudes, values, and feelings held by members of a particular society or culture.

story of freedom in the United States. Instead, he referred to elements of that story to call forth the full mythos of freedom in a democratic society for his audience:

In a sense we've come to our nation's Capital to cash a check. When the architects of our republic wrote the magnificent words of the Constitution and the Declaration of Independence, they were signing a promissory note to which

Public Speaking and Service Learning: Engaging Community

Sarah Cresalia, a public speaking student at Colorado State University, completed her service learning project at a therapeutic equine-riding organization called Hearts and Horses. She quickly learned how much her help was desperately needed by this organization. Its need and lack of volunteers influenced Sarah to reflect on a lack of cultural motivation for people to voluntarily help one another. In her persuasive speech, she challenged the mythos of "pull yourself up by your bootstraps" as a way to motivate her audience to action.

Volunteering is an opportunity that everyone should take advantage of. It allows you to give back to your community and see the difference that you are making not only in others but also in yourself. That said, I do not feel that volunteerism is culturally valued enough here in the United States. Society does not function as individuals on their own; it functions only when we join together to better our community. My service learning work has taught me all of this in a matter of months.

Hearts and Horses is a therapeutic riding center that strives to help participants accomplish more than they ever thought they could, both mentally and physically. Hearts and Horses is a large operation and it relies heavily on volunteers. Recently, I joined the "turn in/turn out" team, which means that I help take the horses out of their stalls and move them to a paddock so they can get some exercise, and then I bring them back to their stalls. During this time, there should be another team that goes through and cleans out the horse stalls. However, there are not enough volunteers for that job, and so this task has fallen on my team to complete.

> **"THERE ARE MANY COMPETING MYTHOS PEOPLE CAN USE TO JUSTIFY THEIR ACTIONS, AND PEOPLE SHOULD BE AWARE OF THE WAYS SUCH VALUES CAN AFFECT OTHERS."**

In my persuasive speech, I decided to talk about this general lack of "lending a helping hand" in our highly competitive culture by challenging some of the common mythos that guide our culture. I feel there are many competing mythos that people can use to justify their actions, and people should be aware of the ways such values can affect others in society. By incorporating this concept into my speech, I feel I gained additional speaker credibility, and made stronger arguments, as it showed that I cared for not only the clients, volunteers, and employees of Hearts and Horses but greater American society as a whole.

Tips for Incorporating Service Learning into Public Speaking

- Your service learning assignment can be a rich source of evidence for your persuasive reasoning. When you pull evidence from your service experiences, you help establish your derived credibility for your audience.

- When you urge your audience to take action, be careful not to shame your audience into taking any action you promote. Instead, persuade ethically by motivating them to reflect on their values and actions (like our culture's mythos) and then empower them to make a rational change for themselves.

- Common phrases like "pull yourself up by your bootstraps" can be used to motivate an audience. But phrases like these reveal a culture's mythos and also can be used to contradict the mythos. Challenge mythos carefully and consider also using stories and quotations that support your challenges.

every American was to fall heir. This note was a promise that all men—yes, black men as well as white men—would be guaranteed the unalienable rights of life, liberty, and the pursuit of happiness.

When speakers rely on mythos, they don't tell just any story. They refer to an intensely familiar story, one that has been repeated over the years and is part of the common sense of a culture.

Mythos Has a Logic

Although a culture's myths may be as much legend as fact, they do contain a logic that rings true for that culture. They're like the fairy tales, folklore, and science fiction we grow up with. Although these myths are filled with larger-than-life heroes and villains, incredible adventures, death-defying feats, and supernatural powers, they reflect the logic, or common sense, of their culture. For example, consider the story of George Washington and the cherry tree. Washington probably never chopped down a cherry tree, but the logic of the story rings true: It is wrong to tell lies.

The power of mythos in a persuasive speech is that it allows you to tap into the logic of a culture. When you use mythos, think carefully about what logic you are appealing to and how that logic "makes sense" to your audience.[16]

Different Cultures Have Different Myths

Because all cultures have a unique history, they all have unique myths. When you appeal to mythos in a speech, stay audience centered and keep in mind that members of your audience may have different cultural myths.

For example, Native Americans recognize communication with nonhuman entities, such as the rivers or the wind, as completely normal and even necessary for human survival. However, people from other traditions may have difficulty accepting this perspective. Similarly, many African Americans tell a story of two worlds, one in which African Americans live and another inhabited by white people. In contrast, many white people tell a story of only one world, inhabited equally by all, in which all are equally free to move about and make choices. Each culture has a different mythos, and you must recognize these differences or risk alienating rather than persuading your audiences.

Using evidence effectively and appealing to credibility, emotion, and mythos will help you build a strong case for your position. Another strategy that will help you craft persuasive messages is to build sound arguments. By avoiding the common fallacies in reasoning discussed next, you can make sure your arguments are accurate and strong.

Practicing the Public Dialogue

16.2

Consider Appeals to Emotion and to Mythos

In small groups, discuss your preparation for the next persuasive speech you'll give in class. Identify the appeals to emotion and to mythos you plan to make in your speech. As a group, help one another strengthen these appeals and ensure that they are audience centered. Discuss whether these appeals are appropriate and how you plan to make them in an ethical way.

Online Resources

CourseMate To see an example of a speaker appealing to emotion in a persuasive speech, watch the video of Mary Fisher's address to the 1992 Republican national convention. Notice how she appeals to powerful emotions but does so in an audience-centered way. You can find this speech under the Chapter 16 resources in your CourseMate for *Invitation to Public Speaking*. To hear a speaker appeal to mythos, access **Web Connect 16.1: Appealing to Mythos** and read or listen to American labor leader Cesar Chavez's 1984 address to the Commonwealth Club. Chavez often appealed to mythos to inspire and persuade his audiences. For example, he related the Mexican American mythos of pilgrimage, penance, and revolution to the fight for the rights of the poor. What cultural mythos can you identify in his speech?

Fallacies

Whether you intend to or not, you can make inaccurate arguments, called fallacies. A **fallacy** is an argument that seems valid but is flawed because of unsound evidence or reasoning. Fallacies are a problem in persuasive speeches not only because they undermine speakers' arguments but also because, despite their factual or logical errors, they can be quite persuasive. Fallacies can seem reasonable and acceptable on the surface, but when we analyze them, we see that their logic is flawed (Toulmin's model of reasoning from Chapter 7 is an excellent tool for analyzing arguments). Although there are more than 125 different fallacies, a discussion of the most common types is adequate for beginning public speakers. These are ad hominem, bandwagon, either-or, false cause, hasty generalization, red herring, and slippery slope.[17] At the end of the discussion of these fallacies, also see Table 16.1, which provides brief descriptions of other fallacies often heard in speeches.

Ad Hominem: Against the Person

Ad hominem is a Latin term that means "against the person." Perhaps one of the most familiar fallacies, an **ad hominem fallacy** is an argument in which a speaker attacks a person rather than that person's arguments. By portraying someone with an opposing position as incompetent, unreliable, or even stupid, you effectively silence that person and discredit her or his arguments or ideas. Here are some other examples of ad hominem fallacies:

> Of course Obama worked so hard to pass the health-care bill—he's a liberal democrat who only wants to create a socialist country.

> Well, sure, Bush wanted to open up lands for drilling. Isn't that how he got into office, with the financial support of his oil buddies?

Ad hominem fallacies are persuasive because they turn the audience's attention away from the content of an argument and toward the character and credibility of the person offering that argument. They cloud an issue, making it hard for an audience to evaluate the ideas the speaker challenges. But more important, ad hominem fallacies make erroneous claims. The argument against Obama's character clouds the issue of whether providing health care for American citizens is the right thing to do. Similarly, Bush may have indeed received campaign financing from oil companies, but that fact does not prove his drilling policy was suspect.

Listen carefully for arguments against a person's character and avoid them in your own speeches. They do little to build your credibility or help your audience see that your ideas are preferable to someone else's.

Bandwagon: Everyone Else Agrees

When you fall prey to the **bandwagon fallacy**, you are suggesting that something is correct or good because everyone else agrees with it or is doing it. In public speaking, this translates to making statements like these:

> Many other communities are adopting this nonsmoking ordinance in restaurants. It's a perfect solution for us as well.

Good to Know!

fallacy: Argument that seems valid but is flawed because of unsound evidence or reasoning. **ad hominem fallacy:** Argument in which a speaker attacks a person rather than that person's arguments. **bandwagon fallacy:** Argument that something is correct or good because everyone else agrees with it or is doing it.

How can we allow gays and lesbians in our organization? They've not been allowed in the military or scouting organizations, so why should we accept them in ours?

The bandwagon fallacy works a little like group pressure: It's hard to say no to something everyone else is doing. But the logic of the bandwagon is flawed for two

Civic Engagement in Action

"TO CARE IS TO ACCEPT RESPONSIBILITY"

On August 8, 1988, several thousand unarmed civilians demonstrating for democracy in Burma (now called Myanmar) were gunned down by troops loyal to Ne Win, Burma's repressive leader. This event, known as the Massacre of 8–8–88, led prodemocracy activist Aung San Suu Kyi to realize, "I could not, as my father's daughter, remain indifferent to all that was going on."

Dr. Suu Kyi was only two when her father, General Aung San, was assassinated by political rivals. Revered as a national hero for negotiating Burma's independence from the United Kingdom in 1947, Aung San inspired not only his country but also his daughter, who as an adult decided to step forward and carry on his tradition of "selfless courage and his vision of a free and democratic Burma." In 1990, Dr. Suu Kyi and her party, the National League for Democracy, won 80 percent of the vote over the military regime that had called the election. But having expected to win themselves, the regime refused to relinquish power and ordered Dr. Suu Kyi to leave the country. She refused, knowing that she would never be allowed to return to her country if she left. The military placed her under house arrest, and she remains imprisoned to this day, prevented from seeing her family and other supporters.

In 1991, Aung San Suu Kyi was awarded the Nobel Peace Prize in recognition of her nonviolent struggle for democracy and human rights. She continues to speak out against oppression despite the difficulties she has endured for more than two decades. "It is undeniably easier to ignore the hardships of those who are too weak to demand their rights than respond sensitively to their needs," she says. "To care is to accept responsibility, to dare to act in accordance with the dictum that the ruler is the strength of the helpless." For her, the struggle for democracy is not simply about ideals; it is about what

David Longstreath, FILE/AP Photo

affects us in our everyday lives. It "is about our job and your children's education; it's about the house you live in and the food you eat; it's about whether or not you have to get permission from somebody before you visit your relatives in the next village; it's about whether or not you can reap your own harvest and sell it to the person you want to sell it to." And although the current government of Burma actively works against her efforts, Dr. Suu Kyi is committed to seeing democracy in Burma. "Running away is not going to solve any problems," she explains. "The nightmare of Burma must be resolved through dialogue with the Burmese government."[18]

You Can Get Involved

CourseMate If you'd like to learn how you can get involved in the U.S. democratic process, access **Web Connect 16.2: E-Democracy** with your CourseMate for *Invitation to Public Speaking*. This resource provides links to political news, unbiased information about candidates running in current elections, and resources that allow you to become part of our country's dialogue about politics and democracy. For information about how you can act in support of democracy farther afield, access **Web Connect 16.3: Freedom House**, an organization founded by Eleanor Roosevelt that works to promote democracy and freedom around the world. Both of these resources are nonprofit, nonpartisan organizations.

reasons. First, even though a solution or a plan might work well for some, it might not be the best solution for your audience. You need to do more than argue "it will work for you because it worked for others." You need to explain exactly why a plan might work for a particular group of people, community, or organization. Second, just because "lots of others agree" does not make something "good." Large groups of people agree about many things, but those things aren't necessarily appropriate for everyone. When you hear the bandwagon fallacy, ask yourself two questions: If it is good for them, is it good for *me*? Even if many others are doing something, is it something I support?

Either-Or: A False Dilemma

A dilemma is a situation that requires you to choose from options that are all unpleasant or that are mutually exclusive. When we're facing a dilemma, we feel we must make a choice even if it is not to our liking. In persuasive speeches, an **either-or fallacy**, sometimes called a *false dilemma*, is an argument in which a speaker claims our options are "either A or B," when actually more than two options exist. To identify a false dilemma, listen for the words "either-or" as a speaker presents an argument. Consider these two examples:

> Either we increase access to our before- and after-school meal programs or our students will continue to fail.

> Either we increase our candidate's appeal to women or we don't get elected.

In both examples, the audience is presented with a false dilemma. Intuitively, we know there must be other options. In the first example, there are other ways to respond to poor student performance—better nutrition is only one part of the solution. In the second, there likely are other ways to increase a candidate's appeal and chances of success. Sometimes, it's hard to see the other options immediately, but they are usually there.

Either-or arguments are fallacious because they oversimplify complex issues. Usually, the speaker has created an atmosphere in which the audience feels pressured to select one of the two options presented. Even if those options may be good choices, an either-or argument prevents us from considering others that may be even better.

False Cause (Post Hoc): Mistaking a Chronological Relationship

A **false cause fallacy** is an argument mistaking a chronological relationship for a causal relationship. There are two types of false cause fallacies. The first type occurs when a speaker assumes that one event *caused* the second to occur. Notice how the speaker in the following example mistakenly assumes that the first event caused the second:

> After the state passed legislation in favor of the death penalty, violent crimes decreased. The new legislation has deterred criminal activity.

> Criminal activity may have declined after the state implemented the new legislation; however, it does not prove that the legislation caused the decline. Other

Good to Know!

either-or fallacy: Argument in which a speaker claims our options are "either A or B," when actually more than two options exist. Sometimes called a *false dilemma.* **false cause fallacy:** Argument mistaking a chronological relationship for a causal relationship.

factors may have influenced the decline, such as methods of reporting violent crimes, rehabilitation programs in prisons, and even educational opportunities for individuals at risk to commit violent crimes.

The second type of false cause fallacy is known as a *single cause fallacy*. This fallacy occurs when speakers oversimplify and assume a particular effect has only one cause. This is misleading because many problems are complex, resulting from multiple causes. Notice how the example below blames only one cause for childhood obesity:

> The number of obese children in the United States has significantly increased over the past decade. According to pediatric experts, approximately 30 percent of children under the age of thirteen are obese. This problem is caused by the

Ethical Moment

WHAT ARE GOOD REASONS?

In 2010, the New York City Department of Health and Mental Hygiene angered some New York City residents after publishing a pamphlet for drug users. Since accidental drug overdose is reportedly the fourth leading cause of early adult death in New York City, the agency hoped the pamphlet would help save lives. The pamphlet consists of ten tips to help users reduce the harms associated with injecting drugs. These tips included information about how to "prepare drugs carefully" and advised people to use new syringes every time and to make sure to find a vein before injecting drugs. This detailed advice left some NYC residents questioning whether the pamphlet was a help or a how-to guide.

John P. Gilbride, a Drug Enforcement Administration official, "expressed his concern that the pamphlet could send a message that leads individuals to believe they can use heroin in a safe manner" and that "heroin can never be safe." Similarly, New York City Council Representative Peter F. Vallone Jr. said he was unhappy that taxpayer money was used to produce the pamphlet and asked the health commissioner to stop circulating it.

Don Des Jarlais, a research director for the Chemical Dependency Institute, offered a different view of the pamphlet. He believes it can save lives. Des Jarlais claims that after New York City implemented a needle exchange program, the city saw an 80 percent reduction of HIV reported among new drug users. He believes

10 Tips for Safer Use
1. Prevent Overdose
2. Treat Overdose
3. Don't Share
4. Use New Syringes
5. Prepare Drugs Carefully
6. Take Care of Your Veins
7. Know Your HIV Status
8. Get Tested and Treated for Hepatitis
9. Get Help for Depression
10. Ask for Help to Stop Using

New York City Department of Health and Mental Hygiene

the advice in the pamphlet could reduce the number of deaths associated with heroin overdose.[19]

What Do You Think?

1. Are there good reasons to try to prevent HIV infections or deaths among drug users, even though users engage in an illegal activity? What are those reasons?

2. Do you think the pamphlet is unethical and a misuse of taxpayer money? Why or why not?

3. Are there other ways the Health Department could use ethos, pathos, and logos to inform drug users about the risks associated with drug use? What other kinds of evidence could the Health Department use to reduce rates of HIV infection and overdose?

4. Log on to **Web Connect 16.4:4. NYC Heroin Pamphlet** to see a portion of the pamphlet and some of its visual images. Are there other images or ways of communicating visually that the Health Department could use to ethically make their arguments about safety? What might those look like? **CourseMate**

unhealthy school lunches being served in schools across the nation. We need legislation mandating more nutritious lunches to solve the obesity epidemic.

This example assumes that there is only one cause to the problem of childhood obesity—unhealthy school lunches. In fact, there are a number of reasons American children are obese: fast food, junk food, and trans fats consumed outside of school; lack of physical exercise inside and outside school; and possibly genetic factors.

Hasty Generalization: Too Few Examples

A **hasty generalization fallacy** is an argument based on too few cases, or examples, to support a conclusion. For example, when speakers rely only on personal experiences to draw conclusions, they may fall into the trap of a hasty generalization because personal experiences often are not enough to prove a claim is true. Notice how the following speaker relies only on her personal experience to support a larger claim:

> The School of Business and Finance is the hardest program to be accepted into at our university. I have applied three times and still have not been admitted.

Although this particular speaker may have been denied admittance into the School of Business and Finance many times, it does not prove that the program is the toughest for *all* students.

In addition to relying solely on personal experience, hasty generalization fallacies also consist of too few external cases, or examples, to support a claim. The following example illustrates an argument based on too few examples:

> Bilingual teachers will be hired before monolingual teachers. After all, Mr. Montoya and Ms. Morale were both recently hired, and they speak two languages.

This example relies on too few examples at only one school to prove that bilingual teachers are hired before monolingual teachers. Speakers using examples to support a claim must provide enough specific instances to convince their audience that the claim is true (Chapter 7).

Red Herring: Raising an Irrelevant Issue

The term *red herring* comes from the fox hunting tradition in England. Before a hunt began, farmers often dragged a smoked herring around the perimeter of their fields. The strong odor from the fish masked the scent of the fox and threw the hounds off its trail, keeping the hounds from trampling the farmers' crops. Although this worked well for the farmers, trailing the equivalent of a red herring around an argument is not such a good idea. When we make use of the **red herring fallacy**, we introduce irrelevant information into an argument to distract an audience from the real issue. The following example illustrates the red herring fallacy:

> How can we worry about the few cases of AIDS in our town of only 50,000 when thousands and thousands of children are dying of AIDS and AIDS-related illnesses in other countries?

Good to Know!

hasty generalization fallacy: Argument based on too few cases, or examples, to support a conclusion. **red herring fallacy:** Argument that introduces irrelevant information to distract an audience from the real issue.

In this example, the speaker turns the argument away from her own community and toward the international problem of AIDS. The audience then becomes more concerned about AIDS in other countries. Undoubtedly, this is an important issue, but it is not the one under discussion, which is equally important. Because of the red herring, the audience is less inclined to move toward a solution for the local situation.

Red herring arguments are fallacious because they turn the audience's attention from one issue to another. This type of fallacy can be hard to spot because both issues usually are important, but the audience feels pulled toward the most recently raised issue. As an audience member, listen carefully when a speaker introduces a new and important topic in a persuasive speech; you might be hearing a red herring fallacy.

Slippery Slope: The Second Step Is Inevitable

A **slippery slope fallacy** is an argument in which a speaker claims that taking a first step in one direction will inevitably lead to undesirable further steps. Like a skier speeding down a hill without being able to stop, a slippery slope fallacy suggests the momentum of one decision or action will cause others to follow. Here is an example of a slippery slope fallacy:

> If we allow our children to dress in any way they want at school, they soon will be wearing more and more outrageous clothing. They'll start trying to outdress one another. Then it'll be increasingly outrageous behaviors inside and outside the classrooms. Soon they'll turn to violence as they try to top one another.

The speaker is making a slippery slope argument by suggesting that if one unwanted thing happens, others certainly will follow. The audience gets caught up in the momentum of this "snowball" argument. Slippery slope arguments can be persuasive because the speaker extends the first claim (for example, the dress codes) to a larger issue (violence) when the two may not even be linked. Before you accept the full claim made with a slippery slope argument, stop and consider whether the chain of events really is inevitable.

As you listen to speeches, and as you put your own arguments together, keep in mind that a fallacy is an error in logic. When we persuade others, we want to be sure our logic is sound and not based on error or deception. The fallacies that commonly occur in persuasive speeches are easy to spot if you understand how they work. Those discussed in this chapter and presented in Table 16.1 on page 352, as well as the errors in reasoning identified in Chapter 7, are easy to avoid if you take time to lay out your arguments carefully. By avoiding fallacies, you will enhance your persuasive efforts, increase your credibility, and contribute positively to the public dialogue.

Practicing the Public Dialogue

16.3

Considering Logical Fallacies

Using your speech topic and research for your next persuasive speech, convert the arguments you plan to make in your speech to logical fallacies. Write one example of seven of the logical fallacies you've just read about. Bring your fallacies to class and present each of them to your classmates. See if they can identify the type of fallacy you are committing. After every student has presented her or his fallacies, discuss which were the hardest to spot and which were the most "persuasive." Now revise those fallacies, correcting their flawed reasoning.

Online Resources

CourseMate To help you identify the different types of logical fallacies so that you can avoid using them—and being used by them—access **Web Connect 16.5: Understanding Fallacies** through your CourseMate for *Invitation to Public Speaking*.

Good to Know!

slippery slope fallacy: Argument in which a speaker claims that taking a first step in one direction will lead to inevitable and undesirable further steps.

Table 16.1

Additional Fallacies Often Heard in Speeches

Fallacy	What It Does	Example
ad populum ("to the people")	Convinces the audience that because something is popular, it must be correct or right.	Nearly 75 percent of children in our community take advantage of YMCA programs. The Y programs must be the best for keeping children active and safe.
appeal to fear	Seeks to gain support based on deception or a threat.	Even though you told me that your class is full, I would like to take it this semester. I spoke to my mother, who is one of the university's attorneys, and she said overrides can be granted.
appeal to ignorance	Assumes that a lack of evidence proves (or disproves) the speaker's claim.	Because there is no concrete evidence that civilizations exist on planets other than Earth, they must not exist.
appeal to tradition	Argues for the continuation of a practice because it has always been done that way.	The college should continue to require that students have 120 credits to graduate because the college has always required students to take 120 credits.
begging the question	Makes a circular argument whereby the speaker uses the same argument as both the evidence and claim.	Hormone-free meat products are the healthiest because they do not contain hormones.
false analogy	Presents an analogy based on two things that are not essentially alike.	Since the state banned texting while driving to reduce accident rates, the state should also ban eating while driving.
false authority	Cites a well-known person rather than evidence to prove a claim.	The NBA commissioner said that athletes drafted into the NBA right out of high school will not face any future repercussions for not having a college degree. He must be right.
non sequitur ("it does not follow")	Makes a conclusion that does not follow logically from the premises.	The federal government needs to raise the national minimum wage if it wants to help put unemployed workers back into the workforce.
straw man	Attributes a weak argument to the opposition and then demolishes it (rather than addressing the opposition's real argument).	Politicians who want to tax candy and soda are not concerned about the working class. These politicians are only worried about making money, not about how struggling families will be impacted by the additional tax. We need to help working class families, not hurt them by creating another tax!

Preparation Outline with Commentary

You Have My Deepest Sympathy: You Just Won the Lottery

by Maria DiMaggio

Specific Purpose: To persuade my audience that winning the lottery is not as great as it's perceived to be and that they should invest their money in alternative ways

Thesis Statement: Lottery participants could avoid the financial and personal problems that often accompany lottery winnings by finding alternatives to this form of gambling.

CourseMate *Now that you've explored how to use logos (evidence), ethos (credibility), pathos (emotion), and mythos (cultural beliefs) in persuasive speaking, how to avoid some common fallacies, and how to persuade audiences effectively and ethically, create your own persuasive speech. Use the following speech as a model. Go to your CourseMate for* Invitation to Public Speaking *to watch a video clip of this speech and see Maria's transcript and speaking outline. Maria gave this speech in an introductory public speaking class. The assignment was to give a five- to seven-minute persuasive speech with a minimum of four sources cited. Students were also asked to create a preparation outline that included a Works Cited section. (You can use your CourseMate to access videos of other persuasive speeches, including "Colorado Prison Reform: A Solution to Reduce Recidivism and Overcrowding" by Jessica Fuller, "Fat Discrimination" by Carol Godart, and "Stop Animal Testing" by Amanda Konecny.)*

Introduction

I. You have my deepest sympathy; you just won the lottery. *(catch attention)*
II. Most of us would be shocked if someone said we'd won $20 million and then offered us condolences; however, hundreds of lottery winners have discovered the downside of winning big.
III. I used to think I'd be the happiest person in Brooklyn if I could just win a million dollars, but my research about the lottery winners convinced me to spend my money elsewhere—and I hope you'll follow my example. *(establish credibility)*
IV. Lottery participants can avoid problems that often accompany lottery winnings by finding alternatives to this form of gambling.
V. Today I'll explain that the lottery is a form of gambling that raises money for good causes; however, winners often end up with financial and personal problems, and you are better off spending your money elsewhere. *(preview main points)*

Body

I. Lotteries are a form of gambling that raise money for good causes.
   A. The *World Book Encyclopedia* identifies lotteries as a popular form of gambling.

Commentary

Maria begins her speech by combining antithesis with an intriguing statement. She then reveals the topic and problem of her speech.

   She creates common ground by telling her audience that she used to think she'd be happy if she won the lottery, a common dream. She also establishes her credibility by stating that she's researched her topic.

   Maria hopes to persuade her audience to immediate action. She alludes to her solution throughout her introduction and states it explicitly here: People should seek happiness in other ways and find alternative ways to spend their money.

   Maria uses her first main point to describe the evolution of lotteries. She defines lotteries as a form of gambling, evoking a negative connotation. However, she takes her definition from a highly credible source.

Persuasion and Reasoning

In her subpoint I.B, Maria acknowledges that lotteries also generate revenue for good causes. The examples touch on two iconic American events, the American Revolution and France's gift of the Statue of Liberty. These examples and Maria's acknowledgment that lotteries are used for good causes set the stage for her appeal to mythos later in the speech.

Reasoning deductively, Maria makes a broad claim that supports her thesis: "Unexpected problems arise for lottery winners." Her supporting examples establish her claim as viable.

Organized according to the problem-solution pattern, Maria's speech focuses on a question of policy. In her second main point, she states the problem: Winning the lottery often causes misery. By appealing to emotions and citing statistics and examples from her research, she establishes the scope of the problem.

In her third main point, Maria explicitly proposes her solution: Invest your disposable income in ways that will generate a greater return or that will be more fulfilling. Her suggestions are reasonable, and her audience will probably

1. Winners pay to participate, generally by purchasing tickets at a uniform price.
2. According to a 2002 article in *The Detroit News*, winners are determined by random drawings; unfortunately, you are sixteen times more likely to get killed driving to buy the ticket than you are to win a record amount.
3. Lotteries were popular in the United States in the 1700s.
4. However, several states made them unconstitutional in the 1880s due to fraud by lottery companies and pressure from social reformers.
5. New Hampshire reinstated the lottery in 1963; now, more than half the states have state-run lotteries.

B. Lotteries generate revenue for good causes.
1. The earliest lottery, organized in London in 1680, raised money for a municipal water supply.
2. A French lottery helped pay for the Statue of Liberty.
3. Closer to home, a national lottery helped support the American Revolutionary War.
4. In 1772, one lottery's proceeds were divided among a Presbyterian church, a German Lutheran church, the Newark Academy, and three Philadelphia schoolmasters.
5. Current lotteries in New Hampshire and Oregon, among other states, provide educational funding.

Transition: Now that we know a bit about the history of lotteries, you'd think your life would be great if you could only win big. Right? Well, there can be major problems for winners and their heirs.

II. Unexpected problems arise for lottery winners.
   A. First, their dreams of instant riches are not always fulfilled.
   1. Unless winners take a much lower lump sum, funds are distributed over twenty to twenty-five years.
   2. A lottery "millionaire" is really a "thousandaire" who gets about $50,000 annually before taxes, delinquent taxes, past-due child support, and student loans are taken out.
   3. Winners cannot draw cash from winnings, use them as collateral for loans, or liquidate future payments.
   B. In addition, many suffer personal loss and rejection.
   1. William "Bud" Post won $16.2 million but watched his brother go to jail, convicted of hiring a hit man to kill him.
   2. Debbie won $6.58 million but lost contact with her sisters, who stopped speaking to her when she declined to pay their debts.
   3. Bernice took a day off work to claim her $1 million; her job was given to someone else.
   4. Daisy won $2.8 million but went through a painful lawsuit.
      a. Her son's friend sued for half the winnings because she asked the friend to pray that she'd win.
      b. He prayed, she won, so he thought he was entitled to some of her money.
      c. The court ruled against him, saying he couldn't prove his prayers caused her to win.
   C. Lottery winnings don't necessarily bring happiness.
   1. A study conducted by the *Journal of Personality and Social Psychology* of people with the best of luck and those with the worst of luck supported this conclusion.

2. Accident victims weren't as unhappy as expected; however, lottery winners were unhappier and took less pleasure in life than expected.
   D. Finally, heaven help the heirs if a lottery-winning relative dies and leaves them with a fortune.
      1. They must immediately pay estate taxes on the unpaid total, with monthly penalties added after nine months.
      2. According to the book *Lottery Players and Winners*, Johnny Ray Brewster won $12.8 million, taking it in annual payments. His sister Peggy inherited the payments, but upon inheritance she immediately owed $3.5 million in taxes.

Transition: Given the low probability of winning and the many problems winners face, there surely must be other solutions if you have money to burn.

III. Use your extra money in far more profitable expenditures.
   A. Invest in the stock market; investing just $10 to $20 monthly can pay off immensely by the time you retire.
   B. Donate your extra money to a charitable organization and claim a tax deduction.
   C. Indulge yourself: buy cable, eat lobster occasionally, buy season tickets to a sporting or a cultural event, or get an exotic pet.
   D. Finally, if you like to think your lottery money supports education, you can donate to my college fund!

Conclusion

I. I hope I've convinced you that playing the lottery is not all it's advertised to be.
II. I've explained what the lottery is, the problems it can cause, and some alternative ways to get rid of the money.
III. So the next time you see a new lottery millionaire, consider sending your sympathies rather than your congratulations.

Works Cited

Associated Press. "Compare the Odds." *The Detroit News.* [Electronic version]. 2002. Retrieved June 2, 2005, from http://www.detnews.com/2002/metro/0204/16/b01–446437.htm.

Beyer, G. W., and Petrini, J. D. *Lottery Players and Winners: Estate Planning for the Optimistic and the Lucky.* 2002. Retrieved June 2, 2005, from http://www.professorbeyer.com/Articles/Lottery.htm.

Brickman, P., Coates, D., and Janoff-Bulman, R. "Lottery Winners and Accident Victims: Is Happiness Relative?" *Journal of Personality and Social Psychology,* 36(8), 1978: 917–927.

Findlay, J. M. *People of Chance.* New York: Oxford University Press, 1986.

Goodman, E. *8 Lottery Winners Who Lost Their Millions.* November 18, 2004. Retrieved June 2, 2005, from http://moneycentral.msn.com/content/Savinganddebt/Savemoney/P99649.asp.

Sanford, R. *Jackpot! What to Do before and after You Win the Lottery.* 1996. Retrieved June 2, 2005, from www.note.com/note/pp.jackpot.html.

Von Herrmann, D. *Their Big Gamble: The Politics of Lottery and Casino Expansion.* Westport, CT: Praeger, 2002.

Also notice that she makes an indirect appeal to mythos by asking her audience to spend money on pursuits that define the American way of life: endorsing capitalism by investing in the stock market, supporting altruism by donating to charity, and indulging in luxuries that we've earned through our hard work.

Maria could have strengthened this portion of her speech by spending as much time discussing her solution as she did discussing the problem. For example, she could have told a brief story about how spending her own money on small luxuries has brought her fulfillment. Overall, she could have provided much more evidence to convince her audience that her solutions would result in happiness.

She uses a common phrase to signal the end of a speech. She then provides a nice, succinct summary of her main points, and she reinforces her thesis.

Maria concludes her speech by circling back to the intriguing statement she made in her introduction.

Chapter Summary

Persuasive speaking requires carefully preparing and framing your arguments.

- Carefully prepared arguments allow you to respectfully request change rather than badger or manipulate your audience into agreeing with you.
- Frame your arguments by using evidence, credibility, emotion, and mythos. Logos (the careful use of evidence), ethos (appeals to your credibility), pathos (appeals to emotion), and mythos (stories based on cultural beliefs and values) represent four ethical ways to enhance the public dialogue.

In persuasive speaking, three aspects of the effective use of evidence are especially important.

- Use specific rather than general evidence.
- Use novel information more often than what the audience already knows.
- Be sure your sources are credible.

Credibility, attributed to a speaker based on his or her competence and character, evolves during a speech.

- You can add to your initial credibility by explaining your competence to the audience and establishing common ground with them.
- You can build derived credibility through your delivery, which should be energetic, moderately fast, and comfortable.
- If you are successful, you will end with high terminal credibility.

Emotional appeals can be one of the most challenging, but effective, aspects of persuasion.

- Appeals to emotions help catch your audience's attention, reinforce an idea, move your audience to action, or show your audience how deeply you feel about the topic.
- The six primary emotions (fear, anger, surprise, sadness, disgust, and happiness) are expressed similarly across cultures.
- However, the three secondary emotions (pride, guilt, and shame) are expressed differently across age, gender, and culture.
- One additional emotion appealed to in persuasive speaking is reverence.

- Present your appeals to emotion with vivid language.
- Balance your appeals to emotion with appeals to reason so your audience is exposed to both aspects of the issue.

Appeals to mythos help you persuade by using the stories told within a culture that reflect its folk knowledge and ideals.

- Appeals to mythos tap into a culture's common sense and call to mind its shared values, attitudes, and patterns of behavior.
- When we appeal to mythos, we rely on a story or myth that reminds our audience of shared principles.
- Although our culture's myths may not be factually true, their logic is meaningful.
- Different cultures have different myths based on their different experiences and histories.

Fallacies are errors in an argument that result from flawed reasoning. The most common fallacies are

- Ad hominem (against the person)
- Bandwagon (everyone else does it)
- Either-or (false dilemma)
- False cause (mistaking a chronological relationship)
- Hasty generalization (providing too few examples)
- Red herring (raising a distracting new issue)
- Slippery slope (one step will lead to others)

There are several things to keep in mind to use persuasive reasoning ethically.

- When using evidence, provide enough information about your sources so that your audience can assess their credibility and select sources your audience will see as trustworthy and fair.
- When you appeal to emotions in persuasive speeches, stay audience centered to avoid overly graphic and violent appeals, overly frightening or threatening appeals, and overly manipulative appeals.
- When appealing to mythos, stay audience centered and use stories that speak to your audience's shared beliefs and values.
- Make sure your arguments don't include logical fallacies. Fallacies are unethical and confusing for audiences because they cloud the central argument.
- Manipulating an audience's emotions through threats or overly graphic images is unethical.

Invitation to Public Speaking Online

CourseMate Now that you have read Chapter 16, use your Speech Communication Course-Mate for *Invitation to Public Speaking* for quick access to the electronic resources that accompany this text. These resources include

- **Study tools** that will help you assess your learning and prepare for exams (*digital glossary, key term flash cards, review quizzes*).
- **Activities and assignments** that will help you hone your knowledge and build your public speaking skills throughout the course (*Practicing the Public Dialogue activities, review questions*).

- **Media resources** that will help you explore public speaking concepts online (*Web Connect links, Enhanced eBook*), develop your speech outlines (*Speech Builder Express 3.0*), watch and critique videos of sample speeches (*Interactive Video Activities*), upload your speech videos for peer reviewing and critique other students' speeches (*Speech Studio online speech review tool*), and download chapter review so you can study when and where you'd like (*Audio Study Tools*).

This chapter's key concepts and review questions are also featured on the following pages.

Key Concepts

ad hominem fallacy (346)
bandwagon fallacy (346)
character (336)
common ground (338)
competence (336)
credibility (336)
derived credibility (337)

either-or fallacy (348)
ethos (335)
fallacy (346)
false cause fallacy (348)
hasty generalization fallacy (350)
initial credibility (337)
logos (335)

mythos (343)
pathos (335)
red herring fallacy (350)
slippery slope fallacy (351)
terminal credibility (337)

Review Questions

1. You have been asked to give a speech on the topic of living wills to your classmates. Your position is that living wills are good, and you want to persuade audience members to arrange for their own living wills regardless of their age. How will you establish ethos, or credibility, on this topic? How will you make appeals to pathos, or emotion? How will you make this topic relevant to the younger members of your audience? What ethical considerations do you think you'll have to grapple with in this speech?

2. Using the topic you have selected for your in-class persuasive speech, review Chapter 7 to identify three of the five possible types of arguments you might make in a persuasive speech (inductive, deductive, cause, analogy, and sign). Then use the suggestions from this chapter's section on evidence and persuasion to find ways you might make these patterns of reasoning more effective.

3. Using the topic you have selected for your in-class persuasive speech, list the appeals to mythos you might make in the speech. After you've identified these appeals, consider your audience carefully. Determine which appeals likely will resonate strongly with your audience and which may not be appropriate, given their cultural backgrounds.

4. Bring a copy of the morning newspaper or your favorite magazine to class. In groups, identify as many different types of fallacies as you can find. Now that you recognize these fallacies, evaluate the strength of the argument being advanced.

5. As a class, select a topic that is given considerable attention nationally or locally. Identify several positions or perspectives on this issue and divide into groups, with each group taking a different position or perspective. In your groups, develop five fallacious arguments in support of your position. Present these to the class and see if they can find the fallacies and identify or name the type you are using.

6. Check out Speech Studio to see how other students use reasoning in their persuasive speeches. Can you spot instances where they rely on logical fallacies? Or record a speech you're working on, upload it to Speech Studio, and ask your peers for their feedback. What feedback could you use to fine-tune the reasoning in your persuasive speech before you give it in class? ☑Studio

Speaking on Special Occasions

David Young-Wolff / PhotoEdit

People give special occasion speeches when they come together to celebrate, reflect, remember, or establish a common purpose or goal. We give these speeches when we want to acknowledge someone's accomplishments or celebrate events or transitions. We also give them when we come together after difficult events. Special occasion speeches are given at weddings, awards ceremonies, banquets, and funerals. These speeches often bring an audience together and remind people of what they have in common. They also mark certain occasions as special, as unique from the familiar events of our lives.

This chapter introduces you to four types of special occasion speeches: speeches of introduction, speeches of commemoration, speeches of acceptance, and speeches to entertain. Each of these speeches recognizes a different kind of special occasion. Therefore, each has a slightly different goal. You will learn about these different goals as well as specific guidelines to help you prepare and deliver effective special occasion speeches.

- **Speeches of Introduction**
- **Speeches of Commemoration**
- **Speeches of Acceptance**
- **Speeches to Entertain**

IN THIS CHAPTER, YOU WILL LEARN TO:

- Describe the four types of special occasion speeches
- Identify at least four tips for giving effective special occasion speeches

Speeches of Introduction

When you give an **introductory speech**, you provide an audience with a unique perspective on the person you are introducing. Introductory speeches are given for two reasons: to introduce yourself, such as at a job interview or in a newly formed group, or to introduce someone else, usually at a formal event before that person gives a speech. Regardless of whom you're introducing, introductory speeches tend to be brief and tightly organized. The principle of "less is more" applies because the audience is often more interested in what follows the introduction than in the introduction itself.[1] Listeners want you to be brief and to give them specific, interesting, and useful information. Introductory speeches are organized around three goals:

- Acquaint the audience with a person.
- Establish the credibility of the person.
- Generate enthusiasm for the person.

To accomplish these goals, do the following in your speeches of introduction:

Introducing Yourself
- State your name and any of your credentials or titles.
- Identify any qualifications, experiences, or expertise you possess that relates directly to why you're giving your speech. ("I've worked in the insurance business for four years as a . . . during which I learned . . . ")
- State your pleasure at being invited to speak or for the opportunity to participate in the task at hand.

Introducing Another Person
- State your own name and credentials. ("Hello, I'm Mary Brown, director of the Office of Volunteer Programs.")
- Indicate that you will introduce the other person. (For example, "It is my privilege tonight to introduce our speaker, Dr. Robert Gonzales.")
- Provide accurate, relevant details about the person, including credentials, accomplishments, activities, personality traits, personal stories, or even a quote from something the person has said. ("Dr. Gonzales holds a Ph.D. from Harvard University and currently is working as a consultant for . . . He also has experience in . . . He has received numerous awards, some of which include . . . He describes his life as . . . ")
- Identify the topic of the person's speech by describing the general topic or simply by giving the title of the presentation. ("The title of Dr. Gonzales's presentation this evening is . . . He plans to share with us some highlights of his most recent research in . . . ")
- Provide closure to your remarks and welcome the person to the podium or the front of the room. ("Please join me in welcoming Dr. Robert Gonzales.")

To see these tips applied in an introductory speech given by Caroline Kennedy at the 2008 Democratic national convention, access **Web Connect 17.1: Convention Introduction** through your CourseMate for *Invitation to Public Speaking*.

CourseMate

Good to Know!

introductory speech: Speech that provides an audience with a unique perspective on the person introduced.

When you introduce yourself or another person, your goal is to create a sense of respect, an eagerness to hear more, and an understanding of what to expect. To give an effective speech of introduction, consider the following guidelines.

Be Brief

When you introduce yourself, be brief and concise. It can be tempting to share a lot of details about yourself, recount past experiences, and tell personal stories, but doing so can take a lot of time. A successful introductory speech rarely lasts more than three to four minutes. If you do opt to share a past experience or personal story, make sure you can tell it within a minute or two and that it clearly relates to the subject of the introduction.

When you introduce another person, remember you are giving an introduction, not a full-length speech. Avoid lengthy stories and drawn-out explanations. Try, instead, to share enough information so the audience is eager to hear from the speaker but not so much information that they feel overwhelmed.

Be Accurate

Introductory speeches can require considerable background information on the person being introduced. If you are introducing yourself, you already have the information you need. If you're introducing someone else, there is a good chance you will need to do some research on the person unless you are already well informed about him or her. If you must conduct research on a person, you have a number of options. You can do your research on the Internet or at the library, interview the person you are introducing, or obtain a copy of his or her résumé or biography to get the information you need. Being accurate in your speech means that you state all dates, titles, and awards the person has received correctly and you cite the original source of all quotes and personal stories. Being accurate also means you pronounce all information correctly, right down to the speaker's name. If you take time to get your details correct, you not only show respect for the person you introduced, but you also enhance your own credibility.

Bob Daemmrich / PhotoEdit

When introducing another speaker, acquaint your audience members with this person and generate their enthusiasm for hearing his or her speech. If you could introduce anyone for any type of speaking occasion, whom do you think you'd like to introduce? What could you say in your speech to help your audience get excited about hearing what this person has to say?

Be Appropriate

Use your skills at analyzing an audience to present a speech that is appropriate to the occasion. Remember, your goal is to enhance your own or another person's credibility and build enthusiasm for what's to come. If your remarks are too personal, irrelevant to the occasion, or too informal, you will not only affect your own image but also damage the credibility of the person you are introducing. Share only information that fits the occasion.

Ask for permission before you share anything personal about the person you are introducing. What may seem like trivial details or interesting anecdotes to you may embarrass or disturb the person you are introducing. If the person asks you not to share that information, don't do so, even if it's one of your favorite stories.

Speeches of Commemoration

Commemorative speeches praise, honor, recognize, or pay tribute to a person, an event, an idea, or an institution. The two most common types are speeches of tribute and speeches of award. A **speech of tribute** is given to honor someone. A **speech of award** is given to present a specific award and describe why that person is receiving the award. Both highlight a person's exceptional value, qualities, contributions, or accomplishments. Commemorative speeches are usually given in formal settings, such as banquets, receptions, retirement parties, special birthdays, memorial services, and rallies. Speeches of commemoration are organized around two goals:

- Help an audience appreciate the importance of a person, an event, an idea, or an institution.
- Illustrate for an audience a person's unique achievements or the special impact of an event, idea, or institution.

To accomplish these goals, a speech of commemoration should do the following:

- Identify who or what you are commemorating. Name the person, event, idea, or institution being celebrated.
- Identify and describe the qualities or activities that make this person, event, idea, or institution special. Clearly state the unique characteristics or actions being commemorated.
- Identify and describe the contributions made by the person, event, idea, or institution.
- Identify and describe any obstacles the person, event, idea, or institution had to overcome to be successful.
- Identify and describe your relationship to the person, event, idea, or institution being commemorated.

Effective commemorative speeches also include a specific kind of language. Commemorative speakers tell compelling stories and anecdotes, use rich language that brings to mind vivid images, and when appropriate, express deep emotion. They also recite special phrases, sayings, or quotations used by the person being commemorated or attributed to an event, idea, or institution.

In the next example, Molly Botswick commemorates her friend, Samantha Spady, a young college student who died from drinking too much alcohol:

"A memory is what is left when something happens and does not completely unhappen." This quote by Edward de Bono makes me think of one girl. A girl like no other, a girl so beautiful she captured the attention of every person she passed, a girl that changed my life in countless ways, without even knowing it. That girl was Samantha Spady. I'm sure many, if not all of you have several thoughts running through your mind when you hear her name. Unfortunately, those who weren't touched with the presence of Sam in their lives only know

Good to Know!

commemorative speech: Speech that praises, honors, recognizes, or pays tribute to a person, an event, an idea, or an institution. **speech of tribute:** Speech given to honor someone. **speech of award:** Speech given to present a specific award to someone and describe why that person is receiving the award.

her through the media. I'm here today to tell you that Sam isn't just a statistic; she isn't the girl who drank too much, or the college student who made a deadly mistake. Maybe you knew her, maybe you didn't, but one thing is for sure, Sam was a person with incredible beauty, God-given talents, and an unexplainable innocence that touched the lives of thousands.[2]

Notice how Molly uses a powerful quotation to begin her speech. She also uses descriptive and emotional language to highlight Samantha's positive affect on those around her.

The next example illustrates a speech of award. In 1999, Representative Bobby Rush, a U.S. congressman from Chicago and a former Black Panther, encouraged his audience to support legislation to award the Congressional Gold Medal to Rosa Parks for her remarkable role in the civil rights movement.

Mr. Speaker, I rise today in support of legislation to award a Congressional Gold Medal to Rosa Parks.

Occasionally in our nation's history there are pivotal moments and indispensable individuals that move America away from its divisive past and closer to its imagined promise. December 1, 1955, produced such a moment and such a person.

Rosa Parks grew up in segregation. Every day she was forced to deal with the violation of America's constitutional guarantees. On December 1, 1955, this American woman exacted of this country the freedom and equality the Constitution promises.

Marmaduke St. John / Alamy

Tired, like most citizens after a hard day's work, Rosa Parks refused to obey a shameful law that required her to sit at the back of a Montgomery, Alabama, bus. Her actions set the stage for the civil rights movement of a people who were unfairly and unjustly living under racist law.

Because of this brave American woman, segregation laws around the nation began to crumble and our nation began to respond to the call for African-American equality. Because of her invaluable contribution to our nation, every American lives a better life today. For that reason, it is quite appropriate that Mrs. Rosa Parks receive the Congressional Gold Medal.

But I must add, Mr. Speaker, that today, our nation continues to call for equality and freedom. There are still issues in our America that were issues in 1955. There are still Americans who do not enjoy the promises enumerated in the Constitution.

So, if we are to truly honor this great woman, we must do so, not only with a Gold Medal, but also with actions that further her purpose. We must all become individuals working to end the discrimination and inequalities that exist in our great nation.

A speech of tribute is a common type of commemorative speech used to honor a particular person or a group, such as fallen soldiers. Think about a particularly moving speech of tribute you've heard. What about it was special and inspirational? What would you like to hear in a speech of tribute given for you?

I urge my colleagues to support this legislation and honor the mother of the civil rights movement, Mrs. Rosa Parks. Thank you.[3]

When you give commemorative speeches, you become responsible for conveying the significance of a person, event, idea, or institution to an audience. And if you're commemorating a person, you also want him or her to feel a sense of pride for having been praised and commemorated. To give an effective commemorative speech, consider the following guidelines.

Share What Is Unique and Special

Do not assume the audience already knows the exceptional qualities of who or what you are commemorating. It is your job to inform your listeners of these qualities by offering specific praise for your subject that consists of representative examples of successes, talents, accomplishments, special characteristics, and significant impacts. Be specific about the importance and meaning of who or what you are commemorating.

Express Sincere Appreciation

Express sincere appreciation for all that a person, event, idea, or institution has given or made possible. Speeches of commemoration, whether tributes or awards, praise and honor some person or some thing. Include in your speech sincere recognition of the ways in which who or what you're commemorating has affected a community. Your words should be genuine and express respect and gratitude.

Tell the Truth

Be certain the facts, stories, and traits you attribute to the subject of your commemoration are all accurate. Do not alter the truth to make a story more exciting. Instead, make an effort to find unique and special qualities and experiences that make your speech especially compelling.

When you commemorate a person, share your personal experience with that person so your audience can appreciate his or her exceptional qualities. When you commemorate an event, idea, or institution, share the characteristics that make your subject special in a way that appeals to your audience. Remember, when you give a commemorative speech, you want your audience to feel inspired and appreciative and to respect and admire who or what you are honoring.

Speeches of Acceptance

In an **acceptance speech**, you express your gratitude, appreciation, and pleasure at receiving an honor or a gift. Speeches of acceptance are organized around three goals:

- Thank the audience and the organization that has presented you with the award.
- Show your awareness of the significance of the award.
- Acknowledge the people who helped you accomplish what you're being honored for.

When film director Kathryn Bigelow received an Oscar in 2010 for her film *The Hurt Locker*, she used her acceptance speech to express her gratitude not only to those who helped make the film but also to the women and men in the military:

> This really is—there's no other way to describe it; it's the moment of a lifetime. First of all, this is so extraordinary to be in the company of such powerful—my fellow nominees—such powerful filmmakers who have inspired me and I have admired for, some of whom, for decades. And thank you to every member of the Academy. This is, again, the moment of a lifetime. I would not be standing here

Cengage Learning

CourseMate

To see student speaker Tara Flanagan share what is unique and special about her grandfather in a commemorative speech, use your CourseMate for *Invitation to Public Speaking* to watch the video, respond to analysis questions, and compare your answers to those provided by the author.

Good to Know!

acceptance speech: Speech that expresses gratitude, appreciation, and pleasure at receiving an honor or a gift.

Chapter 17

if it wasn't for Mark Boal, who risked his life for the words on the page and wrote such a courageous screenplay that I was fortunate enough to have an extraordinary cast bring that screenplay to life. And Jeremy Renner, Anthony Mackie, and Brian Geraghty. And I think the secret to directing is collaborating, and I had truly an extraordinary group of collaborators in my crew: Barry Ackroyd and Kalle Júlíusson and Bob Murawski, Chris Innis, Ray Beckett, Richard Stutsman. And if I could just also thank my producing partners, Greg Shapiro, Nick Chartier, and my wonderful agent, Brian Siberell, and the people of Jordan, who were, such a . . . so hospitable to us when we were shooting. And I'd just like to dedicate this to the women and men in the military, who risk their lives on a daily basis in Iraq and Afghanistan and around the world. And may they come home safe. Thank you.[4]

Sometimes, speakers use the significance of an award to call attention to a larger issue. For example, Adam Horovitz, member of the hip-hop group Beastie Boys, included in his acceptance of the 1999 MTV Video Vanguard Award a call to address the serious problem of sexual assault at some large music festivals, particularly the 1999 Woodstock festival. "They [the sexual assaults at the festival] made me feel really sad and angry," he said as he accepted the award. "I'm talking to all the musicians here—I think we can talk to the promoters and make sure they do something about the safety of all the women and girls who come to all of our shows."[5]

Although the main focus of a speech of acceptance is to express your thanks for receiving an award or a gift, it has other purposes as well. To give an effective speech of acceptance, consider the following guidelines.

Understand the Purpose of the Award

Be familiar with the background, history, and unique characteristics of the award. To receive an award is to receive an honor. Be certain you understand the honor you are receiving so you can speak intelligently about what the award means to you. You may even choose to organize your acceptance speech around the specific qualities of the award, or you can use your understanding of the meaning and purpose of the award to encourage others to act, to remind the audience of larger social issues, or simply to reinforce shared values and principles.

Recognize Others

Although you are being recognized as an outstanding individual, give credit and thanks to those who have contributed to your success. Verbally acknowledge their influence, support, and the ways they helped you succeed. Use caution here because it is tempting to try to thank everyone to whom you are close. Avoid this pitfall and thank only those people or groups who have been especially supportive, helpful, or pivotal to your success.

Practicing the Public Dialogue

17.1

Design a Speech of Commemoration

Choose a person, event, idea, or institution you would like to commemorate. In class, design a one-minute speech of commemoration. Begin by making a list of the accomplishments, qualities, or influences you wish to recognize. Select two or three that you feel you can talk about comfortably and make them the main points of your speech. Decide how you will describe these characteristics, paying special attention to the language you will use. Be sure your descriptions and praise are specific, your speech expresses sincere appreciation and respect, and your facts are accurate. Now deliver this speech to your classmates and ask them to give you feedback. Did your speech follow the guidelines outlined in this chapter?

Online Resources

CourseMate For advice about giving a common type of commemorative speech, a wedding toast, access **Web Connect 17.2: Tips for Making a Wedding Toast**. To see examples of another common type of commemorative speech, a speech given at a memorial service, use your CourseMate for *Invitation to Public Speaking* to access videos of Professor Nikki Giovanni's inspiring convocation address at the memorial held for the victims of the shootings at Virginia Tech and Oprah Winfrey's eulogy for civil rights activist Rosa Parks.

Respect Time Limitations

The length of your acceptance speech will vary depending on the situation. When you are invited to receive an award and give a speech, ask how long your speech should be. If the award committee requests a short speech, plan to be brief. If they want a longer speech, respect this request. A longer speech suggests your audience is interested in hearing a little more about you. For example, they may want to hear what you plan to do with a monetary award or what your future plans are.

Practicing the Public Dialogue

17.2

Design a Speech of Acceptance

Design a one- to two-minute speech of acceptance for an imaginary award you've just received—be creative (and appropriate). In your speech, express your gratitude for receiving the award, acknowledge the purpose of the award, and recognize the people who helped you achieve the award. Conclude by explaining what you will do with the award and what your future plans are. Now deliver this speech to your classmates and ask them to give you feedback. Did your speech follow the guidelines outlined in this chapter?

Online Resources

 CourseMate To see examples of acceptance speeches for all types of occasions, access **Web Connect 17.3: YouTube Acceptance Speeches** with your CourseMate for *Invitation to Public Speaking*. When you get to the YouTube website, search on "acceptance speeches." Which of these speeches appeal to you the most? Why? Did the speeches follow the guidelines outlined in this chapter?

Speeches to Entertain

Sometimes called *after-dinner speeches*, speeches to entertain are often given after a formal meal, usually a dinner, but also after a lunch or a breakfast meeting.[6] Those who give speeches to entertain usually are more experienced at speaking. However, even a novice speaker may be asked to deliver a speech to entertain at a luncheon for a service group or after a formal dinner at a club. A **speech to entertain** is lighthearted and addresses issues or ideas in a humorous way. But don't mistake these speeches for comedic acts. They do more than just provide the audience with a series of jokes, and they follow many of the basic principles of other special occasion speeches. Speeches to entertain have a specific purpose, thesis statement, and main points. They may be informative, invitational, or persuasive and are organized in specific patterns, just like other speech types. Speeches to entertain have two goals:

- Entertain the audience.
- Make the audience think.

When you give a speech to entertain, you want to make the audience laugh and smile as you give your speech. You also want the audience to "entertain" the issue—to look at it carefully and explore its implications. This balance between humor and presenting issues can be a tricky one. Let's take a closer look at each of these components of a speech to entertain.

Humor is perhaps one of the most complicated communication phenomena. What is funny to one person isn't always funny to another. You might tell a joke or story to two people and only one laughs. Then there are times when you tell a joke in the right environment and everyone thinks it's funny. If you repeat that joke in the wrong context, no one will find it the least bit amusing. And if subjectivity and context weren't enough to consider, delivery is also a tricky matter. If you rearrange the wording of a joke just a bit or forget to tell a line, no one will understand what is supposed to be so funny.

Good to Know!

speech to entertain: Lighthearted speech that addresses issues or ideas in a humorous way.

Predicting what will make people laugh is a bit like predicting the weather—we're often wrong. However, research tells us that what makes something funny is a combination of these elements:

- Timing
- Your objective in telling the joke
- The members of your audience

Timing is the way you use pauses and delivery for maximum effect. Research suggests that timing is a critical element in humor.[7] Personal experiences also tell us that timing is integral to how a joke is received and understood. Pauses to set a mood, before punch lines, or before key phrases can make the difference between a successful joke and one that falls flat. In a now-famous joke, Barbara Bush, in

Speaking Visually

What Does Place Say?

In 1955, Claudette Colvin (in March) and Rosa Parks (in December) protested discrimination against African Americans by refusing to give up their seats on a bus to white men. In 1968, students at Columbia University protested the university's and the United States' involvement in the Vietnam War by barricading the administration building, entering and exiting only through the windows of the president's office. In 1971, Mary Daly, the first woman invited to preach at a Sunday sermon in the history of the Harvard Memorial Church, led an exodus of women and men from the church to protest patriarchal religion. In 1984, Ronald Reagan spoke at Pointe de Hoc, Normandy, the site of a famous World War II battle, commemorating the soldiers who fought in that battle. And from December 1997 until December 1999 (738 days), Julia Butterfly Hill lived in an old-growth redwood tree in California to protest and prevent loggers from cutting it down.

These speakers, and others like them, blend their verbal messages with visual communication. The places in which they speak and take action communicate to their audiences the seriousness of their ideas. As professor of rhetoric Maureen Daly Goggin argues, people who have been denied access to material spaces can make a powerful statement by claiming those spaces as their own, as Colvin, Parks, and the Columbia students did.[8] In the case of Hill, occupying the tree communicated to others the inability of the tree to speak for itself and her willingness to call attention to that.[9] Finally, Reagan's choice of the actual space in which an important battle occurred called to mind powerful cultural memories and images and gave his commemoration of the soldiers enormous emotional and political power.[10]

AP Photo/Marty Lederhandler

Good to Know!

timing: Way a speaker uses pauses and delivery for maximum effect.

her 1990 speech to the graduating class of Wellesley College, told her audience, "Who knows, somewhere out in this audience may even be someone who will one day follow in my footsteps and preside over the White House as the president's spouse." She paused and added, "I wish him well."

Sometimes, *not* using a pause when you ordinarily might can also be funny because it can catch the audience off guard. When Ellen DeGeneres delivered the 2009 commencement address at Tulane University, she didn't pause at all when she said, "Follow your passion. Stay true to yourself. Never follow someone else's path unless you're in the woods and you're lost and you see a path. Then by all means you should follow that."[11] She got a big laugh from her audience when she suddenly switched gears from talking about a metaphorical path to giving advice about a very literal one.

The second aspect of successful humor is the objective of the joke. Appropriate jokes for speeches to entertain should strive to make light of something, remind us of our humanity, highlight the silly or the bizarre, tease others playfully, and even relieve tension in difficult times. Humor can also be used to make fun of others and put them down.[12] Avoid this type of negative humor, as it will likely offend audience members. Appropriate humor stands a greater chance of truly entertaining the audience.

AP Photo/Dan Steinberg

The third component of successful humor is the audience. Of course, no two audiences will respond to the same joke in the same way. Still, when you know your audience well, you should have a better sense of what your listeners will find funny. Remember, one of the most common reasons a joke backfires is that a speaker may have failed to consider the group memberships as well as the individual or collective experiences of the audience.[13] This can lead to you telling a joke that "isn't funny" or that "goes too far" for the members of your audience.[14] So before you select the amusing stories and jokes for your speeches to entertain, consider the master statuses, standpoints, values, and background of your audience carefully.[15]

When giving a speech to entertain, carefully consider how your audience will receive your humor. In her role as a comedian, Kathy Griffin uses risqué, gossipy humor that appeals to her fans. But when she speaks at other events for more general audiences, she tries to use humor that appeals to a group of widely diverse people (although she often doesn't succeed and gets in trouble for it). How could you incorporate humor into a speech to entertain so it would be well received by your audience?

Research over the past twenty-five years suggests a number of interesting differences related to master statuses. Although men often find humor that shows contempt for others to be funny, women are far less likely to appreciate jokes of this sort. In contrast, women tend to find self-directed humor funnier than do men—but not when it's too harsh. Additionally, ethnic minorities may enjoy in-group humor but often take offense at out-group humor. That is, when people from a particular group make jokes about their own group, those jokes may be seen as funny. However, when people outside that group make jokes about the group, those jokes are far less likely to be perceived as funny and may be considered offensive.[16] As a rule, then, when the master statuses of your audiences are quite varied, try to avoid jokes that make fun of people or groups in harsh or mean-spirited ways.

Although funny, speeches to entertain are also about issues that are relevant to a particular audience or community. Some issues that might be relevant to audiences today are how the government spends, or doesn't spend, tax dollars; the environment; and family life in the new millennium. Speeches to entertain help an audience make sense of what is happening around them or come to terms with issues and dilemmas that affect their lives.[17] They often put things into a new perspective and add humor to situations that may have been difficult or drawn out.

They can also introduce new ideas, giving the audience something to think about that may not have occurred to them before.

As you consider the issues you might address in your speech to entertain, identify those topics that may be particularly relevant to members of the audience.

Public Speaking and Service Learning: Engaging Community

Anna Casper, a sophomore public speaking student at Colorado State University, completed her service learning project at Adaptive Recreation Opportunities (ARO), which aids adults with developmental disabilities with a variety of recreational events in the community. Anna's project was to help facilitate a bowling league for five months. She got to know her eight participants well and decided to briefly commemorate each of them in her final speech to the class.

After several months of bowling every Saturday, ARO held an awards ceremony for the participants. As a facilitator, I was asked to give a short commemorative speech about each of the eight participants I worked with throughout the season. For each individual, I made a point of saying something unique about him or her. After spending so much time with all of them, I got to know each of them personally. Therefore, sharing a short story about the participants was easy for me to do.

I also informed the audience—made up of other ARO facilitators, ARO participants, and their friends and family—about my specific relationship with each participant. I then thanked them genuinely for being a part of the bowling league and presented each of them with a certificate of completion and a recognition of their highest score of the season. It was a great experience to see how the activities that ARO provides help people with developmental disabilities.

I found out a few weeks later that the final speech in the public speaking class was going to be a commemorative speech, so I decided to simply expand on the speech I had given at the awards ceremony.

I used some of the same tactics and actually acted out the presentation of the certificates as if the participants were in the classroom. It got a great response. I believe it helped me to have already given the speech once before, in a nonclassroom setting, to the people I was commemorating.

> **"I BELIEVE IT HELPED ME TO HAVE ALREADY GIVEN THE SPEECH ONCE BEFORE, IN A NONCLASSROOM SETTING, TO THE PEOPLE I WAS COMMEMORATING."**

Tips for Incorporating Service Learning into Public Speaking

- When choosing a subject for a commemorative speech, reflect on your service learning experiences as a whole. Remember that although commemorative speeches are often about people, they can also acknowledge special memories, concepts, rites of passage, or remarkable objects that have made an impression on you.

- When you use your service learning experiences for your commemorative speech, it can help to pick a theme of comparison and stick with it throughout your speech. For example, compare your subject with another praiseworthy object that your audience is familiar with. That way, in case they have not shared your exact experience, they can still easily relate to your topic.

- Often, a special occasion speech is the final speech of the semester. If so, use your service learning experience and everything you've learned in class to try something courageous that truly reflects the praiseworthiness of your subject. For example, you could compose a poem about your subject, sing a song, give your speech from a new position in the room, walk around, act out dialogue with the characters in your speech, or the like. Find an innovative approach to your final speech.

Once you've identified several possibilities, narrow these general topics and formulate a thesis statement. Check to be sure your approach has a humorous side to it and will appeal to your audience. From there, you can begin to develop the main points of your speech.

To help you balance the delivery of humor and relevant information to your audience and give a speech that entertains rather than offends or bores, consider the following guidelines.

Use Humor Carefully

Always err on the side of caution when you use humor in your speech. Although it is easy to get caught up in the moment, don't let your jokes run away from you. Remember, jokes often have more than one interpretation, and what may be funny to some can be offensive to others.[18] Most people don't find being made fun of publicly to be humorous. If you think a joke might offend or put someone down, leave it out of the speech. Remember, your goal is to entertain, not to alienate, the audience. When you offend an audience, you lose credibility and respect, which are difficult to regain.

Speak about Meaningful Issues

Remember, a speech to entertain is also about issues. Although it is meant to be funny, your goal is not to provide the audience with a continual stream of jokes. Rather, your goal is to develop an argument or an idea in an amusing way. As you select your topic and decide how you will frame it, consider your audience carefully. Although they do want to be entertained, they also want to hear a speech that is interesting and insightful. Before you finalize the topic of your speech, make sure it truly is relevant, is appropriate, and will hold the interest of your audience.

Pay Careful Attention to Your Delivery

Although delivery is a key component of any speech, a skilled delivery is paramount in a speech to entertain. Practice your speech many times so you can deliver your stories, jokes, and anecdotes smoothly and flawlessly. Work out the timing of your jokes well in advance and practice them until they feel like second nature. Your words and ideas will be even funnier if you can deliver your humor eloquently, in a relaxed style, and with the appropriate timing.[19]

Practicing the Public Dialogue

17.3

Design a Speech to Entertain

Identify three local or national issues you think would be appropriate topics for a speech to entertain. Is there a lighter side of these topics, something that makes them humorous or conveys them in a humorous light? Now consider a possible audience for each topic. Be sure that what you find humorous about these topics also will be funny to the audience. Select one of the three topics you feel has the strongest potential to be a successful speech to entertain and prepare a thesis statement and an outline for it. Share these with your class and ask them to give you feedback. Does the class feel your speech would be appropriate and interesting for its intended audience?

Online Resources

CourseMate Politicians often use humor to address (or deflect) issues for particular audiences. Access **Web Connect 17.4: The President Makes Fun of Himself** to see an example of President George W. Bush using humor at the 2001 Radio and Television Correspondents Dinner. Humor is also often used in speeches meant to criticize politicians. A good example is the speech comedian and satirist Stephen Colbert gave at the 2006 White House Correspondents' Association Dinner, which you can access at **Web Connect 17.5: Colbert Makes Fun of the President**. Why did each of these speakers use humor in their speeches? What was the effect of their humor? If you'd like some tips for using humor in your own speeches, access **Web Connect 17.6: Tips for Using Humor Effectively**. You can access these resources through your CourseMate for *Invitation to Public Speaking*.

SAMPLE SPEECH with Commentary

Water

by Brandon Perry

Specific Purpose: To commemorate the strength, flexibility, and beauty of water
Thesis Statement: I'm thankful for all that water's enduring strength, everlasting flexibility, and exciting beauty have done for us and given us.

CourseMate *Are you ready to give a special occasion speech? Use the following speech as a model. Brandon gave this speech in an introductory public speaking class. The assignment was to give a three- to five-minute speech commemorating a special person, place, or thing in the speaker's life. In addition, use your CourseMate for* Invitation to Public Speaking *to access video clips of other commemorative speeches, such as Tara Flanagan's "My Grandfather, John Flanagan Sr."*

It is in the sky. It is on the ground. It is in us. Do you know what IT is? Father Time has no control over it, weapons weep at its power, and like an architect, it chisels and creates. Do you what IT is? Water is what I speak of, and nowadays we view water passively—nothing more than a convenience—but it is more than that. Every day I see the strength of water in how it shapes the landscape of this earth. I see its flexibility in giving me the ability to shape snow to throw. And I see a beauty that competes with the most beautiful sunset.

Discovering the amazing strength of water doesn't require going halfway across the Earth. Think about the strange and mysterious creatures of the deep blue sea. Turn your head toward the purple majestic skyscrapers of the West. Listen to the sounds of a roaring old-man-winter blizzard in Colorado. Take a walk down the hallway, then a right, arrive at the fountain, and take a nice long relaxing cool drink. Water, like a lifelong friend, is the regenerator, the reviver, the reliever of your life that you can't live without.

Water is uniquely flexible to many contexts. Little kids throwing water balloons and running through sprinklers would be unheard of without water. College students, enjoying a day off from classes, throwing snowballs at each other and building snowmen, would be unimaginable without water. The clouds that crowd and bustle through our bright blue sky, giving inspiration to artists and kids alike, would be unthinkable without water. The water we use every day once quieted the cries of an early Earth, quenched the thirst of a dinosaur, and gave blood to the mighty trees of the past and present of our world.

Commentary

By asking a series of questions, Brandon piques his audience's curiosity and draws them in. He then reveals the topic of his speech.

In his introduction Brandon indicates how he appreciates his topic by describing some of water's virtues. In addition, by talking about water's "strength," "flexibility," and "beauty," he previews his main points.

He connects to his audience by linking his topic to human senses—he asks his audience to think about, move toward, and listen to the sounds of water.

The use of alliteration ("the regenerator, the reviver, the reliever") helps make the speech appealing to listeners.

Brandon includes an anecdote about playing

in the snow to relate to his audience of college-aged students.

In using personification ("the clouds that crowd and bustle . . . , giving inspiration"), he helps bring life to his topic.

Notice the vivid imagery and rhythm Brandon uses in this paragraph to describe water's beauty.

In his conclusion, Brandon provides a short summary of the three virtues he admires most about water.

Beauty, they say, is in the eye of the beholder. But for those who claim they cannot see water's beauty, they need to look again. The glistening songs of blooming flowers in a midday spring afternoon are water's beauty transformed. Stand by a remote mountain lake, and a perfect, clear reflection of the mighty trees and peaks in the crystal clear water might just say hello. What makes water's beauty more unique and special, though, than any other is its ability to pass it on. The mighty Amazon rainforest or slopes covered in twenty feet of snow are just a couple examples. This beauty also allows all of us to view ourselves in a different light, like a mirror—it tells no lies. So when you stop and stare into a reflection that water gives you, do you see just yourself, or can you see deeper things, deeper ideas, deeper emotions?

Water was here long before and will be here long past our deaths, on this planet or the next. Life without water's enduring strength, everlasting flexibility, and exciting beauty would be all but impossible for most living things on this Earth. Be thankful for all that water has done for us; it has given us ALL that we see before us, in one form or another.

Chapter Summary

Generally, there are four types of special occasion speeches.

- Speeches of introduction
- Speeches of commemoration
- Speeches of acceptance
- Speeches to entertain
- Each of these speeches contributes to the public dialogue by calling attention to meaningful and honorable traits or encouraging audiences to reflect on issues in lighthearted ways.

Speeches of introduction provide an audience with a unique perspective on the person introduced.

- The person introduced can be either the speaker or another person.
- When you give a speech of introduction, remember to be brief, accurate, and appropriate.

Speeches of commemoration praise, honor, recognize, or pay tribute to a person, event, idea, or institution.

- When you give this type of speech, share what is unique or special about who or what you are commemorating.

- Also express your sincere appreciation and tell the truth about the person or thing you are commemorating.

In speeches of acceptance, the speaker expresses gratitude, appreciation, and pleasure at receiving an award, honor, or gift.

- The main goal of an acceptance speech is to express thanks.
- However, speakers also should understand the purpose of the award, recognize others for their assistance, and respect any time limitations that have been placed on the speech.

Speeches to entertain are lighthearted speeches that address issues and ideas in humorous and appropriate ways.

- Because what makes people laugh is quite complicated, be sure to use humor carefully in your speeches to entertain.
- Also speak about meaningful issues and pay careful attention to your delivery.

◯ Invitation to Public Speaking Online

CourseMate Now that you have read Chapter 17, use your Speech Communication CourseMate for *Invitation to Public Speaking* for quick access to the electronic resources that accompany this text. These resources include

- **Study tools** that will help you assess your learning and prepare for exams (*digital glossary, key term flash cards, review quizzes*).
- **Activities and assignments** that will help you hone your knowledge and build your public speaking skills throughout the course (*Practicing the Public Dialogue activities, review questions*).

- **Media resources** that will help you explore public speaking concepts online (*Web Connect links, Enhanced eBook*), develop your speech outlines (*Speech Builder Express 3.0*), watch and critique videos of sample speeches (*Interactive Video Activities*), upload your speech videos for peer reviewing and critique other students' speeches (*Speech Studio online speech review tool*), and download chapter review so you can study when and where you'd like (*Audio Study Tools*).

This chapter's key concepts and review questions are also featured on the following pages.

Key Concepts

acceptance speech (364)
commemorative speech (362)
introductory speech (360)

speech of award (362)
speech of tribute (362)

speech to entertain (366)
timing (367)

Review Questions

1. Pair up with someone in class you do not know well. Talk with each other for ten minutes to discover answers to these questions: Who is this person? What are his or her accomplishments? What makes those accomplishments significant? Now write a one-minute speech to introduce your partner. Share your speeches with each other and discuss whether your introductions are accurate and appropriate.

2. Identify an award you would like to receive during your lifetime. What is the purpose of this award? If you were to receive this award, whom would you identify as playing a significant role in assisting you in getting the award?

3. Identify your favorite public figure and write an outline for a speech to commemorate this person. Check that your outline identifies the traits that make this person unique and special. Identify the places in your speech where you express your sin-

cere appreciation for this person. Finally, check to be sure your representation of this person is true and that your facts and stories about him or her are correct.

4. Bring a newspaper or magazine to class. In groups, select a topic from one of these sources and use it to write an outline for a speech to entertain. Identify your audience and the occasion, and then make a list of the ways you could remain audience centered by using humor carefully and appropriately. Make another list of the ways the topic you have selected is meaningful to your audience and the public dialogue.

5. Check out Speech Studio to see special occasion speeches given by other students. Or record a speech you're working on, upload it to Speech Studio, and ask your peers for their feedback. What feedback could you use to fine-tune your special occasion speech before you give it in class? ☑ Studio

Appendix

Speaking in Small Groups

In this appendix, we take a look at how speakers come together in small groups to create and organize presentations. A great deal of the public dialogue occurs in small group settings as people come together to discuss issues and dilemmas that affect them. Consider these examples:

- Local activist groups often start as small groups of people concerned about some aspect of their community. Through discussions, planning, and presentations, they use their voices to influence issues and policies.

- In business settings, teams of coworkers pool their abilities to complete projects. As they work together, they use their voices to communicate ideas and ways of implementing their ideas.

- Local city councils hear concerns from residents, discuss those concerns, and then make decisions they hope are in the best interest of the community.

As these examples indicate, small group speaking is an important part of the public dialogue. As environmentalist and entrepreneur Paul Hawken noted in his commencement address at University of Portland in May 2009, small group speaking allows us to connect with one another about issues that are important to us:

- **What Are Small Groups?**
- **Why Do People Speak in Small Groups?**
- **Formats for Small Group Speaking**
- **Question-and-Answer Sessions in Small Group Formats**
- **Tips for Speaking Effectively and Ethically in Small Groups**

IN THIS APPENDIX, YOU WILL LEARN TO

- Explain what small groups are and why people speak in them

- Describe the six most common formats for small group speaking

- Use the reflexive thinking method to solve problems in a group

- Conduct a productive meeting

- Identify at least five tips for managing question-and-answer sessions

- Identify at least five tips for speaking effectively and ethically in small groups

What I see everywhere in the world are ordinary people willing to confront despair, power, and incalculable odds in order to restore some semblance of grace, justice, and beauty to this world. . . . Humanity is coalescing. It is reconstituting the world, and the action is taking place in schoolrooms, farms, jungles, villages, campuses, companies, refugee camps, deserts, fisheries, and slums. You join a multitude of caring people. No one knows how many groups and organizations are working on the most salient issues of our day. . . . This is the largest movement the world has ever seen. Rather than control, it seeks connection.[1]

Small group speaking is speaking to give a presentation to a small collection of individuals or speaking as part of a small group of people. You can find yourself engaged in this form of speaking when you deliver oral reports, participate in panel discussions, present at symposiums, give team presentations, solve problems as a team, conduct meetings, or participate in question-and-answer sessions. Your speaking goals in these situations may include informing, inviting, or persuading, but the unique setting of your speech requires that you give special consideration to your listeners and your interaction with them. When speaking to a small group, you must attend to group processes and dynamics, ethically facilitate disagreements, promote inclusive dialogue, and accomplish whatever task you and the other members of your group have been asked to complete. In this appendix, we look closely at these dynamics, beginning with a discussion of small groups and why people speak in them. We then examine the six most common formats for small group speeches.

What Are Small Groups?

A **small group** consists of three to fifteen people who must work together to achieve a common goal and who have the ability to influence one another through verbal and nonverbal communication.[2] Let's take a closer look at the defining characteristics of small groups.

The first characteristic of small groups is their size. To constitute a small group, the group must include at least three but not more than fifteen members. Although not everyone agrees on the upper limit of small groups, three members is the minimum, and when a group has more than fifteen members, it usually isn't "small" any longer, and the interactions among the members change significantly.

The second characteristic of small groups is open verbal communication among group members. Small group dynamics require that all members must be able to express their ideas freely and communicate openly with one another. In small groups, even though a leader may guide the group's interaction, each group member should be able to participate in the group's dialogue easily.

The third characteristic of small groups is the importance of nonverbal communication. Gestures, facial expressions, and even a person's unique habits and styles are just as important as the words that are said. Group members sometimes get the wrong idea about another person's nonverbal communication, which can affect a group's overall communication and performance negatively. To complicate matters, much small group interaction today takes place through mediated channels, such as video conferencing, Internet chat, or satellite television. Thus,

Good to Know!

small group speaking: Speaking to give a presentation to a small collection of individuals or speaking as part of a small group of people. small group: Three to fifteen people who must work together to achieve a common goal and who have the ability to influence one another through verbal and nonverbal communication.

as technology is used more and more, groups will need to use more effective verbal communication to compensate for the lack of nonverbal communication.

Finally, the fourth characteristic of small groups is that they have a common goal that group members work together to achieve. This common goal binds group members together in a shared purpose, makes them interdependent, and keeps them communicating with each other. Ideally, members of a group must think of themselves as a group rather than as individuals. Thus, group members must recognize that they can achieve more working together as a group than if they act alone.

Why Do People Speak in Small Groups?

Public speaking occurs in different contexts (Chapters 1 and 3). Speakers decide to speak, are asked to speak, or are required to speak. These same contexts influence speaking in small groups.

Deciding to Speak in Groups

Important issues can motivate us to speak individually, but they also can cause us to decide to speak in groups. Sometimes, an issue is so important that we join with people who also have decided to speak out about an important matter. For example, Susan Love, Susan Hester, and Amy Langer joined together in 1991 to create the National Breast Cancer Coalition (NBCC). Although each had been speaking about breast cancer alone, by joining together, they found they had more influence and were successful in getting Congress to approve funding for breast cancer research. Love, Hester, and Langer have spoken on television shows, testified at congressional hearings, and addressed survivor and activist groups. Today, the NBCC oversees more than 600 organizations interested in breast cancer advocacy and touches the lives of tens of thousands of individuals.

Being Asked to Speak in Groups

You might also be asked to speak as a member of a group because you have experiences or expertise in a particular area. In the workplace, you might be asked to give a speech because you have certain experiences or training that others want to hear about. You might also be asked to speak in an informal group (for example, a club) to provide information or new insights. Similarly, members of Congress are often asked to join committees because they have experience in a particular area. For example, the U.S. Senate Committee on Agriculture, Nutrition, and Forestry includes members who come from agricultural states and have experience with agricultural issues. Senators who join this group have experiences and expertise they wish to use to shape the nation's farming and forestry policies. They speak in small groups to other members of Congress, the media, and even their own constituents.

Being Required to Speak in Groups

Finally, you might be required to communicate in a group context, especially in your work setting. In today's workplace, a great deal of work is done in small groups. In this setting, people meet frequently to give speeches about their ideas, research, or other findings. Additionally, today's workplace often involves working off site, and workers often find themselves giving speeches and sharing information visually with coworkers via mediated communication.

TABLE A.1

Common Formats for Small Group Presentations

Oral report	• Speech given by one member of a group to present findings, conclusions, or proposals to an audience.
Panel discussion	• Informal discussion among group members in which they respond and react to one another's ideas. • Often includes comments and responses from the audience.
Symposium	• Formal presentations on one topic by group members. • Group members do not necessarily have the same goal or purpose. They may disagree with one another.
Team presentation	• Well-coordinated, formal presentations on one topic by group members. • Each presentation builds support for the goal of the team presentation.
Problem-solving session	• Discussion among group members that uses the reflective thinking method to identify solutions to a problem.
Meeting	• A formal gathering of a group to discuss an issue or solve a problem. • When you conduct a meeting, you facilitate communication among the group members attending the meeting.

Formats for Small Group Speaking

There are six common formats for speaking in small groups that you may be asked to follow: oral reports, panel discussions, symposiums, team presentations, problem-solving sessions, and meetings. These types of presentations are briefly described and summarized in Table A.1 and discussed in detail in this section.

Oral Reports

Oral reports are speeches given by an individual that present a group's findings, conclusions, or proposals to other members of the group or to a larger audience. When you present an oral report, use the skills you have learned in earlier chapters for giving a speech. Remember to prepare your general purpose, specific purpose, and thesis statement. Outline your main points and select your pattern of organization. Be sure to prepare an introduction that catches your audience's attention, reveals

Good to Know!

oral report: Speech given by an individual that presents a group's findings, conclusions, or proposals to other members of a group or to a larger audience.

the topic of your report, establishes your credibility, and previews your main points. Include connectives between the major sections of your report and write a conclusion that reinforces your thesis statement and brings your presentation to a close.

Panel Discussions

A **panel discussion** is a structured discussion, facilitated by a moderator, among group members that takes place in front of an audience. When you are part of a panel discussion, you not only share your ideas with the other members of your group, but you also share them with a larger audience. A panel discussion typically begins with brief opening statements by each of the panelists, followed by an informal discussion among them about their ideas. A moderator, who may be a member of the panel, facilitates the discussion. Usually, the discussion becomes more focused as group members learn from each other and the audience. Occasionally, the moderator or panel members may wrap up the discussion and summarize what has been said, but just as often, the discussion ends without resolution or summary. Because the goal of the panel discussion is to react to the ideas of another person, it is an ideal setting for invitational speeches. Group members can present their current thinking on a topic, learn from each other and the audience, and refine their ideas for future decision making.

When you are part of a panel discussion, prepare your opening remarks beforehand, thinking of your speech as a short informative speech that previews what you hope to discuss during the session. Then view your participation in the discussion as a series of short speeches in which you develop a particular idea, invite others to understand your perspective or explore an issue with the other panel members, or encourage others to adopt your views.

Symposiums

A **symposium** is a public discussion in which several people each give speeches on different aspects of the same topic. Unlike panel discussions, which usually feature short opening statements by the participants, symposium speakers usually have fully prepared speeches that are formally presented. At a symposium, either the speakers are experts in a particular subject area, or a topic may be divided into different areas so the audience can learn about many aspects of a single topic. If you are part of a symposium, a moderator usually introduces each speaker and his or her topic and facilitates audience questions and comments if appropriate. Symposiums usually feature three to five speakers, with each person speaking for ten to fifteen minutes. Typically, a symposium session lasts anywhere from one to two hours, with the time divided between the participants and audience questions.

If you are part of a symposium, follow the procedures for giving your speech outlined in this text. You probably will find that you use a manuscript for this presentation or that your speaking outline is quite detailed. Remember to stay within your time limits so other speakers can present their speeches and to ensure time for the question-and-answer session. Typically, a moderator will time the speeches

Good to Know!

panel discussion: Structured discussion, facilitated by a moderator, among group members that takes place in front of an audience. **symposium:** Public discussion in which several people each give speeches on different aspects of the same topic.

and give signals to the speakers as their time reaches the end. Be sure to practice your presentations before you give the speech and to anticipate questions from the audience so you can formulate your answers.

Team Presentations

A **team presentation** consists of several individual members of a group, with each presenting a different speech on a single topic. For instance, you might make a team presentation with other members of your group so you can present a proposal for a new program or product you have developed as a team. Each of the speeches is formal, with speakers addressing different parts of the proposal or product and each speaker using similar delivery styles. The individual speeches in team presentations follow each other without interruption. To make sure the presentation flows smoothly, team presentations usually have one group member acting as the moderator.

If you give a team presentation, it should be well organized using one of the organizational patterns discussed in this book. Ask each group member to give a speech on a single main point and have one member present the introduction and conclusion. This person usually is the moderator, who may introduce each speaker and his or her topic.

Problem-Solving Sessions

At times, you will speak as a member of a group to seek a solution to a problem the group faces. At other times, you may be asked to identify solutions to problems faced by other people or groups. These tasks are typically performed in a **problem-solving session**, a discussion among group members that uses the reflective thinking method to identify solutions to a problem. The **reflective thinking method** is a five-step method for structuring a problem-solving discussion. Developed by philosopher John Dewey, the reflective thinking method is one of the most widely used methods for solving problems.[3] Reflective thinking involves taking a careful, systematic approach to a problem. The five steps of this model are:

1. Identify the problem.
2. Analyze the problem.
3. Suggest possible solutions.
4. Consider the implications of the solutions.
5. Reach a decision about the best solution.

Many researchers have added a sixth step, implementing the solution, which we'll discuss at the end of this section. As you engage in the reflective thinking method, consider taking an invitational approach (Chapter 14), which can help you explore issues openly and freely.

Identify the problem. The first step of the reflective thinking model is problem identification. In this stage of the decision-making process, group participants

Good to Know!

team presentation: Presentation consisting of several individual members of a group, with each presenting a different speech on a single topic. **problem-solving session:** Discussion among group members that uses the reflective thinking method to identify solutions to a problem. **reflective thinking method:** Five-step method for structuring a problem-solving discussion: identify the problem, analyze the problem, suggest possible solutions, consider the implications of the solutions, and reach a decision about the best solution. A sixth step is often added: implement the solution.

identify the nature of the problem, the extent of the problem, who is affected by the problem, and the impact on those affected. Groups often research the problem extensively and may use an invitational approach at this stage to be sure they identify and explore all aspects of the problem. Once the group identifies the problem, it moves on to the next step of the model, problem analysis.

Analyze the problem. It might be natural to jump to a discussion of solutions to the problems that have been identified. Instead, effective group communication starts by discussing why the problem exists. Much like a physician who must diagnose a patient's illness, the reflective thinker must understand the causes of the problem before moving on to discussing solutions. Besides helping the group arrive at a more reasoned solution, this step helps the group present its findings more successfully. At this stage, groups often use an open, invitational approach to ensure they understand the problem as fully as possible. After group members have thought carefully about the reasons the problem exists, they can move on to suggesting solutions.

Suggest possible solutions. A popular method used by groups at this stage of the problem analysis process is **brainstorming**. Brainstorming is the process of generating ideas randomly and uncritically, without attention to logic, connections, or relevance (Chapter 3). When groups brainstorm, they suggest as many ideas as they can think of without judging those ideas. After the group has listed as many ideas as possible, they can do two things. They can go through the list and eliminate ideas that are not suitable until just a few options remain. Or the group may rank a longer list of options and then choose the solution that has the most support.

A potential pitfall for groups as they generate solutions is a concept known as **groupthink**,[4] which occurs when the group conforms to a single frame of mind and chooses a solution without fully and objectively examining other possible solutions. Groups that fall victim to groupthink often are under a tight timeline, are pressured by the leader, or are afraid to question each other's ideas. They also tend to get along well and favor consensus over conflict. Groupthink can be avoided by having several group members take on the tasks of challenging ideas, suggestions, and information; by creating smaller groups to work on the same issues independently, then come back together as a full group; or by holding "second chance" meetings a few days after a decision has been made to give members time to fully evaluate each decision.[5]

Consider the implications of the solutions. After a group has arrived at potential solutions, it studies the implications of those solutions. The discussion in the group should avoid immediately enacting a single solution and instead take time to fully examine its disadvantages or impact on others. This stage requires a good deal of discussion about causes and effects to allow the group to fully explore the implications of each solution.

Reach a decision about the best solution. Groups may use several methods to reach a decision about the best solution. For example, if the group has the time

Good to Know!

brainstorming: Process of generating ideas randomly and uncritically, without attention to logic, connections, or relevance.
groupthink: Act of a group conforming to a single frame of mind and choosing a solution without fully and objectively examining other potential solutions.

and resources to implement a pilot study, it can study the effects of the decision over a period of time. Groups can also use reasoning to choose the solution that has the fewest detrimental effects. Or groups can use a consensus model, which requires all members to agree on a single best solution. Alternatively, they can vote on the best solution and let the majority decide which solution to support.

Implement the solution. Researchers often include a sixth step in Dewey's reflective thinking model: implementing the solution. In this stage, the group determines how to carry out what it has decided. It is important for the group to consider who will be responsible for the different parts of the solution and when the solution should be implemented.

When you work in groups, you will be faced with a variety of problems to solve and issues to sort through. When you use these steps for solving problems, you can help your group arrive at a solution that will actually solve the problem and that should benefit all involved.

Meetings

One of the most common forms of public speaking in groups is the **meeting**, a formal gathering of a group to discuss an issue or solve a problem. When you conduct a meeting, you facilitate communication among the group members who attend. You prepare an agenda so people stay focused, and you manage the flow of conversation so people stay on track. Here are some guidelines for conducting a successful meeting.

Provide an agenda in advance. Several days before the meeting, provide participants with an agenda. The **agenda** lists what topics will be discussed and for how long. If possible, gather topics for the meeting from group members before you prepare and distribute the agenda. Make sure the progression of items is logical (for example, follow a chronological pattern that moves from old business to new business or another organizational pattern that helps the group stay focused). If you cannot distribute a copy of the agenda to the group before the meeting, pass it out at the start of the meeting so the group can follow your plan as the meeting unfolds.

Specify the time and location of the meeting. Clearly state the start time, end time, and location of the meeting. Include this information on the agenda, or post it where group members will see it. Although it sometimes is difficult to specify an end time, meetings that have one typically stay on topic, and groups are more likely to solve problems within the time frame they are allowed. In addition, group members need to know how long a meeting will last so they can schedule other meetings and events more accurately.

Be prepared for the meeting. The best meetings are those in which both you and the group members are prepared. When group members have not read meeting materials or have not thought about issues that will be discussed, an

Good to Know!

meeting: Formal gathering of a group to discuss an issue or solve a problem. **agenda:** List of topics that will be discussed in a meeting and for how long.

ineffective meeting often results. To avoid this, distribute important materials to group members beforehand so they have time to read and think about them. Be sure you read the materials ahead of time. Think carefully about the issues and how you will manage the discussion around them. Prepare any visual aids beforehand and check your equipment. Notify group members in advance if you want them to report on their activities to the group so they can prepare their presentations. Plan to follow the five steps for reflective thinking to help the group solve problems and stay focused.

Use an effective procedure for conducting meetings. Group members must know the group's rules for conducting meetings, such as the rules for governing who may speak, how decisions will be made, and how votes will be taken. Many groups have an established procedure for conducting meetings that is pretty easy for new group members to pick up as they attend a few meetings. Here's a general procedure for conducting a meeting:

- Open the meeting by stating what is to be discussed and what the group should try to accomplish by the end of the meeting.
- Appoint someone to take the minutes, or notes, of the meeting or ask a volunteer to do so.
- If any group members have been asked to present information to the group, ask them to do so.
- At this point, the group should have the information it needs to begin discussing the topics of the meeting. Open up the meeting to discussion, facilitating the conversation so that the group stays focused.
- When the group has concluded its discussion, summarize the main points that were raised and specify how the group should follow up on the meeting.

Distribute the minutes of the meeting to group members. After the meeting, provide copies of the minutes to group members. The minutes of a meeting should clearly identify what the group discussed and any action taken by the group. Be sure to identify group members who are responsible for certain tasks and assignments. Provide reports of these actions at future group meetings.

Question-and-Answer Sessions in Small Group Formats

Small groups are common and excellent formats for exploring issues with question-and-answer sessions. These sessions provide an opportunity for group members and their audiences to explore an idea or proposal in more detail, ask for clarity, and share their own perspectives. Even though you won't know for sure what to expect during question-and-answer sessions, there are ways you can prepare for them, and advanced preparation can make the difference between a mediocre question-and-answer session and a stimulating one. Ensuring a good question-and-answer session has two steps: preparing for potential questions beforehand and managing the discussion during the session.

Preparing for Questions

There are several ways to prepare for the question-and-answer session. First, take time to identify the questions you think might be asked. Then, prepare your answers to the questions.

Identify potential questions. As you think about the topic under discussion, keep a log of the questions you think group members or your audience might ask. Pay attention to the controversies or disagreements raised by the issue you are discussing to help you identify potential questions. If you can discuss the topic with others before the session, they can help you identify likely questions. Add these to your log of questions.

Formulate and practice answers. After you've identified the questions you might be asked, prepare your answers as thoroughly as you can. Write out your answers, outline them, and record pertinent quotes, statistics, examples, or other data that support each answer. Although this may seem like a lot of extra work, it can give you the confidence you need to respond to your audience in respectful and audience-centered ways.

Although you cannot always anticipate the exact questions you will receive, you often can come close. You should be able to answer a question that is similar to one you anticipated by making minor adjustments to the answer you formulated. If some of the questions are likely to be controversial, practice your answers in front of other people. They can help you with wording and organization as well as with adding or subtracting details.

As a rule, your answers to simple questions should be brief—between ten and sixty seconds in length. Answers to complex questions may take longer, but remember, you are answering questions, not giving a speech. Remember, too, that others are waiting to ask questions. If you spend all your time on one question, you will prevent others from raising important issues.

Managing the Question-and-Answer Session
Several techniques will help ensure a productive question-and-answer session. They can help you manage the flow of conversation as well as keep an audience-centered perspective.

Explain the format. It's a good idea to establish the format of the question-and-answer session during the introduction of the session. You might want to establish a few rules, such as time limits for each question, the number of questions a person may ask, or rules to ensure that as many sides of an issue as possible are raised and discussed. Setting the rules will help all involved know what to expect and help you manage the flow of discussion ethically and effectively. Selecting a "process person," someone who monitors the session and the rules you have established, can help ensure that the group follows the format you have set.

Listen and clarify. One of your most important tasks when managing a question-and-answer session is to listen thoughtfully to each question before answering in a respectful manner. This can be a difficult task if the question is unclear or hostile. When a group member asks you an unclear question, try to listen carefully for the keywords and important points. Then, using this information, restate the question so it is clear to you and ask the person if this is what he or she meant. Use such language as, "If I understand the question, you are asking me . . . Is that correct?" or "I think what you're asking is . . . Am I right?" If you simply cannot make sense of the question, you can always ask the person to repeat it for you.

When you are faced with a hostile question, it can be hard to understand what the person is asking. Hostile questions usually come from someone who feels threatened or believes you have not addressed his or her needs and concerns. Sometimes, you can respond to the content of the question as well as acknowledge the emotion. This takes practice. Here are some tips:

1. Don't take the hostility personally. If you can, establish goodwill and common ground by identifying points of agreement, shared experiences, or common background with the members of your group.
2. Display an audience-centered perspective and communicate with civility as you respond. Responding civilly is more likely to decrease the hostility than an uncivil response.
3. Listen to the content as well as the emotional components of the questions being asked. Separate out the emotions and determine the facts or information you are being asked to provide.
4. Address your answer to the content of the question, not the emotion. Offer information that will clarify your ideas or position. In responding, also strive to reinforce an invitational environment (Chapter 14) so you can explore an issue and get as many perspectives on it as you can. Try to explain rather than argue.
5. Offer evidence for your position. Use the skills you learned in Chapter 6 to present your ideas logically and reinforce your own credibility. Sometimes, the hostility can be reduced when you respond with strong evidence to support your claims.[6]

After you have tried these strategies, if you feel confident enough to do so, you can acknowledge the emotion attached to the issue. You want to be careful here, though, because many people do not like to be told how they feel. If you say something like "I understand the anger attached to this issue," the person may either appreciate the recognition or snap back with a retort about not being angry. As a rule, use caution when answering emotionally charged questions.

Keep a positive mind-set. Some beginning speakers are uneasy about question-and-answer sessions. One way to feel more confident about this part of a speech is to frame it positively. Most questions are signs of interest and curiosity; your listeners genuinely want to know more about a subject. A question-and-answer session gives people a chance to ask for additional information, and you have the opportunity to provide it.

Address the entire group. Even though a specific person in the group has asked a question, keep your answer audience centered. First, restate the question so all in the room can hear it. Second, deliver the answer to the entire group, not just to the person asking the question. These two actions bring the full group into the conversation and help keep everyone interested. Usually, a question asked by one group member is a question that others have, too. However, you occasionally receive a question whose answer applies only to the person asking it. When this happens, respond that the question seems to address the needs of only one person, and you will be glad to speak with him or her after the presentation. In doing so, you acknowledge the importance of the person, but not at the expense of the larger group.

Answer with honesty. At some point in your speaking career, you will be asked a question for which you do not have an answer. Rather than trying to fake an answer or justify why you don't have one, be honest. Admit you don't know the answer. Then acknowledge the importance of the question, refer it to someone who may know the answer, or offer to try to find the answer after the session if it seems appropriate to do so.

Stay focused. Unlike a speech, which has a specific purpose and thesis statement, question-and-answer sessions can cover a wide range of ideas and perspectives, some of them only remotely related to the topic at hand. Additionally, with many people asking questions, keeping track of time and the flow of ideas can be difficult. However, you can do several things to keep the dialogue focused.

1. State how much time you have for the question-and-answer session. This will help group members and your audience gauge the number of questions they can ask and the amount of detail you can provide in your answers.
2. You occasionally will get a few people who try to dominate the session. They either ask repeated questions or use their question to engage in an extended monologue. When you can regain the floor, thank those people for their interest and ideas and explain that it's important to hear from a variety of group members. Then turn to other people with questions to keep the discussion moving.
3. Keep track of time, alerting the group and audience when the question-and-answer session has reached its midpoint as well as when the session is nearing its end. At these points, refocus the discussion, stating, "We've had a number of questions related to [this aspect of the topic]. Do we have any questions on topics we haven't covered yet?" In this way, you can create an opportunity for people who have not yet been able to ask their questions.

Tips for Speaking Effectively and Ethically in Small Groups

Whatever type of small group speech you make, keep in mind some general tips. These tips will help you organize your ideas and work together with other group members so each of you can participate effectively and ethically in the group's dialogue.

- **Consider the group's purpose and audience when selecting a presentation format.** If the group is in the preliminary stages of identifying a problem, the problem-solving session or panel discussion may be the best format. Later, the group may wish to use the symposium format to air ideas for a more particular audience. When finished with the task, the group may choose to make a team presentation or an oral presentation to the audience that will enact the group's solution. Whatever format you choose, consider including a question-and-answer session if members of the group or the audience would benefit from the opportunity to engage in open dialogue. Throughout your presentation, and your question-and-answer session if you include one, remain faithful to the group's stated purpose and format. Switching to a new purpose or format during a presentation is unethical, conveys a lack of organization, and can communicate dishonesty and an unwillingness to listen to what audience members wish to say.

- **Use appropriate delivery style and skills.** Panel discussions, problem-solving sessions, and meetings usually consist of impromptu and extemporaneous speeches. Symposiums and team presentations are usually extemporaneous, delivered from a manuscript, or even memorized. In addition, group members must remember that even when they are not speaking, they still are communicating with the audience. Facial expressions, body language, or gestures that contradict another speaker's message send confusing signals to the audience. Note that small group formats often foster invitational speaking, so make sure your nonverbal and verbal messages reflect this approach.
- **Organize your presentation.** For panel discussions, symposiums, and team presentations, one group member should introduce the speakers. Likewise, one group member should offer concluding remarks. Organize the rest of the presentation in a format consistent with the purpose of the presentation and the type of format used. Panel discussions will have a looser organization than symposiums; remain ethical during these discussions and allow time for each presenter to speak. Team presentations and oral reports will be highly structured so the group can achieve its goal and present its information effectively. For meetings and problem-solving sessions, be sure to explain the format and, to stay ethical, follow the agenda or established rules throughout the presentation. If you include a question-and-answer session with any of these speaking formats, remember that the session is more likely to be successful if you prepare for questions likely to be asked.
- **Use effective visual aids as needed.** If visual aids are used, all members of the audience should be able to see them, and they should reflect the guidelines for effective and ethical visual aids discussed in Chapter 12. For a team presentation, in particular, coordinate visual aids between all of the team members so each member's visual aids employ a style that is consistent across the team.

Practicing the Public Dialogue

A.1

Design a Group Presentation Speech

In class, divide into four different small groups. Select a topic about a current issue of interest on your campus or in your local community. Assign each group one of the following small group speaking formats: a panel discussion, a symposium, a team presentation, a problem-solving session, or a meeting. Following the guidelines presented in this appendix, design a thirty-minute small group presentation on the topic you've chosen. After your presentation is planned and organized, elect one person from your group to give an oral report to the class describing your presentation. As a class, discuss the strengths, weaknesses, and ethical aspects of each type of small group presentation planned by the groups in your class. Which formats best get at the heart of your topic while remaining ethical and why?

Appendix Summary

As you participate in the public dialogue, you likely will find yourself speaking in small groups.

- When you *speak* in a small group, you are speaking to an audience of three to fifteen people.
- When you *work* in a small group, you are working with three to fifteen people toward a common goal.
- People speak in small groups for the same reasons they give other types of speeches: They decide to speak, they are asked to speak, or they are required to speak.

There are six common formats for making group presentations.

- An oral report is a speech given by a single individual.
- A panel discussion allows several people to discuss issues and give presentations.
- A symposium is a public discussion in which several people, usually experts, give a formal presentation on different aspects of the same topic.
- A team presentation is made by several members of a group, with each person presenting a different speech on a single topic.
- A problem-solving session is an approach to small group communication that uses the five-step reflective thinking method to identify solutions to a problem.
- A meeting is a formal gathering of a group to discuss an issue or solve a problem. When you conduct a meeting, you facilitate the communication of group members during the meeting.

There are five steps in the reflective thinking method.

1. Identify the problem.
2. Analyze the problem.
3. Suggest possible solutions.
4. Consider the implications of the solutions.
5. Reach a decision.
6. Many researchers have added a sixth step, implementing the solution.

When you conduct a meeting, there are five things you can do to help improve its effectiveness.

1. Provide an agenda.
2. Specify a time and a location.
3. Prepare for the meeting.
4. Use an effective procedure for running the meeting.
5. Distribute minutes after the meeting.

Question-and-answer sessions allow group members and their audiences to communicate in three key ways.

- Explore an idea or proposal in more detail.
- Ask for clarity.
- Share their own perspectives.

There are three things you can do to prepare for question-and-answer sessions.

- Identify potential questions.
- Formulate answers ahead of time.
- Practice a calm, nondefensive delivery of your answers.

During your speech, there are five things you can do to manage a question-and-answer session.

- Explain its format and time frame before you begin taking questions.
- Carefully listen to and clarify questions.
- Respond to the content of questions rather than to the emotion of the person asking the question.
- Address the entire group or audience when you answer questions.
- Be honest when you don't know an answer, and stay focused so a range of topics is included in the session.

There are five key tips for speaking effectively and ethically in small groups.

- Consider the group's purpose and audience when selecting a presentation format.
- Remain faithful to that purpose and format throughout your presentation.
- Use the appropriate delivery style and skills.
- Organize your presentation.
- Use effective visual aids as needed.

Invitation to Public Speaking Online

CourseMate Now that you have read this appendix, use your Speech Communication CourseMate for *Invitation to Public Speaking* for quick access to the electronic resources that accompany this text. These resources include

- **Study tools** that will help you assess your learning and prepare for exams (*digital glossary, key term flash cards, review quizzes*).
- **Activities and assignments** that will help you hone your knowledge and build your public speaking skills throughout the course (*Practicing the Public Dialogue activities, review questions*).

- **Media resources** that will help you explore public speaking concepts online (*Web Connect links, Enhanced eBook*), develop your speech outlines (*Speech Builder Express 3.0*), watch and critique videos of sample speeches (*Interactive Video Activities*), upload your speech videos for peer reviewing and critique other students' speeches (*Speech Studio online speech review tool*), and download chapter review so you can study when and where you'd like (*Audio Study Tools*).

This chapter's key concepts and review questions are also featured on the following pages.

Key Concepts

agenda (382)
brainstorming (381)
groupthink (381)
meeting (382)

oral report (378)
panel discussion (379)
problem-solving session (380)
reflective thinking method (380)
small group (376)

small group speaking (376)
symposium (379)
team presentation (380)

Review Questions

1. Working in a small group, give a twenty-minute team presentation on an issue affecting the nation today. How will you divide the presentation and structure your speeches? What kind of delivery style will you use? What kind of visual aids will you use? Why do you think your presentation will be a success? In what ways can you strengthen the presentation?

2. Share the topic and specific purpose of your next speech with the class. Let them ask you questions about your topic and purpose, and practice answering those questions as though you were conducting a question-and-answer session.

3. Check out Speech Studio to see student groups speak in various small group settings. Or record a speech you're working on, upload it to Speech Studio, and ask your peers for their feedback. What feedback could you use to fine-tune your small group speech before you give it in class? ✅**SPEECH Studio**

Impromptu
Speaking

Cindy L. Griffin
Colorado State University

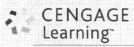

Australia • Brazil • Japan • Korea • Mexico • Singapore • Spain • United Kingdom • United States

Impromptu Speaking

An impromptu speech may be the most common type of speech you will give. An **impromptu speech** is a speech you deliver that is not planned or prepared in advance. Impromptu speeches usually last only a few minutes and are given in the workplace, in community meetings or gatherings, and at social events. You give an impromptu speech when someone asks you to explain what you know, share your experience or perspective, or when you decide to speak out spontaneously about some issue, person, or idea. At school, you might be asked to summarize a section of your assigned reading or restate the main points of a discussion. Or you might attend a meeting held by student government and decide to speak out on an issue. In the workplace you might be asked to share what you know about an item on a meeting agenda, or you might decide to speak out about an issue under discussion. Socially and at community meetings and gatherings, you give impromptu speeches when you are asked to share what you know or an experience you've had, and when you decide to speak up to praise someone, challenge a claim or suggestion made, or add your voice to a conversation, discussion, or debate.

Because impromptu speeches are unplanned, researchers have a hard time gathering systematic data about them. However, common sense tells us that impromptu speeches follow many of the rules and formulas we use for planned speeches. Thus, they use almost all the skills you are learning in your public speaking class. Impromptu speeches also rely on some of the techniques used in improvisation. In this chapter, we'll explore what impromptu speeches have in common with planned speeches, what makes them unique, and how some theories of improvisation can help with impromptu speaking. You'll then be asked to practice different kinds of impromptu speeches so that you can develop skills and strategies you need to give this common type of speech outside the classroom.

Similarities between Planned and Impromptu Speeches

Let's look at what some of the similarities are between planned speeches and impromptu speeches. Like planned speeches, impromptu speeches:

- Have an audience, so you will use your skills of audience analysis.
- Have a purpose, so you will have a thesis statement (central idea) and a main point or points.
- Rely on accurate information, so you will develop your ideas using your knowledge, previous research, and expertise.
- Also use the various types of supporting evidence you've learned about (examples, narratives, statistics, testimony, definitions) and sometimes even provide abbreviated citations for them.
- Rely on effective reasoning (inductive, deductive, causal, analogical, reasoning by sign).
- Also should avoid logical fallacies, such as false cause and hasty generalizations.
- Require a clear organizational pattern, and you will select the one that best fits your purpose, speaking environment, and time constraints.
- Have introductions and conclusions, although they usually are single words or simple phrases rather than longer narratives.
- May use signposts and connectives to help you express your ideas and keep your audience involved.

As this list shows, there are many similarities between planned and impromptu speeches, which is to your advantage because you've already learned how to practice and deliver a planned speech.

Differences between Planned and Impromptu Speeches

There are important differences between planned and impromptu speeches, and understanding those differences can help you develop the skills you need for giving effective impromptu speeches. Unlike planned speeches, impromptu speeches:

- Won't give you time to narrow or focus you topic before the speech, so when you work on your planned speeches, practice focusing your topics.

- Won't give you time to organize your main points before the speech, so develop a strategy for organizing your points quickly.
- Are usually short, so choose your evidence and patterns of reasoning carefully and with an impromptu speech's short time frame in mind.
- Require that you think of an introduction and a conclusion quickly, so develop strategies for coming up with these speech elements quickly.

Some of the strategies you can learn to assist you with impromptu speaking can be compared to the techniques used by jazz musicians or actors in improvisational theatre, so let's turn to those now.

Impromptu Speaking and Improvisation

Organizational scholars, as well as students of jazz and improvisational theatre, have studied improvisation in order to better understand what it means to "think on your feet." In what seems like a contradiction, these scholars and practitioners have concluded that there is "much preparation and study behind effective improvisation."[1] But actually, both jazz music and improvisational acting rely on "grammars" and "rules" that are practiced ahead of time.[2] This practice is described as "prepare to be spontaneous"[3] and "rehearse spontaneity." So, although improvisation is often thought of as unplanned and random creativity, definitions and research suggest that improvisation relies on "available material, cognitive, affective, and social resources," and that it is a "response to the moment" as well as a "composing while executing."[4] Those who excel at improvisation are people who possess expertise in their subject area, are present in the moment, draw from a familiar set of rules or grammar, and train or practice for their performances.[5] If we translate these skills to the public speaking arena, we can see that to give successful impromptu speeches speakers need the following:

© 2011 Thinkstock

- *Expertise:* a knowledge base of their topic, something they have studied and practiced.
- *Presence in the moment:* the ability to pay attention to a discussion or situation so that they can contribute appropriately and meaningfully.
- *Rules or grammar:* an understanding of the basic elements of public speaking and audience analysis.
- *Training:* opportunities for practicing impromptu, or spur-of-the-moment, speeches.

Expertise

Expertise is very contextual. You may have considerable experience and knowledge of certain topics, but you may not for others. When you know a good deal about a topic, it is much easier to speak about it. However, you still can be an "expert," even when you aren't familiar with a topic. Your expertise may come from asking several questions about the topic, raising concerns as someone who does not know much about it, and even urging others to clarify their arguments and positions. Using these techniques, you can give an impromptu speech on a topic you are less familiar with, because your "expertise" comes from investigating and needing to know more about a topic or an issue before deciding what to say about it.

Presence in the Moment

Being present in the moment means that your attention is "wholly on the task" and your "awareness extends beyond the immediate space" to your audience and to the larger social environment.[6] For example, being present in the moment at work or a community event means that when you give an impromptu speech, you not only are paying attention to the conversation going on around you, but you also are paying attention to who is in the room with you and what is happening in your workplace or community as a whole. Presence in the moment relies on audience analysis skills as well as on recognizing that your voice is one among other members of your group, team, organization, or community.

Rules or Grammar

Because you have studied various types of planned speeches, you already have a basic set of rules, or a grammar, for giving speeches. As such, you also have a grammar you can rely on when giving impromptu speeches. You know you need such speech elements as a specific topic, an organizational pattern, main points, arguments, evidence, and an introduction and a conclusion. You understand the impact of time limits and of your audience on the amount of information you can present as well as how you can best present it. You also recognize the need to speak clearly and make eye contact with your audience. These rules constitute the grammar of public speaking, and they can be applied to impromptu speeches.

© 2011 Thinkstock

Training

Just like a musician getting ready for a concert or an actor rehearsing for a play, you too will benefit from practice in giving impromptu speeches. Outside of the classroom you won't know when an opportunity for an impromptu speech will come your way, but by practicing and training throughout your public speaking course, you will develop various skills that will help you give successful impromptu speeches. Because training and practice are so important, the remainder of this chapter will be focused on those tasks.

Training for and Practicing Impromptu Speeches

Lori Gracey and Megan Moe-Lunder developed a technique that involves our hands to help students practice giving impromptu speeches. Gracey and Moe-Lunder suggest the following steps.

1. Hold up your hand with your palm facing you.

2. Visualize your topic printed in the palm of your hand.

3. Close your hand to "seize" your topic.

4. Extend your thumb. This is your introduction.

5. One at a time, extend your fingers, visualizing one word written on each.

a. Index finger: first point supporting your topic

b. Middle finger: second point supporting your topic

c. Ring finger: third point supporting your topic

6. Extend your pinkie. This is your conclusion.[7]

As this list shows, there are many similarities between planned and impromptu speeches, which is to your advantage because you've already learned how to practice and deliver a planned speech.

1. From where you are sitting or standing, focus on the center of the room and visualize your topic there.

2. Look straight ahead at the wall in front of you. Begin your introduction.

3. Look at the corner of the room to your right. This is your first main point.

4. Look at the corner of the room to your left. This is your second main point.

5. Look back at the center of the room. This is your conclusion.

A third technique involves visualizing a house.

1. Visualize a house. This is your topic.

2. Visualize entering the door. This is your introduction.

3. Visualize walking into the first room. This is your first main point.

4. Visualize walking into a second room. This is your second main point.

5. Visualize walking into a third room. This is our third main point.

6. Visualize walking out the back door. This is your conclusion.

If you are asked to give an impromptu speech and you have a minute or so before you actually speak, try this technique:

© 2011 Thinkstock

1. Jot down your topic near the top of a piece of paper or on your notes.

2. Make a quick list of your main points under your topic.

3. Off to one side, write a word to help you with your introduction.

4. On the opposite side, write a word that will help you conclude your speech.

5. If there is something you want to be certain to share but are afraid you will forget, write down a word that will help you remember that idea or argument.

Practice giving impromptu speeches with each of these techniques to see if one works better for you. You can also modify them to fit your style and situation, adjusting them to the length of time you have for the speech and the complexity of your topic.

Impromptu Speeches to Practice

Using the techniques described in the previous section, use any of the following situations to practice giving impromptu speeches. Some of these activities are meant for public speaking instructors to use in class, but you can modify them as you like and use them to practice impromptu speaking outside of class.

Pull Out an Object

1. Reach into your backpack, pocket, or purse. Pull out an object. Give a one-minute speech to the class explaining how to use the object, why the object is necessary to have, or the ways in which the object could be improved.

2. Have everyone in the class remove an object from their backpack, pocket, or purse. Put all the objects in a container at the front of the room. Ask each student to go to remove an object from the container, and give a speech to commemorate the item. (Students can also give informative, persuasive, and invitational speeches about the objects.)

One Topic, Three Minutes

1. Bring a stack of index cards with random topics written on one side to class. Place the stack at the front of the room, face down. Ask students to come to the front of the class, select a card, and deliver a three-minute impromptu speech related to that topic. Each speech should include an appropriate organizational pattern, well-developed arguments and points, and effective introductions and conclusions.

2. Bring a stack of index cards to class and brainstorm one-minute to three-minute impromptu speech topics with the class. Select the best speech topics and write one topic on each card. Place the stack face down, or in a bag or box, and ask students to select a card and give an impromptu speech on the topic indicated on the card.

This Weeks' Events

1. Bring several copies of the school paper to class. Discuss events written about in the paper that may be controversial, have a strong impact on the student or school, or be of human interest. Ask students to identify an issue from the paper and deliver a speech about that issue.

2. Select several media, such as YouTube clips, that represent current events or local, national, or global issues. Show the clips to the class. Ask students to give one-minute speeches on those issues.

Multiple Perspectives

1. Select a topic that is complex or an issue that is difficult to resolve. Ask each member of the class to give a speech on that topic, with the requirement that each person must present a different element or perspective on that topic. Ask students to begin their speeches with a connective that links the speech before theirs to the speech they are about to give.

2. Brainstorm five controversial topics that would be suitable for an impromptu speech. Write those topics on a set of index cards or the board. Make a list of the organizational patterns commonly used for speeches and

place that list either on the board or on another set of index cards. Ask a student to come to the front, and have the members of the class choose a topic and an organizational pattern for the student. Ask the student to give an impromptu speech on the chosen topic using the chosen organizational pattern. Continue until all the topics and patterns are combined.

You Can't Say _____

1. Bring a variety of objects to class, or generate a list of possible impromptu topics and write them on index cards. Ask a student to select an object or a card and to give a speech on that item or topic without every using the name of the item or the word on the card.

2. As a class, generate a list of common slang words used in everyday speech (including fillers) or in transitions and connectives (first, next, now that). Using the index cards or objects from activity 1 above, ask students to give impromptu speeches without using any of those words identified by the class.

Vote for Me/Us/Them

1. Hold a mock election for class officers. Randomly select students to come to the front and give impromptu speeches on why they should be elected to office.

2. Randomly select three or four students to act as a slate of candidates. Give them two to five minutes to work as a group to identify their platform. Ask the students speak about their platform and why that slate should be selected. Hold a question-and-answer session after each speech to practice impromptu discussions.

3. After the students in activity 2 (i.e., the candidates) give their speeches (and perhaps conduct a question-and-answer session), randomly select several students to come to give speeches that either support or reject the candidates as viable candidates for office.

Tell Us a Story

1. Ask students to come to the front of the class and share one of their favorite moments, experiences, or lessons in life. As a part of this speech, ask the students to introduce the story, tell it, and then explain why the event, moment, or lesson is important to them.

2. Get into pairs. With your partner, share a story of a "first" for you (first day of school, first time you ate something new, first time you skied). Then give an impromptu speech to the class that describes your partner's "first" and explain what the lesson or importance of that "first" might be.

Give Us Some Reasons

1. Review the types of reasoning commonly used in speeches. Ask each student to use one of the types of reasoning in an impromptu speech that persuades or invites his or her audience to select or explore one type of reasoning as the "best" type of reasoning to use.

2. Ask a student to identify one thing she or he is especially good at or wants to become good at. Using the types of reasoning reviewed in activity 1, ask the student to give a short speech explaining why she or he is good at that thing or should become good at it.

3. Brainstorm five or more controversial topics that would be suitable for an impromptu speech. Write those topics on a set of index cards or the board. Make a list of the patterns of reasoning commonly used for speeches and write that list either on the board or on another set of index cards. Ask a student to come to the front of the class and have the members of the class choose a topic and one or two patterns of reasoning for the student. Ask that student to give an impromptu speech on that topic using those patterns of reasoning. Continue until all the topics and patterns are combined.

Can You Find the Fallacies?

1. Bring a variety of silly and unrelated objects to class. Review the most common fallacies used in public speaking. Ask a student to select one of the items and present a fallacious argument about that item. Ask the class to identify the fallacy used.

2. Select a topic that is current and controversial. Ask each student to give an impromptu speech on that topic, using fallacious reasoning. Once each speech is finished, ask the audience to identify the fallacies they heard in the speech and replace them with credible and ethical reasons.

Impromptu Speeches and the Public Dialogue

Recall from Chapter 1 that when you enter the public dialogue, you engage in an ethical and civil exchange of ideas and opinions. When you give an impromptu speech, you enter that dialogue relying on the skills you have learned and practiced in your speech class. As you enter that conversation, you won't have the usual time to prepare a formal speech. However, you can still give ethical and effective impromptu speeches using the tips, strategies, and ideas of improvisation discussed in this chapter.

References

1. Dusya Vera and Mary Crossan, "Improvisation and Innovative Performance in Teams," *Organization Science*, 16, May/June 2005, p. 203.
2. Robert M. Keller and David R. Morrison, "A Grammatical Approach to Automatic Improvisation," *Proceedings SMC '07, 4th Sound and Music Computing Conference*, July 2007, Lefkada, Greece, pp. 330–337.
3. Vera and Crossan, 203.
4. Adapted from Vera and Crossan, p. 205.
5. Vera and Crossan; Keller and Morrison.
6. Vera and Crossan, p. 208.
7. Lori Gracey and Megan Moe-Lunder, "The Handi-Speech: Teaching Impromptu Speaking," G.I.F.T.S. Submission, National Communication Association, November, 2008. http://www.allacademic.com//meta/p_mla_apa_research_citation/2/5/9/3/0/pages259307/p259307-1.ph

Civic Engagement

Supplemental Chapter

for

Invitation to Public Speaking

Contents

Section I: Civic Engagement in Public Discourse

Introduction: What Is Civic Engagement?

As you grow, your family values and beliefs are what influence your perceptions. When the time arrives for you to head off to college, you carry with you many of those values and beliefs. An important and critical part of our society is for an individual to become an active and informed part of the community. As you evolve and become more informed, your perspectives may change and your actions will reflect that change. Your actions are shaped by the campus community, but you still engage with others around you and work to make change or stand up for what you believe in. Action can be on a larger scale, taking part in the community itself. Regardless of how you choose to engage with the surrounding community, *the challenge is to engage.*

"Democratic societies rely on the active and informed participation of their citizens," notes the Center for Communication and Civic Engagement at the University of Washington. It has always been considered a privilege in the United States to take part in an election and have your voice heard. In recent years, it seems as though our citizens have become apathetic both at the national and local level. A new generation shows the promise of engaging with local issues, while considering a larger entity—the world.

There is no single definition for the term *civic engagement*; however, the following two definitions may help you better understand the concept:

1. Individual and collective actions are designed to identify and address issues of public concern. Civic engagement can take many forms—from individual volunteerism to organizational involvement to electoral participation. It can include efforts to directly address an issue, such as working with others in a community to solve a problem or interacting with the institutions of representative democracy. Civic engagement encompasses a range of activities, such as working in a soup kitchen, serving on a neighborhood association, writing a letter to an elected official, or voting. (Pew Charitable Trusts)
2. A morally and civically responsible individual recognizes himself or herself as a member of a larger social fabric and therefore considers social problems to be at least partly his or her own. Such an individual is willing to see the moral and civic dimensions of issues, to make and justify informed moral and civic judgments, and to take action when appropriate. (*American Democracy Project,* Introduction, p. xxvi)

Brainstorming Civically Engaged Speech Topics

1. Recall a time when you have witnessed an injustice. What emotions did it raise in you? How did you react? Was intervention an option? What did you wish would change about the situation? If this were a reoccurring problem, what, if anything, could have been done in your community to resolve this problem? Is this topic one which your classmates would benefit from knowing about? How could focusing on this topic work to change that injustice?

2. What are some local environmental or energy concerns in your community? Is there disagreement on how to designate, protect, and better utilize and conserve local water, open space, parks, and wind or solar power? What are the key arguments involved in these disagreements? Do you feel your classmates could become more informed advocates and voters if your topic centered on a local environmental or energy issue?

3. Consider the local economy in your community. Locally owned businesses directly benefit the local population economically and environmentally. How many stores, which you frequent, are locally owned? Are there any farmer's markets in your community that offer locally grown seasonal products? Could delivering a speech on an aspect of your local food economy help your classmates to become more empowered over the power of their dollar?

4. Does the size of your community seem to be growing and expanding, remaining stable, or shrinking? What physical or emotional clues do you see in your community that enable you to justify your answer to the prior question? What attitudes and actions do you believe your community should take toward growth? How could a speech on community growth help your classmates to understand their own attitudes about the future of their community?

5. Consider your rights and privileges as a student at your school. Have you witnessed an instance where you felt a student's voice was being intentionally ignored? If you have been part of such a situation, might it be possible that your fellow students have as well? How could a speech on a particular student issue motivate your classmates to become advocates for student rights?

6. Think about the relationship between your school and the greater community. Do both entities view each other with respect? Are there instances of unjustified stereotypes? Do any local laws or ordinances exist that seem unfair to their entity? How could you help your classmates to understand their role in either compliance or helping to change any local ordinances that might be unfair to either part of the community?

7. Recall a time when you were surprised to learn about a little-known right or privilege of which you were entitled. How did that right or privilege benefit you? What feelings did it evoke in you? Do you feel that a majority of your classmates could benefit from knowing about this right or privilege?

8. How many of your neighbors do you know? Is your community (your classroom, cafeteria, library, dormitory, local neighborhood, workplace, etc.) an environment where people take time to learn each other's names? Are there attitudes, spaces, or groups that you avoid within your own community? How do these aspects of your neighborhood affect you on a daily basis? Are there any topics you could explore that could improve the quality of life and sense of community for you and your neighbors?

Section II: Fostering Civic Engagement through Narrative Forms

What Is the Narrative Form in Public Discourse?

As Cindy L. Griffin illuminates throughout the text, narratives are a powerful form of communication that create connections between speakers and audiences. The author also notes that narratives help personalize important points, challenge audiences to think in new ways, and create strong emotional responses.

The use of narrative is a common communicative practice across cultures. In U.S. culture, orators and rhetoricians rely on narrative forms in political, religious, educational, and professional contexts in order to incite responses and in many cases to call audiences to action. Narratives can be a useful springboard for encouraging audience members to become engaged in broader issues of importance.

Consider the following examples:

> ➤ Have you been a student in a class where an instructor's effective use of narrative allowed you to access course material on a more meaningful level, thus prompting you to become more interested in a global, interactive approach to a topic and/or discipline?
> ➤ Have you witnessed discourse in a free speech zone on your campus where personal narratives or anecdotes were used to provide strong support for a particular cause or persuasive agenda?
> ➤ Have you interacted with spiritual leaders in your lifetime who rely on narratives to engage theological perspectives and encourage religious or spiritual involvement and participation?
> ➤ Have politicians used narratives in debates or campaign speeches that cause you to react or interest you in a particular political issue?

These are only a sample of ways that orators use narratives to engage audiences and motivate audience members toward a particular course of action. The following list of activities can be used as individual exercises or within small cooperative learning groups to further your understanding of the ways in which narratives can serve as part of public discourse that promotes and enhances civic engagement.

1. As you plan for your next speech in a public speaking course or in another public speaking context, brainstorm ways in which you could insert narratives that would help connect you with your audience and encourage them to begin thinking actively about your topic. If your speech is designed to call your audience to action, consider telling a compelling story that shows your investment in the cause so that your audience can begin to personalize the issue.

2. During a local or national election period, track the use of narratives among political candidates so that you can assess ways in which candidates use narrative as a rhetorical strategy to promote their platform issues. Discuss your assessments with peers, colleagues, friends, and family so that larger conversations may be held regarding significant political issues and the ways in which issues are presented in public forums.
3. The next time you find yourself in a conflicting interpersonal exchange, consider re-approaching the conflict from the perspective of narrative. Use storytelling to convey emotions and key issues, and encourage other parties to express issues through the use of narratives as well. Once resolution is reached, discuss how using narrative helped you achieve a peaceful resolution and changed the dynamics of the disagreement.
4. Encourage your instructors to use narratives in their pedagogical practices. Affirm their teaching strategies by acknowledging how narrative forms deepen your understanding of course content. Suggest ways to integrate service-learning or experiential models of education into the curriculum so that students can begin to connect course material with the "stories" of the world outside the classroom.
5. Stay up to date with current events so that you may be a contributing voice in your community and in personal or social groups who help others become aware of major issues that affect citizens at the local, national, and global levels.
6. Seek out ways to be active in your community as a mentor to younger students. Using your storytelling skills, offer your time as a tutor or as a volunteer with a youth mentoring program so that young people can be encouraged and guided through critical decisions and life stages.

Creating Narrative Comparisons

When composing a narrative, it is important to consider the ways your audience can relate to your story, particularly if your story recognizes a rare event that took place in your life. This helps create an engaging story as well as reducing your potential public speaking anxiety. One way to approach narrative speechwriting is to first lay out a list of comparisons to which most of your audience members can relate. This list then becomes a helpful list from which to create imagery devices such as metaphors, similes, idioms, etc.

For example, imagine you are recreating a story about a skydiving experience. This might be a story of great excitement, bravery, and conquering a lifelong fear. However, you must assume that a very small percentage of your audience have experienced a similar event. To help them understand such an emotion, you will need to compare this experience to something they are likely to have experienced—perhaps riding on a rollercoaster, moving out on their own, starting the first day of high school, etc.

Complete the following exercise before writing your narrative as a means of brainstorming helpful comparisons that you might want to include in your story.

	Your Narrative	**Helpful Comparison**
Main emotion of narrative		
Roles of people		
Sensory experiences:		
Sights		
Smells		
Tactile senses		
Tastes		
Sounds		
Moral or lesson learned		

Story Mapping

Story mapping can be a great help when it comes to writing a narrative speech. Try filling out a chart similar to the following before creating any text in paragraph form.

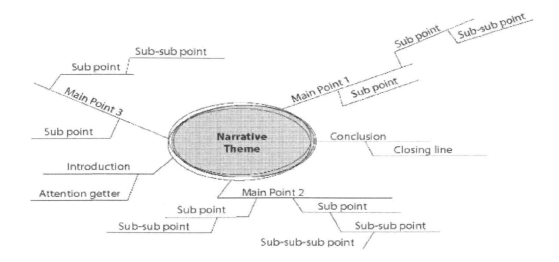

Create categories and subcategories to chart the many different directions of your story. This process often helps visual learners see what is involved in the story and develops the appropriate framework before writing sentences and paragraphs.

Another option is to create a story map centering around the five senses to get a sense of all the details happening during a particular event. The following illustrates this type of story map.

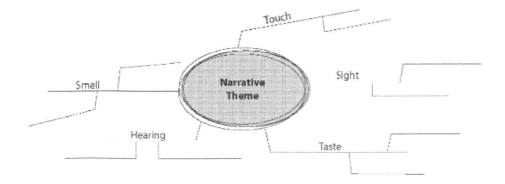

Section III: Civic Engagement Reconsidered

Audience Centeredness

What does it really mean to be audience-centered? Every time you have the opportunity to speak in public you must look to your audience for inspiration. Your audience will aid you in the speaking process in many ways. Considering your particular audience will tell you, among other things:

- What topic to choose.
- What sources to use.
- What form your speech should take.
- How to order your points.
- What terminology to explain more fully.
- What visual aid to use.
- How much extemporaneousness to display.

Your audience is a valuable tool for speech preparation. If you spend a great deal of time thinking of your speech topic, your speech will probably go badly. If you prepare a great visual aid and practice over and over but never think about your audience, your speech will not likely be successful. If you did all of that and you loved the speech but your audience never heard a word, what is the point of speaking in public? Public speaking is very much about the *audience*. To be a successful speaker, ask yourself:

- Who are you speaking to?
- Is it a voluntary audience?
- Will they have some interest in your speech topic?
- What level of knowledge will they possess regarding this topic?
- What points will need more explanation?
- What level of formality will they expect?
- How much time will you have for dialogue?

Audience centeredness does not stop here but continues through the delivery of the speech, where you are committed more to helping the audience understand than finishing your speech in the way you planned. Through the dialogue and/or question and answer session, your audience is still your top priority. We use to conceive of public speaking as a one-way mode of communication. I talk, you listen. Now we know that it is a much more dynamic process and that the audience is every bit as important as the speaker. With this knowledge you will be a much more effective speaker.

Service Learning and Civic Engagement

During a fall semester I had the good fortune to enroll in a Basic Public Speaking course. I call it good fortune now but at the time I certainly did not feel that way. I had waited several semesters to take the class most students take as freshman. I decided that since it was a requirement for graduation I had better not put it off any longer. I thought, it cannot be that bad. However, my outlook changed drastically. The professor wasted no time stressing that this course was a service-learning course. At first I was uncertain what that meant, but she went on to explain that we would be required to complete at least 20 hours of service in the community as a partial requirement for the course. I could not believe that I had to take a course with this sort of ridiculous requirement. I mean, who has 20 extra hours in 16 weeks? Certainly not me; with work and 18 credits, I was busy enough. However, I decided to stay in the class because I needed the credits to graduate.

About one week into the class the professor invited representatives from the agencies we would be working with to come in and give a short presentation. I listened to each and chose the one that seemed the most flexible and the least painful. After signing a contract where I swore to complete at least 20 hours of meaningful service for the agency, I began my work at the Family Center where I tutored children who attended the afterschool program. On the first day, which came about 8 weeks into the semester, because I had procrastinated so much, I was still not convinced that this was going to be a useful experience. I decided that I needed to go. Quitting was not an option, so I decided to make the best of it. I put my best foot forward and continued to do that for seven other days as I completed more than the minimum hours of required service. In that time I began to see classroom principles come to life. Concepts that were just theory in the classroom were real at my agency. I could identify them in my interactions with the children, which allowed me to know that they were more than just conjecture. In addition, I was able to remember these things more easily because they were no longer just words on the page in my notebook.

That was not the end of the benefits I reaped from my service-learning experience. Another, and perhaps far more important, thing that I learned in that organization was the immense need of those children for the services the agency provided. I was taken aback at the sheer number of children crowded into that small space. I also became aware of the shortage of volunteers. I could not believe that all of this was going on in the community where I lived without my even noticing it. Because I loved working with those children, I decided to stay with the organization and continue volunteering my time after the semester was over. Since taking that class, which has changed my life, I have been involved with service learning in some way every semester. I have taken training through the Office of Service Learning and Volunteer Programs, served as a service-learning assistant, and taken several other service-learning classes. I have attended graduate school where I focused on service learning, and this year I will have the opportunity to teach three sections of Introduction to Public Speaking with service learning as a partial requirement just like the course I took that changed my life.

Finding the Right Fit: Community Partners

Civic engagement is a mind, body, and voice activity. For it to occur you must be present both mentally and physically. There are many great community partners, but not all will be right for you. Here are questions to consider when choosing a community partner.

- ➢ *Location:* Will I be able to get there on time whenever I am scheduled to serve?
- ➢ *Hours:* Will the hours they have available fit into my schedule?
- ➢ *Clientele:* Do they serve a demographic that I am interested in working with?
- ➢ *Structure:* Will this be a highly structured service placement? Do I require structure to be productive?

Your instructor has gone to great lengths to ensure that you have a variety of quality service-learning options. Whether civic engagement occurs or not is up to you. Please treat community partners with care. They will come to depend upon your work and greatly appreciate your time and effort. So, go have fun, learn much, and utilize your mind, body, and voice in your university without walls. It will be well worth it.

Ways to Be Engaged Every Day

Civic engagement does not always occur during some monumental speech or nerve-racking process. Sometimes it happens in small ways, in our day-to-day decisions. Here are some ideas about how you can be an engaged citizen every day.

- ➢ Use alternative modes of transportation (walk, take a bus, ride your bike, or carpool)
- ➢ Bring your own coffee cup to the coffee shop
- ➢ Sign a petition
- ➢ Listen to a protestor
- ➢ Have conversations
- ➢ Buy locally
- ➢ Seek out a farmer's market
- ➢ Bring your own grocery bags
- ➢ Turn off lights
- ➢ Consider buying a hybrid car
- ➢ Do product research
- ➢ Attend a political rally
- ➢ Pick a speech topic this semester that will raise awareness
- ➢ Volunteer your time
- ➢ Become knowledgeable about community needs
- ➢ Become knowledgeable about community decision-making processes
- ➢ Vote
- ➢ Use a refillable water bottle
- ➢ Recycle
- ➢ Buy secondhand clothing

Values Survey

When listening to speeches centered around controversial topics, audience members have a tendency to do much more *hearing* than *listening*. Less critical audience members often superficially categorize the content of a speech. This categorization often utilizes popular political opinion and labels that make it easy to reduce the content into dismissible stereotypes. However, did you ever stop to think that most people—regardless of political, religious, or ethnic background— actually share many values? Even though many democratic political campaigns often highlight one or two major actions, most competitors share common values. Often the difference lies in the ways these values are prioritized. To see just how difficult it is to prioritize important human values, try the following survey.

Values Survey

Name: _____

Rank the following values with 1 being the most important and 20 being the least important.

_____ A comfortable life	_____ Mature love
_____ An exciting life	_____ National security
_____ A sense of accomplishment	_____ Pleasure
_____ A world at peace	_____ Self-respect
_____ A world of beauty	_____ Social recognition
_____ Equality	_____ True friendship
_____ Family security	_____ Personal health
_____ Freedom	_____ Wisdom
_____ Happiness	_____ Wealth
_____ Justice	_____ Living in a pleasant community

When You Might Need an Invitational Discussion

Imagine that you are home for break. It is Sunday morning and you decide to attend church with your parents. You have been attending the same small church for most of your life and know many of the people who attend. When you arrive you make a beeline for the coffee and stand by yourself while your parents join a nearby group of friends. While you pour cream in your coffee, you overhear a gentleman in your parents' group make a racial joke. This joke is followed by chuckles and laughs, and the conversation rapidly moves on. At first, you don't think much of this; after all, the joke was very mild and may not even be offensive to some. However, you did notice your parents joining in the laughter, and after thinking about it you decide this action was wrong and you are going to talk to your parents on the ride home after church. The more you think about it, the more nervous you become. You know that they will say, "It was nothing, just a harmless joke." You convince yourself to have the conversation anyway because you know that it is not usually the big things that make the world a better place but the small things that people do and say daily. As you think about how to raise the issue with your parents, you realize that you do not know how to talk with them about their behavior without causing a confrontation.

Have you ever been in this kind of situation? You know that something should be said; you know a conversation should take place, but you don't have the skills to follow through. In *Invitation to Public Speaking* you learn about invitational speaking. This type of speaking is ideal for controversial topics, situations, and conversations, especially those that would benefit from a broadening of opinions, an opening of conversation, and a sharing of ideas. Invitational speaking is, at first, contrary to your normal pattern of conversation and may be somewhat difficult to grasp, but once you understand and can practice it you will possess a tool to help you facilitate these tough conversations that should not be left unspoken.

Invitational Speech Outline

This outline is meant to be a first step in helping you to bring an invitational discussion to life. Use it to begin placing your thoughts in a constructive order that will promote a sense of equality, value, and self-determination.

Name: _____ _____

Speech topic: _____

Are you discussing an issue or position? _____

Describe what body posture you will be using to nonverbally convey a sense of open-mindedness:

_____

_____

Name three language choices (actual words) you will use to promote a sense of equality, value, and self-determination:

_____

_____

_____

Why is this issue or position really important to you? *(personal feelings are encouraged here)*

_____

_____

_____

What aspects of your life (age, race, sex, gender, class, preferences) influence your interest or position regarding this topic? Reflect on this and please name as many as you can.

_____

_____

_____

_____

Body: Research is required (passion and intellect need to join here). Review the factors, opinions, legislations, etc. surrounding this issue or position. Please give a **complete** source citation and a two to three sentence summary of what information the source provided you.

1. Citation:

_____

_____

Summary:

_____

_____

_____

2. Citation:

_____

_____

Summary:

_____

_____

_____

3.Citation:

_____

_____

Summary:

_____

_____

_____

Create three main points to introduce your audience to this issue and/or position. Remember to keep this simple and short to leave room for group discussion.

1. Main point:

_____

_____

_____

Transition:

_____

2. Main point:

_____

_____

_____

Transition:

_____

3. Main point:

_____

_____

_____

_____

Create an invitation for discussion:

_____

Discussion: List 3 open-ended questions you will use for prompting discussion if the audience members do not voluntarily respond?

1. _____

_____

2. _____

_____

3. _____

_____

▼ ▼ ▼

Civic Engagement Wrap-up

In closing, we hope the brief writings and exercises in this chapter help in your quest to become a more civically engaged individual, newly trained in the art of public speaking. Once you have decided to open the door to civic engagement, seeing all the pressing needs of your community can be daunting. Remember, small acts such as reading the local newspaper, getting to know your neighbors, and making use of your local rights and privileges serve to keep you actively engaged in your community. Start with your everyday life first. Observe how small actions can create a tighter web of community. And always, realize that your voice is a vibrant part of the civic fabric that weaves all of our democratic ideals together.

Best of luck in your public speaking endeavors!

Elizabeth Sink
Kristin Slattery
Beth Meyers-Bass
Sonja Modesti

Glossary

Glossary

abstract language: Language that refers to ideas or concepts but not to specific objects.

abstract: Summary of the text in an article or publication.

acceptance speech: Speech that expresses gratitude, appreciation, and pleasure at receiving an honor or a gift.

ad hominem fallacy: Argument in which a speaker attacks a person rather than that person's arguments.

affirmations: Positive, motivating statements that replace negative self-talk.

alliteration: Repetition of initial sounds of two or more words in a sentence or phrase.

analogical reasoning: A process of reasoning by way of comparison and similarity that implies that because two things resemble each other in one respect, they also share similarities in another respect.

antithesis: Placement of words and phrases in contrast or opposition to one another.

argument: Set of statements that allows you to develop your evidence to establish the validity of your claim.

articulation: Physical process of producing specific speech sounds to make language intelligible.

attitude: General positive or negative feeling a person has about something.

audience centered: Acknowledging your audience by considering and listening to the unique, diverse, and common perspectives of its members before, during, and after your speech.

audience centered: Considerate of the positions, beliefs, values, and needs of an audience.

audience: Complex and varied group of people the speaker addresses.

audience: Complex and varied group of people the speaker addresses.

balance: Visual relationship between the items on a visual aid.

bandwagon fallacy: Argument that something is correct or good because everyone else agrees with it or is doing it.

bar graph: Graph that compares quantities at a specific moment in time.

behavioral objectives: Actions a speaker wants the audience to take at the end of a speech.

belief: Person's idea of what is real, not real, true, or not true.

bias: Unreasoned distortion of judgment or prejudice about a topic.

bibliographic database: Database that indexes publishing data for books, periodical articles, government reports, statistics, patents, research reports, conference proceedings, and dissertations.

Boolean operators: Words you can use to create specific phrases that broaden or narrow your search on the Internet.

brainstorming: Process of generating ideas randomly and uncritically, without attention to logic, connections, or relevance.

brief narrative: Short story or vignette that illustrates a specific point.

call to action: Explicitly request that an audience engage in some clearly stated behavior.

careful listener: Listener who overcomes listener interference to better understand a speaker's message.

causal pattern: Pattern of organization that describes a cause-and-effect relationship between ideas or events.

causal reasoning: Process of reasoning that supports a claim by establishing a cause-and-effect relationship.

channel: Means by which the message is conveyed.

character: Audience's view of a speaker's sincerity, trustworthiness, and concern for their well-being.

character: Audience's view of a speaker's sincerity, trustworthiness, and concern for the well-being of the audience.

chronological pattern: Pattern of organization that traces a sequence of events or ideas.

claim: Assertion that must be proved.

closed-ended question: Question that requires the respondent to choose an answer from two or more alternatives.

cognitive restructuring: Process that helps reduce anxiety by replacing negative thoughts with positive ones, called affirmations.

colloquialism: Local or regional informal dialect or expression.

commemorative speech: Speech that praises, honors, recognizes, or pays tribute to a person, an event, an idea, or an institution.

common ground: Similarities, shared interests, and mutual perspectives a speaker has with an audience.

communication apprehension: Level of fear or anxiety associated with either real or anticipated communication with another person or persons.

comparative advantages organization: Organizational pattern that illustrates the advantages of one solution over others.

competence: Audience's view of a speaker's intelligence, expertise, and knowledge of a subject.

competence: Audience's view of a speaker's intelligence, expertise, and knowledge of a subject.

conclusion: Logical outcome of an argument that results from the combination of the major and minor premises.

concrete language: Language that refers to a tangible object—a person, place, or thing.

condition of equality: Condition of an invitational environment that requires the speaker to acknowledge that all audience members hold equally valid perspectives worthy of exploration.

condition of self-determination: Condition of an invitational environment that requires the speaker to recognize that people know what is best for them and have the right to make choices about their lives based on this knowledge.

condition of value: Condition of an invitational environment that requires the speaker to recognize the inherent value of the audience's views, although those views may differ from the speaker's views.

confirm: To recognize, acknowledge, and express value for another person.

connective: Word or a phrase used to link ideas in a speech.

connotative definition: Subjective meaning of a word or phrase based on personal experiences and beliefs.

considerate speech: Speech that eases the audience's burden of processing information.

context: Environment or situation in which a speech occurs.

conversational style: Speaking style that is more formal than everyday conversation but remains spontaneous and relaxed.

coordination: Process of arranging points into successive levels, with the points on a specific level having equal importance.

counterarguments: Arguments against the speaker's own position.

credibility: Audience's perception of a speaker's competence and character.

credibility: Audience's perception of a speaker's competence and character.

critical listener: Listener who listens for the accuracy of a speech's content and the implications of a speaker's message.

culturally inclusive language: Language that respectfully recognizes the differences among the many cultures in our society.

database: Collections of information stored electronically so they are easy to find and retrieve.

decoding: Translating words, sounds, and gestures into ideas and feelings in an attempt to understand the message.

deductive reasoning: Process of reasoning that uses a familiar and commonly accepted claim to establish the truth of a very specific claim.

definition: Statement of the exact meaning of a word or phrase.

delivery: Action or manner of speaking to an audience.

demographic audience analysis: Analysis that identifies the particular population traits of an audience.

demonstration: Display of how something is done or how it works.

denotative definition: Objective meaning of a word or a phrase you find in a dictionary.

derived credibility: Credibility a speaker develops during a speech.

dialect: Pattern of speech that is shared by an ethnic group or people from specific geographical locations.

dialogue: Interaction, connection, and exchange of ideas and opinions with others.

direct quotation: Exact word-for-word presentation of another's testimony.

drawing: Diagram or sketch of someone or something.

either-or fallacy: Argument in which a speaker claims our options are "either A or B," when actually more than two options exist. Sometimes called a *false dilemma*.

empathy: Trying to see and understand the world as another person does.

encoding: Translating ideas and feelings into words, sounds, and gestures.

ethical listener: Listener who considers the moral impact of a speaker's message on one's self and one's community.

ethical public speaker: Speaker who considers the moral impact of his or her ideas and arguments on others when involved in the public dialogue.

ethnocentrism: Belief that our own cultural perspectives, norms, and ways of organizing society are superior to others.

ethos: Speaker's credibility; the second of Aristotle's three types of proof.

ethos: Speaker's credibility; the second of Aristotle's three types of proof.

etymology: History of a word.

euphemism: Word or phrase that substitutes an agreeable or inoffensive expression for one that may offend or suggest something unpleasant.

evidence: Materials that speakers use to support their ideas.

example: Specific instance used to illustrate a concept, experience, issue, or problem.

expert testimony: Opinions or observations of someone considered an authority in a particular field.

extemporaneous speech: Speech that is carefully prepared and practiced from brief notes rather than from memory or a written manuscript.

extended narrative: Longer story that makes an evolving connection with a broader point.

eye contact: Visual contact with another person's eyes.

facial expression: The movement of your eyes, eyebrows, and mouth to convey reactions and emotions.

fallacy: Argument that seems valid but is flawed because of unsound evidence or reasoning.

false cause: Error in reasoning in which a speaker assumes that one event caused another simply because the first event happened before the second.

false cause fallacy: Argument mistaking a chronological relationship for a causal relationship.

fear appeal: Threat of something undesirable happening if change does not occur.

feedback: Verbal and nonverbal signals an audience gives a speaker.

flow chart: Chart that illustrates direction or motion.

font size: Size of the letters in a particular font measured in points.

font: Type or style of print.

full-text database: Database that indexes the complete text of newspapers, periodicals, encyclopedias, research reports, court cases, books, and the like.

gain immediate action: Encourage an audience to engage in a specific behavior or take a specific action.

gain passive agreement: Ask an audience to adopt a new position without also asking them to act in support of that position.

gender-inclusive language: Language recognizing that both women and men are active participants in the world.

general purpose: Speech's broad goal: to inform, invite, persuade, introduce, commemorate, or accept.

gestures: Movements, usually of the hands but sometimes of the full body, that express meaning and emotion or offer clarity to a message.

global plagiarism: Stealing an entire speech from a single source and presenting it as your own.

graph: Visual comparison of amounts or quantities that show growth, size, proportions, or relationships.

group communication: Communication among members of a team or a collective about topics such as goals, strategies, and conflict.

hasty generalization: Error in reasoning in which a speaker reaches a conclusion without enough evidence to support it.

hasty generalization fallacy: Argument based on too few cases, or examples, to support a conclusion.

hearing: Vibration of sound waves on our eardrums and the impulses then sent to the brain.

hypothetical example: Instance that did not take place but could have.

idiom: Fixed, distinctive expression whose meaning is not indicated by its individual words.

impromptu speech: Speech that is not planned or prepared in advance.

incremental plagiarism: Presenting select portions from a single speech as your own.

index: Alphabetical listing of the topics discussed in a specific publication, along with the corresponding year, volume, and page numbers.

inductive reasoning: Process of reasoning that uses specific instances, or examples, to make a claim about a general conclusion.

inferences: Mental leaps we make when we recognize that a speaker's evidence supports his or her claims.

inflection: Manipulation of pitch to create certain meanings or moods.

information overload: When we take in more information than we can process but realize there still is more information we are expected to know.

informative speaking environment: Environment in which a speaker has expertise or knowledge that an audience needs but doesn't already have.

informative speech: Speech that communicates knowledge and understanding about a process, an event, a person or place, an object, or a concept.

initial credibility: Credibility a speaker has before giving a speech.

interference: Anything that stops or hinders a listener from receiving a message.

internal preview: Statement in the body of a speech that details what the speaker plans to discuss next.

internal summary: Statement in the body of a speech that summarizes a point a speaker has already discussed.

interpersonal communication: Communication with other people that ranges from the highly personal to the highly impersonal.

intertextuality: Process in which stories reference other stories or rely on parts of other stories to be complete.

interview: Planned interaction with another person that is organized around inquiry and response, with one person asking questions while the other person answers them.

intrapersonal communication: Communication with ourselves via the dialogue that goes on in our heads.

introductory speech: Speech that provides an audience with a unique perspective on the person introduced.

invitational environment: Environment in which the speaker's highest priority is to understand, respect, and appreciate the range of possible positions on an issue, even if those positions are quite different from his or her own.

invitational speaking: Type of public speaking in which a speaker enters into a dialogue with an audience to clarify positions, explore issues and ideas, or articulate beliefs and values.

jargon: Technical language used by a special group or for a special activity.

language: System of verbal or gestural symbols a community uses to communicate.

line graph: Graph that shows trends over time.

listenable speech: Speech that is considerate and delivered in an oral style.

listening: Process of giving thoughtful attention to another person's words and understanding what you hear.

list: Series of words or phrases that organize ideas one after the other.

logos: Logical arrangement of evidence in a speech; the first of Aristotle's three types of proof.

logos: Logical arrangement of evidence in a speech; the first of Aristotle's three types of proof.

main points: Most important ideas you address in your speech.

major premise: Claim in an argument that states a familiar, commonly accepted belief (also called the general principle).

manuscript speech: Speech that is read to an audience from a written text.

map: Visual representation showing the physical layout of geographical features, cities, road systems, the night sky, and the like.

mass communication: Communication generated by media organizations that is designed to reach large audiences.

master statuses: Significant positions occupied by a person within society that affect that person's identity in almost all social situations.

mean: Average of a group of numbers.

median: Middle number in a series or set of numbers arranged in a ranked order.

memorized speech: Speech that has been written out, committed to memory, and given word for word.

message: Information conveyed by the speaker to the audience.

metaphor: Figure of speech that makes a comparison between two things by describing one thing as being something else.

minor premise: Claim in an argument that states a specific instance linked to the major premise.

mixed metaphor: Metaphor that makes illogical comparisons between two or more things.

mnemonic device: Verbal device that makes information easier to remember.

model: Copy of an object, usually built to scale, that represents an object in detail.

mode: Number that occurs most often in a set of numbers.

monotone: Way of speaking in which a speaker does not alter her or his pitch.

Monroe's motivated sequence: Step-by-step process used to persuade audiences by gaining attention, demonstrating a need, satisfying that need, visualizing beneficial results, and calling for action.

multiple perspectives pattern: Organizational pattern that allows the speaker to address the many sides and positions of an issue before opening up the speech for dialogue with the audience.

mythos: Interrelated set of beliefs, attitudes, values, and feelings held by members of a particular society or culture.

narrative: Story that recounts or foretells real or hypothetical events.

noise: Anything that interferes with understanding the message being communicated.

objective: Having a fair, ethical, and undistorted view on a question or issue.

object: Something that can be seen or touched.

open-ended question: Question that allows the respondent to answer in an unrestricted way.

oral style: Speaking style that reflects the spoken rather than the written word.

organizational chart: Chart that illustrates the structure of groups.

organization: Systematic arrangement of ideas into a coherent whole.

parallelism: Arrangement of related words so they are balanced or of related sentences so they have identical structures.

paraphrase: Summary of another's testimony in the speaker's own words.

patchwork plagiarism: Constructing a complete speech that you present as your own from portions of several different sources.

pathos: Emotional appeals made by a speaker; the third of Aristotle's three types of proof.

pathos: Emotional appeals made by a speaker; the third of Aristotle's three types of proof.

pauses: Hesitations and brief silences in speech or conversation.

peer testimony: Opinions or observations of someone who has firsthand knowledge of a topic (sometimes called *lay testimony*).

personal appearance: Way speakers dress, groom, and present themselves physically.

personal testimony: Your own opinions or observations that you use to convey your point.

personification: Figure of speech that attributes human characteristics to animals, objects, or concepts.

persuasive speech: Speech whose message attempts to change or reinforce an audience's thoughts, feelings, or actions.

picture graph: Graph that presents information in pictures or images.

pie graph: Graph that shows the relative proportions of parts of a whole.

pitch: Highness or lowness of a speaker's voice.

plagiarism: Presenting another person's words and ideas as your own.

posture: Way speakers position and carry their bodies.

preliminary bibliography: List of all the potential sources you'll use as you prepare your speech.

preparation outline: Detailed outline a speaker builds when preparing a speech that includes the title, specific purpose, thesis statement, introduction, main points and subpoints, connectives, conclusion, and source citations of the speech.

preview: Brief overview in the introduction of a speech of each of the main points in the speech.

probe: Question that fills out or follows up an answer to a previous question.

problem-cause-solution organization: Organizational pattern that focuses on identifying a specific problem, the causes of that problem, and a solution to the problem.

problem-solution organization: Organizational pattern that focuses on persuading an audience that a specific problem exists and can be solved or minimized by a specific solution.

problem–solution pattern: Pattern of organization that identifies a specific problem and offers a possible solution.

pronunciation: Act of saying words correctly according to the accepted standards of a language.

proxemics: Use of space during communication.

public communication: Communication in which one person gives a speech to other people, most often in a public setting.

public dialogue: Ethical and civil exchange of ideas and opinions among communities about topics that affect the public.

question of fact: Question that addresses whether something is verifiably true or not.

question of policy: Question that addresses the best course of action or solution to a problem.

question of value: Question that addresses the merit or morality of an object, action, or belief.

rate: Speed at which a speaker speaks.

real example: Instance that actually took place.

reasoning by sign: Process of reasoning that assumes something exists or will happen based on something else that exists or has happened.

red herring fallacy: Argument that introduces irrelevant information to distract an audience from the real issue.

referent: Object, concept, or event a symbol represents.

repetition: Repeating keywords or phrases at the beginnings or endings of sentences or clauses to create rhythm.

research inventory: List of the types of information you have for your speech and the types you want to find.

rhetorical question: Question, used for effect, that an audience isn't supposed to answer out loud but rather in their own minds.

rhythm: Arrangement of words into patterns so the sounds of the words together enhance the meaning of a phrase.

signpost: Simple word or statement that indicates where you are in your speech or highlights an important idea.

sign: Something that represents something else.

simile: Figure of speech that makes an explicit comparison of two things using the word *like* or *as*.

slang: Informal nonstandard vocabulary, usually made up of arbitrarily changed words.

slippery slope fallacy: Argument in which a speaker claims that taking a first step in one direction will lead to inevitable and undesirable further steps.

spatial pattern: Pattern of organization that arranges ideas in terms of location or direction.

speaker: Person who stimulates public dialogue by delivering an oral message.

speaking environment: Time and place in which a speaker will speak.

speaking outline: Condensed form of a preparation outline that you use when speaking.

specific purpose: Focused statement that identifies exactly what a speaker wants to accomplish with a speech.

speech about a concept: Informative speech about an abstraction, something you can't perceive with your senses, such as an idea, a theory, a principle, a worldview, or a belief.

speech about an event: Informative speech that describes or explains a significant, interesting, or unusual occurrence.

speech about an object: Informative speech about anything that is tangible, that can be perceived by the senses.

speech about a place or a person: Informative speech that describes a significant, interesting, or unusual place or person.

speech about a process: Informative speech that describes how something is done, how something comes to be what it is, or how something works.

speech of award: Speech given to present a specific award to someone and describe why that person is receiving the award.

speech of tribute: Speech given to honor someone.

speech to articulate a position: Invitational speech in which the speaker invites an audience to understand an issue from her or his perspective and then opens up a conversation with audience members to learn their perspectives on the issue.

speech to entertain: Lighthearted speech that addresses issues or ideas in a humorous way.

speech to explore an issue: Invitational speech in which the speaker attempts to engage an audience in a discussion about an idea, concern, topic, or plan of action.

speech topic: Subject of your speech.

spotlighting: Practice of highlighting a person's race or ethnicity (or sex, sexual orientation, physical disability, and the like) during a speech.

standpoint: Perspective from which a person views and evaluates society.

state or situational anxiety: Apprehension about communicating with others in a particular situation.

statistics: Numerical summaries of facts, figures, and research findings.

stereotype: Broad generalization about an entire group based on limited knowledge or exposure to only certain members of that group.

subordination: Process of ranking ideas in order from the most to the least important.

subpoint: Point in a speech that develops an aspect of a main point.

sub-subpoint: Point in a speech that develops an aspect of a subpoint.

summary: Concise restatement of the main points at the end of a speech.

symbol: Word or phrase spoken by a speaker.

systematic desensitization: Technique for reducing anxiety that involves teaching your body to feel calm and relaxed rather than fearful during your speeches.

terminal credibility: Credibility a speaker has at the end of a speech.

testimony: Opinions or observations of others.

thesis statement: Statement that summarizes in a single declarative sentence the main ideas, assumptions, or arguments you want to express in your speech.

thought, or reference: Memory and past experiences that audience members have with an object, concept, or event.

timing: Way a speaker uses pauses and delivery for maximum effect.

topical pattern: Pattern of organization that allows the speaker to divide a topic into subtopics, each of which addresses a different aspect of the larger topic.

trait anxiety: Apprehension about communicating with others in any situation.

transition: Phrase that indicates a speaker is finished with one idea and is moving on to a new one.

two-sided message: Persuasive strategy that addresses both sides of an issue, refuting one side to prove the other is better.

value: Person's idea of what is good, worthy, or important.

verbal clutter: Extra words that pad sentences and claims but don't add meaning.

visualization: Process in which you construct a mental image of yourself giving a successful speech.

vocalized pauses: Pauses that speakers fill with words or sounds like "um," "er," or "uh."

vocal variety: Changes in the volume, rate, and pitch of a speaker's voice that affect the meaning of the words delivered.

volume: Loudness of a speaker's voice.

References

References

Chapter 1

1. Harold Barrett, *Rhetoric and Civility: Human Development, Narcissism, and the Good Audience* (Albany: State University of New York Press, 1991), p. 147.

2. Deborah Tannen, *The Argument Culture: Moving from Debate to Dialogue* (New York: Random House, 1998), pp. 1–4.

3. See, for example, Stephen Yarbrough, "On 'Getting it': Resistance, Temporality, and the 'Ethical Shifting' of Discursive Interaction," *Rhetoric Society Quarterly* 40 (2010): 1-22; Jennifer Emerling Bone, Cindy L. Griffin and T.M. Linda Scholz, "Beyond Traditional Conceptualizations of Rhetoric: Invitational Rhetoric and a Move Toward Civility," *Western Journal of Communication* 72 (October-December 2008): 434-462; Shawn Spano, *Public Dialogue and Participatory Democracy: The Cupertino Community Project* (Cresskill, NJ: Hampton Press, 2001); William Isaacs, *Dialogue and the Art of Thinking Together* (New York: Currency, 1999); Stephen L. Carter, *Civility: Manners, Morals, and the Etiquette of Democracy* (New York: Basic Books, 1998); Linda Ellinor and Glenna Gerard, *Dialogue: Rediscover the Transforming Power of Conversation* (New York: Wiley, 1998); Jeffrey C. Goldfarb, *Civility and Subversion: The Intellectual in the Democratic Society* (Cambridge: Cambridge University Press, 1998); Josina M. Makau and Ronald C. Arnett, *Communication Ethics in an Age of Diversity* (Chicago: University of Illinois Press, 1997); Ivana Markova, Carl F. Graumann, and Klaus Foppa, eds., *Mutualities in Dialogue* (Cambridge: Cambridge University Press, 1995); Douglas N. Walton and Erik C. W. Krabbee, *Commitment in Dialogue: Basic Concepts of Interpersonal Reasoning* (Albany: State University of New York Press, 1995); Rob Anderson, Kenneth N. Cissna, and Ronald C. Arnett, *The Reach of Dialogue: Confirmation, Voice, and Community* (Cresskill, NJ: Hampton Press, 1994); Harold Barrett, *Rhetoric and Civility: Human Development, Narcissism, and the Good Audience* (Albany: State University of New York Press, 1991).

4. For an excellent discussion of the public dialogue, see Spano, *Public Dialogue and Participatory Democracy*.

5. Adapted from Kenneth Burke, *The Philosophy of Literary Form: Studies in Symbolic Action*, 3rd ed. (1941; reprint, Berkeley: University of California Press, 1973), pp. 110–111.

6. Melbourne S. Cummings, "Teaching the African American Rhetoric Course," in James W. Ward, ed., *African American Communications: An Anthology in Traditional and Contemporary Studies* (Dubuque, IA: Kendall/Hunt, 1993), p. 241.

7. Adapted from Janice Walker Anderson, "A Comparison of Arab and American Conceptions of 'Effective' Persuasion," *Howard Journal of Communications* 2 (Winter 1989–1990): 81–114; Larry A. Samovar and Richard E. Porter, eds., *Intercultural Communication: A Reader*, 10th ed. (Belmont, CA: Wadsworth, 2003); A. J. Almaney and A. J. Alwan, *Communicating with the Arabs: A Handbook for the Business Executive* (Prospect Heights, IL: Waveland, 1982), p. 79.

8. Bonnie Dow, "Ann Willis Richards: A Voice for Political Empowerment," in Karlyn Kohrs Campbell, ed., *Women Public Speakers in the United States, 1925–1993* (Westport, CT: Greenwood Press, 1994), p. 456.

9. Material for this section is from David Niven and Jeremy Zilber, "Elite Use of Racial Labels: Ideology and Preference for African American or Black," *Howard Journal of Communications* 11 (2000): 267-277; Ward, *African American Communications*; Mary Jane Collier, "A Comparison of Conversations among and between Domestic Culture Groups: How Intra- and Intercultural Competencies Vary," *Communication Quarterly* 36 (1988): 122–144; Larry A. Samovar and Richard E. Porter, *Communication between Cultures* (Belmont, CA: Wadsworth, 2007); Anderson, "A Comparison of Arab and American Conceptions of 'Effective' Persuasion"; Samovar and Porter, *Intercultural Communication*; Almaney and Alwan, *Communicating with the Arabs*.

10. Charmaine Shutiva, "Native American Culture and Communication through Humor," in Alberto Gonzalez, Marsha Houston, and Victoria Chen, eds., *Our Voices: Essays in Culture, Ethnicity, and Communication*, 3rd ed. (Los Angeles: Roxbury, 2000), pp. 113–117.

11. Bonnie J. Dow and Mari Boor Tonn, "'Feminine Style' and Political Judgment in the Rhetoric of Ann Richards," *Quarterly Journal of Speech* 79 (1993): 286–302; Julia T. Wood, *Gendered Lives: Communication, Gender, and Culture*, 9th ed. (Belmont, CA: Wadsworth, 2011); Marsha Houston, "When Black Women Talk with White Women: Why the Dialogues Are Difficult," in Gonzalez, Houston, and Chen, *Our Voices*, pp. 98–104.

12. James C. McCroskey, "Oral Communication Apprehension: A Summary of Recent Theory and Research," *Human Communication Research* 4 (1977): 78 (italics added). See also Amber N. Finn, Chris R. Sawyer, and Paul Schrodt "Examining the Effect of Exposure Therapy on Public Speaking State Anxiety," *Communication Education* 58 (January 2009): 92-109; Paul L. Witt, Mendy L. Roberts and Ralph R. Behnke, "Comparative Patterns of Anxiety and Depression in a Public Speaking Context," *Human Communication* 11 (Summer 2008): 219-230; and Jessica J. Winters, Naomi R. Horvath, Myrna Moss, Kate Yarhouse, Chris R. Sawyer and Ralph R. Behnke "Affect Intensity of Student Speakers as a Predictor of Anticipatory Public Speaking Anxiety" *Texas Speech Communication Journal* 31 (Winter 2007): 44-48.

13. Ralph R. Behnke and Chris R. Sawyer, "Milestones of Anticipatory Public Speaking Anxiety," *Communication Education* 48 (1999): 164–172; Amy M. Bippus and John A. Daly, "What Do People Think Causes Stage Fright? Naïve Attributions about the Reasons for Public Speaking Anxiety," *Communication Education* 48 (1999): 63–72; Thomas E. Robinson II, "Communication Apprehension and the Basic Public Speaking Course: A National Survey of In-Class Treatment Techniques," *Communication Education* 46 (1997): 190–197.

14. Michael J. Beatty, "Situational and Predispositional Correlates of Public Speaking Anxiety," *Communication Education* 37 (January 1988): 29–30; Bippus and Daly, "What Do People Think Causes Stage Fright?"

15. Paul L. Witt and Ralph R. Behnke, "Anticipatory Speech Anxiety as a Function of Public Speaking Assignment Type," *Communication Education* 55 (April 2006): 167–177; Shannon C. McCullough, Shelly G. Russell, Ralph R. Behnke, Chris R. Sawyer and Paul L. Witt, "Anticipatory

Public Speaking State Anxiety as a Function of Body Sensations and State of Mind," *Communication Quarterly* 54 (February 2006): 101-109; and Murray B. Stein, John R. Walker, and David R. Forde, "Public-Speaking Fears in a Community Sample: Prevalence, Impact on Functioning, and Diagnostic Classification," *Archives of General Psychiatry* 53 (1996): 169–174.

16. John A. Daly, Anita L. Vangelisti, and David J. Weber, "Speech Anxiety Affects How People Prepare Speeches: A Protocol Analysis of the Preparation Processes of Speakers," *Communication Monographs* 62 (December 1995): 383–397.

17. See Tony E. Smith and Ann Bainbridge Frymier, "Get 'Real': Does Practicing Speeches Before an Audience Improve Performance?" *Communication Quarterly* 54 (February 2006): 111-125; Karen Kangas Dwyer, *Conquer Your Speechfright: Learn How to Overcome the Nervousness of Public Speaking* (Fort Worth, TX: Harcourt, 1998); Karen Kangas Dwyer, "The Multidimensional Model: Teaching Students to Self-Manage High Communication Apprehension by Self-Selecting Treatments," *Communication Education* 49 (2000): 72–81; James C. McCroskey, "The Implementation of a Large Scale Program of Systematic Desensitization for Communication Apprehension," *Speech Teacher* 21 (1972): 255–264.

18. Joe Ayres and Theodore S. Hopf, "Visualization: A Means of Reducing Speech Anxiety," *Communication Education* 34 (1985): 318–323; Joe Ayres and Theodore S. Hopf, "Visualization: Is It More Than Extra-Attention?" *Communication Education* 38 (1989): 1–5; Joe Ayres and Theodore S. Hopf, "The Long-Term Effect of Visualization in the Classroom: A Brief Research Report," *Communication Education* 39 (1990): 75–78; Joe Ayres, Tim Hopf, and Debbie M. Ayres, "An Examination of Whether Imaging Ability Enhances the Effectiveness of an Intervention Designed to Reduce Speech Anxiety," *Communication Education* 43 (1994): 252–258; Robert McGarvey, "Rehearsing for Success: Tap the Power of the Mind through Visualization," *Executive Female* (January–February 1990): 34–37.

19. Adapted from Ayres and Hopf, "Visualization: Is It More Than Extra-Attention?" pp. 2–3.

20. Joe Ayres, "Coping with Speech Anxiety: The Power of Positive Thinking," *Communication Education* 37 (October 1988): 289–296.

21. William J. Fremouw and Michael D. Scott, "Cognitive Restructuring: An Alternative Method for the Treatment of Communication Apprehension," *Communication Education* 28 (1979): 129–133.

22. Compiled from http://www.convergingvoices.com/oband (accessed June 12, 2007) and http://www.orangeband.org/ (accessed April 23, 2010).

Chapter 2

1. Martin Buber, in Rob Anderson, Kenneth N. Cissna, and Ronald C. Arnett, eds., *The Reach of Dialogue: Confirmation, Voice, and Community* (Cresskill, NJ: Hampton Press, 1994), p. 23.

2. See L. A. Janusik and A. D. Wolvin, 2006, *24 Hours in a Day: A Listening Update to the Time Studies.* Paper presented at the meeting of the International Listening Association, Salem, OR (2006).

3. Richard Emanual, Jim Adams, Kim Baker, E. K. Daufin, Coke Ellington, Elizabeth Fitts, Jonathan Himsel, Linda Holladay, and David Okeowo, "How College Students Spend Their Time Communicating," *The International Journal of Listening* 22 (2008): 26.

4. Lyman K. Steil, Larry L. Barker, and Kittie W. Watson, *Effective Listening: Key to Your Success* (New York: McGraw-Hill, 1993), p. 51.

5. Michael P. Nichols, *The Lost Art of Listening* (New York: Guilford Press, 1995), p. 3.

6. This definition is adapted from Donald L. Rubin, "Listenability = Oral-based Discourse + Considerateness," in Andrew D. Wolvin and Carolyn Gwynn Coakley, eds., *Perspectives on Listening* (Norwood, NJ: Ablex, 1993), pp. 261–281.

7. Compiled from http://www.alasthemovement.org/default_en.asp; http://www.barefootfoundation.com/index_en.php; Dan Kimpel, "Shakira's Songs Are the Heart of Her Success," BMI.com, 30 July 2007, http://www.bmi.com/news/entry/535199; Maegan La Mala, "Slim and Buffett Donate to Shakira's ALAS," VivirLatino.com, 16 May 2008, http://vivirlatino.com/2008/05/16/slim-and-buffett-donate-to-shakiras-alas.php; Shakira, "The Democratization of Education," speech to the Oxford Union, 8 December 2009, http://www.shakira.com/news/title/the-democratization-of-education; and Amy Turner, "Shakira: Every Little Thing She Does Is Magic," The Sunday Times, 1 March 2009, http://entertainment.timesonline.co.uk/tol/arts_and_entertainment/music/article5802815.ece.

8. Adapted from Arthur K. Robertson, *Listen for Success: A Guide to Effective Listening* (New York: Irwin Professional Publishing, 1994), pp. 25–26.

9. Available: http://www.urbandictionary.com/define.php?term=college+morning (accessed April 26, 2010).

10. Available: http://www.urbandictionary.com/define.php?term=awesome%20sauce (accessed April 26, 2010).

11. Diana K. Ivy and Phil Backlund, *Exploring GenderSpeak: Personal Effectiveness in Gender Communication*, 2nd ed. (Boston: McGraw-Hill, 2000), p. 174.

12. Adapted from Amy Einsohn, *The Copyeditor's Handbook: A Guide for Book Publishing and Corporate Communications*, 2nd ed. (Berkeley: University of California Press, 2006), pp. 404–416.

13. Julia Wood, *Gendered Lives: Communication, Gender, and Culture*, 9th ed. (Belmont, CA: Wadsworth, 2011), p. 118.

14. Wood, *Gendered Lives*, p. 118.

15. Ivy and Backlund, *Exploring GenderSpeak*, pp. 175–176.

16. See Manuel Carreias, Alan Garnham, Jane Oakhill, and K Cain, "The Use of Stereotypical Gender information in Constricting a Mental Model: Evidence from English and Spanish, *Quarterly Journal of Experimental Psychology* 49 (1996): 639-666; Friederike Braun, Anja Gottburgsen, Sabine Sczesny and Dagmar Stahlberg, "Konned Geophysider Frauen sein? Generische Personenbezeichnungen im Deutschen [Can Geophysicians be Women? Generic Terms in German]" *Zeitschrift fur Germanistische Lingistic* 26 (1998): 265-283.

17. Pascal Gyagz, Ute Gabriel, Oriane Sarrasin, Jane Oakhill and Alan Garnham, "Generically Intended, but Specifically Interpreted: When Beauticians, Musicians, and Mechanics are all men," *Language and Cognitive Processes* 23 (2008): 464-484.

18. U.S. Department of Labor, Bureau of Labor Statistics, "Earnings of Women and Men by Race and Ethnicity, 2007," *TED: The Editor's Desk*. October 30, 2008. Available: http://bls.gov/opub/ted/2008/oct/wk4/art04.htm (accessed April 26, 2010).

19. Compiled from "George Allen's America: Whom It Includes and Whom It Doesn't," Editorial, *The Washington Post*, August 15, 2006. http://www.washingtonpost.com/wp-dyn/content/article/2006/08/14/AR2006081401114.html. Retrieved March 10, 2010.

20. Andrew Wolvin and Carolyn Gwynn Coakley, *Listening*, 5th ed. (Madison, WI: Brown & Benchmark, 1996), p. 232.

Chapter 3

1. "The New Student Politics" [Online]. Available: http://www.actionforchange.org/getinformed (accessed May 7, 2007).
2. Alfred Rosa and Paul Escholz, *The Writer's Brief Handbook*, 2nd ed. (Scarborough, Canada: Allyn & Bacon, 1996), p. 7.
3. Compiled from http://www.AMillionThanks.org; "Camp Pendleton," *City News Service*, May 19, 2005, n.p.; "Million Thanks," *City News Service*, March 31, 2004, n.p; "Greetings from Heart, Home: More Mail Pours in for Teenager Who Gave Troops A Million Thanks," *The Daily News of Los Angeles*, January 14, 2005, p. SC1; "High School Student Organized Letter-writing Campaign for Military," *The Associated Press State and Local Wire*, March 31, 2004, n.p.; "America Supports You: Top Enlisted Service Member Gets Milestone Letter," *American Forces Press Service*, February 1, 2007; and http://www.dosomething.org/project/a-million-thanks-how-say-thank-you-men-and-women-serving-our-country (accessed April 29, 2010).
4. Compiled from Collins, Lauren, "Banksy Was Here: The Invisible Man of Graffiti Art," The New Yorker, 14 May 2007; "Picture Gallery: Banksy Art in Big Easy," Sky.com, 28 August 2008; and Langley, William, "For the Gauguin of Graffiti It Was All about Tagging. Now He's into Six-Figure Price Tags," Telegraph.co.uk, 18 March 2007.
5. Compiled from Harmanci, Reyhan, "Above the Fold," San Francisco Chronicle, 11 July 2007, and interviews with Above in Graphotism Magazine 29, October 2002, and Bant Magazine 31, February 2007.
6. Adapted from J. Anthony Blair, "The Rhetoric of Visual Arguments" in Charles A. Hill and Marguerite Helmers, Eds. Defining Visual Rhetorics, Mahwah, New Jersey: Lawrence Earlbaum, 2004. 41-62.

Chapter 4

1. For an excellent summary and discussion of the various theories that attempt to explain social development, see Julia T. Wood, *Gendered Lives: Communication, Gender, and Culture*, 7th ed. (Belmont, CA: Wadsworth, 2007), pp. 37–59.
2. Gordon Marshall, ed., *The Concise Oxford Dictionary of Sociology* (New York: Oxford University Press, 1994), p. 315.
3. See, for example, Samia Ula Nur Alhabib and Roger Jones, "Domestic Violence Against Women: Systematic Review of Prevalence Studies." *Journal of Family Violence* 25.4 (2010): 369-382; "Demographics" United States Department of Labor, Bureau of Labor Statistics, http://www.bls.gov/cps/demographics.htm#race; Alex Kingsbury, "Fighting Violence With Words and Deeds." *U.S. News & World Report* 146, no. 10 (November 2009): 53; "A Policy Maker's Guide to Hate Crimes," Bureau of Justice Assistance, US Department of Justice, http://www.ncjrs.gov/pdffiles1/bja/162304.pdf; "Victims," Office of Justice Programs, Bureau of Justice Statistics, http://bjs.ojp.usdoj.gov/index.cfm?ty=tp&tid=9; and William B. Weeks and Amy E. Wallace, "Race and Gender Differences in General Internists' Annual Income," *Journal of General Internal Medicine* 21 (November 2006): 1167-1171.
4. Alice H. Eagly, and Shelly Chaiken, "The Advantages of an Inclusive Definition of Attitude," *Social Cognition* 25.5 (2007): 582-602; Egly and Chaiken, "Attitude Structure and Function," in *Handbook of Social Psychology* 1

(1998): 323–390; and James M. Olson and Mark P. Zanna, "Attitudes and Attitude Change," *Annual Review of Psychology* 44 (1993): 117–154.
5. Rushworth M. Kidder, *How Good People make Tough Choices: Resolving the Dilemmas of Ethical Living*, NY: Harper Collins, 2003 (original work published in 1995); Kidder, *Shared Values for a Troubled World* (San Francisco: Jossey-Bass, 1994); Milton Rokeach, *Beliefs, Attitudes and Values: A Theory of Organization and Change* (San Francisco: Jossey-Bass, 1970); Milton Rokeach, *The Nature of Human Values* (New York: Free Press, 1973); Shalom H. Schwartz and Wolfgang Blisky, "Toward a Theory of the Universal Content and Structure of Values: Extensions and Cross-Cultural Replications," *Journal of Personality and Social Psychology* 58 (1990): 878–891.
6. His Holiness the Dalai Lama and Howard C. Cutler, *The Art of Happiness: A Handbook for Living* (New York: Riverhead Books, 1998), pp. 1–2.
7. Kenneth Burke, *Counter-Statement* (Berkeley: University of California Press, 1968), p. 31.
8. Lyman K. Steil, Larry L. Barker, and Kittie W. Watson, *Effective Listening: Key to Your Success* (New York: McGraw-Hill, 1993), p. 91.
9. Compiled from Lisa D. Moraes, "Kanye West's Torrent of Criticism, Live on NBC," The TV Column, *The Washington Post*, September 3, 2005 [Online]. Available: http://www.washingtonpost.com/wp-dyn/content/article/2005/09/03/AR2005090300165.html (accessed May 13, 2010); Lisa Respers France, "Anger over West's Disruption at MTV Awards," CNN.com/entertainment, September 14, 2009 [Online]. Available: http://www.cnn.com/2009/SHOWBIZ/09/14/kanye.west.reaction/index.html (accessed May 13, 2010); and Karen Valby, "The Ego Has Landed," *Entertainment Weekly*, January 28, 2006.
10. Compiled from http://www.un.org/works; "Angelina Jolie on Her UN Refugee Role," *National Geographic News*, June 18, 2003 [Online]. Available: http://news.nationalgeographic.com/news/2003/06/0618_030618_angelinajolie.html and "UNHCR Goodwill Ambassadors" [Online]. Available: http://www.unhcr.org/cgi-bin/textis/vtx/home (accessed August 2007 and June 2010).

Chapter 5

1. Alvin Toffler, *Future Shock* (New York: Random House, 1970), p. 350.
2. Patricia Senn Breivik, *Student Learning in the Information Age* (Phoenix, AZ: Oryx Press, 1998), p. xi.
3. Adapted from Myrtle S. Bolner and Gayle A. Poirier, *The Research Process: Books and Beyond*, 2nd ed. (Dubuque, IA: Kendall/Hunt, 2002), pp. 144–145; Shirley Duglin Kennedy, *Best Bet Internet: Reference and Research When You Don't Have Time to Mess Around* (Chicago: American Library Association, 1998), pp. 144–145.
4. Bolner and Poirier, *The Research Process*, p. 248.
5. Adapted from Bolner and Poirier, *The Research Process*, p. 168; Christine A. Hult, *Researching and Writing across the Curriculum* (Boston: Allyn & Bacon, 1996), pp. 28–29.
6. Adapted from Charles J. Stewart and William B. Cash Jr., *Interviewing: Principles and Practices*, 11th ed. (Boston: McGraw-Hill, 2006), p. 1.
7. Larry King, *The Best of Larry King Live: The Greatest Interviews* (Atlanta, GA: Times, 1995). Review this book and notice the depth of knowledge King possesses over a wide range of subjects and topics. His preparation enables him to ask relevant, informed questions of each of his interviewees.
8. Adapted from George Killenberg and Rob Anderson, *Before the Story: Interviewing and Communication Skills*

for Journalists (New York: St. Martin's Press, 1989).

9. Elder, Gerri, "100 Obscure and Remarkable CD Covers," *Smashing Magazine,* 13 May 2009. Available: http://smashingmagazine.com/209/05/13/100-obscure -and -remarkable.

10. Rothman, Wilson, "Cool Album Art and Packaging: Records, Cassettes, CDs Then Nothing," Gizmodo.com, 16 April 2009. Available: http://i.gizmodo.com/5215258/cool-album-art-and-packaging-records-cassettes-cds -then-nothing.

11. Walsh, Bill, quoted on the Album Cover Network website. Available: http://www.albumcovers.net/.

12. Paul Martin Lester, *Visual Communication: Images with Messages,* 4th ed. Boston: Wadsworth/Cengage, 2006, vii.

Chapter 6

1. Compiled from http://www.care.org/carework/emergencies/sudan/; http://www.eyesondarfur.org/conflict.html; "George Clooney and Don Cheadle Receive Summit Peace Award," TheCommunity.com, n.d.; http://notonourwatchproject.org/; Barbara Slavin, "Powell Accuses Sudan of Genocide," USA Today, 9 September, 2004; "10 Questions for Don Cheadle," Time .com, 17 May 2007.

2. Adapted from Edward S. Inch and Barbara Warnick, *Critical Thinking and Communication: The Use of Reason in Argument*, 3rd ed. (Boston: Allyn & Bacon, 1989), pp. 194–197.

3. Walter R. Fisher, *Human Communication as Narration: Toward a Philosophy of Reason, Value, and Action* (Columbia: University of South Carolina Press, 1987), p. 58.

4. Kathleen Hall Jamieson, *Eloquence in the Electronic Age: The Transformation of Political Speechmaking* (New York: Oxford University Press, 1988), p. 140.

5. Victoria Moore, "Christian, the Lion Who Lived in My London Living Room," *The Daily Mail,* May 4, 2007 [Online]. Available: http://www.dailymail.co.uk/femail/article-452820/Christian-lion-lived-London-living-room .html (accessed May 22, 2010).

6. Cynthia Crossen, *Tainted Truth: The Manipulation of Fact in America* (New York: Simon & Schuster, 1994), p. 42.

7. Reza Fadaei, ed., *Applied Algebra and Statistics* (Needham Heights, MA: Simon & Schuster, 2000), pp. 544, 545.

8. Compiled from http://detnews.com/article/20100106/SCHOOLS/1060325/Dearborn-students—sweatshirts -stir-outrage and Eric D. Lawrence, "Hundreds Attend Dearborn Meeting about Twin Towers Shirts." *Detroit Free Press,* January 6, 2010 [Online]. Available: http://www .wzzm13.com/news/news_story.aspx?storyid=117250.

9. Barbara Kantrowitz and Pat Wingert, "Teachers Wanted," *Newsweek,* October 2, 2000, p. 40.

10. Adapted from Inch and Warnick, *Critical Thinking and Communication*, p. 154.

11. Alex Pasternack, "China Makes Celebrity Spokespeople Liable for Unsafe Food," *The Huffington Post,* March 21, 2009 [Online]. Available: http://www.huffingtonpost.com/alex-pasternack/china-makes-celebrity-spo_b_177704 .html (accessed May 22, 2010).

12. Adapted from bell hooks, *Talking Back: Thinking Feminist, Thinking Black* (Boston: South End, 1989), pp. 3, 107, 109, 110.

13. The discussion over the type of language used by Truth, and whether or not she actually did repeat the phrase "ain't I a woman," is nicely summarized in Suzanne Pullon Fitch and Roseann M. Mandziuk, *Sojourner Truth as Orator: Wit, Story, and Song* (Westport, CT: Greenwood Press, 1997).

14. I. A. Richards, *The Philosophy of Rhetoric* (New York: Oxford University Press, 1965) (original work published 1936); C. K. Ogden and I. A. Richards, *The Meaning of Meaning: A Study of the Influence of Language upon Thought and of the Science of Symbolism* (New York: Harcourt, Brace & World, 1923).

15. Sanjay Kali, "Definition of Feminism," n.d. [Online]. Available: http://ezinearticles.com/?Definition-of -Feminism&id=1697184 (accessed May 22, 2010).

Chapter 7

1. For a discussion of the importance of maintaining Aristotle's distinction between logos and logic, see Joseph Little, "Confusion in the Classroom: Does Logos Mean Logic?" *Journal of Technical Writing and Communication* 29 (1999): 349–353. Aristotle suggested that logos refers to the process of reasoning as well as establishing credibility, or ethos, and using emotional appeals, or pathos. See also George Kennedy's translation of *Aristotle: On Rhetoric: A Theory of Civic Discourse* (Oxford: Oxford University Press, 1991), p. 37.

2. See Chaim Perelman and Luce Olbrechts-Tyteca, *The New Rhetoric: A Treatise on Argumentation,* John Wilkinson and Purcell Weaver, trans. (Notre Dame, IN: University of Notre Dame Press, 1969), pp. 31–35, for a discussion of the universal audience, or that group of imagined listeners to whom we submit claims and test their "logic."

3. Adapted from Stephen Toulmin, Richard Rieke, and Allan Janik, *An Introduction to Reasoning* (New York: Macmillan, 1979).

4. Perelman and Olbrechts-Tyteca identify approximately twenty-two different argument schemes in *The New Rhetoric*, and Douglas N. Walton offers twenty-five different argumentation schemes in *Argumentation Schemes for Presumptive Reasoning* (Mahwah, NJ: Erlbaum, 1996). Although all of these schemes are important, students in a beginning public speaking course do well to rely on the five basic types discussed in this chapter and in most other public speaking texts.

5. Aristotle, *Rhetoric*, II, 20, 1394a, cited in Perelman and Olbrechts-Tyteca, *The New Rhetoric*, p. 358. See also Aristotle, *The "Art" of Rhetoric*, John H. Freese, trans. (Cambridge, MA: Harvard University Press, 1982), p. 265, for a slightly different translation of Aristotle's view on examples.

6. The material in this section and the section on deductive reasoning is from Lester Faigley and Jack Selzer, *Good Reasons* (Needham Heights, MA: Allyn & Bacon, 2000); Howard Kahane and Nancy Cavender, *Logic and Contemporary Rhetoric: The Use of Reason in Everyday Life*, 11th ed. (Boston: Wadsworth, 2010); Stephen Toulmin, *The Uses of Argument* (London: Cambridge University Press, 1969).

7. See, for example, David Vancil, *Rhetoric and Argumentation* (Boston: Allyn & Bacon, 1993), p. 134, who suggests that argument by example is "one of the archetypal forms of the inductive process"; David Zarefsky, *Public Speaking: Strategies for Success* (Needham Heights, MA: Allyn & Bacon, 2002), pp. 153–154

8. For an excellent compilation of women's speeches related to their right to vote, as well as other rights, including Anthony's speech, see Karlyn Kohrs Campbell, ed., *Man Cannot Speak for Her: Key Texts of the Early Feminists* (New York: Praeger, 1989).

9. See Faigley and Selzer, *Good Reasons*; Kahane and Cavender, *Logic and Contemporary Rhetoric*; Edward S. Inch and Barbara Warnick, *Critical Thinking and*

Communication: The Use of Reason in Argument, 3rd ed. (Boston: Allyn & Bacon, 1998).

10. T., Buddy, "White House Launches Anti-Meth Campaign," About.com Guide to Alcoholism, 15 October 2009. Available: http://alcoholism.about.com/b/2009/10/15/white-house-launches-anti-meth-campaign.htm; MethResources.gov, "2009 Anti-Meth Ad Campaign," n.d. Available: http://www.methresources.gov/2009antimeth.html.

11. http://www.lifeormeth.com/.

12. Australia's Life or Meth organization reports a 45 percent reduction of meth use in teens and a 75 percent reduction in adults. See Mary K. Casey, Lindsay Timmermann, Mike Allen, Sarah Krahn, Katie LaPlant Turkiewicz, "Response and Self-Efficacy of Condom Use: A Meta-Analysis of this Important Element of AIDS Education and Prevention" Southern Communication Journal [serial online]. January 2009; 74 (1):57-78. Available from: Academic Search Premier, Ipswich, MA. Accessed May 27, 2010; Donna C. Jessop and Jennifer Wade, "Fear appeals and binge drinking: A terror management theory perspective," British Journal of Health Psychology [serial online]. November 2008; 13 (4):773-788. Available from: Academic Search Premier, Ipswich, MA. Accessed May 27, 2010; Robin L. Nabi, David Roskos-Ewoldsen, and Francesca Dillman Carpentier. 2008. "Subjective Knowledge and Fear Appeal Effectiveness: Implications for Message Design." Health Communication 23, no. 2: 191-201. Academic Search Premier, EBSCOhost (accessed May 27, 2010); Patricia A. Rippetoe and Ronald W. Rogers, "Effects of Components of Protection-Motivation Theory on Adaptive and Maladaptive Coping with a Health Threat," Journal of Personality and Social Psychology 53 (1987): 596-604. Connie Roser and Margaret Thompson, "Fear Appeals and the Formation of Active Publics," Journal of Communication 45 (1995): 103-121; Carol L. Schmitt, Thomas Blass, "Fear Appeals Revisited: Testing a Unique Anti-smoking Film." 2008. Current Psychology 27, no. 2: 145-151. Academic Search Premier, EBSCOhost (accessed May 27, 2010) and; Norman C.H Wong and Joseph N. Cappella. "Antismoking Threat and Efficacy Appeals: Effects on Smoking Cessation Intentions for Smokers with Low and High Readiness to Quit," Journal of Applied Communication Research [serial online]. February 2009; 37 (1):1-20. Available from: Academic Search Premier, Ipswich, MA. Accessed May 27, 2010.

13. Compiled from http://dotearth.blogs.nytimes.com/2009/09/15/the-ultimate-green-technology-condoms/, http://mediamatters.org/mmtv/200910200020, and http://dotearth.blogs.nytimes.com/2009/10/20/thought-experiments-on-sex-and-death/.

14. False causes are also known by their Latin name, post hoc, ergo propter hoc, which means "after this, therefore because of this." For a succinct discussion of false causes, see Inch and Warnick, Critical Thinking and Communication, pp. 208–209.

15. Compiled from Claudia Kalb, "Culture of Corpulence: American Innovations in Food, Transportation, and Technology are Threatening to Supersize Us All," Newsweek, March 22, 2010, pp. 42-48; and Michelle Obama, 'Michelle on a Mission: How we can Empower Parents, Schools, and the Community to Battle Childhood Obesity," Newsweek, March 22, 2010, pp. 40-41.

16. Cited in Paul Rogat Loeb, Soul of a Citizen: Living with Conviction in a Cynical Time (New York: St. Martin's Griffin, 1999), pp. 68–69.

17. Compiled from Wangari Maathai, The Green Belt Movement: Sharing the Approach and the Experience

(New York: Lantern Books, 2003); Wangari Muta Maathai, Unbowed (New York: Knopf, 2006); "Wangari Maathai Quotes" [Online]. Available: http://womenshistory.about.com/od/quotes/a/wangari_maathai.htm; and http://www.greenbeltmovement.org.

18. Jerry Alder and Mary Carmichael, "The Tsunami Threat," Newsweek, January 10, 2005, p. 42.

19. Inch and Warnick call reasoning by sign "coexistential" reasoning, suggesting "an argument from coexistence reasons from something that can be observed (as a sign) to a condition or feature that cannot be observed." See Inch and Warnick, Critical Thinking and Communication, p. 201.

20. Alder and Carmichael, "The Tsunami Threat," p. 42.

21. Toulmin, The Uses of Argument; Toulmin, Rieke, and Janik, An Introduction to Reasoning. See also Mary M. Gleason, "The Role of Evidence in Argumentative Writing," Reading & Writing Quarterly 14 (1999): 81–106.

22. For a discussion of the characteristics of credibility, see James B. Stiff, Persuasive Communication (New York: Guilford Press, 1994), pp. 89–98.

Chapter 8

1. For a historical overview of the research on organizing speeches, see Ernest Thompson, "Some Effects of Message Structure on Listeners' Comprehension," Speech Monographs 34 (1967): 51–57; James C. McCroskey and R. S. Mehrley, "The Effects of Disorganization and Non-Fluency on Attitude Change and Source Credibility," Communication Monographs 36 (1969): 13–21; Arlee Johnson, "A Preliminary Investigation of the Relationship between Organization and Listener Comprehension," Central States Speech Journal 21 (1970): 104–107; Christopher Spicer and Ronald E. Bassett, "The Effect of Organization on Learning from an Informative Message," Southern Speech Communication Journal 41 (1976): 290–299. For more recent discussions of the importance of organization in speeches, see Patricia R. Palmerton, "Teaching Skills or Teaching Thinking," Journal of Applied Communication Research 20 (1992): 335–341; Robert G. Powell, "Critical Thinking and Speech Communication: Our Teaching Strategies Are Warranted—Not!" Journal of Applied Communication Research 20 (1992): 342–347.

2. Compiled from Caroline Kennedy, "Power of One: Zainab Salbi Helps Women Recover," Time.com, 1 May 2008, available: http://www.time.com/time/magazine/article/0,9171,1736706,00.html; Pati Poblete, "Profile: Zainab Salbi: One Mission, Thousands of Lives," San Francisco Chronicle, 27 January 2002, page E-5; and Women for Women International, http://www.womenforwomen.org/.

Chapter 9

1. Bas A. Andeweg, Jaap C. de Jong, and Hans Hoeken, "'May I Have Your Attention?' Exordial Techniques in Informative Oral Presentations," Technical Communication Quarterly 7 (1998): 281.

2. Lineberry, Cate, "Tattoos: The Ancient and Mysterious History," Smithsonian.com, 1 January 2007. Available: http://www.smithsonianmag.com/history-archaeology/10023606.html#ixzz0pX08ZUVx.

3. Lineberry, "Tattoos: The Ancient and Mysterious History." Available: http://www.smithsonianmag.com/history-archaeology/tattoo.html?c=y&page=5#ixzz0pX6bzr4s.

4. Pew Research Center for People and the Press, "A Portrait of 'Generation Next': How young people view their lives, futures, and politics, 9 January 2007. Available:

http://people-press.org/report/300/a-portrait-of-generation-next.

5. Lineberry, Cate, "Today's Tattoos," Smithsonian.com, 1 January 2007. Available: http://www.smithsonianmag.com/people-places/tattoo_modern.html.

6. Mindy Fenske, "Movement and Resistance: (Tattooed) Bodies and Performance," *Text and Performance Quarterly* 4 (2004), 51–73.

7. Mark L. Knapp, Roderick P. Hart, Gustav W. Friedrick, and G. M. Shulman, "The Rhetoric of Goodbye: Verbal and Nonverbal Correlates of Human Leave-Taking," *Speech Monographs* 40 (1973): 182–198.

Chapter 10

1. The debate over the role of language in constructing or reflecting reality is centuries old, beginning with Plato and Aristotle. For a summary of this debate and the implications of the many positions, see Gill, *Rhetoric and Human Understanding, Prospect Heights, Illinois, Waveland, 1994.* James L. Golden, Goodwin F. Berquist, and William E. Coleman offer an anthology of some of the primary texts in this debate in their book *The Rhetoric of Western Thought*, 6th ed. (Dubuque, IA: Kendall/Hunt, 1997).

2. C. K. Ogden and I. A. Richards, *The Meaning of Meaning: A Study of the Influence of Language upon Thought and of the Science of Symbolism* (New York: Harcourt, Brace, 1930) (original work published 1923).

3. For an excellent discussion of signifying, see Henry Louis Gates, *The Signifying Monkey: A Theory of Afro-American Literary Criticism* (New York: Oxford University Press, 1988); Geneva Smitherman, *Talkin and Testifying: The Language of Black America* (Boston: Houghton Mifflin, 1977).

4. Jennifer Steinhauer "Verdict in Myspace Suicide Case" *New York Times*, November 26, 2008 [Online]. Available: http://www.nytimes.com/2008/11/27/us/27myspace.html.

5. The material in this section is from Khosrow Jahandarie, *Spoken and Written Discourse: A Multi-Disciplinary Perspective* (Stamford, CT: Ablex, 1999), pp. 131–150; Eckart Scheerer, "Orality, Literacy, and Cognitive Modeling," in Boris M. Velichkovsky and Duane M. Rumbaugh, eds., *Communicating Meaning: The Evolution and Development of Language* (Mahwah, NJ: Erlbaum, 1996), pp. 211–256; M. A. K. Halliday, "Spoken and Written Modes of Meaning," in Rosalind Horowitz and S. Jay Samuels, eds., *Comprehending Oral and Written Language* (New York: Harcourt Brace Jovanovich, 1987), pp. 55–82; Wallace Chafe and Jane Danielewicz, "Properties of Spoken and Written Language," in Horowitz and Samuels, eds., *Comprehending Oral and Written Language*, pp. 83–113.

6. Eric Partridge, *Usage and Abusage: A Guide to Good English* (New York: Norton, 1995), p. 182 (original work published 1942).

7. Rigoberta Menchú, "Five Hundred Years of Sacrifice before Alien Gods," *Interview*, 1992 [Online]. Available: http://www.indigenouspeople.net/menchu2.htm.

8. Richard Lederer, *The Bride of Anguished English: A Bonus of Bloopers, Blunders, Botches, and Boo-Boos* (New York: St. Martin's Press), pp. 33, 44.

9. Audley "Queen Mother" Moore, in Toyomi Igus, ed., *Book of Black Heroes: Vol. 2, Great Women in the Struggle: An Introduction for Young Readers* (Orange, NJ: Just Us Books, 1991), p. 12.

10. Complied from http://www.hsan.org: "Hip-Hop Setting the Beat in First: Black Artists Hold Billboard's Top 10," *Boston Globe*, October 4, 2003, n.p.; "Industry Insiders Call for Limits on Rap Lyrics: Group Seeks Voluntary Standards for Language," *The Houston Chronicle*, April 25, 2007, p. 2; "Zip Un-Hip Lyrics: Rap Bigs Say Industry Should 'Bleep' Out Three Dirty Words," *Daily News* (New York), April 24, 2007, p. 4; and The Smiley Group, *The Covenant with Black America* (Chicago: Third World Press, 2006).

11. Partridge, *Usage and Abusage*, p. 14.

Chapter 11

1. Herbert W. Hildebrant and Walter W. Stevens suggest that no one method is better than another. Rather, "it is the ability of the individual speaker in using a particular method" that is influential. See Hildebrant and Stevens, "Manuscript and Extemporaneous Delivery in Communicating Information," *Speech Monographs* 30 (1963): 369–372.

2. Robert J. Branham and W. Barnett Pearce, "The Conversational Frame in Public Address," *Communication Quarterly* 44 (1996): 423.

3. Peter A. Andersen, Michael L. Hecht, and Gregory D. Hoebler, "The Cultural Dimension of Nonverbal Communication," in William B. Gudykunst and Bella Moody, eds., *Handbook of International and Intercultural Communication* (Thousand Oaks, CA: Sage, 2002), pp. 89–106; Larry A. Samovar and Richard E. Porter, *Communication between Cultures* (Belmont, CA: Wadsworth, 1991), pp. 205–206.

4. Stephen E. Lucas, *The Art of Public Speaking*, 7th ed. (New York: McGraw-Hill, 2001), p. 290.

5. Paul L. Soper, *Basic Public Speaking*, 2nd ed. (New York: Oxford University Press, 1956), p. 151. Soper also cites Ambrose Bierce as suggesting, with regard to too high a pitch, that positive is "being mistaken at the top of one's voice." See Soper, *Basic Public Speaking*, p. 150.

6. Adapted from Soper, *Basic Public Speaking*, p. 143.

7. Nicholas Christenfeld, "Does It Hurt to Say Um?" *Journal of Nonverbal Behavior* 19 (Fall 1995): 171–186. Christenfeld's study also found that audiences prefer no pauses to empty pauses.

8. See, for example, Stephanie Martin and Lyn Darnley, *The Teaching Voice* (San Diego, CA: Singular Publishing Group, 1996), p. 60; Patsy Rodenburg, *The Need for Words: Voice and the Text,* New York: Routledge, 2001; Linda Gates, *Voice for Performance* (New York: Applause, 2000); Richard Dowis, *The Lost Art of the Great Speech: How to Write One, How to Deliver It* (New York: American Management Association, 2000).

9. Many communication scholars define nonverbal communication as all aspects of communication other than words. In a public speaking course, the distinction between vocalized communication as verbal and nonvocalized communication as nonverbal seems pedagogically useful. A similar distinction is made in many other public speaking texts.

10. Ray Birdwhistell, *Kinesics and Context* (Philadelphia: University of Pennsylvania Press, 1970); Albert Mehrabian, *Silent Messages: Implicit Communication of Emotion and Attitudes*, 2nd ed. (Belmont, CA: Wadsworth, 1981).

11. See, for example, April R. Trees and Valerie Manusov, "Managing Face Concerns in Critics: Integrating Nonverbal Behaviors as a Dimension of Politeness in Female Friendship Dyads," *Human Communication Research* 24 (1998): 564–583; James C. McCroskey, Aino Sallinen, Joan M. Fayer, Virginia P. Richmond, and Robert A. Barraclough, "Nonverbal Immediacy and Cognitive Learning: A Cross-Cultural Investigation," *Communication Education* 45 (1996): 200–211; Mary Mino, "The Relative Effects of Content and Vocal Delivery during a Simulated Employment Interview," *Communication Research*

Reports 13 (1996): 225–238. See also Julia T. Wood, *Interpersonal Communication: Everyday Encounters*, 2nd ed. (Belmont, CA: Wadsworth, 1999), p. 148.

12. For an excellent discussion of variations in nonverbal expectations across cultures, see Gudykunst and Moody, eds., *Handbook of International and Intercultural Communication*.

13. For example, see "Good-Looking Lawyers Make More Money, Says a Study by Economists," *Wall Street Journal*, January 4, 1996, p. A1; Patricia Rozell, David Kennedy, and Edward Grabb, "Physical Attractiveness and Income Attainment among Canadians," *Journal of Psychology* 123 (1989): 547–559; Tracy L. Morris, Joan Gorham, Stanley H. Cohen, and Drew Huffman, "Fashion in the Classroom: Effects of Attire on Student Perceptions of Instructors in College Classes," *Communication Education* 45 (1996): 135–148.

14. Arthur J. Hartz, "Psycho-Socionomics: Attractiveness Research from a Societal Perspective," *Journal of Social Behavior and Personality* 11 (1996): 683.

15. Paula Morrow writes that even though physical attractiveness is difficult to "quantify," "people within a given culture tend to agree with each other regarding whether a person's facial appearance is physically attractive or not and they tend to be consistent in their judgments over time." See Morrow, "Physical Attractiveness and Selection Decision Making," *Journal of Management* 16 (1990): 45–60, esp. p. 47. See also Ruth P. Rubinstein, *Dress Codes: Meanings and Messages in American Culture*, 2nd ed. (Boulder, CO: Westview, 2001); C. Peter Herman, Mark P. Zanna, and E. Tory Higgins, *Physical Appearance, Stigma, and Social Behavior: The Ontario Symposium, Vol. 3* (Hillsdale, NJ: Erlbaum, 1986).

16. Mark T. Palmer and Karl B. Simmons, "Communicating Intentions through Nonverbal Behaviors," *Human Communication Research* 22 (1995): 128–160.

17. Steven A. Beebe, "Eye Contact: A Nonverbal Determinant of Speaker Credibility," *Speech Teacher* 23 (1974): 21–25; Steven A. Beebe, "Effects of Eye Contact, Posture and Vocal Inflection upon Credibility and Comprehension," *Australian Scan Journal of Nonverbal Communication* 7–8 (1979–1980): 57–70; Martin Cobin, "Response to Eye Contact," *Quarterly Journal of Speech* 48 (1963): 415–419.

18. See, for example, Peter E. Bull, *Posture and Gesture* (New York: Pergamon, 1987).

19. See, for example, Gilbert Austin in Mary Margaret Robb and Lester Thonssen, eds., *Chironomia or A Treatise on Rhetorical Delivery* (Carbondale: Southern Illinois University Press, 1966) (original work published 1806); John Bulwer, in James W. Cleary, ed., *Chirologia: Or the Natural Language of the Hand, and Chiromomia: Or the Art of Manual Rhetoric* (Carbondale: Southern Illinois University Press, 1974) (original work published 1644).

20. "Complete List of 2008 Peabody Award Winners." The 2008 Peabody Awards were awarded April 1, 2009, at the University of Georgia. Available: http://www.peabody.uga.edu/news/event.php?id=59.

21. YouTube Fact Sheet. Available: http://www.youtube.com/t/fact_sheet.

22. Geier, Thom, et al, "The 100 Greatest Movies, TV Shows, Albums, Books, Characters, Scenes, Episodes, Songs, Dresses, Music Videos, and Trends that Entertained Us over the Past 10 Years," *Entertainment Weekly* 1079/1080 (2009, December 11), 74–84.

23. Aucoin, Don, "For Young Activists, Video Is Their Voice," *The Boston Globe*, March 5, 2010, page A1.

24. Aucoin, Don, *The Boston Globe*, page A12.

Chapter 12

1. Will Linkugel and D. Berg, *A Time to Speak* (Belmont, CA: Wadsworth, 1970), pp. 68–96. See also Elena P. Zayas-Bazan, "Instructional Media in the Total Language Picture," *International Journal of Instructional Media* 5 (1977–1978): 145–150; Emil Bohn and David Jabusch, "The Effect of Four Methods of Instruction on the Use of Visual Aids in Speeches," *Western Journal of Speech Communication* 46 (1982): 253–265.

2. Raymond S. Nickerson, "Short-Term Memory for Complex Meaningful Visual Configurations: A Demonstration of Capacity," *Canadian Journal of Psychology* 19 (1965): 155–160.

3. Bohn and Jabusch, "The Effect of Four Methods of Instruction on the Use of Visual Aids in Speeches," p. 254.

4. William J. Seiler, "The Effects of Visual Materials on Attitudes, Credibility, and Retention," *Speech Monographs* 38 (1971): 331–334.

5. Joe Ayres, "Using Visual Aids to Reduce Speech Anxiety," *Communication Research Reports* 8 (1991): 73–79.

6. Myles Martel, *Before You Say a Word: The Executive Guide to Effective Communication* (Upper Saddle River, NJ: Prentice Hall, 1984).

7. Wilma Davidson and Susan J. Klien, "Ace Your Presentation," *Journal of Accountancy* 187 (1999): 61–63.

8. For a nice discussion of using lists as visual aids, see Margaret Y. Rabb, *The Presentation Design Book: Tips, Techniques and Advice for Creating Effective, Attractive Slides, Overheads, Multimedia Presentations, Screen Shows and More* (Chapel Hill, NC: Ventana, 1993).

9. For example, see Lynn Kearny, *Graphics for Presenters: Getting Your Ideas Across* (Menlo Park, CA: Crisp, 1996); Claudyne Wilder, *The Presentations Kit: Ten Steps for Spelling Out Your Ideas* (New York: Wiley, 1994); Rabb, *The Presentation Design Book*.

10. For example, see Rabb, *The Presentation Design Book*; Wilder, *The Presentations Kit*; Russell N. Baird, Duncan McDonald, Ronald H. Pittman, and Arthur T. Turnbull, *The Graphics of Communication: Methods, Media and Technology* (New York: Harcourt Brace Jovanovich, 1993).

11. Hans Biedermann, *Dictionary of Symbolism: Cultural Icons and the Meanings behind Them*, trans. James Hulbert (New York: Facts on File, 1992).

Chapter 13

1. Conversation with Jennifer McMartin, student at Colorado State University, June 6, 2001.

2. John R. Johnson and Nancy Szczupakiewicz, "The Public Speaking Course: Is It Preparing Students with Work Related Public Speaking Skills?" *Communication Education* 36 (1987): 131–137.

3. See, for example, Deanna P. Dannels, "Time to Speak Up: A Theoretical Framework of Situated Pedagogy and Practice for Communication across the Curriculum," *Communication Education* 50 (2001): 144–158; Sherwin Morreal, Michael Osborn, and Judy Pearson, "Why Communication Is Important: A Rationale for the Centrality of the Study of Communication," *Journal of the Association for Communication Administration* 29 (2000): 1–25; and Andrew D. Wolvin, "The Basic Course and the Future of the Workplace," *Basic Communication Course Annual* 10 (1989): 1–6; National Association of Colleges and Employers, *Job Outlook 2010* survey.

4. Compiled from Sandy Miller, "For the Love of Animals: Everyday People Making a Difference," *Best Friends*

Magazine, March/April 2010; Denise LeBeau, "Saving America's Dog," 29 October 2008, available: http://network.bestfriends.org/groups/conferences/news/archive/2008/10/29/saving-americas-dog.aspx; Lori Weise, "Downtown Dog Rescue Needs Your Support—Letter Writing Camp," posted to Ashleyandhobie.com, Animal Rescue for Southern California Message Boards, 27 December 2009, available: http://ashleyandhobie.com/board/viewtopic.php?f=26&t=15481&p=58682; Animal Planet, "Meet Shorty Rossi," accessed 28 October 2010, available: http://animal.discovery.com/tv/pit-boss/bios/shorty-rossi.html; and Shorty's Pit Bull Rescue, http://animal.discovery.com/tv/pit-boss/bios/shorty-rossi.html.

5. Compiled from "Rep. Wilson Shouts, 'You Lie' to Obama during Speech," CNNPolitics.com, September 10, 2009 [Online]. Available: http://www.cnn.com/2009/POLITICS/09/09/joe.wilson/ (accessed April 5, 2010); and "House Passes Resolution Criticizing Wilson," CNNPolitics.com, September 15, 2009 [Online]. Available: http://www.cnn.com/2009/POLITICS/09/15/wilson.resolution/index.html (accessed April 5, 2010).

Chapter 14

1. The theory of invitational rhetoric was initially proposed by Sonja K. Foss and Cindy L. Griffin in "Beyond Persuasion: A Proposal for an Invitational Rhetoric," *Communication Monographs* 62 (1995): 1–18. That theory has been modified here so it is applicable to public speaking practices.

2. This excerpt comes from Jennifer Emerling Bone, Cindy L. Griffin, and T. M. Linda Scholz, "Invitational Rhetoric: Myths, Misunderstandings and the (Re)Making of Theory," unpublished manuscript, 2005. Thanks go to Jennifer Emerling Bone for her work on this portion of the manuscript.

3. "World Trade Center Site Memorial Competition Jury Statement," *New York Times*, November 19, 2003 [Online]. Available: http://www.nytimes.com/2003/11/19/nyregion/19WTC-JURY-TEXT.html.

4. "Memorial—*Reflecting Absence*: WTC Memorial Jury Statement for Winning Design," Lower Manhattan Development Corporation, January 13, 2004 [Online]. Available: http://www.renewnyc.com.

5. "Memorial—*Reflecting Absence*: WTC Memorial Jury Statement for Winning Design."

6. Lower Manhattan Development Corporation, January 2, 2003 [Online]. Available: http://www.renewnyc.com.

7. For more discussion on the conditions of equality, value, and self-determination, see Harold Barrett, *Rhetoric and Civility: Human Development, Narcissism, and the Good Audience* (Albany: State University of New York Press, 1991); Seyla Benhabib, *Situating the Self: Gender, Community, and Postmodernism in Contemporary Ethics* (New York: Routledge, 1992); Linda Ellinor and Glenna Gerard, *Dialogue: Creating and Sustaining Collaborative Partnerships at Work* (New York: Wiley, 1998); William Isaacs, *Dialogue and the Art of Thinking Together* (New York: Currency, 1999); Paul Rogat Loeb, *Soul of a Citizen: Living with Conviction in a Cynical Time* (New York: St. Martin's Griffin, 1999); M. Scott Peck, *The Different Drum: Community-Making and Peace* (New York: Simon & Schuster, 1987); Carl R. Rogers, "The Interpersonal Relationship: The Core of Guidance," *Harvard Educational Review* 32 (1962): 416–429; M. U. Walker, "Moral Understandings: Alternative 'Epistemology' for a Feminist Ethics," *Hypatia* 4 (1989): 15–28.

8. My thanks to Marko Mohlenhoff, former campaign associate at the Fort Collins Area United Way, for sharing his approach to public speaking and working with me on this example.

9. bell hooks, *Outlaw Culture: Resisting Representations* (New York: Routledge, 1994), p. 241.

10. Compiled from http://www.un.org/Dialogue/heroes.html; http://www.messagestick.com.au/awareness/jbeetson/index.html; http://www.smh.com.au/articles/2002/09/20/1032054956049; and http://news.sbs.com.au/livingblack/index.php?action=proginfo&id=345, May 24, 2006, Series 5, Episode 12.

Chapter 15

1. Compiled from http://www.labucketbrigade.org; The Smiley Group, *The Covenant with Black America* (Chicago: Third World Press, 2006); "Watchdog Group to Protest Refinery: Activists to Mix with Exxon Stockholders," *Times-Picayune* (New Orleans), May 24, 2005, p. 1; "Two Groups Suing Refinery: They Claim Plant Violates Clean Air Act," *Times-Picayune* (New Orleans), February 13, 2004, p. 1; "Group Plans to File Suit against Refinery: They Allege Pollution Violations," *Times-Picayune* (New Orleans), December 5, 2003, p. 1; "Refinery Emissions Too High, Groups Say: Chalmette Residents Fear for Their Health," *Times-Picayune* (New Orleans), September 24, 2003, p. 1; "Residents to Learn to Test Air Quality: Devices to Check for Chemicals on Display," *Times—Picayune* (New Orleans), October 18, 2002, p. 1; and "Neighbors Seeking Proof of Pollution," *Times-Picayune* (New Orleans), July 20, 2000, p. 1.

2. Adapted from Bruce E. Gronbeck, Raymie E. McKerrow, Douglas Ehninger, and Alan H. Monroe, *Principles and Types of Speech Communication*, 11th ed. (Glenview, IL: Scott, Foresman/Little, Brown Higher Education, 1990), pp. 180–205.

3. Numerous scholars, beginning with Aristotle, define persuasion as a process, as something that takes place over time. For example, see Gerald R. Miller and Michael E. Roloff, eds., *Persuasion: New Directions in Theory and Research* (Beverly Hills, CA: Sage, 1980); Kathleen Kennedy Reardon, *Persuasion in Practice* (Newbury Park, CA: Sage, 1991); James B. Stiff, *Persuasive Communication* (New York: Guilford Press, 1994) for three examples of this processual definition of persuasion.

4. See Stiff, *Persuasive Communication*, pp. 117–119.

5. Compiled from http://www.gargaro.com/ribbons.html; http://www.yellowribbonamerica.org/; http://www.yellowribbon.org/; http://www.blueribboncampaignforme.org/; www.livestrong.org; and http://www.teenhelp.com/teen-sexuality/jelly-bracelets.html.

6. Adapted from Paul Martin Lester, *Visual Communication: Images with Messages*, 4th ed. (Boston: Wadsworth/Cengage, 2004), pp. 111–118.

7. Bryan B. Whaley and Lisa Smith Wagner, "Rebuttal Analogy in Persuasive Messages: Communicator Likability and Cognitive Responses," *Journal of Language and Social Psychology* 19 (2000): 66–84.

8. Connie Roser and Margaret Thompson, "Fear Appeals and the Formation of Active Publics," *Journal of Communication* 45 (1995): 103–121.

9. Patricia A. Rippetoe and Ronald W. Rogers, "Effects of Components of Protection-Motivation Theory on Adaptive and Maladaptive Coping with a Health Threat," *Journal of Personality and Social Psychology* 53 (1987): 596–604; Mary K. Casey, Lindsay Timmermann,

Mike Allen, Sarah Krahn, and Katie LaPlant Turkiewicz, "Response and Self-Efficacy of Condom Use: A Meta-Analysis of this Important Element of AIDS Education and Prevention," *Southern Communication Journal* [serial online] 74, no. 1 (January 2009): 57–78. Available: Academic Search Premier, Ipswich, MA (accessed May 27, 2010); Donna C. Jessop and Jennifer Wade, "Fear Appeals and Binge Drinking: A Terror Management Theory Perspective," *British Journal of Health Psychology* [serial online] 13, no. 4 (November 2008): 773–788. Available: Academic Search Premier, Ipswich, MA (accessed May 27, 2010); Robin L. Nabi, David Roskos-Ewoldsen, and Francesca Dillman Carpentier, "Subjective Knowledge and Fear Appeal Effectiveness: Implications for Message Design," *Health Communication* 23, no. 2 (2008): 191–201. Academic Search Premier, EBSCOhost (accessed May 27, 2010); Patricia A. Rippetoe and Ronald W. Rogers, "Effects of Components of Protection-Motivation Theory on Adaptive and Maladaptive Coping with a Health Threat," *Journal of Personality and Social Psychology* 53 (1987): 596–604. Connie Roser and Margaret Thompson, "Fear Appeals and the Formation of Active Publics," *Journal of Communication* 45 (1995): 103–121; Carol L. Schmitt and Thomas Blass, "Fear Appeals Revisited: Testing a Unique Anti-smoking Film," *Current Psychology* 27, no. 2 (2008): 145–151. Academic Search Premier, EBSCOhost (accessed May 27, 2010); and Norman C. H. Wong and Joseph N. Cappella, "Antismoking Threat and Efficacy Appeals: Effects on Smoking Cessation Intentions for Smokers with Low and High Readiness to Quit," *Journal of Applied Communication Research* [serial online] 37, no. 1 (February 2009): 1–20. Available: Academic Search Premier, Ipswich, MA (accessed May 27, 2010).

10. Hong Chyi Chen, Richard Reardon, Cornelia Rea, and David J. More, "Forewarning of Content and Involvement: Consequences for Persuasion and Resistance to Persuasion," *Journal of Experimental Social Psychology* 28 (1992): 523–541.

11. Vincent R. Waldron and James L. Applegate, "Person Centered Tactics during Verbal Disagreements: Effects on Student Perceptions of Persuasiveness and Social Attraction," *Communication Education* 47 (1998): 55–56.

12. Jack W. Brehm, *A Theory of Psychological Reactance* (New York: Academic Press, 1996); Patricia Kearney, Timothy G. Plax, and Nancy F. Burroughs, "An Attributional Analysis of College Students' Resistance Decisions," *Communication Education* 40 (1991): 325–342.

Chapter 16

1. For a nice discussion of the importance of maintaining Aristotle's distinction between logos and logic, see Joseph Little, "Confusion in the Classroom: Does Logos Mean Logic?" *Journal of Technical Writing and Communication* 29 (1999): 349–353. Aristotle suggested that logos refers to the process of reasoning as well as establishing credibility, or ethos, and using emotional appeals, or pathos. See also Aristotle, *On Rhetoric: A Theory of Civic Discourse*, George Kennedy, trans. (Oxford: Oxford University Press, 1991), p. 37.

2. Awareness, understanding, agreement, acceptance, and enactment are based on William J. McGuire's phases describing the process of persuasion. See William J. McGuire, "Attitudes and Attitude Change," in Gardner Lindzey and Elliot Aronson, eds., *Handbook of Social Psychology*, Vol. 1 (New York: Random House, 1985), pp. 258–261.

3. See John C. Reinard, "The Empirical Study of the Persuasive Effects of Evidence: The Status after 50 Years of Research," *Human Communication Research* 15 (1988): 3–59.

4. Donald Dean Morely and Kim B. Walker, "The Role of Importance, Novelty, and Plausibility in Producing Belief Change," *Communication Monographs* 54 (1987): 436–442.

5. See Edward S. Inch and Barbara Warnick, *Critical Thinking and Communication: The Use of Reason in Argument*, 3rd ed. (Boston: Allyn & Bacon, 1998), p. 159.

6. See, for example, Peter A. Andersen and Laura K. Guerrero, eds., *Handbook of Communication and Emotion: Research, Theory, Applications, and Contexts* (San Diego, CA: Academic Press, 1998), esp. chaps. 16 and 17; Kathleen Kelley Reardon, *Persuasion in Practice* (Newbury Park, CA: Sage, 1991), pp. 108–110; James B. Stiff, *Persuasive Communication* (New York: Guilford Press, 1994), pp. 119–131.

7. Laura K. Guerrero, Peter A. Andersen, and Melanie R. Trost, "Communication and Emotion: Basic Concepts and Approaches," in Andersen and Guerrero, *Handbook of Communication and Emotion*, p. 6.

8. Richard E. Porter and Larry A. Samovar, "Cultural Influences on Emotional Expression: Implications for Intercultural Communication," in Andersen and Guerrero, *Handbook of Communication and Emotion*, p. 452.

9. For a sample of speakers who possess these traits, see "Top 100 American Speeches of the 20th Century," News and Public Affairs, University of Wisconsin–Madison [Online]. Available: http://www.news.wisc.edu/misc/speeches/.

10. See Richard M. Perloff, *The Dynamics of Persuasion* (Hillsdale, NJ: Erlbaum, 1993), pp. 136–155; Stiff, *Persuasive Communication*, pp. 89–106.

11. Stiff, *Persuasive Communication*, pp. 102–104.

12. Perloff, *Dynamics of Persuasion*, pp. 170–179.

13. "Top 100 American Speeches of the 20th Century."

14. Marian Friestad and Peter Wright, "Everyday Persuasion Knowledge," *Psychology & Marketing* 16 (1999): 185.

15. Friestad and Wright, "Everyday Persuasion Knowledge," p. 188.

16. For a nice discussion of the logic of mythos, see Glenn W. Most, "From Logos to Mythos," in Richard Buxton, ed., *From Myth to Reason? Studies in the Development of Greek Thought* (Oxford: Oxford University Press, 1999), pp. 25–47.

17. See Frans H. van Eemeren and Rob Gootendorst, *Argumentation, Communication, and Fallacies: A Pragma-Dialectical Perspective* (Hillsdale, NJ: Erlbaum, 1992); Howard Kahane and Nancy Cavender, *Logic and Contemporary Rhetoric: The Use of Reason in Everyday Life*, 8th ed. (Belmont, CA: Wadsworth, 1998).

18. Compiled from Alan Clements, *The Voice of Hope: Aung San Suu Kyi; Conversations with Alan Clements* (New York: Seven Stories, 1997); and Michael Aris, ed., *Freedom from Fear and Other Writings* (London: Penguin, 1991).

19. Alan Buxbaum, "NYC Heroin Pamphlet—Is It a Help or a How-to Guide?" CNN.com, January 4, 2010.

Chapter 17

1. Architect Ludwig Mies van der Rhoe (1886–1969) is credited with using this phrase to describe his "skin and bones" architecture [Online]. Available: http://www.phrases.org.uk/meanings/226400.html (accessed May 2010).

2. http://www.samspadyfoundation.org/pdf/mollysspeech.pdf (accessed May 2010).

3. Congressman Bobby Rush, "Tribute to Mrs. Rosa Parks," April 20, 1999 [Online]. Available: http://www.house.gov/rush/pr42099s.htm.

4. http://www.altfg.com/blog/awards/kathryn-bigelow-oscar-acceptance-speech-494/ (accessed May 2010).

5. Joal Ryan, "Rock Throws Stones at MTV Video Music Awards," *E! Online*, September 9, 1999 [Online], http://aol.eonline.com/News/Items/0,1,5285,00.html.

6. Stephen E. Lucas, *The Art of Public Speaking*, 7th ed. (Boston: McGraw-Hill, 2001), p. 445.

7. Jerry Palmer, *Taking Humor Seriously* (London: Routledge, 1994), p. 161.

8. Maureen Daly Goggin, "Visual Rhetoric in Pens of Steel and Inks of Silk: Challenging the Great Visual/Verbal Divide" in Charles A. Hill and Marguerite Helmers, eds., *Defining Visual Rhetorics* (Mahwah, NJ: Erlbaum, 2004), pp. 87–110.

9. See, for example, Judith Roof and Robyn Wiegman, eds., *Who Can Speak? Authority and Critical Identity* (Chicago: University of Illinois Press, 1995).

10. See, for example, Carole Blair, "Communication as Collective Memory," in Gregory J. Shepherd, Jeffrey St. John, and Ted Striphas, eds., *Communication as . . . Perspectives on Theory* (Thousand Oaks, CA: Sage, 2006), pp. 51–59; and Carole Blair, "Contemporary U.S. Memorial Sites as Exemplars of Rhetorics Materiality," in Jack Selzer and Sharon Crowley, eds. *Rhetorical Bodies* (Madison: University of Wisconsin Press, 1999), pp. 16–57.

11. Ellen DeGeneres Commencement Address, May 11, 2009, Tulane University [Online]. Available: http://www.graduationwisdom.com/speeches/v0041-4-ellen.html (accessed May 2010).

12. See, for example, Charles R. Gruner, "Advice to the Beginning Speaker on Using Humor—What the Research Tells Us," *Communication Education* 34 (1985): 142–147;

Christie McGufee Smith and Larry Power, "The Use of Disparaging Humor by Group Leaders," *Southern Speech Communication Journal* 53 (1988): 279–292; Elizabeth E. Grahm, Michael J. Papa, and Gordon P. Brooks, "Functions of Humor in Conversation: Conceptualization and Measurement," *Western Journal of Communication* 56 (1992): 161–183; Frank J. MacHovec, *Humor: Theory, History, Applications* (Springfield, IL: Charles C Thomas, 1988); Palmer, *Taking Humor Seriously*.

13. Jeffrey H. Goldstein, "Theoretical Notes on Humor," *Journal of Communication* 26 (1976): 104–112. See also Barry Alan Morris, "The Communal Constraints on Parody: The Symbolic Death of Joe Bob Briggs," *Quarterly Journal of Speech* 73 (1987): 460–473.

14. Even experienced comedians can go too far for their audiences. Consider the example of Joe Bob Briggs in Morris, "The Communal Constraints on Parody."

15. For an interesting discussion of gender differences in humor, see M. Alison Kibler, "Gender Conflict and Coercion on A&E's *An Evening at the Improv*," *Journal of Popular Culture* 32 (1999): 45–57.

16. See Joan B. Levine, "The Feminine Routine," *Journal of Communication* 26 (1976): 173–175; Lawrence La Fave and Roger Mannell, "Does Ethnic Humor Serve Prejudice?" *Journal of Communication* 26 (1976): 116–123; Dolf Zillmann and Holly Stocking, "Putdown Humor," *Journal of Communication* 26 (1976): 154–163.

17. See Palmer, *Taking Humor Seriously*; Joseph Alan Ullian, "Joking at Work," *Journal of Communication* 26 (1976): 129–133.

18. Victor Raskin, *Semantic Mechanism of Humor* (Dordrecht, the Netherlands: D. Reidel, 1985).

19. Sylvia Simmons, *How to Be the Life of the Podium: Openers, Closers and Everything in Between to Keep Them Listening* (New York: AMACOM, 1991).

Index

Index